INSIGHT GUIDES
GREAT RAILWAY
JOURNEYS OF EUROPE

APA PUBLICATIONS L

Part of the Langenscheidt Publishing Group

INSIGHT GUIDE
GREAT RAILWAY JOURNEYS OF EUROPE

Editorial
Managing Editor
Tom Le Bas
Series Editor
Dorothy Stannard
Picture Manager
Steven Lawrence

Distribution

UK & Ireland
GeoCenter International Ltd
Meridian House, Churchill Way West
Basingstoke, Hampshire RG21 6YR
sales@geocenter.co.uk

United States
Ingram Publisher Services
One Ingram Blvd, PO Box 3006
La Vergne, TN 37086-1986
customer.service@ingrampublisher
services.com

Australia
Universal Publishers
PO Box 307
St Leonards, NSW 1590
sales@universalpublishers.com.au

New Zealand
Hema Maps New Zealand Ltd (HNZ)
Unit 2, 10 Cryers Road
East Tamaki, Auckland 2013
sales.hema@clear.net.nz

Worldwide
Apa Publications GmbH & Co.
Verlag KG (Singapore branch)
7030 Ang Mo Kio Ave 5
08-65 Northstar @ AMK
Singapore 569880
apasin@singnet.com.sg

Printing
CTPS – China

©2009 Apa Publications GmbH & Co.
Verlag KG (Singapore branch)
All Rights Reserved

First Edition 2002
Updated 2003, 2005, 2008
Reprinted 2011

CONTACTING THE EDITORS
We would appreciate it if readers
would alert us to errors or out-
dated information by writing to:
**Insight Guides, P.O. Box 7910,
London SE1 1WE, England.**
insight@apaguide.co.uk

www.insightguides.com

ABOUT THIS BOOK

The first Insight Guide pioneered the use of creative full-colour photography in travel guides in 1970. Since then, we have expanded our range to cater for our readers' need not only for reliable information about their chosen destination but also for a real understanding of the culture and workings of that destination. Now, when the internet can supply inexhaustible (but not always reliable) facts, our books marry text and pictures to provide those much more elusive qualities: knowledge and discernment. To achieve this, they rely heavily on the authority of locally based writers and photographers. *Insight Guide: Great Railway Journeys of Europe* conveys both an understanding of how various countries' railway systems developed and what their highlights are today:

How to use this book

◆ The **Features** section, indicated by a yellow bar at the top of each page, covers the historical development of Europe's railways and discusses some current concerns.
◆ The main **Journeys** section, with a blue bar, is a country-by-country review of the most interesting railway routes, including the most worthwhile places to visit en route.
◆ The **Travel Tips** listings section, with an orange bar, is a point of reference for information on travel, hotels, shops, restaurants and more.

The contributors

This book was co-ordinated by managing editor **Tom Le Bas** at Insight Guides' London office; Le Bas also wrote the journeys in Slovakia, Hungary and Poland as well as the

Berlin to Budapest route and the Palma–Sóller journey in Mallorca.

The task of advising on the scope of the coverage and selecting the routes to be included was achieved with the assistance of **Anthony Lambert**, an award-winning writer on railway travel and a committee member of the British Guild of Travel Writers. Lambert wrote and updated all the history and features chapters, the chapters on Switzerland and Germany, all of the Great Britain routes except those entirely in Scotland, the Corsica section and the two Norwegian routes. He also compiled the heritage listings for these countries and contributed many photographs.

The Ireland introduction and Dublin to Tralee journey were written by **David Lawrence**, who also provided the essay on Eating on Trains. **David**

Haydock, editor of several books and magazines on railways, helped update the book for 2009 and wrote all of the France chapter apart from Marseille–Nice, Pyrenean routes, and Corsica. Another award-winning member of the British Guild of Travel Writers, **Gary Buchanan**, provided the account of the classic Orient Express journey as well as the essays on the history of that "train of kings", and on the Royal Scotsman.

Robin McKelvie, also a Guild member, wrote the two Scottish routes as well as Paris–Moscow, Marseille–Nice and Venice–Zagreb. Long-time Insight regular **Marcus Brooke** contributed the entire Italy chapter, as well as many photographs.

Three Insight editors from the series' London editorial office also contributed: **Sylvia Suddes** wrote the Algeciras–Ronda and Madrid–Seville journeys, **Clare Griffiths** wrote the Helsinki–St Petersburg route, and **Martha Ellen Zenfell** wrote the Douro Valley route.

The Transcantábrico route was provided by **Peter Lemmey**. **Nick Inman**, a regular writer for Insight, contributed El Cremallera and Alicante–Dénia in the Spain section, as well as the French Pyrenean routes and Budapest–Istanbul. The Austria section was written by **Roland Beier**. **Donald Wilson** wrote the Inlandsbanan route in Sweden. The two Greek routes were contributed by **Zane Katsikis** and **John Wilcock**. The Travel Tips were compiled by **Jason Mitchell** and **Christina Park**.

Pam Barratt edited the text, and the book was proofread and indexed by **Penny Phenix**.

Map Legend

— ·· —	International Boundary
— — — —	Province Boundary
⊖	Border Crossing
—•—	National Park/Reserve
▬▬▬	Featured Rail Route
⓲	Tourist Information
♜ † ♰	Church/Ruins
†	Monastery
☾	Mosque
✡	Synagogue
♜ ⌂	Castle/Ruins
🛏	Mansion/Stately home
∴	Archaeological Site
⋒	Cave
𝚰	Statue/Monument
★	Place of Interest

The main places of interest in the Places section are coordinated by number with a full-colour map (e.g. ❶), and a symbol at the top of every right-hand page tells you where to find the map.

INSIGHT GUIDE

GREAT RAILWAY
JOURNEYS OF EUROPE

CONTENTS

Maps

European Railways	**76**
VSOE London–Venice	**82**
Paris/Amsterdam–Moscow	**89**
Great Britain and Ireland	**96**
West Highland Line	**98**
Shrewsbury–Swansea	**113**
Middlesbrough–Whitby	**116**
France	**128**
Southeast France	**133**
Eastern Pyrenees	**152**
Corsica	**154**
Spain and Portugal	**164**
Alicante–Dénia	**177**
Douro Valley	**181**
Switzerland	**188**
Italy	**218**
Verona–Innsbruck	**221**
Cagliari–Arbatax	**232**
Austria	**240**
Germany	**262**
Köln–Frankfurt–Trier–Giessen	**265**
Scandinavia	**290**
Bergen–Oslo	**293**
Helsinki–St Petersburg	**304**
North Central Europe	**312**
Venice–Zagreb	**315**
Routes from Dresden and Prague	**318**
Budapest–Istanbul	**333**
Southeast Europe	**335**
Peloponnese	**339**

Inside front cover:
European Railways; Regional Maps
Inside back cover:
European Railways; Featured
Route Maps

Introduction

European Rail Travel	**15**

History & Features

Decisive Dates	**18**
The Growth of Rail Travel	**21**
Engineering Feats	**35**
Station Architecture	**43**
The Pursuit of Speed	**51**
Heritage	**57**

Information panels

The Channel Tunnel	**41**
Railway Hotels	**49**
The Royal Scotsman	**100**
El Transcantábrico	**166**
Swiss Narrow Gauge Lines	**204**
The Sicilian Temple Route	**228**
The Train of Kings	**234**
Meals on Wheels	**258**
Scheduled Steam Trains in Poland	**326**

Railway Journeys

Introduction	**75**

Cross-Continental Routes	**79**
The Venice Simplon-Orient Express	**80**
Paris–Amsterdam–Berlin–Moscow	**87**

Great Britain and Ireland	**95**
The West Highland Line	**98**
Inverness–Kyle (Lochalsh)	**103**
London–Inverness–Wick	**105**
Settle–Carlisle	**109**
Shrewsbury–Swansea	**113**
Middlesbrough–Whitby	**115**
Irish Railways	**117**
Dublin–Tralee	**118**
Museums/Heritage Lines	**120**

France	**127**
Paris–Marseille by TGV	**130**
Clermont Ferrand–Nîmes	**132**
Béziers–Clermont Ferrand	**136**
Clermont–Brive–Aurillac	**138**
Marseille–Grenoble–Geneva	**140**

Travel Tips

European Rail Travel 348
Country by Country A-Z . . . 352
Further Reading 392

♦ Full Travel Tips index
is on page 347

Left: a TGV races through the
French countryside

Marseille–Nice–Monaco **142**
Nice–Digne **146**
Around Mont Blanc **149**
Routes in the French
 Pyrenees **151**
Corsica **154**
Museums/Heritage Lines **158**

Spain and Portugal **163**
Along the North Coast **165**
Algeciras–Ronda...................**171**
Seville–Madrid on the AVE.......**173**
El Cremallera **176**
Alicante–Dénia **177**
Mallorca: Palma–Sóller **178**
Portugal: the Douro Valley.....**179**
Museums/Heritage Lines **183**

Switzerland **187**
Geneva–Milan **189**
Zürich–Chiasso **192**
Zermatt–St Moritz on the
 Glacier Express.................**194**
St Moritz–Scuol–Tarasp.........**200**
St Moritz–Tirano **203**

Luzern–Interlaken
 (Jungfraujoch) **206**
Montreux–Zweisimmen–
 Lenk **210**
Museums/Heritage Lines **212**

Italy **217**
Verona–Innsbruck **219**
Nice–Rome **222**
Naples–Palermo **224**
Sardinia..............................**230**
Museums/Heritage Lines **235**

Austria **239**
Lindau–Innsbruck **241**
Innsbruck–Salzburg–Linz.......**245**
Vienna–Villach.....................**249**
Villach–Salzburg **253**
Museums/Heritage Lines **256**

Germany........................... **261**
Cologne–Frankfurt **263**
Trier–Koblenz–Giessen..........**267**
Harzer Schmals'bahnen........**270**
Innsbruck–Garmisch–Munich.**273**

Munich–Lindau.....................**279**
Dresden–Nürnberg–
 Frankfurt **282**
Museums/Heritage Lines **284**

Scandinavia....................... **289**
Bergen–Oslo **291**
Oslo–Bodø **294**
Sweden's Inlandsbanan.........**299**
Helsinki–St Petersburg **304**
Museums/Heritage Lines **307**

Other European Routes **311**
Venice–Zagreb **313**
Berlin–Budapest...................**317**
Routes from Budapest...........**320**
Slovakia: Zvolen–Kosice **321**
Slovakia: Kosice–Zilina **324**
Kraków–Zakopane **327**
Budapest–Istanbul.................**328**
Thessaloniki–Athens.............**336**
Around the Peloponnese **338**
Museums/Heritage Lines **342**

EUROPE'S BEST RAILWAY JOURNEYS

Europe's railways offer a huge variety of experiences to suit everyone, from tiny, narrow gauge steam locomotives chugging up mountains to sleek, efficient TGVs that glide through entire countries at ever-increasing speeds

CLASSIC JOURNEYS

Appreciate some of Europe's most dramatic scenery from the comfort of a railway carriage.

- **Settle–Carlisle**. Britain's most spectacular main line, through wild, hilly countryside with great walks from stations *(see page 110)*.
- **Seville–Madrid**. The dash across the southern *meseta*, Spain's central plateau, with its olive groves, ends in the splendid station of Atocha with its tropical garden *(see page 173)*.
- **Geneva–Milan**. The train is the best way to enjoy the northern shore and vineyards along Lake Geneva, special enough to be a World Heritage Site *(see page 189)*.

LUXURY TRAINS

- **The Royal Scotsman**. There's no more stylish way to see Scotland than a journey aboard this sumptuous train *(see page 100)*.
- **The Venice Simplon-Orient Express**. Its history, immaculate period carriages, outstanding food and perfectly delivered service make this the most romantic of trains *(see page 80)*.
- **The El Transcantábrico**. Luxury on the narrow gauge railway along the Bay of Biscay on Spain's northern coast *(see page 165)*.

LEFT: old-fashioned luxury on board the Royal Scotsman. **ABOVE AND RIGHT:** take in the wonderful views whilst dining in style on the Orient Express.

SCENIC BYWAYS

- **Shrewsbury–Swansea**. Linking a succession of spa towns, this line traverses some of Wales' finest landscapes *(see page 113)*.
- **Clermont Ferrand–Nîmes**. This meander through the Cévennes mountains and the valleys of the Massif Central called for impressive engineering works *(see page 132)*.

- **Trier–Koblenz–Giessen**. Both parts of this journey astride the Rhine follow rivers but the landscapes are very different *(see page 267)*.
- **Sweden's Inlandsbanan**. Few railways in Europe traverse such remote country as this seasonal line up the spine of the country *(see page 299)*.

ABOVE RIGHT: Mallorca's delightful narrow gauge railway line from Palma to Sóller.
BELOW RIGHT: the Glacier Express in Switzerland.

MOUNTAIN RAILWAYS

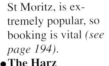

- **Le Train Jaune**. Yellow narrow gauge trains clatter across the hills of the Cerdagne with the mountains of the Pyrenees seldom out of sight *(see page 152)*.
- **The Glacier Express**. Europe's finest mountain railway journey, between Zermatt and

St Moritz, is extremely popular, so booking is vital *(see page 194)*.
- **The Harz Mountains**. The narrow gauge network that threads the historic landscapes of the Harz is one of the most characterful in Europe *(see page 270)*.

ISLAND RAILWAYS

- **Corsica**. An efficient metre gauge railway runs through spectacular mountains and valleys, and is the best way to see the island *(see page 154)*.
- **Mallorca**. The island has a developing and efficient railway system, but the most scenic journey

remains the link between the capital and Sóller *(see page 178)*.
- **Sardinia**. The astonishingly circuitous 4½ hour journey between Arbatax and Cagliari takes you through the tangled *macchia* and ancient woods of the Seulo Mountains *(see page 230)*.

PRACTICAL TIPS

Decide what sort of holiday you want, and whether the train services match your plans, before buying a pass or tickets. Train frequencies in rural France often require more careful planning than those in Switzerland, for example, where hourly services make rail travel perfect for walkers and cyclists.

If time is no object, secondary routes may be more interesting and scenic than a high-speed line.

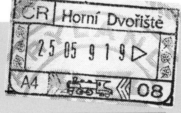

If you're freewheeling around Europe with an InterRail Pass, the Thomas Cook European Rail Timetable is indispensable.

Try to reserve seats at busy times on intercity routes, though this is unnecessary in some countries, such as Switzerland.

Overnight trains are usually cheaper than a hotel room and allow more time for sightseeing during the day. Book your bed well in advance on popular routes. Earplugs help induce sleep, but you may need a loud alarm call.

The opportunity to enjoy a three-course meal in a proper dining car is, regrettably, a rare pleasure *(see page 258)*; take it when you can! Book as early as possible, as places at tables are always in demand.

EUROPEAN RAIL TRAVEL

The magic of train travel lies in its ability to provide an endlessly changing procession of landscapes and cultures

"**D**ear Victoria, gateway to the world beyond England. How I love your continental platform, and how I love trains anyway. Snuffing up the sulphurous smell ecstatically, so different from the feint, aloof, distantly oily smell of a boat. But a train, a big snorting hurrying, companionable train with its big puffing engine, sending up clouds of steam and seeming to say impatiently, 'I've got to be off, I've got to be off, I've got to be off', is a friend."

This book is for those who can identify with these words of the writer Agatha Christie, or think they might be able to, given the chance. Of the various modes of travel, only sailing ships and the grand liners have rivalled the train in the affections of their users and the wider public. For a century and a quarter, their appeal was bound up with the atmosphere and character of the steam railway, which artists, composers and novelists sought to capture. Yet even today, with the romance of steam confined to heritage railways and the occasional forays of museum locomotives, railways continue to exercise an immense appeal.

Even at its most basic, in the utilitarian units of the suburban commute, the train remains the most civilised form of mechanised land transport, provided the supply of seats matches demand and the management is competent. The freedom train travel gives to work, read or stare out of the window with one's thoughts is, for millions each day, a welcome hiatus. As the playwright Stephen Poliakoff has said, one of the joys of train travel is the way the landscape rolls past the window like a film at the cinema.

For travellers intent on exploring and experiencing a country, train travel has its rewards. Robert Louis Stevenson said that the best way to see a country was from the window of a train. After all, what can you learn from the window of a plane? For Paul Theroux "A train isn't a vehicle. A train is part of a country. It's a place." Although European trains are not the mobile souks of a country such as India, they still offer the opportunity to meet people, and only the most reclusive of rail travellers are without their stories about people met and conversations enjoyed.

This book suggests some of the great European railway journeys and provides advice on the use of the railway networks, including the invaluable range of passes that make train travel both simpler and cheaper. Most of the journeys have been selected for the scenery that passengers enjoy, though some are included as important links between other journeys or as epic transcontinental migrations that call for a couple of nights' rest and recuperation at their end. Though air travel has whittled away the number of overnight trains, there

PRECEDING PAGES: a blur of speed; admiring the view on the Glacier Express; the Orient Express restaurant car. **LEFT:** crossing the Landwasser viaduct on the Chur to St Moritz line.

are still enough left to create that unrivalled sense of anticipation that accompanies the late evening departure of a long train of sleeping cars from beneath a dark vault of ironwork. By dawn it may have crossed several borders, and the passenger awakes to quite different landscapes and architecture, soon appreciated, one hopes, from a seat in the restaurant car for breakfast. Part of the magic of European rail travel is the variety of landscapes and cultures encountered in such a compact area. In just a few hours the train can have migrated from western affluence to eastern influences, from northern chill to southern warmth.

In travelling by train rather than plane or car, you are making a major contribution to minimising the environmental impact of travel. As tourism is growing faster than any other global industry, it is ever more important that less-polluting forms of transport are chosen by individuals and encouraged by governments if we take seriously the goal of sustainable tourism.

How we chose the journeys

The routes in the book have been chosen either for their scenic merit or because they are notable in other ways – for instance, the Paris–Marseille and Seville–Madrid high-speed lines are included because of the remarkable speed and smoothness of the journey. Others, such as Paris–Moscow, have to be considered "great" journeys for their romance and history. Obviously, this is a subjective exercise.

With such a huge number of routes to choose from, and with limited space, we have focused on regular, scheduled services that appear in national rail timetables (and the Thomas Cook European Timetable). In a few instances, other, privately operated, routes have been included; these vary from the five-star luxury of such famous "cruise trains" as the Venice Simplon-Orient Express and El Transcantábrico, to small mountain railways such as La Rhune in the French Pyrenees. Heritage railways, however, have not generally been described: selected listings of these, together with railway museums, can be found at the end of each "journeys" chapter.

Where possible, we have included journeys that can be completed in daylight hours, and without changing trains. The "Essentials" panel in the margin at the start of each route explains the journey times and other details, including a cross-reference to the Thomas Cook European Timetable, published monthly and an essential component of any European rail journey.

The decision was made to concentrate on the journeys themselves rather than the start and end points of the route. A brief list of essential sights has been included for the major cities where the routes begin or end or through which they pass. ❑

RIGHT: steam locomotive maintenance, King's Cross, 1931.

Decisive Dates

1758 First railway authorised by the British Parliament, from Middleton Colliery to Leeds.
1778 First railway built in France, at the mouth of the Loire.
1794 First use of flanged (wooden) rails, at Otaviga mines in Hungary.
1804 First locomotive successfully hauls load at Merthyr Tydfil, South Wales.
1812 Matthew Murray's engine begins work at Middleton Colliery in England.
1825 Stockton & Darlington Railway opened.

1827 First railway opened in Austro-Hungarian Empire, Linz–Budweiss (Ceske Budejovice).
1828 First public railway in France opened, St-Étienne–Andrézieux.
1829 Stephenson's *Rocket* achieves 46 km/h (29 mph) at the Rainhill trials in England.
1830 Canterbury & Whitstable Railway opened. Liverpool & Manchester Railway opened.
1834 First railway opened in Ireland, from Dublin to Kingstown (Dun Laoghaire).
1835 First railway in Belgium opened between Brussels and Malines. First railway in Germany opened, Nuremberg to Fürth.
1836 First London railway (Spa Road to Deptford). First railway in Russia opened, running from St

Petersburg through Tsarskoe Selo to Pavlovsk. World's first narrow gauge railway opened, Festiniog Railway, North Wales.
1838 Electric telegraph first used, on the Great Western Railway from London.
1839 First railway in Italy opened, from Naples to Portici.
1841 First Thomas Cook-organised excursion train.
1842 Queen Victoria's first railway journey. First major rail crash, when 48 died on the Versailles–Paris express.
1844 First railway in Switzerland opened, from Basel to St Louis. J.M.W. Turner paints *Rain, Steam and Speed, the Great Western Railway.*
1848 First railway opened in Spain, from Barcelona along the Costa Brava to Mataró.
1849 First railway opened in the Netherlands, running from Amsterdam to Haarlem.
1851 Moscow–St Petersburg line opened.
1854 First railway opened in Norway, between Christiana (Oslo) and Eidsvoll.
1855 The world's first special postal train travels between London and Bristol.
1856 First Portuguese railway opened, Lisbon to Carregado. First railways opened in Sweden, Gothenburg to Joosered and Malmö to Lund.
1862 William Frith paints *The Railway Station at London Paddington.*
1863 First underground railway opened, from Bishop's Road to Farringdon Street, London. Gas lighting introduced in carriages on North London Railway.
1869 First railway opened in Greece, between Athens and its port, Piræus.
1871 Europe's first rack railway opens in Switzerland, climbing to Rigi from Vitznau.
1874 First use of Pullman cars in Britain, on the Midland Railway. First Pullman car sleeping service in England, St Pancras to Bradford.
1878 First Tay Bridge opened.
1879 First run of dining car with kitchen in England, London King's Cross to Leeds. Collapse of first Tay Bridge. First practical electric railway, Berlin Trades Exhibition.
1882 Gotthard Tunnel opens, becoming the first railway link through the Alps.
1883 Britain's first public, electric railway opened, at Brighton. Orient Express introduced.
1886 Severn Tunnel opened in Britain.
1887 Second Tay Bridge opened in Scotland.
1890 Forth Bridge opened in Scotland. World's first underground electric railway opened, the City & South London.

1893 First elevated railway opened, in Liverpool.
1895 First film of moving train, shot by Louis Lumière at La Ciotat.
1898 Switzerland opens the world's first electric rack railway, between Zermatt and Gornergrat.
1900 First section of Paris Metro opened.
1904 *City of Truro* reaches 164 km/h (100.2 mph) (disputed).
1906 Simplon Tunnel opened.
1915 Britain's worst rail disaster, at Quintinshill, with 227 killed.
1921 German railways nationalised as Deutsche Reichsbahn.
1922 Grouping of Britain's railways into "Big Four".
1924 Arthur Honegger wrote symphonic movement, *Pacific 231*.
1926 *Golden Arrow (La Flèche d'Or)* introduced, London–Paris. Nationalised Société Nationale des Chemins de Fer Belges (SNCB) created.
1928 World's longest non-stop run inaugurated, London–Edinburgh 629 km (393 miles).
1932 *Flying Hamburger*, first high-speed diesel train, enters service, Berlin–Hamburg.
1934 Agatha Christie's *Murder on the Orient Express* published.
1938 World speed record for steam, 202 km/h (126 mph) by *Mallard*, England. Nationalised Société Nationale des Chemins de Fer Français (SNCF) created.
1939 World record set for diesel-electric traction in Germany, 213 km/h (133 mph).
1945 German railways split into Deutsche Reichsbahn (DR) in East Germany and Deutsche Bundesbahn (DB) West Germany.
1948 British Railways created, following nationalisation by the Labour government.
1950 Irish railways nationalised.
1951 World's first preserved railway reopened, Talyllyn Railway in Wales.
1955 World electric speed record set in France, 331 km/h (205.7 mph).
1968 British Rail withdraws standard gauge steam.
1976 Introduction of High Speed Trains (HSTs) capable of 200 km/h (125 mph), between London and Bristol/South Wales.
1981 First Ligne à Grande Vitesse (LGV), Paris–Lyon. New world speed record set in Germany, 406.9 km/h (252 mph).
1989 Inauguration of LGV Atlantique, Paris–Le Mans/Tours. New world speed record set in

France, TGV-Atlantique, 482.4 km/h (301.5 mph). Introduction of InterCity Express (ICE) trains.
1990 Introduction of X2000 trains in Sweden. New world speed record set in France, TGV-Atlantique, 513.3 km/h (319.5 mph).
1991 Introduction of ICE Hamburg–Munich trains.
1993 Start of TGV Nord services, Paris–Nord-Pas de Calais.
1994 Formal merger of DB and DR, reuniting German railways. Channel Tunnel opened, 6 May.
1996 Introduction of Thalys, Paris–Brussels.
2000 Øresund Bridge opened linking Denmark and Sweden, 1 July. Opening of the LGV Méditerranée, Valence–Avignon–Marseille.

2003 Opening of first stage of Channel Tunnel rail link in England.
2004 Madrid–Lleida high-speed line opens.
2005 Implementation of Bahn 2000 timetable in Switzerland.
2006 New Berlin Hauptbahnhof opens, Europe's largest multi-level railway station.
2007 World speed record set by TGV, at 574.8 km/h (359 mph), 3 April. LGV Est opens for Paris–Strasbourg/Basel TGV services, 10 June. Lötschberg Base Tunnel in Switzerland opens, 15 June. Full opening of Channel Tunnel Rail Link/HS1 into London St Pancras, 14 November.
2008 Madrid–Barcelona high-speed line inaugurated, 20 February. ❏

LEFT: Robert Stephenson, railway pioneer.
RIGHT: a Eurostar en route from London to Paris.

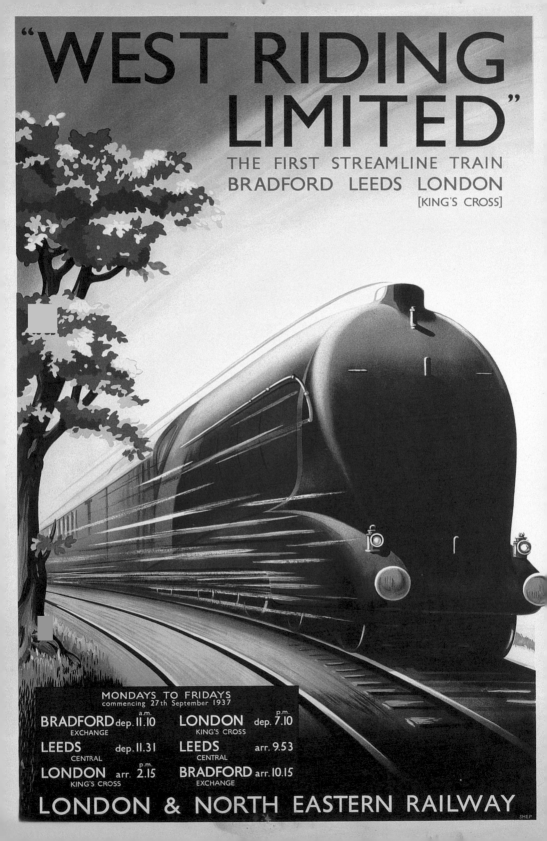

THE GROWTH OF RAIL TRAVEL

The impact of the railways was enormous. They opened the world to commerce, widened social perspectives and facilitated military campaigns

It is not often that the likely impact that an invention will have on the fabric of society is immediately apparent. The steam locomotive was one exception. Few in Britain who witnessed the opening of the Stockton & Darlington or Liverpool & Manchester railways can have been in much doubt that they were witnessing a turning point in world events. The same cannot be said even of the motor car: the Caledonian Railway of Scotland commissioned a photograph in the early 1900s showing its largest express engine dwarfing a car, ridiculing the pretensions of this flimsy conveyance.

The sense of an historical watershed was encouraged by the rapid development of this new form of locomotion. Writing in the late 19th century, the American Charles Francis Adams pointed out that "the great peculiarity of the locomotive engine, and its sequence, the railroad, was that it burst rather than stole or crept upon the world. Its advent was in the highest degree dramatic."

Immediate benefits

The hyperbolic rantings of some early sceptics, denouncing the very concept of railways as "a dupe of quackery", were soon made to look absurd by such simple and irrefutable evidence as a reduction in the price of coal in Leicester from 18 to 11 shillings a ton following the opening of the Leicester & Swannington Railway in 1832–33.

What is more, most people found railway travel agreeable: a friend of Sir Walter Scott wrote in 1838 that the speed of 28 mph (45 km/h) was attained so smoothly that he had "felt more dizzy when whirled along by four horses at the rate of ten or eleven miles in the hour". When Queen Victoria made her first railway journey, from Slough to London in June 1842, she described herself as "quite charmed".

LEFT: 1930s advertisement for the London North Eastern Railway (LNER).

RIGHT: Sankey viaduct, near Bury, 1831.

Reactions to the steam locomotive itself varied. Except for those who had worked in textile mills or watched a steam engine pumping water out of mines, no one had seen a machine on this scale, and certainly not one that moved or was so physically expressive of its purpose. The British radical MP John Bright

described his response to the first sight of a locomotive at Rochdale in 1839: "It was a new thing and I think the power, speed and the grandeur of these great locomotive engines can never grow old, and that we can never regard them without wonder and without admiration."

The children's author Beatrix Potter was enthralled by them: "To my mind there is scarcely a more splendid beast in the world than a large Locomotive… I cannot imagine a finer sight than the Express, with two engines, rushing down this incline [from Kingswood Tunnel to Dunkeld on the Highland Railway line]."

In contrast, the parish clerk of a Wiltshire clergyman was quite overcome when he was taken to witness the passage of a train on the newly opened Great Western Railway: "he fell prostrate on the bank-side as if he had been smitten by a thunderbolt! When he had recovered his feet, his brain still reeled, his tongue clove to the roof of his mouth, and he stood aghast, unutterable amazement stamped upon his face. It must have been quite five minutes before he could speak, and when he did it was in the tone of a Jeremiah. 'Well, Sir, that was a sight to have seen; but one I never care to see again! How much longer shall knowledge be allowed to go on increasing?' "

If that seems far-fetched, it should be remem-

Building the networks

The speed with which European rail networks were built reflects how quickly most governments, businessmen and entrepreneurs realised that this was an invention that would have a major impact on economic, social and political life throughout the world. At a local level, towns that rejected the chance to be on a mainline railway soon stagnated or atrophied, and manufacturers without easy access to a railway were soon at a severe commercial disadvantage. Most countries had varying periods of feverish railway construction, as well as the inevitable financial crises and scandals.

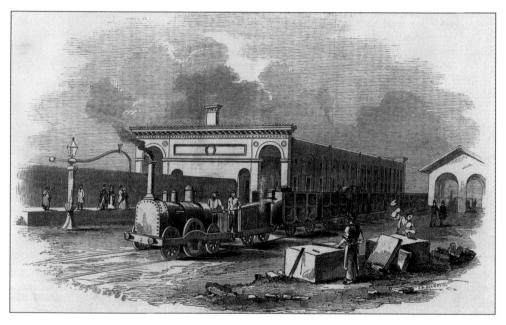

bered that when the first film of a moving train, shot by Louis Lumière at La Ciotat in southern France, was shown to the public in 1895, some people in the front row leapt to their feet in fear that they were about to be crushed.

But it was not just the locomotive that inspired awe. Over a century before Bright saw his first steam engine, the largest single-span bridge in Britain had been constructed across a remote burn in County Durham to carry a waggon-way linking a coal mine with the River Tyne. Opened in 1727, the Causey Arch was hailed as a feat comparable with the Via Appia; people came from far and wide to see it, and it was commemorated in published prints.

The approach adopted by governments towards the railway routes themselves varied enormously. At one extreme was Great Britain, with a *laissez-faire* policy in which competition was encouraged; at the other was the autocratic decision of Tsar Nicholas I to link Moscow and St Petersburg by a straight line, ignoring the needs of the historic towns of Torzhok, Valday and Novgorod, through which the railway could easily have been routed.

Prudent governments learned from the mistakes of others and adopted a more cautious approach. Leopold I of Belgium sought the advice of George and Robert Stephenson in devising a rational network. After some years of cantonal bickering, the Swiss government asked Robert Stephenson to plan a system. The French government came up with a Paris-focused network and the novel idea of building the infrastructure, including stations, and leaving private companies to lay the track and undertake all operations. Slow progress by these companies due to financial problems compelled the government to guarantee a minimum rate of return.

Europe understandably looked to Britain, the pioneer, for practical help – not only with

nationals of other European countries, most of which quickly developed the workshops and skills to build most of their own equipment.

ROMANCE OF STEAM

The great steam age was romanticised – and immortalised – by J.M.W. Turner's painting, *Rain, Steam and Speed*, in 1844.

Grand openings

The scale of most official openings reflected the importance attached to railway transport during the second half of the 19th and the early 20th century: they were an opportunity for a free ride, verbose speeches, sumptuous banquets and possibly the conferring of some awards if a monarch or prime minister was present.

planning, surveying, financing and building railways, but also with the provision of locomotives and other equipment. It was a measure of the standing in which British engineers were held that the Piedmontese were unwilling to buy shares in their own Turin–Novara railway until they heard that the Cheshire-born contractor Thomas Brassey had taken a large number of shares as part payment for the work.

But British engineers and contractors were soon joined, and gradually displaced, by

LEFT: an engraving of Cambridge station.
ABOVE: work in progress – laying new rails at London King's Cross, 1930.

If the drawings and lithographs of early French and Italian openings are to be believed, they eclipsed anything staged in Britain. For the celebrations in Nantes of the inauguration of the railway to Angers in 1852, pavilions fronted by classical columns were erected alongside the line and plinthed statues placed between the running lines along which four locomotives moved in parallel. There was more pomp at Strasbourg the same year: four locomotives were positioned before an immense dais with steps up to a canopied altar, so they could be blessed by the city's archbishop.

This trend reached its zenith with the 1862 opening of the first railway in the Papal States, between Rome and Velletri. Inclement weather kept the Pope away, but the train was blessed by his chaplain, the Archbishop Prince of Hohenlohe, surrounded by the prelates of the Apostolic Court, the musicians of the Sistine Chapel and regiments from Rome and France.

The distinguished guest list at these prestigious events was often international. When Thomas Brassey's railway between Cherbourg and Caen was opened, not only were Louis Napoleon and Empress Eugénie present, but

> ### A TRAGIC EVENT
>
> William Huskisson, President of the Board of Trade, was hit by a train and killed while officiating at the opening of the Liverpool–Manchester line in 1830.

so was Queen Victoria. The tradition continues for the few railway openings of major consequence: on 6 May 1994, Queen Elizabeth II and French President François Mitterand formally opened the Channel Tunnel.

The impact of the railways

The substantial reduction in transport costs brought about by railways had far-reaching consequences. Lower prices for all kinds of products combined with the opening up of new markets to increase the demand for manufactured goods. The commuter train removed the limits to urban growth, and rail links led to a major increase in trade between nations.

Railway construction also played a significant role in the 19th-century unification of disparate kingdoms and duchies into nation states – notably in Germany and Italy. Even in long-established countries, construction of the railway system engendered nationalist feelings. In Switzerland, for example, disapproval of the leading role of French and German financiers in Swiss railways led to strong public pressure for the system to be nationally controlled. The railways were nationalised in 1902 after a public referendum.

From the use the Prussians made of the railways in suppressing the uprisings of 1848 or the dispatch of 30,000 troops from Russia to Hungary the following year, it was evident that railways would play a major role in future conflicts. However, the Franco-Prussian War of 1870–71 emphasised the limitations: in speeding mobilisation, railways were only as efficient as the co-ordination between railway and military authorities, and this was often poor. Distribution from railheads was weak; and railways were susceptible to sabotage.

Inevitably, lines built for political rather than economic reasons were unprofitable, often barely able to cover their running costs. State guarantees to pay the interest on loans to fund construction were a common way of ensuring that marginal lines – intended to foster unity or encourage development of rural areas – were built. Many of the railways in the Balkans were planned for geo-political reasons.

Running on economic lines

Perhaps the major instance of state construction of railways for economic and social benefits took place in France, where over 20,000 km (12,500 miles) of minor lines were built as feeders to the principal routes under an act of 1880 embodying the Plan Freycinet. This incorporated a plan of desired secondary lines together with a poorly-devised financial framework under which they would be built and operated.

Many of the rural metre or narrow gauge networks – like those of other European countries – were routes of great character. Penetrating quiet corners of the French countryside, such railways had an immense impact on areas that had remained more or less unchanged for centuries. Suddenly there was more than a local market for produce, thanks to cheaper and faster transport to nearby towns. To meet the extra demand, better farm equipment and fertilisers were brought in by train.

While this cheaper "imported" equipment threatened the livelihood of local tool makers, new job opportunities were created by the ease with which villages and towns could be reached. This broadened social circles and offered the chance to look beyond the immediate community for employment. The range of goods in village shops increased, and daily newspapers broadened the focus of people's interest and concerns.

The growth of travel and tourism

The speed of train travel compared with that of a horse-drawn coach, coupled with the middle classes' ability to pay long-distance fares, opened up opportunities that would have been unthinkable to previous generations. As the Maine-born poet Edna St Vincent Millay put it:

My heart is warm with the friends I make,
And better friends I'll not be knowing,
Yet there isn't a train I wouldn't take
No matter where it's going.

Before the railways, most people scarcely travelled a day's walk from their birthplace, and the only ones who could visit other countries were the very rich on a Grand Tour, or men willing to risk the uncertainties of life as a sailor or soldier. The railway opened up unprecedented opportunities, although it was to be several decades before the middle classes started venturing abroad in large numbers; first came the day excursion.

Thomas Cook claimed to have run the "first public excursion train" (a special train at reduced fares) in England when he organised a temperance outing from Leicester to Loughborough in July 1841. In fact, such trains are almost as old as the railways, and the first instance is thought to have been an excursion on the Bodmin & Wenford Railway in June 1836. What is beyond question, however, is the impact of Cook's excursion, for he went on to arrange more special trains to further the cause of temperance, in which he passionately believed, gaining unrivalled experience in their

organisation. In the summer of 1845 he applied his knowledge to a commercial excursion, and produced for the journey the first in a long line of handbooks. These had a "threefold advantage – they excite interest in anticipation; they are highly useful on the spot; and they help to refresh the memory in after days".

Although Cook's first conducted tour to Scotland in the following year was something of a disaster, it "transformed me from a cheap Excursion conductor to a Tourist Organiser and Manager". After coming perilously close to bankruptcy, Cook recovered and went on to build up the business that remains a byword in

THE FLYING SCOTSMAN

One of the world's most famous trains, the Flying Scotsman, began the 393-mile (629-km) run between London King's Cross and Edinburgh in 1862. After dining cars were added in 1900 (previously the train had stopped for a 20-minute lunch break at York), the Scotsman's journey became the longest non-stop run in the world when even the break for a locomotive and/or crew change was eliminated in 1928 by the provision of corridor tenders, allowing a crew change on the move. In 1934 the train made the world's first 100-mph (160-km/h) run. The *Flying Scotsman* locomotive still runs today, under the auspices of its owner, the National Railway Museum.

LEFT: Gustave Eiffel, one of the great engineers.
RIGHT: Thomas Cook pioneered the railway excursion in the name of temperance.

tourism. It was a short-lived decision by Scottish railways in 1862 to stop issuing cheap tourist tickets that compelled Cook to expand his operations to the Continent, leading holidays to Paris and Switzerland the following year. By the end of the century, there were few places in Europe served by railways that Thomas Cook did not cover: in 1894 he added the "almost undiscovered country" of Herzegovina, and in 1899 the first group arrived in St Petersburg for a journey on the newly opened Trans-Siberian Railway to Vladivostok.

The event that made the railway excursion a part of British life was the Great Exhibition of

The earliest recorded works excursion was in 1840, when the marine and steam engine builder R & W Hawthorn of Newcastle chartered a train for its workers and their families to have a day in Carlisle. But it was the restorative air of the seaside that attracted most day-trippers, and works outings enabled many to see the sea for the first time. Sporting fixtures also generated good business: 82 special trains were run for the 1887 St Ledger Day race in Doncaster, for example.

The demand for tickets often exceeded expectations, requiring additional carriages and locomotives: an excursion to Brighton in 1844 ended

1851. People went to great lengths to save the money for a visit, and over 6 million admission tickets were sold. For many, it was their first long-distance train journey, and 165,000 of them travelled by Cook-organised excursions.

Holidays for all

Gradual reductions in working hours from the mid-19th century went hand-in-hand with the idea of the excursion train and a growing ability to pay the fares. In 1871 the British government created four bank holidays, and within a decade a week's holiday at the seaside was the goal of many families. Blackpool doubled in size in each decade between 1870 and 1900.

up with 60 carriages and six locomotives. Even scheduled holiday trains, like the Cornish Riviera Express, would sometimes run in several portions, so great was the demand for tickets.

By the final quarter of the 19th century, the middle classes were starting to venture abroad in considerable numbers, leading to unkind caricatures in satirical publications. As places were popularised by the middle class, aristocratic patrons moved to pastures new. By the beginning of the 20th century, tourism was becoming an international phenomenon – as indicated by the cosmopolitan guest list at popular resorts.

At Hotel Schreiber, on Mt Rigi in Switzerland, for example, on 8 August 1903, 237 people from 17 countries were staying: 72 Germans, 47 French, 30 Americans, 21 Russians, 12 Dutch, 11 Swiss, 10 Austrians, 9 Italians, 6 Belgians, 5 English, 4 Poles, 2 Egyptians, 2 Spanish, 2 from semi-independent Trieste, 2 Danes, 1 Brazilian and 1 Czech.

A different class of travel

The provision of three classes of carriage by the Liverpool & Manchester Railway set a pattern for rail travel around the world. Some made do with two; the Prussians offered a choice of four, with a special class for military use; and the Montpellier–Sète Railway in

before relief arrived in the form of mineral oil. Some French railways sold spectacles to protect the eyes of passengers travelling third class or in one of the curious, double-decker suburban carriages with open upper seats. The witty cartoons of French caricaturist Honoré Daumier are a testament to the tribulations of such travel.

Even when third-class passengers were afforded a roof and upper sides to carriages, they were denied a view because the use of expensive glass was restricted to a few tiny windows to provide light at a high level. But even this was an improvement on slow and uncomfortable coach travel, whose services

became redundant once a parallel railway line was opened for business.

France felt a need for five classes. As the surviving Bodmin & Wenford Railway carriages of 1834 in the National Railway Museum in York testify, passengers in third (or lower) class at first had to make do with roofless, open wagons, some without so much as a bench to sit on. Holes were drilled in the floor to act as drains. Besides the coal smuts and smoke, wind and rain, passengers would have to endure the stench of rendered animal fat or vegetable oil that was used as a lubricant for axle bearings,

For early first-class passengers, railway travel was far more agreeable. The skills of the stage-coach builders were developed to provide comfortably upholstered seats with arm- and head-rests. Yet it took many decades for passengers to receive the facilities now taken for granted: for much of the 19th century the only heating came from metal foot-warmers hired from stations; the absence of toilets spawned a variety of contraptions allowing people to relieve themselves with some decorum; and not until 1879 was it possible to eat in a restaurant car on a British train.

LEFT: LNER camping coaches came equipped with "every requisite for a camping holiday".
ABOVE: first-class carriage, 1838.

Railways were unwilling to add amenities that would increase the weight of trains, in turn requiring more powerful locomotives that burned more coal. They often had to be coerced by governments into raising standards.

In Europe the carriage divided by internal walls was quickly adopted as the usual layout, following construction of the first compartment carriage in 1834; during the 20th century many European railways began to move away from compartment stock.

RAILWAYS & ROYALTY

Most 19th-century monarchs had trains built specially for them. The first carriage designed for royalty was adapted for the Dowager Queen Adelaide by the London & Birmingham Railway in 1842.

port's interest was primarily in day saloons rather than the sleeping cars with which Pullman was associated, so when the first Pullman-car train on a revenue-earning journey in Europe left Bradford for London St Pancras on 1 June 1874, it comprised four carriages with a mixture of open saloons and compartments and a single sleeping car.

In the same month, the Pullman Palace Car Co., as the European subsidiary was entitled, signed the first contracts with railways in Italy. Although

Luxury carriages

George Mortimer Pullman, born in New York State in 1831, had a huge effect on the improvement of railway carriages. His train journeys, selling furniture made by his cabinet-maker brother, gave him the idea for carriages that would make travel by train a pleasure rather than an endurance. Although Pullman's carriages made his name synonymous with luxurious style and service, many contemporary accounts suggest that the reality was very different. Nonetheless, Pullman's ideas attracted the attention of a man who shared his objectives. James Allport, General Manager of the Midland Railway, met Pullman during a tour of America in 1872. All-

the Pullman company later provided carriages for such British trains as the Southern Belle and Harrogate Pullman, most of the opportunities in Europe were lost to a company founded by the other great name behind the development of luxury carriages, the Belgian Georges Nagelmackers.

Touring America, Nagelmackers was unimpressed by what the Pullman company offered, but was quick to see that the real value of their services was "through running". At that time, trains generally terminated at borders or at the end of a company's line, requiring frequent changes on long journeys. Nagelmackers believed that luxury-carriage services that crossed national and commercial boundaries would promote international travel. He would attach carriages to trains, railway companies would charge a normal fare in return for free haulage, and Nagelmackers would make money from a surcharge for use of his carriages.

Setbacks and opportunities

Plans to launch a Paris–Berlin train were stymied by the outbreak of the Franco-Prussian War in 1870, but Nagelmackers quickly seized the initiative and used his five new carriages for an Ostend–Brindisi service for Britons catching Peninsular & Oriental

Cenis Tunnel. Having built it, the French wanted to hold on to the revenue it generated.

Nagelmackers was in trouble. No one was willing to offer a route for the 10 carriages of his newly-registered Compagnie Internationale des Wagon-Lits et Grands Express Européens (CIWL). He was saved by the arrival in Britain from America of Colonel William Mann, with two boudoir cars, superior to Nagelmackers' carriages. The two men formed a partnership and gradually won business, helped by the fact that the Prince of Wales (later Edward VII) travelled in one of the cars to his brother's wedding in St Petersburg. In due course, Mann

Steamship vessels bound for Alexandria and Bombay through the newly opened Suez Canal. "The P&O Express" was such a success that Nagelmackers ordered five more carriages and, together with P&O, built a luxury hotel in Brindisi where passengers could await the boat in comfort.

As soon as the Franco-Prussian war ended, P&O abandoned Nagelmackers, after the French had refused to allow his coaches to use the much faster new route through the Mont

LEFT: Edward VII's sleeping car on the Royal Train.
ABOVE: *Ione*, one of the Pullman carriages used on the current Venice-Simplon Orient Express.

became homesick for America and sold out to Nagelmackers, leaving him to complete the rout of Pullman's European efforts and dominate luxury international train services.

The Orient Express

The most famous train created by CIWL was undoubtedly the Orient Express, which first ran on 4 October 1883 from Gare de Strasbourg (now Gare de l'Est) in Paris to Constantinople (Istanbul). The thickly-carpeted, gas-lit carriages were panelled in teak, walnut and mahogany and decorated with Gobelins tapestries. Passengers sat on leather upholstery, slept in silk sheets, ate with silver cutlery and drank out of crystal glasses. On the first run, brass bands greeted the train at intermediate stations, and after Bucharest the King of Romania invited the passengers to break the journey at his new summer palace.

Other long-distance or international trains followed: by 1914 CIWL had 32 luxury trains in service. None, however, captured the public imagination like the Orient Express, helped by the many novels and, later, films which used it as a setting. For more on the history of the Orient Express, *see page 238.*

For more on the history of the Orient Express, *see page 238.*

> ## JOY RIDER
>
> King Boris III of Bulgaria not only loved riding on the Orient Express but also used his regal prerogative to take over as driver and run it at full throttle while travelling through his realm.

more than seven boxes and five small parcels for the longest journey". The 3rd Duke of Sutherland had an entire train when he migrated between his Staffordshire and Highland homes.

Another reason for several luggage vans on international trains was that those who could afford to travel to other countries often did so for much longer than a fortnight's holiday, partly of course because it took them longer to get there. Families would often stay for months on end, like the characters

Portmanteaus and parasols

Travelling light is a necessity imposed by air travel. Until habits began to change, or standards fall, depending on your point of view, it would have been unthinkable for men to have appeared for dinner at a smart hotel in anything less than a suit. For women, a different dress and hat for each day was *de rigeur.* Cartoonists, and paintings such as Frith's *The Railway Station,* give some idea of the huge quantities of luggage with which people travelled.

The 1859 *Official Guide to the London & North Western Railway* advised that travellers should "take as little luggage as possible; and ladies are earnestly entreated not to indulge in

in some of Thomas Mann's novels and short stories, bringing with them governesses or nannies to look after the children. Noël Coward was particularly fond of long trans-continental railway journeys, and when he set off for the Far East in 1929, he took 27 pieces of luggage and a gramophone.

The golden age

For those with the wherewithal to pay for the best, the quality of carriages and service on the Trains de Luxe from the late 19th century to the outbreak of World War II has never been surpassed. Between the wars, the railway companies introduced many new amenities:

telephones and secretarial services on some German trains; a hairdressing salon on the Flying Scotsman; chromium-finished cocktail bars; observation saloons with armchairs.

More routes were added beyond the borders of Europe, making possible comfortable rail travel to the Middle East and Asia. The Simplon-Orient Express offered connections with the newly introduced Anatolia and Taurus expresses, so that from Paris one could reach Baghdad in 6½ days, Tehran in 8 and Karachi in 12. International sleeping and dining cars continued to be operated mostly by CIWL, although Germany had its own operating company, Mitropa.

d'Azur. This had through coaches for Interlaken, Bucharest, Vienna and Constantinople, which were attached to other expresses at Paris, although in summer there were enough passengers to justify a direct train, avoiding Paris and stopping only for locomotive changes. In 1936 the Night Ferry, composed of specially-built Wagons-Lits coaches, made its first journey between London Victoria and Gare du Nord in Paris via the Dover–Dunkerque rail ferry.

The pioneering work by Swiss and Italian railway engineers on the use of electric traction before World War I was expanded into progressive electrification schemes in most

Many of the most famous trains were introduced between the wars. The well-known La Flèche d'Or between Calais Maritime and Paris began operation in 1926; it was made up entirely of Wagon-Lits Pullmans and covered the 294 km (184 miles) in 190 minutes. The English Pullman equivalent between Dover and London Victoria, also known as the Golden Arrow, began in 1929. Another train from Calais was the equally famous Train Bleu, a colloquial term for the all-blue stock of the train that served the Côte

European countries, and diesel traction, too, was developed. Germany's *Flying Hamburger* became one of the best-known examples of the latter, the two-car articulated unit averaging 124 km/h (77 mph) over the 285 km (178 miles) between Berlin and Hamburg.

War and decline

The railways had suffered during World War I but the damage inflicted during World War II was even greater and more widespread. Some lines were so badly damaged that they never reopened. As happened after 1918, large numbers of army lorries were sold off, giving a boost to road haulage at the expense of the

LEFT: the *Mallard*, the world's fastest steam locomotive, departs for Scarborough and Hull.
ABOVE: heritage charter train.

railways. The rapid growth of the car industry also helped to foster the idea that the age of the railways was over.

By the 1930s wealthy, long-distance travellers were starting to go by plane. For three decades the railways fought a losing battle. The road lobby had become much more influential and some politicians stood to benefit financially from the decline of the railways.

The mostly nationalised railways did what they could to modernise with the funds granted them, but motorway and road building received a higher priority. Gradually the classic names of rail expresses began to disappear. Throughout

Europe, steam traction was being replaced by electrics and diesels. Few countries executed the process with greater haste or waste than Britain, where locomotives with only eight years' working life were sent for scrap (it was not unusual for steam locomotives on the Continent to become centenarians, although 40–50 years was more usual).

The demise of steam was heralded by British Railways' 1955 Modernisation Plan, outlining a major electrification programme supplemented by diesels. Dozens of untried diesel designs were ordered, some proving so disastrous that they survived for less than five years. In 1963, Dr Beeching produced his infamous

plan, ordered by a government that clearly saw road transport as an evolutionary successor to railways. The plan envisaged widespread closures of rural and duplicated railways, including – with customary myopia – the only north–south main line built to accept continental-sized rolling stock. The electrification programme was scaled back to keep the diesel fleet occupied, and between January 1963 and December 1968, the steam locomotive fleet went from 8,767 to three, and British track mileage fell from 47,543 miles (76,068 km) to 33,976 miles (54,361 km).

The shock of the 1973 oil crisis, coupled with growing concern about the damage to health and to the planet from pollution, prompted a review of transport thinking. With new roads becoming badly congested almost as soon as they were built, it became obvious that greater mobility did not mean greater accessibility. It was time to rethink the role of the railways.

The renaissance of rail

Few inventions enjoy a second life, but the congestion and pollution produced by road vehicles have prompted a re-evaluation of the role of rail transport. Central to this change of thinking has been a realisation that it is impossible to build a way out of congestion. US cities such as Los Angeles have failed to reduce congestion however much land and money are thrown at road building, and the result has been air quality so bad that on some days children and the elderly are advised to stay indoors.

Consequently, forward-thinking cities have revived or built tram (or light rail) networks, and high-speed railways are helping to reduce long-distance car travel as well as relieving pressure on airports by eliminating the need for internal flights – very few have operated between Paris and Lyon since the opening of France's first Ligne à Grand Vitesse in 1981.

The high-speed trains that run on these routes are not as luxurious as the grand expresses of the inter-war years, but they are nonetheless smooth and comfortable. A higher proportion of transport investment by national governments and the European Commission is now being directed at railways, helping to raise standards of comfort and operational reliability. ❏

LEFT: shelter from the Blitz in the London underground.
RIGHT: looking north on the Forth Bridge.

ENGINEERING FEATS

The building of the railways required extraordinary feats of engineering – viaducts, tunnels and bridges that allowed the tracks to surmount all obstacles

Railway engineering was the wonder of the 19th century. Canals had produced some outstanding aqueducts and tunnels, but because barges were used almost entirely for freight traffic, few people were aware of such achievements as Pontcysyllte Aqueduct in Wales or the 17th-century Canal du Midi in southern France, linking the Mediterranean to the Atlantic. Passenger trains enabled people to see for themselves the magnificent structures that were soon the subject of paintings, aquatints, lithographs and engravings, reproduced by such publications as the *Illustrated London News* as well as national and local newspapers.

Impressing the famous

It was as much the civil as the mechanical engineering that impressed the actress Fanny Burney when she accompanied George Stephenson on the footplate of the *Northumbrian* for a journey along the Liverpool & Manchester Railway: "You can't imagine how strange it seemed to be journeying on thus, without any visible cause of progress other than the magical machine, with its flying white breath and rhythmical, unvarying pace, between these rocky walls, which are already clothed with moss and ferns and grasses; and when I reflected that these great masses of stone had been cut asunder to allow our passage thus far below the surface of the earth, I felt that no fairy tale was ever half so wonderful as what I saw. Bridges were thrown from side to side across the top of these cliffs, and the people looking down upon us from them seemed like pigmies standing in the sky."

Admiration for the achievements of leading civil engineers gave the profession a new standing. Portraits were commissioned and honours were bestowed on the most successful. This esteem was reflected in the willingness of royalty to open new railways or bridges. Queen Victoria was in Newcastle two years running

for such occasions: to open Robert Stephenson's High Level Bridge in 1849, and the magnificent Central Station a year later.

The need for extensive civil engineering works was due to the limited ability of the adhesion steam locomotive to climb gradients. Anything steeper than 1 in 40–50 would require

a banking or pilot engine, and a gradient of 1 in 100 – the stipulation for the Settle & Carlisle railway – was considered an ideal maximum. Standard gauge railways cannot follow the contours of hills in the way canals do, and engineers realised that speeds would soon increase, making gentle curves even more important. Consequently, railways required earthworks on a scale far exceeding anything in the canal age.

Building the formation

For most of the 19th century, mechanical aids to railway construction were limited. The majority of railways were built using picks, shovels and wheelbarrows wielded by vast

LEFT: the construction of the Channel Tunnel took six years and billions of pounds.
RIGHT: Isambard Kingdom Brunel.

armies of itinerant workers, nicknamed navvies after the canal-building "navigators" of the 18th century. Living in basic, temporary accommodation thrown up by contractors, often in shanty towns miles from the nearest settlement, navvies soon developed a reputation for hard drinking and violence. The fear they instilled in local residents was generally unjustified, but there were occasional riots that required military as well as police force to quell.

Apart from bridges and tunnels, the two basic elements of a railway were the cutting and the embankment. Wherever possible, the spoil from the former was moved via a rudimentary

line built by Thomas Brassey. The cuttings attracted many Frenchmen, one of whom was heard to exclaim: *"Mon Dieu! les Anglais, comme ils travaillent!"* The use of a foreign workforce was a continuing feature of railway construction: many of Switzerland's railways relied heavily on Italian labour.

Viaducts and bridges

The early railway engineers could draw on the experience of road bridges and canal aqueducts for the railways. What was remarkable was the proliferation of designs using the basic materials of stone, brick, iron and wood in

waggon-way to create the latter, but where no embankment was needed the spoil was removed by barrow runs. These were crude wooden inclines up the cutting sides to allow spoil to be spread on surrounding land. Haulage was usually by means of a horse-pulled rope mounted over a pulley at the top of the embankment; a man at the rear of the barrow steered it up the boards. It was dangerous work, as both horses and men sometimes slipped in muddy conditions; if the barrow fell on the same side as the navvy, he could easily be injured.

British navvies had a reputation for hard work, and they were sometimes employed on early continental railways, such as the Paris–Rouen

varying combinations, usually determined by the location of the structure and the availability of materials. Provided good stone and mortar are used, such structures are probably the most durable, requiring little maintenance. Wooden structures were cheap and quick to build, and there are still a few major ones in use, such as the 830-yard (759-metre) Barmouth Bridge across the Mawddach Estuary in Wales.

The study of metallurgy was still in its infancy, and some limitations were discovered the hard way: the problems of cast iron were tragically highlighted in 1847 when Robert Stephenson's skew bridge across the River Dee at Chester collapsed as a train was crossing, with the loss of five lives. The use of cast iron in spans of over 33 yards (30 metres) was blamed. Insufficient allowance for the effect of wind, coupled with shoddy workmanship, was held responsible for one of the most tragic railway disasters, when all 13 of the high girders of Scotland's Tay Bridge fell into the water during a storm in 1879, taking a train and 75 lives with it. Its designer, Thomas Booch, had failed to address the problem of vertical cracks in the wrought-iron piers. He merely bound them with hoops rather than cur-

ENDLESS LABOUR

The expression "It's like painting the Forth Bridge" has entered the English language as a way of describing any interminable task.

beautifully situated, 13-arch Knucklas Viaduct in Wales is a classic example of the way railway companies were happy to spend money on decoration. The crenellated parapet is supported by corbels and at each corner of the viaduct is a semi-circular castellated turret with arrow slits. Other examples include the lattice girder bridges over the River Kinsig at Offenburg, north of Freiburg in Germany, and the crossing of the Garonne at Bordeaux, both approached by turreted, crenellated gateways with neo-Gothic arches.

ing the cause – the pressure exerted on the cylinders by the Portland cement with which he had filled them.

Aesthetic requirements

Most engineers intended their structures to make a positive contribution to the landscape through the use of sympathetic materials, elegant design or embellishment. Sometimes the last was forced on the company by conditions attached to the sale of land. The

LEFT: dismantling a gantry at Waterloo in London to make way for a new electric signal box, 1936.
ABOVE: Britannia Bridge, linking Anglesey with Wales.

A bridge that relies entirely on its form is the graceful, cantilever and lattice-girder Forth Bridge across the Firth of Forth in Scotland. Opened in 1890, the bridge was one of the first major structures to use steel rather than wrought iron; over 50,000 tons of steel held together by 8 million rivets were used on the 2,766-yard (2,529-metre) long bridge. This was the world's largest cantilever bridge until 1917 when it was overtaken by the Quebec Bridge in Canada. For a century, until Railtrack altered the maintenance arrangements, the task of keeping the steelwork protected from the elements required a full-time team of 29 painters (see box above).

Some record holders

One of the most famous steel viaducts in the world is the Garabit Viaduct designed by Gustave Eiffel over the River Truyère on the scenic line between Béziers and Neussargues *(see page 137)*. Opened in 1884, it has the seventh-highest arch in the world at 112 metres (122 yds) and is now painted in a surprising shade of pink. For 67 years France had the highest railway bridge in the world: Fades Viaduct, across the Sioule River in the Puy-de-Dôme on the railway between Clermont-Ferrand and Montluçon via Volvic, has four unequal spans on masonry piers at a maximum height of 132.5

RACK RAILWAYS

The ability of trains to climb steep gradients varies according to the type of traction – electric traction can cope with steeper gradients than steam locomotives – the nature of the railway and the radius of curves. To allow trains to climb mountains, various engineers have developed an original idea of John Blenkinsop, superintendent of Middleton Colliery near Leeds, for a cog mounted on the engine to engage a toothed rail. Blenkinsop's toothed rail was positioned outside the two running rails, whereas all subsequent systems have had the rack rail placed centrally between them. Most rack systems have been the work of Swiss engineers.

metres (145 yds). It was built between 1901 and 1909. This record was held until 1976 when Serbia's five-span Mala Rijeka Viaduct opened, eclipsing the Fades Viaduct by almost 50 percent, at 198 metres (216 yds).

One of the most complex bridge types is the swing bridge, which allows shipping to pass "through" a bridge where there would otherwise be insufficient height. One of the largest in Europe is the Caronte Bridge across the Marseille–Rhône canal just to the west of Marseille.

The title for Europe's longest railway bridge (with road deck above) passed to the Øresund Bridge linking Denmark and Sweden on its opening on 1 July 2000. In addition to the 7,243 metres (7,921 yds) of the bridge is a 4,055-metre (4,435-yd) artificial island created from the spoil produced by boring a 3,510-metre (3,839-yd) tunnel at the western (Danish) end.

The Alpine tunnels

The Alps were the greatest challenge to Europe's railway engineers. Tunnels were needed, but the sheer height of the mountains made it impossible to adopt the usual tunnelling methods, whereby the sinking of a number of shafts would enable headings (tunnelling faces) to be established at several points in addition to those at each end. Spoil could be taken up, and equipment and lining materials lowered down the shafts, which would finally be lined to act as ventilation shafts. This greatly increased the speed of boring, as well as making train operation in steam days less smoky.

The principal drawback of working without intermediate shafts was that it reduced the engineers' knowledge of the rock strata that were likely to be encountered. There was no knowing where poor rock might be met, leading to rock falls that could crush the tunnel workings, or where an explosive charge might release a torrent of underground water. Second, there was greater room for error in making sure the two workings met in the middle. Yet so skilled did the engineers become that the two centre lines of the 14.6-km (9.1-mile) Lötschberg Tunnel met with an error of just 25.7 cm (10 in) horizontally and 10.2 cm (4 in) vertically.

Although it was the Swiss who inevitably gained the most experience in tunnelling, with a greater percentage of its route kilometres in tunnel than any other country, it was a tunnel between France and Italy that first penetrated the Alps. Construction of the Mont Cenis Tunnel took 14 years (1857–71). The 13.6-km (8.8-mile) bore was built by Thomas Brassey, but much credit must go to his agent, Thomas Bartlett, who improved a pneumatic drill designed by Germain Sommeiller, driven by water-powered compressors that hammered the rock face at 300 strokes a minute. The compressed air helped ventilate the torrid workings.

The first link between Italy and central Europe was provided by the 14.99-km (9½-mile) Gotthard Tunnel, which began immediately to the south of Göschenen station. For almost eight years, from June 1872, labourers

when a drill of the southern section suddenly shot through into empty space. The sounds of the other team's workings had been heard for two months, so they were prepared for this moment. The section engineer on the southern side handed through the tiny opening a tin box containing a photograph of Favre – the "*Capo*" or boss, who was always meant to be the first to pass through the tunnel.

The human cost

The human cost of tunnel boring was huge. On the Gotthard, deaths caused by accidents averaged about 25 a year, with casualties in the

drawn mostly from northern Italy toiled night and day with compressed-air rock drills and explosives to meet the punishing schedule agreed by the engineer, Louis Favre.

Accepting severe penalties in the event of failure, he committed himself to having the tunnel open in eight years; it took 10, but by that time Louis Favre was resting in the graveyard by Göshenen church, having died of a heart attack in the tunnel workings in 1879, aged 53.

With teams naturally working from both ends, the breakthrough came in February 1880,

LEFT: rack railway at Pilatus, Switzerland.
ABOVE: a stiff climb up Schynige Platte, Switzerland.

hundreds. Even if workers emerged externally unscathed, they might have contracted one of the illnesses that stem from breathing rock dust, explosive fumes and stale air.

The two single-bore Simplon tunnels were the second major Swiss Alpine tunnels to be built, the first between 1898 and 1906, the second brought into use in 1921. Tunnellers worked in extreme discomfort: 8 km (5 miles) from the north portal of the Simplon Tunnel, the temperature was 52.8°C (127°F). When additional fans proved ineffective in reducing the temperature, engineers resorted to spraying ice-cold water around the rock face. To allow flexible train working when repairs were required, the two tunnels were enlarged at the midway point into a large, single chamber with crossovers between tracks. Until around 1960, when remote control from Brig was set up, the signal box at this extraordinary location deep in the mountain was manned 24 hours a day.

The Lötschberg Tunnel

Last of the major tunnels to be built, and the most difficult, was the Lötschberg Tunnel between Kandersteg and Goppenstein on the line between Spiez and Brig in the Bernese Oberland. Boring began in 1906 using about 4,000, mostly Italian workers, housed in huge camps at each end. The southern work camp was buried by an avalanche one February night in 1908, killing 12 men, but worse was to come inside the tunnel workings. The engineers were confident that with at least 183 metres (200 yds) between the tunnel and the floor of a valley under which they were tunnelling, they would meet nothing but rock. However, on 24 July 1908, a charge was detonated which released so much glacial debris and water into the workings that 1,554 metres (1,700 yds) of the tunnel were filled, killing 25 workers.

After months of trial borings and discussion it was agreed that there was no alternative but to

EUROPE'S HIGHEST AND WIDEST

● The world's highest railway bridge, at 198 metres (216 yds/650 ft), spans Serbia's Mala Rijeka gorge near Kolašin on the scenic line between Belgrade and the Adriatic coast at Bar, in Montenegro.
● The world's greatest span is on the Salzburg–Villach line in Austria. The Pfaffenberg–Zwenberg Bridge has a concrete arch span of 200 metres (219 yds).
● The world's longest brick viaduct, on the London & Greenwich Railway, was opened in 1836. The 878 arches stretched for 6 km (3¾ miles) and used 60 million bricks.
● The highest masonry bridge in Europe is near Corte on Corsica, at 100 metres (109 yds/328 ft).

block off the affected section and all the inundated equipment with a wall 10 metres (33 ft) thick, and divert the tunnel to the east. The two bores met in March 1911, and the tunnel was opened to traffic in 1913, creating one of Europe's last, and most spectacular, main arteries.

The Austrian Alps are penetrated by a shorter tunnel, although it is still the third-longest in Europe: the Arlberg Tunnel, which opened in 1884 and is 10.25 km (6⅓ miles) long, was built for traffic between France and Austria via Switzerland and lies on the impressive line between Bludenz and Innsbruck. ❑

ABOVE: the Eurostar terminal at London St Pancras.

The Channel Tunnel

The first recorded suggestion of a tunnel under the English Channel was made in 1802 by a French mining engineer, who envisaged tunnels linking the shores, with a central island where horses would be changed. For over 20 years from the 1830s, another French engineer, Aimé Thomé de Gramond, studied the geology of the Channel, but, even with the backing of the successful English civil engineer Sir John Hawkshaw, nothing came of his proposals.

The first official agreement between the British and French governments over the idea was signed in 1875, and in 1881 the visionary railway manager Sir Edward Watkin initiated work through the Anglo-French Submarine Railway Company. Before British military authorities got the jitters the following year and persuaded parliament to cancel the project, a total of 4 km (2½ miles) had been excavated from Shakespeare Cliff and at Sangatte in the Pas de Calais. Work was not to resume for almost a century: in 1973, trial borings began, but two years later the recently-elected Labour government again stopped work at the moment the first boring machine was ready.

The scheme was revived under Margaret Thatcher, and after a tendering process Eurotunnel emerged as the successful consortium. Construction work commenced soon after the Channel Tunnel Act was passed in July 1987. Boring began in February 1988 to create two parallel rail tunnels and between them a smaller service tunnel.

Underwater tunnels pose particular difficulties because of the steep gradients needed at each end to take the track well below the floor of the water, and because of the need for pumping if there is an ingress of water. With these and other obstacles to contend with, and in common with so many major civil engineering projects, costs for the Channel Tunnel soon escalated way beyond the estimates, leading to acrimonious disagreements between the contractors and Eurotunnel. The strain on Eurotunnel's financing was immense, and it was a great achievement of co-Chairman, Sir Alastair Morton, that the consortium of banks was held together, not only during construction but through the difficult first few years before operations made a profit.

RIGHT: at times it seemed as if the project would never be completed.

The tunnel finally opened in May 1994, well behind schedule. Almost inevitably, things got off to a bad start when a train full of journalists got stuck mid-tunnel. There were various operational difficulties and a serious fire in 1996, though without loss of life. But soon the system was running smoothly. For the first time it was possible to travel from the UK into Europe quickly and comfortably without having to suffer the tedious travails of air travel; Paris was now just 3 hours from London, Brussels 2 hours 40 minutes. With further journey time reductions, the train has become the obvious choice, reducing the demand for air services between these cities.

The 49.4-km (30¾-mile) tunnel is used by three different types of train: passenger-carrying Eurostars between London St Pancras and Paris/Lille/Brussels; Eurotunnel's shuttle trains carrying cars and lorries; and through rail freight services. Through passenger trains are also operated from London to Disneyland Paris and to Bourg-St-Maurice during the skiing season.

The high-speed line linking Paris and the tunnel was ready for the 1994 opening; on the British side work had not even begun. Only in 2003 was the first stage of the Channel Tunnel rail link opened. Its full opening in late 2007 allowed journey times between the capitals of 2 hours 20 minutes at speeds of 300 km/h (186 mph). ❏

STATION ARCHITECTURE

So imposing were many Victorian stations that they were called "Cathedrals of Steam". Some have been preserved and adapted for innovative purposes

The advent of railways produced a whole new area of work for architects. In contrast to canals, where nothing more innovative was required than lock-keepers' cottages and warehouses, railways called for an entirely new range of buildings. Stations, goods sheds, locomotive depots, carriage sheds, signal-boxes and water towers were all unprecedented types of structure.

With so many hundreds of thousands of examples, it is hardly surprising that quality varies enormously, ranging from some of the finest buildings of any kind in the urban landscape to some that are little more than ersatz bus shelters. Most countries have a rich variety of well-designed station buildings that add enormously to the pleasure of railway travel.

The principal reason for this diversity is that, for the most part, railways were built and maintained by private companies, before amalgamation reduced their numbers or nationalisation brought state ownership. Inevitably, most effort and money went into station buildings, but even some of the more utilitarian structures were embellished with decorative details. Many buildings were standardised, none more so than minor station buildings in France, where a station in Normandy looks much the same as one in Corsica.

Adapting and harmonising

As the new railway transport system required buildings with a whole set of new requirements, it was seldom feasible to adapt existing buildings. There are very few examples of railway stations occupying adapted structures, but a few stand out. Britain's impecunious Eastern Counties Railway adapted a Georgian mansion for its station at Enfield in 1849, and the Great Northern Railway devised the grandest residence for its stationmaster at Bourne, in Lincolnshire, by converting the early 17th-

LEFT: ornate touches at Antwerp station.
RIGHT: Brunel's roof supported by slender columns at London's Paddington station.

century Red House, also used as a ticket office. In Switzerland, a Graubünden chalet of 1720 became the station of Celerina Staz.

Some railway companies were conscious of their responsibilities to an historic town and tried to harmonise their station buildings with the prevailing style or materials. Others adopted

standard designs and brought in bricks of a different hue from those made by the local works, or used brick where stone predominated. But most railways used an eclectic mix of styles for their stations that reflected both local circumstances and the preferences of the architect and, occasionally, the client. Ghent St-Pierre was built to reflect the medieval architecture of the Belgian town, while the neo-Gothic of Battle station in Sussex echoes nearby Battle Abbey. In important cities and towns, railway companies often went to great lengths to create a building that would engender civic pride, as well as reassure those wary of rail travel by the solidity of their buildings.

Creating the right impression

The first company to lavish money on buildings to impress and inspire confidence was the London & Birmingham Railway. Its stations at each end of the line were "to the modern city what the city gate was to the ancient city" to quote Carroll Meeks. At Euston, a massive Doric portico was erected as the entrance; when built in 1837 its columns were the tallest in London. Both this and the Ionic-columned equivalent at Curzon Street in Birmingham were designed by Philip Hardwick, who later worked with his son on the equally magnificent Great Hall and Shareholders' and Direc-

roof (a fourth was added in 1916) look as impressive today as they did on their completion in 1854. They are helped by the unusual transepts that were created for long-discarded operating practices. The Moorish decorative scheme was devised by Matthew Digby Wyatt.

The outstanding London terminus, however, is newly restored St Pancras, on account of the immense Gothic-Revival hotel and station designed by Sir Gilbert Scott, and the great train shed roof by W.H. Barlow. The two exemplify the 19th-century contrast between the atavism of station façades and the cutting-edge technology employed to build the monumental coverings of

tors' rooms at Euston. The application of classical architectural precepts to station design set a pattern in which earlier styles were used to mask the functionality of the station.

With his customary attention to detail, the engineer of the Great Western Railway, Isambard Kingdom Brunel (1806–59), designed many of the railway buildings between London, Bristol and the West Country. Tudor styling was applied to his masterpiece, the station and train shed at Bristol Temple Meads, which opened in 1841, with a magnificent hammer-beam roof reminiscent of Westminster Hall.

The second station at Paddington is another of Brunel's triumphs. The three spans of his

platforms and trains. The immense cast-iron ribs of the train shed were made by the Butterley Iron Company in Derbyshire and extend far below the platforms. They meet to form a depressed Gothic arch 36½ yds (33.5 metres) above the platforms.

Beneath the platforms, in the once dark undercroft, barrels of Burton beer were stored, and Barlow had to design it to accommodate the maximum number of barrels. Few stations have been designed using a barrel of beer as the unit of measurement.

Today St Pancras receives Eurostars after their sprint from the Channel Tunnel over the new high-speed line, and the long-empty rooms and corridors of the Midland Grand Hotel are being returned to life. The building is being restored to use as a hotel and for flats, which calls for sensitive design in a Grade I listed building.

Parisian greats

Of Paris's outstanding terminals, the Gare St-Lazare is the largest, with 27 platforms. The station will always be associated with the series of 12 paintings commissioned from Claude Monet in 1877. The novelist Emile Zola praised them as "terrific views of railway stations. You can hear the trains rumbling in, see the smoke billow up under the huge roofs". The Gare du Nord was reconstructed in 1889 to produce the

Political statements

In some countries the station was a political or nationalist statement. The classic example of the former is Milan Central station. Opened in July 1931, it is one of the most grandiose in the world. Designed on the monolithic scale favoured by totalitarian regimes, it has a façade 185 metres (202 yds) long and platforms covered by five steel arches, the central one having a span of 72 metres (79 yds). The public spaces are decorated with 2,400 tons of marble.

An emphatically modern, Nordic style was employed by Eliel Saarinen for his design of Helsinki Central station in 1918, at a time when

station seen today, and most recently adapted to act as the terminal for Eurostar trains from London and Thalys trains from Brussels.

The Gare de Lyon was transformed around 1900 with the tall, ornate clock tower. Someone familiar with these stations a century ago would have no difficulty recognising them today, and it is this sense of continuity – alone among the various categories of railway buildings – that partly explains their ability to evoke the sense of romance many still associate with rail travel.

LEFT: the Gothic grandeur of London St Pancras, designed by Sir Gilbert Scott.
ABOVE: Milan Centrale's imposing facade.

Finland was still under Russian dominance. On either side of the round-headed entrance stand four pink-granite giants holding globes that light up at night.

The chandeliered stations of the Moscow Metro were designed to impress visitors as well as Muscovites with the achievements of the Soviet Union. Foreigners are often surprised by the generous space of the public areas as well as their palatial decoration, with marble walls, stucco work and murals.

Stations and society

Stations became imbued with all kinds of associations that developed because the railway station soon began to rival the market as the focal point of the community. People out for a stroll would wander down to the station to watch the arrival of a train or two. The Railway Children of Edith Nesbit's eponymous novel were doing nothing unusual by taking in their Yorkshire country station during walks.

Meetings and partings invested stations with emotional connotations: the trysts under the station clock; the anticipation of going on holiday; the sadness of setting off for war, wondering if the receding view of a waving handkerchief would be the last sight of a loved one; the different aura of a station at the beginning and end

Stations on celluloid

Countless films have used stations as important components in the plot or as a motif, and some have been the fulcrum of the story, as in *Brief Encounter*, the poignant tale of doomed love that is forever associated with Rachmaninov's *2nd Piano Concerto*; or in Vittorio de Sica's *Indiscretion of an American Wife*, set almost entirely in Rome's Stazioni Termini. The fictional station of Buggleskelly on the equally fictional and delightfully named Southern Railway of Northern Ireland was the setting for one of the most successful inter-war British comedies, *Oh! Mr Porter*, starring the

of school term. These themes were increasingly picked up by poets, novelists, painters, photographers and film-makers.

The French novelist and poet Théophile Gautier (1811–72) wrote: "These cathedrals of the new humanity are the meeting-points of nations, the centre where all converges, the nucleus of huge stars whose iron rays stretch out to the ends of the earth." After the more or less conventional depiction of stations during the 19th and early 20th centuries came the work of painters such as Giorgio de Chirico and Paul Delvaux, for whom the station became a symbolic setting for the depiction of emotional states of mind or a metaphor in a dream-like composition.

familiar team of Will Hay, Moore Marriott and Graham Moffat. A Czech country station was the scene for the film *Closely Observed Trains*, based on the wartime story by Bohumil Hrabal about an adolescent's longing for sexual initiation, obligingly provided by a member of the resistance movement as his reward for taking part in the destruction of an ammunition train.

Decline and wrecking ball

The sense during the immediate post-World War II decades that the railways' loss of market share was an inexorable process did nothing to help those fighting to prevent the destruction of landmark railway buildings. Thousands of kilometres of line have been closed throughout Europe, stripping stations of their function. Some main lines have become secondary routes, making today's passengers wonder at the lavish scale of remaining buildings.

The greatest single loss in Britain was, perhaps, the Euston Arch. Its destruction in 1962 was made all the more regrettable by the dullness of the station that replaced the old one, as well as by the fact that the arch could easily have been incorporated in the new station plan. Its destruction did, however, alert many people to the value of Victorian buildings, and a wide cross-section of railway structures are among

torn down in 1963 to make way for a skyscraper, despite public protest. None the less, Britain, in particular, has suffered some major losses, such as Nottingham Victoria, Birmingham Snow Hill, Glasgow St Enoch and Manchester Central (though the train shed has been converted to an exhibition hall). Countries ravaged by war have had many older structures destroyed. France lost 100 large and almost 1,000 smaller stations during World War II.

Renaissance

Since the nadir of the 1960s, most railway administrations have taken progressively bet-

the many 19th-century buildings now given statutory protection.

A similar fate almost befell Zürich's Hauptbahnhof, designed by Jakob Friedrich Wanner and completed in 1871. A proposed office development above the concourse was scrapped in the face of a public outcry, and the station has now been sensitively restored.

Europe has lost nothing on the scale of New York's magnificent Pennsylvania Station, based on the Baths of Caracalla in Rome, which was

ter care of their legacy of historic buildings, encouraged by the clear preference of passengers for a refurbished historic building with character rather than the bland, utilitarian replacement that seemed the usual alternative.

Besides providing improved facilities for passengers, restored stations often have surplus space that can be rented out, sometimes for a complementary activity such as a café or cycle hire agency. This provides an income for the railway and enhances the feeling of security if a station is unstaffed at any time.

In Britain, the work of the Railway Heritage Trust, set up in 1985 to award grants for conservation work, has helped to save hundreds of

LEFT: a postcard of Luzern station, 1903.
ABOVE: Liverpool Street station in London, a successful and sensitive update of the Victorian original.

buildings. In Portugal the stations decorated with *azulejos* tiles in many parts of the country are being given the care they deserve. In Finland, agreement was reached between various organisations in 1998 that 872 different railway buildings at 85 locations should be preserved; they range from locomotive depots to railway staff housing as well as stations.

Innovative new designs

As governments and the EU recognise the need to increase use of railways if the quality of life in towns and cities is to be improved, money for imaginative station designs is being found.

Some of the most exciting work has been by Spanish-born architect Santiago Calatrava. In Portugal he designed Lisbon Oriente station, adjacent to the Expo '98 site, covered by a striking, delicate roof supported by 60 symmetrical steel and glass 25-metre (82-ft) high "trees". Calatrava has also designed buildings for Zürich Stadelhofen and the TGV station at Lyon Satolas airport.

In Britain, the reconstruction of London's Liverpool Street station showed how an unwieldy and impractical edifice built piecemeal during the Victorian era could be adapted and enhanced without sacrificing its character. British Rail's own architects not only created a station that is a pleasure to use, but designed the scheme around the need to keep the busy commuter station open. Another triumph has been the elegant, curving new roof for Waterloo International, designed by Nicholas Grimshaw, which was widely praised when it was completed in 1993 for the start of Channel Tunnel services (now transferred to St Pancras).

Saved by conversion

A range of ingenious uses has been found for 19th-century stations, largely in order to save them from demolition. Some of the grander stations have made outstanding art galleries and museums. The best-known example is the Gare d'Orsay in Paris, which has been adapted brilliantly to become the city's principal gallery for 19th-century art, the Musée d'Orsay. Where better to hang Monet's paintings of Gare St-Lazare than a former cathedral of steam?

Other examples include Berlin's oldest station, the Hamburger Bahnhof, which became the city's Museum of Modern Art in 1996; the oldest terminal station in the world, Manchester Liverpool Road, which has been incorporated into the Museum of Science & Industry; and Brunel's original train shed and station at Bristol housed the British Empire and Commonwealth Museum until its move to London.

Smaller stations often make splendid homes: signal-boxes can become summer-houses; the goods shed a garage and store; the gap between a twin-platformed station can become a swimming pool or sunken garden. Modest-sized stations are easy to adapt to commercial uses such as restaurants, hotels, offices, banks, tourist information centres, bookshops and craft workshops. The station at Pocklington on Humberside became a sports centre. Appropriately for a village with strong religious connections, Little Walsingham's station was converted into a Greek Orthodox church.

Even old locomotive depots have been adapted: in France, the roundhouses at La Rochelle, Metz Frescaty and Béthune have been converted into retail accommodation, while in Britain the London & Birmingham Railway roundhouse at Camden has been put to various uses, including a theatre. The imagination applied to their rescue is also a tribute to the original quality of construction. ❑

LEFT: innovative regeneration; the Musée d'Orsay.

Railway Hotels

In common with the railway itself, the railway hotel began in Britain. The first purpose-built hotel was at Euston station, occupying two facing buildings on either side of the former Doric Arch and linked by an underground passage. On one side the Victoria Hotel was a "dormitory" for third-class passengers, while on the other, the Euston was suitably appointed for first-class passengers. Opened in September 1839, it was leased four years later by a Corsican named Zenoni Vantini, who went on to create the first railway refreshment room, at Wolverton.

Other hotels soon followed at the railway junctions of Derby, Swindon and Normanton. The Midland Hotel at Derby was to establish a pattern for railway and other hotels in the way it emulated a country house by being set in its own grounds with an ornamental fountain in the forecourt. Opened in 1840, it has the distinction of being the oldest purpose-built station hotel in continuous use as a hotel.

It spawned a number of country-house establishments such as the West Country hotels of the Great Western Railway, at Tregenna Castle near St Ives and North Bovey Manor near Moretonhampstead. Golf provided the principal attraction at some country hotels, such as Gleneagles and Turnberry. The railways also used hotels to bolster passenger takings on trains serving resorts, such as the Zetland Hotel at Saltburn-on-Sea where the Stockton & Darlington Railway made sure there was an entrance door almost opposite the place where carriages halted.

Other hoteliers sometimes complained of the threat railway hotels represented to their businesses, as happened prior to the opening of the North Eastern Railway's first hotel in York in 1853.

In the days when some railway companies operated their own steamship services, hotels designed to serve passengers changing between train and ship were a natural extension of their business operations. The first was the Royal Pavilion Hotel at Folkestone, built by the South Eastern Railway (SER) and opened in 1843 for passengers using the steam packet service to Boulogne. Charles Dickens was a regular guest at the SER's Lord Warden Hotel in Dover.

RIGHT: the luxurious Hotel Schreiber perched on Mount Rigi, Switzerland.

Despite the success of the Euston hotels, it was another 15 years before another railway-owned hotel opened in London, although over a dozen followed before the end of the century. The French Renaissance edifice at Paddington exemplified the tendency of railway hotels to be at the forefront of architectural and technical developments, the Great Western Royal Hotel having fireproof staircases, electric clocks and an elaborate bell system. It was the first of many large hotels. The zenith of the railway hotel as far as opulence – and rates – were concerned was reached in the magnificent Midland Grand Hotel at St Pancras, which closed in 1935 but is being reopened.

Other railways in Europe followed the British example and set up their own hotels, but not on anything like the same scale. It was far more usual for hotels adjacent to stations to be built by independent hotel companies. Not even the Canadian Pacific Railway matched British railway companies in the scale and extent of its hotels, although Ireland had a good number, such as those of the Great Southern & Western Railway at Killarney, Dublin, Limerick Junction, Caragh Lake, Cork and several others.

In Switzerland, some hotels atop mountains or near stations were railway-owned, while others, like the outstanding Hotel Schreiber on Mount Rigi, were independently financed and operated. ❑

THE PURSUIT OF SPEED

*Speed has always held a fascination. In today's world it is essential
for commercial success but must always be balanced against safety concerns*

Speed has been a major objective of railway engineers since the 1829 Rainhill Trials, the contest to decide on the motive power for the Liverpool & Manchester Railway. The ability of a locomotive to reach a speed of 10 mph (16 km/h) was regarded as essential. The trial was won by the Stephensons' entry, the *Rocket*, which amazed everyone but its builders by reaching the "very high velocity" of just over 29 mph (46.4 km/h).

Within two decades, speeds of 60 mph (96 km/h) were being achieved in daily service on the Great Western Railway, confounding those who had predicted dire consequences for human health if the body was subjected to speeds much higher than the gallop of a horse.

The business of speed

The average speed of trains has always had an intricate relationship with railway economics. Raising average speeds requires an investment in better track and faster locomotives which consume more fuel; journey times fall and more passengers or freight are attracted on to trains, and revenue rises. However, the correlation – and the trade-off with the higher costs – is imprecise and naturally varies with time and place. Today the competition is with air and road transport, and the dramatic impact on market share as a consequence of slashing rail journey times by high-speed lines and trains has been perhaps the dominant driving factor in railway investment since the 1980s.

But human nature being what it is, it is speed records that capture the public imagination, and railway managers have used this fascination to maximise publicity almost from the start.

In Britain the principal battleground has been the Anglo-Scottish routes: in 1888 and 1895 the east and west coast lines (operated by the Great Northern, North Eastern and North British companies on the east coast, and the

London & North Western and Caledonian on the west coast) indulged in racing bouts to reach the remote Scottish junction where the two routes converged for the final section to Aberdeen. Newspapers carried excited daily reports on the previous night's runs and lauded the victor.

Railway rivalry

The rivalry resumed in the 1930s, with the two railways adopting streamlining for locomotives and carriages in an effort to capture the world speed record for rail transport. The London & North Eastern Railway (LNER) finally secured a lasting victory with the *Mallard*'s achievement of 126 mph (201.6 km/h) between Grantham and Peterborough in 1938. During this period of public rivalry, crowds gathered by the linesides to see each new contender for the headline-grabbing timings; cinema newsreel film crews added to the coverage.

Although it was these exploits that attracted media attention, neither route was served by

LEFT: replica of Trevithick's first steam locomotive.
RIGHT: a rider tests her prowess against the Carlisle Express at Tring, Hertfordshire, 1938.

the train with the fastest average speed. That distinction went to the Great Western Railway's *Cheltenham Flyer*, which in 1932 averaged an astonishing 71.4 mph (114.2 km/h) over the 77 miles (123 km) between Swindon and London Paddington, making it the fastest train in the world. That record, however, did not remain with Britain for long.

In 1935 German Railways introduced an articulated, two-car diesel train with open seating and a tiny bar on the *Flying Hamburger* service between Berlin and Hamburg, averaging 123.8 km/h (77.4 mph) and taking 138 minutes for the journey. This was only four minutes less than the fastest InterCity Express (ICE) until December 2004 when trains were accelerated to cover the 285 km (177 miles) in 90 minutes.

A few years before *Mallard* set the standard, efforts had been made to capture the steam record from the current holder in Britain, the LNER's Pacific *Silver Link* with a speed of 112.5 mph (181 km/h), by streamlining a Class 05 4-6-4. In 1936 this rather sinister-looking machine, now in Nuremberg Transport Museum, achieved 200.4 km/h (124.5 mph) at Neustadt an der Dosse, just west of Berlin. It held the world record until it was eclipsed by *Mallard* in 1938.

PUSHING TECHNOLOGY TO THE LIMIT

Whatever the stage of development or form of traction, pushing locomotives to their design limits and beyond entails risk. This has been brought home on a number of occasions during official or semi-official attempts to break records or cut journey times. In 1896 a northbound sleeping car train was derailed at Preston through running too fast. Timings were immediately eased and a ban put on any resumption of racing.

Competition between two railways to whisk disembarking transatlantic passengers from Plymouth to London resulted in disregard of a speed restriction and a serious accident at Salisbury in 1906, when 28 people were killed. In 1937 the press run of the London Midland & Scottish Railway's new Coronation Scot came within a hair's breadth of disaster when it entered a series of 20 mph (32 km/h) cross-overs at almost 60 mph (96 km/h), causing the train to lurch so violently that people were thrown to the floor and crockery sent flying. Luckily the train just kept to the rails.

In 1955 French Railways' record-breaking run with electric BB9004 very nearly came to grief when the track was severely distorted by fierce hunting (oscillation) of the locomotive's bogies. A new world record of 331 km/h (205.7 mph) was set, but a photograph taken of the buckled track was suppressed and did not appear in print until 1981.

Electrics and dedicated lines

Electric traction had held greater promise than steam since the extraordinary run in 1903 of a German AEG rail car which reached 210.2 km/h (130.6 mph) on a military railway between Marienfelde and Zossen, an astonishing speed for the time. This remained the world record for electric power for half a century until, in 1954, French Railways began a series of remarkable runs that were to help the country become the first in Europe to enjoy dedicated high-speed lines and trains.

The move towards high-speed lines has been one of the principal post-World War II devel-

of track cant (angling to allow higher speed) and signal spacing that have to be made on a mixed-use railway.

Tilting trains

The only alternative (and a cheaper one) is a tilting mechanism that allows trains to run through curves at a higher speed. During the 1970s it looked as though Britain would assume a commanding lead in tilt technology, as British Rail worked on the Advanced Passenger Train (APT), which was intended to take over inter-city routes. A successful outcome held the promise of healthy exports, as great

opments in railway operation, pioneered by Japanese National Railways with the opening of the Tokaido line between Tokyo and Osaka in 1965. Its immediate commercial success in doubling the number of passengers within a year convinced others that this was the way to achieve a renaissance of rail travel.

The Japanese had chosen to build new lines laid out for speed, with gentle curves and an absence of slower-moving, local passenger or freight trains. This avoided the compromises

LEFT: the *City of Truro*, the fastest locomotive of its day.
ABOVE: a line-up of Gresley A4 locomotives at the National Railway Museum, York.

interest surrounded the project, not least from the United States and Canada.

Unfortunately, it was not to be: a combination of Treasury parsimony, delays due to the sheer number of technical innovations designed into the train, industrial disputes and an exaggerated fear of tilt mechanism failure, causing the train to foul the loading gauge, were the prime factors that put paid to the APT in 1981. Development work was abruptly halted and the train put into store. By mid-1986 most of the APT vehicles were in a scrap yard.

Yet, as so often with British-invented technology, others were able to develop it commercially. A Talgo tilting train entered service between Madrid and Zaragoza in 1980, and was later extended to Barcelona, while in Italy Fiat developed a successful, active tilt system, allowing tilting Pendolino trains to enter commercial service in Italy in 1988.

These operate over conventional lines as well as sections of high-speed line, while striking, Pininfarina-designed, non-tilting, high-speed trains, the ETR 500 class, have been built for services over Italy's growing high-speed network, with routes operating east–west from Turin through Milan to Venice and north–south from Milan to Naples via Bologna, Florence and Rome.

Another two lines are being built: from Perpignan to Figueres in Spain; and an extension of the Paris–Lyon route from Dijon to Mulhouse known as Rhine-Rhône.

ICE services

German Railways originally opted for non-tilting, high-speed trains for its new high-speed lines, known as Neubaustrecke, on which construction began in 1973. ICE services began in 1991 between Hamburg and Munich via Hanover, Frankfurt, Mannheim and Stuttgart. Attractively-styled, new generation ICEs, including diesel tilting versions, have been brought into use, gradually taking over

The TGV

France has eschewed tilting trains, developing the longest network (1,700 km/1,062 miles) of dedicated high-speed lines (Ligne à Grande Vitesse), following the opening of LGV Méditerranée in 2001 and LGV Est in 2007. The Train à Grande Vitesse (TGV) has been able to set many new records since the first orange, grey and white sets entered service in 1981 with the opening of the first LGV between St-Florentin near Paris and Lyon. The LGV network from Paris also extends to Le Mans and Tours in the west and the Channel Tunnel in the north, and the latest generation of TGVs include double-decker coaches.

more main line services. A first generation ICE briefly captured the world record in 1988, reaching 406.8 km/h (252.8 mph) before commercial services began. In May 1990, France won back the record, but even that new record of 515.3 km/h (320.2 mph) was eclipsed by a TGV reaching 574.8 km/h (359 mph) in 2007.

Yet despite the maxima being reached on new high-speed lines elsewhere, in 1991 British Rail had more trains running at averages over 100 mph (160 km/h) than any other European country. That position has been steadily eroded as ever more generous levels of investment in other western European countries have raised performance of their flagship services.

The European High-Speed Network

Today France boasts the fastest European average speeds. The LGV Méditerranée allowed an hour or more to be slashed from the schedules of many trains between Mediterranean coast stations and northern France. It is possible to leave Marseille at 5.15pm and be in London before midnight. But the fastest average speed is over LGV Est opened in 2007. A TGV covers the 167.6 km (104.75 miles) in 36 minutes at an average speed of 279.3 km/h (174.56 mph).

The success of the TGV has encouraged other European countries, which are now rapidly catching up with France. Spain is currently in third place, with the Alta Velocidad España (AVE) trains, based on the French TGV design. Over 46 AVE trains a day average more than 200 km/h (125 mph), the fastest being train 3211 on the 580 km (362½ miles) between Madrid's Atocha station and Barcelona Santis, at an average of 266.5 km/h (166.6 mph). Spanish Railways are so confident about the dependability of its AVE services that passengers receive 100 percent refunds if trains are more than five minutes late.

Germany's ICE trains offer the third fastest timings, with ICEs averaging 233.5 km/h (146 mph) between Frankfurt Flughafen and Siegburg/Bonn. These top three countries are followed by Britain, Sweden, Italy and Finland.

Norway takes the laurel for the fastest link between a capital city and its national airport, which is provided by the Gardermobanen line between Oslo Sentral and Gardermoen Airport. The current fastest service covers the 52 km (32 miles) at an average speed of 164.2 km/h (103 mph).

Extensions and prospects

Further extensions are under construction on the high-speed networks of France, Germany, Italy and Spain. However, the upgrade of the West Coast main line in Britain, intended to allow Virgin tilting trains to travel at a maximum of 225 km/h (140 mph), has been scaled back to 200 km/h (125 mph) and there is no prospect of a north-south high-speed line until at least the late 2010s.

LEFT: 1950s photo shoot with the world's fastest train.
RIGHT: today's European expresses run at speeds of over 300 km/h (186 mph).

The prospects for speeds much higher than 350 km/h (219 mph) are limited by the steel wheel/steel rail interface, which has led Central Japan Railway (JR Central) to invest large sums in magnetic levitation (MAGLEV) technology; a test track has been built in Yamanashi prefecture.

Although a world record has been established with a speed of 581 km/h (361 mph), a programme of intensive trials and research to reduce construction and operating costs cannot overcome the fundamental problem that integration with conventional trains is bound to be difficult and limited. ❑

A LACK OF INVESTMENT

For almost a century and a quarter Britain's railways were at the forefront of technical development, reflected in the country holding the world speed record for steam traction. Although the launch of the InterCity 125 in the 1970s was a boost, the fragmented model for the privatisation process of the late-1990s weakened an industry already suffering from decades of under-investment by central government. The most recent blow to industry prestige has been the abandonment of plans for the operation of tilting trains at 140 mph (225 km/h), following the 2001 collapse of Railtrack. Government support for a high-speed north–south line is needed.

HERITAGE

Early railway engineers and entrepreneurs had little thought for posterity, but the preservation and appreciation of historic railways is now big business

Railway preservation in its various forms is now so well established in Europe that it is hard to imagine how slowly the idea took hold. Today, when collecting all manner of things has become the focus of many people's lives, we almost take it for granted that either an institution or an individual, somewhere, will save significant items of our cultural past for future generations. Yet for a century or more after the opening of the Stockton & Darlington Railway in 1825, few countries had any sort of policy to safeguard their railway heritage.

Preservation begins

Most of the early efforts to preserve railway artefacts came from either the museum world or from prescient figures in the railway industry. In Britain, it was the former, and began with the opening in 1857 of London's South Kensington Museum, the institution that would later become the Science Museum. It took charge of the remains of the Stephensons' *Rocket* in 1862. In most other European countries it was the railway staff themselves who took the initiative.

The catalyst for popularising the concept of preservation was the celebration of various anniversaries marking the founding of railway companies. In 1875, for example, the North Eastern Railway organised events to mark the jubilee of the Stockton & Darlington Railway, which it had taken over in 1863. Yet even then, no consideration was given to the future of any of the celebrated locomotives that took part. Only when its successor, the London & North Eastern Railway (LNER), organised the centenary would things be different.

Austria leads and Norway follows

In Austria, as early as 1885, Dr Baron von Röll, a senior officer of the newly created State Railways, suggested forming a collection of relics that would commemorate the achievements of the railway pioneers. The board approved and

von Röll was given the job of setting up a museum. In 1893, an exhibition was opened to the public in the administration building opposite Vienna West station. The State Railway Museum contained some choice early items, such as an 1834 horse wagon and the narrow gauge locomotive *Gmunden,* dating from 1854.

Donations from Austrian private railways and contracting firms flooded in, encouraging ideas of a new and larger building. In 1896 the museum was placed under the Presidential Office, but it was not until 1914 that space was found in the new Technical Museum for Trade & Industry for some of the full-size locomotives and rolling stock. The outbreak of war delayed the opening until 1918, but the collection survived World War II. Today most of the exhibits have been moved to the Eisenbahnmusem at Strasshof *(see page 254).*

In Norway the idea for a railway museum came from the Norwegian Stationmasters' Association in 1896, and work started at once

---

LEFT: rail memorabila at Shackerstone station.
RIGHT: the Talyllyn Railway, original heritage line.

to collect suitable material. Initially housed in a room at Hamar station on the Oslo–Trondheim line, the collection later found a new home nearby where old railway buildings were re-erected and opened to visitors in 1930. In time this was outgrown, and the museum moved to its present site 3 km (2 miles) north of Hamar, beside Lake Mjøsa, in 1955 *(see page 307)*. The site has been laid out as a railway station with running lines for demonstration. Locomotives of three gauges are on display. Some of the rooms in the reconstructed buildings have been restored to their original condition, while others house themed exhibitions.

(see page 284) has adapted the workshops and roundhouse locomotive depot outside the old Anhalter station in an imaginative way. The collection contains 27 steam, 14 diesel and 12 electric locomotives and numerous smaller exhibits.

The latecomers

Despite its international importance, Britain was slow to recognise its early railway history. There were a few isolated instances of companies preserving a particularly historic item, such as the South Eastern Railway's saving of the Canterbury & Whitstable Railway's 1830 *Invicta*, but no national guidance. Not until after

Preservation in Italy and Germany

The National Museum of Science & Technology in Milan *(see page 235)*, housed in the former Olivetan convent of San Vittore, contains locomotives that had been stored in Rome for many years. Some 13 steam locomotives and various electrics are on display.

In Germany the legacy of the pre-unification states has led to a number of museums being devoted to railways and transport, or having sections on the subject. One of the oldest is the Deutsches Museum Verkehrzentrum in Munich *(see page 284)*, which first opened in 1925 and displays artefacts that have been collected since 1903. In Berlin, the Deutsches Technikmuseum

World War I was there much effort by the railway companies to take account of their past, and even then some railway officials behaved like philistines when it came to history.

Two eminent chief mechanical engineers scrapped historic locomotives that had been laid to one side by their predecessors. In 1906, G. J. Churchward cut up the magnificent, broad gauge *North Star* and *Lord of the Isles*, and in 1932 Sir William Stanier ordered the same fate for a collection of engines that had been assembled at Derby on the London Midland & Scottish Railway.

It was not until the LNER organised a splendid cavalcade of locomotives, many hauling carriages or wagons, to mark the centenary of the Stockton & Darlington Railway (SDR) in 1925 that serious thought was given to establishing Britain's first railway museum. This opened in a former locomotive works in York in 1928, and was soon broadened by locomotives that came from non-LNER constituent railways.

Nonetheless, for years it remained a small regional museum. Things began to change with the opening of the British Transport Museum at Clapham in London in 1963, which included artefacts from all parts of the country, although it was light on Great Western Railway (GWR) material because a museum devoted to the GWR had been opened at Swindon the year before.

There was no room for expansion at Clapham so the museum was superseded by the National Railway Museum (NRM; *see page 120*) which opened in 1975 in a former locomotive roundhouse at York; this received the contents of the older York railway museum, which was then closed. The NRM has become an immensely successful enterprise, attracting half a million visitors a year.

Another country that had been rather slow in creating a national museum was France. Its National Railway Museum *(see page 158)* opened in 1976 in the Alsatian town of Mulhouse, close to the border with Switzerland. A standard gauge, engineering bias is evident, with only modest displays devoted to the social and economic aspects of railways compared with the large collection of steam and electric locomotives and rolling stock. There is almost nothing about the extensive narrow gauge railways that once served vast areas of rural France.

The amateurs take over

People are often quite emotional about railways. Many who never set foot on a train all year would be among the first to be upset by the idea that their local train service might be axed. When the Lynton & Barnstaple Railway was threatened with closure in 1935, for example, almost everyone came to the protest meeting in Barnstaple by car. Whatever the reasons for the feelings that railways generate, this emotional attachment has induced hundreds of thousands of people all over the world to give

up large amounts of their spare time and money to preserve something they value.

For most people, the steam locomotive has always been at the heart of railways' appeal, and it was to save some notable examples that the first voluntary efforts were made. It is a measure of the allure of steam that these unofficial preservation schemes would, in time, eclipse the work of the official sector and become the custodians of far more artefacts than the formal museum sector.

One of the earliest instances of a group of individuals preserving a locomotive occurred in 1927 when the Stephenson Locomotive

Society took the decision to buy from the Southern Railway a condemned Stroudley 0-4-2 dating from 1882, No. 214 *Gladstone*. It was placed on loan at the LNER's museum in York, where it was joined in the early 1930s by one of the first locomotives thought to have reached 100 mph (160 km/h), *City of Truro*. This began to give the museum a national rather than a merely regional scope.

Preserving working railways

The idea of preserving a working railway appears to have had its origin in the United States, where, in 1937, the Save the Bridgton Narrow Gauge Railroad Club suggested buying

LEFT: the Douglas C-47B "raisin bomber" atop the Deutsches Technikmuseum in Berlin.
RIGHT: vintage tickets.

one of the delightful narrow gauge railways in Maine. Regrettably, the owners preferred to see it scrapped rather than kept for posterity, but the scrap merchant had a greater sense of history than the railroad company and set aside the locomotives and carriages. These were later used on the now-closed Edaville Railroad in Massachusetts, which was created by a fruit farmer after the war.

The idea of preserving an entire working railway resurfaced after World War II, when the Welsh narrow gauge Talyllyn Railway *(see pages 62 and 123)* was under threat of closure. A meeting was called, resulting in the

lines, to operate passenger trains. This arrangement is common in Germany, Switzerland and France. Another accepted form has been the establishment of a railway museum in a former locomotive works or depot, with a short running line for demonstration purposes. Sometimes these have become bases for locomotives operating over the national railway network.

Some countries now have hundreds of heritage railways and museums, ranging from small, family concerns in converted stations or goods sheds, to major tourist enterprises employing dozens of people and playing a major role in the regional tourism industry.

formation of the Talyllyn Railway Preservation Society in 1950, which took over and reopened the line the following year.

Standard gauge railway preservation soon followed, with successful attempts in 1960 to save the historic Middleton Railway in Leeds and the picturesque country branch line in Sussex, now well-known and loved as the Bluebell Railway *(see page 120)*.

Since then, "amateur" railway preservation throughout Europe has taken different forms. Besides those societies that have assumed ownership of a railway, others have taken advantage of light passenger traffic at weekends, or an absence of traffic on freight-only private

A distinction should also be made between tourist railways – those lines that have been preserved solely because they pass through attractive scenery – and heritage railways that have been saved for overtly rail-related reasons. The latter often aim to give visitors an experience of travel in a different age, perhaps recreating stations to look as they did before World War I or in the 1930s and with their staff (often volunteers) dressed in appropriate uniforms. Some railways have enough stations to restore each one to reflect a different period.

The principal museums and preserved railways are listed at the end of each chapter, but some deserve a second mention.

Austria

Two of the country's outstanding railway attractions are not heritage railways in the more usual sense of being closed lines saved by third-party efforts, since neither of Austrian Railways' metre gauge rack railways has ever been closed. Both the Puchberg–Hochschneeberg and the St Wolfgang–Schafberg lines continue to use steam power by choice, with a mixture of century-old and recently built locomotives.

Britain

Britain has more heritage railways operating daily services over a longer season than any other European country. Many are now substantial businesses, offering lunch and dining trains, engine-driving courses, themed weekends and Christmas "Santa Specials" to attract more visitors. Yet each has an individual character, influenced not only by its surroundings but also by the interests of those who created and run it. Some try to preserve the atmosphere of

> ### THE RAILWAY CLUB
>
> An amateur interest in railways is almost as old as the railways themselves. The Railway Club, founded in 1899, spawned hundreds of imitations catering for myriad specialist interests.

The small town of Jenbach on the main line to the east of Innsbruck has long been a mecca for railway enthusiasts. To the north is the rack railway up to the Achensee *(see page 245)*, worked by three steam engines dating from 1899; to the south is one of Europe's oldest independent railways, the Zillertalbahn *(see page 245)*, which uses steam traction for its tourist trains over the 32 km (20 miles) to Mayrhofen. Besides the traditional black tank engines, it has a former Yugoslavian 0-8-2, built in 1909.

LEFT: the Great Hall at York's National Railway Museum.
ABOVE: Strathpeffer station is now an arts and crafts centre.

a Great Western branch line with Brunswick green locomotives and chocolate-and-cream coloured carriages, barrows of period suitcases or milk churns on the platforms, and posters of West Country resorts to admire while warming your hands before the fire blazing in the waiting-room grate.

Some of the best known heritage railways are the "Great Little Trains of Wales", narrow gauge lines with immense appeal, thanks to the glorious scenery through which they pass and the perennial appeal of smaller gauges. The Ffestiniog Railway *(see page 121)* provides a valuable transport link between the National Rail terminus at Blaenau Ffestiniog and

Porthmadog, situated on the scenic line between Shrewsbury and Pwllheli. The Ffestiniog line played such an important part in the development of narrow gauge railways worldwide that in 1870 the Russian Tsar sent emissaries to witness one of its innovations – the trial runs of double-boilered, articulated steam locomotives.

Another railway, this time linking Porthmadog with the North Wales coast, is the Welsh Highland Railway *(see page 123)*, a 25-mile (40-km) line being rebuilt south from Caernarfon. By 2009 it will be fully reopened, using Manchester-built articulated Beyer Garratt locomotives repa-

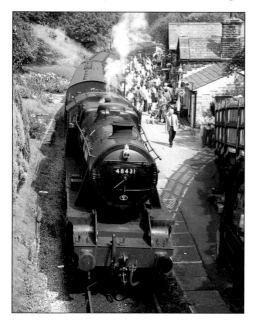

triated from South Africa. The railway serves the start of several walks up the highest mountain in Wales, Snowdon, and also winds through the precipitous Aberglaslyn Pass.

Further south, the pretty journey up the Afon Fathew valley from Tywyn to Abergynolwyn, and on to Nant Gwernol at the foot of the old slate quarries, will always remind anyone associated with railway preservation that this is where it all began. It was the example of the Talyllyn Railway pioneers that inspired others to believe that such schemes could be made to work. Even when the railway's prime function was conveying slate, Britain's favoured roofing material, the tourist potential of the line was apparent, as people used it to reach the impressive Dolgoch waterfalls.

A few favourites

It is almost invidious to select a few of the dozens of preserved standard gauge railways in Britain, as each one has individual qualities to attract visitors. For the pleasure of riding in superbly restored period carriages between stations renovated to look as they did in 1900, in the 1930s and the 1950s, it is hard to better the Bluebell Railway in Sussex *(see page 120)*. Its multi-platformed, intermediate station at Horsted Keynes still has the atmosphere of a deeply rural junction, where one might have half an hour to linger over a pint of draught beer by the refreshment-room fire while waiting for an onward connection. Its fleet of locomotives and carriages reflects the fact that it had plenty of choice during its formative years in the 1960s.

Another early venture was the Keighley & Worth Valley Railway *(see page 122)*, always seeming much longer than the 4¾ miles (7.6 km) between the main line junction at Keighley and the village of Oxenhope. It, too, has plenty of carriages that would have been lit by oil or gas when new, as well as half a dozen engines that were in use when Victoria was on the throne. The line passes through Haworth, famous as the home of the Brontë sisters, who shared the vicarage with their father and brother.

For a dramatic setting and the authentic appearance of a North Eastern Railway branch line, the North Yorkshire Moors Railway *(see page 122)* is outstanding. Running south from a junction with the Esk Valley line at Grosmont, the railway climbs at a steep gradient up into the moors at Goathland and through lovely

---

SNOWDON'S RACK RAILWAY

Great Britain is not over-endowed with high mountains, and the only historic rack railway it possesses provides an alternative means of reaching the summit of Mt Snowdon, in Wales. Using the technology that the Swiss made their own, after a pioneering effort by Americans, the Snowdon Mountain Railway *(see page 123)* has taken millions to the 3,563-ft (1,086-metre) peak since the operation began in 1897. Seven steam and four diesel locomotives propel trains slowly up the 4¾ miles (7.6 km) of track, the mountain falling away on both sides above Rocky Valley and providing views as far as the Isle of Man, and even Cumbria on a clear day.

Newtondale to the market town of Pickering. The goods shed at Goathland has been imaginatively restored as a café, retaining a sense of its original function by using open wagons for seating areas and barrels as seats.

The distinctive character of the branch lines that served West Country holiday resorts is captured by several railways *(see pages 122 and 123)*: the West Somerset between Bishops Lydeard and the sea at Minehead; the Paignton & Dartmouth running alongside the Dart estuary and through Devon woods to rejoin the sea at Torbay; the South Devon along the Dart Valley from Totnes; and the Swanage Railway. The last performs a useful public transport function by relieving traffic congestion around popular Corfe Castle by operating trains from a park-and-ride station at Norden. In due course it is hoped to extend services northwards to connect with National Rail services at Wareham.

Almost every preserved railway is single track, not least because most of them are based on branch lines or secondary routes that never had need of more. A notable exception is the Great Central Railway *(see page 121)* in the east Midlands, running over what was a double track main line between Loughborough and Leicester. Following reopening with a single line, a second track has been relaid for much of the 8 miles (12.8 km), offering the rare sight of steam trains passing at speed.

Eastern Europe and Greece

Most of the small number of tourist and heritage railways in eastern Europe have their origins in state activity rather than individual initiatives. Many of these are former forestry and mining railways which have been resurrected as heritage lines since the fall of the Iron Curtain. Examples are the Hronec Forest Railway in Slovakia *(see page 322)*, the Szalajka Forest Railway in Hungary *(see page 320)*, and the 600-mm (1 ft 11⅝-in) gauge Zuin Railway *(see page 343)* from Znin to Wenecja and Gasawa in Poland.

Undoubtedly the most remarkable enterprise is the Wolsztyn experience in Poland *(see page 326)*, offering the opportunity to drive and fire steam locomotives under the eye of the

regular crew on service trains between Wolsztyn and Poznan.

In Yugoslavia, the remarkable series of spirals and tunnels on the 760-mm (2 ft 5⅞-in) gauge line from Mokra Gora to Sargan has been rebuilt, having lain derelict since closure in 1974. The Sargan Mountain Railway *(see page 343)* is the heart of a tourism development scheme that also includes a 600-mm (1 ft 11⅝-in) gauge line into the forest.

One of the most notable revivals in the late 1990s was the enchanting Volos Railway in Greece *(see page 337)*, running through olive groves along the flank of Mt Pilion, with views

over the Pagasitic Gulf. The trains, with open-balconied wooden coaches, were initially hauled by the original French-built tank engines dating from before World War I, but these have been replaced on most trains by diesel-powered, steam-outline affairs.

France

Many of France's private lines are tourist rather than heritage railways, focusing on provision of a train service over a particularly scenic stretch of railway rather than trying to recreate or preserve a period railway experience. Probably the best-known heritage railway in France is the Chemin de Fer (CF) du

LEFT: picturesque Haworth Railway, the Yorkshire Dales.
RIGHT: the museum at Cierny Balog on the preserved Hronec Forest Railway, Slovakia.

Vivarais *(see page 158)*, running through the hills of the Ardèche between the Rhône-side town of Tournon and Lamastre, noted for its gastronomy. The founder of the society which saved the Vivarais took his inspiration from a visit to the Talyllyn Railway.

Operated mostly by Swiss-built, articulated steam locomotives, the Vivarais also has some inter-war railcars whose remarkable ugliness exudes character. The railway follows the River Doux past the St-Josephe vineyards, which produce one of the best Côte du Rhônes, and a medieval stone-arched bridge that was once the largest arch of its kind in the world.

Historic and military links

Very different is Le Chemin de Fer de la Baie de Somme in Picardy *(see page 158)*, which runs along both sides of the Somme estuary, past willow-lined streams and bird-filled marshes. It perfectly conveys the character of the myriad networks of narrow gauge railways that once meandered through much of rural France. It serves the historic seaside towns of Le Crotoy, Cayeaux-sur-Mere and St-Valery-sur-Somme, from where William the Conqueror set sail for England in 1066.

The battlefields of World War I were supplied by networks of quickly laid, narrow gauge rail-

Another section of the old Réseau du Vivarais is gradually being opened between Dunières and St-Agrève to the west of Lamastre. Using steam locomotives from other narrow gauge systems as well as some venerable diesel railcars, the railway runs through alpine foothills and an impressive gorge.

Further east, to the south of Grenoble, vintage electrics take visitors to the Chemin de Fer de La Mure *(see page 141)* into largely inaccessible mountain scenery, the highlight of which is the dramatic defile of the Drac gorge. The line teeters along a ledge and a series of bridges and viaducts at a dizzying height above the steep slopes down to the river.

ways that could bring men, munitions and supplies to the front. One of these forms the basis of the remote CF Froissy–Cappy Dompierre *(see page 159)* to the east of Amiens. After the war these networks became part of the local transport infrastructure, carrying agricultural produce as well as raw materials to, or products from, brickworks, quarries and sugar refineries. Some of the steam locomotives that work most trains have World War I connections, and there is a museum explaining the origins of the line and its historical significance.

The most successful standard gauge railway in France is the Train à Vapeur des Cévennes *(see page 158)*, from Anduze to St-Jean du

Gard, thanks to its daily service over a long season. Trains climb nearly all the way from Anduze across some fine viaducts and past a park of oriental plants at La Bambouseraie.

Germany

The survival in East Germany of some steam-worked narrow gauge railways until the reunification of Germany in 1990 has been a helpful legacy for tourism in those areas. Their retention and development makes them the principal destination for visitors in search of regular steam operations *(see page 284)*, supplemented by new heritage railways such as the Preßnitz-

steam locomotives. One of the shortest but most delightful railways is the 2-km (1¼-mile) Chiemseebahn in Bavaria *(see page 285)*, between the Munich–Salzburg line at Prien and the pier at Stock, where boats leave for Ludwig II's castle at Herrenchiemsee. Its principal locomotive is a tram engine of 1887, and its appropriate rolling stock is four-wheeled.

A good example of co-operation between preservation groups and railway owners is the series of trains that operates on some weekends between Kassel-Wilhelmshöhe and Naumburg, terminus of a part-industrial 33-km (21-mile) branch to the west of the Hessian town.

talbahn between Jöhstadt and Steinbach. In western Germany there is a strong tradition of regionally-owned railways, often operated by surprisingly modern trains. Some accommodate local preservation societies and allow them to run special trains at weekends, although few operate more than one or two days a month.

The country's first museum line was an 8-km (5-mile) metre gauge operation between Bruchhausen-Vilsen and Asendorf *(see page 285)* to the south of Bremen, which has 12

LEFT: beautifully crafted tram at the Utrecht Railway Museum, the Netherlands.
ABOVE: music and refreshment, Stainz line, Austria.

One of Germany's finest working museum collections is the Eisenbahnmuseum Bochum-Dahlhausen *(see page 284)*, near Essen. There is an elevated signal box and administration building containing various exhibitions. A shuttle railcar links the S-bahn station and museum on operating days, and trains also run between nearby Hattingen (terminus of S-bahn line 3), Wengern Ost and Hagen.

Switzerland

One of the two remarkable Swiss developments of the 1990s was the construction of a batch of new rack steam locomotives in Winterthur for the lines up the Rothorn and to Rochers-de-

Naye. Overlooking lakes Brienz and Geneva respectively, the two railways were the only Swiss rack lines using steam on a daily basis until the latter sold its locomotive to the former. The new locomotives are capable of one-person operation, and even have a timing device to light themselves up in the morning. The Brienz Rothorn Bahn already used steam as well as diesel traction.

The other impressive initiative was the gradual reopening of the former metre gauge line over the Furka Pass *(see page 195)*, using locomotives repatriated from Vietnam. The line runs from a junction with the Brig–Chur line

at Realp and climbs over the summit in tunnel to drop down to Gletsch and (from 2009) Oberwald. The railway has a shorter operating season than the Brienz Rothorn Bahn.

The Blonay–Chamby line *(see page 212)* above Montreux and Vevey is Switzerland's principal heritage railway, with a large collection of well-maintained steam and electric traction, and a wonderfully scenic line on which to demonstrate them. Luzern's Verkehrshaus der Schweiz *(see page 212)* is Europe's largest transport museum, where the railway section provides a fascinating insight into the particular challenges faced by those building and operating railways in such a mountainous country.

Excursions on national railways

Most railways have programmes of excursions organised by national or private operators, using sets of every-day carriages or privately-owned rakes (strings of carriages) of historic vehicles hauled by steam, diesel or electric traction. Probably the best-known private operator is the Venice Simplon-Orient Express *(see page 80)*, but there are many others, taking passengers to special events such as sporting fixtures, or running over scenic routes.

Many are aimed specifically at railway enthusiasts. In Britain the first example of a railway enthusiasts' special train using a preserved locomotive on the main line was in 1938, when the Railway Correspondence & Travel Society chartered the recently restored Great Northern Railway "Single" No. 1 and its historic train. Since then charter trains have become common in most countries, commemorating the passing of a particular class of locomotive, the closure of a line or the anniversary of a notable event in railway history.

The most elaborate events are German "Plandampfs", which entail preserved locomotives taking over both passenger and freight service trains on one or more secondary lines, sometimes over several days. They attract people from all over Europe to ride behind and photograph steam engines on "ordinary" trains rather than special workings.

The future of heritage railways seems rosy, given the perennial appeal of steam and railway travel, although they have to overcome occasional obstacles raised by officials in national governments or the EU – the latter even proposed that all hot surfaces on a steam locomotive should be painted a fluorescent colour. It was to counter such absurdities, and represent their collective interests, that the European Federation of Museum & Tourist Railways (FEDECRAIL) was formed in 1994.

But heritage railways have become such big business in many parts of Europe that they now represent a powerful element of the tourism industry. In Britain alone, in 2007, they turned over £58 million, employed 1,640 people supported by over 14,700 volunteers, and attracted 5.7 million passengers. ❏

LEFT: immaculately dressed attendants on the Orient Express.
RIGHT: springtime on the Talyllyn Railway.

JOURNEYS

*A detailed guide to Europe's best railway journeys,
with routes traced on the accompanying maps*

Choosing fewer than 100 railway journeys from the tens of thousands offered by the railways of Europe is obviously a subjective affair. If there is a bias, it is probably towards routes through hills and mountains; the appeal of a railway line is often related to the degree of difficulty of its construction, reflected in the tunnels and viaducts as well as the impressive views that usually accompany the most heroic conquests of the railway builders.

Rail travel allows one to cover high mileages by the fastest trains, or slow the pace by taking a stopping train and breaking the journey at some promising place. The journeys have been written to encourage such diversions; most rail passes allow enough flexibility for the indulgence of such whims, being valid for a given number of days a month. Those seeking advice on the best ticket or pass options, or looking for help devising an itinerary from the timetables, should contact a specialist booking agent *(see page 348)*. Timetables are generally much easier to read than is commonly supposed, some being models of clarity, such as the Swiss railway and bus timetables. For anyone travelling in more than one country, the Thomas Cook European Timetable, published monthly, is indispensable, though it omits some minor railways.

The best journeys combine splendid landscapes with interesting towns and villages and the character of the railway itself. Although some of the most delightful byways have gone – such as the marvellous narrow gauge railway that linked Belgrade and Sarajevo, which had overnight trains equipped with sleeping and dining cars, as well as dawdling trains linking every hamlet with the nearest market – many still survive. The metre gauge lines that variously thread their way across the top of Spain, link two of Switzerland's most famous resorts, or twist through the mountains of Corsica, are each very different but equally engaging.

For people wishing to discover something of the history of a country's railways or to experience what it was like to ride a steam-hauled narrow gauge train through the forests of Finland, each chapter is concluded by a listing of the principal railway museums and heritage railways. Inevitably the timing of operations on the latter vary from year to year, dependent as most of them are on volunteer labour. It is therefore important to check with the railway concerned to avoid disappointment.   ❏

PRECEDING PAGES: Le Train Jaune in the French Pyrenees; crossing the Invershin Bridge in the Sutherland Highlands between Inverness and Wick; Alpine splendour at Les Tines between Chamonix and Martigny.
LEFT: precipitous scenery on the Brienz–Rothorn Bahn, Switzerland.

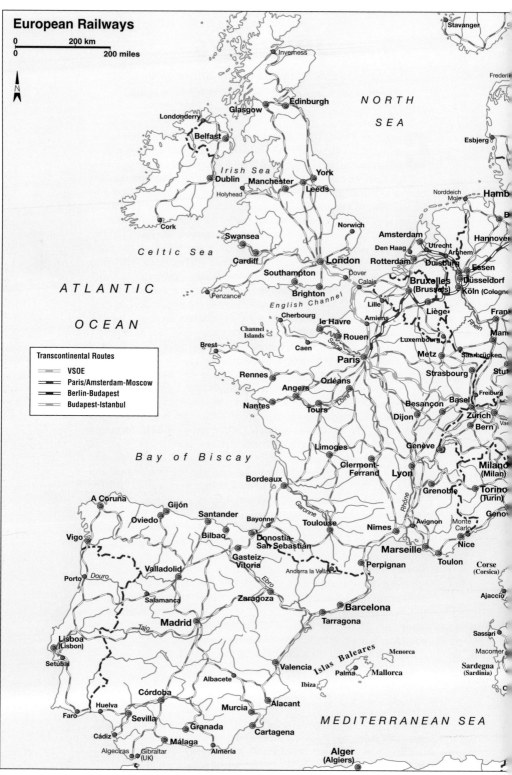

European Railways

```
0        200 km
0           200 miles
```

Transcontinental Routes

- VSOE
- Paris/Amsterdam-Moscow
- Berlin-Budapest
- Budapest-Istanbul

The GOLDEN ARROW
ALL PULLMAN TRAIN

DAILY BETWEEN

LONDON   CALAIS   PARIS

Departs: LONDON 10.45 a.m.   Arrives: PARIS 5.40 pm.
Departs: PARIS 12 noon   Arrives: LONDON 7.15 pm.

CROSSING THE CONTINENT

Crossing Europe by long-distance express train remains the epitome of romantic travel; although the Golden Age may be long gone, today's express trains are mostly smooth, fast and comfortable

Map on page 76/77

The idea of boarding a train and striking out across the Continent to reach a distant destination has appealed to romantics since the dawn of the railway age. As the European network evolved through the 19th century, the concept of international train travel took hold; the first international train travelled the relatively short journey between Strasbourg and Basel in 1841, but it wasn't long before fast express trains were covering much greater distances.

Thomas Cook was at the forefront of the new form of travel, and in part thanks to his pioneering vision, the concept of the Grand Tour on the railways gradually became fashionable. Soon the well-to-do were boarding the boat train from Victoria to link with Wagons Lits services on the Continent. Often the development of long-distance railways was linked with the shipping company routes to India and the Orient; the railways transported mail and passengers to meet the liners, firstly to Spain, and, after the opening of the Suez Canal in 1869, to Brindisi, Athens and Port Said.

Modern long-distance rail travel

In modern Europe, the ultra-fast trains operating between such cities as London and Paris, Madrid and Seville will get you to your destination as quickly, if not quicker, than a plane. Longer journeys, such as Paris to Madrid and Rome, are obviously quicker by air, but travelling overnight in the supreme comfort of the new class of "Train Hotels", which feature single- and double-occupancy cabins with en suite showers, is an infinitely preferable option.

Europe's longest rail journey on one single train is the Paris to Moscow run, which departs twice weekly (three times in summer) and takes 46 hours. Other epics include Berlin to Kiev, and the Budapest to Istanbul route *(see page 328)*. The Yugoslav war of the 1990s severely disrupted the routes leading southeast from Western Europe to Greece and Turkey, and there are still no direct trains from Vienna to Athens. The Olympus service travels between Ljubljana and Thessaloniki, and on to Athens from June to October. The Trans-Balkan connects Budapest and Thessaloniki via Romania and Bulgaria. The line between Croatia and Sarajevo, severely damaged in the war, re-opened in 2001.

The perennially popular Inter-Rail pass (Eurail for non-Europeans) means that many cross-continental routes are heaving with backpackers in summer. The most popular routes radiate out from the tourist hubs of Paris, Prague, Rome, Florence and Barcelona. In the following chapter are two classic rail journeys that cross Europe; north to south on the Orient Express, and west to east on the Paris to Moscow route.

LEFT: Wagons-Lits was *the* way to travel.
BELOW: an Inter-Rail pass gives the freedom to explore Europe.

ESSENTIALS

Distance: 1,703 km
(London–Venice)

Duration of journey:
28 hrs 30 mins
(2 days, 1 night)

Frequency of trains:
2 per week March to
November
(London–Venice
departures on
Thursday and
Sunday;
Venice–London on
Wednesday and
Saturday)

THE VENICE SIMPLON-ORIENT EXPRESS

London's grubby Victoria Station may seem an incongruous place to set off on a 1,703-km (1,058-mile), 28½-hour journey in consummate luxury to La Serenissima – that most emotive name for the timeless city of Venice. The mêlée of tourists consulting the destinations boards; commuters rushing hither and thither; perplexed travellers listening to inaudible announcements; all are soon left behind at the specially-reserved check-in lounge at the eastern side of the station, just before the entrance to Platform One.

Baggage is tagged, your seat assignments in the British Pullman cars are noted on your boarding card, and the number of the allocated Wagons-Lits on the continental portion of the train marked on your ticket. Almost unnoticed, the 10 chocolate and cream Pullman cars have arrived at Platform 2, and smartly uniformed personnel are standing beneath the individual carriage name signs to welcome their guests.

Your fellow passengers collect their belongings and make their way towards the train. The *frisson* is tangible. Perhaps their Pullman carriage will be that in which Grace Kelly travelled after she became Princess Grace of Monaco; or the one in which the *beau monde* once rode to the Casino at Monte Carlo; or the special car in which members of European nobility were carried to the Coronation of Queen Elizabeth II in 1953.

Audrey, *Cygnus*, *Ibis*, *Ione*, *Lucille*, *Minerva*, *Perseus*, *Phoenix*, *Vera* and *Zena*; the classical names of the carriages hark back to a more distinguished era and rekindle the golden age of railway travel. Each one is shining and polished like a new toy and has a style entirely its own. *Phoenix* and *Zena* (used in the

BELOW: photo call
before departure
from Victoria.

1976 film *Agatha*) are distinctly Art Deco; *Ione* and *Ibis* have an Edwardian feel to their marquetry, with a frieze of roses and Greek dancing girls. They are even more opulent now than they were when they ran in such famous trains as the Brighton Belle, the Queen of Scots and the famous Cunarder boat trains.

Bon voyage

At 11.15am precisely, the electric locomotive takes the strain and this idiosyncratic train takes its leave from London's busy terminus. Within seconds you are crossing the Thames, past the imposing chimneys of Battersea Power Station on the left, before being plunged into the sprawling urbanisation of the metropolis, epitomised by Brixton with the bronze statues of commuters on the Y-shaped platform. Inside your *coupé* or table for two, the champagne corks have popped and the time has come to toast this journey in time, space and splendour.

Bromley South, Orpington, Chelsfield, the unremarkable leafy suburbs flash past your window. By now you're finishing the first of three courses of the lunch that is served en route to Folkestone. Heads turn to the left, and then across the carriage, attempting to glimpse the apple and cherry orchards of Kent – not for nothing is this county called the Garden of England. Another Limoges china plate is filled with poached salmon, accompanied by mint-flavoured new potatoes and a variety of salad leaves. The scene outside is now punctuated by white-capped oast houses – testimony to the ancient art of brewing, although most have now been converted into private homes.

The chalk hills of the North Downs lie off to the left, as does the new high-speed line for Eurostar trains bound for France and Belgium. You are now approaching the vast array of marshalling yards that lead to the Channel Tunnel,

Map on page 82

The "real" Orient Express is still in service, just; since 2001 it runs only as far as Vienna. Future plans remain unclear.

BELOW: the Paris to Constantinople Orient Express pauses at Salzburg.

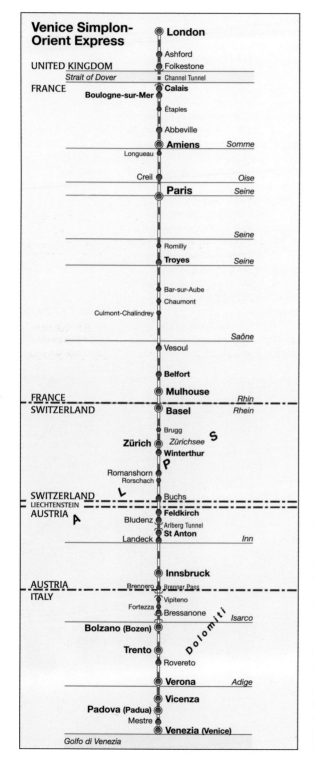

Venice Simplon-Orient Express

- London
- Ashford
- Folkestone

UNITED KINGDOM
Strait of Dover
Channel Tunnel

FRANCE
Boulogne-sur-Mer
- Calais
- Étaples
- Abbeville
- **Amiens** *Somme*
Longueau
Creil *Oise*
- **Paris** *Seine*

Seine
- Romilly
- **Troyes** *Seine*
- Bar-sur-Aube
- Chaumont
Culmont-Chalindrey
Saône
- Vesoul
- **Belfort**
FRANCE — **Mulhouse** *Rhin*
SWITZERLAND — **Basel** *Rhein*
- Brugg
Zürich *Zürichsee* **S**
- **Winterthur**
Romanshorn **P**
Rorschach
SWITZERLAND **L** — Buchs
LIECHTENSTEIN
AUSTRIA **A** — **Feldkirch**
Bludenz *Arlberg Tunnel*
- **St Anton**
Landeck *Inn*
- **Innsbruck**
AUSTRIA — Brennero — Brenner Pass
ITALY — Vipiteno
Fortezza — Bressanone *Isarco*
Bolzano (Bozen) *Dolomiti*
Trento
- Rovereto
- **Verona** *Adige*
- **Vicenza**
Padova (Padua)
Mestre
- **Venezia (Venice)**
Golfo di Venezia

and before long the train slows as it passes Folkestone Central – on the right, this ramshackle town slopes down to the grey-blue sea. After some jolting the train reverses and descends the steepest incline on British railways. Sailing boats and fishing dinghies bob gently as you cross a low-slung bridge to the almost defunct harbour station. In the distance, the White Cliffs of Dover set the scene.

For the next hour you are divorced from the romance of the rails as you board a coach for the 35-minute journey through the Channel Tunnel aboard Le Shuttle. On French soil, you head for Courcelles on the outskirts of Calais, and there, standing among a panoply of railway vehicles like a cardinal among curates, is Europe's most elegant train.

The Orient Express

Drawn up like Grenadier Guards in gleaming royal blue and gold livery, stand the 17 carriages of the Compagnie Internationale des Wagons-lits et des Grands Express Européens. Waxed mirror-bright, they make up the longest passenger train in Europe at slightly over 400 metres (1,320 ft). Formalities are brief, before passengers are shown to their compartments in the 11 sleeping cars – the most sumptuous and spacious ever to have run in Europe.

The information booklet beside the ubiquitous, fringed Pullman lamp in your carriage lists the many and varied histories of these carriages, dating back to 1926. Unlike the British Pullmans with their exotic names, the *wagon-lits* have numbers – but their history is no less colourful. Sleeping car 3,309, built in 1926, was decorated by René Prou, and ran in the Simplon-Orient Express from 1928 to 1939, and again after the war until 1958, when it was transferred to the Sud Express. Another car, 3,425, built in Birmingham in 1929, saw service in Turkey, running in the Anatolia Express and the Aegean and Taurus expresses after the war. Also British-built, car 3,473 – typified by its "flower garland" marquetry – ran in the famous Train Bleu between 1929 and 1937.

Shortly before 5pm the Venice Simplon-Orient Express slips quietly away on the first portion of its journey through five European countries. Paris will be reached in around three hours. This allows ample time to familiarise yourself with your compartment, which at this stage is made up for day use, with a couch and cushions as well as head-rests. Behind the door is a cabinet within which is secreted a washbasin adorned with a hand-painted motif reflecting the marquetry decoration of the compartment.

A discreet knock at the door and your white-gloved steward introduces himself. He takes care of passport and customs formalities, ensures you are familiar with the various lighting and heating controls, and hours later reappears to convert the entire compartment into its bedtime configuration. Moments later the maitre d' is in attendance to take reservations for dinner in the *Chinoise*, *Etoile du Nord* or *Lalique* dining cars.

By now you've left the sand dunes and marshland of the Pas de Calais behind. The forest of Crécy near Le Touquet is famous as the battlefield where King Edward III of England and his son the Black Prince overcame the might of the French in 1346. The train whizzes past farmhouses painted in faded colours and cafés with flower-filled window boxes. As you take turns to refresh and dress for dinner, the train follows the course of the River Somme – site of some of the fiercest fighting of World War I and, long before, the Battle of Agincourt in 1415 when Henry V forded the river with his army to defeat the French.

Dinner in Paris

The first dinner sitting is completed before the train pulls into the Gare de l'Est (to allow guests disembarking in Paris to enjoy a memorable meal), while the second sitting takes place after departing from the city. The restaurant cars await their guests in all their finery, while feverish activity goes on in the galleys. The epicurean delights of chef Christian Bodiguel are served in the magnificent surroundings of the Salon Pullman with its priceless Bacchanalian Maiden panels by Lalique. Lobster with *foie gras* followed by *mignon* of lamb with a ginger sauce are a precursor to the elaborate cheese course, which includes a signature creamy variety infused with Calvados. All choices on *Le Menu* are included in the fare, while a superb collection of fine wines are additional, as is the small *à la carte* selection.

Those awaiting the later sitting enjoy cocktails in the Bar Car – recreated from a first-class restaurant car dating from 1931. The immaculate interior, with small stools and convenient tables, is dominated by the baby grand piano adjacent to the curved bar.

As the train negotiates the loop line around Paris, the dome of Sacré Coeur reflects the setting sun and the Eiffel Tower pricks the evening sky. A bevy of anonymous Corail trains act as chaperones to their elegant older sister nudging into the Gare de l'Est. Those who dined at the early sitting take this opportunity to stretch their legs. As the train is stationary for almost 40 minutes there's even the chance to visit the station buffet, although their evening dress looks somewhat incongruous among the backpackers.

Map on page 82

ORIENT-EXPRESS
TRAINS & CRUISES

Crest and crown indicate what a superior train this is.

BELOW: afternoon tea delivered to your compartment.

Departing at 9.40pm from this terminus, the train makes a sprightly escape through inky-black Parisian suburbs. At Romilly, the line joins the Seine and follows the river upstream as far as the medieval town of Troyes.

By now the Bar Car is in full swing. The pianist is playing familiar melodies from Broadway and West End musicals; this party often continues into the small hours. At whatever time you go to bed, you'll find your sleeping car has been converted to its nightime configuration. The profusion of linen and blankets deadens noise from the tracks and a relaxed sleep usually ensues.

Celebrating the journey of a lifetime on the Orient Express.

Breakfast in the Alps

Early risers are rewarded as the long, narrow **Zürichsee** is unravelled from the tissue of mist. Winterthur, Romanshorn and Rorschach, archetypal Swiss towns one and all, start to come to life; neat, freshly-mown lawns, flower beds ablaze with colour, quaint shop windows, not a curtain out of place, nor a graffiti inscription in sight.

Sargans comes into view with its 11th-century castle on top of one hill, a church on the other. Moments later the train swings into the frontier station of **Buchs**. It's time for breakfast – served in the privacy of your cabin by the ever-attentive steward. Croissants that came on board a couple of hours ago, Colombian coffee to kick-start the day and freshly-squeezed orange juice to assuage the excesses of the night before.

With the snow-capped peaks of **Liechtenstein** looking down on the right-hand side of the train, you strain skywards to catch a glimpse of this tiny principality's capital of Vaduz, with its castle. A few miles further, there's another neck-craning moment; you had better get used to looking out of both sides of the train, as from now on the scenery can only be described as sensational.

BELOW: a table for two in the restaurant car.

Mighty Schattenberg Castle towers above the Austrian border town of Feldkirch, then the fortified town of **Bludenz**, with a 15th-century church, comes into view. Climbing ever more steeply through the Vorarlberg you pass high pastures dotted with immaculate, slope-roofed chalets. Such is the incline, the train now requires not just two locomotives in front, but one behind as well, to ensure a smooth journey up the precipitous track towards the **Arlberg Tunnel**.

Opened in 1884, the third longest tunnel in Europe at 10.2 km (6⅓ miles) separates the Vorarlberg from the Tyrol. The summit – at 1,802 metres (5,945 ft) – is reached inside the tunnel. After being plunged into darkness for seven minutes the train emerges into an amphitheatre of snow-capped mountains. At the famous alpine resort of **St Anton** you can see the filigree ski lifts stretching up the mountain on the left-hand side of the train during its brief pause.

Gathering speed, the descent towards Innsbruck crosses the mighty, single-span Tressana Bridge, past Landeck with a massive fortified castle standing sentinel to the Inn Valley. A 30-minute stop at **Innsbruck** allows time to stretch your legs before lunch. The Tyrolean capital was a favourite with Emperor Maximilian in the 1500s, and remains a popular base for touring Austria's beautiful Tyrol region.

Another reversal of the train and another ascent, this time towards the **Brenner Pass**, whose summit is at 1,375 metres (4,357 ft). A gourmet lunch is enjoyed as the train criss-crosses the spectacular alpine roads heading south, gliding past the cars and lorries backed up at the border customs post. High above the serpentine roads, castles perch like eyries as the train negotiates tight twists and turns through the rocky crags of the Dolomites.

Map on page 82

Descent into Italy

Soon the conifers of the higher elevations are replaced with an increasingly gentle scene of patchwork vineyards and orchards. There are little villages with attractive, ancient churches, and medieval towns with famous names like Fortezza and Bolzano. The picture-postcard moated castle, former residence of the ruling Prince Bishops, signals your arrival at **Trento**, capital of Trentino. Now the railway line follows the Adige River downstream towards Rovereto.

The setting for the ill-fated romance between Shakespeare's tragic lovers, Romeo and Juliet, the Etruscan city of **Verona**, with its attractive tiled roofs, can be seen in the distance. Some passengers alight here, especially during July, when spectacular open-air performances of Verdi's operas are held in the Roman amphitheatre, the Arena.

As the train glides across the **Veneto**, ripe and burnished by the afternoon sun, a decadent afternoon tea is served in your compartment. The vineyards of Soave and Valpolicella stretch out to the horizon. Ochre-hued **Vicenza** – home to Palladio, the great Renaissance architect – precedes the city of **Padua**, which will always be inextricably linked with Galileo (1564–1642), the great astronomer who was professor of mathematics at the city's university.

BELOW: passengers awake to glorious Apine scenery.

A visit to Venice during Carnival (late winter) is to see the city at its most exciting and atmospheric.

Journey's end

Shortly before 5.30pm the train finally crosses the long causeway that connects Mestre, on the mainland, with the island setting of **Venice**, that unique Italian contribution to civilised city life. To the right you can glimpse several *campanile* (bell towers) rising skyward from a profusion of terracotta dwellings abutting the open reaches of the Guidecca – the large sea lane that so many cruise ships follow during their visit to the city of Titian, Tintoretto, Tiepolo and, perhaps the greatest exponent of the Venetian scene, Canaletto.

The main station, Santa Lucia, houses a frenzy of porters ready to whisk your baggage to waiting motorboats. For passengers continuing on to **Rome** (occasionally scheduled during late spring and autumn) the train departs mid-morning the following day, arriving in Rome's Ostiense Station late afternoon. The king of trains has arrived at the Eternal City.

Other routes

It is possible to recreate this "magic carpet to the East" on twice-weekly (Mar–Nov) scheduled runs from London and Paris to Venice, as well as occasional journeys to Prague, Vienna, Budapest, Krakow, Rome and that Holy Grail of Orient Express destinations, Istanbul. The **Istanbul** journey starts in Paris (normally in late August or early September). After travelling east to **Budapest**, the Hungarian capital, for a tour of this historic city and overnight stay, the train heads east into Romania. There is a stop at Sinaia in the Transylvanian Alps, and a visit to the famous **Peles Castle**. The journey continues to **Bucharest** where you stay overnight before continuing to Bulgaria, arriving on the fifth day at Istanbul.

PARIS/AMSTERDAM/BERLIN–MOSCOW

Map on page 89

In the days of the Cold War, travelling on the Ost–West express from Western Europe right into the heart of the Soviet bloc was always one of Europe's most daunting rail experiences. Passengers were officially warned by the British Foreign Office against travelling on what they deemed to be one of the most dangerous train routes in Europe. Buying tickets in Britain, nervous travellers were presented with a British Rail International caveat that read, "Standards on this service may not be as high as those normally associated with European train travel."

The old Ost–West express officially ran from Paris to Moscow's Belorusskaya, but in reality it gathered passengers and carriages from all over Western Europe with connections from London Victoria, the ferry port of Ostende, and Paris. The engine and the majority of the carriages were Russian stock, as were the guards and train crew.

The old train may no longer officially exist, but the rail journey from Paris (or Amsterdam) to Moscow is still of great interest to rail enthusiasts, or indeed anyone of an adventurous nature. The pan-European route opens up a swathe of great cities and sweeping countryside, as well as offering an insight into the political map of Europe as the rail traveller ventures from the comfort of Western Europe into the harsher world of post-communist Russia.

High-speed lines from London St Pancras to Paris and Brussels make it more feasible than ever to take the train east. In fact, these days it is possible to travel from London to Hong Kong by rail, with just three changes of train (in Brussels, Moscow and Beijing); the entire journey can be done in ten or eleven days.

ESSENTIALS

Thomas Cook timetable no. 24

Distance: 3,450 km (Paris–Moscow)
Duration of journey: (Paris–Moscow): 45 hrs 49 mins (1 day, 2 nights) Amsterdam–Moscow 37 hrs 56 mins (1 day, 2 nights)
Frequency of trains: Paris–Moscow: 2 weekly, 3 weekly in summer Amsterdam–Moscow 1 daily

BELOW: Russian conductress.

Route options

The twice-weekly (three weekly in summer) Paris–Brussels–Berlin–Moscow train has been joined by the Jan Kiepura, a daily service from Amsterdam (it previously started in Brussels) travelling via Cologne, Berlin and Warsaw to Moscow. Both are a big improvement compared to the old Ost–West express, with friendly staff and comfortable berths. Alternatively, you could start your journey to Moscow further east, on the Moskva Express (Thomas Cook timetable no. 56) from Berlin, or on a direct sleeper train from Vienna (timetable no. 95).

From Paris the train travels to Brussels and arrives in Berlin the following morning, when it stops for around seven hours, giving passengers the chance to explore the city. The Jan Kiepura service stops at Cologne (where the impressive cathedral can be seen from the station platform) but passes through Berlin at 4am, and only stops for 20 minutes. **Frankfurt (Oder)**, Germany's less-illustrious Frankfurt that has none of the shiny skyscrapers of the megalopolis further west, is the last German station before Poland and functions as the border stop.

In the old days it was always after the train had pulled out of Berlin's Ostbahnhof that the fun really started, as it passed beyond the Iron Curtain into Eastern Europe. The contrast between east and west

is still there, but is far less marked these days – particularly now that Poland is a member of the European Union.

Across the North European Plain

The scenery across the North European Plain through Poland, Belarus and Russia is an almost endless procession of thick, dark-green forest, punctuated by fields and small towns and villages. The Moscow route is by no means as scenic as many of Europe's great train journeys, despite the best efforts of a number of rivers and low lying hills, but it is the sense of history and the feeling of riding across the new political map of Europe that is the real attraction.

A couple of hours after entering the vast rural expanse of Poland the train reaches the first major Polish city, **Poznań**. The area around Poznań is a true rail buff's paradise. Old Polish steam locomotives – the last regular scheduled steam trains operating in Europe *(see page 326)* – run the 60 km (38 miles) southwest to the town of Wolsztyn.

Northeast of Poznań, a totally different rail experience awaits. The Biskupin Railway is a perfectly preserved narrow gauge railway that trundles across the Wielkopolska countryside. It originates in the town of **Gasawa** and rumbles on to **Znin**. This line is very much geared towards tourists, who provide the necessary money to keep the narrow gauge trains running. There is also a network of narrow gauge trains that connects small communities throughout the Wielkopolska region that few visitors ever take the time to discover.

Around 3½ hours after leaving Poznań the train arrives in the city of **Warsaw**; it's best to stay on the train for the 10-minute stop because Warszawa Centralna is one of Europe's less salubrious stations. The train stops again at

The Paris to Moscow line runs across the middle of Poland, Belarus and European Russia, through vast tracts of rural land far removed from the modern age.

BELOW: a snowy platform at Moscow.

Warsaw Wschodnia, on the other side of the River Wisla, before travelling onwards to Belarus.

Border break

Belarus is one of the few ex-Soviet countries that chose to stay with Mother Russia and the remote Belarussian border outpost still retains some of its Cold War chill. Passengers should be wary at this stop of taking too many photos or getting off and on the train, as this often riles the border guards, whom it is best to avoid. These days, the atmosphere at **Brest** is far less threatening and the main interest is the changing of the train bogies that is necessary for travelling on the wider Russian gauge tracks. The whole process of changing the bogies takes around two hours as each carriage has to be done individually. Travellers who have taken the Trans-Siberian Express across Russia to China or Mongolia will be familiar with this operation; the uniquely wide gauge is a legacy of the paranoia of the former Soviet leadership, who were concerned about the possibility of foreign armies using the rail network to invade from the West.

Once fitted to the correct gauge, the train rolls on towards Moscow on the classic invasion route that ultimately crippled the ambitions of both Napoleon and Hitler in their attempts to conquer Moscow and defeat Russia. While the flat landscape and its gentle hills may look innocuous enough during the summer months, the long winters are a harsh, bitter affair that stopped both the French and German armies in their tracks. Today the plains are best enjoyed from the warmth and comfort of the train.

The Belarussian capital, **Minsk**, which sprawls across the banks of the Svisloch and Nerniga rivers, is unappealing on first sight. Minsk is Soviet-era planning on a grand scale with most buildings erected since 1945. Delving beyond the concrete façades, the tragic story emerges of a city that in 1941 had 270,000 inhabitants. By the end of the war, and a savage attack by the Germans and equally brutally recapture by the

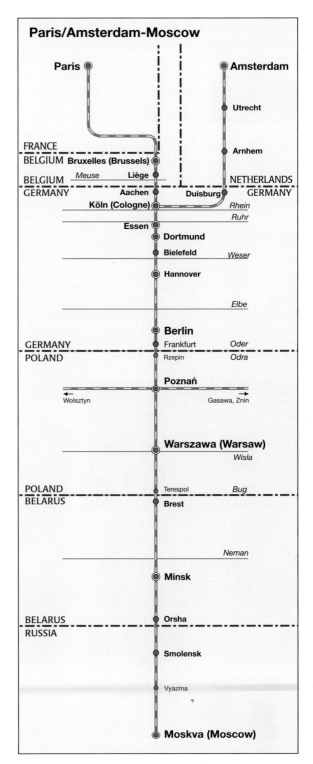

Journey's end is Moscow's grand Belorusskaya station.

Russians, 80 percent of the buildings had been destroyed and the shattered population had dwindled to under 40,000. It is this story that fires the imagination, with a number of museums given over to the war years, from heroic martyr displays to simple places that recall personal suffering. To delve into this forgotten aspect of World War II, and for a unique insight into life behind the Iron Curtain, Minsk is well worth a one- or two-day stop.

Smolensk to Moscow

The first Russian city en route is **Smolensk**, which is approached through a sprawl of goods yards where engines can be seen shunting around freight and passenger carriages. Smolensk suffered catastrophically during World War II when all but 300 of its houses and the entire Jewish population were obliterated by the Nazis. The city had long been on the front line, with Germans, Poles, French and Russian forces vying for control through the centuries. Today much of Smolensk's architecture is a throwback to Soviet times, but the city is worth exploring to unravel the layers of its eventful history. Highlights include the impressive town walls, the 17th-century Uspensky Cathedral and a monument to General Kutuzov, the brilliant strategist and field marshal who distinguished himself in the 18th-century wars against Turkey and commanded the Russian opposition to Napoleon.

BELOW: Siberian portrait. **RIGHT:** the romance of long-distance rail travel.

The final run from Smolensk and on to **Moscow** seems to take an eternity as the train crawls through the Stalinist-era housing estates and numerous suburban rail stations before it rolls into Moscow's impressively grand Belorusskaya station (at 8.30pm on the Paris train, 11am on the Jan Kiepura). A high-speed journey that began in Western Europe has come to an exciting finale in the endlessly fascinating Russian capital. ❑

ONWARDS TO ASIA

Moscow is a rail hub extraordinaire, with links to China and Japan via the Trans-Siberian express, and Central Asia on the "Turk–Sib" line.

There are in fact three Trans-Siberian trains, all of which head east from Moscow, out over the Urals (where the line crosses into Asia) and across the forests of Siberia. To the east of Irkutsk and beautiful Lake Baikal, the Trans-Mongolian route splits off from the main Trans-Siberian line, cutting south to the Mongolian border, and passing through the Mongolian capital of Ulan Bator on its way to Beijing. The Trans-Manchurian branches off further to the east, heading south across Manchuria to Beijing. The Trans-Siberian itself continues eastwards until it reaches the Pacific at Vladivostok, where ferries operate to Nakhodka in Japan.

The Turk–Sib route runs south-east from Moscow, across the steppes to Kazakstan and Uzbekistan, where it stops at the capital, Tashkent. From Tashkent there are easy connections to the stunning Silk Road cities of Samarkand, Bukhara and Khiva. Trains also run to the Kazak city of Almaty, from where it is possible to catch a train across the Chinese border to Urumqi and from there to other parts of China.

GREAT BRITAIN AND IRELAND

Map
on page
96

*Britain's railway heritage is second to none, and there is no shortage
of attractive journeys – from the bucolic delights of the Shrewsbury to
Swansea route to the scenic splendour of the West Highland line*

Britain gave railways to the world. Crude wagons had been used on track-
ways using wood, stone and iron for rails since at least the early 17th
century, but it was the work of Richard Trevithick and George and Robert
Stephenson in the first quarter of the 19th century that made possible the successful application of steam power to the railway.

The opening of the Stockton & Darlington and the Liverpool & Manchester
railways, in 1825 and 1830 respectively, are two of the most portentous events
in modern history. Britain's railway network grew rapidly, from 6,084 miles
(9,734 km) in 1850 to 15,563 miles (24,901 km) in 1880, reaching its greatest
extent in 1926 with 20,267 miles (32,427 km). A combination of sensible
pruning and foolish amputation has since whittled the network down to little
over 10,000 miles (16,000 km).

A colourful heritage

A visit to the National Railway Museum at York or one of the heritage railways
with a good stock of older locomotives gives an insight into how colourful
Britain's railways were until the 1920s. Few other countries invested so much
money and effort into making sure that their locomotives, in particular, were an
aesthetic pleasure. Yet with the 1922 grouping of 120
railway companies into four, followed by nationalisation in 1948, variety and colour diminished.

For the past half century railway managers have had
other concerns. Myopic governments and Treasury parsimony have resulted in decades of under-investment in
the method of transport of most value in a densely populated country. Today, Britain's railways compare
unfavourably with other European networks, with passengers paying higher fares for an inferior service.

It was hoped that the re-privatisation of the railways
in 1994 would generate the sustained levels of investment necessary for Britain's railways to reach continental standards. Regrettably, this has not proved to
be the case. Railtrack, the owner of the track, stations
and signalling, found itself in serious difficulties,
which had a deleterious effect on train performance
as well as delaying improvement projects. In 2001,
Railtrack was deemed unviable and collapsed.

However, Britain's chronic traffic congestion means
that train travel is usually faster than the alternatives,
much safer and generally less stressful. The ambience
for railway passengers has improved as billions of
pounds-worth of new trains have been introduced. As
one would expect from a network with over 20 different train operating companies, standards and pro-
cedures across the network vary, but efforts are
continuing to make the network seamless to the user.

PRECEDING PAGES:
steaming out of
Porthmadog
station.
LEFT: the narrow-
gauge Snowdon
Mountain Railway.
BELOW: the
observation coach
on the Royal
Scotsman.

Great Britain and Ireland

0 ————— 100 km
0 ————— 100 miles

N

ATLANTIC
OCEAN

Shetland
Yell Unst
Foula⚬ Mainland
Lerwick

⚬ Fair Isle

Westray
Mainland
Stromness Orkney
Hoy Islands
Thurso South
Ronaldsay
Wick

Helmsdale

Lewis
Stornoway

The Minch

Ullapool

Harris
North
Uist
South Uist Skye
Kyle of
Lochalsh Achnasheen Dingwall Moray Firth Elgin
Inverness
Barra Rum Ben Nevis W. Highlands Scotland Huntly
Mallaig 1344 40
Aviemore Aberdeen
Coll Fort William
Grampian Mountains Pitlochry
Tiree Mull Criaolarich Montrose
Firth of Lorn Oban Perth Dundee
Jura Stirling Firth of Forth
Weyhas 10 North Berwick
Islay Bay Greenock 2
Largs Glasgow Edinburgh Berwick-upon-Tweed
Arran Carstairs
Ayr Southern Uplands UNITED KINGDOM
Portrush Lockerbie
Coleraine Dumfries Morpeth
Londonderry Larne Hexham Newcastle upon Tyne
Ballymena 43 Durham
Donegal Northern Antrim Carlisle Middlesbrough
Enniskillen Ireland Bangor Stranraer The Pennines Whitby
Portadown Belfast Whitehaven Scafell 33 Scarborough
Ballina Pike Penrith Darlington
Sligo Newry Isle of 35 977 England
Carrick-on- Man Windermere 26 Kendal Bridlington
Westport Shannon Dundalk Barrow-in- Settle York
Castlebar Longford Drogheda Ferness Lancaster 5
Le Corrib IRISH 18 Kingston
IRELAND SEA Blackpool Preston Leeds upon Hull
Athlone Anglesey Liverpool 16 Manchester Doncaster Grimsby
Galway Dublin Llandudno Chester 4 Sheffield
Lough Holyhead Stoke-on- 14 Skegness
Derg Portarlington Snowdon 1085 27 38 Trent 30 King's 32 Great
Ennis Kildare Blaenau 6 Crewe 13 Nottingham Lynn Yarmouth
Thurles Wicklow 19 46 Ffestiniog Derby 21 Peter- 12
Limerick Kilkenny Carlow Mtns Pwllheli 28 Shrewsbury borough Norwich
Tralee Tipperary Clonmel Arklow Cardigan 42 47 Leicester 7 31 Ely Lowestoft
Mallow Enniscorthy Bay Wales Birmingham Coventry Cambridge
Killarney Wexford 45 Cambrian 37 44 Colchester Ipswich
Carrantouhill Rosslare Aberystwyth Mtns Worcester Stratford- Milton Chelmsford
1038 Cobh Fishguard 22 Hereford upon-Avon Keynes Southend
Cork Waterford Milford Gloucester 20 Watford 25 Margate
Haven Carmarthen 11 Newport Oxford Reading London 36
St George's Channel Swansea 15 Swindon Basingstoke Guildford Maidstone Dover
Cardiff Bristol 17 Salisbury Gatwick 8 Hastings
CELTIC Bristol Channel Taunton 29 Southampton Brighton Folkestone
SEA Barnstaple Bournemouth 23 Eastbourne
Exeter Weymouth 41 Portsmouth
Newquay 9 39 Isle of Wight
Truro 34 Torquay English Channel
Penzance Plymouth Dieppe
Land's Falmouth Fécamp
End Isles of FRANCE
Scilly Cherbourg

● ❶ Museums and
Heritage Lines
——— Featured route

Scenic highlights

There is no shortage of delightful journeys to add to those described in detail in the following pages. Away from the industrial areas, it is difficult to find a train journey in Scotland that is not a pleasure to the eye. South of the border, the historic line between Carlisle and Newcastle follows the only gap between the north Pennines and the foothills of the Cheviots, twice crossing the route of Hadrian's Wall and serving a series of attractive market towns, some with names dating back to Roman times.

For miles travelled beside the sea, few lines can hold a candle to the Carlisle–Barrow–Carnforth journey, which is seldom out of sight of water once the train has reached Maryport, with its 18th-century coal port and planned town. Both Maryport and Whitehaven have much of maritime and architectural interest to detain the visitor. The only competitor for sea views is the Dovey Junction–Pwllheli section of the railway west of Shrewsbury, which also serves Aberystwyth. For miles the railway is cut into a ledge in the cliff face, and Britain's longest timber viaduct across the Mawddach estuary provides a magnificent view of Cader Idris.

The narrow-gauge Ffestiniog Railway links the Pwllheli line at Minffordd with one of Wales's last rural branch lines, a cross-platform interchange at Blaenau Ffestiniog allowing passengers to head north along the beautiful Conwy valley to Llandudno Junction on the Holyhead–Chester line. Also offering continual sea views, this main line along the north coast of Wales has two of Britain's finest engineering structures, the Conwy and Menai bridges.

The other two groups of branch lines that should be considered for a rail-based tour of Britain are in East Anglia and in the West Country. In East Anglia is the East Suffolk line from Ipswich to Lowestoft, from where it is possible to take a train through the Norfolk Broads to Norwich. If time permits, savour the all-too-rare experience of changing trains at a country junction by stopping at Reedham to catch a train to Great Yarmouth and reach Norwich via Acle.

Devon and Cornwall used to be a warren of branch lines serving the numerous seaside resorts. Today one can still leave a London to Penzance train to take a branch to Exmouth, Barnstaple, Gunnislake, Looe, Newquay, Falmouth and St Ives. All the area's secondary cross-country lines have gone except for Bristol–Bath–Weymouth service which links some of Britain's loveliest market towns.

The good old days

Britain is rich in railway history, which feeds a peculiarly British nostalgia. Although the last regular steam services were phased out in 1968, there are plenty of heritage lines running today to satisfy the enthusiast, with highlights including the West Somerset Railway, the Vale of Rheidol Railway in mid-Wales, and the Bluebell Railway in Sussex. The Golden Age of luxury travel is remembered in the form of the Royal Scotsman *(see page 100)* as well as in numerous specialist services using original rolling stock. A full listing of heritage railways and railway museums appears on pages 120–23.

Map on page 96

A young enthusiast on the Severn Valley Railway.

BELOW: a new-style Virgin express train.

ESSENTIALS

Thomas Cook
timetable no. 218

Distance: 164 miles

Duration of journey:
5 hrs 10 mins

Frequency of trains:
3–4 per day (direct)

Star Attractions:
Glasgow
● **Buchanan Street**
● **St Mungo**
    Cathedral
● **Glasgow Art**
    Gallery & Museum
● **Barras Fleamarket**

THE WEST HIGHLAND LINE

Standing in the bowels of Glasgow's subterranean Queen Street Station, it comes as no surprise to learn that the old steam trains had to be cable-hauled up the Cowlairs Incline (the slope leading out of the station) by stationary steam engines. This is only the first of many challenging ascents on the West Highland Line, "The Iron Road to the Isles", an epic rail adventure that takes travellers through some of Europe's most beautiful landscapes. The sedate pace – trains take over five hours to cover the 164 miles (264 km) – allows time to appreciate the majestic mountain scenery.

Echoes of the past

The first hour of the journey is spent trying to shake off the sprawling suburbs of Glasgow and the debris of its industrial past. While the city may have gone through something of a renaissance over the last decade or so, the journey from Queen Street to Helensburgh tumbles through the rusting remnants of an era when many of the world's great ships were Clyde-built. In those days many of the world's finest engineers were Scots, a tradition of excellence carried over into the construction of the West Highland Line.

The line was built to serve two main industries – tourism and fishing – shuttling tourists between central Scotland and the Western Highlands and bringing them back along with the marine cargo.

Originally the rails only extended as far as the old garrison town of Fort William, which was reached in 1894. It was not until 1901 that the railway finally made it to the open sea at the bustling fishing port of Mallaig.

Just after Helensburgh at Craigendoran Junction, the West Highland Line splits off from the main line and begins its ascent into the Highlands. The old piers and urban clutter are soon replaced by the peaceful shores of Loch Long, Loch Goil and the Gare Loch as the four-carriage Sprinter diesel unit struggles up the first gradients. The most impressive loch of them all is **Loch Lomond**, the largest stretch of fresh water in Britain, which the line skirts for 10 miles (16 km), winding through the wooded slopes with occasional glimpses across the cold waters. This is Rob Roy country, where the legendary outlaw evaded the authorities among the ramble of glens and lochs, a tale immortalised by 19th-century novelist Sir Walter Scott.

The train climbs more than 500 ft (150 metres) in just 5 miles (8 km) before arriving at **Crianlarich**, where it divides; two carriages head west for the town of Oban, gateway to the islands of Mull and Islay. The remaining two carriages edge further north as expansive views of the mountains and Caledonian forests open up. One of the most dramatic set pieces of the West Highland Line is the **Horseshoe Viaduct**,

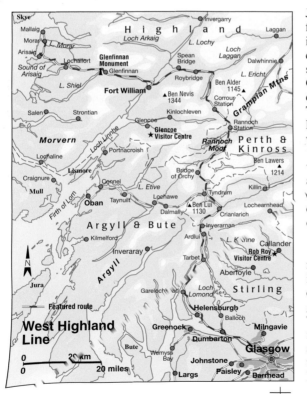

a sweeping curve and small viaduct that were only built as a cash-saving measure. Journey times would have been reduced if the glen had been crossed by a single, much larger viaduct, but financial limitations meant that this glorious loop took shape between the solid masses of Beinn Odhar and Beinn Dorain.

In contrast to the winding track and steep gradients of much of the route, **Rannoch Moor** is a wide, open plateau that the train rolls across with seemingly little effort. This illusion belies the difficulty of laying a track across the sodden, inhospitable moor that Robert Louis Stevenson so dramatically immortalised in his novel *Kidnapped*. The initial attempt to lay solid foundations was a disaster as the bog swallowed up all the spoil laid on it. The eventual solution was to "float" the track across, to lay it directly on top of the sodden moor.

Remote Rannoch

Rannoch station stands in spectacular isolation, a tiny dot in a bleak netherworld, miles from the nearest human settlement. In summer this is a great jumping off point for walkers, ramblers and climbers; in winter the dramatic surrounding mountains are a place for serious and experienced mountaineers only, as the regular call-outs for mountain rescue services testify.

Soon after Rannoch, at **Corrour**, the West Highland Line reaches its highest point. This is the station where the four protagonists from Irvine Welsh's *Trainspotting* decamped with the idea of doing some Highland walking, but were quickly deterred by Leum Uilleim's imposing slopes.

Impressive mountains shadow the West Highland Line for much of its journey, but the granddaddy of them all is **Ben Nevis**, Britain's highest peak at 4,406 ft (1,344 metres), which looms over the town of **Fort William**. Ben

Map on page 98

The ornate badge of the Royal Scotsman harks back to an earlier age of rail travel.

BELOW: grand scenery on the West Highland Line.

Royal Scotsman

Since its inaugural run in 1985, the Royal Scotsman has redefined luxury train travel in Britain. From April to November, guests assemble at Edinburgh's Waverley station as a kilted bagpiper sets the scene. Drawn up like guards on parade, the Royal Scotsman's nine gleaming carriages, resplendent in purple livery and gilt lettering, evoke the sense of a truly grand occasion. This is home for the next five days.

The ambience is truly luxurious. Champagne and hors d'oeuvres are served as you mingle in the Observation Car. Seating all 36 passengers in comfortable, two-person sofas and roomy, upholstered armchairs in muted tones of blue, this carriage contains an open veranda.

Guests are then escorted to their state sleeping car. These are the most stylish accommodation to be found within the limits imposed by European railway carriages. Originally Pullman day cars, they have since been completely rebuilt in the style of the

Edwardian era. The beds are all lower berths and there is an en suite bathroom with shower, wash-basin and toilet.

Slowly and sedately this most regal of trains makes its way onto the scenically stunning West Highland Line. Loch Long, Loch Lomond and Rannoch Moor offer a magical mosaic of mountains, lochs, pine and birch-wood forests, a perfect backdrop as you settle down to the first of many memorable meals.

The two dining cars convey a wonderfully old-fashioned character, and the harmonious combinations of local Scottish produce, varied during the tour to satisfy eye and taste-buds alike, are worthy of a Michelin star. Stewardesses in tartan skirts and nattily-attired stewards ensure that the country house party atmosphere never palls. The theme continues in the off-train arrangements where the team of well-informed guides, as well as the train's own liveried motor coach, form an integral part of this encounter with centuries of heritage and tradition.

At the Inverawe Smokehouse you see how a range of locally-caught fish are smoked to perfection before they are dispatched to Harrods. Ballindalloch Castle, home of the Macpherson-Grant family since 1546, affords the chance to have a close encounter with a herd of Aberdeen Angus cattle, as golden eagles fly high in the sky.

At Kyle of Lochalsh, after a visit to the mystical Isle of Skye, traditional Gaelic melodies are played on the *clarsach* during an after-dinner recital in the Observation Car. During the coming days, Scotland's highest mountain, Ben Nevis, offers an impressive backdrop to the Caledonian Canal; Eilean Donan, the most romantic of all Scottish castles, where the clans fought and the MacRaes found refuge, appears straight off a calendar cover; while at the Dalmore Distillery you learn the art of whisky blending whilst enjoying a "wee dram".

As the train returns south via the ancient Scottish capital of Perth, the magnificent Highland scenery gives way to a more gentle terrain. Having crossed the century-old Forth Railway Bridge, it is just a few more miles to journey's end at Edinburgh. ❏

LEFT: enjoying a wee dram at the bar on the Royal Scotsman.

Map
on page
98

Nevis's sturdy shape manages to disguise its height from many angles on the approach from Corrour, but the snow that usually cloaks its upper reaches indicates its lofty altitude. Travellers with time to spare could take a room in one of the many bed-and-breakfasts and hotels in Fort William and make their own challenge on the summit. Reaching the top is possible even for relatively inexperienced walkers on a good day, but it should always be approached with caution, as the weather can change from fair to atrocious in seconds.

Heading out of Fort William the train hugs the shores of **Loch Linnhe**, a sea loch that is the first sign that we are now close to the open sea. The track now struggles through the demanding terrain of the West Highland Line Extension, which celebrated its centenary in 2001. The 39-mile (62-km) route is a major feat of railway engineering, necessitating a mass of rock cutting and drilling, the building of 11 tunnels and five major viaducts. In summer the Jacobite steam train runs along the extension line all the way from Fort William to Mallaig and back, serving up large helpings of nostalgia along with its day-trip refreshments. While more casual tourists admire the views from the old carriages and buy a video souvenir of the journey, the rail enthusiasts crane their necks out of windows to snap photos of the steam engine pummelling its way seawards.

A selection of whisky from the Highlands.

Breathtaking Glenfinnan

The most stunning section of the extension, and arguably the greatest rail vista in the British Isles, is at **Glenfinnan**. Here the train squeals around the 21 arches of Glenfinnan Viaduct, one of the finest examples of engineering from the great golden age of Britain's railways. Initial objections that the viaduct would spoil the breathtaking beauty of Glen Finnan quickly dissolved when it became

BELOW: Bonnie Prince Charlie's Monument, Glenfinnan.

EATING AND SLEEPING EN ROUTE

Glenfinnan station is a shining testament to one man's love for the golden age of the railways. John Barnes fondly remembered Glenfinnan from his youth and when hatchet plans threatened its future he acted to preserve the station and turn it into a museum.

Today his dream has exceeded all his expectations. The station now incorporates a bunk house – a sleeping car that has been converted for use as comfortable self-catering accommodation for travellers – and a beautifully restored dining car serving food and its own real ale brew. The sleeping car is open all year round, is heated during the winter and has cooking and washing facilities (tel: 01397 722295).

Elsewhere on the West Highland Line there is another railway bunk house, at Tulloch. The original station building has been impressively revamped in Swiss chalet style. The bunk house also has a dining room and a small shop. The surrounding area is good walking country with a number of easily accessible munros (the name given to a Scottish peak in excess of 3,000 ft/915 metres).

Railway-themed dining in the region continues with the Station House Restaurant at Corrour and the Station Tearoom in Crianlarich.

Glenfinnan Viaduct was one of the first structures on this scale to be built of concrete. Its use gave the nickname "Concrete Bob" to its builder, Robert McAlpine. The viaduct was featured in the second film of the Harry Potter saga.

obvious that the curl of the viaduct only enhanced the dramatic scene. At the foot of the glen the viaduct snakes around as the River Finnan runs down in search of the salt waters of Loch Shiel, a shadowy sea loch that itself is dwarfed by the towering Highland massif. At the centre of it all is a **monument to Bonnie Prince Charlie** and his brave Highlanders who advanced as far as Derby in 1745 on their Jacobite quest, before they were finally forced to retreat north, only to be massacred on the brutal moor of Culloden.

After the overwhelming drama and sense of history of Glenfinnan the landscape now opens up with the first views of the "Small Isles" – **Rum**, **Eigg** and **Muck** – which hang tantalisingly close offshore, and tease in and out of view on the run seawards to Mallaig. This part of the line includes the Leachabhuidh Tunnels, the Gleann Mama Viaduct and the impressive **Borrodale Viaduct**, as the train slides through rock cuttings and around hillsides. In a final scenic flourish before Mallaig the white sands of **Morar** and **Arisaig** twinkle into view, impossibly starched against the clear blue waters on a sunny day. Morar is another great stopping-off point, with impressive beaches ideal for bracing strolls, as well as Scotland's shortest river, the Morar, and deepest loch, Loch Morar. Local legend holds that Loch Morar has its own monster, Morag, who has so far attracted none of the tourist hype of her famous sibling in Loch Ness.

Journey's end is reached at **Mallaig** with the squawk of seagulls and the tang of salty sea air. The busy fishing harbour bustles with life as visitors set off on forays to unspoiled islands and fishermen tuck into "fish suppers" they helped catch. It all feels a million miles away from the big city life and post-industrial residue of Glasgow, but soon the Sprinter will be turning tail and heading back over the tracks on one of the world's most spectacular railway journeys.

BELOW: the Jacobite steam special at Glenfinnan.

INVERNESS–KYLE OF LOCHALSH

Map on page 96

The Inverness to Kyle of Lochalsh line takes passengers through some of Scotland's most rugged and spectacular scenery. The Skye Railway, as it is better known, stretches from the chilly waters of Scotland's east coast and the nation's newest city, Inverness, right up over the Highland mountains, and down to the west coast waters of Kyle of Lochalsh, where the Isle of Skye lies just across the water.

Originally the Dingwall & Skye Railway Company, the enterprise behind building the line, intended to extend the track all the way from Inverness to Kyle, but when it opened on 10 August 1870, financial problems meant it only went as far west as Strome Ferry. It was not until 1897, when competition from the newly opened West Highland Line forced the successor Highland Railway to extend the line, that trains ran the 82 miles (132 km) between Inverness and Kyle.

Along the Moray Firth

After the train leaves Inverness station it spends the next half hour winding through the growing suburbs and towns that dot the banks of the **Moray Firth**. The flats of the Firth are home to grey herons, swans and geese, and there is also a colony of bottlenose dolphins that the eagle eyed may be lucky enough to spot. The line also crosses the **Caledonian Canal**, a feat of engineering on a similarly impressive scale to the Skye Railway, forming a link between Inverness and the old garrison town of Fort William at the other end of the Great Glen, 60 miles (97 km) away. In summer boats can be seen queuing up to use the Ocean Lock that connects the canal to the North Sea.

Soon after the town of **Dingwall**, supposed birthplace of Macbeth, the Skye Railway finally shakes off the companion Far North Line, which breaks away in search of the top of mainland Britain. This is where the impressive scenery really starts as the North Sea is left behind for good and voluminous mountains start to loom on the horizon. There are four lochs to negotiate on this stretch: Garve, Luichart, Auchuillin and Achanalt, and also the chance to spot herds of wild red deer.

The diesel engines face hard work as the line struggles up towards **Achnasheen**, the highest station on the route at 646 ft (197 metres), marking the watershed between the Atlantic and the North Sea. In summer this is a popular jumping-off point for walkers and climbers. Even in July and August there is often snow on the highest peaks, while a journey in winter takes the train through a snowy wilderness that frequently overworks the snow plough fitted to the front of the train.

Achnasheen is one of the many romantically named stations en route, translating as "The Field of Storm". The names of the stations themselves, many of them signposted in both Gaelic and English, give an insight into the complex and tumultuous history of the Highlands. There is the French-named town of Beauly, Attadale ("Valley of Fighting" in Norse) and the Gaelic Loch Luichart ("Loch of the Holly Tree") and Achnashellach ("Field of Willows"). The Gaelic name for Kyle of Lochalsh translates as "Narrows of the Rolling Waves".

ESSENTIALS

Thomas Cook timetable no. 226

Distance: 82 miles

Duration of journey: 2 hrs 25 mins

Frequency of trains: 3–4 per day westbound, 3–4 per day eastbound

BELOW: crofting is still a way of life in remote parts of the Highlands.

The scenery starts to change markedly once again as the line drops down and around the west coast sea lochs. The route is at its most spectacular on the 10-mile (16-km) Strome Ferry–Kyle extension, which took four years and £250,000 to build, a fortune by 19th-century standards. The train scythes through a series of rock cuttings (some as deep as 80ft/24 metres) and tunnels as it skirts the loch edge. The views are stunning, as island-dotted sea lochs shimmer on the right-hand side of the train and shadowy peaks loom in the background.

Many Highland stations have information centres as well as opportunities to buy souvenirs.

Picturesque Plockton

Soon after the treacherous tidal Strome Narrows, the picture-postcard village of Plockton appears. This dreamy collage of whitewashed houses and multi-coloured boats rests right on the waterfront and makes an ideal stop, with a couple of hotels, a sprinkling of bed-and-breakfasts and the odd loch-side pub to serve the needs of rail travellers. In Plockton there is little to do bar relax by the waterfront breathing in the fresh air and admiring the panoramic views. Evenings are best spent in Off the Rails, an excellent restaurant housed in the old railway station building, that serves Scottish cuisine with a modern twist, using fresh ingredients from the surrounding hills and sea lochs.

From Plockton the line cuts through swathes of rock and heather as it flirts with views of the islands that dot the west coast. Soon the horizon in the west is filled with the craggy peaks of Skye's Cuillin mountains. Journey's end comes as the train slips into Kyle of Lochalsh station. A new concrete bridge across the narrow channel to Skye has done little to tame the wild beauty of what many rate as Scotland's most attractive island, a fittingly dramatic end to a rail journey that eases passengers through some of Scotland's most impressive scenery.

BELOW: a view of Plockton from the Inverness–Kyle train.

LONDON–INVERNESS–WICK

Map
on page
96

This 734-mile (1,181-km) journey to the northernmost reach of the British mainland requires at least two days. London to Inverness takes a little over eight hours on the fast day-time train, but a more relaxed schedule would allow exploration of some outstanding cities. The journey requires a change of train at Inverness.

King's Cross to Peterborough

The journey starts at **King's Cross** station, perhaps the most austere of London termini, with only the Italianate clock tower embellishing the functional brick façade to the twin-span roof of the train shed. Opened in 1852, it is in marked contrast to St Pancras next door, the most ornate railway terminus in Britain. The line north through Gas Works and Copenhagen tunnels used to be a smoky, noisy business in steam days, as locomotives struggled up the steep bank on rails often wet from flooding. The north London suburbs flash past the window for the first miles. Soon the train is racing through undulating Hertfordshire farm-land; the East Coast main line, as the route is known, was built for speed, helped by the relative flatness of much of the countryside through which it passes.

In winter, **Hatfield House** can be seen on the hill beyond the tower of the parish church; the 16th-century house was home to Robert Cecil, 3rd Marquess of Salisbury who was three times prime minister in the 19th century. **Welwyn Garden City** was one of the low-density "garden cities" advocated by Ebenezer Howard around 1900. Just to the north, a 40-arch viaduct built with 13 million bricks provides a grandstand view over the Mimram valley.

ESSENTIALS

Thomas Cook
timetable nos.
185/186/221/226

Distance: 734 miles

Duration of journey:
London–Inverness
8 hrs 7 mins (day), 11 hrs 25 mins (night);
Inverness–Wick
3 hrs 52 mins

Frequency of trains:
London–Inverness
1 direct day train and
1 direct night train;
Inverness–Wick 3–4
per day

BELOW: the GNER express at Berwick.

Star Attractions: York

● York Minster
● Jorvik Viking
  Centre
● Castle Museum
● National Railway
  Museum
● Treasurer's House

Once past the original garden city of Letchworth, the line leaves Hertfordshire for Bedfordshire and miles of market gardens. Approaching **St Neots** and the pinnacled church tower of St Mary's, the line passes the water-meadows of the River Ouse to the west and skirts the Fens to the east, "where sky and Lincolnshire and water meet" as the poet Philip Larkin put it. The major junction of **Peterborough** is preceded by a bridge across the River Nene and a view east of the Barnack-stone cathedral; largely built in the 12th century, it is one of the country's finest Norman buildings.

Built for speed

North from Peterborough the line climbs towards **Stoke Summit**. It was on the southbound descent from Stoke Tunnel that the world record for steam traction was set in 1938 by the streamlined Pacific *Mallard*, which can be seen in the National Railway Museum in York.

The well-wooded landscapes for much of the way to Grantham are the most pleasing between London and York. **Grantham**'s skyline is dominated by the graceful spire of St Wulfram's, a largely 13th-century creation with a later library of chained books above the porch. The flat landscape still has the feel of the Fens as the train reaches **Newark**, with a magnificent market square and the castle where King John died in 1216. A long stretch of woodland precedes the major railway junction of **Doncaster**, chosen by the Great Northern Railway for its locomotive, carriage and wagon works, although most people know the town for its racecourse and the St Leger race, inaugurated in 1778. A succession of murky river and canal crossings and some of the country's largest coal-fired power stations do little to relieve the landscape until **York** comes into view.

BELOW: the National Railway Museum in York is one of the world's largest transport museums.

The station befits the city; its 1870s curving, four-span roof with the elegantly decorated supporting ironwork is a masterpiece. Outside is the Royal Station Hotel, which retains some of its original features. The station is only a short walk from the River Ouse and the city centre, which is compact enough to explore on foot.

Passing the National Railway Museum on the left, trains quickly accelerate along the straight stretch of line along the Vale of York to Darlington with the growing outline of the Hambleton and Cleveland hills to the northeast. On the right, just before **Thirsk**, is a sign marking the midway point between London and Edinburgh. Further north, **Durham** is entered by a 10-arch viaduct that offers a fine view of the Norman castle and cathedral and the River Wear.

More industrial scenes are passed on the way to one of the great moments on the journey, the crossing of the River Tyne by the **King Edward VII Bridge**, which the monarch opened in 1906. From it six other bridges can be seen, most notably Stephenson's High Level Bridge of 1849. It is Grade I listed, as is John Dobson's glorious classical station and train shed at **Newcastle-upon-Tyne**, regarded by some as the finest station in the country. The nearby Museum of Science and Engineering has plenty of information on the Stephensons' works.

As the distance between railway and coast narrows, gorgeous snatches of white sandy beaches and castles flash by. There is a lovely view of the small town and harbour at **Alnmouth** and later of Holy Island, topped by the outline of Lindisfarne Castle. The 28-arch Royal Border Bridge was the last link to be opened between London and Edinburgh, in 1850. **Berwick-upon-Tweed**, on the north bank, retains the most unusual Italian-designed fortifications, built during the late 16th century.

North of the border

The line passes a string of enticing sandy beaches as it crosses into Scotland, before turning inland to skirt the Lammermuir Hills. Bypassing the station at the former garrison town of **Dunbar**, the line regains the coast near **Longniddry** with occasional views over the Firth of Forth. The volcanic rump of Arthur's Seat overlooks the railway as it works its way through suburbs to arrive at **Edinburgh Waverley**, one of the best-sited major stations in Britain, conveniently placed in an inconspicuous trench between the old and new towns.

Trains for Perth take an inland route rather than crossing the Firth of Forth on the spectacular Forth Bridge. Passengers are compensated by a run through the lovely valley between the Ochil Hills in the east and southern outliers of the Grampians to the west. First stop is **Stirling**, where the largely 15th-century castle towers over the town on an immense rock. Beside the farms of Strathallan the railway makes its way to **Gleneagles**, famous for its golf course and former railway hotel, and into Strathearn for **Perth**, where the kings of Scotland used to be crowned.

The route of the old Highland Railway cuts right through the Grampians, reaching the highest summit of a British mainline railway at **Druimuachdar** (1,484 ft/ 452 metres). Lowland farms gradually give way to forests and heather-covered moors and granite-grey rock. Even in driving rain, it is country that stirs the soul of all but the incorrigibly unromantic. There is

Map on page 96

Star Attractions: Edinburgh
● The Castle
● The Royal Mile
● Royal Museum of Scotland
● St Giles Cathedral
● Palace of Holyroodhouse
● National Gallery
● New Town

BELOW: Edinburgh's Waverley station, with the Balmoral Hotel behind.

Dunrobin Castle is the Scottish home of the Dukes of Sutherland, one of whom played a leading role in the Highland Clearances.

BELOW: wintry scene south of Helmsdale.

plenty to detain those with the time to savour the small towns and villages linked by the railway: **Dunkeld & Birnam** for the ruined cathedral and the wood made famous by Shakespeare's *Macbeth*; **Pitlochry** to see the salmon pass at a dam, the theatre and Queen's View of Loch Tummel; **Blair Atholl** for the castle; **Kingussie** for the Highland Folk Museum; **Aviemore** for the Strathspey Railway.

At Aviemore the Cairngorms are seen in the distance before the train tackles the climb to the last summit before Inverness, at Slochd (1,315 ft/401 metres). Dropping down across the viaduct over the Findhorn river and the 28-arch structure over Strath Nairn, the line passes west of the infamous battlefield where in 1746 the last hopes of the Jacobites were crushed without mercy at Culloden, the last battle fought on British soil.

Views over the Moray Firth precede arrival at the unusual, triangular station at **Inverness**, where the fine museum nearby provides a good introduction to most facets of the Highlands. There are three trains a day between Inverness and Wick/Thurso, with trolley refreshments. This is a much-underrated journey, and offers a variety of landscapes: Beauly Firth with the Black Isle on the northern shore following departure from Inverness; Cromarty Firth after leaving the junction for Kyle of Lochalsh at **Dingwall**; the climb through increasingly wild country to the sheep sale centre of **Lairg**; the gentler section beside the coast through **Dunrobin**, where the castle of the railway's great patron, the 3rd Duke of Sutherland, can be visited; the turn inland at **Helmsdale** to pass up the gloriously beautiful Strath Kildonan; the desolation of the inhospitable moors between the bird-watching centre at **Forsinard** and Britain's most northerly junction at **Georgemas**; followed by the final sections through pastoral fields to Caithness's only towns of **Wick** and **Thurso**.

LEEDS–SETTLE–CARLISLE

Map
on page
96

Ask ten railway buffs to nominate the most scenically dramatic railway journey in England and there would probably be a unanimous response: the Settle & Carlisle line. The reason is simple: no other route can match the grandeur of the Pennine landscapes through which the railway forced a passage.

It is a railway of ironies. It should never have been built in the first place: it was proposed by the Midland Railway (MR) as a way of relieving delays to its Anglo-Scottish traffic on the West Coast line, owned by the rival London & North Western Railway (LNWR), which had a policy of making things awkward for MR traffic. However, alarmed at the prospect of losing business to the new line, the LNWR became more co-operative. In light of this improvement, the MR was on the point of deciding against building such an obviously costly route. But Victorian railway politics intervened, ever eager for more competition, and Parliament forced it to proceed.

Once the die was cast, the Midland Railway proceeded to build one of the best-engineered mainline tracks in the country, despite the inhospitable terrain. When the Settle & Carlisle (S&C) opened to passengers in 1876, it had cost the then prodigious sum of £3.8 million. But there was little in the way of passenger traffic, and it is a final irony that it took the threat of closure in the 1980s to boost traffic figures to levels unknown for many decades.

Today the railway is in good health. Its value as a diversionary route to the West Coast main line has been properly recognised, large volumes of freight traffic are routed over it, hundreds of walkers use it on sunny weekends, and it is a popular route for steam-hauled excursions. Stations have been reopened and restored, some by the Friends of the Settle & Carlisle Line, which played a major part in the successful fight against closure proposals.

ESSENTIALS

Thomas Cook
timetable no. 174

Distance: 114 miles

Duration of journey:
2 hrs 40–45 mins

Frequency of trains:
7 per day (8 on Sat;
3 on Sun)

BELOW: a guard
on the Embsay &
Bolton Abbey
Railway, Skipton.

Leeds to Settle Junction

The northbound journey on the Settle & Carlisle begins at the recently rebuilt Leeds station, where the imposing 1938 North Concourse has been brought back into use. As far as Skipton, S&C trains share the line through Airedale with electric stopping trains; the S&C proper begins at Settle Junction, where Leeds to Lancaster trains turn west to the sea. Between Leeds and Skipton, S&C trains stop only at Shipley and Keighley, but there is much to see en route.

After the triangular junction at **Shipley**, the train passes through **Saltaire**, the model town built around a huge mohair and alpaca mill by the enlightened entrepreneur Sir Titus Salt. Part of the mill now houses the largest collection of paintings by Bradford-born artist David Hockney. **Keighley** is the junction for the mostly steam-operated Keighley & Worth Valley Railway, which climbs into Brontë country at Haworth and on to Oxenhope. The once important junction town of **Skipton** has a well-preserved medieval castle and attractive main street.

Pausing today at the restored, Grade II-listed station of **Hellifield**, where the line from Blackburn trails in from the southwest, it is hard to believe that this

station once had a uniformed staff of 60 with first- and third-class refreshment rooms. After passing the signal box at Settle Junction the S&C begins, and the line almost immediately starts to climb. It is not so much the gradient – 1 in 100 is not too severe – as the length of the climb that earned the 15 miles (24 km) to Blea Moor Tunnel the nickname of "the long drag". For the fireman of steam days it meant an almost continuous shovelling of coal.

Settle to Carlisle

As the train approaches the first station, **Settle**, the green dome of Giggleswick school chapel can be seen to the west. An attractive market town with a couple of local history museums and some good vernacular buildings, Settle is easily explored on foot from the station. Continuing north through a narrow, wooded valley, the line enters the Yorkshire Dales National Park and, near the village of Stainforth, crosses twice in quick succession a loop in the River Ribble.

The valley broadens on the approach to **Horton-in-Ribblesdale**, allowing extensive views across dry-stone-walled fields to the northeast and the jelly-mould outline of Pen-y-ghent. All of the stations in the National Park offer access to good walking, and though most are unstaffed, a telephone is provided to check that trains are running to time – a welcome facility in poor weather when a wait in a local pub would be preferable to a station shelter.

The country becomes steadily wilder with only the occasional farm building and wind-blown tree rising above the moorland that displaces the pasture. To the west is the 2,375-ft (724-metre) summit of Ingleborough, reached by a series of distinctive steps and crowned by an Iron-Age fort with part of the walls still standing. A terrace of quarry workers' cottages heralds the approach

BELOW: Moorcock Viaduct, to the north of Garsdale.

to **Ribblehead**, the best-known place on the S&C, thanks to the **viaduct** to the north of the station, the longest on the railway at 443yds (405 metres).

Map on page 96

Today the station has a visitor centre and provides access to the Dales Way, which passes underneath the viaduct. The station was once a focal point of life for the isolated community that used it; from 1880 to 1956 the booking hall was used for church services, stone was dispatched from the adjacent sidings until the mid-1980s, and from 1938 the stationmaster had to file an hourly weather report from 7am to 9pm.

Looking north from the station drive, it is hard to imagine that the hollow now filled by the viaduct was once what served as home to about 2,000 navvies, who toiled on the viaduct and on Blea Moor Tunnel. Batty Moss camp, as it was known, was in existence for seven years and had a post office, library, school, mission house, hospital and public houses, augmented by carts supplying milk, meat and vegetables.

The double track becomes single to pass over the spectacular 24-arch stone viaduct, which was the principal reason for the closure proposals in the 1980s: British Rail said it would take between £4¼ and £6 million to repair the structure; in the end it cost £3 million. Wind speeds of over 90 mph (145 km/h) have been recorded by the anenometer at Ribblehead; cars have been blown off trains, and railway workers have been forced to cross on their hands and knees to take advantage of the shelter provided by the parapet.

On the east side of the railway as the train leaves the viaduct is the lonely signal box of Blea Moor, almost a mile from the nearest road. The sight of the deepening cutting that precedes Blea Moor Tunnel was a relief to those working on the steam engines, for the line levels off soon after entering the tunnel and then begins to fall towards the northern portal. Every inch of the 2,629-yd (2,404-metre) tunnel had to be blasted, so solid was the rock, and its cost was about one-third of the total for the entire line.

As the sign proudly proclaims, Dent is the highest mainline station in England.

Britain's highest station

Emerging from the tunnel, the line crosses the 10-arch Dent Head Viaduct and hugs a shelf along the flank of Great Knoutberry Hill, with magnificent views to the west over Whernside. A glimpse can be had of lovely **Artengill Beck** to the east as the train crosses the eponymous 11-arch viaduct on the approach to **Dent**, the highest mainline station in England, at 1,150 ft (350 metres) and now available for weekly rental. To the south stands a row of stone cabins that once housed snow-clearing gangs; during the arctic winter of 1947, it was conditions around Dent that prevented the line being used as a through route for almost two months. The best views are also to the west as the train leaves Rise Hill Tunnel, to Baugh Fell and along Garsdale. One of the few sections of level track on the line allowed the building of water troughs to replenish the tanks of steam locomotives; the only set on the S&C, they had to be steam-heated to prevent them freezing in winter. There are hopes that **Garsdale** could again become a junction: a scheme exists to rebuild the railway through Wensleydale that closed in 1959.

BELOW:
high and isolated;
Dent station.

As at Ribblehead, the waiting room at Garsdale was used for church services, while a library occupied the ladies waiting room and the base of the water tower formed what was probably Britain's most bizarre community hall. Just north of the station the train crosses the 12-arch Moorcock Viaduct with the historic Moorcock Inn below the line to the east. This was the scene of an annual cattle and sheep fair as well as a welcome and rare place for refreshment for those crossing the moors by horse or mountain pony.

Ais Gill and Wild Boar Fell

A few miles north of Garsdale the line crosses the northern boundary of the National Park as it nears the last summit at **Ais Gill**, situated under the lowering bulk of **Wild Boar Fell**. From here the line is on a falling gradient nearly all the way to Carlisle, first winding along the pastoral Eden Valley to the market town of **Kirkby Stephen**. Although the landscapes here may lack the scale and bleak beauty of the higher stretches of the line, the countryside is still delightful, and there are views to the west that extend on a clear day as far as the Lake District peaks.

The former county town of Westmorland, **Appleby** is dominated by its 12th-century castle, now a major attraction for visitors that incorporates a rare breeds farm. The final highlight of the line is the picturesque, wooded gorge north of the villages of **Lazonby** and **Kirkoswald**, which can be best appreciated by walking through it to the next station at **Armathwaite**.

After a final view of the River Eden from one of the S&C's largest embankments, the line veers away from the river and reaches the border city of **Carlisle**. Visits to the castle and Tullie House Museum and Art Gallery are the best way to appreciate the town's role during the years of constant cross-border raiding.

BELOW: a "Santa special" nears Otterburn.

SHREWSBURY–SWANSEA

Map below

This 122-mile (196-km) journey on the Heart of Wales line passes through some of the most unspoilt scenery in Wales. Now a branch line with only four trains a day, the Heart of Wales line once had through coaches from London Euston, Liverpool, Manchester and York to serve a string of fashionable spas.

The route begins at the grand, Grade II-listed station in **Shrewsbury**, its three-storey mock Tudor façade of 1848 resembling a university college. For the first 20 miles (32 km) trains share a double track line with services bound for Hereford and Cardiff, passing through **Church Stretton** with views over the Long Mynd to the west and Wenlock Edge to the east. At **Craven Arms**, Heart of Wales services leave the Hereford line and curve sharply southwest over a single line, with a view of Stokesay Castle to the left. Running through sparsely populated rolling hills of pasture and coniferous and deciduous woodland, the train passes the halts at **Broome** and **Hopton Heath** and draws up beside the handsome stone building at **Bucknell** with its triple-gabled porch.

Border country

The 8th-century Offa's Dyke and a long-distance footpath run through the market town of **Knighton**; nearby are some earthworks thought to have been raised by the 1st-century British king, Caractacus. A stop at **Knucklas** allows one to admire the magnificent 13-arch Knucklas Viaduct *(see page 37)* just to the south as the train curves towards it. There is a stiff climb through rock cuttings to the tunnel, summit and station at **Llangunllo**, the highest point on the line at 980 ft (299 metres) above sea level and overlooking the village. Extensive views can be had along the valleys of the river Lugg and Cwm Aran as the train drops down through **Llanbister Road**, flower-bedecked **Dolau** and **Pen-y-Bont** halts.

Although the Romans probably knew of the waters at **Llandrindod Wells**, their exploitation was facilitated by the opening of the railway in 1865 and the town grew tenfold in the 50 years after 1861, becoming a popular spa attracting up to 80,000 visitors a year. The county town of Powys has the National Cycle Museum and the local museum has a collection of Roman antiquities from nearby Castell Collen. At the once-busy interchange of **Builth Road** the railway crosses over the remains of an equally lovely north–south journey between Brecon and Three Cocks and Moat Lane junctions, the latter on the Shrewsbury–Aberystwyth line.

Crossing the River Wye, the train pauses at **Cilmery** where Llewelyn the Last (the last indigenous prince of Wales) was killed in a skirmish in 1282. The reputed spot is marked by a monument on a hill to the right which is visible from the train. After **Garth**

ESSENTIALS

Thomas Cook timetable no. 146

Distance: 122 miles

Duration of journey: 3 hrs 57 mins–4 hrs 24 mins

Frequency of trains: 4 per day (2 on Sun)

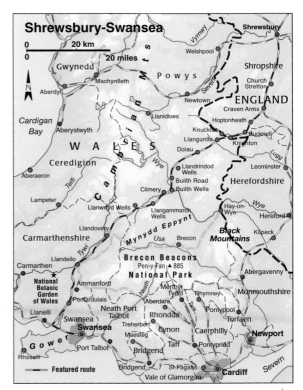

Wales is well known for its heritage lines; the Vale of Rheidol Railway runs from Aberystwyth to Devil's Bridge.

and two crossings of the River Irfan, the railway reaches the next spa at **Llangammarch Wells**, the only place in Britain that offered a source of barium chloride to those with cardiac and rheumatic complaints. In 1912 the German Kaiser and his family came here, travelling incognito. Today the pump house is silent. The smallest town in Britain, **Llanwrtyd Wells**, has successfully adapted from a spa to a centre for outdoor holidays. It has an historic clothing factory dating from the 1820s which reopened after World War I to employ men disabled in the war. The Cambrian Woollen Mill still functions on similar lines.

The wild moorland scenery continues during the climb up to the 1,000-yd (914-metre) Sugar Loaf Tunnel, named after the strikingly shaped mountain through which it burrows. The tunnel emerges onto a shelf in the hillside with dramatic views to the southeast, soon taking in the Black Mountains. From here the line drops sharply at a gradient of 1 in 60 across the curving 18-arch Cynghordy Viaduct to **Llandovery**. The railway then follows the course of the River Tywi through much flatter country with little of interest until **Llandeilo**, where the National Trust estate of Dinefwr Park can be seen to the west. Within the grounds landscaped by "Capability" Brown is a 17th-century house with a Gothic façade and a deer park with the famous Dinefwr White Park cattle.

It is easy to detect increasing evidence of former industrial activity as the train passes **Ammanford**, the area once home to tin-plate and other heavy engineering works. Soon after **Pontardulais** the railway comes alongside the sandy expanses of Loughor estuary which has been a source of cockles since the Romans established a station here on a strategic site later chosen by a Norman lord for his castle. At the industrial town of **Llanelli**, trains reverse and retrace their route beyond Loughor to **Swansea**.

BELOW: a typical pastoral scene in central Wales.

MIDDLESBROUGH–WHITBY

Map on page 116

Standing at Middlesbrough station, it is hard to believe that this is the start of a rural railway journey. The townscape is a scene of chemical works, factory estates and dock cranes as well as the town's most famous landmark, the transporter bridge, with its 190-yd (174-metre) span across the River Tees. Before leaving, spare a moment to admire the station's elegant ticket hall with its hammer-beam roof resting on stone corbels, constructed in 1877.

Yet within 10 minutes of leaving Middlesbrough station the train for Whitby has entered the North York Moors National Park. Before it does so, it pauses at **Marton** where Captain James Cook was born in 1728 – this is the first of several links with the great explorer that you'll find at various points along the line. As urban housing gives way to pasture, the vaguely volcanic outline of Roseberry Topping comes into view. Its craggy western side was caused by a collapse into iron workings beneath; the splendid views the summit offers of the coastline can be reached by a short walk from **Great Ayton** station. The village has a small museum devoted to Cook in the school he attended, and the obelisk that hoves into view to the east was erected to mark the centenary of his birth.

A sharp curve to the west brings the train into what is left of the country junction of **Battersby**, once a conduit for iron ore from the mines of Rosedale to the south. There are few scars to suggest that over half a million tons of ore was extracted each year from the green hills above the junction, but a pretty route up the old incline takes walkers up to join the Lyke Wake Walk, which follows part of the old mineral railway.

Along the Esk Valley

The train reverses at Battersby and heads due east along the Esk Valley, criss-crossing the course of Sleddale Beck and then the broadening River Esk down to the sea at Whitby. Grazing land gives way to bracken, gorse and heather as the valley slopes steepen. In common with all stations on the line, **Commondale** offers a choice of various footpaths across the hills, some following routes taken by the trains of ore-laden pack-ponies that preceded the railway.

One mile from the stone houses and station at **Danby** are the remains of the palace fortress of the Latimer family where Henry VIII is believed to have courted Catherine Parr, his sixth and last wife. The cricket field beside the line at **Glaisdale** was once the site of three blast furnaces, although their fires were extinguished in 1876 and only photographs survive to convince sceptics that such an idyllic spot could once have been an ironworks.

River and railway are hemmed together by steep valley sides, restrained by massive masonry walls, as the train descends to **Egton**, famous locally for its gooseberry show, and the junction of **Grosmont**. Here the steam trains of the North Yorkshire Moors Railway *(see page 122)* begin their steep climb south, across the heart of the moors to Pickering.

As the train leaves Grosmont, an impressive gorge can be seen to the north. Curves so sharp that wheel

ESSENTIALS

Thomas Cook timetable no. 211

Distance: 35 miles

Duration of journey: 1 hr 26 mins

Frequency of trains: 4 per day

BELOW: Whitby is one of England's most unspoiled seaside towns.

The stark, beautiful remains of Whitby Abbey mostly date from the late Middle Ages.

flanges squeal herald arrival at **Sleights**, where the river becomes broad and placid, with rowing boats moored to the banks. The train weaves its way around the hills and suddenly the immense form of Larpool Viaduct comes into view. This Grade II listed, 13-arch viaduct towers 120 ft (37 metres) above the Esk and used to carry what was then the coastal line north from Scarborough. Today, after recent restoration work, it carries the Dover–John O'Groats route of the National Cycle Network.

Whitby

Passing underneath the viaduct and with the Esk estuary on the right, the train rolls into **Whitby** station, a fine stone building dating from 1847, with a five-arched *porte cochère* on the street. The tourist information centre occupies part of the station, which is perfectly sited to explore the most delightful town on the northeast coast. Its harbour is surrounded by tiers of red-tiled buildings, reaching up to the West Cliff and some of the most elegant townhouses, while the East Cliff is dominated by the imposing remains of **Whitby Abbey**, reached by a flight of 199 stone steps. Originally founded in 657, the abbey was destroyed by the Danes in 867 but refounded in 1078, and most of the remains date from the 13th and 14th centuries.

The respect James Cook developed for the products of Whitby's shipyards while he was apprenticed to the coastal and Baltic trades encouraged him to buy a collier originally built here. The ship was rechristened the *Endeavour* and was made famous by Cook's first major voyage in 1768–71, carrying the Royal Society expedition to Tahiti. The house where he lodged in the attic when he was an apprentice is now the **Captain Cook Memorial Museum**.

Whitby is synonymous with jet ornaments and jewellery and also has a number of artistic and literary connections. A century after Cook's famous voyage, a local portrait photographer, Frank Meadow Sutcliffe (1853–1941), began to create what became perhaps the finest contemporary photographic record of any coastal town in Britain. Whitby is also renowned for inspiring Bram Stoker (1847–1912) with the idea for *Dracula*, and a stroll along Whitby Sands may evoke a picture of the walrus and the carpenter, since Lewis Carroll (1832–98) is said to have been inspired to write the poem while he was here. You could also follow the White Rabbit Trail, a walk devised by the Whitby Civic Society.

So popular is the Magpie Café fish-and-chip restaurant that you may have to queue to find out why it is so highly regarded. The white-fronted house overlooking the harbour has been a café since the 1930s and serves a wonderful variety of locally caught fish.

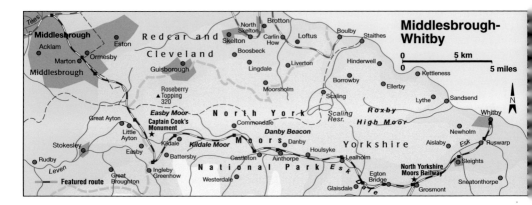

Map
on page
96

IRELAND

The fact that the whole of Ireland was part of the United Kingdom when the railways were built means that the system developed along British lines. The first line, from Dublin to the port of Dunleary (later Kingstown and now Dun Laoghaire), opened to passengers in 1834 and was constructed to the British gauge of 4 ft 8½ in (1435 mm). Subsequent main lines were, in general, laid down at the 5 ft 3 in (1602 mm) gauge. Towards the end of the 19th century numerous rural lines (often at the side of roads) were built to a 3 ft (914 mm) gauge; all of these are now closed but something of their atmosphere can be gained by a ride on a short reconstructed stretch of the Cavan & Leitrim Railway at Dromod, immediately adjacent to the Irish Rail station on the line to Sligo.

As in much of Western Europe, the heyday of the Irish railways was coming to an end in the years after World War I; line closures were underway around 1930. The amount of track in the country has dropped by more than half, from 3,500 miles (5,632 km) in the early 20th century to around 1,385 miles (2,230 km) today.

To get the best overall view of Ireland the route described from Dublin to Tralee is superb, but there are other scenic lines. Belfast to Londonderry skirts the north coast for some miles, while the Dublin to Wexford line runs high above the sea south of Bray, weaving in and out of tunnels through the headlands, followed by lush river scenery. Other lines have good views of distant mountains which look so much better with the clear Irish air giving tones of purple and green according to the season.

BELOW: Irish landscape on the Dublin to Cork line.

ESSENTIALS

Thomas Cook
timetable no. 245

Distance: 207 miles

Duration of journey:
4 hrs 25 mins

Frequency of trains:
2 per day (direct)

DUBLIN–TRALEE

Since the 1930s closures of the beautiful lines through the mountains of the west to Kenmare, Dingle, Valentia, Clifden, Killybegs and Burtonport, it is the Dublin–Tralee route that gives the best overview of the timeless Irish landscape. Tralee itself makes an excellent base from which to explore County Kerry. This is the longest journey on one train in Ireland, with one through train every day and extras on Friday and Sunday, plus other opportunities involving a change at Mallow. There is no main line electrification in Ireland (just the suburban coast railway in Dublin) and trains to and from Tralee are thus diesel hauled with USA-built locomotives, named after Irish rivers. The carriages are comfortable with the provision of a good restaurant car.

The journey passes through so much that is typical of Ireland, following the double track main line to Cork as far as Mallow (144 miles/232 km) where it branches off to the west through mountainous country to Tralee. Speeds, by European standards, are not fast, but at a leisurely 70 mph (112 km/h), there is plenty of time to take in the countryside.

Dublin to Limerick

Trains depart from Heuston station in **Dublin**, about a mile (1.6 km) or so west of the city centre (the tram runs frequently from Connolly Station, which is on the DART electric suburban railway and the terminus for trains from Belfast and Sligo). Heuston station (known as Kingsbridge in earlier days) has a magnificent classical frontage, built in 1844 by the English architect, Sancton Wood, with good modern shopping and catering facilities inside.

BELOW:
a windy perch on
the Dublin GPO.

The train climbs steeply out of Dublin, then through miles of expanding suburbs (served by a recently re-established suburban train service to Kildare) but soon levels out. The line is then essentially straight as far as Mallow. On the left are huge granite milestones indicating the mileage travelled from Dublin. Out in the open country, there are glimpses of the Grand Canal, with an especially fine aqueduct at **Monasterevan** (36 miles/57 km).

For much of the first part of the journey the train travels through lush countryside, with good views of the distant Wicklow Mountains. At **Kildare** (the 30 Milestone is on the platform) the old cathedral is visible, with a magnificent round tower adjoining it to the left. These towers are still common in Ireland; with their doors mounted well clear of the ground they were easy to defend.

Soon the train is moving across the central plain of Ireland, an area of poor soil with large tracts of countryside where the terrain is mostly bog. In these marshy regions the turf (peat) is dug commercially, and small railways were often utilised to get the produce to its destination – sometimes to specially built power stations.

The railway passes numerous small towns such as **Portarlington** (with a magnificent station, recently restored), Portlaoise, Ballybrophy and Thurles before arriving at **Limerick Junction** (107 miles/171 km), the changing point for the city of Limerick. Most of these small backwater towns have little in the way of 'sights', but they are pleasant places to stroll and experience the Irish way of life, which, despite huge changes in the last 20 years or so, still continues at an unhurried pace.

Castles are a feature of this area, with many of them located close to the railway. These structures were often fortified homes rather than national defences and therefore have far more window openings than are usually found in castles. From **Thurles** onwards, the track runs increasingly close to the mountains and, after especially fine views of the distant ranges around Thurles (on the right), the scenery becomes more majestic until it reaches the Killarney area, set in the midst of grand landscapes.

Mallow to Tralee

After Mallow, the train travels at a more leisurely pace with much wilder scenery until, at **Killarney**, the highest range of mountains in Ireland come into view. MacGullycuddy's Reeks, as they are called, lie to the southwest, with Carrauntouhill (at 3,408 ft/1,038 metres) being the highest in Ireland. Killarney is a popular stopping-off place and there are numerous hotels to accommodate visitors, including the luxurious Great Southern (once owned by the railway company). This was built in Victorian times and stands proudly just outside the station entrance.

At Killarney, the train reverses and then sets off up the continuation of the line above the town. Tralee is reached in about 35 minutes. This final section again has wonderful mountain views and the clear air gives a rare atmosphere if you are lucky enough to come here on a sunny summer evening. ❏

Map on page 96

Star Attractions:
Dublin
● Temple Bar
● Guinness Storehouse
● Trinity College Library
● National Gallery
● Phoenix Park
● National Museum
● National Writers' Museum

BELOW: a rugged coastline in southwest Ireland.

Museums and Heritage Lines

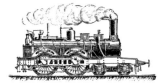

No country in the world can match Britain for the density of its heritage railways and museums or for the intensity of their operating seasons. The numbers relate to the map on page 96.

Museums

Bressingham Steam Experience ❶; Thetford Road, Diss, Norfolk IP22 2AB
Café, shop, museum, carousel
Open: Apr–Oct daily 10.30am–5.30pm
Features: three narrow gauge lines run through lovely gardens
Nearest station: Diss
Tel: 01379 686903
www.bressingham.co.uk

Glasgow Museum of Transport ❷; Kelvin Hall, 1 Bunhouse Road, Glasgow G3 8DP
Café, shop
Open: daily 10am–5pm, Fri and Sun open from 11am
Features: collection of Scottish locomotives and artefacts
Nearest station: Kelvin Hall (Underground)
Tel: 0141 287 2720

London Transport Museum ❸
Covent Garden, London WC2E 7BB
Café, shop
Open: daily 10am–6pm, Fri 11am–9pm
Features: collection of London's over- and underground trains
Nearest station: Covent Garden (Piccadilly Line)
Tel: 020 7379 6344
www.ltmuseum.co.uk

Musuem of Science & Industry ❹; Liverpool Road, Castlefield,

Manchester M3 4FP
Café, shop
Open: daily 10am–5pm
Features: collection of Manchester-built locomotives
Nearest station: G-Mex (Metrolink from Manchester Piccadilly or Victoria)
Tel: 0161 832 2244
www.msim.org.uk

National Railway Museum ❺
Leeman Road, York Y02 4XJ
Restaurant, shop, bookshop, video theatre
Open: daily 10am–6pm
Features: one of the world's great railway collections
Nearest station: York
Tel: 08448 153139
www.nrm.org.uk

Heritage lines

Bala Lake Railway ❻
(Llanuwchllyn–Penybont)
Llanuwchllyn, Bala, Gwynedd LL23 7DD
Café, shop
Open: Apr–Sept daily except some Mon and Fri
Features: lake views
Nearest station: Ruabon (bus link)
Length:4½ miles (7.2 km)
Gauge: 1 ft 11⅛ in (600 mm)
Tel: 01678 540666
www.bala-lake-railway.co.uk

Battlefield Line Railway ❼
(Shackerstone–Market Bosworth–Shenton)
Shackerstone Station, Shackerstone, Nuneaton, Leicestershire CV13 6NW
Café, shop, museum
Open: Easter–Oct weekends and some weekdays
Features: Shenton adjacent to battlefield of Bosworth
Nearest station: Nuneaton
Length: 5 miles (8 km)
Gauge:4 ft 8½ in (1,435 mm)
Tel: 01827 880754

Bluebell Railway ❽
(Sheffield Park–Kingscote)
Sheffield Park Station, Uckfield, East Sussex TN22 3QL
Restaurant, pub, café,

shops, museum
Open: May–Oct daily; weekends all year
Features: outstanding stations, period coaches, dining trains
Nearest station: East Grinstead
Length: 9 miles (14.1 km)
Gauge: 4 ft 8½ in (1,435 mm)
Tel: 01825 720800
www.bluebell-railway.co.uk

Bodmin & Wenford Railway ❾
(Bodmin Parkway–Bodmin–Boscarne)
Bodmin General Station, Bodmin, Cornwall PL31 1AQ
Café, shop
Open: June–Sept daily; various weekends and weekdays
Features: woodland walks from Colesloggett Halt
Nearest station: Bodmin Parkway
Length: 6½ miles (10.4 km)
Gauge: 4 ft 8½ in (1,435 mm)
Tel: 01208 73666

Bo'ness & Kinneil Railway ❿
(Bo'ness–Birkhill)
Bo'ness Station, Union Street, Bo'ness, W. Lothian EH51 9AQ
Cafés, shop, museum
Open: Mar–Oct most weekends; early July–Aug daily
Features: Birkhill Clay Mines
Nearest station: Linlithgow
Length: 3½ miles (5.6 km)
Gauge: 4 ft 8½ in (1,435 mm)
Tel: 01506 822298
www.srps.org.uk

Brecon Mountain Railway ⓫
(Pant–Pontsticill)
Pant Station, Dowlais, Merthyr Tydfil CF48 2UP
Cafés, shop, workshop
Open: April–Oct almost daily
Features: overseas locos
Nearest station: Merthyr (bus to Pant Cemetery)
Length: 3½ miles (5.6 km)
Gauge: 1 ft 11¾in (603 mm)
Tel: 01685 722988
www.breconmountainrailway.co.uk

Bure Valley Railway ⓬
(Wroxham–Aylsham)
Aylsham Station, Norwich Road,

Aylsham, Norfolk NR11 6BW
Restaurant, café, shop
Open: Easter–early Oct daily;
other weekends
Features: combined train and boat
excursions on Broads
Nearest station: Wroxham
Length: 9 miles (14.4 km)
Gauge: 15 in (381 mm)
Tel: 01263 733858
www.bvrw.co.uk

Churnet Valley Railway ⓭
(Leekbrook–Kingsley & Froghall)
The Railway Station, Cheddleton,
Staffordshire ST13 7EE
Café, shop, museum, flint mill
Open: Mar–Oct Sun; Apr–Sept
Sat and various other days
Nearest station: Stoke-on-Trent
Length: 5¼ miles (8.4 km)
Gauge: 4 ft 8½ in (1,435 mm)
Tel: 01538 360522

Crich Tramway Village ⓮
Crich, Near Matlock, Derbyshire
DE4 5DP
Restaurant, shop, bookshop, pic-
nic areas, video theatre, museum
Open: Apr–Oct daily; other days
and weekends
Features: one of the world's great
operating tram collections in period
setting over a 1-mile (1.6-km) line
Nearest station: Whatstandwell
Tel: 01773 854321
www.tramway.co.uk

Dean Forest Railway ⓯
(Lydney Junction–Parkend)
Forest Road, Lydney, Gloucester-
shire GL15 4ET
Café, shop, museum
Open: Mar–Oct and Dec, various
days
Features: riverside walk, forest trail
Nearest station: Lydney Junction
Length: 4¼ miles (6.8 km)
Gauge: 4 ft 8½ in (1,435 mm)
Tel: 01594 845840
www.deanforestrailway.co.uk

East Lancashire Railway ⓰
(Heywood–Bury–Rawtenstall)
Bolton Street Station, Bury,
Lancashire BL9 0EY
Café, shops, museum
Open: weekends and Bank Holi-
days all year; various weekdays
Features: walks from stations,
wine and dine trains
Nearest station: Bury
Length: 12 miles (19.2 km)
Gauge: 4 ft 8½ in (1,435 mm)
Tel: 0161 764 7790
www.east-lancs-rly.co.uk

East Somerset Railway ⓱
(Cranmore–Mendip Vale)
Cranmore Railway Station, Shep-
ton Mallet, Somerset BA4 4QP
Café, shop, museum
Open: Mar–Oct most weekends,
some weekdays
Features: exhibition of David
Shepherd paintings
Nearest station: Castle Cary/
Frome
Length: 2¾ miles (4.4 km)
Gauge: 4 ft 8½ in (1,435 mm)
Tel: 01749 880417
www.eastsomersetrailway.com

Embsay & Bolton Abbey Steam Railway ⓲
(Embsay–Bolton Abbey)
Bolton Abbey Station, Bolton
Abbey, Skipton, North Yorkshire
BD23 6AF
Cafés, shop
Open: Sun all year; Apr–Oct Sat;
mid-July–Aug daily
Features: specialist collection of
industrial locomotives
Nearest station: Skipton (bus link)
Length: 4½ miles (7.2 km)
Gauge: 4 ft 8½ in (1,435 mm)
Tel: 01756 710614
www.embsayboltonabbeyrailway.
org.uk

Ffestiniog Railway ⓳
(Porthmadog–Blaenau
Ffestiniog)
Harbour Station, Porthmadog,
Gwynedd LL49 9NF
Cafés, shops, museum
Open: mid-Mar–Oct daily
Features: glorious scenery, walks
from stations, slate museums
Nearest station: Porth-
madog/Blaenau Ffestiniog
Length: 13½ miles (21.6 km)
Gauge: 1 ft 11½ in (597 mm)
Tel: 01766 516000
www.festrail.co.uk

Gloucesteshire Warwickshire Railway ⓴
(Toddington–Cheltenham)
The Station, Toddington,
Cheltenham, Glos GL54 5DT
Café, shop, narrow gauge railway
Open: Mar–Nov weekends,
various weekdays
Nearest station: Cheltenham (bus
link)
Length: 10 miles (16 km)
Gauge: 4 ft 8½ in (1,435 mm)
Tel: 01242 621405
www.gwsr.com

Great Central Railway ㉑
(Loughborough–Leicester North)
Loughborough Central Station,
Great Central Road, Loughbor-
ough, Leicestershire LE11 1RW
Cafés, shops, museum
Open: weekends and Bank
Holidays all year; May–Sept
some weekdays
Features: double track section,
dining trains
Nearest station: Loughborough
Length: 8 miles (12.8 km)
Gauge: 4 ft 8½ in (1,435 mm)
Tel: 01509 230726
www.gcrailway.co.uk

Gwili Railway ㉒; (Bronwydd
Arms–Llwyfan Cerrig); Bronwydd
Arms Station, Bronwydd Arms,
Carmarthenshire SA33 6HT
Café, shop
Open: Mar–Oct, various days
Nearest station: Carmarthen (bus
link)
Length: 2½ miles (4 km)
Gauge: 4 ft 8½ in (1,435 mm)
Tel: 01267 230666
www.gwili-railway.co.uk

Isle of Wight Steam Railway ㉓
(Smallbrook Junction–Wotton)
Haven Street, Ryde, Isle of Wight
PO33 4DS
Café, shop, museum
Open: June–mid-Sept daily;
various other days
Features: period coaches
Nearest station: Smallbrook Jct
Length: 5 miles (8 km)
Gauge: 4 ft 8½ in (1,435 mm)
Tel: 01983 882204
www.iwsteamrailway.co.uk

Keighley & Worth Valley Railway ❷❹
(Keighley–Oxenhope)
Haworth Station, Keighley, West Yorkshire BD22 8NJ
Cafés, shops, museums
Open: weekends and Bank Holidays all year; July–Aug daily
Features: walks from stations, Brontë Museum nearby
Nearest station: Keighley
Length: 4¾ miles (7.6 km)
Gauge: 4 ft 8½ in (1,435 mm)
Tel: 01535 647777
www.kwvr.co.uk

Kent & East Sussex Railway ❷❺
(Tenterden Town–Bodiam)
Tenterden Town Station, Tenterden, Kent TN30 6HE
Café, shop, museum
Open: Apr–Oct weekends; end July–early Sept daily
Features: Bodiam Castle, dining trains
Nearest station: Ashford (bus link)
Length: 10½ miles (16.8 km)
Gauge: 4 ft 8½ in (1,435 mm)
Tel: 01580 762943
www.kesr.org.uk

Lakeside & Haverthwaite Railway ❷❻
(Haverthwaite–Lakeside)
Haverthwaite Station, Nr Ulverston, Cumbria LA12 8AL
Café, shop, museum
Open: late Mar–early Nov daily
Features: steamer connections at Lakeside
Nearest station: Ulverston
Length: 3½ miles (5.6 km)
Gauge: 4 ft 8½ in (1,435 mm)
Tel: 01539 531594

Llanberis Lake Railway ❷❼
(Llanberis–Penllyn)
Gilfach Ddu, Llanberis, Gwynedd LL55 4TY
Café, shop
Open: Easter–May, Sept Sun–Fri; June–Aug daily; Oct Sun–Thur
Features: mountain scenery, Slate Museum, Country Park
Length: 2½ miles (4 km)
Gauge: 1 ft 11½ in (597 mm)
Tel: 01286 870549
www.lake-railway.co.uk

Llangollen Railway ❷❽
(Llangollen–Carrog)
The Station, Abbey Road, Llangollen, Denbighshire LL20 8SN
Cafés, shops
Open: May–Sept daily; Oct–Apr many weekends and other days
Features: beautiful scenery, lunch and dining trains
Nearest station: Ruabon (bus link)
Length: 7½ miles (12 km)
Gauge: 4 ft 8½ in (1,435 mm)
Tel: 01978 860951
www.llangollen-railway.co.uk

Mid-Hants Railway ❷❾
(Alresford–Alton)
The Railway Station, Alresford, Hampshire SO24 9JG
Cafés, shops, museum
Open: Jan–Oct weekends; many weekdays in summer
Features: real ale trains
Nearest station: Alton
Length: 10 miles (16 km)
Gauge: 4 ft 8½ in (1,435 mm)
Tel: 01962 734866
www.watercressline.co.uk

Midland Railway Centre ❸❶
(Hammersmith–Riddings Junction/Pye Bridge)
Butterley Station, Ripley, Derbyshire DE5 3QZ
Cafés, shops, museum, park railways
Open: most weekends, various weekdays
Features: country park, farm museum, canal, dining trains
Nearest station: Derby (bus link)
Length: 3½ miles (5.6 km)
Gauge: 4 ft 8½ in (1,435 mm)
Tel: 01773 570140
www.midlandrailwaycentre.co.uk

Nene Valley Railway ❸❶
(Wansford–Peterborough)
Wansford Station, Stibbington, Peterborough PE8 6LR
Café, shops, museum
Open: Easter–Oct weekends, various weekdays
Features: many continental locomotives, country park adjacent to Orton Mere station
Nearest station: Peterborough

Length: 7½ miles (12 km)
Gauge: 4 ft 8½ in (1,435 mm)
Tel: 01780 784404
www.nvr.org.uk

North Norfolk Railway ❸❷
(Sheringham–Holt)
Sheringham Station, Sheringham, Norfolk NR26 8RA
Cafés, shops, museum
Open: Apr–Oct most days
Features: sea views
Nearest station: Sheringham
Length: 5¼ miles (8.4 km)
Gauge: 4 ft 8½ in (1,435 mm)
Tel: 01263 820800

North Yorkshire Moors Railway ❸❸
(Grosmont–Pickering)
Pickering Station, Pickering, North Yorkshire YO18 7AJ
Cafés, shops, museum
Open: mid-Mar–early Nov daily
Features: beautiful scenery, walks from stations, dining trains, trains to Whitby
Nearest station: Grosmont
Length: 18 miles (29 km)
Gauge: 4 ft 8½ in (1,435 mm)
Tel: 01751 472508
www.nymr.co.uk

Paignton & Dartmouth Railway ❸❹
(Paignton–Kingswear)
Queen's Park Station, Paignton, Devon TQ4 6AF
Cafés, shop
Open: Easter–Oct daily
Features: sea views
Nearest station: Paignton
Length: 7 miles (11 km)
Gauge: 4 ft 8½ in (1,435 mm)
Tel: 01803 555872

Ravenglass & Eskdale Railway ❸❺; (Ravenglass–Eskdale Green)
Ravenglass, Cumbria CA18 1SW
Cafés, shops, museum, mill
Open: late Mar–early Nov daily; other weekends
Features: glorious scenery, walks
Nearest station: Ravenglass
Length: 7 miles (11 km)
Gauge: 15 in (381 mm)
Tel: 01229 717171
www.ravenglass-railway.co.uk

Romney Hythe & Dymchurch Railway ㊱; (Hythe–Dungeness)
New Romney Station, Kent
TN28 8PL
Cafés, shops, toy and model museum, model railway
Open: late Mar–early Nov daily; other weekends and days
Features: observation coaches
Nearest station: Folkestone (bus link)
Length: 13½ miles (21.6 km)
Gauge: 15 in (381 mm)
Tel: 01797 362353
www.rhdr.org.uk

Severn Valley Railway ㊲
(Kidderminster–Bridgnorth)
Railway Station, Bewdley,
Worcestershire DY12 1BG
Cafés, shops, model railway
Open: every weekend; early May–early Oct daily
Features: Kidderminster Railway Museum, lunch and dining trains
Nearest station: Kidderminster
Length: 16½ miles (26.4 km)
Gauge: 4 ft 8½ in (1,435 mm)
Tel: 01299 401001
www.svr.co.uk

Snowdon Mountain Railway ㊳
(Llanberis–Summit)
Llanberis, Gwynedd LL55 4TY
Cafés, shops
Open: mid-Mar–early Nov daily
Features: glorious scenery, walks from stations
Nearest station: Betws-y-Coed (Snowdon Sherpa bus)
Length: 4⅝ miles (7.6 km)
Gauge: 2 ft 7½ in (800 mm)
Tel: 0871 720 0033
www.snowdonrailway.co.uk

South Devon Railway ㊴
(Buckfastleigh–Totnes)
Buckfastleigh Station,
Buckfastleigh, Devon TQ11 0DZ
Café, shop, museum
Open: Apr–Oct daily
Features: adjacent butterfly and otter farm
Nearest station: Totnes
Length: 7 miles (11 km)
Gauge: 4 ft 8½ in (1,435 mm)
Tel: 0845 345 1420
www.southdevonrailway.org

Strathspey Railway ㊵
(Aviemore–Broomhill)
Aviemore Station, Dalfaber Road,
Aviemore, Inverness PH22 1PY
Cafés, shops, museum
Open: mid-Mar–Oct weekends; early June–Sept daily
Features: osprey viewing
Nearest station: Aviemore
Length: 10 miles (16 km)
Gauge: 4 ft 8½ in (1,435 mm)
Tel: 01479 810725
www.strathspeyrailway.co.uk

Swanage Railway ㊶; (Swanage–Norden); Station House,
Swanage, Dorset BH19 1HB
Cafés, shops, model railway
Open: Apr–late Oct daily; most weekends and various weekdays
Features: Corfe Castle
Nearest station: Wareham
Length: 6 miles (9.6 km)
Gauge: 4 ft 8½ in (1,435 mm)
Tel: 01929 425800
www.swanagerailway.co.uk

Talyllyn Railway ㊷; (Tywyn–Nant Gwernol); Wharf Station,
Tywyn, Gwynedd LL36 9EY
Cafés, shops, museum
Open: mid-Mar–early Nov daily
Features: scenery, walks
Nearest station: Tywyn
Length: 7¼ miles (11.6 km)
Gauge: 2 ft 3 in (686 mm)
Tel: 01654 710472
www.talyllyn.co.uk

Tanfield Railway ㊸
(Andrews House–East Tanfield)
Marley Hill Engine Shed, Marley
Hill, Gateshead, NE16 5ET
Café, shop
Open: Jan–Nov Sun and Bank Holidays; summer Wed–Thur
Features: Causey Arch, 1854 engine shed, period carriages
Nearest station: Newcastle
Length: 3 miles (4.8 km)
Gauge: 4 ft 8½ in (1,435 mm)
Tel: 0191 388 7545
www.tanfield-railway.co.uk

Tyseley Locomotive Works ㊹
670 Warwick Road, Tyseley,
Birmingham B11 2HL
Café, shop, museum, frequent

steam excursions; open weekends
Nearest station: Tyseley
Tel: 0121 707 4696
www.vintagetrains.co.uk

Vale of Rheidol Railway ㊺
(Aberystwyth–Devil's Bridge)
The Locomotive Shed, Park
Avenue, Aberystwyth,
Cardiganshire SY23 1PG
Cafés, shops
Open: late Mar–Oct almost daily
Features: scenery, walks
Nearest station: Aberystwyth
Length: 11¾ miles (18.8 km)
Gauge: 1 ft 11½ in (597 mm)
Tel: 01970 625819
www.rheidolrailway.co.uk

Welsh Highland Railway ㊻
(Caernarfon–Rhyd
Dhu[–Porthmadog in 2009])
Harbour Station, Porthmadog,
Gwynedd LL49 9NE
Café, shop
Open: mid-Mar–early Nov daily
Features: locos from South Africa
Nearest station: Bangor (bus link)
Length: 12 miles (21 km)/ (25 miles [40 km])
Gauge: 1 ft 11½ in (597 mm)
Tel: 01766 516000
www.festrail.co.uk

Welshpool & Llanfair Light Railway ㊼; (Welshpool–Llanfair
Caereinion); The Station, Llanfair
Caereinion, Mid-Wales SY21 0SF
Cafés, shops
Open: Easter–Oct weekends, daily in school holidays
Nearest station: Welshpool
Length: 8 miles (13 km)
Gauge: 2 ft 6 in (762 mm)
Tel: 01938 810441

West Somerset Railway ㊽
(Bishops Lydeard–Minehead)
Railway Station, Minehead,
Somerset TA24 5BG
Cafés, shops, museum
Open: Apr–Oct almost daily
Features: longest heritage railway
Nearest station: Taunton (bus link)
Length: 20 miles (32 km)
Gauge: 4 ft 8½ in (1,435 mm)
Tel: 01643 704996
www.west-somerset-railway.co.uk

FRANCE

France was the pioneer of high-speed trains in Europe, but the country also has an extensive network of quiet rural railways winding through memorable mountain scenery

Map on page 128/9

It was in 1827, three years after the first public rail service in Britain, that the first railway opened in France, from St-Etienne to Andrézieux. This and other lines built to Lyon and Roanne by 1836 were designed to transport coal to the Loire and Rhône rivers. Carrying passengers, who were initially accommodated in coal wagons, was a mere by-product. By 1837 the first Parisian suburban railways had opened, to be followed in 1841 by the Strasbourg to Basel line. This was not only the first French long-distance line, but also the first international railway in Europe. Today's national railway museum, the Cité du Train, at Mulhouse *(see page 158)* is situated on this historic route.

The French government encouraged the development of a wider rail network by granting longer concessions and financial aid, and dozens of small companies were created to build and operate isolated lines. But by 1860, seven large networks dominated the scene – the Nord, Est, Paris-Lyon-Méditerranée (PLM), Paris-Orléans (PO), Ouest, Midi and the state-run Etat. This was the situation that applied until the network was nationalised on 1 January 1938, when the Société Nationale de Chemins de Fer Français (SNCF) was formed.

While today's rail network was largely complete by 1870, the government of 1879 agreed on the construction of numerous minor lines, often built to metre gauge, with little or no economic justification. These limped on with massive state aid until the formation of the SNCF, after which a closure programme took the network back to something like that of 1870. Traces of these narrow gauge railways remain all over France, mainly in the form of preserved lines.

Many railways running along borders, especially the German border, were built for strategic reasons; the lines in Alsace-Lorraine ended up in German territory after the Franco-Prussian War in 1871. Railway buildings here are very Germanic – the station at Metz is a superb example – and operating practices are different from those in the rest of France. Trains still run on the right instead of the left, so there are flyovers near the old border to allow trains to change sides.

Reconstruction and speed

After World War II, massive reconstruction of the railways was necessary, and SNCF embarked on a programme of main line electrification. Around 85 percent of all traffic today is electric, the main exceptions being on cross-country routes, especially in the Massif Central. Then, from the early 1950s, came the quest for speed. While trains struggled to maintain speeds of 120 km/h (75 mph), new electric locomotives were gradually taken beyond 200 km/h (124 mph) and in an astonishing week in March 1955, two locomotives reached 331 km/h (206 mph) in the Landes region

PRECEDING PAGES: the Loulla viaducts, Chemin de Fer de La Mure. **LEFT:** advertisement for the Wagons-Lits service between Paris and Amsterdam. **BELOW:** Thalys units at the Gare du Nord.

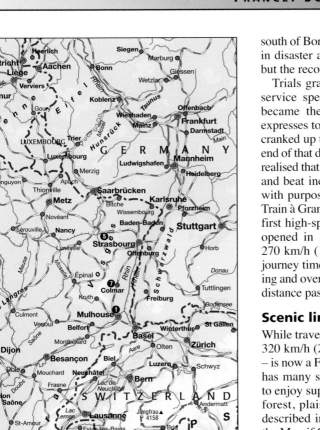

south of Bordeaux. The trials nearly ended in disaster as track started to deteriorate, but the record stood until the 1980s.

Trials gradually translated into higher service speeds – 160 km/h (100 mph) became the norm in the 1960s, while expresses to Bordeaux and Toulouse were cranked up to 200 km/h (124 mph) by the end of that decade. During the 1970s, SNCF realised that the only way to go even faster, and beat increasing air competition, was with purpose-built, high-speed lines: the Train à Grand Vitesse (TGV) was born. The first high-speed line, from Paris to Lyon, opened in 1981, with trains running at 270 km/h (168 mph), halving the 4-hour journey time. The network is still expanding and over three-quarters of SNCF's long-distance passengers now travel by TGV.

Scenic lines

While travelling at 300 km/h (186 mph) – 320 km/h (200 mph) on the new LGV Est – is now a French passion, the country still has many slower, scenic lines with time to enjoy superb views of mountain, river, forest, plain or coast. Apart from those described in this book, any line through the Massif Central, the Pyrenees, the Alps or the Jura turns up beautiful vistas.

Apart from the TGV, there is a great deal of investment in new trains, mostly with air conditioning, much-improved comfort, and more frequent services. Where lines were closing 10 years ago, they are now reopening, although village stations are still losing services.

The wave of rail privatisation throughout Europe has not yet reached France and is not seen as necessary. However, some may see the need for a little more entrepreneurship. Visitors may be surprised to find that many lines have long periods without trains (if you miss your service the next one may not be for hours) and many long-distance trains have no catering of any sort (take sandwiches). On the other hand, trains are very punctual and connecting services are usually held when a train is a few minutes late. Cancellations are almost unheard of, except in the Paris suburbs where trains are, anyway, very regular. Strikes (grèves) are frequent but often at a local level only.

ESSENTIALS

Thomas Cook
timetable no. 350

Distance: 750 km

Duration of journey:
3 hrs (some services
take 10 to 20
minutes longer)

Frequency of trains:
16–18 per day

PARIS–MARSEILLE BY TGV

The Train à Grande Vitesse is a high-speed train designed to run both on purpose-built new lines at 300 km/h (186 mph) and on existing railway lines. All TGVs consist of a power car – a single-ended locomotive – at each end and (for lower weight and better stability) a set of articulated coaches between. The latest generation are the double-decker **TGV Duplex** sets which mainly operate on this route. Although incredibly fast, TGVs are also very safe – no passenger has been killed as a result of a TGV crash in 26 years of operation. On the high-speed lines, drivers do not observe signals but are told at what speed to drive, taking into account the state of the track and the other trains on the line.

A grand station

Before boarding the TGV, cast an eye around the **Gare de Lyon**, built at the height of the belle époque. Apart from the fine clock tower, the station has one of the best restaurants in Paris, the Train Bleu, a listed monument, with walls and ceiling decorated by artists of the time. Most of the high-speed trains running hourly from Paris to Marseille are known as TGV Duplex as they are double-decker. When booking your seat, ask for the top deck for a better view.

The TGV leaves Paris behind and slowly builds up speed, passing many of its sister trains being cleaned in the depot to the west. After seven minutes, the train swings east onto the high-speed line and starts to accelerate. By the time it leaves the tunnel, it has reached over 160km/h (100 mph) and has left the suburbs behind. At Crisenoy the line is joined by the motorway to the east and the train reaches 300km/h (186 mph); despite the speed, the ride remains

BELOW: hurtling through the French countryside.

astonishingly smooth. The line runs across the plain of **Brie**, famous for its cheese but also a major cereal-producing area, crossing the **River Seine** at Montereau, an industrial town to the west.

We now enter **Burgundy**, although few of the vineyards that make the region famous throughout the world are visible. Soon after Montereau the distant 12th-century cathedral of **Sens** is visible to the west. The terrain gradually becomes more wooded and around an hour from Paris the cereal-growing region blurs into an area of pasture with buff Charolais cattle grazing peacefully between villages of warm brown stone. To the west, is **Cluny**, a centre of pilgrimage with its octagonal-spired Romanesque church and ruined abbey dating from 1088.

At this point it is possible to sense how hilly the railway line is, as it climbs to the Col du Bois Clair parallel with the local highway. The TGV makes light work of the steep gradient, which allowed the engineers to avoid building expensive tunnels. Around 1½ hours from Paris there is a glimpse of Mâconnais vines as the train rushes past **Mâcon-Loché** station, crosses the River Saône and turns southwards along its flood plain towards Lyon. The line turns eastwards, avoiding this superb Roman city, and after a tunnel emerges to cross the Rhône Valley railway, the motorway and the river itself.

There may be a pause at **St-Exupéry** station (serving Lyon's airport) with its magnificent, winged station building designed by Spanish architect, Santiago Calatrava. Just a couple of hours from Paris, orchards start to appear as the climate is now warm enough for peaches and apricots. Passing through **Valence** TGV station, the limestone Vercors area of the Alps forms a rugged background to the east while to the west lie the foothills of the Ardèche.

Approach to the Mediterranean

The train passes close to **Montélimar**, famous for nougat made from local almonds. The vegetation becomes Mediterranean as the line climbs over the motorway and into the valley of the Rhône, which will be crossed four times. This is an important wine-producing area, with stout Côtes-du-Rhône and Châteauneuf-du-Pape reds produced around the Roman town of **Orange**.

After a brief climb out of the valley, there is a superb view of **Avignon** and the Papal palace to the north, before the train plunges downhill on a magnificent double bridge back over the Rhône into the new Avignon TGV station. The line now follows the river Durance to **Cavaillon**, famous for its melons, then cuts through limestone hills near **Vernègues**, a village completely razed by an earthquake in 1909.

The TGV crosses the line's longest viaduct (1,733 metres/1,895 yds) at **Ventabren**, then the **Roque-favour Aqueduct**, built in 1847, is briefly visible to the south. To the north, beyond Aix-en-Provence, is the wedge-shaped **Montagne Ste-Victoire** immortalizeed by Cézanne in many of his paintings.

We pass through **Aix-en-Provence** station, then plunge into the longest railway tunnel in France (7,834 metres/8,567 yds). As the TGV emerges, there's a brief glimpse of the port, the Frioul islands and the Château d'If before we reach **Marseille**'s St-Charles station.

Map on page 128/9

Star Attractions:
Marseille

● Vieux Port
● La Canebière street
● Opéra
● Notre-Dame de la Garde

BELOW: the route passes through several famous wine-producing regions.

ESSENTIALS

Thomas Cook
timetable no. 333

Distance: 303 km

Duration of journey:
5 hrs 5 mins (Le
Cévenol 4 hrs 45
mins)

Frequency of trains:
3 per day (direct)

CLERMONT FERRAND–NÎMES

As an alternative to the 3-hour dash by TGV from Paris to Marseille described in the preceding pages, those who have the time can take the scenic route on Le Cévenol, which departs Paris at 08.47 to reach Marseille, via Clermont Ferrand and Nîmes, 10½ hours later. The scenery through the Cévennes mountains between Clermont and Nîmes is worth anyone's time (although the Paris–Clermont journey itself is relatively unexceptional).

Clermont Ferrand is capital of the Auvergne region and home of Bibendum, the plump Michelin man made of tyres. Michelin's ugly factories on the edge of town do not detract from the beauty of the city centre. Clermont's 13th-century cathedral is a fine Gothic pile with double spires, the only French cathedral built out of black volcanic rock.

Along the River Allier

After passing through the suburbs of Clermont, the railway joins the valley of the River Allier which it follows, almost to its source, for the next 180 km (112 miles). At this point, there are ancient volcanic plugs *(puys)* on both sides of the valley. To the west is the **Plateau de Gergovie** where Julius Caesar was beaten back by Vercingétorix, king of the Gauls, in 52 AD, while to the east is the **Puy St-Romain**, rising to 779 metres (2,556 ft). In its shadow lies **Vic-le-Comte** (6 km/3½ miles from the station), a little town founded by Benedictine monks in the 8th century. The railway now winds along the narrow Allier valley to **Issoire**, a small town with one of the biggest Romanesque churches in the Auvergne region. Issoire is the first of many towns and villages along this route

BELOW: hiking
in the Cévennes.

LE PUY

Le Puy-en-Velay is perhaps the most astonishing natural site in France. In a depression in the Velay plateau, two volcanic plugs *(puys)* rise out of the surrounding earth. On the steep-sided St-Michel *puy*, the Romanesque chapel of St-Michel d'Aiguilhe was built in the 11th century, probably replacing a temple to Mercury. You have to climb 268 steps to visit the chapel. The second *puy*, Rocher Corneille, which is less abrupt, is topped by a 16-metre (53-ft) cast-iron statue of the Virgin and Child, Notre-Dame de France, which was erected in 1860. The statue is hollow and it is possible to climb to the crown for a superb view of the surrounding countryside.

However, Le Puy's attractions are not limited to the physical environment. The town's houses tumble down the sides of the Rocher Corneille, while the Romanesque 12th-century Cathédrale Notre-Dame, which has Byzantine influences in its architecture, lies at its foot. Unsurprisingly, the town has been a centre of pilgrimage for hundreds of years. The area is also well known for its exquisite lace.

There are three daily direct trains to Le Puy from Clermont Ferrand, taking just over 2 hours, and six from Paris (4 hours 20 minutes) involving one change in St Etienne or Lyon Perrache.

associated with the struggle between Protestants, whose French stronghold is still in the Cévennes, and Catholics. Issoire suffered badly in the Wars of Religion, when the Protestant fanatic Captain Merle led an orgy of torture and demolition of church towers in 1575, before the Catholic Duke of Anjou retook the town two years later, sacking and burning the houses in the process.

Soon after Issoire the 856-metre (2,808-ft) **Puy d'Ysson** is visible to the west and above **Le Breuil sur Couze**, the remains of Nonette Castle dominate a bend of the Allier. The line then leaves the river behind to reach the ancient town of **Brioude** whose Basilique St-Julien is the largest Romanesque church in the area. The church owes its name to a Roman legionnaire, converted to Christianity, who was martyred here in 304 AD.

The railway now joins the Senouire Valley, rejoining the Allier just before **Langeac**. Shortly before this, the Le Puy branch splits off at St-Georges d'Aurac *(see panel)*. Langeac itself is an old town nestling on a hillside at the start of the Allier Gorge, whose snaking curves the train is obliged to follow for the next 85 km (53 miles). The river here is subject to unpredictable floods and no road or settlement has ever been built in the valley. Construction of the railway, which involved 12,000 workers, was extremely problematic; on the 67-km (42-mile) section to Langogne, there are 64 tunnels, 12 large viaducts and many retaining walls. In many places there are wires to detect rock falls onto the line. Just before the plunge into the gorge, the village of **Chanteuges** has an imposing Romanesque church and the remains of an abbey to the east. There follows a series of villages – **Prades**, **Monistrol d'Allier** – shoe-horned into the valley, while the line avoids some tight river bends by tunnelling through promontories. At **Chapeauroux**, the railway curves on a 28-arch viaduct through the beautifully situated village.

Map below

Bibendum, the ubiquitous Michelin man, hails from Clermont Ferrand.

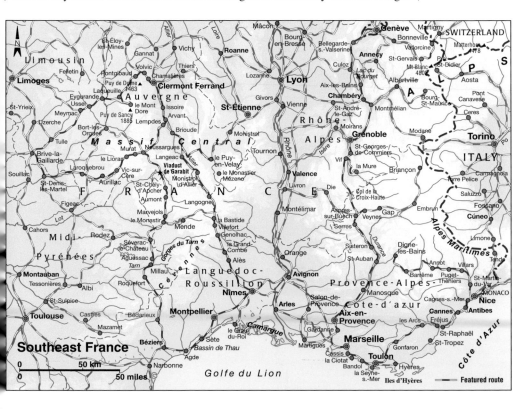

Star Attractions:
Nîmes
● **Roman arena**
● **Maison Carrée**
● **Carrée d'Art**
● **Jardin de la**
  Fontaine
● **Castellum**
● **Porte Augustus**
● **Musée des Beaux**
  Arts

The next town is **Langogne**, a small centre but an important one, given the sparse local population. Here, houses were built in a circle around the church in medieval times. The railway line is nearer the summit of a plateau now and views expand over greater distances until **Luc** where the Allier Valley closes in again. At **La Bastide**, the summit of the line (1,023 metres/3,356 ft) is reached. The Allier rises just east from here on the watershed that separates rivers flowing into the Atlantic at Nantes and Bordeaux and into the Mediterranean.

The Stairway of Giants

For the train, it is all downhill from here, on what is known as the "Stairway of Giants", with the track clinging to hillsides as it slowly descends towards the coastal plain. First the tracks cut through a forest, mainly in tunnel, before reaching **Prévencheres** with its 12th-century bell tower, and heading across the artificial Lac de Rachas on the Altier Viaduct. This was a massive 72 metres (236 ft) high when built, but over half is now hidden by water. The train passes through more tunnels before skirting the Lac de Villefort and stopping at **Villefort** itself. Apart from the attractions of the lake, the town is a centre for visiting the Chassezac Gorges and the Cévennes National Park. The railway continues to twist and turn, passing the red-roofed village of **Concoules** to the west, before halting at **Genolhac**, a pretty town decked with flowers in summer.

The sun often appears at this point as the line leaves the Cévennes and approaches the Mediterranean, passing through a thickly forested area, before crossing the Luech valley on the **Chamborigaud Viaduct**. This is 47 metres (154 ft) high, has 41 arches and describes a near semi-circle. The train then passes through the line's longest tunnel before reaching **Ste-Cécile d'Andorges**

BELOW: an overview of Nîmes, clearly showing the magnificent Roman arena.

and entering the Gardon Valley. The line quickly runs into an area of abandoned coal mines, with settlements strung along the valley to **La Grand-Combe**. As the train leaves the industrial area, there is a little more savage beauty before the large town of **Alès**, which grew up on the back of the silk and, later, coal industry. For the rest of our journey to Nîmes, the countryside opens out, and the railway roughly follows the Gardon and crosses vineyards producing Costières du Nîmes.

Map on page 133

Nîmes–Béziers

The short trip between these two Mediterranean towns initially passes through vineyards then runs close to the coast with views of the sea. Thirty minutes from Nîmes is **Montpellier**, capital of the Languedoc – not as old as neighbouring towns from the Roman era, but with a great deal of charm all the same. As well as many superb old buildings in the city, there is the Musée Fabre, an art museum with a rich collection of paintings.

From Montpellier, the railway nears the coast, with views over several *étangs* – stretches of salt water enclosed by long sand spits. The largest is the **Bassin de Thau**, to the north after Sète, where oysters and mussels grow fast in the warm water. **Sète** itself is an attractive old fishing port, famous for its "nautical jousting" in which jousters with 3-metre (10-ft) lances try to knock each other off the bows of opposing rowing boats.

Béziers is a centre of wine production founded by the Romans around 35 BC on the banks of the River Orb. Today, the fortified cathedral of St-Nazaire, dating back to 760 AD, dominates the river and presents a fine sight from the Pont Vieux. The town has three museums, including one devoted to wine, which has examples of Greek, Etruscan and Roman vessels for carrying the valuable liquid.

On the Ligne des Causses between Beziers and Neussargues.

BELOW: Robert Louis Stevenson.

STEVENSON AND THE BEAST

In September 1878, the writer Robert Louis Stevenson embarked on a 12-day tramp through the Cévennes. Starting from Le Monastier-sur-Gazeille, 20 km (12 miles) south of Le Puy, his route criss-crossed the Clermont–Nîmes railway at Langogne, Luc and La Bastide. The line was under construction at the time. Indeed, Stevenson met engineers engaged on the project and swore they were the most civilised people he encountered on his trip. There is now a Stevenson Historic Trail following his eventful journey.

After spending a night in Langogne, Stevenson was forced to bed down in a wood the following night as no-one would open their doors to him, being petrified of the "beast of Gévaudan". The Cévennes region was still imbued with tales of a massive beast that had first spread terror throughout the Gévaudan area over a century earlier. In three years in the 1760s, the beast was purported to have killed over 100 people and injured hundreds more. When eventually shot, however, the "beast" turned out to be a wolf of modest size – a "Napoleon amongst wolves" according to Stevenson. Yet fears persisted; there were reports of another large beast killing 20 people in nearby Limousin around 1815, while "rabid wolves" prowled the mountain forests at the time of Stevenson's visit.

ESSENTIALS

Thomas Cook
timetable no. 332

Distance: 394 km

Duration of journey:
6 hrs 45 mins

Frequency of trains:
1 per day (direct)

BÉZIERS–CLERMONT FERRAND

This line is one of the most spectacular in France, crossing some of its wildest territory, with very little in the way of settlements – in places the population density is a mere 14 people per square kilometre. The largest town, Millau, has just 22,000 inhabitants. Unlike the Clermont-Nîmes route *(see pages 132–35)*, where the tracks climb almost continuously from either direction to La Bastide, the Béziers line is a switchback ride of successive climbs and descents.

Vineyards and orchids

Leaving **Béziers**, wine production is much in evidence for the first half hour of the journey. The Languedoc region produces more wine than anywhere else in France – and although much of this is decidedly *ordinaire*, there is quality, too; Côteaux du Languedoc and Faugères are the local specialities. The train then cuts through hills to reach **Bédarieux**, in the Orb valley. Following the river to Le Bousquet d'Orb, the line twists through the Monts d'Orb, passing through a short tunnel at the Col de l'Homme Mort (Dead Man's Pass). We then descend onto the **Causse de Larzac**, which give the line its nickname, the *Ligne des Causses*. the first of several bare, arid, limestone plateaux in this region, known to naturalists for their unique ecosystems; orchids thrive in this environment.

Just after **Tournemire** station, the village of **Roquefort** hugs the ridge to the west, on a hillside created by the collapse of a limestone plateau, riddled with caves used to age the village's famous, blue, ewe's milk cheese. The railway soon descends to the Tarn Valley to reach **Millau**, passing the magnificent new viaduct, the world's highest – but, sadly, for road traffic only. The town dates back to the 1st century AD when it was a thriving market and pottery centre; it is now more famous for making gloves from local sheepskin. The local museums display both skills and the old town is pleasant for a stroll. Millau makes a good base for exploring the Grands Causses and the gorges of the Tarn and other rivers.

The tracks now run north along the Tarn Valley then turn northwest at **Aguessac** to climb to 839 metres (2,750 ft) before dropping down to **Séverac-le-Château**, a village of superb old houses, dominated by a rock on which stand the ruins of the eponymous castle. Here lived Louis d'Arpajon, a national military hero who disgraced himself by murdering his son and wife out of jealousy. The train continues its tortuous descent over the **Causse de Séverac** before dropping into the valley of the Lot near **Banassac-La Canourgue**, close to the beautiful old village of La Canourgue. Continuing alongside the Lot, then north along the Colagne Valley, we reach **Marvejols**, a centre for health cures. The village still has three ancient gates and a statue representing the "beast of Gévaudan" *(see page 135)*. The obsession with this animal has led to the establishment of the Parc du Gévaudan, famous for its wolves, 4 km (2½ miles) north of the town. Wolves and bears were eliminated from this wild region long ago, and attempts to reintroduce them have been resisted by local farmers. However, bison and vultures have both been reintroduced here recently, with great success.

BELOW:
Roquefort cheese.

Map
on page
133

The line now climbs continuously due north through wild uplands, the 1,179-metre (3,868-ft) **Roc de Peyre** visible to the west before **Aumont-Aubrac**. The Aubrac area, to the west, is volcanic and covered with woods or open pasture punctuated by rocks and stone walls. To the east is the granite mass of the Margeride. Soon after St-Chély d'Apcher, the train reaches the highest point on the line at 1,053 metres (3,454 ft), then crosses the Truyère River on the line's *pièce de résistance*.

The **Garabit Viaduct** *(see page 38)* was built in 1884 and designed by Gustave Eiffel. The 448-metre (490-yd) central section rests on a single arch carrying the railway 123 metres (405 ft) above the river. In order to visit the viaduct, you must continue to St-Flour from where a special train runs in summer. **St-Flour** itself is a lovely village perched on top of a hill overlooking the River Ander, with a 15th-century Gothic cathedral dominating the site. The train crosses another harsh plateau before arriving at **Neussargues**, where it meets the line from Aurillac *(see page 139)* and joins the route from Nîmes *(see page 132)* at Arvant.

Protestantism in the Cévennes

Away from the German border region, the hills of the Cévennes are traditionally the most Protestant area of France. The ideas of Luther and Calvin started to gain ground here early in the 16th century and within decades conflict was rife, with churches burned down and whole families massacred. The Edict of Nantes in 1598 brought greater tolerance but its Revocation in 1685 reawoke the conflicts. The richest Protestants fled to Switzerland or Germany while those who remained rebelled between 1702 and 1704 in the War of the Camisards, a nickname taken from the shirts worn by Protestant rebels.

BELOW: Garabit Viaduct, designed by Gustave Eiffel.

ESSENTIALS

Thomas Cook
timetable nos.
326/317/331

Distance:
(1) Clermont–Brive
197 km
(2) Brive–Aurillac
102 km
(3) Aurillac–Clermont
168 km

Duration of journey:
(1) 3–3 hr 30 mins
(2) 1 hr 40 mins
(3) 2 hrs 20 mins

Frequency of trains:
(1) 3 daily
(2) 4–5 daily
(3) 6–8 daily

BELOW: sweeping landscape around the Puy de Dôme.

CLERMONT FERRAND–BRIVE–AURILLAC (CIRCUIT)

This three-stage journey, which is now very difficult to do in one day, covers parts of the Massif Central known as Auvergne and Limousin, the latter after the home of France's finest pottery, Limoges. The line to Brive, instead of heading directly southwest out of Clermont, curves around the town and heads northwards, climbing rapidly. Before leaving the town, it passes through the elegant suburb of **Royat**, a spa resort straggling along the cool Tiretaine Valley; the river tumbles in waterfalls over lava flows spewed out by now-extinct volcanoes. Auvergne's geological history means that there are innumerable sources of mineral water, many of which have been exploited since Roman times.

Presidential connections

The railway heads north, skirting around the **Volcans d'Auvergne** national park, with its two dozen extinct volcanoes *(puys)* forming a remarkable string of craters, the highest of which is the **Puy de Dôme**. This peak rises to 1,463 metres (4,800 ft) and, crowned by a television mast, is clearly visible from the railway line. The view of the other *puys* from the summit is tremendous – although now rounded by the passage of time and covered with grass, many clearly show the remains of craters. Until now it has been necessary to drive or walk to the summit of the Puy but by 2012 a rack-railway will be built to relieve the heaving car park.

The next station on the line serves the suburb of **Chamalières**, fief of former French President, Valéry Giscard d'Estaing, who supported construction of the "Vulcania" theme park in the national park. The line continues north, gaining height rapidly through a series of curves and tunnels. Twenty minutes out of Clermont is the station of **Volvic**, where one of France's best-known mineral waters is drawn. Just past Volvic the Montluçon railway peels off to the north (a short distance along this line is the **Fades Viaduct**, Europe's highest railway bridge until 1976). After passing through **Pontgibaud**, close to a 12th-century castle, the Brive line follows the Miouze Valley to the junction of Laqueuille where a branch line turns southeast to the spa resorts of **La Bourboule** and **Le Mont-Dore**, the latter situated near the source of the River Dordogne and at the foot of the Puy de Sancy.

Turning due west into the Limousin region, the train snakes along the Clidane Valley to Eygurande-Merlines, a junction with a minor line to Paris. This once continued south to Bort-les-Orgues and Aurillac but was abandoned when the Dordogne was dammed to form a substantial lake. The train soon arrives at **Ussel**, a small town where Jacques Chirac was mayor for 26 years before being elected president. A little further on is **Meymac**, a town with a fine group of old houses around the St-André abbey, founded in 1085. **Tulle** is a town that developed along the Corrèze Valley and its lace has given the town's name to gauzy fabric used for veils.

The train reverses at Tulle and heads southwest along the narrow gorge of the River Corrèze. Halfway to Brive, it passes through a short tunnel directly under the remains of a castle at Cornil. **Brive-la-Gaillarde** is the largest town in the Corrèze *département*, a centre for the local fruit and vegetable industry and home to a strong rugby team. If this journey is not to be completed in a single day, Brive is a good place to stop. There are many local trips to be made from this busy centre, the most striking, perhaps, to the village of **Collonges-la-Rouge** – the suffix refers to the local red sandstone which brings harmony to this picture-book village.

Map
on page
133

The return leg

The return to Clermont starts off due south, the line cutting through a ridge in tunnel before following the River Tourmente. The station at **Turenne** lies some distance from the ancient village, crowned by a ruined castle; this was once the fiefdom of Huguenot Henri de la Tour d'Auvergne. After **St-Denis-lès-Martel**, a three-way junction, the line to Aurillac turns due east, following the wide valley of the Dordogne, and past **Bretenoux-Biars** it plunges into the narrow Cère Valley, criss-crossing the river through the gorge until **Laroquebrou**.

At **Aurillac** a change of train is necessary; this is the largest town on the route to Clermont, and has an historic centre. The railway twists through the town then runs along the foot of the Monts du Cantal. At **Polminhac**, a castle dominates the village and **Vic-sur-Cère**, with its spring and waterfall, has many picturesque old houses. From here, the Cère Valley again closes in and the scenery becomes increasingly spectacular, with the Puy Griou and Puy Mary to the north and 1,858-metre (6,096-ft) Plomb du Cantal to the south. **Le Lioran** is a modern ski resort at over 1,100 metres (3,600 ft). From here we follow the gorge of the Alagnon, amid thick pine forests. The gorge opens out from **Murat** to **Neussargues** then closes in again and the line follows it to **Lempdes**. At **Arvant**, our branch joins the main line from Nîmes to reach Clermont.

BELOW: the Clermont–Bordeaux express, 1926.

ESSENTIALS

Thomas Cook
timetable nos.
362/365

Distance:
(1) Marseille–Veynes
206 km
(2) Veynes–Grenoble
109 km
(3) Grenoble–Geneva
165 km

Duration of journey:
(1) 2 hrs 35 mins
(2) 1 hr 55 mins
(3) 2 hrs 10 mins

Frequency of trains:
(1) 4 daily
(2) 6 daily
(3) 2 daily

BELOW: one of
several viaducts
between Marseille
and Grenoble.

MARSEILLE–GRENOBLE–GENEVA

Enjoying the wonderful Alpine scenery on the Marseille–Geneva route was once an easier proposition than it is today; since the inception of the TGV Mediterranean line, direct services between the two cities now only operate over high-speed lines via Lyon. To follow the old route via St-Auban and Grenoble involves two changes of train, at Veynes and Grenoble, but this scenic line makes it worth the effort.

The train takes the same route between Marseille and St-Auban as the return from Digne *(see page 148)*, following the Durance Valley for much of the way. The valley narrows in the Défilé de Mirabeau then opens out again before arriving at **Manosque**, with its attractive old centre. **Sisteron** is situated in a remarkable defile cut by the Durance through a mountain ridge, and is dominated by a citadel to the west and a chapel to the east. Settlement here dates back 4,000 years. From Sisteron, the railway branches northwest along the Buëch Valley, where the landscape becomes increasingly rocky – the village of **Serres** is a lovely sight with its colourful houses clustered around the Pignolette rock peak.

Veynes to Grenoble

From Veynes the train turns north to **Aspres-sur-Buëch**, then starts to climb along the narrowing Grand Buëch Valley following the river and main road as the mountains become increasingly wild and grandiose. At **La Rochette**, a ridge cut into teeth by erosion juts into the valley and the remains of a feudal castle can be seen to the east. At **Lus-la-Croix-Haute**, the landscape opens out into an amphitheatre of rolling alpine country surrounded by peaks, and to the the northwest is the astonishing **Mont Aiguille**, a flat-topped mountain towering to 2,086 metres (6,843 ft), where climbers, possibly under the influence of local mushrooms, have claimed to see angels' clothes. From Lus the line makes the last climb to the pass at **Col de la Croix Haute** (1,167 metres/3,828 ft), past houses built to withstand severe weather. Snow fences are increasingly evident. After the tunnel, the line descends gradually, hugging the mountain slopes above a profound valley. This opens out to reveal an alpine plain studded with glacial *roches moutonées*.

More amazing views of the Mont Aiguille are to be had at **Clelles-Mens**, then the train crosses to the other side of a depression at **Monestier-de-Clermont**. The line slowly descends the mountainside and follows a double loop in order to drop quickly to **Vif** before arriving at **St-Georges-de-Commiers**, where the **Chemin de Fer de La Mure** *(see panel)* begins.

The industrial suburbs we pass next means we are coming into **Grenoble**, a high-tech city with a superb location at the foot of the Chartreuse mountains where the Drac and Isère rivers meet. The best way to see the city is to take the bubble-like cable cars from the old town across the river to the Fort de la Bastille, 500 metres (1,540 ft) up the mountainside. The city has an excellent modern art museum and it is possible to visit the home of the writer, Stendhal (1783–1842), who was born in the city.

North to Geneva

The train now follows the Isère Valley northwards between the Chartreuse mountains to the west and the Belledonne chain to the east. This corridor, known as Grésivaudan, was cut by a glacier and is sheltered enough to be a major fruit growing area. As the line turns west at Montmélian, it passes vineyards producing the local Chignin white and Mondeuse red wine, before arriving in **Chambéry**, the old capital of Savoie, a region that once extended well into the Italian Alps. The old town includes a 15th-century cathedral and an 18th-century castle. Following the valley, the train arrives at **Aix-les-Bains**, a spa town dating back to Roman times, with one cold and two hot springs. A few Roman remains can be seen, as can elegant hotels from the 19th-century boom in health cures.

Aix lies on the shore of the **Lac du Bourget**, which the train now skirts. On the opposite shore stands the **Abbaye de Hautecombe**, where 42 of the Savoie royal family are buried. Usually calm, France's biggest and deepest inland lake can become very stormy. Above the lake stretches a wild upland area, the Bugey, where lynx, originating from Switzerland, are successfully re-establishing themselves.

At **Culoz**, the line crosses the Rhône then joins its valley and heads north towards Switzerland. After the industrial town of Bellegarde, at the exit to a tunnel, the river and railway push between the Montagne du Grand Colombier to the west and the Montagne du Gros Foug to the east before the landscape opens out as the line enters Switzerland. **Geneva** itself, birthplace of Calvinism, sits in a superb site between mountains and lake, where the city's symbol, the Jet d'Eau fountain, the highest in the world, springs 145 metres (476 ft) into the air. The city has a wide variety of old and new buildings, world-class museums and enough lakeside parks to rest the weariest traveller after this long journey.

Map on page 133

The scenic stretch of line between Veynes and Grenoble.

BELOW: slow progress on the Chemin de Fer de La Mure.

CHEMIN DE FER DE LA MURE

The La Mure metre gauge railway was opened in 1888 to carry anthracite from the mines around La Mure to the standard gauge line at St-Georges-de-Commiers. The line follows a tortuous route (the two villages are 16 km/10 miles apart as the crow flies; the track runs for almost twice that distance) of tight curves, viaducts and tunnels, and became a tourist attraction after the last mine closed in 1988. From St-Georges, there is a steep ascent to 875 metres (2,870 ft). After Notre-Dame-de-Commiers, the line hugs the mountainside with a splendid view over Lac de Monteynard, some 300 metres (1,000 ft) below, formed by damming the River Drac. Above the lake, the train makes a stop to allow passengers to admire the breathtaking view. The line then turns north and climbs by means of loops, including two parallel viaducts on different levels at Loulla. After a halt at La Motte d'Aveillans station, where a museum of bee-keeping has been established, is the "tunnel mystérieux" where pictures projected by lanterns on the tunnel wall describe the work of the now-closed coal mines. Finally, before the descent to La Mure, La Pierre Percée, a rock through which a hole has been cut by erosion, is visible to the north. Trains run from April to October (Thomas Cook timetable no. 397).

ESSENTIALS

Thomas Cook
timetable no. 360

Distance: 241 km

Duration of journey:
2 hrs 25 mins
(Marseille–Nice), 25
mins (Nice–Monaco)

Frequency of trains:
18 per day to Nice;
numerous local trains
operate between
Nice and Monaco

MARSEILLE–NICE–MONACO

The writer Somerset Maugham once called the French Riviera a "shady place for shady people" and nowhere is this more true than at Marseille's St-Charles station. The blue riband TGV extension line may have opened in summer 2001, cutting journey times from Paris to Marseille to just three hours, but the station remains a raffish affair – colourful, vibrant, but still on the shady side.

Hills and fishing villages

After leaving the suburbs, the train passes through **Aubagne**. The countryside around here was made famous by Marcel Pagnol, whose books *Jean de Florette* and *Manon des Sources* were turned into successful films. The train turns south to **Cassis**, a beautiful little fishing port (2 km/1 mile from the station), once popular with artists such as Matisse and Dufy. The limestone coast to the west is cut with superb coves known as *calanques*, popular with hikers, divers and rock climbers.

A few minutes later, the train arrives at **La Ciotat** station, where the Lumière brothers, pioneers of cinema, made one of the first motion pictures (of a train arriving) in 1895. The coast is now fleetingly in view as we pass through **St-Cyr-sur-Mer**, where a 1st-century AD Roman villa has been turned into a museum, and **Bandol**, an attractive port frequented by writers Thomas Mann and Katherine Mansfield in the early 20th century. Both the Cassis and Bandol areas produce good wine.

BELOW: en route through the Massif des Maures.

After a glimpse of the fort at **La Seyne**, the train reaches **Toulon**, France's premier military port, situated on a fine natural harbour. While the rocky coast stretches eastwards to such famous places as St-Tropez, the railway now turns

inland towards the rugged, forested mountain ranges of the Massif des Maures, following a wide valley full of olive groves, fruit trees and vines. These produce Côteaux Varois and Côtes de Provence wines, for which the village of **Les Arcs** is the centre, while **Gonfaron** produces corks.The Massif itself is composed of oddly-shaped, orange-hued hills, dry and dusty in comparison to the spine of the Maritime Alps that runs further to the north. The Massif looks more like the landscape of the Grand Canyon than anything else on the French Riviera, with thinly-forested slopes only heightening the barren feel of the landscape.

Along the Corniche

The twin resort towns of Fréjus and St-Raphaël bring respite from the harshness of the hinterland, painting the archetypal Riviera scene of bronzed bodies lazing across the sands, seas of parasols as far as the eye can see, with swathes of pavement cafés lining the streets. Like many of the towns in this part of France, though, a richer past is buried beneath the tourist gloss of today. **Fréjus** was settled by the Massiliots, before Julius Caesar's men swept into town in 49 BC, leaving behind extensive ruins. The old Roman port is now occupied by the gardens seen shortly after the station, with remains of the town walls, an arena, an aqueduct and a theatre, glimpsed just before the station.

Fréjus's beach leads to **St-Raphaël**, a modern resort with a wide, sandy beach. The most eventful period of St-Raphaël's history occurred during World War II, when this was one of the main landing beaches for Allied troops, in August 1944. Today the jumble of wartime wrecks is very popular with scuba divers, with the highlight being the well-preserved American minesweeper that lies just off the St-Raphaël coastline.

Map
on page
133

Star Attractions: Nice
● Vieux Ville
● Château
● Promenade des
Anglais
● Musée Matisse
● Musée Chagall

LEFT: the Carlton Hotel, Cannes.
BELOW: public pool in Monaco.

The railway hugs the coast east of St-Raphaël, giving superb views along the **Corniche de l'Esterel** at every twist and turn, as well as inland, where the **Massif de l'Esterel** is formed of pink rock partially covered with *maquis*, cork-oaks and pines. At **Agay** and **Anthéor**, viaducts curve round bays, giving plunging views of sandy beaches. After passing a series of creeks, the line takes a tunnel to cut through a cape and reach **Théoule-sur-Mer**, a small resort at the start of the Golfe de la Napoule – the Bay of Cannes.

Festival centres

Cannes is a superb resort, famous for its film festival each spring. A walk along the Boulevard de la Croisette is a must, for its elegant hotels, restaurants, boutiques and luxurious cars. But do not miss the old port, the superb villas and the view from the Cap de la Croisette. The railway continues along the coast, now largely built up, but with some excellent views of the sea, through the legendary names of **Juan-les-Pins**, famous for its jazz festival, and **Antibes**, which has conserved an historic old town and fort as well as hosting a museum devoted to Picasso in the old Château Grimaldi, visible from the station.

From Antibes, the railway skirts the long, straight beach before reaching **Cagnes-sur-Mer**, a long-established artists' colony; one of its most famous residents was Renoir, whose home, just east of the town, is now a museum.

Nice dates from Greek occupation, four centuries before Christ, and has a wonderful array of attractions – Roman remains, no fewer than six art museums, a wonderful market and enough other sights and sounds to occupy several days.

The city makes a great base for exploring the region as it is well-equipped with hotels in all price ranges as well as tour companies, car hire firms and

BELOW: Monaco and its marina.

large shops. The pebble beach may not be as impressive as some others on the French Riviera, but a stroll along the **Promenade des Anglais** at sunset is still a quintessential Riviera experience. Nice was once home to many of Europe's finest modern artists with such luminaries as Marc Chagall, Henri Matisse and Pablo Picasso flocking here to seek inspiration from the unique qualities of the local light. Today their legacy lingers in the cluster of first-rate art galleries in town, making a stop here essential for anyone with even a passing interest in art.

Rail buffs are well catered for, too, with Les Chemins de Fer de la Provence offering a popular day trip from Nice, with two-carriage diesel trains leaving the Gare du Sud bound for the Provençal town of Digne-les-Bains *(see page 146)*.

Millionaires' row

It is only a short journey up the line to the principality of **Monte Carlo**, with its glittering capital of **Monaco**. This glamorous oasis for Europe's rich and famous offers a tax-free haven for those who can afford the high cost of living. The state-of-the-art rail terminal feels more like a slick airport than a railway station, but it is well worth leaving the train and spending a day in this enclave. Accommodation is expensive, and almost impossible to find during the annual Grand Prix, but there are plenty of inexpensive places to eat along the seafront, where the most popular pastimes are people-watching and posing. The best view of Monaco is from the terrace of the Grimaldi Palace, which rests on a steep promontory to the west of the main city. One unusual attraction is the public swimming pool, which is open to visitors. It is one of the few egalitarian places in town where it is difficult to differentiate between cash-strapped backpackers and the ultra-rich residents of one of the world's wealthiest playgrounds.

Map on page 133

Marinas on the French Riviera accommodate over a third of the world's luxury yachts.

BELOW: the TGV Méditerranée has made the Riviera more accessible than ever.

ESSENTIALS

Thomas Cook
timetable no. 361

Distance: 166 km

Duration of journey:
3 hrs 15 mins

Frequency of trains:
4 per day

NICE–DIGNE

The magnificent Nice–Digne line is one of the few remaining metre gauge railway lines in France. It is also one of even fewer that is privately operated, by the appropriately named Chemins de Fer de la Provence (CP). Trains leave from the unassuming modern CP station, 10 minutes' walk north from Nice Ville. Sadly, the superb Gare du Sud across the street from the new station, where CP trains used to terminate, has been empty and neglected since it was commandeered by the city authorities for redevelopment in the 1990s.

Nice to Entrevaux

The CP train clatters out of Nice, snaking between buildings and stopping at traffic lights guarding level crossings before climbing through pretty suburbs until it turns north after **Lingostière** to reach the valley of the River Var. The line then works its way northwards for 20 km (12 miles) between the wide, stony Var and a dual carriageway, serving shopping centres and dormitory villages. After **St-Martin-du-Var**, the valley starts to close in, and after **La Vésubie**, the line crosses the river from the deep Gorge de la Vésubie and enters the equally deep **Défilé de Chaudan** with the surrounding crags becoming increasingly dramatic. Next there is a long tunnel, then the line turns northwest, still following the Var, with remarkable rock strata in view.

Villages cluster on the steep valley sides; one of them is **Villars-sur-Var**, a haven of peace (because cars are banned) surrounded by vineyards. Ten minutes later, we come to **Touët-sur-Var**, a tiny village hugging a rock face, where the church is built on an arch over a torrent. Touët is also the starting point for exploration of the monumental **Gorges du Cians** to the north.

About 10 minutes from Touët is **Puget-Théniers**, an important market centre, where an attractive old town hides behind the less appealing modern district. A joyous statue of a plump nude – *L'Action Enchainée* – caused a conflict between church and anti-clerical opinion. Dedicated to the revolutionary, Blanqui, the statue had to be removed from its place in full view of the church after protests from clerics. Puget-Théniers is the starting point for the **Train des Pignes** *(see panel on page 148)*.

After a further five minutes, the train arrives at the delightful village of **Entrevaux**, which huddles at the foot of a rock in a meander of the Var. On top stands a citadel, perched 156 metres (512 ft) above the town and reached via a slope that zigzags 800 metres (2,624 ft) up the rock face, passing through no fewer than 20 gates on the way. The quarter-hour slog up the hill is well worth the effort for the views.

Flood damage

Back on the train, the line continues to follow the Var. The river was almost the undoing of the CP in 1994, when violent floods washed much of the railway embankment and even a major bridge away. Repairs were certainly not justified on economic grounds alone but it is a vital lifeline to many villages.

BELOW: picturesque Entrevaux.

Reconstruction took a whole year. A few minutes from Entrevaux, the line turns southwest to thread the narrow valley of the Coulomp, which joins the Var at Pont de Gueydan where the view is now ruined by quarry workings. Around this point olive groves start to give way to hay meadows and stands of sweet chestnuts, as the climate becomes harsher. After exiting a short tunnel, the train passes the **Pont de la Reine Jeanne** to the south, a bridge dating back to Roman times but rebuilt after floods in 1682.

After another five minutes we arrive in **Annot**, a village surrounded by enormous sandstone outcrops. The line now starts to climb even more steeply, needing two horseshoe curves to gain height near **Le Fugeret**. To the east, the line passes **Méailles**, a village just visible on a limestone outcrop known for its caverns, then cuts through the mountain in a long tunnel and turns southwest along the Verdon Valley. **St-André-les-Alpes** is situated between peaks at the north end of the Lac de Castillon, just visible to the south, a lake created behind a dam in 1947 in order to tame the wild Verdon River.

Along the Route Napoléon

At Barrême the line joins the Asse Valley and the N85 road, better known as the **Route Napoléon**, which comes up from the southeast. This was the route taken by Napoléon (avoiding the Rhône Valley) as he marched north after his escape from the Isle of Elba on 1 March 1815.

Barrême station itself contains an interesting exhibition of fossils, reflecting the fact that the mountains to the west are a geological reserve. The train now snakes between outcrops of limestone at the Clue de Chabrières, then reaches journey's end at **Digne-les-Bains**. As its name proclaims, Digne is a spa town,

Map on page 133

BELOW:
Annot station.

A good place to stop for refreshment when taking the Train des Pignes.

beautifully located at the confluence of three valleys in an area famous for its pungent lavender. The town has retained the elegance of a spa resort and has numerous monuments of note, including the 11th-century Cathédrale Notre-Dame du Bourg.

Although plans exist to extend the CP line to meet the Marseille–Veynes SNCF line at Château-Arnoux-St-Auban, it hasn't happened yet, so at present a bus ride is necessary. Nice–Digne–Marseille–Nice circuits (also Nice–Marseille–Digne–Nice) are possible in summer – in winter there are fewer trains running between Marseille and St-Auban.

St Auban to Marseille

From St-Auban, the SNCF line follows the wide valley of the River Durance for 45 minutes. The Durance has been systematically dammed and tapped to irrigate local orchards, with canals branching off at several points. After crossing the river on a long bridge just before Meyrargues, the line cuts through a forest then nears Aix-en-Provence with the Montagne Ste-Victoire, often painted by Cézanne, omnipresent to the east.

Aix-en-Provence dates back to the third century BC and was once the capital of Provence. Aix has retained much of the elegance of the past in its avenues, fountains and buildings, and is now classed a World Heritage Site by UNESCO. The city has such a collection of beautiful buildings, squares and museums that half a day at least is required to explore all of its corners.

The train now becomes a suburban commuter shuttle, trundling through the altogether different industrial town of Gardanne before descending slowly but surely through the rather ugly northern suburbs of Marseille.

BELOW: the Train des Pignes at La Vesubie Gorge.

THE TRAIN DES PIGNES

Puget-Théniers is the starting point for the steam train to Annot, known fondly as the Train des Pignes. The name recalls the use of pine cones, which regularly replaced coal as fuel when times were hard. In May 1951 the last steam locomotives on the Nice–Digne line were replaced by diesels. As tourism in the area grew, a group of enthusiasts got together with the aim of bringing steam traction back. On 19 July 1980, their goal was achieved. Since 1981, the formula has been the same – tourist services operate on summer weekends along the most scenic part of the line – from Puget-Théniers to Annot, with connections from Nice at 8.50am, returning at 8.57pm. See www.gecp.asso.fr.

Trains are formed of restored coaches dating back to between 1888 and 1912. Two quite different steam locomotives are the stars. The more modest, turned out in shining green and black, is number E-327, a 2-3-0 tank engine built in 1909 and once used on a large network of country lines in Brittany. The other is loco E-211, an unusual "Mallet" 2-4-0 + 0-6-0 tank. The loco sits on two chassis, an arrangement allowing high power but short wheelbases advantageous when it was used on the sinuous lines of the Douro Valley in Portugal.

AROUND MONT BLANC

Map
on page
133

The SNCF standard gauge line from Lyon and Paris reaches St-Gervais, at the foot of Mont Blanc, but then gives way to the metre gauge Ligne de Savoie which continues into Switzerland, while other private lines take visitors closer to the peaks. Given the mountainous nature of the area, it is not surprising that there is some fantastic scenery en route.

The world's steepest railway

The Ligne de Savoie was built by the Paris-Lyon-Méditerranée railway to Chamonix in 1901 then was extended to Argentière and Vallorcine by 1908. At Vallorcine, on the Swiss border, it meets the Swiss Martigny-Châtelard railway (MC) end on and, thanks to new trains, some services run all the way through to Martigny. Try to take the Mont Blanc Express train, well worth it for the observation cars which allow some unsurpassed views.

The line leaves St-Gervais, passing an ugly aluminium plant before climbing steeply from Chedde to Servoz, where it gains 381 metres (1,250 ft) in height in only 9 km (5 miles). This necessitates a 1 in 11 gradient – the steepest in the world worked by trains without rack equipment (while the Swiss part relies on racks to help climb the steep gradients, the SNCF does not). On this section, the little train is dwarfed by a massive but elegant motorway viaduct that takes traffic through the Mont Blanc road tunnel into Italy. The tunnel was closed for two years in 2000/2001 after a tragic fire in a truck killed 39 people. The line then follows the pretty Arve Valley between towering mountains to Chamonix. At Les Bossons, the Bossons glacier can be seen to the south as it reaches right down to the roadside.

One of the world's foremost mountaineering centres, **Chamonix** itself is a pleasant town nestling in the valley and is the point from which travellers can experience another world record – the world's highest cable car, which at times hangs 500 metres (1,640 ft) above ground on its way to the Aiguille du Midi, a 3,842-metre (12,600-ft) peak extending the Mont Blanc range. It is also the terminal for the Chamonix-Montenvers line, described on the following page.

The SNCF line continues up the valley to Argentière where it passes through the Aiguille Rouge mountain range in a tunnel, emerging at Le Buet. Some SNCF trains terminate at Chamonix; others continue to Vallorcine and Le Châtelard, where there is a connection with the Swiss MC line. A few trains each day run right through to Martigny and one popular trip is to continue from Martigny along the shores of Lac Léman (Lake Geneva) through Montreux and Lausanne to Geneva (see page 189). From Geneva's Eaux Vives station, it is possible to return to St-Gervais on an SNCF service.

Tramway du Mont-Blanc

Before continuing on the SNCF tracks, cross the station forecourt at St-Gervais to where the Tramway du Mont Blanc (TMB) begins. This is France's highest railway, climbing from 584 metres (1,916 ft) to the

ESSENTIALS

Thomas Cook
timetables nos.
572/393

Distance: 56 km (St-Gervais–Martigny)

Duration of journey:
2 hrs 20 mins

Frequency of trains:
3 per day St-Gervais–Martigny (Mt Blanc Express), 4 per day (change at border)
Extra trains run in tourist season

BELOW: the Mer de Glace at Montenvers.

Nid d'Aigle (Eagle's Nest) terminus at 2,372 metres (7,782 ft). The line first runs through the streets of **Le Fayet**, a spa resort where people still come to take the waters at the famous baths. The line then becomes a true rack railway, the cogs on the small electric train engaging in the teeth of the rail between the tracks. The first stretch of rack takes the train to **St-Gervais** itself, a health and ski resort. The line then traverses a wood and emerges onto alpine meadows where the air is full of jangling cow bells. From Bellevue station, over the final 2 km (1 mile), the line climbs 600 metres (1,970 ft) along narrow ledges and through tunnels hewn in the rock. The Nid d'Aigle terminus was reached in 1914; it was meant to be temporary, but the funds were never found to continue to the Bionnassay glacier on the north face of Mont Blanc and the Aiguille du Gouter, just under the summit. For now, the only solution is to continue on foot.

Chamonix–Montenvers

Just over the footbridge from Chamonix SNCF station is the terminus of the Montenvers line, whose little red trains climb from the base station at 1,042 metres (3,417 ft) to the terminus at **Montenvers** (1,913 metres/6,275 ft). This rack rail line, built in 1909, climbs through forests, two major tunnels and innumerable avalanche shelters that allow it to operate all year round.

At the top there are tremendous views over the 200-metre (660-ft) thick **Mer de Glace**, a vast sea of ice where the Leschaux, Tacul and Talefre glaciers meet to form the second biggest glacier in the Alps. The ice slides downhill at a rate of 8 mm (⅓ in) an hour. A cable car carries passengers from the station down to the edge of the ice from where a tunnel has been cut into the glacier. It is an enjoyable hour-long walk back to Chamonix from here.

BELOW: a bird's-eye view of Chamonix from the Aiguille du Midi cable car.

ROUTES IN THE FRENCH PYRENEES

Map
on page
128/9

Compared with the Alps, the Pyrenees has a little less to offer rail lovers. Main lines cross the border on the flat at either end of the range, although a more scenic line runs between France and Spain via Latour-de-Carol, which connects with the little "Yellow Train" coming up from the east. There are also two quaint rack railways that climb the steep Pyrenean gradients – to the summit of La Rhune, where you can cross the frontier on foot for a magnificent view (weather permitting), and to the shrine of Núria in Spain *(see page 180)*.

La Rhune

La Rhune, the westernmost peak of the Pyrenees, can be ascended by an old-fashioned cog railway that sets off from a mountain pass, the Col de St-Ignace (169 metres/554 ft), between Ascain and Sare. The lower station is connected by bus with St-Jean-de-Luz on the coastal main line.

An alternative to the round trip is to take the train to the top of the mountain and follow the marked footpath down (allow at least two hours). Either way, wear warm clothing as the train doesn't have glass in the windows and conditions on the mountain top can be changeable.

The four wooden trains are shunted up 25-percent (1-in-4) inclines by electric locomotives in which two large cogs engage with a toothed middle rail. The frequency of services varies according to demand but you will be told how long you will have to wait when you buy your ticket. The trip takes about 35 minutes each way, with the train jerking along at only 8 km/h (5 mph). The first part of the route is an abrupt ascent, pushing you back into your seat. Half

ESSENTIALS

Thomas Cook
timetable no. n/a
www.rhune.com

Distance: 4.2 km

Duration of journey:
35 minutes

Frequency of trains:
varies with demand;
every 35 mins in
summer

BELOW:
wooden carriages
on La Rhune.

way up the mountain the track levels, divides to let trains cross and goes into another steep incline, passing the tree line to reach the summit. On the way up you have good views back over the French countryside and towards the resorts of the Atlantic coast. The slopes beside the track are grazed by wild ponies, and vultures can often be seen soaring above.

The summit of La Rhune (905metres/2,969 ft) is a curious no-man's land. You disembark from a French railway, climb some steps and arrive at three Spanish bar-restaurant-souvenir shops after crossing an invisible international frontier. On a clear day you have a 360 degree view from here, stretching to horizons some 100 km (60 miles) away and taking in a large sweep of the Basque Country, both Spanish and French.

Le Train Jaune

Le Train Jaune (the Yellow Train) runs along 63 km (39 miles) of narrow gauge track from Villefranche-de-Conflent (connected by SNCF train to Perpignan) to Latour-de-Carol on the Pyrenean plateau of the Cerdagne. There are three through trains all year plus extra short workings to Fort Roman in July and August.

Most of the 20 stations en route are request stops (*arrêts facultatifs*) but they are only worth getting off at if you intend to go hiking. Mont Louis is a good place to wait for a return train if you are travelling with children and don't want to go too far. Continuing to the less interesting Bourg-Madame, however, gives you an opportunity to see more of the Cerdagne countryside. It's only really worth going on to Latour de Carol, an international station with three gauges of rail (French, Spanish and the Yellow Train's narrow gauge), if you are a real train buff. The best views are to be had from the open carriage, which kids love, but

ESSENTIALS

Thomas Cook
timetable no. 354

Distance: 63 km

Duration of journey:
2 hrs 55 mins

Frequency of trains:
4–5 per day (June–Sept); 2–3 per day at other times, bus replacement frequent in winter

BELOW: at Bourg-Madame station on Le Train Jaune.

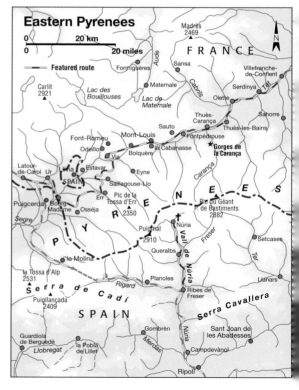

on busy summer days you need to arrive at Villefranche early in order to get a place and you should be armed with plenty of suncream and a hat.

The first part of the route is up the steep-sided Têt Valley. Shortly after **Thuès-les-Bains** station you will see below you the spa of the same name which has the hottest naturally-heated waters in France (over 80°C/175°F). Pulling out of the next station, Thuès-Carança, look left for a glimpse of the picturesque **Gorges de la Carança**. A few minutes further on, the line strides across the Têt Valley on the granite Séjourné Viaduct. After Sauto station the train goes through a series of tunnels before crossing the Têt again by way of the magnificent **Gisclard Suspension Bridge** which is 80 metres (262 ft) high.

An hour out of Villefranche the train climbs out of the Têt Valley and onto the upland plateau of the Cerdagne. The landscape is suddenly quite different: forest and scrub give way to lush pastures filled with Pyrenean wild flowers. The next halt is **Mont-Louis-La Cabanasse**, protected by the highest fort in France. The line continues to climb and reaches its zenith at the inconspicuous **Bolquère-Eyne**. At 1,593 metres (5,226 ft), this is the highest SNCF station in France. Leaving **Font-Romeu-Odeillo-Via** station you can see the back of the **Four Solaire d'Odeillo/Font-Romeu**, a solar oven powered by a bank of mirrors, that is used for scientific research.

Immediately after Estavar station there is a tight bend with views over **Llívia**, an island of Spanish territory marooned in France by an accident of history. The frontier town, **Bourg-Madame**, has little to offer except a walk over the River Rahur for coffee in the outskirts of its Spanish counterpart, Puigcerda. The train continues for 15 minutes to **Latour-de-Carol**, a route node at 1,231 metres (4,038 ft) from where there are main-line trains to Toulouse and Barcelona.

Map on page 152

Waiting for the Train Jaune at Villefranche-le-Conflent station.

BELOW: the train includes an open carriage.

ESSENTIALS

Thomas Cook
timetable no. 379

Distance:
(1) Bastia–Ajaccio
152 km
(2) Ponte Lec-
cia–Calvi 73 km

Duration of journey:
(1) 3 hrs 34 mins
(2) 1 hr 45 mins

Frequency of trains:
(1) 4 per day
(2) 2 per day

BELOW: Corsica's
most famous son.

CORSICA

Corsica's metre gauge railways form a lopsided "Y", with the branch from Calvi in the northwest meeting, at Ponte Leccia, the main line from Bastia in the northeast, to force a dramatic passage through the mountains to Ajaccio. The lines were built with immense difficulty – which is, of course, part of the reason for their appeal to travellers today: the main line has 32 tunnels and 51 major bridges or viaducts, yet was built with a skill and speed that is a tribute to their 19th-century engineers.

State-sponsored construction began at various points between Bastia and Corte in 1883, opening five years later, and today's 232-km (145-mile) system was completed by 1894. Only one branch, running along the east coast from Casamozza near Bastia to Porto-Vecchio, was a protracted business, opened in stages from 1888 to 1935. Sadly, it was so badly damaged during World War II that it never reopened.

Apart from the modern diesel railcars that operate all services, little has changed since construction: the station buildings are still mostly original, and even the water towers and columns for steam locomotives remain, almost half a century after the last whistle was heard.

The idiosyncratic delays to Corsica's trains described by some guide books are largely a thing of the past, and travelling by rail is an excellent way to gain an impression of the island and to visit some of its principal attractions. Even where a parallel road exists, it is generally at a lower level, with diminished views. During the summer months, trains are well patronised, and passengers should not arrive at the last minute expecting to get a seat.

Bastia to Corte

Located only a few minutes' walk from Place St-Nicolas, **Bastia** station is conveniently sited for a walk through the old streets around the harbour and the various places of interest within Terra Nova (or Citadelle). Once on the train, the passage through the suburbs and beside a busy dual carriageway is uninspiring, but once past the railway's workshops at **Casamozza**, the scenery improves dramatically as the railway swings west. It climbs through woods, rock cuttings and a series of short tunnels up the valley of the River Golo, crossing the crystal clear waters three times on substantial viaducts, the first offering a glimpse of the picturesque remains of a Genoese bridge.

The characteristic location of Corsican villages soon becomes apparent: most were built high up on hillsides to escape the malarial mosquito (eliminated just after World War II), but were seldom positioned on the ridge itself. A well still stands beside the station at **Ponte Nuovo**, close to the bridge where Corsican nationalists were heavily defeated by the French in 1769.

On the approach to the island's only railway junction at **Ponte Leccia**, the train crosses the River Asco and runs alongside the Calvi line for the last 500 metres (547 yds) into the station. An adventure tourism company occupies a redundant railway building, its clients often joining the train to reach one of the more remote stations in the mountains. From Ponte Leccia the valley broadens as the train presses south, with more signs of agriculture than on any other stretch of line, even if these are sometimes cows sheltering from the sun on the verandas of abandoned farmhouses or barns.

The line soon starts to climb, and after **Francardo** the railway describes the first of many horseshoe-shaped loops. Ahead can be seen a viaduct at a higher

Map on page 154

Star Attractions:
Corsica
● Bonifacio
● Calanche cliffs
● Restonica and
Tavignano gorges
● Maison Bonaparte,
Ajaccio
● Palais Fesch,
Ajaccio
● Bastia old port
● Corte

BELOW: train cleaning.

level, giving a graphic idea of the gradient. The slopes are covered by the *maquis* for which the island is famous, an aromatic and varying mix of arbutus, heather, juniper, laburnum, lavender, myrtle and rosemary that gave its name to French resistance fighters during World War II (because they often hid out in such terrain). Remains of neglected terracing bear witness to the rural depopulation that has affected Corsica, while ruined towers are reminders of the centuries of Genoese rule. The line reaches its summit in a tunnel under the Col de San Quilico before dropping down to the old capital of **Corte**. It is less than 10 minutes' walk from the station up to the old town, and access by train obviates the struggle for parking space in a town disfigured by traffic in high season. The labyrinth of narrow streets and cobble-stepped alleys below the citadel is best explored on foot.

Mountain paradise

Leaving Corte, the climb resumes, affording wonderful views over unbroken forest as the train twists endlessly round a confusing series of loops and disorienting tunnels before arriving at the well-sited station at **Venaco**. Flying buttresses brace the arched stone walls of a deep cutting as the train briefly descends towards the **Pont du Vecchio**, the stone and steel girder bridge designed by Gustave Eiffel that spans the River Vecchio at a height of 80 metres (262 ft). There is hardly time to appreciate the structure before the train dives into an unlined tunnel. Soon after emerging, the track ahead can to seen high up on the right, with the twin water towers at the station of **Vivario**; the line describes such an immense loop to reach it that a straight line between kilometre posts 91 and 98 measures just 200 metres (656 ft).

BELOW: hiking in Corsica's central mountains.

There follows the most spectacular part of the journey as the train weaves a course through the mountains, with dizzying views down into the gorges of the Vecchio and Manganello rivers and over to Monte Rotondo (2,622 metres/ 8,602 ft) in the distance. A glimpse may be had of the extensive remains of Fort de Pasciolo above the line. After **Savaggio** there is a long section of Larico pine woods and fern-filled cuttings before the train reaches **Tattone**, one of several places where fire crews are stationed in summer to deal with the frequent forest fires.

The climb is over as the railway attains a summit of 906 metres (2,974 ft) at **Vizzavona** station, where there is a restaurant and bar catering to the many walkers who use the station. Immediately to the south the train enters a dead straight tunnel, the longest on the system at 4 km (2½ miles). The village at **Bocognano** can be seen below long before the train reaches it, and further ahead is a viaduct at a much lower level. Descending through forests of chestnuts the railway joins the valley of the River Gravona and follows it all the way to the sea and along the front to the terminus at **Ajaccio**.

The administrative centre of the southern département of Corsica, Ajaccio is situated on a wide south-facing bay. The town is famous as the birthplace of Napoleon Bonaparte in 1769, and his family home is open to visitors.

Map on page 154

Ponte Leccia–Calvi

Apart from the two trains a day that run the entire stretch of line, there is also an almost-hourly summer service between Calvi and Ile Rousse to serve the resorts and beaches along the coast. Leaving the junction at Ponte Leccia the railway turns away from the Bastia line and follows the Navaccia Valley through barren, sandstone countryside almost devoid of habitation or trees. Although still operating, the station at **Pietralba** matches the terrain in its dereliction. Once through the summit tunnel there is a magnificent view across to **Novella** station, which has been converted into a *gîte*, and the terraces around the village. The line passes the derelict station building at **Palasca** and through a deep rock cutting towards the strangely-named station of **PK79 + 800** where extensive views open up over the coastal plain and its occasional splashes of irrigated green in summer. From **Belgodere** a string of hillside villages follow the contour line.

Emerging from one of the many rock cuttings, there is a panorama over the sea and the popular resort of **Ile Rousse**, named after the causeway-linked island that glows red in the evening sun. The train runs beside the beach, past the old town and through the old wall to the station. From here to Calvi the line is seldom out of sight of the sea, as the train rattles around the headlands and past the tiny beach-side halts served by the "Tramway de Balagne" railcars. Corsican pines fringe the beaches and shelter the many camping grounds to the south of the railway. A glimpse can be had of the Foreign Legion base at Camp Rafelli opposite **Calenzana-Lumio**.

Passing hundreds of sizzling, sun-soaked bodies, the train runs past the sands towards the distinctive outline of the Genoese-built citadel around which huddles the station and lovely old town of **Calvi**. ❑

BELOW: the citadel at Corte.

Museums and Heritage Lines

Preserved railways are much less developed in France than in Britain or Germany, as there are fewer enthusiasts to run the lines and fewer people interested in visiting them. Most are open in summer only. The numbers relate to the map on pages 128–129.

Museums

Cité du Train – Musée Français du Chemin de Fer ❶

2 rue Alfred de Glehn, 68200 Mulhouse
Open: daily 10am–6pm; Oct–Mar closes 5pm; Jan weekdays closes 2pm
Restaurant, shop
Features: France's national railway museum
Nearest station: Mulhouse Ville
Tel: 03 89 42 83 33
Fax: 03 89 42 41 82
www.citedutrain.com

Musée du Chemin de Fer de Longueville ❷

AJECTA, Dépôt des Machines, Rue Louis Platriez, 77650 Longueville
Open: July–Aug Sat–Sun 10.30am–6.30pm; otherwise usually open weekends, contact beforehand
Features: museum in old round-house depot, 1 hour from Paris; open day with live steam in mid-September
Nearest station: Longueville
Tel: 01 64 60 26 26
www.ajecta.org

Heritage lines

Chemin de Fer de la Baie de Somme ❸

La Gare, BP 80031, 80230 St-Valéry-sur-Somme
(Noyelles-sur-Mer–Le Crotoy, Noyelles-sur-Mer–Cayeux-sur-Mer)
Features: shop, coastal views, nature reserve
Nearest station: Noyelles-sur-Mer
Length: 27 km (17 miles)
Open: Apr–Sept most days; other weekends
Gauge: 1,000 mm
Tel: 03 22 26 96 96
Fax: 03 22 26 85 66
www.chemin-fer-baie-somme.asso.fr

Chemin de Fer du Vivarais ❹

Avenue de la Gare
07300 Tournon-sur-Rhone
(Tournon–Lamastre)
Café, shop at Lamastre
Features: superb gorge scenery
Nearest station: Tain l'Hermitage (20 minutes' walk)
Length: 33 km (20 miles)
Open: services have been suspended for 2008
Gauge: 1,000 mm
Tel: 04 75 08 20 30
www.ardeche-train.com

Chemin de Fer Forestier d'Abreschviller ❺

2 Place Prévot, 57560 Abreschviller
(Abreschviller–Grand Soldat)
Souvenir shop
Features: steam, forest scenery
Nearest station: Sarrebourg
Length: 6 km (4 miles)
Open: July–Aug daily; Apr–Oct most weekends
Gauge: 700 mm
Tel: 03 87 03 71 45
Fax: 03 87 03 79 12
www.train-abreschviller.fr

Chemin de Fer Touristique de la Vallee de l'Aa ❻

CFTVA, 3 rue des Cuvelots, 62380 Bayenghem-les-Seninghem
(Arques–Lumbres)
Café, restaurant
Features: access to canal boat lift and V2 rocket museum
Nearest station: St-Omer
Length: 15 km (9 miles)
Open: June–Aug Sat–Sun and holidays, May and Sept Sun and holidays
Gauge: Standard
Tel: 03 21 93 45 46 or 03 21 12 19 19
Fax: 03 21 12 15 87
http://cftva.free.fr

Chemin de Fer Touristique du Rhin ❼

26 rue des Cordiers, 68280 Andolsheim
(Volgelsheim–Sans Souci)
Features: line along River Rhine, possible boat trips
Nearest station: Colmar
Length: 12 km (7½ miles)
Open: May–June Sun; July Sun–Mon; Aug Fri–Sun; Sept Sat–Sun
Gauge: Standard
Tel/Fax: 03 89 71 51 42
http://cftr.evolutive.org

Chemin de Fer Touristique du Vermandois ❽

BP 152, 02104 St Quentin
CEDEX
(St-Quentin–Origny Ste-Benoîte)
Restaurant car
Features: cathedral town, valley scenery
Nearest station: St-Quentin
Length: 23 km (14 miles)
Open: Mar–Dec selected weekends
Gauge: Standard
Tel/Fax: 03 23 64 88 38
www.trains-fr.org/cftv

Petit Train d'Artouste

Etablissement Publique des
Stations d'Altitude, Avenue
Messier, 64260 Iseste
(La Sagette–Lac d'Artouste)
Shops, restaurant, cafés
Features: climb through
Pyrenees to mountain lake;
highest panorama in Europe at
over 2,000 metres (6,500 ft)
Nearest station: Pau
Length: 9 km (6 miles)
Open: late May–late Sept daily
Gauge: 500 mm
Tel: 05 59 05 36 99
www.train-artouste.com

Petit Train de la Haute Somme ⑩

APPEVA, BP 70106, 80001
Amiens
(Froissy–Dompierre)
Shop, bar
Features: steam on former
narrow gauge railway serving
Allied trenches in WW1, plus
museum
Nearest station: Albert
Length: 7 km (4 miles).
Open: July–Aug Tue–Sun;
May–Sept Sun
Gauge: 600 mm
Tel: 03 22 83 11 89
www.appeva.org

Petit Train de La Rhune *(see page 151)* ⑪

Col de St-Ignace, 64310 Sare
Shop, restaurant
Nearest station: St-Jean-de-Luz
Length: 4.2 km (2½ miles)
Open: Mar–Nov daily
Tel: 05 59 54 20 26
www.rhune.com

Train à Vapeur des Cévennes

(see picture, right) ⑫; CITEV,
Place de la Gare, BP 50, 30140
Anduze
(Anduze–St-Jean du Gard)
Shops, bar
Features: mountain terrain,
bamboo forest

Nearest station: Alès
Length: 13 km (8 miles)
Open: Apr–early Sept daily;
Sept–Oct Tue–Sun
Gauge: Standard
Tel: 04 66 60 59 01
www.trainavapeur.com

Train à Vapeur de Pithiviers ⑬

AMTP, Musée des Transports de
Pithiviers, rue Carnot, 45300
Pithiviers (Pithiviers–Bellébat)
Shop
Features: narrow gauge line and
museum
Nearest station: Malesherbes
Length: 4 km (2½ miles)
Open: May and Oct Sun,
June–Sept Sat–Sun
Gauge: 600 mm
Tel: 02 38 30 50 02
www.lafrancevuedurail.fr/
pithiviers

Train Touristique du Cotentin ⑭

BP 28 50230, Agon-
Coutainville
(Carteret–Portbail)
Features: fishing port, coastal
views
Nearest station: Carentan
Length: 10 km (6 miles)
Open: July–Aug Tue, Thur, Sat,

Sun; Jun, Sept Sun and holidays
Gauge: Standard
Tel: 02 33 45 93 47
http://ttcotentin.monsite.
wanadoo.fr

Train Touristique des Monts du Lyonnais ⑮

18 Place Sapéan
(L'Arbresle–Ste Foy l'Argen-
tière)
Features: scenic ride near Lyon
Nearest station: L'Arbresle
Length: 20 km (12½ miles)
Open: June–Sept Sun and holi-
days
Gauge: Standard
Tel: 04 74 01 48 87
http://cftb.free.fr

Train Touristique Livradois-Forez ⑯

AGRIVAP, Train Touristique,
La Gare, 63600 Ambert
(Courpière–Sembadel)
Features: ride through regional
park, paper and tractor muse-
ums, abbey at La Chaise Dieu
Nearest station: Thiers
Length: 85 km (53 miles)
Open: July–Aug weekends
Gauge: Standard
Tel: 04 73 82 43 88
http://pagesperso-orange.fr/
..agrivap

SPAIN AND PORTUGAL

Map on page 164

A massive investment programme has brought Spanish railways to the forefront of Europe's high-speed network, but there are also slower, scenic routes to explore both here and in Portugal

Spain's rail infrastructure has always been subject to strong state intervention, although before the foundation of the state-controlled RENFE in 1941 the network was made up of private companies. The first Spanish line opened in 1848, from Barcelona to Mataró on the Costa Brava. Seven years later, the Railroad Bill stipulated that the only tracks that could be laid were those that began or ended in Madrid; this has resulted in the awkward radial nature of the network still evident today. Another lasting problem has been the gauge size, which is broader than that used in the rest of Europe. Nevertheless, by 1867 a basic network running to 4,649 km (2,889 miles) of track had been laid.

Today, the limitations of the original network are being rectified by several high-speed lines. The link between Madrid and the Andalucian cities of Córdoba and Seville now extends south to Málaga, and construction of the high-speed line between the capital and Barcelona is complete, finally overcoming years of technical problems and making reducing travel times between Spain's two largest cities to just two hours and 35 minutes. Passengers can now relax on reclining seats (which can be turned around to face the direction of travel), while the sleek new trains glide through the countryside at 354 km/h (220 mph). The line will eventually be extended to Perpignan in France. Another high-speed link now runs from the capital to Valladolid in the north, which will soon continue to Bilbao and San Sebastián. A similar line between Madrid and Lisbon is underway.

Spanish National Railways (RENFE) operates the vast majority of track, half of which is electrified. Government-owned Ferrocarriles del Estado de Via Estrecha (FEVE) controls a small network, mainly in northern suburban areas. Some 918 km (570 miles) is privately owned. There are several wonderful stretches of line crossing the wide open spaces of the Spanish interior. Other than those featured in the following pages, highlights include the route from Burgos to Madrid across the high *meseta* plateau of Old Castile, and the Granada–Almería line that traverses Europe's only desert on its way to the Mediterranean coast. The luxury Al Andalus Express between Seville and Granada is due to resume operations in 2009.

Portuguese railways

The Portuguese have had a railway since 1856. By 1877 there was a rail link between Lisbon and Porto, its highlight the laced-metal bridge designed by Gustave Eiffel, spanning the Douro River. The Companhia dos Caminhos de Ferro Portugueses came into being in 1951, and now operates a network totalling 3,100 km (1,940 miles).

Trains reach smoothly across the country – north to Valença and Spanish Galicia, south to the Algarve

PRECEDING PAGES: tile décor at the National Rail Museum, Entroncamento, Portugal. **LEFT:** the Modernist façade of Bilbao's Santander station. **BELOW:** stationmaster with baton.

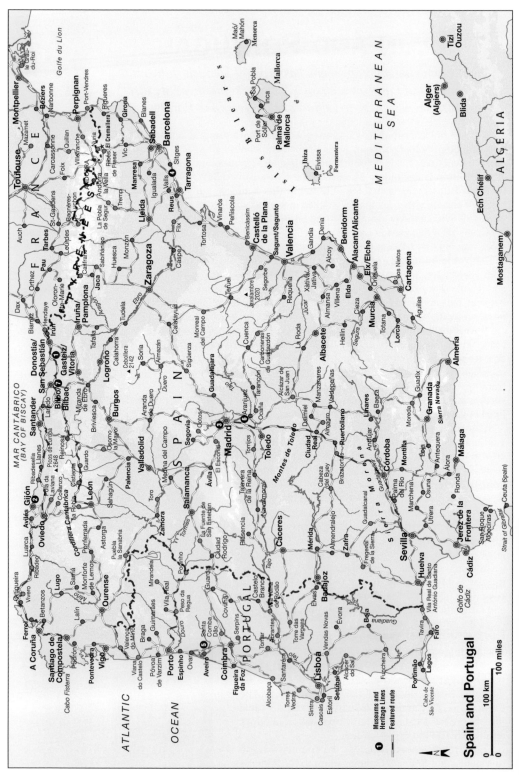

Spain and Portugal

◉ Museums and
Heritage Lines
══ Featured route

| 0 | 100 km |
| 0 | 100 miles |

coast, across the Alentejo plains to the wonders of Évora. From Lisbon an electric train runs west alongside the Tagus River to Estoril and Cascais; at Belém station there are grand sights relating to the Age of Discovery. Other discoveries, as you travel, might include the fascinating variety of stations – the little tiled ones along the northern rivers, the mock-Manueline façade to Lisbon's Rossio station and the stunning architecture of the ultra-modern Oriente station in the Parque das Nações, a major transport hub east of the city.

THE TRANSCANTABRICAN ROUTE

The Biscay coast of Spain stretches for hundreds of kilometres from the border with France to reach Spain's northwesternmost point at Cape Finisterre (Cabo Fisterra). This long coastline sees far fewer holiday visitors than Spain's warmer Mediterranean shores, yet it fronts a fascinating and varied region, full of history and with some of Europe's most delightful countryside where the slopes of the Cordillera Cantábrica run down towards the sea.

A metre gauge railway runs almost the entire length of the Biscay coast; known as the Transcantabrican line, this is one of Spain's most memorable rail journeys. Even at its fastest the run takes three days, transporting the traveller through a variety of landscapes and cultural traditions; however, each section of the journey is worth savouring rather than rushing straight through, and a week is not too long to set aside for the whole route.

Travelling east to west, the Transcantabrican journey starts at Hendaye on the French frontier, takes in San Sebastián, Bilbao, Santander and Oviedo along the way and eventually makes its way to the port of Ferrol on the distant coast of Galicia. This route was once a linked system of independent railway companies whose names can still be seen on some station buildings, but today it is all part of the state-run, light railway group FEVE and its Basque-country operating subsidiary, Eusko Tren (ET). The cheerfully painted stations, modern trains and helpful staff all combine to make the journey a real pleasure.

Along the Basque coast

Hendaye, where we meet the easternmost extremity of the Transcantabrican route, is in fact just within France. Our journey starts on a suburban electric train which will take us over the border and then rattle along through numerous stations and even more numerous tunnels to San Sebastián, 22 km (15 miles) along the coast. The Hendaye–San Sebastián line has been electrified since its inception although the current rolling stock of blue, two-car units, dates only from 1991. Because of all the tunnels, the service is nicknamed *El Topo* (The Mole).

San Sebastián, a city of 200,000 people, is the capital of Guipuzcoa, a stylish seaside resort that merits at least one night's stop. The ET terminus, the Amara station, is on the left bank of the River Urumea. The old town, with a plethora of restaurants and bars, is about a kilometre's walk to the north. While there are several places on the Transcantabrican route that pride themselves on their gastronomy, San Sebastián is second to none.

Map on page 164

ESSENTIALS

Thomas Cook timetable nos. 689/686

Distance: 780 km

Duration of journey:
(1) Hendaye–San Sebastián 36 mins
(2) San Sebastián–Bilbao 2 hrs 35 mins
(3) Bilbao–Santander–Oviedo 7 hrs
(4) Oviedo–Ferrol 6 hrs 25 mins

Frequency of trains:
(1) every 30 mins
(2) hourly (3) 2 daily (change at Santander)
(4) 2 daily direct

BELOW: the beach at San Sebastián.

El Transcantábrico

Luxury land-cruise trains are an established feature on several of Europe's standard gauge rail networks, but it has taken the FEVE railway along Spain's Biscay coast to adapt the concept to the slimmer metre gauge, with its successful El Transcantábrico operation. The train's long rake of blue and white coaches is a familiar sight on the tracks that snake along between the coastline and the Cantabrian mountains.

What El Transcantábrico offers is essentially a well-appointed mobile hotel in traditional Wagons-Lits style, a base for excursions during the day. With the re-opening of the Robla line to passenger trains, the route now runs either from León via Bilbao to Ferrol, then on to Santiago de Compostela by coach, or does the same journey in reverse. The countryside lends itself to this sort of upmarket touring – green valleys and mountain vistas, eminent museums and historic towns, fine food and

famous restaurants. The Transcantábrico melds these facets of Cantabria, Galicia and the Basque country in the course of its 8-day run.

Hauled by a powerful diesel engine, the train makes its way out of the historic Castilian city of León after lunch on Saturday and heads northeastwards through the Cantabrian mountains towards Bilbao. The first night is spent at Cistierna, the passengers retiring to their two-bed or single-suite rooms. The suites, with double beds and showers, are very well appointed indeed. Next morning it's breakfast in the dining car. After excursions to Saldaña and the caves at Sotoscueva, Bilbao is reached on the Monday. Passengers spend the morning here – most will want to see the amazing Guggenheim Museum – before the train departs for Santander, where it stops for the night.

This blend of nights on the train, days touring the countryside and splendid meals in picturesque surrounding, carries travellers on for five more days and nights. The next day, starting at Santander, provides three highlights: the wonderful neolithic paintings in the caves at Altamira; the medieval village of Santillana de Mar; and dinner in the historic town of Cangas de Onís.

As the programme unfolds, passengers gain a multi-faceted impression of northern Spain. The coach trip from Arriondas station high up into the Picos de Europa National Park makes a particularly memorable day, as does the run along the coast west of the Asturian capital of Oviedo, where the railway glides across estuaries and inlets on high viaducts. Very pleasant in summer, Oviedo is located on the north side of the Cantabrian mountain range and is approximately 24 km (15 miles) from the coast, a gateway to both beach and skiing resorts. The line's highlights include the picturesque fishing village of Cudillero, the port of Ribadeo with its steep cobbled streets, and the walled town of Vivero. Ferrol is the end of the line; from here a coach runs the final 80 km (50 miles) to the pilgrimage centre of Santiago de Compostela, with its marvellous cathedral *(for booking information, see page 350.)* ❏

LEFT: time for an apéritif before dinner on El Transcantábrico.

From San Sebastián, hourly trains run along the coast towards **Bilbao**, 111 km (70 miles) away, taking just over 2½ hours. The trains are three-car electric units in blue and grey livery with a good turn of speed between stations, although their spartan interior reflects their original role in short-haul suburban services. This route was originally operated by the Ferrocarriles Vascongados but it, too, is now owned by FEVE and operated by ET.

From San Sebastián, a run of 27 km (17 miles) along the built-up coastal strip brings us to at **Zumaia**, which has a picturesque, half-timbered station building; there is a bus connection here for the Basque Railway Museum at Azpeitia in the hills to the south. The train speeds through attractive rolling countryside with occasional glimpses of the Bay of Biscay, until **Deva**, where the line turns inland. From here to Durango the railway heads southwards, away from the coast, winding uphill into the mountains along narrow valleys lined with plane trees, stopping here and there at busy industrial towns with factory chimneys protruding among the wooded hills.

Map on page 164

The picturesque station at Zumaia, jumping-off point for the Basque Railway Museum.

Gernika and Bilbao

At Amorbieta, some two hours west of San Sebastián, a branch line heads north to **Bermeo**, a colourful port where the train comes to a halt beneath the prows of the fishing craft. However, it is **Gernika**, the largest town on this line, that makes it really notable. This is the same Guernica razed by the 1937 *blitzkrieg* by the Condor Legion at the start of the Spanish Civil War (1936–39), the market-day massacre commemorated by Picasso's famous painting. A walk round the rebuilt town is a thought-provoking experience.

Back on the main route to Bilbao, the line – double track now – winds on from Amorbieta through wooded hills. On either side we pass numerous examples of the *caserio*, the characteristic Basque country farmhouse with an enormous gabled roof, very much a hallmark of the region. Soon the railway begins the descent to Bilbao, entering the suburbs after the long tunnel at Usansolo.

Bilbao is a fascinating city from many points of view – its Guggenheim Museum and fine galleries, its political and industrial history; the bars and restaurants in the old town – and well worth a day or two's stay. The public transport network is complex: four rail termini, two funicular railways, metro and tram systems, and a 19th-century transporter bridge.

The train from San Sebastián arrives at **Atxuri** station, a superb stone building designed for the Vascongados line by Manuel Smith in 1912 in the style of a medieval Basque tower-house: look out for the huge roof beams in the vast, spotless booking hall. Atxuri is a terminus, but it is less than a 2-km (1-mile) walk to **Concordia** station on the other side of the Ria Bilbao, where we pick up the Transcantabrican route again. Concordia, with its superb 19th-century iron and glass façade, is no less impressive than Atxuri, although in a quite different architectural style. It still proclaims the name of its original owners, the FC Santander-Bilbao company, over the entrance. The booking hall is at street level, the trains on the floor above in an elegantly pillared train shed. Between the

BELOW: Bilbao's Guggenheim Museum.

Star Attractions:
Bilbao
● Guggenheim
  Museum
● Hanging Bridge
● Casco Viejo (the
  old town)
● Mercardo de la
  Ribera
● Catedral de
  Santiago

BELOW: stunning
stained glass at
Abando station
in Bilbao.

platforms upstairs stands the preserved 0-4-0T steam engine, and in the lively Café FEVE early-morning travellers mingle with home-going night-clubbers.

West to Cantábrica

The next leg of the Transcantabrican line is more like a serious cross-country journey than the trip on the busy ET inter-urban route from Hendaye and San Sebastián. The FEVE diesel railcar waiting at Bilbao Concordia is well appointed and comfortable but it lacks a buffet: bring your own food and drink for the journey.

The Santander train – usually made up of several railcars coupled together – roars away from Bilbao Concordia in spirited fashion, first through a tunnel under the city and then along the river for a couple of kilometres before heading into the hills. Beyond **Aranguen**, the junction for La Robla route *(see page 170)*, the train starts to climb into the wooded upland country that divides the Basque region from the province of Cantábrica. The growl of the diesel power unit deepens as the gradient starts to bite: the route must have been a real challenge to the drivers of the small steam engines, 4-4-0 tank locos built in Glasgow in the 1880s, that ruled the roost before diesels first arrived in the 1950s.

A succession of tunnels takes the train over the line's summit and into **Cantábrica** itself. As the line starts to wind downhill, meadows fill the valley on either side and rocky crags rise in the background; this is an enchanting tract of country, especially in the spring when the fields are ablaze with wild flowers. Progress is unhurried, with the train making frequent stops at the red-roofed villages, their stations old-fashioned brick or stone buildings smart with FEVE's yellow paint: the leafy station at **Limpias** is especially picturesque.

The hills fall back as the train approaches the coast, and three hours after leaving Bilbao we arrive at Santander's centrally-located metre gauge terminus, positioned right alongside the RENFE station. **Santander**, a modern port and resort as well as the provincial capital, has excellent sandy beaches; walk up the Península de la Magdalena to admire the view of the city across the bay, framed by the green Cantabrican mountains.

Map
on page
164

Asturias

The journey from Santander to the city of Oviedo is another good day's run. The Cordillera Cantábrica is a continuing presence to the south, the track itself keeping to the coastal strip for the first two hours and serving a string of coves, fishing villages and seaside towns. The station gardens along this section are full of rose bushes, lemon trees and palms, sometimes all of them together. Medieval **Llanes**, almost two hours out of Santander, has a pretty harbour and makes a good stop if you want to break the journey for lunch.

Modernist detail
at Bilbao's
Santander station.

Half an hour further on, at **Ribadesella**, the train turns away from the sea and heads inland along another wooded valley. In the old days, the steam locomotives of the Económicos de Asturias railway were renowned all over Europe for their immaculate paintwork and polished brass. They must have looked splendid racing through the landscape on the route up to Oviedo.

At **Norena**, shortly before Oviedo, the line makes a 90-degree flat crossing with the Langreo metre gauge route heading down to the coast at Gijon. The vast hangars in the angle of the two lines house FEVE's new, centralised workshops.

Like Bilbao, **Oviedo** is an industrial city with an improved image: both the 14th-century cathedral and the stone *palacios* in the old squares are superb. Try

BELOW: Puerto de Panderruedas in the Picos de Europa.

a traditional Asturian *fabada* (bean stew) in one of the many excellent restaurants. Oviedo is a convenient centre for visiting the Gijón Railway Museum, 33 km (21 miles) north, with a large collection of steam engines *(see page 183)*.

The Costa Verde

Oviedo's main RENFE station at the end of the Calle de Uria caters to the metre gauge lines as well as the broad gauge. The FEVE side has its own buffet above the platforms, which is a good place to stock up with provisions for the journey in another of the modern railcars, to the sea port of El Ferrol. This will be the final leg of our journey, a run out to the far northwest of Spain along the wild Galician Costa Verde, the aptly named Green Coast.

This is another long run, lasting over six hours. The train starts by taking what was until recently a broad gauge line along to **Trubia**, then heading through the populous Asturian hills towards the sea. The stretch after **Pravia** is the most scenic part of the entire journey. For mile after mile the view is constantly changing; there are deserted beaches with surf crashing on the shore, sweeping vistas across a wide estuary from a high viaduct, shafts of sunlight illuminating an eucalyptus forest, people working in the fields next to tiny, red-roofed hamlets. All these images occur and recur. The fishing ports of **Ribadeo** and **Vivero** are both picturesque little spots to break the journey.

At last, after a final hour where the railway switchbacks through glades of chestnuts and gum trees, the train arrives at the spacious terminus of **El Ferrol**. The city of Santiago de Compostela, a pilgrimage site since the Middle Ages, is only 80 km (50 miles) further on, and many travellers will choose to take the bus or RENFE broad gauge train to Santiago and finish their journey there.

Bilbao's transporter bridge was built in 1893 to link the two sides of the Ría Bilbao estuary while still permitting tall ships to sail upstream. The bridge operates every few minutes during the day, and pedestrians can use a walkway in the gantry to cross the span.

BELOW:
La Robla railway cuts through difficult terrain.

LA ROBLA RAILWAY

At Aranguan junction, outside Bilbao on the Santander route, La Robla line diverges from the Transcantabrican route and heads off southwest towards the mountains. This lengthy, metre gauge railway, opened in stages before 1915, weaves to and fro through the heart of the Cordillera Cantábrica, at times in sight of the Picos de Europa, eventually reaching León and La Robla on the Castilian side of the mountains. Although always used for freight, the line was also once the route of the famous Correo mail train, which took 11 hours from end to end. The Correo was hauled in latter years by gleaming, green Pacific locomotives built by the Société Alsacienne: real thoroughbreds.

The major part of the line from Balmaseda to Guardo, now part of the FEVE empire, was closed to passenger trains from the early 1990s until 2003 because of the state of the track, although freight traffic continued to use it. However, passenger trains are again operating from Bilbao to León (Thomas Cook timetable no. 683). FEVE has introduced a fleet of excellent modern railcars, and runs one service per day in each direction – trains depart Bilbao Concordia station at 2.30pm and arrive at León 7¼ hours later at 9.45pm.

ALGECIRAS–RONDA

Map on page 164

The Algeciras to Ronda *ferrocarril* was built by the Algeciras (Gibraltar) Railway Company Ltd in 1892, and it remains a useful – and scenic – gateway to the hinterland from the southwest coast of Spain. A century ago, the journey took a full day and could be highly dangerous, with highwaymen hiding out in the hills; nowadays it takes only 1½ hours, and the only danger is likely to be heatstroke; temperatures in July and August can be around 40°C (104°F), although there is air-conditioning of sorts on most trains. The trains have only two or three carriages and are usually full to bursting with local people, who greet each other with great familiarity while a smattering of perspiring tourists look on.

ESSENTIALS

Thomas Cook timetable no. 673

Distance: 106 km

Duration of journey: 1 hr 50 mins

Frequency of trains: 6 per day

San Roque

The track follows the course of four rivers all the way from the coast up to Ronda. Algeciras is an ugly, industrial sprawl best avoided; a more pleasant starting point is **San Roque**, a short distance inland, where the Spanish ended up after escaping the clutches of the British in the battle for Gibraltar in 1704. The station is 6km (4 miles) below the ancient town itself. San Roque, dramatically set in the foothills of the Sierra Bermeja, has a beautiful old centre, with steep streets lined by houses with iron-work balconies.

Shortly after leaving San Roque the train pulls into **Almoraima**, where the hills are covered in cork-oaks; cork is a major business in these parts. Further on, cypresses and wild flowers cover deep ravines and the ever-present sparkle of the river wends its way beside the track, sometimes a trickle running over small pebbles, in other places widening out and bubbling lazily over bleached rocks. The atmospheric remains of the once-grand castle that gives its name to **Castellar de la Frontera** is reached by a narrow climbing road.

BELOW: a sun-bleached, rocky landscape.

Rural images

The train lurches off again with a blast on the horn, and before long it is announcing its arrival in **Jimena**. From the station you can see a typical Moorish tower, and white houses spilling down the hillside. As the train makes its way through the countryside, the scenes are truly memorable: steep, densely wooded hills and valleys; near-perpendicular fields of golden wheat that surely no tractor could access; the ever-present slopes of cork- and dwarf-oak trees; sugar cane and banana trees shimmering in the heat; tan-coloured cows and glossy horses; nimble-footed goats accompanied by their equally fleet-of-foot goatherds.

Tiny stations (where do the passengers come from?) with lacy clapboard trimmings follow one another: San Pablo, Gaucín, Cortes de la Frontera, Jimera de Líbar, Benaoján, Morales,

Arriate – the names chug along to the rhythm of the engine. It shuttles through a dozen or so tunnels, giving passengers fleeting glances of oddly shaped mountains and a vast, blue firmament as well as brief respite from the heat. The train enters a viaduct for several kilometres, with each archway a nano-second window onto the gully. Bushes of pink blooms grow in profusion beside a river that is little more than a stream in places.

Each station is unbelievably pretty; each village appears worthy of a visit – if only to walk in the fields and enjoy a cooling drink at the local bar. As the train nears its destination, the trees are grown not for commerce, but sprinkled around haphazardly as nature intended – offering shade from the intense heat.

The Cave of the Cat

A welcome sight in a hot arid land.

At **Benaoján**, you can visit the nature study information centre behind the station, where you will find directions to the **Cueva del Gato** (Cave of the Cat), a couple of kilometres away via a path through fields and olive groves. Although the cave is only accessible to experienced potholers, the site is out of this world, with gushing waterfalls and the craggy Sierra de Grazalema towering above. The Cueva de la Pileta (Pileta Cave), about 4 km (2½ miles) south of Benaoján, was discovered by a local farmer early last century and has fabulous stalactites and stalagmites, as well as Palaeolithic animal paintings dating from around 25,000 BC. The view from the entrance, over undulating valleys, is itself worth the trip.

Shortly after Benaoján, **Ronda** appears to the left of the train. A rocky escarpment shoulders the town, 180 metres (600 ft) above the Guadalevín Valley. The river cleaves the escarpment in two, with the 18th-century Puente Nuevo (New Bridge) spanning the cleft. The old town sits on the southern side of the bluff,

BELOW:
flamenco dancer
at Ronda's *feria*.
RIGHT: the famous
gorge in the middle
of Ronda.

Map
on page
164

the new town is perched on the northern side. There is another, older bridge further upstream which has Moorish origins. Ronda was the capital of an independent Muslim sovereignty until 1485, when Isabela and Ferdinand, the Catholic monarchs, reclaimed the area for Christianity. Churches and monasteries began to make an appearance after the Reconquest, many converted from or built on the sites of existing mosques. Only one 14th-century Moorish tower remains in the town. This is now an integral part of a church – albeit with the Moorish architectural influences that created the style known as Mudéjar.

There are beautiful Moorish baths, ancient palaces and ramparts, museums, gardens and churches, but the star of Ronda is the ravine itself.

SEVILLE–MADRID ON THE AVE

Seville's impressive Santa Justa station is the starting point for this journey aboard RENFE's pride and joy: the Alta Velocidad Española (the acronym, AVE, translates as "bird" in Castilian). From the outset it is obvious that the *mañana* attitude prevalent in Spain does not apply to this quicksilver baby.

In the early 1990s, the Spanish Government was keen to keep up with the rest of Europe in modernising its railway network. With Madrid as an obvious departure point, Seville was chosen as the destination for the first high-speed line – the city was due to host the huge trade fair of Expo '92. Much of the 365 km (228 miles) of track from Madrid to Córdoba was completely new; the final 127 km (79 miles) between Córdoba and Seville runs parallel to existing tracks.

The AVE rolling stock comprises an engine at each end, with three first-class, four standard-class *(turista)* coaches and a buffet car. It holds 325 passengers.

ESSENTIALS

Thomas Cook
timetable no. 651

Distance: 471 km

Duration of journey:
2 hrs 30 mins

Frequency of trains:
roughly every hour

BELOW: view from
Ronda over the
Serranía.

Star Attractions:

Córdoba
● **Mezquita (Mosque)**
● **Sinagoga**
● **Museo Provincial de Bellas Artes**
● **Alcázar de los Reyes Cristianos (palace and gardens)**
● **Palacio de Viana**

Seville
● **Barrio Santa Cruz**
● **Catedral & Giralda**
● **Alcázar**
● **Archivo General de Indias**
● **Mus. de Bellas Artes**

BELOW: the AVE is one of Europe's fastest trains.

AVE is by far the best rail performer in Europe, with a money-back guarantee if the train is late by just five minutes. The European standard gauge of 1,435 mm has been used on 471 km (294 miles) of AVE track, in place of Spain's own railway gauge of 1,674 mm. On the standard gauge track, trains reach speeds of 300 km/h (186 mph); for the remainder of the 12,187 km (7,617 miles) of track, the AVEs have been converted to run on the broader gauge, where speed is limited to 220 km/h (138 mph).

At **Santa Justa** station, proceedings resemble an airport's customs control point: bags are processed through an x-ray machine as stewards check ticket numbers at a booth on the platform. The AVE itself snakes majestically beside the platform, its long, sleek, bullet-nose reminiscent of Concorde. At the appointed departure time to the second, it purrs into life and glides – there is no other word for it – silently into the northeastern suburbs of Seville as a steward's voice comes over the tannoy welcoming everyone aboard, in both Spanish and English.

Style and comfort

The seats are comfortably upholstered – the AVE logo with its superimposed "wings" stamped in blue on a grey background – the aisles are wide and thickly carpeted and the toilets spacious, with shiny chrome 1950s-style soap dispensers. In the buffet car there is an ergonomic free-standing bar with plenty of standing space in which to enjoy a pizza, sandwich or beer.

The ride is silent and smooth as stewards hand out headphones for the film about to be shown; any number of international newspapers are offered, too. Air-conditioning is, of course, paramount in a country where summer temperatures regularly exceed 35°C (95°F). In no time, we are sliding through the country-

Map on page 164

side, with grand *cortijos* (farm estates) dotting the flat, buff-coloured plains and far-off mountains colliding with a big sky. The landscape becomes more hilly, with undulating fields of cereal unfurling into the distance and dry river beds flash by in a blur.

The train streams into **Córdoba**'s modern station 40 minutes later. All is orderly and calm on the glossy platforms and there are security officials weaving their way among passengers, ensuring that everything is running smoothly.

Once out of the station, the suburbs whizz by and in no time we are in the heart of the *campo* (countryside) once again. Hostesses hand out *caramelos* (sweets) to combat ear-popping as the altitude rises. There are glimpses of retreats shaded by pine trees and the play of light on water between hillocks covered in silvery olive trees. This is tunnel time on the AVE, as it rushes through and around the majestic **Sierra Morena**, negotiating several viaducts en route.

Onto the *meseta*

The sierra is left behind as we enter the *meseta*, Spain's vast central plateau and the landscape becomes drier and emptier. The train speeds past the town of **Villanueva de Córdoba**, surrounded by holm-oak woods. Gradually, the gentle hills become more jagged as the train enters the foothills of the Sierra de la Alcudía to the west and the Sierra Madrona to the east, and the AVE crosses a beautiful viaduct. North of here are grassy yellow plains fringed by the far-off Puertollano mountains as we pass through the Valle de Alcudía. This will be the view all the way to the capital, enlivened by a couple of towns: at **Puertollano** there is a glut of disused red-brick industrial buildings. Ugly electricity generators mar an otherwise pleasant, red-earthed and craggy landscape, along with

**Star Attractions:
Madrid**
● **Museo del Prado**
● **Plaza Mayor**
● **Palacio Real**
● **Teatro Real**
● **Parque del Retiro**
● **Ermita de San Antonio de la Florida**

BELOW: the tropical garden at Madrid's Atocha station.

the ubiquitous olive groves. Nearer the capital, rows of huge *jarras* (pitchers once used for storing oil or wine) lie on their sides beside boggy marshland.

The AVE speeds into the outskirts of **Madrid**, where lines of washing are strung across balconies and tower blocks are shuttered against the heat. Within minutes, the train is gently braking as it enters beautiful **Atocha** station. Built 1889–91, it was modernised when this high-speed link was needed for Seville's Expo '92. There is now a lush tropical garden set within a spacious atrium.

EL CREMALLERA

The rack railway affectionately known as El Cremallera ("The Zip") climbs from the town of Ribes de Freser to the Santuari de Núria in the Catalan Pyrenees. The line was opened in 1931, making it the last of Europe's rack railways to be built. **Ribes Vila** station is the best departure point if you arrive by car, but if you are coming by rail, the station at the bottom, **Ribes-Enllaç** connects with the mainline RENFE train from Barcelona. There are nine blue and white trains each way a day (11 at weekends) powered by 1500 volts from overhead cables. Choose a seat on the right-hand side of the train for the best views.

The entire line is only 12.5 km (7¾ miles) long, and the toothed middle rail only starts after 5 km (3 miles) just before the mid-way station of **Queralbs**. Thereafter the severe gradients begin and you climb quickly above the valley. Just in case it is not obvious that you are ascending to almost 2,000 metres (6,560 ft), there are a series of small signboards beside the track giving comparable altitudes in other parts of Spain and Europe.

Shortly after Queralbs, the track enters the attractive gorge of the River Núria, which is here a series of gushing waterfalls. In spring and early summer, if you look carefully among the trees you will see the bright yellow flowers of the Yellow Turk's-Cap Lily *(Lirium pyrinaicum)*, which is used as the symbol of this area, the Vall de Núria.

Spain's highest station

The train emerges from the ninth tunnel into a bowl in the mountains which has a double role – this is one of Catalonia's most holy places as well as being a magnet for hikers and climbers. **Núria** is the highest station in Spain at 1,964 metres (6,444 ft), fully 1,000 metres (3,280 ft) higher than your starting point. From the train you step into a visitor complex that includes a shop, bar, restaurant and hotel. There are also exhibitions about the Cremallera train itself, and the wildlife in the Vall de Núria. The nucleus of the complex is a church dedicated to the Virgin of Núria, which attracts pilgrims all year round – it was the main reason for building the railway up here in the first place.

From spring to autumn Núria is a hiking and outdoor leisure centre, and in winter it's a ski resort. A series of summits (rising to over 2,700 metres/almost 9,000 ft) screens Núria to the north and forms the border with France. You can gain a little more height yourself by following one of the hiking trails up from the town, or by taking a ride on the cable car (which is included in the price of the train ticket).

ESSENTIALS

Thomas Cook
timetable no. 658

Distance: 12 km

Duration of journey:
40 minutes

Frequency of trains:
6 to 12 per day

BELOW: the
Virgen de Núria.

There are only two ways down from Núria: the train, or a beautiful walk down through the gorge to Queralbs station (allow two or three hours for this).

In the south of Catalonia a pair of rack railways run to the spectacular monastery at Montserrat (it can also be reached via a vertigo-inducing cable car.

Maps
on pages
164, 177

ALICANTE–DÉNIA

The resorts of the Costa Blanca are linked by a picturesque narrow gauge railway built by a French company in 1914–15 to transport fruit, vegetables, wine and fish from Dénia to Alicante and return with imported *guano* (fertiliser), grain and flour. The line is worth travelling for its views alone but it also gives access to beaches and several interesting towns on the way.

For the first few kilometres out of Alicante the Tramlink train runs adjacent to the beach; at Palmeral, Carrabiners and Sant Joan the sand is only separated from the track by a main road. The resort of **El Campello** is the first major halt. Following the coast, the line crosses a long, iron girder bridge, the first of seven viaducts, to reach **Villajoyosa**, after which it swings inland under the shadow of Puig Campana (1,410 metres/4,626 ft), and back towards **Benidorm**, giving good views of the skyscraper resort. From Benidorm station the Limón Exprés, a tourist train with antique wooden carriages, sets off five days a week for Gata de Gorgos.

Drawing into **Altea**, the old town can be seen gathered around the blue and white dome of the church. The train runs beneath the town via two tunnels before climbing steeply through luxuriant vegetation. It then edges along a corniche, passes through a tunnel and emerges above the clear green sea. Another tunnel feeds

ESSENTIALS

Thomas Cook
timetable no. 666

Distance: 94 km

Duration of journey:
2 hrs 17 mins

Frequency of trains:
7 per day

BELOW: sun and sand on the Costa Blanca.

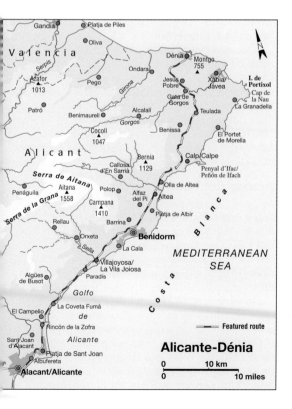

Alicante-Dénia

the line abruptly onto a metal bridge, which, at 105 metres (345 ft), is the highest on the line. There is only a second to take in the precipitous **Mascarat gorge** before the train disappears into yet another tunnel.

For the next few kilometres there are views of the **Penyal d'Ifac**, the mighty rock which rises from the sea in great vertical cliffs; the nearest station is Calp. Leaving Calp, the line turns away from the coast and rattles around a large curve and over another high viaduct. This is the most scenic stretch of line, and the track is fringed with wild flowers. In every ravine there are reeds and oleanders, thirsty century plants keel over on embankments while thistles, chicory and valerian poke out of the grass. After Teulada the train crosses the River Jalón and comes to **Gata de Gorgos** where the station is a minute's walk from the town centre and five minutes from numerous craft and souvenir shops specialising in wicker, raffia and basket work. It is only a short distance through the orange groves to the terminus of **Dénia**. The station here is close to the bars and restaurants of the harbour and the attractive town centre. The only forward connection is by bus, the nearest mainline station being Gandía.

PALMA–SÓLLER

The antique electric train from Palma de Mallorca to Sóller departs from the *fin de siècle* station on Palma's Plaça d'Espanya and climbs over the mountains to descend into the lovely Sóller Valley. The narrow gauge line opened in 1912 and has changed little since. The scenery is still wonderful, and the train itself a delight – the rolling stock is original, and the electric power units date back almost as far (the line was initially steam operated).

Palma is a small city, and soon the train is amid the olive groves of the gently sloping plain, a riot of wild flowers in spring (beginning in late January). Before long the land begins to rise and the craggy peaks of the Serra de Tramuntana appear. The train stops at tiny stations, many of which were built to service the *possessiós* (country estates) visible across the fields. By the time it arrives at **Bunyola** it is approaching the main ridge of the Tramuntana. Bunyola is a pleasant little town, a base for hikers, and has a fine example of Modernist architecture in the Villa Francisca, whose tall yellow spire can be seen from the train.

Across the Tramuntana

Much of the steep section leading to the summit of the line is negotiated in a series of tunnels, but after a few minutes the train emerges onto the northern side of the ridge and a tremendous panorama of Sóller, its valley, and the mountains beyond – including the bare crags of Puig Major, at 1,445 metres (4,740 ft) the highest on the island. The 10.50am departure from Palma stops for 10 minutes at the **Mirador del Pujol den Banya** to allow time to enjoy the view. Be warned that this train is very popular, and it can be difficult to get a seat.

Gradually the track descends to the valley, with more beautiful views and glimpses of the sea. Once on the valley floor the train passes through the famous Sóller citrus groves and past small town gardens to

ESSENTIALS

Thomas Cook
timetable no. 674

Distance: 23 km

Duration of journey:
55 mins

Frequency of trains:
5 per day

BELOW: vintage transport on the island of Mallorca.

reach **Sóller** railway station on the Plaça d'Espanya. From here you can either walk the block or two into the picturesque town centre, or take the open-carriaged *tramvia*, similar to the train in its wood-panelled low-tech charm, from its starting point in front of the station to **Port de Sóller** a short distance away.

Maps
on pages
164/181

PORTUGAL: THE DOURO VALLEY

The Douro railways are the end of the line. There is nothing to do except take them and ride back. This area of northern Portugal, little visited by tourists, is served by one train, plus three commuter narrow gauge railways that plunge deep into the hills, then come to an abrupt stop before returning along the same route. Think of a broken comb with three jagged teeth. The spine of the comb is the Douro line, running from Porto on the west coast to Pocinho in the east, near the Spanish border. It hugs the Douro River as it curves along the bottom of a steep valley of green, terraced fields. Each tooth of the comb is a narrow gauge line that follows a tributary of the Douro northwards through hamlets with hard-to-pronounce names, serving isolated communities not found on any map. Throughout, the scenery is gorgeous, the people polite but remote. Little English is spoken. It is hard to believe that this is Western Europe.

Leisurely progress

With scrupulous attention to the timetables, Porto to Pocinho could be accomplished in 3½ hours. It is possible in theory to return to Porto on the same day. But then again, it might not be. Portugal's railways are run in ways which often seem mysterious to foreigners. This is the charm of the Douro railways, and the bane

ESSENTIALS

Thomas Cook
timetable no. 696

Distance: 175 km
(Porto–Pocinho)

Duration of journey:
3 hrs 30 mins or
3 hrs 50 mins (one
change at Régua)

Frequency of trains:
4 per day

BELOW: vineyards
along the Douro.

Star Attractions:
Porto
● **Sé (Cathedral)**
● **Cais de Ribeira area**
● **Casa Museu de**
   Guerra Junqueiro
● **Port lodges**

of the clock-watcher. Some trains stop at certain destinations, others do not. Some run on Saturday, some do not. Occasionally trains do not run at all, or run on different tracks, or start and stop at stations which may or may not be on the schedules. To travel on all four Douro Valley lines will take several days.

Porto, the departure point for the Douro line is the only large city in northern Portugal. São Bento station makes a grand *entrada* to any journey. Built on the site of an earlier monastery, it was completed in 1916 and beneath its soaring ceilings is a feast of blue and white *azulejos* (painted tiles) by artist Jorge Colaço. Peasant girls with baskets of grapes, and scenes showing early modes of transport signal the change from busy city life to the tranquillity of the countryside just a short journey away. Three arches of stained glass lead to the platforms.

The departure from Porto is equally delightful. The train plunges into a series of tunnels, only to re-emerge high above the town. Below is the gleaming river, the travellers' companion throughout the Douro journey, spanned by Gustave Eiffel's famous bridge and, among others, the graceful two-tier Ponte de Dom Luís I, designed in 1886 by Teófilo Seyrig, who gained his inspiration from the Eiffel bridge.

The Amarante branch line

Little happens between Porto's Campanhã and **Livracão**, the jumping-off point for the first and most popular narrow gauge journey, a half-hour trip to the town of Amarante. Livracão is a typically attractive two-storey station, with a long shaded platform. The train (built in 1948) is only one carriage long, jaunty with red and white stripes. A cab at either end avoids the need for a turn-around. Inside are 18 benches, four of them first class. Initially, it's difficult to see the

BELOW: crossing the Douro on the way out of Porto.

distinction, but when the train shudders into action, first-class passengers are very grateful for the padding between them and the bone-jarring vibrations.

The route climbs the hills above the Tâmega River in ever-increasing increments, tooting and shunting its way past arbours ripe with red grapes, groves of pine trees and a few villages both old and new. Although passing many stations along the way, the train stops only if a passenger wants to get on or disembark. The Tâmega line used to carry on past Amarante, and its station, large and decorative, seems too grand for its currently reduced circumstances. A band of British train buffs called the Portuguese Traction Group are lobbying the government to reopen the Tâmega line in its entirety *(see box on page 182)*.

Amarante is a lovely town, with views of the city and the Ponte de São Gonçalo (1790) reminiscent of Florence. The bridge leads to the Convento de São Gonçalo, dating from 1540. The patron saint is the protector of marriages, and the church is booked up with nuptials much of the year. Beside the rear cloister is a Tourist Information Centre and the clean, modern Museu Municipal Amadeo de Souza-Cardosa, devoted to the work of locally-born Cubist painter, Souza-Cardosa, a contemporary of Picasso's.

River views and the Vila Real line

Back on the Douro line heading east, the train enters the longest tunnel in the valley. Climbing steadily, it emerges from the darkness into sparkling sunlight and a relatively steep 1 in 70 descent towards **Mosteirô**. Keep eyes firmly right for the most exhilarating sight of the trip: a view of a town far below beyond the mighty Douro River, washing flapping and a wedding often in progress. From this point, the river is a constant, a fat, grey ribbon dancing and curving in sinuous moves. At times the train parallels the river, at times the road above, where women balancing baskets of corn or grapes on their heads seem to re-enact scenes from the painted railway tiles of São Bento.

Azulejos tiles brighten up Sao Bento station, Porto.

Régua (also called Peso da Régua) is a big town, best described as a transport hub. A hot, dusty place, it has a tourist information centre, but little of interest. Régua is the departure point for the narrow gauge to **Vila Real** which follows the Corgo River. The best seats are on the left-hand side, facing backwards to watch the valley floor slip away. The landscape on the Corgo line is a mosaic of dizzying shades of green: the yellow-green of terraced vineyards – so steep, grapes can only be harvested by hand; the moss-green of the river far below; the silver-green of olive trees, and the dark-green of pine trees.

The journey takes about 50 minutes each way. Vila Real has one site of inter-est: the **Casa de Mateus**. Pictured on the labels of Mateus Rosé wine, this

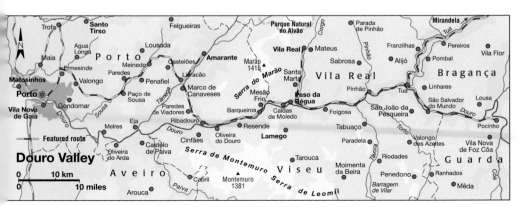

Preserved steam engine at Entroncamento station.

baroque mansion was built in the early 18th century, and still houses the descendants of the family. Visitors can tour part of the house and the grounds, but if time is tight, opt for the flamboyant gardens only, full of fountains, flowers and topiary. The most celebrated feature is a fragrant cedar tunnel 35 metres (38 yds) long, and so tall that the gardeners need specially-made ladders to trim it.

East to Pocinho

From Régua to **Pocinho**, the Douro runs so close to the track that the only things visible are water and the river bank opposite, with steep, vine-covered terraces dotted with port warehouses and handsome *quintas* (manor houses). Before Pocinho is **Tua**, departure point for the 2-hour narrow gauge trip to **Mirandela**. Stock up on supplies in the old-fashioned café across the tracks.

The Tua line – established in 1906 – is not for the squeamish. Its track hangs on a cliff shelf 1,800 metres (5,900 ft) above the Tua Gorge, and its country commuters like to ride with the doors wide open, the better to pick grapes off vines or cool their feet in the mountain air as the train climbs higher and higher. The landscape is starkly beautiful: kingfishers and herons dart and swoop in the gorge; rocks have split open to reveal shades of ochre, yellow and lime green. This line, the last of the narrow gauge journeys, is also the most dramatic.

Back on the Douro line, a pleasant way to end the day is to alight from the Régua train to admire the small station of **Pinhão**. This is one of the most attractive in Portugal, its handsome façade lined with large panels of hand-painted *azulejos*. While away a couple of hours, then catch the last train back. With luck, you will be heading west in the most westerly country in mainland Europe as the sun sets over the Douro River. ❏

BELOW: the manicured gardens at Casa de Mateus, Vila Real.

ALL ABOARD THE PTG

Puffs of black smoke drift into the sky overhead. Children wave from viaducts and farmers pause in the harvesting of oranges and olives to cast admiring glances when a steam-train trip organised by British enthusiasts, the Portuguese Traction Group, trundles through the hills from Régua to Vila Real. The PTG schedules regular trips throughout the year, using vintage locomotives and carriages. They arrange trips with specific requirements, or allow enthusiasts to join a broader-based tour for just the steam train portion. But the PTG is a campaign group, rather than a tour operator. One aim is to raise funds to purchase vintage trains, something the Portuguese regard as unimportant; another is to raise awareness of the country's fine rail network. Stephen Williams' meticulously researched *Portugal by Rail* booklets are particularly impressive. Graham Garnell, based in Lisbon, has fought almost single-handedly to maintain interest in reopening the Tâmega line from its present terminus at Amarante to the one at Arco de Baúlhe, where there is a railway museum. Like many of Portugal's commuter branch lines, it closed in the 1990s, but all track and most stations are in reasonable repair. If the Tâmega is reopened, it will become one of Portugal's first railway preservation projects.

Museums and Heritage Lines

There are few heritage railway lines in Spain, and none at all in Portugal; there are, however, several excellent railway museums. The numbers relate to the map on page 164.

Museums

Basque Railway Museum, ❶

(Eusko Burnibide Museoa/ Museo Vasco de Ferrocarril) Calle Urola 8, 20730 Azpeitia, Guipuzcoa
Tel: 943 150 677
Open: Tue–Sat 10am–2pm, 4–7.30pm (Oct–June Tue–Fri 10.30am–1.30pm, 3–6.30pm), Sun 10.30am–2pm
Features: rich collection drawn from the region's railway heritage. The tall, imposing station building houses the museum office and small exhibits; spacious sheds and hangars outside contain the full-size exhibits: locomotives, coaches and tram cars. The museum also operates steam trains on most weekends throughout the year on 5 km (3 miles) of relaid metre gauge track as far as Lasao station on the old route north towards Zumaia.
Nearest station: Zumaia (bus link)
www.geocities.com/euskalbml

Museo del Ferrocarril de Asturias ❷

Dionisio Fernández-Nespral Aza, s/n. Antigua Estación del Norte, 33206 Gijón
Tel: 985 308 575

Open: Tue–Sat 10am–2pm, 4–8pm, Sun 11am–2pm, 4–8pm; July–Aug Tue–Sun 10am–2pm, 5–9pm
Features: large collection of steam engines in the old Gijón North station. Themed displays explore the social, political and economic history of the local railways.
Nearest station: Gijón
www.gijon.es/fmc

Museo del Ferrocarril de Madrid ❸

Paseo de las Delicias 61, 28045 Madrid
Tel: 902 22 88 22
Open: Tue–Sun 10am–3pm; closed Aug
Features: housed in the 1880 Delicias station, the museum has collections of steam, diesel and electric locomotives and period carriages as well as rooms dedicated to model railways, railway equipment and clocks.
Nearest station: Delicias. Atocha is within easy walking distance to the north.
www.museodelferrocarril.org/delicias.html

Museo del Ferrocarril Vilanova i la Geltrú ❹

Plaça Eduard Maristany s/n, 08800 Vilanova i la Geltrú (45 km/28 miles west of Barcelona)
Tel: 938 158 491
Open: Tue–Sun 10.30am–2.30pm; Sat also 4–6.30pm; Aug daily 11am–2pm, 5–8pm
Features: located in a historic locomotive depot, the museum has one of the best collections of steam locomotives in Europe. There are steam-hauled trips every first Sunday in the month.
Nearest station: Vilanova i la Geltrú (RENFE)
www.ffe.es/vilanova

Secção Museológica de Macinhata do Vouga ❺

Railway Station, Macinhata do Vouga (Portugal).
Tel: 22 200 2723 or 221 052 403
Open: Mon–Fri 9am–1pm, 2–5pm
Features: narrow gauge locomotives, coaches and an array of other period vehicles. The national rail museum at Entroncamento is due to be housed in a new building by 2004; when this happens most of the stock from other Portuguese railway collections will be moved there.
Nearest station: Macinhata (near Aveiro)
www.cp.pt/outros/museus/macinhata/macinhata.htm

Heritage Lines

Tren de la Fresa

❻ (Madrid–Aranjuez)
The train, run by the Museo Ferrocarril in Madrid, departs from Madrid's Atocha station. The line once ferried strawberries from Aranjuez to the capital. Tickets include a coach from Aranjuez station to the main sights, guided visits of the Palacio Real at Aranjuez and the Jardin de las Islas, and entrance to the Museo de Falúas.
Operates: Tue–Sun 10am–3pm; closed Aug
http://www.museodelferrocarril.org/tren_fresa/informacion.html

Bilbao–Gernika ❼

Tel: 94 433 9500
Steam-hauled train operating on two itineraries:
Bilbao–Guernica–Bermeo–Mundaca, and San Sebastián–Zumaya–Deva–Zarautz
Departures are from Estación de Atxuri, Bilbao, every Sunday in July and August.
www.euskotren.es

SWITZERLAND

Switzerland offers some of the world's most spectacular train journeys, on a user-friendly railway system that is run with clockwork efficiency

Map on page 188

Swiss public transport is among the best in the world, and for many visitors its quality and ease-of-use are a revelation. Trains are clean and punctual, stations have a good range of facilities, and information systems are exceptionally clear. But the key to the success of the system is the way each mode of transport is integrated to provide seamless connections and to avoid wasteful and damaging competition between bus and train.

Almost every line, whether operated by Swiss Federal Railways (Schweizerische Bundesbahnen/SBB) or one of the many other operators, has a minimum of a train an hour for at least half the day. The smaller railways run their trains to connect with SBB, and buses, funiculars and lake steamers are almost invariably timed to meet trains or each other. Timekeeping is exemplary, and there is a range of passes for visitors that offers remarkably good value. Couple these factors with the necessity of using mountain railways or cable cars to reach many of the country's finest sights (because there are no roads) and the case for using the Swiss Travel System is overwhelming. It is no wonder that the Swiss people use their railways more than any other nation in Europe. SBB offers many added-value services, some aimed specifically at tourists, such as the Fly-Rail system, by which checked-in cases are not seen again until you reach your station in Switzerland. Luggage can also be sent separately by train. Bicycles can be hired from over 90 stations, and returned to a different station, allowing advantage to be taken of favourable descents.

Mountain challenges

With its abundance of steep terrain, Switzerland makes extensive use of rack railways when gradients become too steep for reliance on the normal adhesion of steel wheel on steel rail. There are several different types of rack system, each named after its inventor, but all rely on a cogwheel fitted to the train engaging a slotted metal bar fitted centrally between the rails. This both allows the train to climb when the conventional wheel would simply slip and helps the train's braking systems on the descent.

Switzerland has several truly spectacular railway journeys – in fact it is almost impossible to find one that does not offer something to the visitor: even the commuter lines of Zürich take one into pleasant countryside, or up the city's local mountain, the Uetliburg. The speed and frequency of trains means that the country can be traversed easily: St Gallen to Geneva is only 4 hours and Basel to Chiasso under 4½ hours. With a Swiss Pass, offering unlimited travel over much of the Swiss Travel System, it is easy to explore the country if one wishes to see as much as possible in a short time.

PRECEDING PAGES: on top of the world on the Gornergratbahn. **LEFT:** crossing the Langweis viaduct between Chur and Arosa. **BELOW:** French flavour in Geneva.

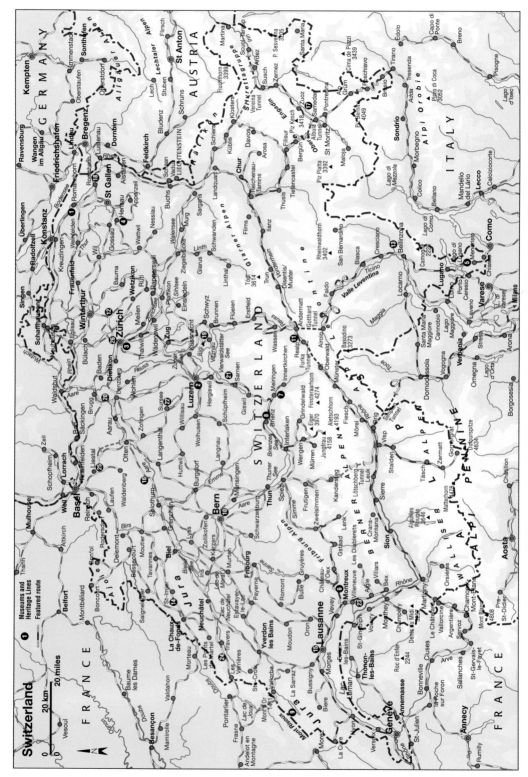

GENEVA–MILAN

Map on page 188

Thanks to the technology employed on the tilting Cisalpino trains, it takes less than 4½ hours to travel across the Alps from Switzerland's most cosmopolitan city to Italy's industrial capital. Yet speed is almost a handicap to enjoying this journey, and the larger windows of conventional trains allow a wider panorama of the splendid views over Lake Geneva (Lac Léman) and the Alps. The route links a dozen places that deserve a day or more to appreciate.

Geneva has accepted exiles and refugees for centuries, from English regicides to Russian anarchists, and the many international organisations based here continue this cosmopolitan tradition. Today almost a third of the population is non-Swiss. This spirit, coupled with the scenic splendours offered from the north side of the lake, has encouraged the rich and famous to make their homes along the lake shore between Geneva and Montreux (see box, page 194). Even the railway line you travel on was built by a foreigner, the Irishman Charles Vignoles.

The exit from Geneva is a delight, passing the Botanical Gardens and the wooded grounds surrounding the venerable mansions of the city's early élites. Before long the trees thin out to reveal the sickle-shaped Lake Geneva, which is seldom out of view to the right until it comes to an end at Villeneuve. Vineyards cover many of the northern slopes along the lake and along the Rhône Valley to Brig.

Nyon, with its five-towered castle, was founded by Julius Caesar in 45 BC and is now the junction for the narrow gauge line to La Cure, serving the closest ski resorts to Geneva. Another fine castle guards the shoreline at **Morges** and today houses the military museum of Canton Vaud.

Lakeside vistas

Lausanne has proved a productive setting for many writers including Edward Gibbon, Charles Dickens, Arnold Bennett and T.S. Eliot, and it still has a thriving artistic life, reflected in the many galleries and museums. The town has a 12th–13th-century cathedral that many regard as the finest Gothic building in the country, as well as the award-winning Olympic Museum, celebrating the movement and the work of the International Olympic Committee, based here since 1915. The streets tumble down to the lake at so steep an angle that the city has Europe's steepest metro, and it is on leaving the station at Ouchy that passengers enjoy some of the best views of the French Alps and the string of lakeside villages on the southern shore. Their piers are served by the lake's mix of screw-steamers and paddle-steamers, some of which are being restored to steam propulsion.

The metro descends to the lakeside to pass the small harbour at **Cully**, sharing the foreshore with vines and tiny private gardens built on headlands that are reached by footbridges across the tracks. The lakeside towns of **Vevey** and **Montreux** are excellent centres for walking, and the start of other great railway journeys (see page 212). Charlie Chaplin lived in Vevey for the last 25 years of his life, commemorated in a new museum, while Montreux is known for its jazz festival. For rail-

ESSENTIALS

Thomas Cook timetable nos. 82/570

Distance: 368 km

Duration of journey: 4 hrs 28 mins

Frequency of trains: 6 per day (direct)

BELOW: Switzerland has more rack railways than any other country.

Star Attractions:
Geneva

● Cathedral of
  St-Pierre
● International
  Red Cross Museum
● Museum of
  Art and History
● Museum of the
  Swiss Abroad
● A boat trip
  on the lake

BELOW: Charlie
Chaplin is
remembered
at Vevey.

way buffs, it is one of the world's few stations with three different track gauges. The railway and the lovely lakeside footpath between Vevey and Villeneuve both run past the walls of one of the world's most famous and romantically situated castles, the **Château de Chillon**, immortalised by Byron's The Prisoner of Chillon.

Into the Rhône Valley

Once past **Villeneuve**, formerly an important staging post for the road over the St-Bernard Pass, the character of the landscape changes dramatically as the lake ends and the railway enters the Rhône Valley, its northern slopes covered in vines and the valley floor home to the occasional heavy industrial plant. **Aigle** is a centre of the wine industry, and the magnificent late 15th-century castle to the north of the line houses a wine museum. The station marks the start of three delightful narrow gauge railways serving resorts in the surrounding mountains, and a fourth line, to the ski resort of Villars, begins at **Bex**.

The train races along the valley to **Martigny**, once the Roman capital of the region. Though little remains of the 5,000-seat amphitheatre, the nearby Pierre Gianadda Foundation is an astonishing art gallery and museum for such a small town, hosting exhibitions in conjunction with the likes of the Metropolitan Museum of Art in New York. A spectacular narrow gauge line heads southwest from Martigny to Chamonix and St-Gervais in France (see pages 149–50).

The Rhône, accompanied by the railway, now swings round to the east. The modern appearance of **Sion** from the railway belies its interesting old centre, with a pair of finely sited castles, one containing what is claimed to be the oldest playable organ in the world, built in the 14th century, on which occasional

FAMOUS RESIDENTS

There can be few areas of the world that have attracted as many famous foreign residents as Geneva and the northern shore of Lake Geneva. In the 1550s, the Scots reformer John Knox chose the city as his home, becoming its first British pastor. Several of those who signed Charles I's execution warrant fled here in 1649. Geneva was later home to French philosopher Jean Jacques Rousseau (who was born here in 1712). The Enlightenment writer, Voltaire, spent many years in and around the city in the mid-18th century, and composed his satirical tale, *Candide*, here.

Countless writers, composers and artists have since found peace and inspiration for their work in the area: Goethe, Byron, Corbet, Dickens, Dostoyevsky, Tolstoy, Tchaikovsky and Stravinsky being among the most famous. More recent celebrities have included the artist Oscar Kokoschka, soprano Dame Joan Sutherland, Charlie Chaplin (when his political sympathies forced him to leave America), Sir Nöel Coward, actors Richard Burton and Peter Ustinov, and rock star David Bowie.

In the 1990s the German magazine *Stern* ran an article claiming that Geneva had more millionaires than unemployed people – for every two people out of work, there were three millionaires. Quite a record.

concerts are given. The town is a great centre for walking, with numerous bus routes into surrounding valleys, many of which are threaded by ancient bisses (irrigation channels). Some of these have been incorporated into the 7,000 km (4,375 miles) of footpaths in the region. Europe's largest underground lake, discovered only in 1943 at St-Léonard, can also be reached by bus from Sion.

Visp, Brig and the Simplon Tunnel

As the railway nears the junction of **Visp**, it is joined by the line from the new Lötschberg Base Tunnel and the southern ramp from the old Lötschberg Tunnel can be seen descending the northern flank of the valley. At Visp the narrow gauge line from Zermatt (see page 194) joins the formation for the last few miles to **Brig**, a good place to break the journey. The town itself is a pleasure to walk around, its most notable building being the Stockalper Palace, which was Switzerland's largest private building when owned by its creator, Kaspar von Stockalper, in the mid-17th century. Around the arcaded courtyard are storerooms and accommodation and three tall towers topped by onion domes.

Leaving Brig the train enters the famous **Simplon Tunnel**, Europe's third longest railway tunnel at 19.8 km (12½ miles) with the Swiss/Italian border at roughly the halfway point. It was opened in 1906, completing the Simplon railway to Italy. The railway emerges into daylight for the pleasing, isolated station of **Iselle di Trasquera** before plunging into a spiral tunnel down Val Divedro to **Domodossala**, junction for the Centovalli line to Locarno (see page 204). The railway follows the valley of the River Toce to **Verbania-Palanza** and the start of the final scenic delight of the journey, the long stretch beside Lago Maggiore through **Stresa** and **Arona**.

Map on page 188

The ruins of the Château de Tourbillon high above Sion.

BELOW: at work on the heritage line between Blonay and Chamby.

ZÜRICH–CHIASSO

ESSENTIALS

Thomas Cook timetable no. 550

Distance: 242 km

Duration of journey: 3 hrs 19 mins

Frequency of trains: 8 per day (direct)

The most important north–south railway in Switzerland carries a staggering amount of traffic, passenger trains sharing the route with hundreds of freight trains a week. It is also the route of various international expresses running between various points in northern Europe and Italy.

Once the train has threaded the maze of tracks outside Zürich Hauptbahnhof, it passes through almost continuous suburbs to **Thalwil** (or takes the tunnel to Baar), with views overlooking Lake Zürich to the left. A tunnel leads to **Sihlbrugg** – the bridge across the Sihl – and a pleasant stretch beside the broad river. Nothing to be seen from the railway would tempt one to explore **Zug**, but its old town, close to the lake, is delightful, with several streets of shuttered houses with pronounced eaves and linear ribbons of colour in their window boxes.

The railway continues along the hillside, with views across Zuger See towards Mt Rigi before reaching the junction of **Arth Goldau**, the start of the second rack line up Rigi. After curving around tiny Lauerzersee, the line passes **Schwyz**, which gave the country its name in 1315. Appropriately, the Swiss Federal Archives, with all the charters of the Confederacy from 1291, are located here.

Unfortunately for travellers, much of the railway beside the Urner See (the southern extension of Vierwaldstättersee, or Lake Luzern) is in tunnel, but passengers gain sufficient glimpses of the lake to appreciate its beauty, enhanced by the sight of one of the five sleek and beautifully maintained paddle-steamers that ply its waters. The lake ends at **Flüelen**, where a transfer between boat and train takes place as part of the William Tell Express journey from Luzern to Lugano/Locarno.

BELOW: a vintage postcard showing the Gotthard Express, with the Matterhorn in the background.

The train enters the broad valley of the Reuss, passing **Altdorf** where, according to the legend, William Tell shot the apple from his son's head. **Erstfeld** became a railway town because it is here that the northern ascent of the famous Gotthard begins – and needed assisting locomotives in steam days. The railway has to climb a vertical height of 634 metres (2,080 ft) in just 28 km (17¾ miles), requiring a spiral tunnel and two horseshoe curves to gain height before reaching **Göschenen**. Situated in a narrow defile, the lonely station here is a junction for the short rack line up to Andermatt through the Schöllenen Gorge. Andermatt is on the route of the Glacier Express (see page 194).

Just south of the station the train enters the 15-km (9¼-mile) long **Gotthard Tunnel** (see page 39), dead straight but for a slight curve at the southern end where the line emerges at **Airolo** in Ticino, the Italian-speaking part of Switzerland. It takes 10 minutes to pass through the tunnel; before it opened, it took a whole day to travel from Göschenen to Airolo. On the left, near the station buildings, is a monument to the 177 men who died during construction work.

Although the southern descent from the Gotthard Tunnel is less severe than the northern climb, it still calls for some impressive bridge-work and two pairs of spiral tunnels, the first just north of **Faido**, the second to the south. Shortly after the lower spirals, the picturesque village of **Giornico** and its two fine churches can be seen from the railway. The best way to appreciate the extraordinary ingenuity of the railway builders – and to see the 15th-century frescoes of San Nicolao – is to hire bicycles at Airolo station and freewheel down to Biasca station via the old road and farm tracks, which are almost traffic-free.

Southern slopes

As the train arrives at **Biasca**, look up to the left to see a waterfall pouring over the cliff face. It is a fast, straight run along the broadening valley to the capital of the Ticino at **Bellinzona**, a magnet for anyone interested in medieval military architecture since the town has no fewer than three remarkably intact castles, and they are all open to visitors. Shortly after leaving Bellinzona, the Locarno line veers off to the west, while the Chiasso line climbs along the contours to the lakeside resort of **Lugano**.

Besides its enviable position and the mild, sunny climate (nearby Agra is the sunniest place in Switzerland), Lugano is noted for its modern buildings, especially those of local architect Mario Botta. A funicular links the station with the pedestrianised heart of the town, and there are several good museums and galleries such as the collection of local painters at the Giovanni Züst Cantonal Art Gallery. Funiculars take visitors up Lugano's two mountains, San Salvatore and Bré, and boats serve 14 piers at villages around the lake.

Leaving Lugano, the train quickly descends to run along the lake shore and crosses a man-made causeway to reach **Capologo-Riva San Vitale**; Switzerland's oldest surviving ecclesiastical building can be found in the latter village, the baptistry dating from around 500. Immediately beyond the railway yards at **Chiasso** is the tunnel that marks the frontier with Italy; Milan is just 40 minutes away.

Map on page 188

Star Attractions: Zurich
● St Peter's Square and Church
● Fraumünster
● Grossmünster
● Swiss National Museum
● Art Gallery

BELOW: the balmy shores of Lago Maggiore.

ZERMATT–ST MORITZ ON THE GLACIER EXPRESS

ESSENTIALS

Thomas Cook
timetable no 579

Distance: 290 km

Duration of journey:
7 hrs 49 mins to
8 hrs 25 mins

Frequency of trains:
4 per day (mid-May
to mid-October only)

The Glacier Express is Switzerland's best-known train, and deservedly so. Although it takes 8 hours to cover the 290 km (181 miles) between the famous resorts, the marvellous landscapes that roll past the window are constantly changing, the observation cars allow panoramic visibility and the freshly-cooked lunch is surprisingly good. Yet the train is a double misnomer: it is definitely not an express, and it no longer offers passengers sight of the glacier after which it was named. From its inauguration in 1931 until 1982, trains ground their way past the Rhône glacier on the ascent to the Furka summit; now they rush through the Furka Base Tunnel, and anyone intent on seeing the shrinking glacier from a train window will have to take the preserved Dampfbahn Furka Bergstrecke railway from Realp (see page 212). But neither of these facts detracts from a journey that would be in the top 10 of a pantheon of the world's great train journeys.

Zermatt to Brig

The journey begins in **Zermatt**, a remote village that grew to be a town because of its proximity to the Matterhorn and the macabre fate of the first party of climbers to reach the summit, in 1865. Human nature was little different then from now, and tourists in their thousands flocked to see where Edward Whymper's party came to grief. Zermatt remains one of the most popular Alpine resorts, offering skiing until later in the spring than most others. The number of visitors would have destroyed the character of the place but for the enlightened decision to ban cars; electric vehicles ferry luggage and passengers between station and hotel, and parts of the town still have a rustic character.

BELOW: admiring the view from the observation car on the Glacier Express.

The railway north to Visp follows the Matter Vispa River, and the susceptibility of the Mattertal to avalanches is apparent as soon as the train glides out of Zermatt and enters the first of many shelters that protect the line. The sheer scale of the Alps is immediately evident through the tinted roof-glass of the panoramic coaches, giving a worm's eye view of the mountains on either side. It's best to keep looking upwards as the train passes **Täsch**: the place is a vast coach- and car-park for Zermatt, with shuttle trains ferrying back and forth between the two.

There are plenty of views of the river as the railway switches banks, while grazing cows and barns on staddle stones are reminders of the principal activity of these Alpine valleys before the growth of tourism in the 19th century. **Stalden-Saas** is the station for frequent buses to the well-known winter sports resort of Saas-Fee, which is another car-free zone. The railway continues its rack-braked descent to the floor of the Rhône valley at Visp, where it turns east to follow the Geneva–Milan main line into **Brig** (see page 191). Visp station has been rebuilt to become the junction station for trains using the Lötschberg Base Tunnel from Bern/Spiez and the main line from Geneva as well as the narrow gauge Matterhorn–Gotthard-Bahn.

To the Furka Base Tunnel

From Brig the railway climbs to its first summit at the entrance to the base tunnel under the Furka Pass at Oberwald. It is a measure of the difficulty faced by the construction engineers that this section of railway was one of the last significant lines in Switzerland to be finished, finally opening in 1926. At that time, it proved impossible to keep the line up to the original Furka Tunnel

Map
on page
188

For the best view of the Matterhorn without donning crampons, you should take the Gornergratbahn from Zermatt, which climbs 1,484 metres (4,868 ft) in just 9.4 km (6 miles) to a hotel and verandah opposite the peak.

BELOW: the original line past the Rhône Glacier was closed in 1982.

F.O.B.
Rhonegletscher u. Furkastraße

For an awe-inspiring view of the Rhône Glacier, take the preserved Dampfbahn line from Realp to Gletsch (details on page 212).

details on page 212

BELOW: the Matterhorn–Gotthard-Bahn.

open between October and April because the costs of snow clearance and avalanche protection could not be met in the days before winter sports gained mass appeal. The winter weather on the section between Oberalp and Realp was so severe that it even had a bridge that could be dismantled every autumn.

The gradients are not too steep for adhesion working until **Betten**, where the first rack section is announced by the characteristic clunking sound of the rack being engaged by the cog wheels under the train. Here the railway crosses the Rhône, which has seldom been out of sight since Brig, and at **Grengiols** the train crosses the highest viaduct on the FO just before entering a tunnel that spirals inside the mountain to emerge at a higher level, looking down on the viaduct and the confluence of the Rhône and Binna rivers.

For one of the finest vantage points over the **Aletsch Glacier**, Europe's longest at about 24 km (15 miles), it is worth breaking the journey at **Fiesch**. Five minutes' walk from the station is the cable car to Eggishorn, from where you can get an excellent impression of the size of the glacier. The train canters past a succession of pretty villages along the broadening valley, the white-towered churches surrounded by dark-wood chalets and some centuries-old agricultural buildings. **Niederwald** was the birthplace of César Ritz, who managed the Savoy Hotel in London before building the Ritz in Paris and giving his name to the famous London hotel.

The mountains begin to crowd in as the train approaches **Oberwald** and the start of the **Furka Base Tunnel**. From Oberwald the railway used to climb continuously on the rack for almost 9 km (5½ miles) up past the Rhône glacier to a summit tunnel underneath the Furka Pass. This closed in 1982 when the Furka Base Tunnel opened, allowing year-round operation of through trains.

Oberwald is the starting point for two spectacular bus journeys, over the Gotthard Pass to Airolo in Ticino (see page 193) and over the Grimselpass to Meiringen (see page 207).

Map on page 188

Andermatt and the Oberalp Pass

The train emerges from the 15-km (9¼-mile) tunnel at **Realp** to a landscape of gorse-covered hills. Soon after passing a 12th-century tower at **Hospental**, it arrives at the resort of **Andermatt**, junction for the rack line through the Schöllenen gorge to Göschenen (see page 193). There follows one of the most spectacular sections of the journey as the line climbs at 1 in 9 through a succession of four half spirals, three of them in tunnel at the elbow bends, which increases the sense of disorientation. Before the train turns east again, you can look down on Andermatt and back along the Urseren Valley towards Realp.

The line continues to climb, though at gentler gradients, towards the highest point on the Matterhorn–Gotthard-Bahn at **Oberalp Pass** (2,033 metres/6,670 ft), the boundary between Uri and Graubünden cantons. The landscape is desolate – tussock grass and bog, broken by only the occasional farm building. In winter the train is sometimes in a sheer-walled canyon of snow, and sections of the railway are protected by avalanche and snow shelters. **Oberalppasshöhe** is the start of a walk to the source of the Rhine at Toma Lake – where you can jump across the stream – and the beginning of the steep descent towards Disentis. The long tunnel is often the opportunity for the train's head waiter to demonstrate his skill at pouring grappa from a bottle several feet away from the glass, while the steepness of the descent makes diners appreciate the necessity of the angled stems on the wine glasses (which can be bought as souvenirs).

BELOW: lunch on board.

TIP

One of the most unusual experiences Switzerland offers can be had from Preda station on certain winter nights when the road down to Bergün is closed to traffic and given over to tobogganing. The railway obligingly ferries passengers and toboggans up the hill, and the road is lit with lanterns.

BELOW: crossing Landwasser Viaduct.

Twisting down the valley of the Vorderrhein, the train passes a branch line leading to the tunnel workings of the AlpTransit project, which is building a new railway tunnel under the Alps. The town of **Disentis** is dominated by the great Benedictine monastery of St-Martin, thought to have been founded around 700 by an Irish monk. Here the Matterhorn–Gotthard-Bahn ends and a Rhätische Bahn (RHB) locomotive takes over for the rest of the journey to St Moritz.

Along the Vorderrhein

The countryside becomes more pastoral and wooded as the line follows the broadening Vorderrhein to the historic town of **Ilanz**, with a fortified church and some 15th-century houses. Beyond Valendas-Sagogn is the bizarre **Flims Gorge**, its towering white cliffs contorted into such peculiar shapes that it would have made a perfect set for filming Star Wars. The line to St Moritz trails in on the right just before the Vorderrhein meets the Hinterrhein to become the Rhine. Some Glacier Expresses continue through the junction station at **Reichenau-Tamins** to the attractive cantonal capital of **Chur**. An important town since Roman times, Chur was the birthplace in 1741 of portrait painter Angelica Kauffmann, who emigrated to England in 1766 and became a founder of the Royal Academy. An art gallery in Grabenstrasse has some of her paintings.

The Glacier Express for Davos continues east, while the main part of the train reverses direction at Reichenau-Tamins before turning south along the valley of the Hinterrhein. After the scenic delights of the route so far, it is hard to believe that this final stage will not be an anti-climax; but it proves just as varied and interesting as the rest of the journey, and the climb to the Albula Tunnel is regarded as one of the railway wonders of the world.

The Landwasser Viaduct

Several castles guard the flanks of the valley as the train climbs to **Thusis** where the Via Mala can be seen briefly to the right. This 15th-century road passes through a narrow gash in the earth – "the most sublime and tremendous defile in Switzerland" according to Murray's Hand-book, and painted several times by Turner. Beyond the pretty village of **Tiefencastel** the valley becomes wilder, the thickening forests allowing occasional glimpses of waterfalls. After Alvaneu stands one of the world's best-known railway bridges, the **Landwasser Viaduct**, which is approached alongside the river of the same name. It is not so much the structure itself that impresses, though the curving masonry bridge of 5⅔ arches is handsome enough, but rather the exceptional way in which the railway crosses the incomplete arch and dives straight into a tunnel in a sheer wall of rock.

The few hotels in the attractively-sited village of **Filisur** are a good base for walkers: a footpath leads back to the Landwasser Viaduct and another follows the river and railway along the beautiful valley towards Davos. But it is to explore the footpath leading to the **Albula Pass** that many people break their journey: the path is punctuated by boards explaining how the railway climbs a vertical height of 416 metres (1,364 ft) in just 13 km (8 miles) without any rack assistance. It does this by a series of loops and spirals with 14 tunnels and 8 viaducts, making the section even more disorienting to the passenger than the climb out of Andermatt.

Once through the 6-km (3¾-mile) **Albula Tunnel**, the railway begins its descent to the junction with the line from Scuol-Tarasp (see page 200) before **Bever**, where the railway joins the broad valley of the upper Engadin. Leaving **Samedan** there is a delightful view to the left of a picturesque church set amid trees on a low hill. The last station before journey's end, **Celerina**, is near the foot of the Olympic bobsleigh track and the famous Cresta run, built in 1884 by three Englishmen.

After a short tunnel, the Glacier Express draws into the world-famous resort of **St Moritz**. Although the spa here has been used since at least the 16th century, it was only during the second half of the 19th century that it became a popular winter resort, when the enterprising hotelier, Johannes Badrutt, offered a group of British tourists free accommodation to prove how delightful the area could be during the winter months. It convinced them, and thousands followed.

Winter sports apart, St Moritz makes a good base for walking, with excellent public transport by train, bus or cable car to the start of many valley or mountain walks. It is also the start of a delightful cycle route beside the River Inn through the Engadin to Innsbruck. Although the town's status inevitably means higher prices, there are still some excellent hotels, full of character, away from the centre.

The Palm Express postbus journey to Lugano is one of the finest in the country, passing the village of Sils-Maria, where the Giacometti family (Alberto being the most famous member) lived and worked. A museum commemorates them, with examples of their sculpture and paintings. St Moritz is also the start of two other scenic railway journeys, to Scuol-Tarasp and Tirano in Italy (see pages 200 and 203).

Map on page 188

Taking part in a local harvest festival.

BELOW:
St Moritz is famous for its skiing.

ESSENTIALS

Thomas Cook
timetable no. 546

Distance: 60 km

Duration of journey:
1 hr 24 mins

Frequency of trains:
hourly

ST MORITZ–SCUOL-TARASP

It is difficult to define what makes a landscape pleasing, but the gentle valley of the Inn between St Moritz and Scuol-Tarasp, close to the Austrian border, is an unending delight, punctuated by attractive villages whose buildings are often decorated with the painted sgraffiti decoration characteristic of the region. The railway itself was a major civil engineering achievement, with 17 tunnels and 72 bridges, some of great elegance. Its cost was originally justified by the expectation that it would become part of a through route from Austria to Italy.

Attractive stations

The journey from St Moritz entails a change of train at **Samedan** as trains for Scuol now start at Pontresina (see page 203). From **Bever**, they keep to the north flank of the valley for most of the journey. The first station at **La Punt-Chaumes** is, like most stations on the line, a pleasure to look at, with attractive round-topped doors, and windows decorated with colourful window boxes. Some of the larger farm buildings combine houses with barns and other agricultural functions, an arrangement typical of the Engadin region and much of eastern Switzerland.

At the large village of **Zuoz** the distinctive three-storey tower of the once-influential Planta family home can be seen from the train. Surprisingly for such a well-protected country, Switzerland has only one national park (straightforwardly named **The Swiss National Park**); access to its western end can be gained from S-chanf station. At **Cinuos-chel-Brail** the valley narrows and the railway crosses the Inn by a single-span bridge over a deep gorge. The railway describes a large loop to diminish the gradient down to **Zernez**, where there is

BELOW: 1930s poster advertising the Haute Engadin railway.
RIGHT: Susch on the River Inn.

an exhibition about the park in the new National Park House opened in 2008. The uniform character of the houses in the village is the result of a decision to rebuild to a common plan after fire swept through the village in 1872.

After **Susch** is the junction for the Vereina Tunnel line through to Davos, which has reduced the journey time between Zürich and St Moritz/Scuol-Tarasp for those who don't mind missing the scenic pleasures of the Albula Pass route (see page 199). The villages of **Guarda** and **Ardez** have both received awards for the way they have conserved their architectural heritage and are a pleasure to explore on foot.

When the sound of the train indicates the end of the long Tasna Tunnel, look to the right: as it crosses the highest bridge on the line before diving into another tunnel there is a magnificent glimpse of one of Switzerland's most romantic castles, at Tarasp. There is also a good view of the castle from the station at **Ftan**, situated so far below the village that the latter has a bus service from Scuol, a duplication normally regarded as wasteful by Swiss transport planners.

Scuol-Tarasp

The station at **Scuol-Tarasp** is also slightly above the spa town – a legacy of a proposed link with Austria – and a shuttle bus meets trains throughout the working day. There are two parts to Scuol: the upper part is the older, and many houses have deeply recessed windows splayed through the massive walls like gunports; the lower is the more recent, where buildings designed to exploit the "champagne of the Alps", as Scuol's waters are known, were built during the 19th and 20th centuries. The water's health-giving properties have been recognised for centuries, and there is an old fountain in upper Scuol, on La Plazetta,

Map
on page
188

BELOW: hot-air ballooning gives the best view of all.

The 11th-century castle at Tarasp can be seen for miles around.

that offers ordinary water, and reddish, iron-rich water. An even greater variety of water used to be on offer at the Trinkhalle, built in the 1840s beside the river, each type accessible through a separate arched opening.

The town has one of the most attractive spas in Switzerland: the Bogn was built in the 1990s, using marble of different colours and other high-quality materials, to produce a centre that is visually exciting as well as restful. One of the pools leads outside, allowing bathers to enjoy the beauty of the surrounding mountains, and computer-programmed whirlpools complement personal advice on preventive medicine and diet.

In common with the whole of the Engadin, Scuol offers some of the best walking in Switzerland, with thousands of kilometres of footpaths that can be accessed using the railway or postbuses. Postbus is also the best way to reach the enchanting village of **Tarasp**, which would be popular even without the attraction of its 11th-century castle.

Tarasp castle

Built by the lords of Tarasp, the castle was for centuries owned by Austrian families before it was taken over by the canton of Graubünden after the Napoleonic Wars. The cost of upkeep prompted its sale, but a succession of irresponsible owners allowed it to deteriorate and its contents were gradually sold. In 1900 it was bought by Dr Karl Linger, the German inventor of a popular mouth freshener. On his death the castle was offered to a grandson of Queen Victoria, Grand Duke Ernest Ludwig of Hesse. Now in new ownership, the castle is open for guided tours of a number of rooms, including the dining room which has been used for concerts and has some rare, early 16th-century stained glass.

BELOW: the lush pastures of Graubünden canton.

ST MORITZ–TIRANO

Map on page 188

Few railway journeys as short as the 2½ hours of the **Bernina Express** between St Moritz and Tirano can encompass such an extraordinary transition – from glaciers to palm trees. The highest rail crossing of the Alps is made even more spectacular in summer by open-air carriages, which enable photographers to take panoramic pictures of the stupendous landscapes that open up with every twist of this sinuous railway. In figures, this translates into a climb from 1,778 metres (5,833 ft) at St Moritz to 2,256 metres (7,401 ft) at Bernina, followed by an ear-popping descent to 429 metres (1,407 ft) at Tirano in Italy. What is astonishing is that this fall of 1,524 metres (5,000 ft) in less than 40 km (25 miles) is accomplished without any rack assistance – the Bernina railway overcomes by adhesion a greater vertical distance than any Swiss rack railway.

As with all the Swiss journeys, a week or more could be spent exploring the villages the stations serve, walking up some of the valleys and taking cable cars or funiculars up some of the surrounding peaks.

St Moritz to Alp Grüm

The Bernina line leaves **St Moritz** on a different alignment from the Chur/Scuol-Tarasp routes, passing through the line's longest tunnel to race across the lovely triangle of land at the upper Engadin. Passing the 1720-built chalet station of **Celerina Staz** (a rare instance of an older building being adapted for railway use) and **Punt Muragl Staz** (change for the nearby funicular up to Muottas Muragl), the train reaches the junction of **Pontresina**. The town has an Alpine Museum with reconstructed rooms as well as various themed displays.

ESSENTIALS

Thomas Cook timetable no. 547

Distance: 61 km

Duration of journey: 2 hrs 27 mins

Frequency of trains: 10 per day

BELOW: Ospizio Bernina station is the main jumping off point for walkers.

Swiss Narrow Gauge Railways

No other country in the world can match Switzerland for the number and variety of passenger-carrying narrow gauge railways. Narrow gauge lines are preferred for mountainous or remote areas with low population densities, because the difficulty and/or expense of building a standard gauge railway does not merit the investment.

Some of the longer and best-known narrow gauge railways are described in detail in this book, but visitors to Switzerland should not miss the chance to ride on other equally impressive, if shorter, lines. Most remain lifelines for the communities they serve, especially in winter when roads are treacherous, or closed. Some are rack railways, and all have a distinctive character.

Martigny–St-Gervais-les-Bains This international route linking the Geneva–Brig main line with Chamonix and the SNCF line to

Annecy traverses the breathtaking gorge of Le Trient, with vertiginous drops of 426 metres (1,400 ft) to the valley floor.

Bex–Villars–Col-de-Bretaye Notable for the sheer variety of landscapes and the extraordinary contrast between the start of the journey in the Rhône Valley and the tranquillity of the Alpine meadows at Col-de-Bretaye.

Aigle–Les Diablerets The most interesting of the three narrow gauge railways that start at the wine centre of Aigle, it loops around the town's magnificent castle before forging up the lovely valley of the Grand Eau.

La Chaux-de-Fonds–Glovelier/Tavannes The network of lines serves the Jura Mountains, one of the least visited parts of Switzerland. An area of woods and heathland, it offers good walking and unrivalled country for riding.

Yverdon–Ste-Croix After twisting through foothills planted with sugar beet, the train suddenly climbs steeply through woods and along the dramatic Gorges de Coratanne to the world capital of the music box and automata, with two museums to prove it.

Locarno–Domodossola The international railway through the glorious scenery of the Centovalli has the most striking steel viaducts of any railway in the country, crossing the many tributaries of the Melezza River.

St Gallen–Gais–Appenzell–Herisau–Gossau The Appenzellerbahn serves this eponymous area of the country, noted for its cycling and walking, particularly in the mountains around the Ebenalp and Säntis which dominate the landscape.

Luzern–Engelberg This busy railway passes through the historic town of Stans (for the quaint funicular up the Stanserhorn) on its way to the resort of Engelberg. Most people come to take the cable car up Mt Titlis, but there is also an important Benedictine monastery which is open to visitors.

Chur–Arosa The winter and summer resort of Arosa could hardly have a better approach than the railway, high up on a ledge above the Schanfigg Valley with its pretty villages and farms. The line crosses the Langweis Bridge, the longest reinforced concrete span in the world when opened in 1914. ❑

LEFT: skiers at Col de Bretaye, terminus for the line up from Bex.

From **Morteratsch** there is a "climate trail" to illustrate the hastening retreat of the glacier, which can be seen from the train as it describes a loop on its climb towards Bernina Diavolezza. The **Morteratsch Glacier** is a classic example of a by-product of global warming that afflicts the entire Alps – glacial retreat. When the station opened in 1908, Edwardian tourists could walk the 150 metres (164 yds) to the tongue of the glacier in a few minutes; today it is a 3-km (2-mile) hike. More than half the ice in Alpine glaciers has melted since 1850. The thaw of the permafrost imposes huge costs: it acts as a glue to prevent rock avalanches, so measures have to be taken to protect vulnerable settlements, as well as transport infrastructure and winter sports facilities.

A cable car ascends from here to Diavolezza where there is what Baedeker describes as "a view of surpassing grandeur" over the Bernina range. The terrain becomes desolate as the train approaches the summit of the line and skirts the pale-green waters of Lago Bianco, once four separate lakes until dammed for hydroelectric power. Walkers often disembark at the summit station of **Ospizio Bernina**, which looks as though it has been built to withstand being buried in snow. Some take the 2-hour walk down to **Alp Grüm**, where there is a hotel and terraced restaurant by the station with a magnificent view over the Palü glacier.

Map on page 188

The original mountain-rescue kit.

A dramatic descent

There follows one of the world's steepest descents of an adhesion railway, the line dropping at an almost continuous gradient of 1 in 14 (70 percent). To achieve this it loops repeatedly back and forth, with tunnels or viaducts at many of the elbows, so passengers are quickly disoriented when they emerge from a tunnel with the hill rising on a different side. Trees cover many slopes, but they periodically break to give glimpses of Val Poschiavo.

As the train leaves Cadera Tunnel, the flange-squealing eases and speed picks up as the train makes for **Poschiavo**, where the workshops of the Rhätis-che Bahn are passed. Well worth exploring, Poschiavo has a main square with some fine patrician houses and a Spanish quarter, built in 1830 with the savings of returning emigrants. Running along the road on grooved rails embedded in the tarmac, the train reaches Lago de Poschiavo at **Le Prese** and skirts the water to the southern end of the lake at **Miralago**. Looking north, there is a good view of the mountains through which the train has passed.

A variety of crops begins to appear in the fields as the train descends more steeply, with the Poschiavino River on the western side, past the emphatically Italian campaniles at **Brusio** and on to the last engineering flourish of the railway – the nine-arched curved viaduct by which the line spirals under itself. Three modern sculptures have been placed inside the circle of this unusual feature.

Once through the last station in Switzerland at **Campocologno**, the valley broadens and joins the Valtellina. After trundling through orchards and past market gardens, the train again behaves like a tram and clatters along the road into Tirano alongside the standard gauge railway that can take passengers on to Lago di Como and Milan.

BELOW: passing the milky waters of Lago Bianco near the summit of the line.

ESSENTIALS

Thomas Cook
timetable nos.
561/564

Distance:
(1) Luzern–Interlaken
74 km
(2) Interlaken–
Jungfraujoch 32 km

Duration of journey:
(1) 2 hrs
(2) 2 hrs 11 mins
(change trains at
Lauterbrunnen and
Kleine Scheidegg)

Frequency of trains:
both routes have
hourly services

BELOW: the view
from Pilatus.

LUZERN–INTERLAKEN–JUNGFRAUJOCH

In tours that try to cram as much of Europe as they can into a fortnight, the Swiss element is most likely to be a train journey up to **Jungfraujoch**, famous primarily because it is the highest railway station on the Continent, at 3,454 metres (11,333 ft). It is also a spectacular journey, with views better than from the summit itself. The cost of maintaining a railway like the Jungfraubahn is prodigious, so it is not surprising that the otherwise all-encompassing Swiss Pass entitles holders only to a discount on the high fare. Consequently it is worth checking that there is a good chance of clear visibility before setting off (most likely in the morning); warm clothes and sunglasses are essential at any time of year.

The round trip from Luzern can easily be done in a day, perhaps even using a steamer on Brienzer See for part of it. The line between Luzern and Interlaken is the only metre gauge railway operated by Swiss Federal Railways (SBB). The scenery is so good that there are panorama coaches with swivel armchairs on some trains.

Luzern and its lake

Luzern is one of the best holiday bases in Switzerland, with excellent rail links, a host of places to visit via the magnificent fleet of steamers on the lake (five of them paddle-steamers), exceptional museums and galleries for a town of its size, one of Europe's finest concert halls, and a good range of hotels, many of outstanding quality and character.

Interlaken-bound trains soon meet the edge of Lake Luzern, sharing tracks with trains for Engelberg as far as the junction and lakeside resort of **Hergiswil**. A

tunnel masks the transition to the shore of the Alpnachersee and **Alpnachstad** where the world's steepest rack railway begins its ascent of Mt Pilatus. Monumental cliffs rearing out of the lake give way to rolling farmland as the train makes for **Sarnen**, capital of Obwalden canton, where the oldest account of the inception of the Swiss Confederation, written around 1470, is kept in the town hall.

More water comes into view to the west (right-hand side) as the railway skirts the lake of Sarnen, its surface often broken by brightly coloured sailing boats. The pretty village of **Sachseln** on its shore has many fine houses, some dating from the 17th century. The surrounding hills gain in height as the train pauses at **Giswil**, start of the rack-assisted ascent to the Brünig Pass and broadening views back over Sarnersee and then over the turquoise waters of Lungernsee, now a reservoir.

Passing through a delightfully unspoilt valley, with only a few farm buildings amid the trees and fields, the final section of the climb reaches the summit at **Brünig-Hasliberg**. This station is used by hikers who then gain access, by postbus and cable car, to numerous dramatic walks along the ridge. The descent to the floor of the Aare Valley is even steeper than the ascent, breaks in the trees affording a glimpse of the river and railway heading west to Brienzer See.

Meiringen meringues

The train reverses direction at **Meiringen**, which gave its name to the meringue, devised by a local patissier. The town is also famous for its association with Sherlock Holmes, since it was the setting of the nearby Reichenbach Falls that Sir Arthur Conan Doyle chose for the fatal struggle with Professor Moriarty. The connection is commemorated in an imaginatively-designed museum in the basement of the English Church. Besides a funicular to the falls, there is an astonishingly narrow gorge, wide enough only for a footpath, to the east of Meiringen.

The line runs through orchards along the flat valley floor to the eastern end of Brienzer See, of which there are enchanting views as the railway takes the northern shore to reach the woodcarvers' village of **Brienz**. A connecting bus takes visitors to the 80-ha (198-acre) **Swiss Open-Air Museum** at Ballenberg, an outstanding collection of rural buildings rescued from demolition and re-erected in an authentic setting. Opposite the station is the foot of the rack railway up Mt Rothorn; most of the trains are steam-operated, some with locomotives built in the 1990s. The pier at Brienz gives passengers the option of making one leg of the journey to or from Interlaken by boat. The lake has one paddle-steamer, the 1914 Lötschberg.

Interlaken Ost is the interchange between the Brünig line, the standard gauge (with direct trains from places as far afield as Frankfurt and Hamburg), and the Bernese Oberland Railway (BOB). The boat pier is also close by. The yellow and blue carriages of the BOB take passengers for the Jungfrau as far as Lauterbrunnen. It is important to be in the correct part of the train, since BOB trains divide at Zweilütschinen; almost invariably the front section goes to Lauterbrunnen, the rear to Grindelwald.

The train curves round the perimeter of an airfield to reach **Wilderswil**, junction for the rack railway up

Map on page 188

Star Attractions:
Luzern
● Swiss Transport Museum
● Art Gallery & Concert Hall
● A ride on a paddle-steamer
● Bourbaki Panorama
● The old town
● A walk along the old city wall

BELOW: the Swiss Transport Museum, Luzern.

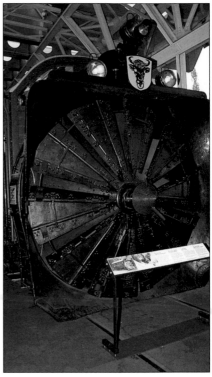

The Regina Hotel at Wengen, overlooking the peaceful car-free village.

Schynige Platte and, curiously, the burial place of two daughters of Schumann and one of Mendelssohn. Just before the junction of **Zweilütschinen** the railway crosses the Black Lütschine, shortly before its confluence with the White Lütschine, which the railway follows up a narrowing valley towards **Lauterbrunnen**. As the village is flanked by two remarkably sheer walls of rock, it is no surprise that there are 72 waterfalls of varying size along the valley, the most famous and spectacular of which are the Staubbach and Trümmelbach.

At Lauterbrunnen there is a cross-platform change to the connecting train of the Wengernalpbahn, which, in a rare display of lack of Swiss foresight, was built to a different gauge from the BOB and the Jungfraubahn, necessitating two changes. As there are no roads that climb above the valley, everything has to be transported by train, with wagons for supplies and large quantities of luggage.

Lauterbrunnen to Kleine Scheidegg

Leaving Lauterbrunnen there is a good view of the Staubbach Falls to the right, while to the left the massif of the Männlichen, Tschuggen and Lauberhorn towers above the line. Gradually the village of Mürren comes into view, situated on a dramatic shelf above a vertical slab of rock. The railway divides, the "old" line now used for goods traffic continuing to the right, while the "new" line (opened in 1910) bears to the left on slightly gentler gradients. The two meet just before the railway reaches the car-free resort of **Wengen**.

The clean air and peace of the compact village are a tonic, and for some a revelation of how pleasant places can be without traffic. Electric vehicles are available to shuttle luggage between hotels and station, or carry those with disabilities. A cable car ascends the Männlichen, from where there is a panorama

BELOW: the Schynige Platte railway, one of several narrow gauge lines south of Interlaken.

BUILDING THE JUNGFRAUBAHN

The construction of a railway to Jungfraujoch was first mooted in the 1870s, but encountered local opposition from farmers who feared it would frighten their cattle, while horse-drawn-carriage operators saw their livelihoods under threat. Despite the opposition, various plans were drawn up and duly rejected, in part due to exorbitant costs. At least one proposal failed because the speed at which it transported passengers to the 3,454-metre (11,330-ft) summit would allow insufficent time to acclimatise to the altitude. In 1893, Adolf Guyer-Zeller came up with the idea of starting the railway at the newly finished summit station of the Wengenbahn at Kleine Scheidegg rather than down in the valley. A breakthrough was the concept of building the line in stages, which could be opened for business one at a time, thereby generating funds for the continuing construction further up the line.

The railway Guyer-Zeller began to build in 1896 was much as he orginally envisaged. The first stretch up to Eiger Glacier opened just two years later. The entire system was finally completed in 1912 (nine years later than planned), after many vicissitudes, including the explosion of a gunpowder store that was reputedly heard as far away as Germany.

of the various valley systems that form this part of the Bernese Oberland. From the summit there is a walk along the ridge to Kleine Scheidegg (see below).

The views from the train above Wengen become progressively more spectacular as it climbs closer to the adjacent peaks of the Eiger, Mönch and Jungfrau. It is no wonder that Byron found the inspiration to write Manfred while staying at **Wengernalp**; even today there is nothing but the station and one of the most peaceful hotels in the world to distract one from the awe-inducing view. Tchaikovsky, Mendelssohn and Richard Wagner were also guests here.

A remote interchange

Situated on a saddle of rock linking the Lauberhorn and the Jungfrau massif, the remote **Kleine Scheidegg** station is full of activity. Trains from Lauterbrunnen and Jungfraujoch exchange passengers and a Grindelwald line feeds in from the north. Several restaurants cater for walkers and skiers who also congregate here.

Shortly after the station and restaurant at **Eigergletscher**, where the huskies that haul sledges at the summit are kennelled, the train enters the 7,122-metre (7,789-yd) tunnel. Stops are made at **Eiger Wall** and **Eismeer** for passengers to de-train and walk along a passage to a viewing window in the side of the mountain before continuing to the underground station at **Jungfraujoch**.

It is advisable to walk slowly on leaving the train as most people feel some effect from the altitude. Lifts ascend to the various levels for restaurants, an audio-visual programme about the mountain and the railway (with English as well as German commentary), exhibition area, sledge rides, open-air verandas and winter garden. A weather station and Europe's highest grid-connected solar power plant also share the mountain.

Map
on page
188

Switzerland has several fine clock and watch museums.

BELOW: pleasure steamer on Brienzer See.

ESSENTIALS

Thomas Cook
timetable no. 566

Distance: 75 km

Duration of journey:
2 hrs 10 mins

Frequency of trains:
hourly

MONTREUX–ZWEISIMMEN–LENK

The metre gauge Golden Pass Express is operated by special panoramic trains with outstandingly comfortable coaches and driving trailers that allow some passengers to enjoy a driver's eye view of the track. Reservations are not obligatory, but they are advisable in season to secure the best seats.

Famous for its jazz festival and nearby Castle of Chillon, **Montreux** makes a good base for walking and exploring the eastern end of Lake Geneva. Its station on the Geneva–Brig–Milan main line is one of the few places in the world where three different track gauges meet, the smaller two being the 800-mm (2 ft 7½-in) gauge of the rack railway up Rochers-de-Naye, the larger one the metre gauge of the Montreux–Oberland Bernois Railway that operates the trains through to Lenk.

The climb up to the 2,045-metre (6,709-ft) summit of Rochers-de-Naye begins as soon as the train leaves Montreux. There is a tremendous view at the top over Lake Geneva and the French Alps. The Swiss Pass is valid as far as Caux, with a 25 percent discount thereafter. There are some great walks from the intermediate stations at **Glion** and **Caux**, and an Alpine garden with over 1,000 species near the summit, which has a restaurant and an audio-visual display to show the views you're missing on cloudy days.

Spiral tunnels and horseshoe curves

The journey to Lenk starts in a U-shaped tunnel that gives a foretaste of the horseshoe curves by which the train gains height to give wonderful views over the lake and into France. **Chamby** is one end of the Blonay–Chamby heritage railway,

Map
on page
188

so a steam locomotive may be glimpsed at weekends. Beyond **Les Avants**, where Nöel Coward lived for 14 years, the gradient reaches its steepest point, at 1 in 13.7 – an astonishing figure for a railway worked solely by adhesion.

The long tunnel under the Col de Jaman marks a complete transition of landscape, into the remote Hongrin Valley with scattered chalets and farm buildings down which the railway drops to the junction of **Montbovon**, for trains to Gruyères and Bulle. Occasionally sheltered from avalanches, the railway climbs again, forging a way through the wooded gorge of the Sarine to enter the Pays d'Enhaut. Pausing at **Rossinière**, where there is a magnificently-decorated chalet dating from 1754 near the station, the railway turns away from the Sarine to reach the area's principal town of **Château d'Oex**.

Alpine cows always like to look their best for visitors.

Ballooning centre

The association of Châteaux d'Oex with hot-air ballooning dates only from 1979, but the area's ideal atmospheric conditions have quickly made it an international centre, and the town hosts the world's leading ballooning championship in the last week of January. At other times of the year visitors can experience the thrill of seeing the Alps from a balloon. The town's Pay-d'Enhaut Museum is an entertaining introduction to this distinctive area and its history.

Continuing along a ledge in the hillside with broad views across the valley, the railway crosses into German-speaking Switzerland at **Rougemont**, where the 11th-century Romanesque church hosts concerts as part of the Menuhin Festival between late July and early September, as does the 15th-century church in **Saanen**. The train takes advantage of the last opportunity for fast running to reach the famous summer and winter sports resort of **Gstaad**, after which the line climbs in earnest. Numerous cable cars and chairlifts can be used for short-cut access to upland walks, of which there are many around Gstaad, with some of the remoter valleys, such as Lauenental, being accessible by postbus.

BELOW: driver's-eye view at Rochers de Naye.

The line describes a semi-circle at a 1 in 25 gradient to cross an impressive three-span viaduct. The white peaks of the Diablerets group can be seen as the train climbs to the summit of the railway at **Saanenmöser**, after which there is a sharp descent into the Simme Valley and the junction with the standard gauge line from Spiez at **Zweisimmen**. The largest village in the Simmental, Zweisimmen also has one of the longest gondola rides in Switzerland – the two-section lift up to Rinderberg, which is 5,102 metres (5,580 yds) in length to gain a vertical height of 1,061 metres (3,481 ft).

Pausing at **Blankenburg** with its baroque castle and covered bridge across the river, the train parallels the river as it heads for the horseshoe of mountains that rings **Lenk** and seals it from any other approaches. The panorama from the town is dominated by the Wildstrubel at 3,243 metres (10,639 ft). Besides being a popular year-round resort, Lenk is also a spa, with the strongest Alpine sulphur springs in Europe. A music academy and a New Orleans Jazz Festival in July swell the summer visitors, many of whom are attracted simply by the walking and the quiet of a town without through routes. ❑

Museums and Heritage Lines

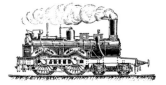

Switzerland has some of the finest heritage railways and museums in Europe. Numbers relate to the map on page 188.

Museum

Locorama ❶
Alte SBB Lokremise, Egnacherweg 1, CH-8590 Romanshorn
Open: Apr–Sept Sun 2–5pm
Features: new museum with collection of historic locomotives and rolling stock. Signal gantry from Romanshorn station.
Nearest station: Romanshorn
Tel: 071 460 24 27
www.locorama.ch

Verkehrshaus der Schweiz ❷
(Swiss Transport Museum)
Lidostrasse 5, CH-6006 Luzern
Open: Mar–Oct daily 10am–6pm; Nov–Feb 10am–5pm
Restaurant, shop
Features: one of the world's great railway collections
Nearest station: Luzern
Tel: 041 370 44 44
www.verkehrshaus.org

Zurich Tram Musuem ❸
Forchstrasse 260, CH-8008
Open: Apr–Oct Wed–Fri 2–5pm, Sat 1–6pm, Sun 1–5pm
Shop, model tramway
Features: tram rides
Nearest stations: Burgweis (Line 11, direction Rehalp)
Tel: 044 380 21 62
www.tram-museum.ch

Heritage lines

Appenzeller Bahnen ❹
Open: daily
Features: buffet car and saloon coach; occasional steam

Nearest stations: St-Gallen, Gossau
Gauge: 1 metre
Tel: 071 354 50 60
www.appenzellerbahnen.ch

Associazione club del San Gottardo ❺
(Mendrisio–Stabio–Valmorea–Cantello–Malnate Olona)
Club del San Gottardo, Casella Postale 1250, CH-6850 Mendrisio
Open: June–Oct first and various Sundays of month
Features: rare international heritage railway
Nearest station: Mendrisio
Length: 12.5 km (7.8 miles)
Gauge: 1,435 mm
Tel: 091 646 57 61
www.clubsangottardo.ch

BC Blonay–Chamby ❻
Open: May–early Oct weekends and some weekdays
Café, shop, museum
Features: largest working collection of historic railway locomotives and vehicles in Switzerland
Nearest stations: Blonay, Chamby
Length: 3 km (2 miles)
Gauge: 1 metre
Tel: 021 943 21 21
www.blonay-chamby.ch

BDB Ballenberg-Dampfbahn ❼
(Interlaken Ost–Meiringen–Giswil)
Open: steam operation on various Sundays
Café, shop
Features: bar coach, rack section
Nearest stations: Interlaken Ost, Giswil
Length: 45 km (28 miles)
Gauge: 1 metre
Tel: 033 828 73 40
www.dampfbahnen.ch

Brienz Rothorn Bahn ❽
(Brienz–Rothorn)
Open: end May–late Oct daily
Cafés, shops, summit hotel
Features: steam and diesel operation

Nearest station: Brienz
Length: 7.6 km (4¾ miles)
Gauge: 1 metre
Tel: 033 952 22 22
www.brienz-rothorn-bahn.ch

Compagnie du Train à Vapeur de la Vallée de Joux ❾
(Le Pont–Le Brassus)
Open: daily; steam on various days
Café
Features: historic carriages
Nearest station: Le Pont
Length: 13 km (8 miles)
Gauge: 1,435 mm
Tel: 024 424 10 70
www.ctvj.ch

Dampfbahn Bern ❿
Verein Dampfbahn Bern, Postfach 5841, CH-3001 Bern
Open: runs on a few Sundays each year
Operates: varied excursions
Features: use of locomotives based in Burgdorf, Laupen, St-Sulpice and Spiez
Nearest station: Bern
Gauge: 1,435 mm
Tel: 031 302 39 68
www.dbb.ch

Dampfbahn Furka Bergstrecke ⓫
(Realp–Gletsch)
Open: late-June–early Oct Fri–Sun; early July–mid-Aug daily
Café, shop
Features: beautiful scenery, long summit tunnel. Extension to Oberwald opening in 2009/10.
Nearest station: Realp
Length: 13 km (8 miles)
Gauge: 1 metre
Tel: 0848 000 144
www.furka-bergstrecke.ch

Dampfbahn–Verein Zürcher Oberland ⓬
(Bauma–Bäretswil–Hinwil)
Open: May–mid-Oct various Sundays
Café, shop
Features: historic coaches
Nearest stations: Bauma, Hinwil
Length: 12 km (7½ miles)
Gauge: 1,435 mm (4 ft 8½ in)
Tel: 052 386 17 71
www.dvzo.ch

Ferrovia Mesolcinese ⑬
(Misoxerbahn)
(Castione–Cama)
Open: June–Aug, various
Sundays
Features: historic electric
vehicles
Nearest station: Castione-
Arbedo
Length: 13 km (8 miles)
Gauge: 1 metre
Tel: 079 262 39 79
www.seft-fm.ch

La Traction ⑭; (CF du Jura)
Open: steam excursions on
various days
Cafés, shops
Features: historic carriages,
Mallet locomotives
Nearest stations: La Chaux-de-
Fonds, Glovelier, Tavannes
Length: 76 km (47 miles)
Gauge: 1 metre
Tel: 032 952 42 90
www.cj-transports.ch
www.la-traction.ch

LEB ⑮; (Lausanne–Echal-
lens–Bercher Bahn)
Open: daily; steam on various
days; reservation necessary
Café, shop
Features: historic carriages
Nearest station: Lausanne
Length: 23 km (14 miles)
Gauge: 1 metre
Tel: 021 886 20 15
www.leb.ch

Oensingen–Balsthal Bahn ⑯
Open: daily; steam on various
days
Café
Features: saloon and historic
coaches
Nearest station: Oensingen
Length: 4 km (2½ miles)
Gauge: 1,435 mm
Tel: 062 391 31 01
www.oebb.ch

Rhätische Bahn ⑰
Graubünden
Open: daily
Operates: occasional programme
of steam and historic electric
excursions

Features: glorious scenery
Gauge: 1 metre
Tel: 081 288 43 40
www.rhb.ch

RHB ⑱ (Rorschach–Heiden–
Bergbahn)
Open: daily; steam on various
Sundays
Café, shop
Features: rack railway
Nearest station: Rorschach
Length: 7.1 km (4½ miles)
Gauge: 1,435 mm
Tel: 071 354 50 60
www.ar-bergbahnen.ch

Rigi Bahnen ⑲
(Vitzau–Rigi)
Open: daily; steam on various
days
Café, shop
Features: glorious scenery,
walks from stations, summit
hotel
Nearest station: Arth-Goldau;
boat service to Vitznau
Length: 6.8 km (4¼ miles)
Gauge: 1,435 mm
Tel: 041 399 87 87
www.rigi.ch

Schinznacher Baumschulbahn
⑳
Open: late-Apr–early Oct,
Sat–Sun
Café, shops, gardens
Features: spectacular narrow
gauge railway around nursery
Nearest station: Schinznach Bad
Length: 2.5 km (1½ miles)
Gauge: 600 mm
Tel: 056 463 62 82
www.schbb.ch

Stanserhorn-Bahnen ㉑
(Stans–Kälti)
Open: Apr–late Nov, daily
Café, restaurant, shop
Features: Switzerland's most
historic funicular, spectacular
scenery
Nearest station: Stans
Length: 1.5 km (1 mile)
Gauge: 1 metre
Tel: 041 618 80 40
www.stanserhorn.ch

Sursee–Triengen-Bahn ㉒
Open: steam on various days
Features: saloon and historic
carriages
Nearest station: Sursee
Length: 8.9 km (5½ miles)
Gauge: 1,435 mm
Tel: 041 921 40 30
www.dampfzug.ch

Swiss Vapeur Parc ㉓
Open: mid-Mar–early Nov most
days 1.30–6pm; mid-May–mid-
Sept 10am–6pm
Café, shop
Features: intricate passenger-
carrying miniature railway
Nearest station: Villeneuve
Length: 1.8 km (1 mile)
Gauge: mixed miniature gauges
Tel: 024 481 44 10
www.swissvapeur.ch

VVT Vapeur Val-de-Travers ㉔
(St-Sulpice–Travers)
Open: various weekends
Café, shop, museum
Features: historic carriages,
occasional longer excursions
Nearest station: St Sulpice
Length: 12 km (7½ miles)
Gauge: 1,435 mm
Tel: 032 863 24 07
www.vvt.org

Waldenburgerbahn ㉕
(Waldenburg–Licstal)
Open: daily; steam on occasional
Sundays
Café, shop
Features: historic coaches
Nearest station: Liestal
Length: 13.1 km (8 miles)
Gauge: 750 mm
Tel: 061 965 94 94
www.waldenburgerbahn.ch

Zürcher Museums-Bahn ㉖
(Zürich Wiedikon–Sihlbrugg)
Open: programme of steam
excursions on various
Sundays
Features: historic coaches
Nearest station: Zürich Wiedikon
Length: 18.6 km (11½ miles)
Gauge: 1,435 mm
Tel: 0848 962 962
www.museumsbahn.ch

ITALY

Many lines in the Italian south and on the islands are old-fashioned and picturesque. Further north, the network connects with its neighbours using some of Europe's smoothest trains

Map on page 218

On 3 October 1839, in the "Kingdom of two Sicilies", the aptly-named locomotive, *Vesuviana*, steamed the 6 km (4 miles) between Naples and Portico to signal the birth of rail travel in Italy. Other Italian states, not wishing to be outdone, quickly ordered tracks to be built, and by 1850 the country had some 2,000 km (1,240 miles) of railway lines. With the desire to link disparate parts of the new nation, following Italian unification in the 1860s, the network really began to take shape, encouraged by the government's offer to refund the cost of construction as soon as a new line was opened. Within four years all Italy's principal cities were inter-connected. The railways were nationalised in 1905, although more than 20 small, privately-run lines still operate to this day.

In the years between the two world wars, particularly under the dictator Benito Mussolini, who is said to have stood at Rome's railway station, stopwatch in hand, to ensure that his trains ran on time, electrification of the rail system proceeded apace, and soon Italian trains were the fastest in the world. With the development of Pendolino tilting trains, first introduced in 1988, Italy remains at the forefront of high-speed rail technology.

The system now has a total length of about 16,000 km (10,000 miles) and covers the entire country, including Sicily and Sardinia. The state-owned company, Ferrovie dello Stato (FS) also has a basic shipping fleet comprising a variety of train-carrying ferries that ply between Calabria and Sicily (passengers and freight) and between Civitavecchia and Sardinia (freight only).

PRECEDING PAGES: Milan Centrale station. **LEFT:** the Rome to Florence express catches the evening rays. **BELOW:** coffee break in Venice.

North and south

The services offered by FS are varied and range from sleek, hi-tech, Eurostar Italia trains, the fastest and most luxurious of the fleet, which include the tilting Pendolinos, to Regionale trains, by way of Eurocity, Intercity, Diretto, Espresso and Interregionale. On the whole, punctuality and comfort of services decrease from north to south.

Other than those routes featured in the following pages, there are numerous attractive railway journeys all over Italy. Many of the lines running across the Apennine mountains in the centre of the country are picturesque, with mountain views and quintessentially Italian villages; Rome to Pescara, and the line from Terni to Sulmona are good examples. Other highlights include the run from Pistoia to Viareggio on the Ligurian coast, which winds through timeless Tuscan countryside; and the narrow gauge mountain route from Catanzaro up to Camigliatello in the beautiful Sila region, a journey through one of Europe's least-known regions.

Neuchâtel
Bern
Thalwil
Luzern
LIECHTEN-
STEIN
Innsbruck
Wörgl
Liezen
Bruck an
der Mur
Szombathely
Székesfehérvár
Lausanne
SWITZERLAND
Chur
Spuol-
Tirano
Schwarzach-
St Veit
AUSTRIA
Graz
Balaton
Zalaegerszeg
HUNGARY
Evian-les-
Bains
Brig
St Moritz
Merano
Spittal-
Millstättersee
Villach
Klagenfurt
Maribor
Balatonszentgyörgy
Dombóvár
Pré
St-Didier
Zermatt
Domodossola
Verbani
Sondrio
Tirano
Bolzano
Pieve
di Cadore
SLOVENIA
Celje
Koprivnica
Pecs
Bourg-
St-Maurice
Matterhorn
4478
Aosta
Biella
Como
Lecco
Edolo
Trento
Belluno
Udine
Gorizia
Ljubljana
Zagreb
Virovitica
Drava
Osijek
Vercelli
Novara
Bergamo
Brescia
Vicenza
Treviso
Pordenone
Sezana
Trieste
Karlovac
Slavonski
Brod
Torino
Asti
Cremona
Verona
Padova
Venezia
Rijeka
Priviaka
CROATIA
Cuneo
Alessandria
Pavia
Piacenza
Mantova
Rovigo
Chioggia
Po
Ferrara
Gospić
Bihac
Tuzla
Genova
Parma
Modena
Ravenna
BOSNIA-
HERZEGOVINA
Savona
Bologna
Knin
Vareš
Nice
Imperia
La Spezia
Massa
Pistoia
Forlì
Rimini
SAN MARINO
Zadar
Šibenik
Split
Sarajevo
MONACO
Ventimiglia
Viareggio
Lucca
Pratovecchio
Stia
Sansepolcro
Ancona
Mostar
LIGURIAN
SEA
Pisa
Firenze
Volterra
Livorno
Cecina
Siena
Arezzo
Pergola
Macerata
Ploče
Metković
Dubrovnik
Corse
(Corsica)
I. d' Elba
Grosseto
Perugia
Ascoli
Piceno
San Benedetto
del Tronto
ADRIATIC
SEA
Calvi
Bastia
Viterbo
Terni
Teramo
I. Trèmiti
Corte
Rieti
L'Aquila
Pescara
Peschici
Calenella
Ajaccio
Civitavecchia
Sulmona
San Vito-
Lanciàno
Termoli
Fiumicino
Roma
Avezzano
Isernia
Campobasso
Manfredonia
Lido di Ostia
Velletri
Frosinone
Piedimonte
Matese
Foggia
Bari
I. Asinara
Palau
Nettuno
Latina
Formia
Caserta
Benevento
Avellino
Matera
Brindisi
Porto Torres
Sorso
Golfo Aranci
Olbia
Napoli
Vesuvio
Salerno
Potenza
Lecce
Alghero
Sassari
Nuoro
Sorrento
Taranto
Macomer
Sorgono
Agrópoli
Sapri
Gallipoli
Oristano
Sardegna
(Sardinia)
Arbatax
Maratea
Sibari
Otranto
Iglesias
Mandas
Páola
Camigliatello
Silano
Carbonia
Cagliari
Cosenza
Crotone
Lamezia
Terme
Catanzaro
Isole Eólie
Tropea
Cinquefrondi
IONIAN
SEA
MEDITERRANEAN
SEA
Palermo
Sicilia
(Sicily)
Messina
Reggio
di Calabria
Isole
Egadi
Trapani
Cefalù
Patti
M.Etna
3323
Giarre-Riposto
Marsala
Enna
Castelvetrano
Caltanissetta
Catania
Agrigento
Licata
Gela
Siracusa
Bizerte
Ragusa
Annaba
L'Ariana
I. di Pantelleria
MEDITERRANEAN
SEA
Jendouba
Tunis
I. di Linosa
MALTA
Valletta
ALGERIA
Sousse
Kairouan
I. di Lampedusa
TUNISIA
I. Kerkenah

Italy

Museums and
Heritage Lines

Featured route

0   100 km

0   100 miles

VERONA–INNSBRUCK

Map on page 221

This is a breathtaking journey with glorious views of Alpine peaks, many of which remain snow-covered throughout the year. Narrow fast-flowing rivers run alongside the tracks, and the landscape is lush with coniferous and deciduous trees, fruit orchards and vineyards. Numerous castles are passed en route, but unfortunately few of them can be seen from the train.

Into the hills

On leaving Verona the track loops northwest along the left bank of the River Adige – the second-longest river in Italy – skirting on the right the vine-planted hillsides of **Valpolicella**, renowned for its sparkling wine. Soon, **Rivoli** and its valley is reached, followed by the wider Val Lagarina and, after 69 km (43 miles), the busy railhead of **Rovereto**, at an altitude of 211 metres (693 ft). Travellers are greeted by three life-sized dinosaurs whose presence is a reminder of the 1991 discovery of 200-million-year-old Jurassic footprints in the area. Eight kilometres (5 miles) beyond, the village of Calliano with the restored Castle Beseno – more of a fortified town than a castle – can be seen.

The train keeps to the left bank of the Adige and after 14 km (9 miles) arrives in **Trento,** the capital of Trentino, sitting in a large natural amphitheatre surrounded by mountains. Immediately across the river from the station a cable car ascends to the lower slopes of majestic Mt Bondone. A private railway, Ferrovia Elettrica Trento-Malè, runs from its own separate Trento station northwest to Marivella at the start of the Brenta Dolomites where, with a great deal of luck, you will see brown bears – only about a score remain. Trains depart about every hour and make the 66-km (41-mile) journey in about 1 hour 40 minutes.

North of Trento, the valley narrows and the intensity of cultivation increases. The vines are strung on wide pergolas – a horizontal trellis supported on posts – a traditional method of viticulture in these parts since Roman times. This permits the breezes blowing up the Adige Valley from Lake Garda to circulate round the grapes, with a beneficial, cooling effect.

At this point the train abandons the River Adige and follows its tributary, the Isarco. The next stop is **Bolzano/Bozen** – from here to Innsbruck all signs are in both Italian and German. Bolzano is the capital of the bilingual province of Alto Adige/Süd Tirol, ceded by Austria to Italy after World War I. In the mountain valleys people use German rather than Italian, and favour dumplings and *schnitzels* rather than *prosciutto* and pasta. With them they drink some of the great wines that are produced in the region – it is estimated there are 40 vines for every inhabitant. Visitors to Bolzano can see the 5,300-year-old remains of "Otzi", found mummified in a glacier 10 years ago.

The Dolomites

To get closer to some superb views of the **Dolomites**, whose improbably jagged peaks soar to over 3,300 metres (10,800 ft), board one of the three cable cars operating from Bolzano (turn right outside the

ESSENTIALS

Thomas Cook timetable no. 595

Distance: 274 km

Duration of journey: 3 hrs 35 mins

Frequency of trains: 6 per day (direct)

BELOW: high-speed 'Eurostar Italia' trains operate as far as Bolzano.

*In the mountains
between Soprabol-
zano and Collalbo.*

BELOW: the
Verona–Innsbruck
line gives some
tremendous views
across to the
Dolomites.

station). Departures are at 20-minute intervals, taking you 1,220 metres (4,000 ft) up the slopes of Mt Renon/Rittner to Soprabolzano/Oberbozen, from where there are stunning views stretching across to Rosengarten. Next to the cable car terminus board the electric tramway (hourly service) – with luck, antique wooden coaches will be in service – for the 20-minute journey to Collalbo/Klobenstein to view the fanciful Longomoso Pyramids, eroded earth pillars capped by stone "hats".

Frequent trains make the 32-km (20-mile) journey alongside the River Adige northwest to **Merano**, a renowned spa with a casino, delightful botanical gardens and splendid views of the mountains. The journey time is 40 minutes.

The South Tyrol

Back on the Innsbruck line, after a long tunnel, the track enters the Isarco (Elsack) Valley and makes a sweeping arc for the next 60 km (38 miles). In doing so, it is following the traditional spine of the South Tyrol which has been a major route between the Germanic and Mediterranean worlds since Roman times. At first the valley is rocky but soon becomes lush with fruit orchards, vineyards and chestnut trees. The river is narrow and fast-flowing, and at several places is crossed by flimsy, covered wooden bridges.

Ponte Gardena/Waidbruck and Castle Trobug, perched high on a crag above Gardena to the right, soon appear. This area is renowned for its wood carvers – there are reputedly 3,000 of them, many of whom speak Ladin (Romansch), a derivative of Latin that has been spoken here since time immemorial. Superb quality pieces, as well as kitsch, are on sale.

The train passes through Chiusa/Klausen, a picturesque little town 28 km (18

miles) from Bolzano, before arriving at elegant **Bressanone/Brixen**, a popular resort with a baroque cathedral and restored royal palace. On leaving Bressanone large gun bunkers can be seen, a reminder that the Tyrol has long been a battleground. A further 11 km (7 miles) takes you to Fortezza/Franzensfeste, where limestone pinnacles shoot skywards from dense pine forests.

The Brenner Pass and Innsbruck

Soon after Fortezza, a long, narrow, wooded valley opens out into a lush green basin and the town of **Vipiteno/Sterzing**, a pretty place grouped around a street lined by typical, white Tyrolean houses with red-tiled roofs and geraniums bursting from over-hanging balconies. And so to the **Brennero/Brenner Pass** which, at 1,375 metres (4,511 ft), is the lowest route across the Alps and the only one crossed in the open by a main railway line. From here the track, hemmed in by trees, runs due north and sharply downhill through the Sill Valley. As the train emerges from a short tunnel, the first sight of the Tyrolean capital, **Innsbruck**, is the solid, red, baroque Stiftskirche (Wilten Abbey Church) backed by the snow-covered Nordkette slopes, rising to 2,334 metres (7,657 ft).

To reach the Altstadt (Old Town) where Innsbruck's major attractions are interspersed with cafés and restaurants, stroll 300 metres down Salurner Strasse, which faces the station, and turn right into Maria Theresien Strasse, then into pedestrianised Herzog Friedrich Strasse. Here stands the 14th-century Stadtturm tower, with grand views from the top. Across the square is the Goldenes Dachl (Golden Roof), composed of 2,657 16th-century, gilded copper tiles. The interior houses a museum devoted to Habsburg emperor, Maximilian I.

Star Attractions:
Verona
- **Roman Arena**
- **Castelvecchio**
- **Basilica de San Zeno Maggiore**
- **Palazzo Maffei**
- **Teatro Romano**
- **Palazzo Maffei**
- **Juliet's House, 23 Via Capello**

LEFT: Innsbruck, the Tyrolean capital.

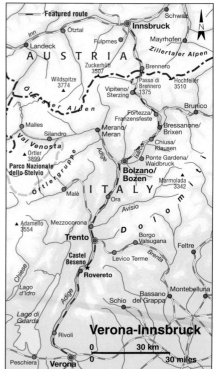

Verona-Innsbruck

ESSENTIALS

Thomas Cook
timetable nos. 90,
360, 580, 610

Distance: 685 km

Duration of journey:
7 hrs 40 mins
(Ventimiglia–Rome)

Frequency of trains:
1 per day
(Ventimiglia–Rome
direct)
3 per day
(Nice–Genoa)
7 per day
(Genoa–Rome)
1 night train only
Nice–Rome direct

BELOW: the
delightful harbour
at Portofino.

NICE–ROME

For the most part, at least until La Spezia, this is a romantic corniche journey with magnificent views of the Ligurian Sea bathing the French and Italian Rivieras. Beyond Pisa, the Ligurian gives way to the Tyrrenhian Sea and the scenery gradually becomes less dramatic. Passengers who board the direct express from Ventimiglia will travel the 652 km (407 miles) to Rome in under 8 hours – for those with more time it is better to travel on the not-infrequent slow trains, even if that entails a number of changes. The route is dotted with ports – Genoa, La Spezia, Livorno, Civitavecchia – from where ferries leave for the islands of Elba, Corsica and Sardinia.

Nice to Genoa

As the train leaves **Nice** on its coast-hugging 33-km (20-mile) journey to the French–Italian frontier, the view is of the foothills of the snow-covered Alps plunging into an azure and turquoise sea. Frequently, however, the glorious scenery is blocked by millionaires' mansions and de-luxe hotels.

No sooner are you settled in your seat than the train arrives at the pretty, resort of **Villefranche**, with colour-washed houses and a station practically on the beach. Next comes the 7-km (4-mile) stretch of villas and sleek white yachts that is the principality of **Monaco**, the heart of the Côte d'Azur. The wealth continues unabated to the final French stop of **Menton**, surrounded by orange and lemon groves, where the station is just a few metres from the sea.

From here it's a short stretch to **Ventimiglia**, and Italy. All the way to La Spezia (240 km/150 miles), the rail route follows the broad, concave sweep of

the Italian Riviera, although FS is gradually rebuilding the line inland, often in tunnels. For now, however, the views over the lush Riviera di Ponente are glorious and, for the first 40 km (25 miles), enlivened with cultivated flowers. On leaving Ventimiglia the train passes plantations of palms whose fronds are used, to the exclusion of all others, by the Vatican during Holy Week. The train soon arrives at **San Remo**, the ageing queen of the Italian Riviera, with elegant old hotels and a palm-lined promenade. **Alassio** heralds a series of more contemporary resorts, and the rail line clings to the sea until **Albenga**, with its medieval wall and Roman ruins. This is succeeded by the resorts of Finale Ligure, Savona and Varazza. After the attractive, prosperous town of **Genoa**, the Riviera di Ponente ends and the Riviera di Levante commences.

Map on page 218

**Star Attractions:
Rome**

● St Peter's and
the Vatican
● Colosseum
● Pantheon
● Trevi Fountain
● Spanish Steps
● Roman Forum
● Raphael Rooms

The Riviera di Levante

The scenery becomes wilder as the train passes the elegant resorts of Santa Margherita and Rapallo. From the former it is just a few kilometres to the fashionable resort of **Portofino**. The next part of the journey is a game of hide and seek as the train pops in and out of tunnels to permit tantalising glimpses of the **Cinque Terre**, five colourful villages perched high above the turquoise sea and virtually unknown until the railway reached them. The train soon arrives in **La Spezia**, set on a wonderful natural harbour whose surrounding hills are dotted with old Genoese castles.

After La Spezia the frontier between Liguria and Tuscany is quickly crossed. This stretch of coast, the Riviera della Versilia, is jammed with disappointingly unattractive resorts, from **Carrara**, where all great sculptors from Michelangelo to Henry Moore have searched for the perfect marble block, to **Viareggio**, the largest Tuscan resort. Gradually the hinterland becomes flatter, and 15 minutes beyond, away from the sea, is **Pisa** with its improbable Leaning Tower and splendid, multi-coloured, four-tiered Duomo. The next stop is **Livorno** (Leghorn), Italy's second largest port.

BELOW: modern station facilities in Rome.

The track, now running across reclaimed swampland, keeps close to the sea as it passes yet another Riviera, the Etruscan, which consists of several overbuilt unattractive resorts. Matters improve at **Cecina**, in the vicinity of which is the WWF reserve of **Bolgheri**, an important feeding ground for migrating birds. Leaving Cecina a glimpse is caught of the promontory of Populonia and of the island of **Elba**. At **Campiglia Marittima**, where the track abandons the coast, the train enters the Maremma, a reclaimed coastal strip that stretches south into Lazio and as far east as Monte Amiata. In classical times this was the northern heartland of the Etruscans.

After **Follonica** the line runs round the foot of the Cape Castiglione massif before reaching Grosseto, the principal town of the Maremma. After the river Ombrone is crossed there is a splendid view of the picturesque Bay of Talamone. As the train enters the region of Lazio, the words of writer D.H. Lawrence come to mind. He described the plain and the low hills that stretch to Rome, over 100 km (60 miles) to the south, as "a peculiarly forlorn coast".

ESSENTIALS

Thomas Cook
timetable no. 640

Distance: 702 km

Duration of journey:
8 hrs 30 mins

Frequency of trains:
2 per day with trains
travelling by ferry
(also 1 night train)

NAPLES–PALERMO

This rail voyage around the Tyrrhenian Sea connects the two largest cities in the southern half of the country. The line stays close to the west coast of the peninsula all the way to Villa San Giovanni on the Strait of Messina, from where a ferry transports the train to Messina, and passengers change trains for Palermo, a further three hours along the Sicilian north coast. This is a fairly demanding trip, but the pleasant, sometimes spectacular, scenery is ample compensation.

The train makes its way through the crowded Neapolitan suburbs, and before long the bulk of **Vesuvius** comes into view, immediately followed, on the right, by the blue waters of the Bay of Naples. The track passes the buried town of **Herculaneum**, followed shortly afterwards by **Pompeii**, before heading eastwards across the plain towards Salerno, reached in around 45 minutes from Naples.

The Circumvesuviana

The state-owned railway scarcely does justice to the Bay of Naples and its attractions, and before boarding it you might like to travel on the private Circumvesuviana railway that skirts the base of Vesuvius and continues to Sorrento. The service is half-hourly and the journey to Pompeii takes about 25 minutes. In Naples the Circumvesuviana has its own ultra-modern station on Corso Garibaldi but all trains stop at the lower level of the Stazione Centrale.

En route there is a constant view of the bay and its islands. Trains stop at **Ercolina** (for Herculaneum and Vesuvius) as well as Pompeii. To visit Vesuvius, board a No. 5 bus outside Ercolina station; this takes you to a car park at the base of the crater from where it is a gentle 40-minute walk over gravel to the rim of

BELOW:
the Amalfi coast.
RIGHT:
crowded streets in
downtown Naples.

the crater, which still emits occasional puffs of smoke (the last eruption was in 1944). To visit the ruins of Pompeii, alight at the Pompei-Villa dei Misteri rather than the Pompeii-Sanatuario station.

Map on page 218

South to the Cilento

Pulling out of **Salerno** the sea is glimpsed as you travel southeast for a short distance to Battipaglia from where a track goes off east to Taranto in the heel of Italy. The train for Palermo turns due south and crosses the plain of Paestum, a sea of plastic hothouses, passing close to the impressive Roman temples at **Paestum** *(see page 228)*. A little further south, past the town of Agrópoli and its ruined castle, it enters the squarish, low massif that juts out from the coast between the gulfs of Salerno and Policastro. This is the **Cilento**, a region of wild, unspoilt beauty where journeys are still made by mule and cart. The coast consists of rugged cliffs, stands of pine and small, pristine coves.

Turning inland and passing through several tunnels, the train emerges into the Alento valley, from where there are tantalising glimpses through olive groves to **Cape Palinuro**, the most beautiful part of this coast. A short distance from the cape the line turns due east, away from the sea, running through tunnels until a steep section of coast is regained at the busy rail junction of Sapri.

The track now runs through olive groves overlooking the beautiful Gulf of Policastro; to the east, sharp-peaked mountains rise to over 1,000 metres (3,300 ft). This tiny slice of coastline (30 km/19 miles long), tucked between Campania and Calabria, belongs to Basilicata, Italy's most backward and undeveloped region. A stop is made at the fashionable resort of **Maratea**, "city of 44 churches" where there is an unusual marble Christ, with hands outstretched.

Star Attractions:
Naples
● **Castel Nuovo**
● **Teatro San Carlo**
● **Museo Archeologico**
● **Palazzo Reale**
● **Castel dell'Ovo**
● **Duomo**

BELOW: among the ruins at Pompeii.

Italy's railways were nationalised in 1905, although over 20 small, independent lines continue to operate around the country.

The toe of Italy

Several tunnels later, the River Noce marks the entrance to **Calabria** – the most southern of Italy's mainland provinces. From here until it reaches the ferry at Villa San Giovanni the track clings fairly closely to the coast as it passes through a landscape of luxuriant vegetation. The first town in Calabria is **Praia a Mare**, a small resort facing the tiny, uninhabited Isola di Dino. Having passed the picturesque town of Scalea, perched on ledges of rock, and the calcified ruins of Cirella, the train arrives at **Páola**, a major junction (for fast trains this is the first stop since Salerno, 220 km/137 miles to the north). St Francis of Páola, Calabria's principal saint, spent most of his life here; in a ravine near the station stands the Santuario di San Francesco.

The line now runs through an intensely cultivated area past a series of small resorts, of which **Amantea** is the largest and liveliest. Rounding Cape Suvero there are tremendous views across the great sweep of the Gulf of Sant' Eufémia, then it's a run across flatlands before we arrive at **Lamezia Terme**.

Tropea to the straits

From Lamezia the main route makes a bee-line for Rosarno, while the historic line follows a 72-km (45-mile) arc along the coast of the **Tropea** promontory before rejoining the main line at Rosarno. To forego the latter, longer route, whose first half between Pizzo and Capo Vaticano is called the Costa Degli Dei (Coast of the Gods) is to deny yourself a glorious journey. There are tantalising glimpses of golden sands, which are easily accessible from several stops – Tropea (known as the Capri of Calabria), Iopollo and Nicótera are three possibilities.

BELOW: endless beaches line the Tyrrhenian coast.

The track runs high above the shore where sparkling seas splash into coves and inlets and the land is a cornucopia of orange groves, prickly pears, palms and oleander. From the magnificent headland of Capo Vaticano, grand views of the Gulf of Gioia can be enjoyed, before the train enters the lush plain of Ravello and soon pulls into **Rosarno** station. All around are groves of century-old, gnarled olive trees.

Back on the main route, the track continues southwards through intensely-cultivated land, passing the beaches (many unseen) of several resorts. **Palmi**, from where the tall television mast on Sicily's northern tip is visible, marks the start of the **Costa Viola** – a name earned from the colour of the sea. A series of tunnels in quick succession blocks out views of beaches until the train emerges just before **Scilla**, a popular resort with an excellent long beach.

On this stretch of coast you may catch sight of small boats with disproportionately tall, ladder-like masts, on which sits one of the crew, and an equally long bowsprit (spar projecting from the bow) on whose tip sits another crew member. These are fishing boats in search of *pesce spada* (swordfish) which abound in these waters: the man atop the mast is the "spotter", the one on the bowsprit the harpoonist.

Across to Sicily

At **Villa San Giovanni** begins the crossing to Messina in Sicily. The voyage itself may take only 20 minutes,

Map
on page
222

but the loading of the train onto the ferry takes well over an hour. This is because the train is much longer than the ferry, resulting in a great amount of shunting: push the first two coaches into the ferry's innards, then back off; push the next two coaches in, and so on.

Not surprisingly, there is always talk of building a suspension bridge – the world's longest – across the Straits. However, the ever-present threat of an earthquake has so far prevented anything progressing past the drawing-board stage. In the 1908 earthquake, 84,000 inhabitants of Messina perished. The latest plan for a bridge, this time well-advanced, was abandoned in 2007.

It is possible to get off the train at Villa San Giovanni while it is being loaded onto the ferry, but the town holds little of interest. However, the much larger town of **Reggio di Calabria**, 13 km (8 miles) and 15 minutes to the south, has in its museum a treasure beyond belief – the *Bronzi di Riace*, two glorious 2-metre (6ft 5-inch), 5th-century BC bronze statues, which fishermen dragged from the sea in 1972. While the train is being loaded onto the ferry, risk-takers might consider boarding a train to Reggio and alighting at Reggio Marittima Stazione from where the museum is a three-minute uphill walk. Bear in mind, however, that trains in this part of Italy are not noted for reliability, so if you want to see the museum it's better to take a taxi.

From **Messina**, the undistinguished, modern, third city of Sicily, which lies on the lower slopes of the Peloritani mountains, the train starts its westward, 3–4-hour journey to Palermo following the coast of the Tyrrhenian Sea for much of the time. Away from the coast the terrain rises slowly to the Nebrodi and, further west, Madonie mountains, both Mafia heartlands. Scattered along the entire route are numerous classical remains. Once the urban sprawl of Messina is left behind, most of the countryside is relatively lush and covered with orange and lemon trees. **Milazzo**, the first stop of note, 36 km (22 miles) from Messina, is situated on a verdant peninsula, unfortunately utterly blighted by a giant oil refinery. The station is far from the port which is the starting point for ferries to the other-worldly **Isole Eolie** (Aeolian Islands), the best known of which are volcanic Stromboli and Vulcano.

From Milazzo to **Cefalù**, the next major stop, the line runs past many small, clean stony beaches backed by extensive citrus groves. From the main square in **Patti** buses make the short journey to Tindari and ancient **Tyndaris**. This was one of the last Greek settlements on Sicily and the beautiful ruins are predominantly Roman rather than Greek. However, what attracts most visitors is not the ruins but the Santuario della Madonna Nera, a modern building that houses a black-faced Byzantine Madonna, said to have miraculous powers.

After passing rocky Cape Calva, we come to the pleasant resort of **Gioiosa Marea**; from here, the island of Vulcano is a mere 20 km (12 miles) offshore. Soon, the windswept peninsula of **Capo Orlando** and the resort of the same name, is reached. It became famous throughout Italy after its shopkeepers defied the demands of the Mafia for their infamous *pizzo* (protection money). **Sant'Agata di**

★

Star Attractions:
Palermo

● **Palazzo dei
Normanni**
● **Via Vittorio
Emanuele**
● **Ballarò Market**
● **Palazzo
Chiaramonte**
● **San Giovanni degli
Eremiti church**

BELOW: loading the rail ferry for Sicily.

The Temple Route

Archaeology enthusiasts visting Sicily, particularly aficionados of classical temples, will delight in the opportunity to explore more than a score of Greek temples on the island, many of which are still in splendid condition. The railway route south from Naples also has more than its fair share of classical wonders, most notably at Paestum, reached in about 35 minutes from Naples (10 trains daily). Three squat, solid, well-preserved, golden Doric temples stand on a flat piece of ground. The oldest is the the Temple of Hera (*circa* 550 BC) which retains its double row of columns, while the best preserved is the Temple of Neptune, 100 years younger. To the north is the Temple of Ceres, the smallest of the trio, which served for a time as a Christian church.

And so to Sicily. From Palermo, a train journey of a little over two hours through lovely countryside to the south leads to Castelvetrano (three direct trains daily, more involving a change), from where a 20-minute bus ride terminates at Marinella. Here, scattered over a large area of sand dunes are eight Doric temples which, with one exception, were built in the 5th and 6th centuries BC. The temples are separated into an eastern group of three and a western group of five. Temple E in the eastern group was probably sacred to Hera and was reconstructed in 1958. Temple G, almost completely in ruins, was one of the largest in antiquity. Cross the depression, Gorgo Crottone, to reach the acropolis and the western group which is dominated by the partially reconstructed Temple C, the oldest temple, whose renowned *metopes* are in the Palermo museum. Glorious views can be enjoyed from the acropolis.

Better known are the temples built between the late 6th and late 5th century BC, which line Agrigento's renowned Valley of the Temples. Agrigento may be reached either directly from Palermo by a train journey of a little over two hours (a dozen trains daily) across the heart of Sicily, or alternatively by bus from Selinunte, which takes the same length of time.

Enter the valley at its eastern end to see the temples of Juno Lacinia. Concord is one of the best preserved in the world; Hercules is probably the oldest of the Agrigento temples; Zeus, if it had been completed, would have been among the world's largest Greek temples; and finally the Sanctuary of the Chthonic Deities which has vestigial remains of four temples. Using these remains part of a temple dedicated to the Heavenly Twins – Castor and Pollux – has been erected.

West of Palermo, standing in chaste solitude atop a hill, is a gem: the unfinished (although this is not evident at first sight) ochre-coloured Doric temple of Segesta (*circa* 420 BC). It is an uphill walk of about 2 km from Segesta Tempio, the unmanned station – more of a restaurant than a station, really – at which passengers alight. This is reached from Palermo by taking the train to Trapani. There are four trains daily. Theoretically, it is possible to visit Segesta and Selinunte by rail and bus on the same day – but don't depend on it. ❏

LEFT: Concord, one of the world's best-preserved Greek temples.

Militello is a good place to alight for those who wish to visit the vast Nebrodi National Park, rich in deciduous trees, especially beech, where foxes and wild cats roam and eagles soar. Unique to the park is the Fratello breed of horses, distinguished by their odd-shaped noses. At **Santo Stefano di Camastra**, further along, some of Sicily's best ceramics, with styles ranging from traditional to contemporary, may be purchased.

Map on page 218

The final stretch: Cefalù to Palermo

Busy, delightful **Cefalù** is second only to Taormina in its popularity as a resort. On leaving the station the train travels directly above the long, lovely beach; looking backwards, the town's renowned Arab-Norman cathedral can be seen. About 20 minutes beyond Cefalù is the large station of Termini Imerese, which owes its importance to the oil refinery that disfigures the landscape. Somewhat surprisingly, there is a beach here and the ubiquitous classical ruins.

Far more attractive is the view from **Bagheria** station. The handsome, cream-coloured, baroque building that can be seen from here is one of several villas built in the 17th and 18th centuries when Bagheria was a summer retreat for the nobility. The Villa Palagonia, 10 minutes beyond the station, is known for its menagerie of grotesque sculptures.

Ahead, jutting out into the sea, is Palermo's limestone promontory of Monte Pellegrino, but before the city is reached the train turns away from the coast to enter a lush plain planted with row upon row of orange and lemon trees. This is the hill-encircled **Conca d'Oro** (Golden Basin) formerly a glorious cornucopia of fruit and other produce, but now much blighted by concrete. **Palermo**'s Centrale station lies just ahead.

The trail up Mt Etna. It is advisable to join a guided tour as conditions can be hazardous.

BELOW: view of Etna from Troina, Sicily's highest town.

THE CIRCUMETNEA

From Messina trains run south for the 3-hour journey to Siracusa. The route is a delight, with the Ionian Sea almost always in view and, for the first part of the route, fine views of the Calabrian coast terminating in Cape Sant'Alessio, a bold promontory of whitish rocks.

Landwards is lush with orange and lemon groves backed by mountains. It is not long before Mt Etna, Europe's highest and most active volcano (3,323 metres/10,966 ft) comes into view. A memorable side trip around the volcano can be enjoyed by alighting from the Messina–Siracusa train at Giarre-Riposto and boarding a train of the narrow gauge Ferrovia Circumetnea. The 114-km (71-mile) loop to Catania takes five hours.

The narrow gauge track climbs up the slopes of the volcano, passing barren stretches of black lava from recent eruptions; there are glorious views of terraced vineyards and almond, hazelnut and orange groves. The train stops at several interesting villages – Linguaglossa, Randazzo, Bronte Adrano, Paterno. Towering above is the threatening presence of Etna, often hidden by the clouds its intense heat tends to create. Alight in Catania at the Ferrovia Circumetnea station and take the FCE metro to the State Railway station, where you can catch a train to Siracusa or back to Messina.

ESSENTIALS

Thomas Cook
timetable no. 629

Distance: 218 km
(Cagliari–Arbatax)

Duration of journey:
6 hrs 40 mins

Frequency of trains:
2 trains daily
mid-June to
mid-September
(Cagliari–Arbatax)

SARDINIA

Sardinia, the second largest island in the Mediterranean, has two railway systems: the Italian state railway, Ferrovie dello Stato (FS) and Ferrovie della Sardegna (FdS), now owned by the regional government. Whereas the FS runs on 1,435 mm standard gauge tracks, the FdS stock runs on 950 mm narrow gauge. On occasions, FS and FdS share the same track, which then consists of three lines of rail. In some towns both share the same station: in others each has its own.

The major FS line runs from Cagliari in the south via Macomer to Chilivani in the north, equidistant from the east and west coasts. At Chilivani it divides, with the eastern branch terminating at Golfo Aranci and the western branch at Porto Torres, having passed through Sassari. However, the Sardinian pearls for the railway buff are those FdS routes on which a tourist service runs during the summer months. In addition to the Cagliari–Arbatax route, on which two trains run daily from June to October, there are less frequent services on the Macomer–Nuoro and the Sassari–Tempio–Palau Marina routes.

The Cagliari to Arbatax route

The train that runs from the rudimentary FdS station at Piazza Repùbblica in Cagliari is a regular year-round commuter service. Leaving noisy, chaotic Cagliari behind the track soon travels through the pleasant rolling hills of Trexenta, where olive and almond trees grow in profusion. At **Mandas**, reached after a couple of hours, passengers transfer to Il Trenino Verde (Little Green Train) – purely a promotional name, as the train scarcely differs from the one from Cagliari – to take them through the mountains for 158 km (99 miles) to Arbatax. The line was inaugurated in 1894, with the aim of opening up the rich mineral deposits and forests in the heart of Sardinia.

A plaque at Mandas station honours D.H. Lawrence (1885–1930), who describes the journey from Mandas to Sorgono in his book, *Sea and Sardinia*. The Sorgono line, running due north from Mandas, traverses similar rugged scenery to the Arbatax line.

Dispel all thoughts of steam engines bellowing smoke and pulling historic wooden carriages. Sensible legislation forbids the use of steam in the dry summer months, and although wooden coaches stand at Mandas they are not normally used. Groups who make prior arrangements and who travel during the "No Fires" period may try to arrange for a steam train pulling historic coaches.

Immediately after setting off eastwards from Mandas the track climbs, twists and turns; the train squawks and screeches and its whistle screams warnings to any animals on the track and to the users of level crossings. These – there are a fair number – are rudimentary affairs, consisting of chains hung across the road.

The 5-hour journey through dramatic mountain landscapes is best described as bone-shaking. So sinuous and convoluted is the route that unless you are carrying a compass you will be at a loss to know in which direction the train is travelling.

BELOW: cool down with an ice cream in Cagliari.

Thirty minutes out from Mandas the train halts at Orroli and then turns north. This is the region known as the **Barbagia**, the home of bandits where vendettas were part of everyday life until not too long ago. The name is of Roman origin, derived from the Latin *Barbaria* – a term used by the Romans for those whose culture and lifestyle differed from their own. About 250 well-preserved *nuraghe*, ancient, squat, circular towers for which Sardinia is renowned, are found in the Barbagia. One of the most famous, the Nuraghe Arrubiu, is a mere 5 km (3 miles) from Orroli. Unfortunately, none can be seen from the train.

Along the Flumendosa

Below Orroli, through a valley covered with fields of barley, flows the Flumendosa, the second longest river in Sardinia. It broadens out to become the attractive Lago dei Flumendosa, a man-made lake formed by one of three dams along the river's journey to the sea. The water remains in sight nearly all the way to **Esterzili**, reached around an hour later. The landscape is well-wooded and the region is especially known for its varieties of oak, including holm- and cork-oak. Higher up the mountains chestnuts, hazelnuts, maples and yews thrive.

Soon we reach the village of **Sádali**, built around the 13th-century church of San Valentino, next to which gushes a sparkling waterfall. As the train enters the tunnel between Sadali and the next stop, Seui, it reaches, at almost 900 metres (3,000 ft), the highest point of the journey. There's a break of about 10 minutes at **Seui** to allow the passage of the down train arriving from Arbatax, and this gives passengers time to make a dash for the simple station café for a cold drink or a shot of espresso.

Map on page 232

Plaque at Mandas station honouring D.H. Lawrence. The writer describes the journey to Sorgono in Sea and Sardinia.

BELOW: FdS rolling stock at Mandas.

Sardinians have a passion for graffiti.

The scented *macchia*

The thick, tangled, heavily-scented vegetation that is so prevalent here is called *macchia* (*maquis* in France) and is not dissimilar to the vegetation on Scottish moors, particularly when it contains yellow-flowering broom, gorse and heathers. Other aromatic plants that make up the *macchia* include rosemary, juniper, myrtle, thyme, rock rose, arbutus (strawberry) trees and mastic shrubs. This is the principal source of food for pigs and goats, and also yields an oil for domestic use. The juniper and myrtle berries are used to make schnapps, and it is from the blossoms of the arbutus that bees collect nectar for the pungent, Sardinian honey, which, it is claimed, is a cure for bronchial asthma. As a result of forest fires, *macchia* is on the increase.

Anulu, the stop after Seui is the highest station in Sardinia, at 865 metres (2,838 ft). All around are the Seulo mountains, dominated to the north by Mt Perdedu. For sheer dramatic beauty the next stretch of line between Seui and Gairo, which crosses a stone and lattice girder bridge over the San Girolamo River, is unsurpassed. The town of **Gairo** was rebuilt after 1951 when its predecessor, Gairo Vecchio, had to be evacuated when torrential rains resulted in a series of landslides.

Hill walkers and nature lovers will want to get off at San Girolamo, midway between Seui and Gairo, and explore the enchanting Montarbu forest to the north. From here footpaths leads to Monte Tonneri (*tonneri* are massive, limestone cliffs) where deer and mouflons (mountain sheep) live among ash, holly and yews. This is one of the best-known sections of the Gennargentu massif.

After Gairo the line turns north and enters the valley of the Flumendosa at the southern end of Lago Alto del Flumendosa. A short distance later, **Villagrande**,

BELOW: wool on the line near Arbatax.

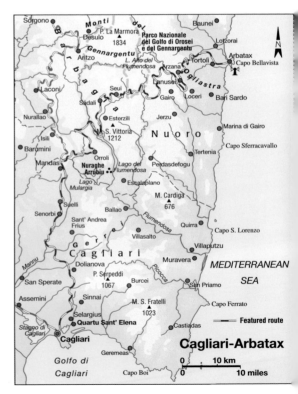

Cagliari-Arbatax

surrounded by reddish granite rocks and renowned for the production of *prosciutto* ham from free-range pigs, is reached. As the train turns south and passes **Arzana**, the track makes a series of sweeping curves including a complete circle, in order to get over a steep slope.

Ultimately the train arrives at **Lanusei**, perched on the eastern slopes of the Barbagia at a height of 555 metres (1,821 ft) and backed by mountains. This was formerly the capital of the region and, because of its salubrious climate, a popular health resort. From here the Tyrrhenian Sea and the large, lush plain which leads to it can be seen.

Descent to the east coast

The train now commences its descent to the east coast, first north and then due east around numerous curves on the steep, rocky hillside. This is the steepest gradient on the route – about 1 in 30. The untamed scenery is gradually replaced by a gentler landscape with groves of olive trees and prickly pears.

The end of the line is the attractive little station at the placid town of **Arbatax**, standing alongside one of the large new marinas that are being built all over the island of Sardinia. For those who intend to spend the night (a morning train departs at 7.50am) or stay longer in the region, it might be better to leave the train at **Tortolì**, which is reached nine minutes before Arbatax and is a much livelier town.

Hardy souls who boarded the early morning train in Cagliari and intend to do the round trip can spend 90 minutes in Arbatax before returning on the 14.30 Trenino Verde which arrives at Cagliari at 20.42. There is also a 12.52 from Cagliari to Arbatax, but the return is the following day. ❑

Map on page 232

BELOW: hiking in the Gennargentu.

The Train of Kings

On 4 October 1883, the official inaugural run of the Orient Express began from the Gare de l'Est in Paris. The passengers embarked under the impression that they would be carried without interruption to Constantinople (Istanbul). This was not to be, as the tracks were not yet built all the way through. Passengers said farewell to the Orient Express at the desolate Romanian village of Giurgiu, from which a ferry took them across the Danube into Bulgaria. From that point a decidedly non-deluxe train continued to the town of Varna, on Bulgaria's Black Sea coast, where they boarded a steam packet to complete their trip to Constantinople. The first complete journey had to wait until 1889.

Over the years the route of the Orient Express changed with the vicissitudes of war, politics and economics. The train was largely superseded in 1919 by a new deluxe Orient Express that travelled through the Simplon

Tunnel. This new, southern route was dictated by the victors of World War I, who wanted to connect western Europe with the emerging states of eastern Europe but bypassing Germany and Austria, their former and possible future enemies.

World War II put much of Europe's train network in the hands of the Germans, who inaugurated a sort of Nazi Orient Express from Berlin to Istanbul. Many Wagons-Lits cars were taken over by the German army to transport officers, and some cars in occupied France were used as stationary restaurants and hostels. One even served as a brothel for Nazi officials. Others were stored in the French countryside, their magnificent, risqué Lalique glass panels and intricate Prou marquetry removed and hidden from harm.

The Paris–Istanbul service resumed after the war, but it was no longer an all-luxury train. Through passage was also hampered by the complexities of crossing the borders of Iron Curtain countries. Air travel further diminished the appeal of international sleeper trains, and the Orient Express made its last regular run with through sleeper service to Istanbul on 22 May 1977 – a shrunken outcast of the hurry-up age.

On 8 October 1977 Sotheby's put five of the original carriages up for auction in Monte Carlo. There were three serious bidders, amongst them James B. Sherwood, chairman of the Sea Containers Group. The first two cars were sold to a decorator representing the King of Morocco, the next two cars were knocked down to Sherwood. With that hammer, began the genesis of the Venice Simplon-Orient Express.

Over the next five years Sherwood scoured Europe for more than thirty 1920's deluxe Wagons-Lits and First Class Pullman cars from the same vintage. A restoration programme, the like of which had never been undertaken before, was instigated and negotiations undertaken with the railway authorities of Britain, France, Switzerland and Italy. On 28 May 1982, Sherwood stood in front of assembled Hollywood stars and socialites at Platform 8 of London's Victoria Station and declared: "The Venice Simplon-Orient Express is resumed." ❑

LEFT: the sumptous dining car.

Museums and Heritage Lines

As in the rest of southern Europe, preserved railways are few and far between in Italy, although there are several railway museums. The numbers relate to the map on page 218.

Museums

Museo delle Ferrovie, Monserrato (Sardinia) ❶
via Pompeo, Monserrato (Cagliari)
Open: weekdays 9am–1pm
Features: exhibits include equipment used by the builders of the earliest railways, a reconstruction of a typical 19th-century railway station with a line linking two stations and a section with period carriage material still in working order
Nearest station: Piazza Repubblica, Cagliari.
Tel: 070 580 246
The most straightforward link on the internet is via www.treninoverde.com

Museo Ferroviario Pietrarsa ❷
Stazione FFSS Pietrarsa, via Pietrarsa, Naples
Open: Mon–Sat 9am–1pm
Features: one of the most important railway museums in Europe, housed in the 19th-century locomotive workshop of Pietrarsa. Displays 38 locomotives, 6 railcars and 10 coaches; of special note is the royal train built in 1929 for the wedding of Umberto di Savoia with Maria José of Belgium. East of Naples city centre on the way to Portici
Nearest station: Pietrarsa S. Giórgio a Cremano
Tel: 081 567 4567

Museo Ferroviario di Trieste Campo Marzio ❸
Stazione di Trieste Campo Marzio, via Giulio Cesare 1, 34100 Trieste
Open: Tue–Sun 9am–1pm
Features: housed in an early 20th-century station, documents the history of railway transport. Displays consist of tools, machinery, railway material, a number of steam, electric and diesel engines, passenger and goods coaches, horse-drawn and electrical trolley-cars from Austria, Hungary and Germany. Monthly tour of the city on vintage trains
Nearest station: Trieste Centrale
Tel: 040 379 4185
Fax: 040 312 756
www.retecivica.trieste.it/museofer

Museo Nazionale della Scienza e della Tecnica ❹
(National Museum of Science and Technology)
Via S. Vittore 21, 20123 Milan
Open: Tue–Fri 9.30am–5pm; weekends and holidays 9.30am–6.30pm; closed Mon
Features: 16th-century monastery housing steam and electric locomotives
Nearest station (metro M2): St Ambrogio (Green Line)
Tel: 02 485 551
Fax: 02 4801 0016
www.museoscienza.org

Heritage lines

Ferrovia Basso Sebino (Treno Blu) ❺
(Bergamo–Paratico Sarnico)
Via Zanica 75, 24126 Bergamo
Open: Mar–Sept weekends; steam trains on various days
Features: links with boat trips to Monte Isola on the Lago d'Iseo
Nearest station: Bergamo
Length: 90 km (56 miles)
Gauge: 1,435 mm
Tel: 030 740 2851
www.ferrovieturistiche.it

Ferrovia Val d'Orcia (Treno Natura) ❻
(Siena–Asciano–Monte Antico)
Contact through the Siena tourist board, tel: 0577-52209.
Features: a vintage train (occasionally steam-hauled) travels south of Siena in the heart of Tuscany, through the Sienese Crete (clay hills) and the Orcia Valley at the foot of Mount Amiata
Open: Sundays and holidays
Gauge: 1,435 mm
Nearest station: Siena
Tel: 0577 207 413
www.ferrovieturistiche.it

Il Trenino verde ❼
(see page 230)
The Ferrovie della Sardegna (FdS) operates four narrow gauge lines, which are of great interest (although not strictly speaking heritage lines) (Mandas–Arbatax; Mandas–Sorgono; Macomer–Bosa; Nulvi–Tempio–Palau)
Via Cugia, 1, Cagliari
Open: runs certain days June–Sept; also possible to arrange specialised itineraries
Gauge: 950 mm
Tel: Cagliari tourist board, 070 651 698/240 200, or FdS office, tel: 070 580 246
www.treninoverde.com

AUSTRIA

*Glorious Alpine scenery, accessed by an extensive network
of rack railways and longer runs make Austria
a favourite destination for train lovers*

Map
on page
240

Austria is a far more varied country than most people imagine. The classic Alpine scenery most associated with it does not extend much beyond Vorarlberg and the Tyrol, the western spur of its territory. The area south of Salzburg has the highest mountains and is more rugged; Carinthia and Styria are lower, drier and heavily forested. The area to the north of the Danube has a distinctly central European feel, while low-lying Burgenland in the east has more in common with Hungary than with the Alps.

The first Austrian railway opened in 1837, running 20 km (12 miles) northeast from Vienna to Deutsch Wagram to form the initial part of the link from the capital to the Silesian coal fields (now in Poland). The ensuing development of the railways was conceived with the grand aim of connecting the far flung territories of the Austro-Hungarian Empire. Unlike many other European countries, Austria has largely retained its network of branch lines serving rural areas; some of these are operated by private railway companies. The major lines are run by Österreichische Bundesbahnen (ÖBB), the national rail operator.

Today the ÖBB network totals 5,656 km (3,515 miles) of track, 3,526 km (2,191 miles) of which are electrified. The backbone of the network is the Vienna–Linz–Salzburg Westbahn, with a branch from Wels to Passau on the German border. Other major lines radiating from Vienna are those to Breclav in the Czech Republic, which continues north to Prague and Warsaw; to Hegyeshalom in Hungary, leading to Budapest; and the Südbahn to Bruck an der Mur, where it splits into a line to Slovenia via Graz and to Italy via Villach.

These lines are supplemented by Bruck an der Mur–Linz, Salzburg–Wörgl, Innsbruck–Bregenz and Salzburg–Villach. Of great importance for freight traffic is the Brenner route south of Innsbruck, which runs over the Brenner Pass to Italy. The construction of railways through Austria's mountainous terrain proved a challenge for 19th- and early 20th-century engineers, and the network has more than its fair share of bridges, viaducts and tunnels, the longest being the Arlberg Tunnel (10.2 km/6⅓ miles) on the Innsbruck–Bludenz line.

PRECEDING PAGES:
road and rail at
Anton am Arlberg.
LEFT: the steam
railway at Stainz.
BELOW: statue on
Beethoven's house,
Heilingenstadt.

Narrow gauge lines

Austria is an extremely beautiful country, and the narrow gauge lines, in particular, promise spectacular journeys. Narrow gauge branches include Waidhofen to Lunz and Ybbsitz, Gmünd to Gross Gerungs, Litschau and Heidenreichstein, Zell am See to Krimml, and St Pölten to Mariazell and Mank. The St Pölten–Mariazell line is electrified, and is considered by many to be the most scenic narrow gauge line in Austria. It is worked with old electrics dating from 1909.

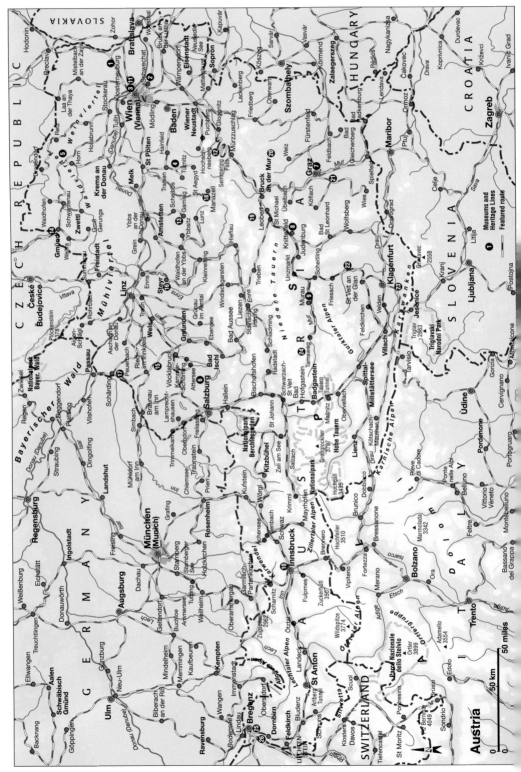

LINDAU–INNSBRUCK

Map on page 240

This 3-hour journey from the German border to the Tyrolean capital takes in some of the best scenery to be found anywhere in the Alps. There are several opportunities to break the journey in attractive towns, many of which have rack railways ascending into the mountains.

The journey begins on the shores of the **Bodensee** (Lake Constance), close to the point where three countries – Austria, Germany and Switzerland – converge. The German town of Lindau is situated just a few kilometres from the Austrian border, on an island linked to the mainland by a long causeway. From Lindau the line runs along the shores of the Bodensee, crossing into Austria before arriving in **Bregenz**, an attractive town that is the capital of Austria's western-most province, Vorarlberg. Bregenz enjoys a privileged location between the lake and Mt Pfänder and although the area close to the shore is fairly uninspiring, further uphill there are some lovely old buildings, including the local church, dating from 1736. The town is famous for its summer festival, the stage for which has been built into the lake. Sadly, the narrow gauge line up **Bezau** has been closed since 1980, and today only a short section near Bezau itself is operated as the Bregenzerwald Museumsbahn *(see page 257)*.

Leaving the Bodensee behind, the next town is **Dornbirn**, an industrial centre, and the largest town in the Vorarlberg region. A few kilometres west of the railway the Rhine marks the border between Austria and Switzerland. Huge dams have been built along the river and these are being maintained by means of a narrow gauge industrial railway, jointly operated by the two countries. Excursions run along the river from Lustenau during the summer months.

After Götzis the main line arrives at **Feldkirch**, a major junction. From Feldkirch to Buchs in Switzerland the railway passes through Liechtenstein, one of Europe's smallest countries; this section is owned and operated by ÖBB, since Liechtenstein does not have its own railway company. Most of the Vienna–Zürich services use this route.

The line to Innsbruck continues eastwards through the mountains to **Bludenz**. At the station you can see electric railcars in yellow and red livery, belonging to the narrow gauge Montafonerbahn, which connects Bludenz with Schruns, a popular resort in both summer and winter. Trains to Schruns operate approximately hourly, taking 20 minutes.

Along the Arlbergbahn

The railway from Bludenz to Landeck is the famous Arlbergbahn, built as a single line and completed in 1884; some sections have now been doubled. The Arlberg Tunnel at the summit is the heart of the line. Construction of this tunnel, at 10,250 metres (33,630 ft) the longest in Austria, only got underway after the Gotthard Tunnel in Switzerland had opened and proved to be a success. As one of the most important lines in the country, the Arlbergbahn was electrified in 1925 (plans for electrification had been made in 1908 but World War I delayed the work). A few electric locomotives from bygone days have been preserved and are used on occasional charter trains.

ESSENTIALS

Thomas Cook timetable no. 951

Distance: 208 km

Duration of journey: 3 hrs 10 mins

Frequency of trains: 2 per day (direct); 8 per day with a change at Bregenz or Feldkirch

BELOW: flowery meadow near Karwendal, Tyrol.

Skiing is big business in the Tyrol and Vorarlberg regions.

The steep gradients demand special methods of operation, and most freight and express passenger trains require the assistance of a second locomotive at the rear of the train. During the winter, the line is threatened by avalanches; the steep slopes have been fortified with anti-avalanche equipment and detectors have been fitted to monitor the track. At times of high avalanche risk, observation posts along the line are staffed around the clock.

The view from the train is splendid, each bend revealing more mountain tops, which often remain covered in snow until late summer. **Langen** is the last stop before we enter the **Arlberg Tunnel**. From the village a mountain road leads to Lech, a well-heeled ski resort. At the far end of the tunnel is St Anton, with its underground station, completed in 2001 for the Alpine Skiing World Championships. There are various opportunities for winter sports and many funiculars and ski-lifts give access to the surrounding mountains. The highest of these are Galzig (2,183 metres/7,162 ft) and Valluga (2,809 metres/9,215 ft). Most of these Tyrolean peaks are covered with Alpine pastures that provide grazing for cattle in the summer months; at the end of summer the return of the livestock to lower levels is marked with a carnival, when the animals are decorated with flowers.

Into the Tyrol

BELOW: a rewarding way to take in the magnificent scenery.

East of **St Anton** the line drops continuously and offers more wonderful views. There is a succession of tunnels along this difficult section of track, and shelters have been built to protect the railway from avalanches and falling stones. A few kilometres west of **Pians** the line crosses a long girder bridge which passes 80 metres (262 ft) above the River Trisanna, just beyond Wiesberg castle. The

ÖTZTAL BY BIKE

The Innsbruck line follows the Inn downstream to the town of Ötztal. At the station you can hire bicycles – you are entitled to a discount if you arrive by train. If you'd prefer to avoid the uphill route, take the bike on one of the frequent bus services from the station up to Sölden or Obergurgl and then coast back down the valley.

The Ötztal Alpine valley is 55 km (34 miles) long, and gains 700 metres (2,300 ft) in height as it leads towards the glacier-covered Ötztal Alps. A short distance up the valley is the stunningly situated village of Ötz with a church dating from the 14th century. Längenfeld is the next village, followed by Sölden, an internationally popular tourist resort during both summer and winter. A few kilometres further up is Zwieselstein, where the Ötztal splits into the Vent and Gurgl valleys. The road to Vent is open in summer only, and is very narrow. Proceeding up the Gurgl valley, you reach Obergurgl – at 1,910 metres/6,266 ft it's the highest village with a church in Austria, and famous for skiing. The road continues up the mountains and crossing into Italy via the Timmelsjoch Pass. South of Obergurgl this road is open from June to October only. The route through the Ötztal is classic Tyrol, with magnificent mountain views. Tourism is well developed, and there is a wide range of accommodation.

valley of the Inn is reached at the large town of **Landeck**. To the south, a mountain road climbs the Reschen Pass into Italy. During the first years of the 19th century plans were made to build a railway along this route, and work was well underway when World War I broke out in 1914; the line was never completed. From here, the track follows the Inn to reach Ötztal, with its beautiful valley running south to the Italian and Swiss borders *(see box)*.

From Ötztal to Innsbruck, the Tyrolean capital

From Ötztal the railway runs along the widening Inn Valley. Just past the town of **Stams** on the right is one of Austria's finest monastery complexes, a 13th-century Cistercian abbey with a superbly restored church. At **Zirl** you can see a steep rock formation to the north – the so-called **Martinswand**, named after St Martin – with the narrow gauge line from Innsbruck to Garmisch-Partenkirchen in Germany threading its way through tunnels beneath it. This line is of special interest since it was the first Austrian electric main line to use single phase alternating current. The success of this new technique in 1912 led to the introduction of this type of electric supply to other lines. Seefeld, 25 km (15 miles) from Innsbruck, is a tourist resort and was the location of the Nordic skiing competitions in the 1964 and 1976 Winter Olympics *(see page 273 for full details of this route)*.

Innsbruck, surrounded by a magnificent ring of high mountain peaks, is the capital of the Tyrol, and makes an excellent base for exploring the region. Its attractions were recognised by Maximilian I, who moved his court here, and the town has managed to preserve the character of its old centre. This is one of the crossroads of Europe, where the east–west route through Austria joins the route from Germany to Italy via the Brenner Pass.

Map on page 240

Star Attractions:
Innsbruck
● **Goldenes Dachl**
balcony
● **Helblinghaus**
● **Hofburg**
● **Hofkirche**
● **Domkirche**
St Jakob
● **Wilten district**
● **Goldener Adler inn**
● **Schloss Ambras**

BELOW: an Italy-bound train near St Jodok.

Early 19th-century metal-working technology at the Blacksmith Museum in Fulpmes.

Innsbruck to Fulpmes

Innsbruck has a metre gauge tramway system and two light railway lines of the same gauge. Whilst the line to Igls, just to the south of Innsbruck, has always been part of the tram system, the 21-km (13-mile) Stubaitalbahn to Fulpmes was constructed by an independent company (in 1904). The Fulpmes railway was originally operated with a/c and only switched to the d/c tram power supply in 1983. Trains to Fulpmes now start at the main railway station and pass via the tram system to Stubaital station, from where the original light railway line starts. There is also the Tiroler Museumsbahnen railway museum *(see page 256)*, and the old shed shelters some of the original a/c railcars. In addition to the regular Innsbruck–Fulpmes trains, there are nostalgic rides on old trams every Wednesday from mid-July to mid-September.

En route to Fulpmes the railway climbs steep slopes which offer good views across Innsbruck and the surrounding mountains. Of these, the Nordkette to the north, have the most impressive peaks: if the view tempts you but you prefer an easy way up, a funicular climbs into the mountains from Hungerberg station in Innsbruck. The Stubaitalbahn continues to the southwest, passing through the villages of Mieders and Telfes with their 18th-century parish churches.

Fulpmes is the pleasant main village of the Stubaital valley, and a good starting point for hiking tours. It has long been known for its iron-workers, and there are still a few riverside workshops today, their hammers powered by the Plövenbach stream: ice axes and crampons from here are highly regarded. The tradition is detailed in the Schmiedemuseum (Blacksmith Museum). From Fulpmes the road eventually reaches the enormous Stubai glacier, a year-round skiing area accessible by funicular from Mutterbergalm, reached by bus from Fulpmes.

BELOW: Innsbruck and its dramatic mountain backdrop.

INNSBRUCK–SALZBURG–LINZ

Map on page 240

This route can be covered in two different ways; the shorter option heads north from Wörgl to take a short-cut through Germany to Salzburg; the scenic route stays within Austrian territory, passing through glorious countryside to Zell am See and Bischofshofen, before turning north to Salzburg. The tracks are reunited for the final stretch to Linz, which traverses the stunning region of Salzkammergut. En route there are various opportunities to take narrow gauge branch lines into the mountains.

The line from Innsbruck to Wörgl is one of Austria's busiest since it is being used both by east–west and north–south traffic flows. Soon after leaving Innsbruck we get to **Hall in Tirol**, where salt was mined until 1968; salt water springs are still used for medicinal treatment. A few kilometres further east, near Baumkirchen, a new railway bridge crosses the river Inn; this is the Innsbruck bypass line which is used by freight trains going directly up the Brenner Pass. After passing Schwaz the train arrives in **Jenbach**, where two scenic branch lines run north and south of the main railway.

The Zillertalbahn

While the Achenseebahn *(see panel below)* runs to the north of Jenbach, the longer 760 mm gauge (and much less steep) Zillertalbahn heads south towards the majestic Zillertal Alps, departing from a separate station adjacent to the ÖBB one. Most of the trains are operated by modern diesel railcars, but certain departures are hauled by steam – these operate up to three times a day during the peak season in summer as well as on certain days during the rest of the year.

ESSENTIALS

Thomas Cook timetable nos. 890, 950, 951, 960

Distance: (1) 382 km (via Zell am See); (2) 323 km (via Rosenheim)

Duration of journey: (1) 5 hrs 4 mins (2) 3 hrs 30 mins

Frequency of trains: (1) 4 daily (change at Salzburg); (2) 6 daily

BELOW: the Achenseebahn rack railway.

THE ACHENSEEBAHN

The metre gauge Achenseebahn rack railway runs 7 km (4 miles) north from Jenbach to the Achensee, at an altitude 400 metres (1,300 ft) higher than the Inn Valley. Journey time is 45 minutes and there are seven daily departures in summer (June–Sept), falling to three in May and October. In 1889 the railway was opened as far as Maurach. Four of the original engines are still used, making them the world's oldest cog-wheel steam locomotives in regular service.

The railway starts outside the main line station and immediately begins to climb steeply. The loco usually pushes one or two antique passenger coaches, some of which have nothing but curtains to cover the open windows. After 4 km (2½ miles) you reach Eben station, where the rack sections ends. Here the loco runs round its train and is coupled to the leading carriage and from here works as an adhesion loco. Passing Maurach, the former terminus, the train follows the line extended in 1916 to reach the boat-cruise pier. The Achensee is the biggest lake in the Tyrol, with a superb mountain setting, and is popular in summer and winter. Maurach is at the southern end of the lake while Pertisau is on the western shore. The train is usually met by a boat that takes passengers for a cruise across the lake.

The Zillertalbahn runs 32 km (20 miles) south from Jenbach to Mayrhofen, through pristine Tyrolean scenery; the journey takes 56 minutes. The line follows the Ziller Valley, hemmed in between the Tux Alps to the west and the Kitzbühel Alps to the east. After passing Fügen and Kaltenbach the train reaches **Zell am Ziller**, centre of the lower Zillertal. Via Hippach the line reaches **Mayrhofen**, the railway's end, from where funiculars offer easy access to the mountains.

Diesel railcar on the Zillertalbahn.

Jenbach to Zell am See

The main east–west line continues east from Jenbach to **Rattenberg**, which has a 15th-century church and a remarkable number of houses of the same age. From the major railway junction at **Wörgl**, the Austrian main line heads to the east, while the Rosenheim and Munich line continues along the River Inn to the north. Be careful when choosing a train to Salzburg: the Innsbruck–Vienna through trains take the shorter route via Germany (ÖBB fares apply) which cuts the journey time by an hour. The line via Zell am See is used by some Innsbruck–Salzburg and Innsbruck–Graz through services and by local trains. If you have time, choose the Zell am See route, the more attractive of the two.

Leaving Wörgl, the railway climbs steadily and passes Hopfgarten and Westendorf. Just before the famous ski resort of **Kitzbühel**, the Schwarzsee can be seen to the north. The Kitzbühler Horn (1,996 metres/6,548 ft) can be reached by a funicular, and offers excellent views all year round. The railway now turns north and as it approaches St Johann you can see the mountains of the Wilder Kaiser to the northwest. The line turns east again and passes Fieberbrunn, marking the start of the climb up the Griessen Pass; many trains need the assistance of an additional locomotive to get over this incline. Having passed the summit, the line drops

BELOW: a steam-hauled train on the Zillertalbahn departs Jenbach for Mayrhofen.

continuously to Saalfelden. To the north there is a good view of the Birnhorn (2,634 metres/8,641 ft). At Saalfelden the track turns south to pass Maishofen, before running along the shores of Zeller See and arriving at **Zell am See** station.

South of Zell am See the main line again turns to the east. **Bruck** is the next major station of interest, where the mountain road to the **Grossglockner** starts. There's a bus to Franz-Josefs-Höhe, from where you can see the top of Austria's highest mountain, the Grossglockner (3,797 metres/12,457 ft). From Bruck the track continues to Schwarzach-St Veit, where it meets the one from Villach, and on to Salzburg via Bischofshofen. The Schwarzach–Salzburg section, and Salzburg itself, are described in the Villach–Salzburg chapter *(see page 253)*.

The Salzkammergut

From Salzburg the main Alpine range is left behind, yet the landscape remains diverting, with smaller mountains and lakes. Several narrow gauge lines meander south into the area of limestone peaks and lakes known as the Salzkammergut, which provided the locations for filming *The Sound of Music*.

The route passes the Wallersee close to Neumarkt and reaches Vöcklamarkt station, beyond Frankenmarkt. Here another narrow gauge railway winds through the hills to Attersee, on the lake of the same name, which is the largest in the area at 20 km (12 miles) long and 3 km (2 miles) wide. The electric railway is run by a private operator, Stern & Hafferl, and connects with boat cruises across the Attersee. Trains run throughout the year, with more frequent services during the peak summer months. Other towns of interest along the shores of the lake are Schörfling in the north, Nußdorf and Unterach in the south.

Back on the main Salzburg–Linz line, Vöcklabruck is a short distance east,

BELOW: street entertainer at Kapitelplatz, Salzburg.

Map on page 240

THE PINZGAUERBAHN

The Pinzgauerbahn narrow gauge line from Zell am See runs for 54 km (34 miles) along the River Salzach, taking 1 hour 45 minutes to reach Krimml. The line is diesel operated but there is a steam-hauled tourist train once a week in summer.

Leaving Zell am See and its picturesque lake, the line heads west, running close to the village of Kaprun, gateway to the year-round skiing paradise of Schmiedinger Kees. Zell am See station rents bikes, and you can take them with you on the train if you don't want to cycle all the way. Mittersill is the centre of the Pinzgau region, with two outstanding baroque churches. The valley now begins to narrow, with good views ahead to the 3,674-metre (12,053-ft) peak of Grossvenediger. From Krimml, take a bus to get to the famous Krimml waterfalls, the highest in Europe. The Krimml River drops about 380 metres (1,246 ft) by means of three cataracts, the most impressive of their kind in Austria. A visit takes around three hours; follow the path through the dense forest to take in each of the seven different viewing points. This line has been damaged by flooding several times in recent years and in mid-2008 was closed for rebuilding between Mittersill and Krimml. Trains were replaced by buses.

Star Attractions:
Salzburg
● **Festung Hohen-**
   salzburg (fortress)
● **Dom (Cathedral)**
● **Residenz (Bishop's**
   Palace)
● **Mozart's birthplace**
● **Mirabell Gardens**
● **Schloss Hellbrunn**

BELOW: the
Schafbergbahn
runs from St
Wolfgang to
Schafbergspitze.

from where another local railway runs south to the Attersee; this line, to Kammer-Schörfling, operates year-round but only runs one passenger train a day, Monday to Saturday. While **Vöcklabruck** is the district's capital, nearby **Attnang-Puch-heim** is the main railway junction. The line north leads to Schärding on the Wels–Passau main line, while that to the south connects to Gmunden and Bad Ischl, joining the main Graz–Innsbruck line at Stainach-Irdning. **Gmunden** is a pleasant town on the Traunsee, while **Bad Ischl** was the summer residence of the Austrian emperors until 1918 and still preserves its imperial atmosphere.

From Attnang-Puchheim the route continues past Schwanenstadt before arriving at Lambach. The latter station has a bypass for fast trains but local trains stop and offer connections to two more local electric railways. The line to the north terminates at Haag while the southern branch ends at Vorchdorf, where you can change trains and continue on a narrow gauge line to Gmunden.

The next major stop on the main line is **Wels**, where trains from Nuremberg and Passau join the Salzburg–Linz–Vienna line. It only takes 15 minutes on an express to complete the final leg to **Linz**, the capital of Oberösterreich province, with a major steel and chemical industry. Fortunately the plants are situated east (downwind) of the centre, and pollution has been greatly reduced in recent years. The centre can be reached easily by tram. Tram route No. 3 crosses the Danube and goes straight to Urfahr, the terminus of one of the steepest adhesion railways in the world. This electric railway goes up the Pöstlingberg, with its large pilgrimage church. The gradient is 10.5 percent and special braking equipment has been fitted for safety reasons. A visit to the Pöstlingberg is highly recommended as it offers a tremendous view across Linz and the River Danube. The line is closed until 2009 for conversion to the same gauge as the city trams.

VIENNA–VILLACH

Map
on page
240

Vienna to Villach trains run on the Südbahn (Southern Railway), opened in stages during the 1840s to link the capital of imperial Austria with the sea ports of the Mediterranean. The line runs along the easternmost slopes of the Alps, the so-called Thermenregion (spa region), famous for its wine as well as its waters.

The old station building at Vienna's Südbahnhof was destroyed in 1945 and its replacement completed in the 1950s. In the central hall stands one of the stone lions surviving from the old station – a San Marco Lion, the symbol of Venice. This will probably be removed during a second rebuilding, designed to integrate the western and southern wings as one through station by 2012. It takes about 10 minutes for an express to emerge from the outskirts of Vienna into open countryside, with vineyards and small villages. It passes through Baden and Bad Vöslau, both of which have hot sulphur springs, before arriving at **Wiener Neustadt**, a major junction 30 minutes from Vienna, and home of the Austrian Military Academy since the days of the Habsburg Empire.

Wiener Neustadt to Hochschneeberg

Several interesting branch lines fan out from Wiener Neustadt, east and south into the Burgenland region, and west to **Puchberg** from where a metre gauge rack railway (the Schneebergbahn) runs up to Hochschneeberg. From Wiener Neustadt hourly departures to Puchberg head into the hills, and you can glimpse Schneeberg rising to 2,076 metres (6,811 ft) ahead. Transfer to the Schnee-bergbahn, where most of the trains are diesel but some steam trains remain. Reservations are obligatory on all services, and can be organised at any major

ESSENTIALS

Thomas Cook
timetable no. 980

Distance: 372 km

Duration of journey:
4 hrs 39 minutes
(fast trains 4 hrs 4
minutes)

Frequency of trains:
11 per day

BELOW: Vienna's
venerable Café
Schwarzenberg.

Star Attractions:
Vienna
● **St Stephen's**
  Cathedral
● **National Opera**
  House
● **Treasury**
● **Belvedere Palace**
● **Spanish Riding**
  School
● **Café Central**

ÖBB station. The track climbs steeply to an intermediate station at Baumgartner, where there is an excellent station buffet. This is where the steam locomotives usually stop to take on water. The final climb leads through a treeless mountain area until you reach **Hochschneeberg**, the highest station in Austria, at 1,792 metres (5,878 ft), with an excellent view. The tracks climb even higher, up to the nearby hotel (Berghaus Hochschneeberg) but are only used to deliver supplies. Various shelters serving meals and drinks are scattered across the Schneeberg, and there are trails down to Puchberg if you want to make your own way back down – allow around 2½ hours for the walk.

The Semmering Pass and trials

From Wiener Neustadt the main line continues southwest to **Gloggnitz**, the starting point of the famous **Semmering Pass**, over which the line gains 457 metres (1,500 ft) in altitude in 29 km (18 miles). When the railway reached Gloggnitz from the north in 1842 and the section from Mürzzuschlag to Bruck an der Mur was opened in 1844, it had still not been decided how to get across the Semmering. Many engineers, including George Stephenson, expressed the opinion that it would be impossible for adhesion locomotives to operate on such a steep slope; possible alternatives included rope inclines (with stationary engines positioned at the summit pulling the wagons up by means of ropes and pulleys), and horse-drawn trams. However, the engineer in charge of completing the line, Carl Ritter von Ghega, was encouraged by his study of the mountain railways of the United States and decided to go ahead with a traditional adhesion railway. Maximum gradients were restricted to 1 in 40, and a total of 16 tunnels and 16 viaducts were necessary to complete the route.

The Semmering line was officially opened on 15 May 1854. Since then the line has been electrified, but otherwise has remained unchanged. Plans to build a base tunnel have long been a subject of political dispute.

Try to get a seat on the left-hand side of the train, for splendid views of the Semmering area. The town of **Semmering** was a well-known resort until the 1930s, but never recovered from World War II. Some of the old hotels, however, have been restored and the town remains popular with skiers.

Mürzzuschlag to Unzmarkt

From Mürzzuschlag to Villach the line runs through the Mürztal region, following the long valley of the Mürz and Mur rivers. This area was industrialised during the 19th century with the help of the railway, and steelworks and other industrial plants are in evidence all the way to **Bruck an der Mur**. At Bruck the main line splits into two, one branch leading to Graz, the capital of the province of Styria, and the other continuing to Villach and on to Italy. On the Villach line, the next stop is **Leoben**, centre of the iron industry. The branch line from Leoben to Vordernberg is now closed to passenger services. A new tunnel – the Galgenberg – has been built west of Leoben and only a few local passenger trains use the original line via Leoben Göss, the home of a famous brand of Austrian beer. From St Michael, fast trains run to Linz and Bischofshofen.

BELOW: Klamm Castle, near the Semmering Pass.

Having passed Bruck, the tracks follow the River Mur through another industrial area, with steel works at Judenburg and Zeltweg, while Knittelfeld is the home of a repair works owned by ÖBB. Fans of motor racing probably already know that the Austrian Formula 1 Grand Prix takes place near Zeltweg.

A few kilometres after passing Judenburg, **Teufenbach** marks the point where the line to Villach leaves the River Mur and begins its ascent into the beautiful southern province of Carinthia. There are several castles in the vicinity of this small village, which dates from the 12th century.

Map on page 240

Along the Murtalbahn

At Unzmarkt, a narrow gauge railway, the Murtalbahn, runs for 65 km (40 miles) along the upper Mur Valley to the town of Tamsweg, through a popular holiday area – the tourist traffic has ensured the survival of the line. The Murtalbahn has been built to the gauge of 760 mm, the standard for most Austrian narrow gauge lines, and is run by the Steiermärkische Landesbahnen, which also operates other branch lines in the province of Styria. Most trains are modern and diesel-powered, although steam trains operate in the summer months between Murau and Tamsweg. In fact, the railway has been among the Austrian pioneers of steam operations on tourist lines, and self-driving courses with steam locos are also on offer.

The upper Mur Valley enjoys a healthy climate, milder than that found further east, and its idyllic villages make an ideal base for hiking in the wooded hills. Having passed Teufenbach *(see above)*, trains pull into **Murau** station, 45 minutes from Unzmarkt. Murau is the capital of this section of the Mur Valley, and a centre for Nordic sports. The line from Murau to Tamsweg is especially scenic, with excellent views. The main point of interest in **Tamsweg**, one hour

Drivers' cabins have become far more comfortable over the years.

BELOW:
a stiff climb up the Semmering Pass.

from Murau (steam trains take an extra 45 minutes), is the pilgrimage church of St Leonhard, with 15th-century stained glass. The railway once continued to **Mauterndorf** but it was neglected and closed down by the authorities several years ago. However, a private society has preserved the line and now operates tourist trains during the summer.

Castles and casinos

At Friesach the main Vienna–Villach line enters Carinthia, Austria's southern-most province, with an almost Mediterranean climate in the summer. At Treibach-Althofen you can see a narrow gauge track along the main line, the first 3 km (2 miles) of which have been preserved as a museum line, leading to Pöckstein castle. As you approach **St Veit an der Glan**, there are views of the spectacular Hochosterwitz Castle, perched on a rock outcrop to the left. At St Veit a secondary line heads directly to Villach along Ossiacher See.

Express trains take the geographically longer (but actually quicker) route via **Klagenfurt**, the capital of Carinthia. This town has an interesting centre with a 16th-century cathedral and the seat of local government which was built at the same time. Klagenfurt is situated at the eastern edge of the **Wörther See**, the most famous of the Carinthian lakes; the waters are particularly warm in summer, making it extremely popular for swimming. The railway runs along the northern shore of the lake, giving great views across the clear waters. Steam-ship tours are available in summer. Resorts line the shore; **Velden** with its casino is the best known. At Velden the lake is left behind; a few minutes later, entering **Villach**, you can see the remains of Landskron Castle up on a hill to the right. It dates from Roman times, and most of its medieval walls still exist.

First-class carriage on the Vienna to Villach express.

BELOW: the resort of Maria Worth on the south shore of the Wörther See.

VILLACH–SALZBURG

Villach is a major railway junction, located at the point where the Vienna–Venice line joins the Salzburg–Ljubljana line for a few kilometres. The journey north to Salzburg passes close to Austria's highest mountains.

The Salzburg line heads northwest from Villach, following the River Drau to **Spittal an der Drau**, where a picturesque line turns west to Lienz in the Osttirol, eventually reaching the Italian town of Fortezza on the main Innsbruck–Verona route. Spittal has an interesting town centre; the major sight, Porcia Castle, is said to be the most important Florentine-style building in Austria. Its court is used for open-air festivals. The **Millstätter See** is situated east of Spittal, and there are splendid views across the lake from surrounding mountains, although, unfortunately, one mountain hides the lake from the view of train passengers.

Spittal to the Tauern Tunnel

Northwest of Spittal the railway leaves the valley of the Drau and starts climbing. This stretch of line began operating in 1909 as a single track, but most sections have now been doubled as far as Mallnitz-Obervellach. Near Oberfalkenstein the train crosses a wide bridge with an excellent view of the remains of Oberfalkenstein Castle. Soon afterwards it enters a new tunnel (opened in 1999), then runs across the Kaponig Viaduct, immediately after which another tunnel extends as far as Mallnitz-Obervellach. The old line via Kaponig has now been abandoned. **Mallnitz**, the last station before the railway crosses the Tauern mountains on its way north, is a winter sports resort and a starting point for hiking tours in the region. For those who want to

Map
on page
240

ESSENTIALS

Thomas Cook
timetable no. 970

Distance: 188 km

Duration of journey:
2 hrs 35 mins

Frequency of trains:
9 per day

BELOW: the
blue waters of
Millstätter See.

Thermal therapy at Bad Gastein, Austria's best-known spa.

spend a day in the mountains without the effort of actually climbing them, there is a funicular railway – reached by a regular bus service from Mallnitz station – towards the Ankogel (3,246 metres/10,649 ft). A few kilometres north of Mallnitz the train enters the 8.5-km (5¼-mile) Tauern Tunnel. Since there are no roads north of Mallnitz, ÖBB operates a car shuttle to Böckstein.

Hot springs and spa towns

The weather is often quite different at the northern end of the tunnel, from where the line reaches the Gastein Valley, well known for its thermal springs. The therapeutic qualities of the springs have been noted since at least the 15th century. **Böckstein**, the first town north of the tunnel, has no hot springs, but in an abortive 1940s attempt to mine gold here it was discovered that the hot and humid atmosphere inside the mountain was a beneficial treatment for rheumatism. Since 1952 the mine tunnel has been used for therapy for those with rheumatic complaints. Trains run to the mine from Böckstein every two hours. The 600 mm gauge line is operated by electric locos.

The most important town in the valley is **Bad Gastein**, which has been a flourishing spa for many decades and these days doubles as a ski resort. The hot springs contain radon gas, again beneficial for treating rheumatic complaints. It is also possible to swim in the Felsenbad pools – both indoor and outdoor (the water is hot enough to make a mid-winter dip tolerable in the latter). As the main centre of the valley, Bad Gastein has numerous well-established hotels. A walk along the Kaiser Wilhelm Promenade is recommended for the fine views it offers across the town and its surroundings.

Further north is the modern thermal resort of **Bad Hofgastein**, followed by Dorfgastein, a village favoured by those who like to get away from the bustle of the spa resorts. North from here the railway descends a steep incline with stunning views over the River Salzach, to reach **Schwarzach-St Veit**, another major railway junction. The line from Villach joins the Wörgl–Saalfelden–Salzburg line, the only rail track that connects the Tyrol with the central and eastern parts of Austria without running through Germany. Its importance has now been reduced, as the European Union has rendered certain borders almost obsolete. The line via Schwarzach-St Veit is still important for freight traffic, however, and the section to Salzburg is part of the route to Villach that plays a major role in traffic from Germany to Carinthia as well as to Slovenia and Croatia.

Schwarzach-St Veit to Hallein

Heading north to Salzburg the train soon reaches the Pongau region, passing the castle of Goldegg on the left before arriving at **St Johann im Pongau**, a small town with one major attraction. Just to the south of the town, the walls of the **Liechtensteinklamm** gorge extend 300 metres (985 ft) but in places are only a couple of metres apart. The word "narrow" does not do it justice. A hiking trail (which takes about 20 minutes), in places blasted through the rock, reaches into the gorge, eventually leading through a tunnel to reach a 65-metre (212-ft) waterfall.

Bischofshofen, 6 km (4 miles) up the line, is the next village; like many other places in the area, it functions as both a summer and winter resort. On the next stretch to Golling the railway runs through an extremely narrow section of the Salzach Valley, the so-called Pass Lueg. The spectacular castle of Burg Hohenwerfen can be seen high above the valley, near the village of Werfen. Close to the village of Golling are the impressive Gollinger waterfalls, plunging 62 metres (203 ft).

Map on page 240

Salt mines to Salzburg

The next major stop is **Hallein**, right on the German border. Salt contributed to the wealth of the region for 3,000 years until mining came to an end in 1989; in the past this was one of the most valuable possessions of the archbishops of Salzburg. The entire mining area has now been converted into a museum (Apr–Oct 9am–5pm; Nov–Dec 11am–3pm; entrance fee) and the railway lines inside the mountain have been retained. The mine entrance can easily be reached by means of a funicular which starts right in the centre of Hallein. The guided tour of the mines is enjoyable and informative, and takes around 90 minutes. Visitors enter the mine complex on the narrow gauge underground railway, slide down a chute on a toboggan (popular with children), and take a boat trip across an illuminated underground lake.

From Hallein it is just 19 km (12 miles) to **Salzburg**, one of Austria's major visitor attractions. It is the birthplace of Mozart (1756–91) and has a prestigious classical music festival. From the Hohensalzburg fortress there are magnificent views across the town and its many churches. *(For a list of the city's main attractions see page 248.)* ❑

BELOW: Mozart souvenirs in Salzburg.

Museums and Heritage Lines

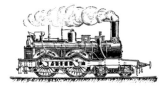

Austria has a large number of railway museums and heritage lines for its size. The numbers relate to the map on page 240.

Museums

Eisenbahnmuseum Strasshof ❶
Sillerstrasse 123, A-2231 Strasshof (25 km/15 miles northeast of Vienna)
Open: Apr–Oct Tue–Sun 10am–4pm
Features: largest Austrian railway museum, national collection, shop, buffet
Nearest station: Silberwald (Line S1)
Tel: 02287 302711
www.eisenbahnmuseum-heizhaus.com

Eisenbahnmuseum Schwechat ❷
Schwechat station, A-2300 Schwechat
Open: May–Oct Sat 1–6pm, Sun 10am–5pm
Features: shop, narrow gauge line with working steam, standard and narrow gauge railway vehicles
Nearest station: Schwechat
Tel: 01 368 15103
www.eisenbahnmuseum-schwechat.at

Wiener Tramwaymuseum ❸
Holochergasse 24, A-1150 Wien
Open: May–Oct Sat–Sun 9am–4pm
Features: shop, biggest tram museum in the world
Tel: 01 786 0303
www.tram.at

Feld- und Industriebahn-museum ❹
Maierhof 8, A-3183 Freiland
Open: Apr–Oct Sun 10am–4pm
Features: shop, buffet, industrial railway museum with working steam on 600-mm gauge
Nearest station: Freiland
Tel: 0664 274 9113
www.feldbahn.at

Waldviertler Eisenbahnmuseum Sigmundsherberg ❺
Bahnstrasse 12, A-3751 Sigmundsherberg
Open: all year daily 9am–4pm
Features: standard gauge rolling stock exhibits
Nearest station: Sigmundsherberg
Tel: 0676 363 2858 or 02983 230 7379
http://195.58.166.60/noemuseen/ansicht_detail.asp?nr=70

Salzkammergut Lokalbahn SKGLB Museum ❻
A-5310 Mondsee
Open: June–Sept weekends 10am–noon, 2–5pm
Features: shop, preserved narrow gauge steam locos
Nearest station: Salzburg Hbf
Tel: 06232 2270
www.ischlerbahn.at.tf

Tramway Museum Graz ❼
Mariatrosterstraße 204, A-8044 Graz
Open: June–Sept Sun 2–6pm
Features: collection of tram vehicles
Nearest station: Graz Hauptbahnhof
Tel: 0316 887 401
www.gvb.at

Eisenbahnmuseum Knittelfeld ❽
Ainbachallee 14, A-8720 Knittelfeld
Open: all year Tue–Sun 9am–5pm
Features: shop, standard gauge exhibits, garden railway (May–Oct Sat–Sun)
Nearest station: Knittelfeld
Tel: 03512 83893
http://members.e-media.at/eisenbahnmuseum-knittelfeld

Club 760, Eisenbahnmuseum Frojach ❾
P.O. Box 51, A-8850 Murau
Open: sporadically; trains run July–Aug Tue–Wed
Features: shop, exhibition of narrow gauge steam locomotives
Nearest station: Frojach-Katschtal
Tel: 06472 7088
www.club760.at

Tiroler Museumsbahnen ❿
Pater Reinischweg 4, A-6020 Innsbruck
Open: May–Oct Sat 9am–5pm
Features: shop, tram and light railway museum
Nearest station: Innsbruck Hauptbahnhof
Tel: 0664 111 6001
www.tmb.at

Heritage lines

Liliputbahn Prater ⓫
Prater 99, A-1020 Wien
Open: Apr–Oct daily; steam Sat–Sun
Features: park railway with steam and diesel locos
Nearest station: Wien Nord
Length: 2.5 km (1½ miles)
Gauge: 381 mm
Tel: 1 7268236
www.liliputbahn.com

Museumsbahn Payerbach-Hirschwang ⓬
ÖGLB, Poschgasse 6, A-1140 Wien
Open: June–Sept Sun
Features: narrow gauge museum railway with diesel and electric locos
Nearest station: Payerbach-Reichenau
Length: 5.9 km (4 miles)
Gauge: 760 mm
Tel: 02666 52423
www.lokalbahnen.at/haellentalbahn

Museumsbahn Kienberg-Gaming-Lunz ⓭
NÖLB, Im Markt 1, A-3292 Gaming
Open: June–Sept weekends

Features: shop, narrow gauge
museum railway
Nearest station: Kienberg-Gaming
Length: 17.4 km (11 miles)
Gauge: 760 mm
Tel: 07416 53087
www.lokalbahnen/bergstrecke

**Waldviertler Schmals-
purverein** ⑭
Bahnhofstrasse 59,
A-3871 Altnagelberg
Open: weekends and Wed,
June–Sept
Features: museum railway
Nearest station: Gmünd
Length: 38 km (24 miles)
Gauge: 760 mm
Tel: 0680 125 3003
www.erlebnisbahn.at/wsv/

**Museumsbahn Ampflwang-
Timelkam** ⑮
ÖGEG, Postfach 11, A-4018 Linz
Open: May–Oct Wed–Sun 10am–
5pm; trains run Sun July–mid-
Sept
Features: shop, restaurant,
museum, steam and diesel trains
Nearest station: Timelkam
Length: 11 km (7 miles)
Gauge: 1,435 mm
Tel: 0664 615394
www.oegeg.at

Steyrtal Museumsbahn ⑯
ÖGEG, as above
Open: May–Sept weekends
Features: shop, buffet, steam
operated museum railway
Nearest station: Steyr
Length: 17 km (10½ miles)
Gauge: 760 mm
Tel: 0664 5087 664
www.oegeg.at

Club Florianerbahn ⑰
Alter Bahnhof, A-4490 St Florian
Open: May–Sept Sun
Features: shop, museum tram to
Pichling (suspended in 2008)
Nearest station: Linz Hbf (then
tram)
Length: 7 km (4 miles)
Gauge: 900 mm
Tel: 664-820 84 81
www.florianerbahn.at

Museumstramway Mariazell ⑱
An der Museumsbahn 5,
A-8630 St Sebastian-Mariazell
Open: July–Sept weekends
Features: shop, museum tram line
to Erlaufsee
Nearest station: Mariazell
Length: 2.5 km (1½ miles)
Gauge: 1,435 mm
Tel: 03882 3014
www.museumstramway.at

**Museumsbahn Vordernberg –
Eisenerz** ⑲
Viktor-Zack Strasse 1,
A-8794 Vordernberg
Open: July–Sept weekends
Features: shop, museum trains
Vordernberg to Eisenerz
Nearest stations: Leoben Hbf
Length: 18.5 km (11½ miles)
Gauge: 1,435 mm
Tel: 03849 832
www.erzbergbahn.at

**Feistritztalbahn Betriebsge-
sellschaft** ⑳
Hauptplatz 13,
A-8190 Birkfeld
Open: mid-June–Oct various
Mon, Thur and weekends
Features: shop, buffet, steam
excursions Weiz–Birkfeld
Nearest station: Weiz
Length: 24 km (15 miles)
Gauge: 760 mm
Tel: 03174 4507-20
www.feistritztal.at

Museumsbahn Stainz ㉑
A-8510 Stainz
Open: May–Oct weekends
Features: shop, buffet, museum
line to Preding-Wieselsdorf
Nearest station: Preding-
Wieselsdorf
Length: 11.4 km (7 miles)
Gauge: 760 mm
Tel: 03463 5500
www.erlebnisbahn.at

**Gurkthalbahn-Kärntner
Museumsbahn** ㉒
A-9330 Althofen
Open: July–Sept weekends
Features: shop, museum line to
Pöckstein-Zwischenwässern

Nearest station: Treibach-
Althofen
Length: 3 km (2 miles)
Gauge: 760 mm
Tel: 0664-17 07 136
www.gurkthalbahn.at

Nostalgiebahnen in Kärnten
㉓
NBiK, A-9028 Klagenfurt,
Postfach 27
Open: July–Sept weekends
Features: shop, restaurant,
museum line to Ferlach
Nearest station: Weizelsdorf
Length: 6 km (3¾ miles)
Gauge: 1,435 mm
Tel: 0463 740368
www.erlebnisbahn.at/nbik

Taurachbahn ㉔
A-5570 Mauterndorf 53
Open: July–Aug weekends
Features: shop, museum line to St
Andrä
Nearest station: Tamsweg
Length: 10 km (6 miles)
Gauge: 760 mm
Tel: 06472 7088 or 7949
www.club760.at/html/
Taurachbahn.htm

**Bregenzerwald
Museumsbahn** ㉕
Nr. 39, A-6941 Langenegg
Open: mid-May–early Oct
weekends
Features: shop, museum line
Bezau-Bersbuch
Nearest station: Bregenz
Length: 6 km (3¾ miles)
Gauge: 760 mm
Tel: 0664 4662330
www.waelderbaehnle.at

Rheinschauen ㉖
Höchster Strasse 4
A-6893 Lustenau
Open: May–Oct Fri–Sun
Features: electric-hauled excur-
sions (occasional steam) on
industrial narrow gauge line
Nearest station: Lustenau
Length: 10 km (6 miles)
Gauge: 750 mm
Tel: 05577 20539
www.rheinschauen.at

Meals on Wheels

The prospect of sitting down to enjoy a proper meal in the restaurant car, with the scenery rolling past the window, is part of the romance and pleasure of train travel. Sadly it is becoming more elusive, as the blinkered outlook of the "profit-centre" mentality insists that nothing can be a loss-leader. Making money by providing a full restaurant service is undoubtedly a challenge, but quality food and service encourages passengers not only to time their journey to avail themselves of a meal, but also to take the train in the first place.

In the days when rail held a virtual monopoly of long-distance travel – an era when people tended to eat more formally – all international and many domestic trains had full dining facilities with white table linen and silver-plated cutlery. Today is the age of the pizza, baguette or burger, but in some countries there are still remarkably good restaurant services on trains. The spirit of the past is still alive and well

on nostalgic luxury trains such as the Venice Simplon-Orient Express and the Royal Scotsman, where passengers pay an inclusive fare for one or more days' journey. Great emphasis is placed, and no expense spared, on dining in style on these trains.

Away from the luxury tourist market, trains throughout Europe tend to fall into four types – high speed (often on dedicated new lines or routes); traditional express trains; semi-fast; and local trains. While the different systems vary enormously in the scope and quality of catering, some provision is usually made in the first three types.

Thomas Cook's European Rail Timetable lists dining facilities under two categories – "Restaurant Car" and "Snacks and Drinks Available" – vague, but a good starting point. Trains in some countries provide nothing but snacks, even on long-distance journeys. It is incredible that France, that land of gastronomic delights, has no restaurant cars of its own. The TGV has an enviable reputation for speed and reliability, but catering remains a weak point: all the TGV, Eurostar and Thalys operations have a small buffet counter, which frequently sells out, and/or a trolley, which does not always reach the far end of the train. Lyria, Eurostar and Thalys – which are effectively TGVs operating from France to Switzerland, the UK, Germany and the Netherlands – serve acceptable meals at tables but only in first class.

Top marks for a full-meal service must go to Austria, Germany and Switzerland, whose catering is of a high standard on a large proportion of trains. The German menus tend to be a little predictable, but the food is well prepared and nicely presented. In all cases, the dining carriages are modern and attractive. The German ICE now runs through to Paris, contrasting with the TGV on a parallel route which serves only snacks.

In Italy, Britain, Spain and Portugal, Cook's timetable will reveal that restaurant cars (as opposed to buffets offering snacks) only operate on a limited number of routes. In Spain the AVE services from Madrid to the south include a meal in the club-class fare. Italy still has a restaurant car service on many services, including Eurostar Italia, InterCity and Cisalpino. Italian railways still usually provide a hand-written daily menu, very much in the

LEFT: table for two on the Orient Express

hands of the chef. In all these countries food is cooked on the train, with the Italians and Austrians probably having the best chefs.

Since the demise of British Rail, dining facilities on British trains have varied greatly. National Express East Coast (London–Leeds–Newcastle–Edinburgh) provides a good menu and tends to be flexible about serving times (not usually a British feature). In most other countries, except Italy, service is "on demand".

First Great Western has several full dining car trains on Monday to Friday between London and Plymouth, and on the London to South Wales service. It is a British peculiarity to serve full meals only on weekdays, as other European countries offer a seven-day service.

Other British rail companies providing dining services include East Midland Trains (London–Sheffield), which offer an all-day menu for first-class passengers, and Virgin Trains on the West Coast line (to and from London's Euston Station), which offer breakfast on morning trains, and afternoon tea and dinner on certain services, again to first-class passengers only. National Express (London–Norwich and London–Glasgow) are more democratic: breakfast, lunch and dinner in their dining cars are available to all passengers.

Places in dining cars are always limited, whichever country you are travelling in.

Less substantial meals are served in Ireland, the Czech Republic, Hungary, Slovakia, Poland and some other ex-communist bloc countries. Finland and Norway both have a limited range of light meals. In all these countries, improvements are taking place but, with the growth of contract catering, the situation can change rapidly.

Trains that cross international frontiers and carry a restaurant car may belong to any of the countries through which they travel. Thus, in France, for example, you may have every confidence in an ICE train which is part of the German network. In the smaller countries such as Belgium, Luxembourg, the Netherlands and Denmark journeys are usually short and a buffet suffices, but international trains serving these countries (except Denmark) may have facilities for meals, and these will be indicated in Cook's timetable. In all cases, where there is a full dining car, lighter refreshments can also be obtained in the restaurant car or from a separate buffet or trolley.

On Europe's overnight trains it was once customary to enjoy a full dinner in the restaurant car before retiring to bed. The gradual withdrawal of dining facilities on such trains has been going on for decades, but the introduction of luxury night trains in recent years has at least partly reversed the trend; on City Night Line (CNL) services in mainland Europe and the Trenhotel system in Spain, a reasonable dinner can be enjoyed in a proper dining car: the overnight hotel trains that operate on the Paris–Madrid and Madrid–Lisbon routes offer full restaurant facilities. City Night Line services operate between Germany, Switzerland and Austria; Trenhotel services run between Madrid, Barcelona and Paris. Again, meals should be reserved in advance.

One of the most sublime railway dining experiences in the world is on the trans-Alpine *Glacier Express* from Zermatt to St Moritz in Switzerland *(see picture on page 197)*, on which a full lunch is served; the wine glasses have bent stems, to compensate for the steep gradients. Wonderful views and excellent food and make this a meal to remember. ❏

GERMANY

Speed, comfort and reliability are hallmarks of the impressive German rail network, complemented on many lines by attractive mountain, forest and river scenery

Map on page 262

From the opening of the first railway in Germany in 1835 (between Nürnberg and Fürth), railway construction proceeded rapidly, and by the end of the century the network covered a total of almost 64,000 km (40,000 miles). Three German states owned their railways from the outset – Baden, Oldenburg and Württemberg – while the private railways in the five others – Bavaria, Hesse, Mecklenburg, Prussia and Saxony – were gradually taken over by their states during the last quarter of the 19th century. The legacy of this individuality can still be seen in the variety of designs of station buildings.

The companies owned by the various states were amalgamated in 1921 to form Deutsche Reichsbahn (DR); the name was retained by East German railways after World War II, those of the West being renamed Deutsche Bundesbahn (DB). The railways had played a central role during the conflict, taking supplies over progressively extended supply routes to the front line. By the end of the war, the damage inflicted on the railways had been severe, but reconstruction and major programmes of electrification quickly restored the network.

Challenges of reunification

Reunification in 1990 presented a huge challenge. There was an urgent need to integrate the two networks, to reinstate east–west links severed by the Iron Curtain. The formal merger of DB and DR as a federally-owned public limited company finally took place in 1994. Limited privatisation is planned.

The greatest changes have been in Berlin, where the separate systems had to be amalgamated. The new interchange between north–south and east–west routes at a new Hauptbahnhof opened in 2006 is one of the most significant changes. Other investment has resulted in impressive new trains for cross-country and branch line services.

The quality of German trains is among the best in the world. Sleek new InterCity Express (ICE) high-speed trains were introduced in 1991 and quickly won traffic from air and road. The next levels of services are InterCity (IC) and InterRegio (IR) trains, supplemented by local trains and tram networks; some operate over railway tracks and lines in city-centre streets. Even on secondary routes trains are of a standard that eclipses the mainline trains of many other countries.

There are plenty of scenic journeys, in addition to those described in this chapter. Others include Arnstadt–Meiningen (through the Thüringer Wald); routes in the southwest around the Black Forest; beautiful river scenery along the Neckar (Heidelberg to Heilbronn); the upper reaches of the Danube (Ulm to Tuttlingen); and coastal scenery near the Danish border (Niebüll to Westerland).

LEFT: Cologne station and Cathedral. **BELOW:** Berlin's ultra-modern Hauptbahnhof.

COLOGNE–FRANKFURT-AM-MAIN

Map
on page
265

Cologne (Köln) takes its name from Colonia Agrippina, third wife of the Emperor Claudius who founded a colony here in AD 51, which later became a prosperous religious, artistic and intellectual centre, thanks to its position on the trade routes around the River Rhine. The station is in the heart of the old town, right next to the famous cathedral.

The section of the Rhine between Cologne and Frankfurt-am-Main is one of the best-known stretches of river in Europe, largely because a railway along each bank provides a marvellous way to appreciate the scenic splendours of this busy waterway. As with the Mosel between Trier and Koblenz, the sky is constantly pricked by the spires, turrets and bartizans of real and mock castles which can often be seen only from the railway on the opposite bank and are therefore described in the "opposite" text *(see Stations for Castles panel, page 266)*. Many of the riverside villages are full of delightful timber-framed houses and inns.

The incessant barge and pleasure-boat traffic – which includes the paddle-steamer *Goethe* – adds to the interest of the journey. The area is also famous for its wine; vineyards predominate on the west- and south-facing slopes.

West Bank route

The exit from Cologne takes the train almost underneath the broadcasting tower and through unremarkable country to the capital of the former West Germany, **Bonn**. Following parliament's move to Berlin, the birthplace of Beethoven (in 1770) still has some ministries and fine museums, including the Rheinisches Landesmuseum which provides a good introduction to the area. The suburb of **Bad Godesberg** is dominated by the ruins of a 13th-century castle.

Remagen is remembered as the place where US troops first crossed the Rhine, over the Erpel Bridge. The bridge collapsed but the remains house a Peace Museum. **Brohl** is the junction for the metre gauge Brohtal-Schmalspureisenbahn line to Engeln, reached by a rack section further up the line *(see page 285)*, and medieval, walled **Andernach** clusters around the Mariendom Cathedral. There is an impressive view of the old town to the east as the train approaches **Koblenz** *(see page 265)*.

Just south of **Königsbach**, the River Lahn joins the Rhine from the east, overlooked by the uninspiring bulk of Lahneck Castle, whose walls were defended by the last of the Knights Templar. The next hill is crowned by the soaring central tower and surrounding buildings of Marksburg Castle, the only Rhenish castle that withstood siege during the Thirty Years War.

Situated on the outer curve of a bend, **Boppard** has fine views of the river and is a good base for walking up the six valleys that converge on the pretty village. Just to the south, on the east bank, are the adjacent ruins of Sterrenberg and Liebenstein castles, known as the hostile brothers. To their south is Deurenberg Castle, nicknamed Maus, immediately followed by Katz Castle, which can be seen as you approach the famous bend at **Loreley** with its tower-

ESSENTIALS

Thomas Cook
timetable nos. 800,
802, 912, 914

Distance: 219 km
(226 km East bank)

Duration of journey:
2 hrs 14 mins
(3 hrs 45 mins East
bank)

Frequency of trains:
hourly (direct);
change at Koblenz on
East bank route

BELOW: Bonn
station *circa* 1900.

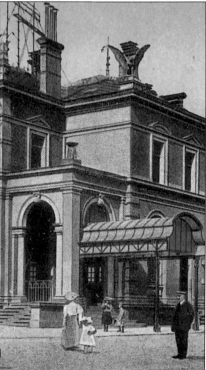

Star Attractions:
Cologne

● **Cathedral**
● **Alter Markt**
● **Rathaus (town hall)**
● **Alte Pinakothek**
● **Roman-Germanic Museum**

ing mass of basalt, 132 metres (433 ft) high. The treacherous currents as the Rhine rounds the Loreley cliffs are notoriously dangerous, and the river has been dredged to create safe channels.

After the attractive town of **Oberwesel** there is a good view of ruined Gutenfels Castle, once taken by the Swedish, above Kaub on the east bank. Inside the town wall of **Bacharach** lies a gem of a medieval village and, above the town, a hostel occupies the 12th-century castle of Stahleck. Above **Niederheimbach** are the remnants of the early 13th-century Fürstenberg Castle, destroyed by the French in 1689. The famous bend at **Bingen** has for a century or more been the place where passengers exchanged the train for a steamer or vice versa. The town is associated with the extraordinary Abbess Hildegard of Bingen – visionary, naturalist, playwright, poetess and composer – who spent most of her 81 years in nearby Benedictine monasteries (a Berlin–Frankfurt express was named after her). Approaching the station, the railway crosses the River Nahe; opposite the town are the twin-towered remains of Ehrenfels Castle.

Leaving Bingen, a large-plinthed statue of Germania stands above the vineyards on the opposite bank. Unveiled in 1883, it commemorates the reunification of Germany in 1871 following the Franco-Prussian War. The railway moves away out of sight of the river, through an area of orchards and market gardens, to **Mainz**, centre of Germany's wine trade. It was here that Gutenberg developed the printing process, commemorated in a museum named after him. The Romanesque cathedral and the old town are also worth visiting.

The short, remaining part of the journey to the immense station serving the country's commercial capital of **Frankfurt-am-Main** is increasingly urban, although the line skirts the forests that lie to the south of the city.

BELOW: Bacharach dates from medieval times.

The scenic east-bank route

The slower east-bank route from Cologne to Koblenz reaches the Rhine at **Bonn-Oberkassel**, where only a cycle path lies between the railway and the water. Vines and orchards replace commuter housing as the train passes the attractive resorts of Königswinter and Bad Honnef. To the south of **Erpel** is the dark stone ruin of Ockenfels. The railway climbs briefly to a higher level near **Linz**, junction for a rack railway up to Kalenborn, but soon returns to river level. As the train passes **Bad Hönningen**, the imposing castle of Rheineck can be seen above the village of Brohl on the west bank.

Approaching the many-spired panorama of **Koblenz**, the projecting spit of land where the Mosel and Rhine meet bears the immense, 36.6-metre (120-ft) equestrian statue of Emperor Wilhelm I, erected in 1897. At **Ehrenbreitstein**, Koblenz's principal east bank station, is the fortress built by the Prussians in 1816 on the site of a castle that dates back to 486 and the time of the Franks.

Shortly after **Niederlahnstein** the line to Giessen turns to the east and the railway crosses the Lahn near its confluence with the Rhine. On the opposite bank is the first of a procession of castles, the huge yellow-ochre bulk of Stolzenfels, where Queen Victoria once stayed. Now a museum, the castle was built in 1244, destroyed in 1689, then restored by Kaiser Wilhelm IV in 1836–42. **Oberlahnstein** has two castles: a small one by the station and a larger, white-walled fortress near the river. The next section of line, following the meander past the wisteria-clad station at **Osterspai**, is one of the loveliest stretches of the journey, with a stone-protected and tree-lined island in the braided river.

At **St Goarshausen** there is a view of the vast ruin of the 13th-century castle of Rheinfels above St Goar on the west bank, once the strongest fortress on the

Map below

TIP

The Drachenfelsbahn is Germany's oldest rack railway, opened in 1883. Take the train to Bonn Hauptbahnhof, then tram line U66 to Bad Honnef. Alight at Königswinter Fahre, from where it is a 10-minute walk to the Drachenfelsbahn in Drachenfelstrasse.

BELOW: the Loreley of legend.

Köln-Frankfurt/Trier-Giessen

Die Loreley.

Die schönste Jungfrau sitzet
Dort oben wunderbar,
Ihr goldnes Geschmeide blitzet,
Sie kämmt ihr goldenes Haar.

Sie kämmt es mit goldenem Kamm
Und singt ein Lied dabei
Das hat eine wundersame,
Gewaltige Melodei.

Star Attractions:

Frankfurt-am-Main

● Römer (town hall)
● Sachsenhausen district
● Historisches Museum
● Palmgarten
● Paulskirche

BELOW: Oberwesel station, access point for Schönburg Castle.

Rhine. After passing a small harbour you get a glimpse of the crenellated portal of Loreley Tunnel, which is followed by Roßstein Tunnel at a bend in the river. Emerging, the multi-turreted castle of Gutenfels looks down on the village of Oberwesel, opposite.

For a change, the next castle is right in the middle of the river, situated on an island at **Kaub**; the 11th-century Pfalz was built to collect customs tolls. A statue of Field-Marshal Blücher, of Waterloo fame, overlooks the main street to commemorate his crossing of the Rhine here in 1813. The partly-habitable castle of Schönburg, with its large cylindrical tower, appears on the opposite bank, south of Oberwesel, followed by the ruined castle of Fürstenberg to the north of Niederheimbach, opposite **Lorch**. North of **Aßmannshausen** and before the bend at Bingen is Rheinstein Castle, built on a prominent rock. Aßmannshausen itself is a pretty village with some good hotels. The cream and ochre-red fort of Mäuseturm stands on an island just north of the confluence of the River Nahe with the Rhine at Bingen, where both railways follow the river in its turn to the east.

Shortly after the popular resort of **Rüdesheim** the railway leaves the river, and the hills of the Rheingaugebirge to the north recede and become lower, allowing the first extensive views since entering the Rhine gorge. East of **Hattenheim**, its handsome station building decorated with coats of arms, is the oldest town of the Rheingau, **Eltville**, with many 16th- and 17th-century townhouses and a castle. Vines cover the gently undulating surrounding countryside.

Trains enter the terminus at **Wiesbaden**, the capital city of Hesse, before reversing for the final part of the journey to **Frankfurt-am-Main**. As the royal spa town in the 19th century, Wiesbaden has numerous fine buildings associated with the thermal waters as well as a novel water-operated rack railway up the Neroberg.

STATIONS FOR CASTLES

Castle (bank)	Station
Ehrenfels (East bank)	Aßmannshausen
Fürstenberg (West)	Niederheimbach
Godesburg (West)	Bad Godesburg
Gutenfels (East)	Kaub
Katz (East)	St Goarshausen
Lahneck (East)	Oberlahnstein
Liebenstein (East)	Kestert
Marksburg (East)	Braubach
Maus (East)	St Goarshausen
Nollich (East)	Lorch
Oberwesel (West)	Oberwesel
Pfalz (East)	Kaub
Reichenstein (West)	Trechtingshausen
Rheineck (Wes)	Brohl
Rheinfels (West)	St Boar
Rheinstein (West)	Trechtingshausen
Schönburg (West)	Oberwesel
Sooneck (West)	Niederheimbach
Stahleck (West)	Bacharach
Sterrenberg (East)	Kestert
Stolzenfels (West)	Koblenz

TRIER–KOBLENZ–GIESSEN

Map
on page
265

The first part of this cross-country journey is on many an itinerary, starting as it does in Germany's oldest city and running through picturesque scenery close to the River Mosel. The second half, however, is one of those neglected byways that is all the more pleasing for being something of a discovery. Between Koblenz and Giessen, the railway and the River Lahn are seldom far apart, except for three large loops in the river, and the valley through which they run is exceptionally beautiful and unspoilt. The journey involves a change of trains at Koblenz; most trains from Trier to Koblenz originate in Saarbrücken, and some continue on to Cologne.

Trier and the Mosel valley

The Romans founded a military base at **Trier** around 20 BC and it is for those remains, rather than later noteworthy buildings, that the city has attained its UNESCO World Heritage Site status. Bahnhofstrasse leads directly to Trier's most notable Roman building, the Porta Nigra, a four-storey sandstone gateway, from which it is easy to walk to all the city's other principal attractions.

Soon after leaving Trier the line crosses over the Mosel, but is then out of sight of the river for the next 40 minutes (sadly, the Moselbahn that once hugged the southern bank of the river to Bullay has closed). To the south, across farmland, are the distant hills and woods of the Hunsrück, immortalised by Edgar Reisz's epic film *Heimat*, while to the north are heavily wooded slopes, broken by the occasional church spire piercing the skyline.

After **Bengel** the first vineyards appear on the south-facing slopes beside the line, which is supported by a long, arched wall. One of the numerous meanders in the Mosel touches the railway just before it dives into Prinzenkopf Tunnel, from which the line emerges to cross the river. **Bullay** is the only junction before Koblenz, with a 10.6-km (6½-mile) branch turning southwest to follow the northern bank of the river to a centre of the Mosel wine trade at Traben-Trarbach.

For most of the remaining journey to Koblenz, there is hardly a moment without a vine in sight and there is plenty of opportunity to admire the way the neat rows are grown on the steepest of slopes and on every available patch of good soil and sun. The beauty of the natural surroundings also made the area a popular place for those with the wherewithal to build a *schloss* on an eminence. With the river briefly to the left, a weir and loch are passed just before **Neef** where there's a tunnel, followed by a return to the north side of the river.

At **Ediger-Eller** the railway enters the Kaiser-Wilhelm Tunnel, one of the country's longest at 4.2 km (2½ miles). In the vineyard chapel at Ediger is an unusual sculpture of Christ being crushed by a wine-press. After **Cochem**, railway and river run side by side all the way to Koblenz, the constant succession of passenger and cargo boats providing continual interest. Reichsburg, one of the most celebrated castles in the Mosel Valley, stands on a vine-

ESSENTIALS

Thomas Cook timetable nos. 915, 906

Distance: 229 km

Duration of journey: 3 hrs 12 mins (change at Koblenz)

Frequency of trains: every two hours

BELOW: the Porta Nigra at Trier is one of Germany's best-preserved Roman buildings.

Star Attractions: Trier
● **Porta Nigra**
● **Roman Baths**
● **Rheinisches**
   Landesmuseum
● **St Peter's**
   Cathedral
● **Hauptmarkt**

covered, conical hill 30 minutes' walk above Cochem; the ruins were rebuilt in 14th-century style during the 19th century. Most of the villages along the opposite bank are of necessity linear in layout, hemmed in by the wooded slopes that rise behind the single street. Occasionally a turn in the river will allow a slope with a sufficiently southerly aspect to be planted with vines, but the majority of vineyards are on the same bank as the railway.

From **Moselkern** it is an hour's signposted walk beside a stream to one of Germany's most stunningly-sited castles. The many pinnacles around the steep roof of **Eltz Castle** rise dramatically from the surrounding forest. It has the kind of art and antiquities that only come from over 900 years of continuous ownership. Sandwiched between the railway and the Mosel near **Kobern-Gondorf** is a Gothic castle, through the grounds of which the road passes. Soaring above the line after the river and railway turn southeast is a functional motorway viaduct, impressive because of its height. The river briefly turns away from the railway before passing underneath it on the outskirts of Koblenz.

Koblenz and the Lahn

Koblenz is situated at an intersection of rivers and hills: the Mosel enters the Rhine almost opposite the Lahn, and from this crossroads four ranges of hills diverge – the Hunsrück to the southwest, the Eifel to the northwest, the Taunus to the southeast and the Westerwald to the northeast. The city is full of historical interest and associations, not least with guidebooks, for it was here that Karl Baedeker set up his publishing business, producing his first guide (to the Rhine) in association with John Murray, in 1834.

BELOW:
quality control
on the Mosel.

The city's oldest building is the Romanesque church of St Castor: founded in 836, it was here that the decision was taken to divide up Charlemagne's empire. Other significant structures include the Romanesque Liebfraukirche, the 13th-century castle, and the imposing equestrian statue of Kaiser Wilhelm I at the confluence of the Mosel and the Rhine, where the Teutonic Knights established their first base, in 1216. The Rathaus (Town Hall) was a Jesuit college until 1794. Take care where you stand to admire the nearby bronze fountain of the spitting boy! On the east bank, reached by ferry, are the immense Ehrenbreitstein Fortress, the birthplace of Beethoven's mother, and the Rhine Museum, largely devoted to ships and river trade.

Trains for Giessen (also spelled Gießen) leave Koblenz in a southerly direction, crossing over the Rhine and turning east off the Frankfurt line at **Niederlahnstein**. Above is the rather ugly pile of Lahneck Castle. The station buildings on this section are often delightful, a good example being the part timber-framed **Friedrichssegen**. Running between valley slopes covered in deciduous woods, the railway reaches **Bad Ems**, passing some fine 19th-century industrial buildings – an age when companies were willing to spend money creating premises with some architectural merit. The station has an overall roof, recalling the time when the hydropathic facilities of Bad Ems were often the choice of royalty. It was here in 1870 – commemorated by a stone on the prom-

Map on page 265

enade – that Wilhelm I's response to the French ambassador resulted in the Franco-Prussian War of 1870–71. The conversation was incorporated in the crucial Ems Telegram. Murray's *Handbook* of 1886 comments that the society patronising the ballroom-equipped kursaal (the spa's social centre) was "usually more select" than could be found at Wiesbaden or Baden-Baden.

In a striking position overlooking the railway on the approach to **Nassau** is an extraordinary pair of buildings associated with the Prussian statesman Baron Stein: the square tower with corner turrets and steeply pitched roof was built by him, and the modern-looking temple below is a monument in his memory. The castle, begun in 1101, was the cradle of the Nassau family which split into two branches in the 13th century, one producing the dukes of Nassau, the other the king of the Netherlands. Emerging from the last of three short tunnels, there is a spectacular view of the Lahn as the track crosses it just before **Obernhof**, which has a very large, dramatically sited church dating from 1359, and the Abbey of Arustein.

Vines appear on the valley slopes, which press in on the line until there is little but the river and railway between them. Above **Laurenburg** stands a chevron-shuttered tower, another home of the Nassau family. Outcrops of grey rock break up the valley sides on the approach to **Balduinstein**, where the ruins of the castle, built in 1320 by Archbishop Baldwin of Trèves, can be seen up a valley to the right. The well-preserved Oranienstein Castle stands on a rocky eminence as the train approaches **Diez**; built in 1672–84, this was one of the ancestral castles of the Nassau-Orange royal house (from which King William III of England was descended) and is now a barracks with a museum open to visitors.

The InterCity Express at Limburg station.

BELOW: Bratwurst sausages are available everywhere.

Limburg to Giessen

Dominating the skyline of the large town of **Limburg** is the Romanesque-Gothic cathedral, surrounded by attractive stone and timber-framed buildings. The character of the countryside has changed by the time the train passes the junction for Frankfurt-am-Main at **Eschhofen**, being much flatter, with distant views to the north. But after **Kerkerbach**, railway and river again share a well-wooded valley. **Runkel** has a magnificent castle with a stone bridge leading to it, followed by an idyllic section running beside the river all the way to **Weilburg**, with its castle on the hill.

After **Löhnberg**, railway and river emerge from the valley and enter a much flatter landscape to reach **Wetzlar**, where 35mm film was invented at the Leitz factory in 1924. It was the emotions Goethe felt in Wetzlar through his unrequited love for Charlotte Buff that led to *The Sorrows of Young Werther*; Charlotte's birthplace, known as the Lottehaus after the fictional heroine, is open to visitors.

The station buildings at **Giessen** in Upper Hesse, are singularly attractive, having been redeveloped in 1904 to incorporate a tall clock tower outside the main hall. Built of red sandstone with decorative carved griffins and lions, the station is a junction on the Frankfurt-am-Main–Kassel line. Giessen's university was founded around the 12th-century castle in 1607, two years before its botanical garden.

ESSENTIALS

Thomas Cook
timetable no. 867

Distance:
(1) Nordhasen–
Wernigerode 61 km
(2) Nordhausen–
Quedlinburg 70 km
(3) Wernigerode–
Brocken 34 km

Duration of journey:
(1) 2 hrs 54 mins
(2) 3 hrs 10 mins
(3) 1 hr 45 mins

Frequency of trains:
2–6 daily; no through
services on routes 1
or 2; change at Eis-
felder or Drei Annen
Hohne (1); Stiege or
Alexisbad (2)

BELOW: high up in
the Harz Mountains.

HARZER SCHMALSPURBAHNEN

The most extensive and scenic of the narrow gauge railways in the former East Germany is the 140-km (87-mile) network of lines known as the Harzer Schmalspurbahn. The main line links the delightful town of Wernigerode with Nordhausen, while the principal branch line leaves the main line at Eisfelder Tahlmühle and heads east, then north to Gernrode. In 2006, the 8 km (5 miles) of standard gauge railway between Gernrode and the World Heritage Site of Quedlinburg was converted to narrow gauge. Of the three other branches, the most important is the remarkable line up the Brocken, a mountain renowned for its literary associations and the saturnalia of Walpurgis Night. Heinrich Heine's book about the Harz made his name, and Goethe set part of *Faust* here.

A large investment

Since unification, large sums have been invested in the railway, improving the facilities and introducing such amenities as cafés and bar cars. The railway attracts hundreds of thousands of visitors to the area each year, and gives walkers access to the densely forested Harz Mountains, a prime hiking area.

The timetable requires careful reading. There are no direct Nordhausen–Wernigerode or Eisfelder Tahlmühle–Quedlinburg trains, so an easy change of train is necessary. Anyone in search of steam workings should note that the Eisfelder Tahlmühle–Stiege section is entirely diesel-operated, apart from occasional special trains. Nearly all trains up the Brocken are steam-hauled.

One of the delights of the locomotive-hauled trains is the opportunity to ride on the open-balcony coaches. Besides enjoying wider views and the cool smell

of the forest, you can stand right by the chimney of a bunker-first working and hear at close quarters the stirring bark of the huge tank engine tackling the steep grades that characterise the system.

The southern terminus of the system, well served by Halle–Kassel trains, is **Nordhausen**. Large enough to have a tram system, the town was badly bombed during World War II but the church still contains much from the 14th-century, including the choir stalls. To the north of the town lies the Konzentratsion-lager-Dora, part of Buchenwald concentration camp, which supplied labour for the construction of V1 and V2 rockets in the 11 km (7 miles) of massive tunnels that were carved out of the mountain of gypsum known as Kohnstein. A grim memorial is open to visitors.

Nordhausen to Wernigerode

Trains stop at several halts on the outskirts of Nordhausen, until after **Ilfeld** the suburbs are left behind. The railway starts to wend its way through the wooded hills that continue all the way to Wernigerode, alternating between narrow valleys with fast-running, tree-shaded streams, beech woods, forests of generously spaced conifers and open meadows ablaze with wild flowers. At **Netzkater** there is a museum of equipment from mining railways and a café in the station.

Many passengers change trains at the junction of **Eisfelder Tahlmühle**, where the lines to Gernrode and Wernigerode split. Heading north to Wernigerode, the wooded station of **Benneckenstein**, 13 km (8 miles) further on, has a railway museum in the goods shed, while the pretty, half-timbered building at **Elend** houses a station café/bar. In the 8 km (5 miles) between **Drei Annen Hohne** and Steinerne Renne there are 72 curves and the line's only tunnel, as the track descends at

TIP

Nordhausen is on the electrified Kassel–Halle line, but connoisseurs of railway byways will not be disappointed by the DB journey between Wernigerode, Halberstadt and Quedlinburg.

BELOW: winter landscape on the Brocken ascent.

THE BROCKEN

One of the last daily steam spectacles in Europe is provided by the succession of well-filled trains to the roadless 1,142-metre (3,747-ft) summit of the Brocken. From the junction at Drei Annen Hohne it is an almost unbroken climb at 1 in 30 to the summit, calling for delightfully demonstrative exertion from the bulky locomotives. The woods are particularly thick as the line climbs to the one intermediate station at **Schierke** for a stop to replenish the water tanks.

Climbing through boulder-strewn, thinning woodland, criss-crossed by walking trails, the line comes out of the trees near the refuge siding at Goetheweg (allowing trains to pass in summer), with views over nothing but unbroken forest for miles.

When the line is busy, descending trains are often diverted into the siding to allow an ascending train an unchecked run up the bank, affording passengers in the waiting train the fine sight and sound of the locomotive storming up the bank. A prominent ski-jump in the distance indicates the popularity of the area for winter sports. Finally, the line spirals round the summit before coming to a halt below a large building housing a restaurant, café and communications equipment.

TIP

Quedlinburg is designated a World Heritage Site for its many streets of timber-framed houses. The circular, medieval centre is a 10-minute walk from the railway station.

gradients up to 1 in 30, providing a challenge for southbound trains. Occasional clearings in the woods give a sense of how vast an area the forest covers. **Steinerne Renne** is a halt and a passing loop in woods, from which the train drifts downhill, past the backs of houses and alongside a stream to **Wernigerode Westerntor**, where the railway's workshops are situated, and the main station at **Wernigerode**. The old town itself seems to be entirely composed of well-restored, half-timbered houses; it also has a splendidly spired 15th/16th-century Rathaus and a multi-turreted *schloss* dating from 1862–85 on the hill. The castle is open to visitors and can even be reached by a miniature railway from the market place in summer. The castle terrace offers splendid views over the Harz and the Brocken.

The Gernrode line

The line from Eisfelder Tahlmühle to Quedlinburg soon leaves the woods and climbs up to a lonely plateau of wild grassland on which the isolated junction of **Stiege** is situated. The line then ambles past a series of attractive villages, birch woods and a willow-fringed river to the spa village of **Alexisbad**, junction for Harzgerode and its 16th-century castle. Passing through deep rock cuttings, the railway comes alongside the road near **Drahtzug** before reaching **Mägde-sprung** with its large collection of old factory buildings. It was here that Prince Frederick Albert of Anhalt, who died in 1796, founded a large ironworks. Among its products were "tasteful articles in cast iron", according to Baedecker, which could be bought from the foundry by passing tourists. Wood-fringed fields border the line before it re-enters the woods at **Sternhaus-Haberfeld** and drops down steeply to **Gernrode**. The town's most notable attraction is the 10th-century St Cyriakus, the oldest Ottonian church in Germany.

BELOW: near Drei Annen Hohne on the Wernigerode–Brocken line.

INNSBRUCK–GARMISCH-PARTENKIRCHEN–MUNICH

Map on page 262

Passengers on the scenic line through the Arlberg between Bregenz and Innsbruck *(see page 241)* may notice on the western side of the Tyrolean capital a track climbing in a most extraordinary manner along the steep northern flank of the valley, weaving in and out of side valleys over viaducts and through tunnels. This is the start of the line that climbs into the mountains of southern Bavaria and continues to Munich (München), reached in under three hours. The southerly section between Innsbruck and Garmisch-Partenkirchen was a late addition, built as an electrified railway between 1910 and 1912; Garmisch-Partenkirchen had been reached from the north in time for the 1890 passion play in Oberammergau.

A vertiginous ascent

Trains for Munich leave Innsbruck in a westerly direction before turning north to cross the River Inn and start the long ascent through the wooded slopes at gradients as steep as 1 in 28. The view (best from the left-hand side of the train) steadily broadens as the train gains height, looking down across the airport to the mountains of the Tyrol and along the Inn Valley. Passengers sometimes have the unusual experience of travelling at the same height as, or even above, an aeroplane. Pausing at tiny halts and wayside stations, the train twists along its ledge and through an avalanche shelter before entering a long tunnel. Those who suffer from vertigo may be thankful that the trees mask the depth of the drop, but occasional openings reveal dizzying chasms of rock.

By **Leithen** the line has curved to the north away from the Inn Valley and reached an area of upland meadows and coniferous forest. Past **Reith**, the sum-

ESSENTIALS

Thomas Cook timetable no. 895

Distance: 160 km

Duration of journey: 2 hrs 50 mins

Frequency of trains: hourly

BELOW: view from the Zugspitzbahn near the Riebersee.

mit is reached and the line dips to the winter sports resort of **Seefeld in Tirol**. The importance of forestry is indicated by wagons loaded with tree trunks at **Scharnitz**, the last station before the train crosses the Austro–German border.

The first station in Germany is the year-round resort and violin-making centre of **Mittenwald**. The musical association stems from 1681 when Mathias Klotz started making violins here after studying the craft with Nicola Amati in Cremona. Prominent in the townscape is the frescoed baroque tower of the fine church of SS Peter and Paul. Cable cars provide access for hiking to four nearby peaks. Soon after leaving Mittenwald the line crosses the Isar Valley, flanked by the steep Karwendel range, and resumes its climb through fields peppered with small farm buildings. **Klais** has the distinction of being the highest station in Germany reached by mainline trains. Beyond it, the valley narrows and trees crowd in on the railway, which soon joins the broad valley of the River Loisach at Garmisch-Partenkirchen, the approach heralded by the ski jump built for the Winter Olympics in 1936.

Garmisch–Partenkirchen, Olympic village

Merged from two villages for the Olympics, **Garmisch-Partenkirchen** was home to the composer Richard Strauss until his death in 1949, and there is a June festival devoted to his work. Attractively decorated houses line some of Garmisch's streets, and it is worth visiting the small pilgrimage church of St Anton for the poignant memorial photographs of soldiers killed in both world wars. To the northwest of the town, and reached by bus, is Ludwig II's jewel-like Schloss Linderhof, one of his smallest creations. Set in a remote valley, the eclectic hunting palace was the only one of his residences to be completed. The

BELOW: early morning at Munich.

formal French gardens are surrounded by parkland in which there is a Moorish pavilion, a Moroccan timber house and a grotto of Venus. Buses from the town also serve two of Ludwig's most ostentatious castles, at Hohenschwangau and – most famously – Neuschwanstein. The area has numerous cable cars providing easy access to mountain walks, as well as the rack railway up the Zugspitze *(see page 276)*. Although the area has the best skiing facilities in Germany, it is an equally appealing summer resort. Whatever the season, it is worth taking the Ausserfernbahn, the cross-country line west from Garmisch-Partenkirchen to Kempten, as it offers exceptional scenery.

The Bavarian foothills

Leaving Garmisch, the train bowls along the broad valley of the Loisach, flanked by gully-riven mountains, to cross the river after **Eschenlohe** and climb at 1 in 45 to the junction for Oberammergau at **Murnau**. Staffelsee comes into view to the west as the contours flatten and market gardening becomes the dominant activity. You can visit the Russian House, where Vassily Kandinsky, Russian-born pioneer of abstract art, lived from 1909 to 1914 (many of his works can be seen at the Lenbachhaus in Munich). The castle museum has exhibitions on local artists and writers, and on life in the Bavarian countryside.

Reaching the outer limit of the Munich S-bahn at **Tutzing**, passengers are denied sight of Starnberger See by intervening woodland until **Starnberg** where there is a lovely view back along the lake. The waters were the scene of an event that continues to exercise a fascination for anyone interested in one of Europe's most colourful monarchs. It was near Berg Castle on the lake that Ludwig II and his physician mysteriously drowned in 1886, following his depo-

Map on page 262

BELOW: the Treasury at Munich's Royal Palace (Residenz).

sition. An impromptu commission had declared the king insane and unfit to rule, and it remains a mystery whether he committed suicide, and the doctor died trying to save him, or whether both were murdered.

You arrive in the Bavarian capital, **Munich**, at the large but uninspiring station built in 1963. You need a long visit to do justice to the city's many attractions. It has dozens of well-presented museums and galleries and many other places of interest reached by the excellent S- and U-bahn or tram/bus network. The best way to explore the pedestrianised centre is on foot, and for English-speakers there is a range of guided tram and walking or cycling tours. Besides architectural visits, there are tours devoted to hops and malt, political history and nature.

The most famous event in Munich's calendar is the 16-day Oktoberfest, beginning in late September. Dating from 1810 and the marriage of the Bavarian Crown Prince, later Ludwig I, to Therese von Saxe-Hildburghausen, the festival has become a major international event, attracting over 7 million people a year. Hotel prices cash in on the high demand, and regulars advise leaving the beer tents at 10.30–11pm, at least an hour before closing time, to avoid the crush later.

The Zugspitzbahn scales the heights

Mechanised access to Germany's highest mountain was first achieved from the Austrian side, by a cable car system opened in 1926. The metre gauge rack railway that takes visitors most of the way up from the German side was built between 1928 and 1930, with a maximum gradient of 1 in 4. The line starts at a small station on the west side of Garmisch–Partenkirchen station. The trains are painted in Bavaria's national colours of blue and white.

Zugspitzbahn trains are painted in Bavaria's colours.

BELOW:
on top of Germany's
highest mountain.

From Garmisch the Zugspitzbahn parallels the scenic cross-country line to Reutte and Kempten, acting as a regular local railway and stopping at small halts. Access to walks in the hills leading up to the Alpspitze is provided by the cable car to Kreuzeck at **Kreuzeckbahn** station. Small wooden huts for hay storage litter the flower-rich grassland, and almost every chalet in the villages seems set on winning a "Bavaria in bloom" award. An immaculately tended cemetery is passed just before the principal intermediate station of **Grainau**, where passengers change to a rack-fitted railcar.

Climbing through mixed woods, the railway reaches **Eibsee** and the foot of a direct cable car from the summit (a ticket allows you to travel by different routes in each direction). The lake comes into view as the climb continues, the shallows around the islands a beautiful crown of turquoise set in the dark blue of the deeper water.

At a height of 1,650 metres (5,413 ft) at **Riffelriß** the line enters the long tunnel that leads to the summit station at **Zugspitzplatt** (2,590 metres/8,497 ft). Here passengers transfer to the cable car for the final ascent to the summit at 2,962 metres (9,717 ft), although many break their journey by walking up to Germany's highest chapel.

The cable car deposits visitors right at the summit in a warren of passageways, stairs, lifts, shops, cafés, restaurants, terraces, a video theatre and an art gallery that has all been built piecemeal over the last century. The original café is the most interesting place to have a warming chocolate, its walls covered in portraits of the men who have scaled the peak. The theatre shows a film of the railway's construction: as one of the last European rack railways to be built, the Zugspitzbahn was rare in having its construction recorded for posterity.

Map on page 262

BELOW: view of Oberammergau.

*The station at
Oberammergau.*

BELOW: fairy-tale
castle at
Neuschwanstein.

Oberammergau, the passion play village

The branch line to the town that performs the world-famous passion play every 10 years is as pleasant a journey as one would wish to such a celebrated place. Distant mountains are usually in view as the train winds round the hills, through woods and farms.

The railway was just finished in time for the 1900 play, and 155,000 people arrived by train. Ten years later it was 224,000. Although the line was electrified, the electric rolling stock could not cope and many steam trains had to be hauled by three locomotives.

The railway climbs as far as **Bad Kohlgrub** and then drops down through a stream-threaded wood to the broad, flat valley that leads to **Oberammergau**. Although very obviously devoted to tourism, the town has some attractive houses; their distinguishing feature is the *trompe l'oeil* decoration known as *Lüftmalerei*. Some of the paintings are old and depict religious subjects, some are new and risible.

Wood-carving keeps some of the population busy between the plays, the origins of which go back to 1633, when plague in southern Bavaria led to the area being sealed off to protect itself against infection. The cordon was penetrated by a local labourer wanting to return to his family; in two days he was dead and so, within three weeks, was a quarter of the village. The survivors vowed that if the pestilence ceased they would stage a passion play every 10 years. The first was performed the following year, but some time around 1680 it was moved to what is commonly regarded as the first year of a decade.

Nearby is Ludwig II's hunting lodge, Schloss Linderhof *(see page 274)*, which can be reached by an hourly bus from the station.

MUNICH–LINDAU

Map
on page
262

The railway from Munich to Lindau is a pleasant way to reach Bodensee (Lake Constance), the second largest expanse of Alpine water after Lake Geneva, with an area of 531 sq. km (205 sq. miles). Direct trains run from Lindau across the border into Switzerland to St Gallen and Zürich, and further international connections are available from nearby Bregenz in Austria, reached by local trains in 10 minutes. Alternatively, this can be made into a circular day trip from Munich, proceeding on to Bregenz and Innsbruck and back to Munich via Garmisch-Partenkirchen *(see page 274)*. Off the Lindau line are numerous cross-country and branch lines, the connecting trains arriving or waiting as your train enters the junction. It is also a line well used by cyclists and walkers to reach the Allgäu Alps. The better views are to be had on the left.

Munich to Kempten

Exits from principal stations are seldom visual treats, and Munich is no exception, although it is surprising how quickly the train reaches coniferous forest interspersed with vast fields of cereals and neat villages with onion-domed church towers and shuttered chalet farmhouses attached to cavernous barns.

Near **Grafrath** a glimpse can be had of Ammersee to the south. The lake can be reached from Munich by the S-bahn line to Herrsching or by a branch line from Geltendorf. Three successive lines branch off the Lindau line to the north towards Augsburg (where Rudolf Diesel developed the engine that is hauling your train), the fastest being the last, from **Buchloe**. As a track trails in to the right from Memmingen, the train arrives at the capital of the Allgäu Alps

ESSENTIALS

Thomas Cook
timetable no. 935

Distance: 220 km

Duration of journey:
2 hrs 13 mins to 2
hrs 54 mins (direct)

Frequency of trains:
12 per day (some
requiring a change
at Kempten)

BELOW: drink and
be merry at the
Oktoberfest.

Star Attractions:
Munich

- Frauenkirche
  (Cathedral)
- Alte Pinakothek
- Neue Pinakothek
- Bavarian National
  Museum
- Royal Palace
  (Residenz)
- Hofbräuhaus
- English Garden

BELOW: Bavarian
generations.
RIGHT: many
Bavarian lakes are
good for swimming.

at **Kempten**. One of the oldest towns in Germany, dating from the Roman occupation, Kempten has remains of the original walls, a fine Roman collection in the Zumsteinhaus in Residenzplatz, and some civic buildings dating from the 17th century. It is also the junction for the scenic line that cuts briefly through northern Austria en route to Garmisch-Partenkirchen.

Immenstadt to the Bodensee

As the train leaves Kempten, the Allgäu Alps rise to the west and south. Nearing **Martinszell**, passengers can look down on a lake fringed by pretty villages to the west before the track joins the River Iller to reach the resort of **Immenstadt**, junction for the branch south to the mountain resorts of Sonthofen and Oberstdorf, once known for their sanatoria. The pedestrianised old town of Immenstadt is very close to the station: worth a visit are the Königsegg Palace, dating from 1620, the 17th-century town hall and the museum, which features the local craft of linen weaving.

The line curves round the east end of Alpsee and hugs its northern shore, the water often skimmed by brightly-coloured sailing boats. The railway was obviously built to a tight budget as it obviates the need for tunnelling by curving around the hills: in only one place did the engineers find it impossible to avoid a tunnel, and that is after the **Thalkirchdorf** halt, where the line enters the 124-metre (136-yd) darkness of Oberstaufener Tunnel to reach the summit of the line at **Oberstaufen**. Noted for its cleansing dietary treatments, which are based on the ideas and research of a local physician, the town makes a good base for walking, with cable cars to assist in the ascent of the nearby peak of Hochgrat (1,833 metres/6,014 ft).

After crossing the viaduct at **Röthenbach**, the train picks up speed as the line takes a straighter alignment through receding hills. Once past the junction at **Hergatz** the enormous expanse of Bodensee comes into view through the trees to the southwest, the railway descending through orchards and market gardens towards the water's edge. It reaches the station at Lindau by a narrow causeway to the island which the station shares with the old town.

Lindau and its environs

Lindau is a truly delightful place, its old centre partly pedestrianised and the area around the station and hotel-ringed harbour also free from traffic. Once a Roman camp and naval base, the island was a free city of the Holy Roman Empire until 1803 when Napoleon made it part of Bavaria. The comings and goings of the lake's steamers in the picturesque setting of the small harbour, with its vaguely Moorish 13th-century lighthouse and huge lion, dating from 1856, at the end of the eastern mole, encourage visitors to linger over a coffee at the many terrace cafés. The first steamer plied Bodensee in 1824, and there is still one paddle-steamer on the lake: the *Hohentwiel*, dating from 1911.

To the west, at a point on the northern shore almost opposite Konstanz, is the small town of **Meersburg**, regarded as one of the best-preserved medieval towns in all Germany. Closer to Lindau, and quickly reached by the railway that parallels the northern shore, is the town famed for its association with the inventor of airships, Graf Ferdinand von Zeppelin. **Friedrichshafen**'s fine museum is actually an extension of the station and is notable not only for the section devoted to Zeppelin and dirigibles, but also for having the largest collection of works by the realist painter, Otto Dix (1891–1969).

Map on page 262

TIP

The Munich–Lindau line is due to be electrified, which may entail occasional line closures at weekends.

BELOW: fishing in the Bodensee.

ESSENTIALS

Thomas Cook
timetable nos. 880,
920

Distance: 628 km

Duration of journey:
7 hrs (change at
Nürnberg)

Frequency of trains:
8 per day

Star Attractions:
Dresden

● **Zwinger Palace**
● **Semperoper**
● **Albertinum**
● **A paddle-steamer**
  trip on the Elbe

BELOW: scenery
west of Dresden.

DRESDEN–NÜRNBERG–FRANKFURT-AM-MAIN

Linking cities of great historical importance and interest, the route begins in southern Saxony, traverses the northern part of Bavaria known as Franconia, and finishes in Hesse. Services are operated by diesel trains because part of the line is still not electrified. There are no through trains from Dresden to Frankfurt; eight daily trains run from Dresden to Nürnberg (Nuremberg), from where there are hourly departures to Frankfurt.

Dresden to Nürnberg

The station at Dresden has a most unusual layout, with S-bahn platforms at a higher level flanking the main terminal platforms. Before the end of the S-bahn and suburbia, the terminus of the 750-mm gauge line to Kurort Kipsdorf, which still uses steam traction, can be seen to the right and at a lower level at **Freital-Hainsberg**. At **Tharandt** the railway leaves the conurbation behind and cuts through the eastern part of the forest of the same name before skirting its southern edge, with good views to the south.

After **Muldenhütten**, the railway crosses the River Freiberger Mulde by viaduct before reaching **Freiberg**, the town that was largely responsible for the historical wealth of Saxony, thanks to its silver mines. The first published book on mining was written by a citizen of Freiburg, and the world's first Mining Academy was established here in 1765.

Panoramic views open up after **Oederan**, followed by the crossing of the River Flöha by the Hertzdorfer Viaduct. On the outskirts of Chemnitz, to the right, is the half-roundhouse railway museum at **Hilbersdorf**. **Chemnitz,**

formerly Karl-Marx-Stadt, was once dubbed the German Manchester on account of its heavy industry, and has a few remaining historical buildings of note, a Renaissance town hall being perhaps the finest.

The large car factory to the left at **Mosel** used to produce the notorious Trabant, but now turns out Volkswagens. A few kilometres to the south is the former coal-mining centre of **Zwickau**, the birthplace in 1810 of composer Robert Schumann, and the house is open to visitors. The Gothic Mariendom and the early 16th-century Gewandhaus, a hall built for the drapers' guild and now used as a theatre, are also worth visiting.

There are lovely views to the west of **Reichenbach** over gently rolling farmland. To the south of **Plauen** the landscape is a painter's dream of farms and woodland stretching for tens of kilometres. Pressing due south through **Hof** before turning west again at **Marktredwitz**, the line reaches **Kirchenlaibach**, junction for nearby Bayreuth – the town synonymous with Wagner.

The final outstanding stretch is between **Neuhaus** and **Vorra**, which affords lovely views up side valleys between a succession of tunnels. The villages of **Hohenstadt** and **Hersbruck** display the distinctive vernacular style of tall-roofed houses with many small windows extending into the steeply pitched gables.

Nürnberg to Frankfurt

The architectural legacy of **Nürnberg**'s medieval heyday was lost during World War II when whole areas of timber-framed houses were destroyed, but the principal public buildings and some areas around them have been painstakingly restored. The German National Museum is exceptional, having the largest collection of German art and culture, and the vast stadium where the Nazis held their rallies is now an exhibition on "Fascination and Terror".

The section of railway from Nürnberg to **Fürth** was the first stretch to be opened in Germany, in 1835, with a locomotive built in Newcastle-upon-Tyne. The line continues through pleasant but unremarkable farmland to **Würzburg**, a good place to break the journey to see the immense baroque palace known as the Residenz (a World Heritage Site), the Hofkirche and the Marien-berg fortress, which can be seen from miles around. It is perched on vine-covered hills and reached from the old town by a bridge with a statue of St Kilian, patron saint of wine. The Residenz was intended as the "palace of all palaces", and the staircase leading up to Tiepolo's frescoes is regarded as one of the most beautiful of the rococo period. Thankfully, it survived the bombs that destroyed much of the old city, which has been rebuilt.

The River Main is on the left of the line for the next 51 km (32 miles), providing some delightful views as the two twist and turn. After leaving the river at **Lohr** the track continues west through forest to **Aschaffenburg**. The principal attraction here is the German Renaissance Schloss Johannisburg, but it also has a replica of a Pompei house built for Ludwig I, in the garden. The castle houses a museum exhibiting German and Dutch old masters and liturgical objects. Just beyond Aschaffenburg is the village of **Dettingen** where, in 1743, George II became the last English monarch to lead his troops into battle. ❑

Maps on pages 262/318

The railway up to Loschwitz from Kornerplatz station in Dresden gives a magnificent view over the Elbe.

BELOW: typical town square architecture.

Museums and Heritage Lines

Germany is unusual in having a number of narrow gauge railways in the eastern part of the country that survived as steam-operated concerns under the GDR. Their historic and touristic value has been recognised and they continue to operate. The numbers relate to the map on page 262.

Museums

Deutsche Dampflokomotiv-Museum ❶
Birkenstrasse 5, 95339
Neuenmarkt/Oberfranken
Open: Tue–Sun 10am–5pm
Features: located in former DB depot, 31 steam locomotives
Nearest station: Neuenmarkt-Wirsberg
Tel: 0 92 27/57 00
www.dampflokmuseum.de

Deutsches Museum Verkehrszentrum ❷
Theresienhöhe 14a,
80339 München
Café, shop
Open: daily (except holidays)
9am–5pm
Features: collection of railway and transport exhibits
Nearest station: Schwanthaler-höhe (U4 and U5)
Tel: 089/50 08 06-762
www.deutsches-museum.de

Deutsches Technikmuseum Berlin ❸
Trebbiner Strasse 9,
D-10963 Berlin
Café, shop
Open: Tue–Fri 9am–5.30pm,
Sat–Sun 10am–6pm
Features: large collection in old roundhouse

Nearest station: (U-bahn) Möck-ernbrücke or Gleisdreieck
Tel: 030/902 54-0
www.dtmb.de

Eisenbahnmuseum Bochum Dahlhausen ❹
Dr -C.-Otto-Straße 191,
D-44879 Bochum
Cafe, shop
Open: Mar–mid-Nov, Tue–Fri,
Sun and holidays 10am–5pm
Features: located in a quarter roundhouse, also operates over Hattingen–Wengern line on some Sundays
Nearest station: Bochum-Dahlhausen (Essen S-bahn, line 3)
Tel: 02 34/49 25 16
www.eisenbahnmuseum-bochum.de

Eisenbahnmuseum Darmstadt-Kranichstein ❺
Steinstrasse 7,
D-64291 Darmstadt
Open: Sun 10am–4pm,
Apr–Sept Wed 10am–4pm
Features: 8-road roundhouse and 5 open tracks, also operates Darmstadt Ost–Bessunger Forsthaus
Nearest station: Darmstadt-Kranichstein/Ost
Tel: 0 61 51/37 64 01
www.museumsbahn.de

Eisenbahnmuseum Neustadt ❻
Hindenburgstrasse 12,
D-67433 Neustadt (Weinstrasse)
Open: Tue–Fri 10am–1pm,
Sat–Sun 10am–4pm
Features: collection of locomotives; also operates Neustadt–Elmstein on various days
Nearest station: Neustadt (Weinstrasse)
Tel: 0 63 21/3 03 90
www.eisenbahnmuseum-neustadt.de

Hamm RLG ❼
(Hamm Süd–Lippborg)
Schumannstrasse 35,
59063 Hamm
Open: Wed 6–8pm, Sat noon–6pm
Features: museum operating over local private line on various days

Nearest station: Hamm Sud and Lippborg-Heintrop
Length: 18.7 km (11½ miles)
Gauge: 1,435 mm
Tel: 02 38 1/54 00 48
www.museumseisenbahn-hamm.de

Lokwelt Freilassing ❽
Westendstrasse 5,
83395 Freilassing
Open: Fri–Sun 10am–5pm
Features: large collection of steam and electric locomotives in half roundhouse
Nearest station: Freilassing
Tel: 08654 771224
www.lokwelt.freilassing.de

Verkehrsmuseum Dresden ❾
Johanneum am Neumarkt,
Augustusstrasse 1,
D-01067 Dresden
Café, shop
Open: Tue–Sun 10am–5pm
Features: good railway section
Nearest station: Dresden Hauptbahnhof
Tel: 03 51/86 44-0
www.verkehrsmuseum-dresden.de

Verkehrsmuseum Nürnberg ❿
; Lessingstraße 6,
D-90443 Nürnberg
Café, shop
Open: Tue–Sun 9am–5pm
Features: large collection of locomotives and rolling stock
Nearest station: Nürnberg/Opernhaus on U2
Tel: 09 11/219-37 40
www.db.de/dbmuseum

Heritage lines

Bergische Museumbahnen Kandertalbahn ⓫
(Kohlfurther Brücke–Greuel)
Strassenbahn-Museum
Kohlfurther Brücke 57,
D-42349 Wuppertal
Open: various days
Features: major tram museum
Nearest station: Wuppertal
Length: 3.2 km (2 miles)
Gauge: 1 metre
Tel: 02 02/47 02 51
www.bmb-wuppertal.de

Berliner Parkeisenbahn ⑫
An der Wuhlheide 189,
D-12459 Berlin-Köpenick
Open: various days
Features: steam and diesel
operation around park
Nearest station: S-bahn Berlin-
Köpenick
Gauge: 600 mm
Tel: 030/53 89 26-60
www.parkeisenbahn.de

**Braunschweigische Landes
Museums Eisenbahn ⑬**
Borsigstrasse 2A,
38126 Braunschweig
Open: Apr–Oct, last Sat of
month
Features: 10 steam locomotives.
Occasional operation over
regional lines
Nearest station: Braunschweig
Tel: 0531/264034-0
www.vbv-bs.de

**Brohtal-Schmalspureisenbahn
Gmbh ⑭** (Brohl–Engeln)
Open: varying days mid-Apr–
late Oct
Features: steam as far as
Oberzissen (12 km/7 miles) on
certain days
Nearest station: Brohl
Length: 17.5 km (11 miles)
Gauge: 1 metre
Tel: 026 36/8 03 03
Fax: 026 36/8 01 46
www.vulkan-express.de

**Bruchhausen-Vilsen–
Asendorf ⑮**
Shop
Open: weekends in summer and
special days
Features: first preservation
society, opened in 1966;
6 steam locomotives
Nearest station: Bruchhausen-
Vilsen
Length: 8 km (5 miles)
Gauge: 1 metre
Tel: 042 52/93 00-21
Fax: 042 52/93 00-12
www.museumseisenbahn.de

Chiemseebahn ⑯
(Prien–Stock)
Café, shop

Open: May–late Sept
Features: links DB and steamer
on Chiemsee
Nearest station: Prien
Length: 1.7 km (1 mile)
Gauge: 1 metre
Tel: 0 80 51/60 90
www.chiemsee-schifffahrt.net

**Dampfbahn Fränkische
Schweiz ⑰**
(Ebermannstadt–Behringers-
mühle)
Postfach 1101, D-91316
Ebermannstadt
Open: May–Oct Sun
Features: steam and diesel
Nearest station: Ebermannstadt
Length: 16 km (10 miles)
Gauge: 1,435 mm
Tel: 0 91 94/79 45 41
www.dfs.ebermannstadt.de

Dampflokfreunde Salzwedel ⑱
Kleinbahnstrasse 8,
D-29410 Salzwedel
Open: Sat 11am–4.30pm and
other days
Features: located in former
DB depot
Nearest station: Salzwedel
Tel: 01 71/4 16 44 77
www.dampflok-salzwedel.de

DBK Historische Bahn ⑲
(Gaildorf West–Backnang
and other lines)
Geschäftsstelle,
Horaffenstrasse 32,
D-74564 Crailsheim
Open: various days
Features: collection of mainline
locomotives at Crailsheim
Nearest station: Gaildorf-West
Length: 30 km (18¾ miles)
Gauge: 1,435 mm
Tel: 0700 325 80 106
www.dbk-historische-bahn.de

Kandertalbahn ⑳
(Kandern–Haltingen)
Open: May–Oct, most Sundays
Features: pleasant river valley
Nearest station: Haltingen
Length: 12.9 km (8 miles)
Gauge: 1,435 mm
Tel: 0 76 26/8 990
www.kandertalbahn.de

**Lemwerder–Delmenhorst
Süd–Harpstedter Eisenbahn-
freunde ㉑**
Postfach 1236,
D-27732 Delmenhorst
Open: various Sundays
Features: steam and diesel
Nearest station: Delmenhorst
Length: 22 km (14 miles)
Gauge: 1,435 mm
Tel: 0 42 44/23 80
www.jan-harpstedt.de

Pressnitztalbahn ㉒
(Jöhstadt–Steinbach)
Café, shop
Open: various weekends
Features: glorious scenery, three
Saxon Meyers
Nearest station: Wolkenstein
Length: 7.8 km (5 miles)
Gauge: 750 mm
Tel: 03 73 43/80 80-7
www.pressnitztalbahn.de

Schwaben Dampf ㉓
Open: various dates
Features: extensive
programme of steam-hauled
excursions
Nearest station: Neuoffingen
Tel: 0 82 24/80 11 40
www.schwabendampf.de

Selfkantbahn ㉔
(Gillrath–Schierwaldenrath)
Display shed
Open: Easter–end Sept Sun
Features: steam tram as well as
locomotives
Nearest station: Geilenkirchen
Length: 5.5 km (3½ miles)
Gauge: 1 metre
Tel: 02 41/8 23 69 or
0 24 54/66 99
www.selfkantbahn.de

Wutachtalbahn ㉕
(Zollhaus-Blumbeg–Weizen)
Open: May–Sept most
weekends, some Wed and Thur
Features: spiral tunnel,
tremendous scenery
Nearest station: Döggingen
Length: 25.6 km (16 miles)
Gauge: 1,435 mm
Tel: 0 77 02/47 76 04
www.sauschwaenzlebahn.de

SCANDINAVIA

*The wide open spaces of Europe's northern wilderness
are penetrated by a few isolated railway lines,
operated by fast, comfortable trains*

Map
on page
290

T he railways of Denmark, Finland, Norway and Sweden are independent,
although their close relationship is reflected in many international services.
However, Finland is handicapped because its former status as a grand duchy
of Russia bequeathed it a 1,524-mm (5-ft) gauge compared with the normal 1,435
mm (4 ft 8½ in), which inhibits through trains. The standard of services in all
countries is high, and the quality of the long-distance trains in Norway and Sweden ranks them among the best in Europe. Networks thin out to the north, with isolated lines penetrating beyond the Arctic Circle in Norway, Sweden and Finland.

As the largest and most populous of the four countries, Sweden predictably
has the largest network (10,000 km/6,215 miles), with tilting X2000 trains over
its busiest southern inter-city routes. The Øresund Link (Tunnel and Bridge)
across to Denmark means that it is possible to travel quickly and comfortably
between Sweden, Denmark and Germany.

A challenging environment

Norway is Europe's most thinly populated country, with a population of only 4.4
million and a mountainous topography, so financing the railway has always
been difficult. Despite these obstacles, Norway has a network of 4,077 km
(2,533 miles). Significant investment has gone into
the construction of tunnels to eliminate particularly
sinuous sections of line and improve journey times.
New, high-quality trains run on main routes: the
Signatur tilting sets are exceptionally comfortable and
well equipped, with a children's play area, a coffee
bar and audio jacks at all seats.

The introduction of Pendolino tilting trains has
reduced journey times between the main cities in
southern Finland, while Danish internal services
received a boost with the opening of the bridge/tunnel
across the Storebælt in 1997, which slashed journey
times between Copenhagen and places on Funen and
Jutland. However, the most important development
of recent years has been the construction of the
Øresund link between Denmark and Sweden, which
consists of the world's longest single bridge carrying
road and rail traffic, and road and rail tunnels. Its
opening on 1 July 2000 allowed for frequent trains
between Copenhagen and Malmö, and a Copenhagen–Stockholm service with journey times cut to
five hours on the X2000 trains.

Routes in the wide open spaces of northern
Scandinavia pass through unspoilt wilderness. Lines
run along the tamer, but still attractive, west coast of
Jutland (Denmark), while the lakes and forests of
eastern Finland have an appeal all their own – the line
from Lappeenranta to Joensuu is particularly attractive.

PRECEDING PAGES:
scenery on the
Bergen–Oslo route,
Norway.
LEFT: the Flåm line,
Norway.
BELOW: Vajkijaur
station, northern
Sweden.

Scandinavia

0 ————— 200 km
0 ————— 200 miles

N

❶ Museums and
    Heritage Lines
——— Featured route

NORWEGIAN
SEA

BARENTS
SEA

Nordkapp

Vardø

Tromsø

Pečanga

Nikel

Murmansk

Inarijärvi

Ivalo

Monchegorsk

Murmanski

Kovdor

Narvik

Torneträsk

Kiruna

Kolari

Alakurti

Kovdozero

Bodø

Fauske

Kebnekaise
2117

Stora
Lulevatten

Løkan
Tekojärvi

Vesterålen

Lofoten

Vestfjorden

Rognan

Gällivare

Rovaniemi

Kemijärvi

Sofporog

Mo i Rana

Jokkmokk

Boden

Tornio

Ozero
Pyaozero

Kemi

RUSSIA

Mosjøen

Uddjaure

Sorsele

Arvidsjaur

Luleå

Oulu

Ozero
Srednee
Kuyto

Grong

Malgomaj

Vilhelmina

Storuman

Jörn

Perämeri
Bottenviken

Kostomuksha

Steinkjer

Lycksele

Kontiomäki

Trondheim

Hornavan

Hoting

Vännäs

Kokkola

Ylivieska

Kajaani

Nurmes

Iisalmi

Lieksa

Hell

Støren

Storlien

Are

Östersund

Långsele

Umeå

Vaasa

Alavus

Pielinen

Kuopio

Joensuu

Oppdal

Storsjön

Storsjön

Seinäjoki

Pieksämäki

Varkaus

Vyanisla

Andalsnes

Dombås

Røros

Bräcke

Härnösand

Jyväskylä

Mikkeli

Kiraa

Savonlinna

Dovre

Ange

Sundsvall

Pori

Tampere

Jämsä

Imatra

Gittertind
2470

Otta

Vinstra

Sveg

Hudiksvall

Söderhamn

Hämeenlinna

Lappeenranta

Priozersk

NORWAY

Flåm

Lillehammer

Bollnäs

Mora

❷

Lahti

Kouvola

Vyborg

Gjøvik

Elverum

Malung

Falun

Turku

Hyvinkää

Kotka

Sankt-
Peterburg

❺

Bergen

Voss

Geilo

Eidsvoll

❸

Hamar

Kongsvinger

Totsby

Borlänge

Gävle

❹

Salo

Helsinki

Labyazhye

Drammen

❻

Moss

❾

Ludvika

Avesta

Sala

Åland

Hanko

Narva

Stavanger

Sandnes

Skien

❼

Karlstad

Frövi

Västerås

Uppsala

Körsta

Tallinn

Tapa

RUSSIA

Nelaug

Halden

Säffle

Örebro

Eskilstuna

❿

Stockholm

Gdov

Egersund

Strömstad

Vänern

Katrineholm

Södertälje

Nynäshamn

Hiiumaa

Riisipere

Tartu

Pskovskoye
oz.

❽

Kristiansand

Arendal

Uddevalla

Vänersborg

Lidköping

⓫

Skövde

Vättern

Norrköping

Linköping

Saaremaa

Pärnu

Viljandi

Pskov

Ostrov

NORTH
SEA

Skagerrak

Skagen

Hirtshals

Göteborg

Kungsbacka

Borås

Nässjö

Jönköping

Västervik

Oskarshamn

Gotland

Ventspils

Gulf of
Riga

Skulte

Valga

Vecumi

Frederikshavn

Varberg

Värnamo

Aseda

Kalmar

Riga

LATVIA

Valmiera

Ostrov

Thyborøn

Thisted

Alborg

Halmstad

Växjö

Öland

Jurmala

Saldus

Ergli

Rezekne

Holstebro

Ringkøbing

Viborg

Randers

Grenå

Helsingborg

Karlskrona

Liepāja

Mažeikiai

Jelgava

Daugava

Daugavpils

Druya

Nørre Nebel

Arhus

Simrishamn

Klaipeda

Šiauliai

Panevežys

Utena

Polatsk

Westerland

DENMARK

København
(Copenhagen)

Lund

BALTIC SEA

Anykščiai

Didžiasalis

Esbjerg

Tønder

Odense
❶

Nyborg

Korsør

Malmö

Ystad

LITHUANIA

Kaunas

Neman

Vilnius

BELARUS

Flensburg

Husum

Nakskov

Nykøbing

Bornholm

Kaliningrad

Chernyakhovsk

Barysaw

Kiel

Rødby

Sassnitz

Łeba

Gdynia

Ustka

Hel

Baltiysk

RUSSIA

Alytus

Minsk

GERMANY

Słupsk

POLAND

Arctic Circle

SWEDEN

Gulf of Bothnia

FINLAND

Gulf of Finland

ESTONIA

BERGEN–OSLO

Map on page 293

The Bergen line is Norway's best-known railway, renowned for its fabulous scenery as well as being celebrated as an outstanding civil engineering achievement. Although the first passenger service left Bergen for Voss in 1883, it was a narrow gauge train, which meant this section had to be reconstructed when work started on the extension to Oslo in 1896. The difficulties of building the railway through precipitous and often frozen mountain terrain were so great that it was not opened through to Oslo until 1907, and it was another year before completion of the snow sheds allowed a winter service.

The builders faced numerous problems: the average snowline in Norway is at about 900 metres (3,000 ft), compared with 2,100 metres (7,000 ft) in Switzerland. A total of 112 km (70 miles) of line was above this height, so extensive work was needed to protect the tracks against snow and ice. Another difficulty was the exceptional hardness of the rock, which is mostly gneiss, granite and crystalline schists. The severe weather conditions, coupled with the absence of even rudimentary roads through the wilder parts of the route, meant that work in the open could proceed for only about three months of the year. Even though tunnelling could continue year-round, the excavated rock could not be removed from the workings in winter because of huge drifts – the men even had to crawl in and out of small tunnels through the snow.

Today the line is 489 km (306 miles) in length, but originally it was considerably longer; successively built cut-offs, often in tunnel, have both shortened the route and made it less susceptible to the winter storms that threaten to block the track and interrupt services.

Bergen to Myrdal

The temptation to catch the first Oslo train from **Bergen**'s imposing 1913 station should be resisted for at least a couple of days in order to do justice to the city, which is on UNESCO's World Heritage list. Although very few medieval buildings survived the fires that periodically ravaged the port, there is plenty to see in this attractive city and good walking in the hills that surround its harbour. To gain an overview of Bergen and to reach walks through wooded hills, take the Fløibanen funicular railway to Fløyen or the cable car to Ulriken.

Almost as soon as the train for Oslo has left Bergen behind, it dives into the 7.6-km (4¾-mile) Ulriken Tunnel, to reach the station at Arna. For much of the first 86 km (54 miles), as far as Voss, the railway is seldom out of sight of fjords, much of the line being built on a shelf blasted out of rock faces rising from the water. Numerous tunnels punctuate the line, mostly hewn out of such solid rock that no lining is necessary. The sheer slopes above the fjord prove no impediment to tenacious conifers, which find a purchase in the most inhospitable of crags as far up as the crown of treeless rock at the summit of the surrounding mountains. The infrequent parcels of land along the foreshore are often occupied by tiny, birch-sheltered wood cabins painted in the distinctive

ESSENTIALS

Thomas Cook timetable no. 780

Distance: 489 km

Duration of journey: 6 hrs 40 mins

Frequency of trains: 3–4 per day + 1 night train

BELOW: the Fløibanen railway above Bergen.

Star Attractions:
Bergen

● **Bryggen**
● **Hanseatiske**
 Museum
● **Grieghallen**
● **Torget Market**
● **Stenersens Samling**
 art gallery
● **The Fløibanen up**
 to Fløyen
● **Grieg's House at**
 Troldhaugen
● **Fantoft Stave**
 Church

BELOW: restored
locomotive on the
Flåm line.

damask that can be seen all over Norway. Boat houses, as common here as suburban garages, reach into the clear water.

Shortly after **Dale** is the longest tunnel on the line – the Trollkona, which is 8.7 km (5½ miles) long. From the tunnel the line drops steeply to follow the River Vossa, its banks periodically linked by tiny, pedestrian suspension bridges, to a large lake, before the skiing centre of **Voss**. After the line begins another long climb through upland farming country, it follows the north bank of the River Raundal into a spectacular canyon, a sheer drop opening up beneath the railway to the south. Near Mjølfjell the first snow shed indicates how high the line has climbed since leaving the coast; once made of timber, most of the snow sheds have been rebuilt in concrete.

At the end of the climb, at gradients of up to 1 in 46 into a barren, almost treeless bowl, the railway enters a long tunnel to reach **Myrdal**, at an altitude of 866 metres (2,841 ft), one of those lonely places that would not exist but for the railway. Sandwiched between two tunnels, the station is famous as the junction for the vertiginous branch to Flåm *(see panel below)*.

The long haul to Finse

Leaving Myrdal on the main line, there is a fine view down over the Flåm line to the north before the train enters a succession of snow sheds, one of which contains Hallingskeid station. From here to Finse is the longest stretch of high mountain railway in Europe. The highest point on the line is at Taugevann 1,303 metres (4,267 ft) above sea level. In winter, sleds drawn by teams of huskies may be spotted on the climb to **Finse**, the highest station on the route at 1,222 metres (4,009 ft), where there is a museum commemorating the navvies who

9. 2063

N S B

THE FLÅM BRANCH LINE

This extraordinary 20-km (12½-mile) line has 20 tunnels and took 17 years to build, opening for five years of steam traction in 1940 before being electrified. Trains depart up to eight times a day for the 55-minute trip. Thoughtfully, the carriages have opening windows and tip-up seats so that passengers can move from side-to-side and take photographs. It is one of the steepest non-rack railways in the world with 16 km (10 miles) at a gradient of 1 in 18, requiring the locomotives to have no fewer than five separate braking systems.

The descent of 863.5 metres (2,833 ft) in such a short journey is accomplished by a spiral tunnel soon after leaving Myrdal. Near Reinunga is a lake of the same name, from which a colossal waterfall drops over a series of walls and slopes into the River Flåm. When the snows melt, the volume of water makes it worth breaking the journey at Kjosfossen to wonder at the noise and power of the cataract. In winter one can only imagine what the petrified columns of ice become in the spring. The small village of Flåm is situated on Aurlandsfjord, a branch of the world's longest fjord, Sognefjord. However, there is little to detain visitors, apart from a small museum to the east side of the station, about the history of the railway.

built this extraordinary railway. It is winter for most of the year at sub-arctic Finse, making it popular with cross-country skiers; it is also an access point for two major trail networks – the Jotunheim to the north and the Hardangervidda to the south. There are no roads at Finse – it is totally remote, yet accessible (even the fastest trains stop here). Because of this, it was chosen for the filming of the initial sequences of *The Empire Strikes Back*, depicting battle scenes on the Ice Planet Hoth. The Blåisen glacier, running down from the Hardangerjøkulen ice cap, is only 5 km (3 miles) along a marked path, and visible from the station. Mountain bikes can be rented from the hotel.

The railway hereabouts is built on a surprisingly straight course across the plateau, enabling the train to bowl along at speed, on grey winter days whipping up the snow into eddying wraiths that mask the view of the monochromatic landscape, broken only by boulders and birch.

The handsome, wooden station building at **Haugastøl** serves another skiing resort which is also popular in summer as a hiking centre. A few kilometres before **Ustaoset** the line crosses the main Oslo–Bergen road (to which it stays close for most of the remainder of the journey) and then follows the north shore of Lake Ustevatn, with good views of the Hallingskarvet mountain ridge. Holiday cabins dot the rolling hills as the train approaches the major winter sports centre of **Geilo**.

Copious rainfall combined with snow-melt makes for fast-flowing torrents on the Hardangervidda.

Along the Hallingdal valley

The train continues its descent through the lovely Hallingdal Valley and its dark coniferous forests, the muffled sound suddenly rising to a metallic roar as the train crosses a river. By **Ål** the line has reached a town large enough to have a few factories, and some passengers reach for a book at this point, although the landscapes rolling past the window remain pleasant enough.

Between Austvoll and **Flå** there is a dramatic stretch where the railway runs along a ledge above the Hallingdalselva River, with great views along the valley, before joining Lake Krøderen and climbing steadily above the water. The line then turns east through sparsely populated hills to burrow through the Haversting Tunnel into a different valley system. This takes the railway down to the junction and sawmill town of **Hønefoss** and through the outlying commuter stations of Oslo. East of **Drammen**, the railway crosses a long bridge over the river mouth, affording views over the branch of the Dramsfjord to the south.

Oslo Sentral station has been skilfully modernised following construction of a tunnel under the city to link previously separate termini; it incorporates the oldest part, which was built in 1877–82.

ESSENTIALS

Thomas Cook
timetable nos. 785,
787

Distance: 1,282 km

Duration of journey:
6 hrs 40 mins
(Oslo–Trondheim),
9 hrs 45 mins
(Trondheim–Bodø)
Frequency of trains:
3 per day Oslo–
Trondheim (+1 night
train); 1 per day
Trondheim–Bodø
(+1 night train)

OSLO–BODØ

Few railways anywhere in the world can have been as long in the building as the line between Oslo and Bodø. The first section to Eidsvoll was opened in 1854 in the presence of Robert Stephenson, who acted as engineer-in-chief. It wasanother 108 years before the final section formally opened, right at the end of the steam era in Norway. Equally, it is one of the few railways to penetrate the Arctic Circle, offering passengers a safe route through landscapes that even today can be treacherous for motorists. It is a journey offering seascapes, mountain panoramas and some of the loveliest valleys in Norway, and one would be unlucky not to have at least one sighting of reindeer, elk or musk. The new Signatur trains are also the most civilised way to reach the old capital of Trondheim.

The section as far as Trondheim is known as the Dovre Railway, after the range of mountains that it crosses at a height of 1,006 metres (3,300 ft). The railway is electrified as far as Trondheim, where diesel traction takes over, and it is best to plan the journey with at least one overnight break in Trondheim in each direction: it takes just over 6½ hours between Oslo and Trondheim, and a further 9¾ hours to reach Bodø. For both sections, the best views are to be had on the left-hand side of the train going north.

North from Oslo

BELOW: Oslo
harbour

Leaving Oslo, trains enter a long tunnel and take the new, high-speed line through an undulating landscape of conifers and birch to **Gardermoen Airport**. The high-speed line continues as far as **Eidsvoll**, where it joins the original tracks to follow the River Vorma to Norway's largest lake, Mjøsa, an important trade route before

the railway arrived in the 1880s. As the train skirts the south-eastern shore, you may catch a first sighting of the lake's *pièce de résistance*, the paddle-steamer *Skibladner*, which has the distinction of being the world's oldest working paddler, built in 1856. Its route and the length of cruises vary from day to day.

From **Tangen**, the line climbs away from the water to give panoramic views to east and west before dropping down to the important railway town of **Hamar**, half way up the eastern side of the lake. Besides the Norwegian Railway Museum *(see page 307)*, the Hedmarksmuseet has 50 or so reconstructed local buildings on a site that incorporates the remains of the cathedral, thought to have been built by the English pope Nicholas Breakspear, who spent two years in Norway before becoming Pope Adrian IV in 1154.

Lillehammer to Dovre

The town at the northern end of the lake, **Lillehammer**, became world famous as a ski resort when it hosted the 1994 Winter Olympics, which gave it world-class sporting facilities. It is a popular resort in summer, too, for cycling, walking, canoeing and fishing. Its main cultural attraction is the largest open-air folk museum in northern Europe, the Maihaugen, which has over 140 buildings brought in from all over the region. The two stocked farms are complemented by displays of rural crafts, and the chance to try your hand at some of them.

The railway follows the much narrower Gudbrandsdal, lined with the usual conifer and birch and punctuated by traditional red-painted farms and side valleys. Leaving **Vinstra**, another station providing access to good skiing country, the train forges along the now broad valley to the forestry centre of **Otta**. Traditional wooden houses are more in evidence as the railway climbs again,

Map on page 290

Star Attractions: Oslo
● Viking Ships & Kon Tiki museums
● National Gallery
● Akershus Castle
● Munch Museum
● Vigelandsparken
● Royal Palace
● Aker Brygge

BELOW: hiking on the Hardangervidda plateau.

Cruise ships have been sailing up the spectacular Norwegian coast from Bergen to the North Cape since 1891.

BELOW: well-ordered, prosperous Trondheim.

along the eastern flank of the valley through a particularly lovely stretch, with views down into an impressive gorge near the town of **Dovre**.

The Rauma railway

The next station – **Dombås** – is the junction for the 114-km (71-mile) **Rauma Railway** to Åndalsnes, which opened in 1924. After Bjorli, this line follows the plunging descent of the river, but despite dropping at gradients of 1 in 50 it is left perched on a shelf of rock on the mountain-side. This is the Trollveggen, one of Europe's tallest cliffs. What appears to be another railway comes into view 137 metres (450 ft) below, reached by a giant S-bend. The semi-circle of Stavem Tunnel reverses the train's direction so that it can cross the River Rauma by the 44.5-metre (49-yd) masonry span of Kylling Bridge, where the rails are 59 metres (194 ft) above the water. Åndalsnes, the terminus of this line, is of little interest in itself, but sits on another fjord and is surrounded by high mountains.

Back on the main Trondheim line, the track turns east and describes a horse-shoe curve to find a passage over the mountains, allowing passengers to look down on Dombås. Having climbed onto a plateau of wilder country, the line takes a straight course, allowing the train to race across a desolate landscape surrounded by mountains before reaching the lonely, attractive station at **Hjerkinn**, a popular stopping-off place for cross-country skiers. The next station, **Kongsvoll**, is an access point for the walks and climbs of the Dovrefjell National Park, which is served by a timber-built inn of 18th-century origin within 10 minutes' walk of the station.

At the end of this bleak stretch, with the 2,286-metre (7,500-ft) summit of Snøhetta, the tallest mountain in the area, to the west, the line descends through a narrow, steep-sided gorge, lined in winter with frozen waterfalls. Past **Oppdal** and its famous slate quarries, forests enfold the line, and one has to be alert to catch a glimpse of the chasm before **Ulsberg** as the train crosses a viaduct over the River Orkla.

Trondheim and the Nordlandsbanen

Trondheim is Norway's third city and former capital, but it has the feel of a small, provincial market town and is easily navigated on foot. The station lies on the northern edge of a triangular peninsula on which much of the old part of the city was built, bordered on its southern side by the River Nidelva. You will find the cluster of principal attractions at the southern point of the peninsula: the cathedral (Nidaros Domkirke), the 12th-century remnant of the Archbishop's Palace and the City Art Museum.

The railway on to Bodø was built as the North Norway Railway (Norlandsbanen) and was not finally opened until as recently as 1962, although it was originally intended to go as far as Narvik (which can be reached on the railway from Kiruna in northern Sweden). A major effort was made by the occupying Germans to finish the line during World War II, to convey iron ore from the mines around Narvik. Over 36,000 Yugoslav, Serb, Soviet, Polish and Norwegian prisoners of war were used as labour, often working in appalling conditions.

The line skirts the Trodheimsfjord for some miles from Trondheim, only the rocky foreshore, decaying boats and copses of hardy birch separating the railway from the water's edge. The line climbs along a shelf in the rock, affording more expansive views over the fjord before dropping down to the famous junction of **Hell**, one of the most photographed stations in Scandinavia, served by local trains from Trondheim to Storlien in Sweden.

From the chalet-style station at **Stjørdal**, the railway veers away from the coast through farming country, offering only distant views of the sea until **Verdal** is reached, where it skirts a shipyard before entering the station. Another stretch of line right beside the water takes the train to Røra, passing small wooden cabins nestling among trees near the shoreline. **Steinkjer** marks the end of the fjord, but a large lake to the north of the line appears soon after the closed station of Sunnan. Trees gradually cover more and more of the rolling hills through which the railway weaves its course, interrupted by occasional clearings with tidy farms and a few fields.

Forest railway

After the end of the lake at **Snåsa**, the line is in forest for much of the way to **Grong**, where several buses meet the train. Two long viaducts take the track into the pretty valley of the River Namsen, which it follows for many miles through deep rock cuttings and short tunnels and across many bridges. The population density is so low that one wonders how many people are served by stops at some of the more remote stations, like **Lassemoen** and **Namsskogan**. Some stand alone in clearings in the trees, reached by a straight, empty road cut through the forest, in winter resembling a scene from *Dr Zhivago*.

Map on page 290

BELOW: Trondheim is a major stop for Hurtigrute coastal steamers.

North from **Majavatn**, the station buildings become noticeably more utilitarian and austere. If possible, move to the right-hand side of the coach for the next 20 minutes or so, to appreciate the gorges through which the river flows along Svenningdal. At **Mosjøen**, the line returns briefly to the sea, negotiating headlands by cuttings or tunnels, before a stretch of rolling farmland and a long, delightful section beside the water, with some picture-postcard views.

This railcar at Bodø is supplied with snow clearing equipment.

Into the Arctic

The River Rana keeps company with the railway through steep-sided Dunderlandsdal. Mid-way between the remote station of **Bolna** and the closed station at Semska, amid a series of snow sheds is the point at which the line crosses the Arctic Circle, marked by a pair of cairns. Visibility in winter can be almost nil, with snow whipped up by the train and the wind creating a white-out. The slopes are barren but for stunted trees and some coarse grass. From **Lønsdal** the train descends steeply through majestic, open country to follow the River Saltelv north to the Saltfjord at **Rognan**. The track now follows the arm of the fjord, though not always within sight of it, all the way to Bodø, pausing at **Fauske**, the last station before journey's end, from where buses run to Narvik for the railway line to Sweden.

It was at a farm near **Bodø** that Louis Philippe (later king of France) was given shelter in 1795 while escaping the Revolution. He was certainly well out of the way: Bodø is so far north it has almost six weeks of midnight sun, from 30 May to 12 July, and a corresponding number of days of mid-winter darkness. At latitude 67° 16', it lies further north than most of Canada, Alaska and Siberia. Much of the 19th-century town was obliterated by German bombing in May 1940, when it was used as a base by British forces.

BELOW: Bodø, in the land of the midnight sun.

SWEDEN'S INLANDSBANAN

Map on page 290

The Inland Railway (Inlandsbanan) – the "trans-Siberian" railway of Sweden – runs from Gällivare, a junction on the main electrified line from Kiruna, to Östersund and Mora, with connections on to Stockholm. The total distance is 1,289 km (806 miles), and the journey offers an unrivalled experience through some of the most remote and beautiful parts of Sweden. It is possible to make stopovers along the route and stay for a night or two in local towns and villages to do some walking in the mountains, or just to enjoy the magnificent wilderness landscapes. Various packages are available combining rail travel with hotel accommodation or trekking.

The history of the line

Plans to lay a line that would open up the endless backwoods of northern Sweden were formulated in the late 1890s, but because of the enormous distances involved, the inaccessibility of the terrain and the difficulty in raising finance, construction did not begin until 1907. One gang started at Östersund, pushing northwards in stages, while another contract undertook the work south from Gällivare – the impetus provided by the need to transport materials to a large hydro-electric power station being constructed near Porjus.

Progress was very slow: the final link between Jokkmokk and Sorsele was not completed until 1937. Meanwhile, south of Östersund, around Sveg, privately-constructed lines were acquired. Link lines were built from the inland track to the main, electrified, parallel route to the east, thus enabling timber to be moved out of the region more quickly.

ESSENTIALS

Thomas Cook timetable no. 762

Distance: 746 km (Gällivare–Östersund)

Duration of journey: 14 hrs 40 mins (Gällivare–Östersund)

Frequency of trains: 1 per day (Gällivare–Östersund; summer only)

BELOW: a common sight on the Inlandsbanan.

In such a sparsely populated area, passenger services were maintained by railcars linking the local towns. Through journeys over the whole line took several days, due to lack of connections and infrequency of service. With the improvement of the local roads and the provision of alternative car and bus transport, passenger services were progressively withdrawn from the mid-1960s and the line seemed doomed, apart from sections maintained for the remaining freight traffic.

However, with the privatisation of much of the Swedish State Railways, a separate company was formed in 1993 to exploit the line's tourist potential and for the last few years it has again been possible to travel over virtually the whole length of the line during the short summer holiday period – early June to the end of August – a great way to experience what is termed "Europe's last wilderness".

Gällivare to Arvidsjaur

The modern town of **Gällivare**, with its fine wooden station building, is the starting point for the journey. As the only departure of the day leaves before 7am, finding a hotel that serves an early breakfast is a necessity – there are no refreshment facilities on the train. A brightly painted, modern diesel railcar is provided for the service and you are welcomed aboard by your hosts, travel-industry students provided through the local Tourist Board, who give a commentary on local places of interest and look after passengers' needs and answer their enquiries. Many of the passengers are members of groups who are only travelling on a section of the line, as part of a coach excursion by road. The independent traveller is very much the exception, but everyone is made to feel welcome.

BELOW: in the dense forests of central Sweden.

On leaving Gällivare, the line runs beside the main line to Kiruna and Narvik before turning southwards and heading off into what will become familiar views for almost the whole of the journey – mile upon mile of forest punctuated by lakes and rivers and the occasional isolated farm. The economical way in which the line was constructed is immediately apparent, with the original, lightly laid track still in use. Heavy engineering works, apart from the bridges across the many rivers, were avoided and the line generally follows the contours, with gradients undulating, although there are also a few short, steep sections.

After about 90 minutes, the train slows for the first refreshment break of the day at **Vajkijaur**, where a small restaurant is conveniently located adjacent to the road and railway. Here you can get a very welcome cup of coffee with delicious home-made buns.

The next station is **Jokkmokk**, where the train pauses briefly. At the north end of the station is a granite pillar that commemorates the official opening of the completed Inlandsbanan by the then Crown Prince of Sweden, Gustaf Adolf, on 6 August 1937. Twenty minutes later the train host announces that you are about to cross the **Arctic Circle**; the train stops to let passengers descend to the small platform at Polcirkeln (Polar Circle) to photograph the signs and the line of white stones that marks the location.

By mid-morning the train has reached the closed station of **Varjisträsk**. The building is now used by local hunters and the old waiting room houses some hunting trophies, including a stuffed eagle with outstretched wings. Near Igge-jaur, your host announces the approach of one of the major engineering features of the line – a combined road and rail bridge over the River Pite. Passengers are invited to walk across the bridge and rejoin the train on the other side, and most people take advantage of this to stretch their legs and view the rushing waters of the wide river below.

A 15-minute refreshment break at **Moskosel** enables passengers to visit the railway museum that has been set up in the station building, dedicated to the workers who built the line. One of the exhibits is a pedal-driven inspection trolley. Here the train host collects lunch orders, which are then telephoned through to the next station, Arvidsjaur, the first town of any size since leaving Gällivare, 274 km (171 miles) to the north.

Arvidsjaur is one of the main tourist centres of Lapland and has a beautiful wooden church dating from 1902. It is worth spending a day or two here, as on Friday and Saturday in July and early August one of Sweden's many preserved steam locomotives comes to life to operate evening tours (departing at 5.45pm) to Slagnäs, 53 km (33 miles) away. Marketed as the "Wilderness Train", the set of original 1930s coaches includes a small restaurant section serving local spe-cialities. It is a very leisurely trip and the train stops on the way for passengers to take photographs and enjoy the cool evening air. No advance booking is necessary.

An unusual day out can be enjoyed by hiring a pedal inspection trolley from the east end of the station to travel over the closed branch line. The tracks run some 75 km (47 miles) to **Jörn** on the main Boden–Stockholm line; in theory you can take your

Map on page 290

BELOW: granite pillar at Jokkmokk commemorating the opening of the line in 1937.

*The Inlandsbanan
has been ferrying
tourists around the
Swedish backwoods
since 1994.*

BELOW: passengers
walk across the
bridge at Iggejaur.

trolley all the way, but most people only venture a few kilometres from Arvidsjaur. The line traverses a sparsely-inhabited forest area and it is possible stop off and have a picnic, the trolleys being light enough to lift off the track to allow others to pass. Trolleys can be hired for periods of up to five hours or, for the real enthusiast, 24 hours.

South from Arvidsjaur

After a lunch of reindeer meat eaten on the station platform, the half-hour stop is soon over and a blast on the train's horn quickly gets everyone back on board. Southbound trains reverse here, and head west for over 80 km (50 miles), passing the southern end of the vast Lake Storavan. The line takes on a different character here, for not only has the track been relaid but it is on proper ballast enabling a faster speed and a less bumpy ride.

Sorsele marks the halfway point on the northern section of the Inlandsbanan to Östersund, and also the point where the daily northbound service passes the southbound train. The stationmaster completes his main job of the day in 15 minutes, supervising the arrival and despatch of his two passenger trains. Sadly, there is no time to do justice to the excellent railway museum in the old station building.

After Sorsele, the track turns south once again and the scenery becomes more desolate and strewn with large rocks. It is here that herds of reindeer are most likely to be seen and, indeed, the driver has to keep a sharp lookout for them as they are very slow to move out of the way, despite constant sounding of the train's horn. **Storuman** is another tourist centre as well as a railway junction for the freight line to Hällnäs. It is also a centre for the timber industry and trainloads of logs are despatched from here. It is worth spending a day in the area as

there is much to see, including the old Railway Hotel, now the town's library, famous for its beautiful paintings and wrought-iron chandeliers. Sweden's largest wooden church is at the nearby village of **Stensele**; built in 1886, it contains a copy of the world's smallest bible, a quarter of the size of a postage stamp.

Soon after leaving Storuman, the line crosses the River Ume on a long girder bridge and begins a steady climb through desolate rocky country to a summit of 450 metres (1,476 ft) near the closed station of Fiandberg, before gradually descending into **Vilhelmina** where there is a 30-minute stop for refreshments.

The area south of here is mainly heathland with scattered clumps of trees and has become a popular area for campers, with stops being made at special halts near the small towns of Dorotea and Hoting to set down passengers who had travelled north on the morning train.

To the south of Hoting the line crosses various river tributaries on three impressive bridges, one of which is made of reinforced concrete – the first of its type in Sweden when it was built. There are views of a series of lakes before the train pulls into the station at **Ulriksfors**. For those passengers who had ordered in advance, a light supper is served here – albeit from the back of an estate car. This station serves the thriving tourist town of **Strömsund**, 4 km (2½ miles) to the northwest. The line then climbs steadily through more thickly forested hills to reach a summit close to the station of Munkflohögen, before descending to the Indalsalven Valley where signs of market gardening and several prosperous farms indicate we have left the wilderness behind and are approaching **Östersund**.

The train now runs parallel to the electrified line from Stockholm to Storlien, on the Norwegian frontier, for the final stretch before terminating at Östersund Central station. Östersund is the largest town in the central Jämtland region, located on the shores of the huge Storsjön lake, Sweden's fifth-largest and the reputed home of the Scandinavian version of the Loch Ness monster.

The railcar to Mora

The southern section of the Inlandsbanan is operated separately on an "out and back" basis from **Mora**, 321 km (200 miles) to the south, where the locomotive and coaches now used for the summer tourist service are based. The daily departure is in mid-afternoon and the train leaves the imposing and well-maintained station and follows the main electrified line to Stockholm for 15 km (9 miles) as far as Brunflo. Here the Inlandsbanan proper diverges and the line heads south, past the ends of two long narrow lakes before reaching **Hackås**. The village is on the southern leg of Lake Storsjön and is famous for its medieval church with wall paintings from the Middle Ages. For the next stretch there are magnificent views across the water to the mountains before the train arrives at **Åsarna**, and a 15-minute stop.

The scenery changes to open moorland interspersed with pine forests against a backdrop of desolate hills. Negotiating this lonely district the line has some quite steep switchback gradients. The line now takes a westerly course and descends to the fertile valley of the River Ljusnan, passing **Älvros** where the landscape opens up and small farms are again in evidence on the approach to **Sveg**. the former junction for the long-closed line to Hede. After a short stop, the line turns south again and climbs to Gratback, at 524 metres (1,700ft) the highest point on the line. The forests in this area are the home of the brown bear and in a clearing in the forest, the train stops for about thirty minutes whilst the guide escorts passengers to visit one of the well-established dens of these elusive animals.

Just before arriving at **Orsa** the train stops on the impressive arched steel bridge above the Helvetes waterfall to enable passengers to take pictures of this scenic location. Soon the train arrives at **Mora**, the terminus for InterCity passenger trains from Stockholm, some 4 hours away. Mora is famous for its handicrafts, in particular the gaily-painted red wooden Dala horses.

The line south to Kristinehamn has been closed since the mid-1960s but the track remains in place. It is a longer term objective of the Inlandsbanan management to reopen this line throughout for freight traffic and for tourist passengers, but until then a replacement bus runs (not Saturday) the 190-km (118-mile) stretch to Nykroppa from where a connecting railcar operates over the final 40 km (25 miles) to Kristinehamn.

Map on page 290

TIP

An excellent way to enjoy Storsjön lake is to take a trip on the oldest steam boat still in service in Sweden, the SS Thomée. Built in 1875, it is now powered by a diesel engine and operates daily excursions from Östersund's small harbour.

BELOW: the attractive wooden station building at Gällivare.

HELSINKI–ST PETERSBURG

ESSENTIALS

Thomas Cook
timetable no. 1910

Distance: 442 km

Duration of journey:
5 hrs 40 mins (new
trains from 2010 are
expected to reduce
this to 3 hrs)

Frequency of trains:
3 per day

*Statues guard the
doors of Helsinki
station, considered a
masterpiece of art
nouveau
architecture.*

The best travelling experiences give an acute sense of departure and arrival; and the train journey from Helsinki to St Petersburg does exactly that. From leaving the civic-minded, organised capital of Finland it takes just under six hours to reach Finlyandsky *vokzal* (Finland Station) and the anarchic streets of St Petersburg's grand but dilapidated candy-coloured world.

Not that Helsinki isn't an impressive town. Take your departure point, the **central station** (Rautatieasema), positioned, as all good stations should be, in the centre of town. Designed by Eliel Saarinen in 1905 (although not completed until 1919), this superb building combines Helsinki's defining National Romantic (art nouveau) architectural style. Travellers can't fail to glance upwards at the granite building's green clock tower, or miss Emil Wikström's brace of impressive, square-jawed statues holding translucent lanterns on either side of the main doors. The interior of the station is also a treat. Clean and well signposted, it is easy to find the ticketing hall, change some money into roubles (Helsinki is one of the few places outside Russia where you can do this) and relax in the Eliel restaurant, its stunning murals overlooked by a large painting by Eero Järnefelt.

Two contrasting trains

There are two trains a day from Helsinki to St Petersburg. The Finnish morning express train, the Sibelius, arrives in St Petersburg in time for a late lunch. The Sibelius is a modern and stylish affair with a dining car, on-board coffee shop and salon compartment for socialising or conferencing. Described in the brochure as "exotic", the journey on the Russian-owned Repin train, which departs daily from Helsinki in the mid-afternoon to arrive at its destination in the late evening, is a more romantic experience. Taking the later train gently eases first-time travellers to Russia into their destination and effectively provides a bridge between the contrasting way of life in Helsinki.

The train's interior gives a taste of the Russian experience to come; shabby but grand, intense and claustrophobic but with elements of the lavish style found in St Petersburg's crumbling, beautiful architecture. First-class cabins comprise two couchettes shaded by dark-green curtains and blinds with matching, worn rugs and blankets. A touch of Russian-style luxury is added by the two pillows and towels per passenger and the complimentary snack served without ceremony on a paper plate. Second-class passengers get a comfy seat in a six-person compartment. The restaurant car, half way along the train, is kitted out

Helsinki-St Petersburg

in yellow and white with blinds and bunches of plastic flowers on the table. Menus are in Russian and, on the back of the menu card, in English. Prices are in roubles and payment is made in either roubles or Euros, depending on the location of the train. No credit cards are accepted.

The route retraces the 1917 journey made by Lenin, who was greeted at Finland station in St Petersburg (later re-named Leningrad) by a crowd of workers and soldiers who lifted him onto the roof of an armoured car, where he ended his first revolutionary speech in Russia with the words, "Long live the socialist revolution!". Six months later the battleship *Aurora* fired the empty shell that heralded the start of the Russian Revolution. Lenin's journey is commemorated by a statue outside the Finland station.

Fields and forests

The train heads northwest out of Helsinki, stopping at the suburban stations of Pasila and Tikkurila before joining the new direct line to Lahti which opened in 2006. Slowly, but surely, the view from the window switches from suburbs to fields, then to the forests of pine, spruce and birch that are the backbone of Finland's paper products industry, the second largest in the world. Some quick ways to identify the different tree species whizzing past your window: pines are the tallest, and tend to have little undergrowth around them; the sun-loving birch has bright, white bark; while spruces can be recognised by their droopy branches and dense, dark-green growth.

Just before the train gets to the station of the winter sports centre of **Lahti** there is an old steam engine to the left. Although you can't see Lahti's famous ski jump from the train, passengers can get a glimpse of part of the deep-blue

Map
on page
304

★

Star Attractions:
Helsinki
● **Cathedral**
● **Kiasma (Museum of**
Contemporary Art)
● **Ateneum (Museum**
of Finnish Art)
● **Finlandia Hall**
● **Esplanade Park**

BELOW:
old-fashioned
comfort on the
Repin train.

Map
on page
304

lake of Päijänne before the line heads east towards the capital of Kymi province, **Kouvola,** a busy junction where freight trains and cargo trucks jostle for position on the tracks next to the station. From Kouvola it is about three-quarters of an hour to **Vainikkala** and the Russian border. On a sunny day the lakeland countryside is breathtaking, the views providing a welcome break from the continuous forests of pine and spruce.

A formidable frontier

The Russian railways were built during the reign of Tsar Nicholas I and, as Finland uses the same wide gauge tracks (a legacy of the days when it was ruled from St Petersburg), travel between the two countries is possible without the time-consuming bogie changing necessary when arriving from countries further south, such as Poland. Remember to adjust your watch, as Russia is an hour ahead of Finland.

The immigration officers on the Russian side of the border have a reputation for being scary. This is justified, but their unsmiling demeanour is more of a hangover from the era of the Cold War than anything to worry about. The unfeasibly large hats that officers wear as part of their uniform unwittingly add to the pantomime exchange with passengers. Next up is customs clearance, which takes place a little way after Vainikkala station. It's a tricky procedure for the uninitiated. All currency, including travellers' cheques, must be declared on a form, along with mobile phones and less obvious items such as "printed editions and information media" which could cover this book if you are reading it on the Repin. Keep hold of your form once it's been scrutinised as it will be checked when you leave Russia. And don't be surprised if your cabin is vigorously searched for stowaways.

As the train picks up speed on the final 2-hour run from Vyborg to St Petersburg, it is possible to change currency and to buy duty-free goods from snazzily attired attendants. Although there are no official smoking areas on board, apart from the desperate, chilly, no-man's-land at the end of the car, passengers often take the opportunity to sample their duty free tobacco in transit and perhaps to celebrate their entry to the romantic city of St Petersburg.

Into St Petersburg

Finland station is an unremarkable building lined with dusty huts selling magazines and food. Go through the station's main doors and you will find a few white taxis waiting to pick up passengers – the station is located north of the River Neva and some way from the main tourist sights and hotels. Taxis are unmetered, and heavy bargaining is essential. Before you start your white-knuckle ride (taxis rule the road in St Petersburg) or take the Metro Ploshchad Lenina into town, take a look at the huge statue of Lenin in front of the station. Unveiled in 1926, it celebrates his triumphant return from Finland *(see previous page)*, and is one of the few remaining statues of Vladimir Ilyich Ulyanov left in St Petersburg – neatly setting the tone for your journey into one of Europe's most compelling cities. ❏

Star Attractions:
St Petersburg
● The Hermitage
● Mariinsky Theatre
● Peter and Paul
  Fortress
● Smolny Cathedral
● Nevsky Prospekt
● Vasiliesky Island
● Alexander Column

BELOW: Lenin's
return to Russia is
commemorated
outside the station.

Museums and Heritage Lines

The numbers relate to the map on page 290.

Museums

Danish Railway Museum ❶
Dannebrogsgade 24,
DK 5000 Odense.
Café, shop
Open: daily 10am–4pm
Features: well-organised and
fascinating displays
Nearest station: Odense
Tel: 66 13 66 30
www.jernbanemuseum.dk

Suomen Rautatiemuseo ❷
(Finnish Railway Museum)
Hyvinkäänkatu 9,
SF 05800 Hyvinkää
Café, shop
Open: Sept–May Tue–Sat
noon–3pm, Sun 12–5pm;
June–Aug daily 10am–5pm
Features: the Imperial train
used by the Romanovs
Nearest station: Hyvinkää
Tel: 0307 25241
www.rautatie.org

Norwegian Railway Museum ❸
Strandvien 163, N-2316
Hamar
Restaurant, shop, narrow
gauge railway
Open: June–mid-Aug daily
10.30am–5pm; rest of year
11am–3pm, Sun until 4pm
Features: one of the world's
oldest railway museums (1896)
Nearest station: Hamar
Tel: 62 51 31 60
www.norsk-jernbanemuseum.no

Swedish Railway Museum ❹
Rälsgatan 1, 80108 Gävle
Café, bookshop
Open: June–Aug daily 10am–
5pm; Sept–May Tue–Sun
10am–4pm
Features: large collection of
locomotives and carriages
Nearest station: Gävle Central
Tel: 026 14 46 15
www.banverket.se/sv/sveriges
-jarnvagsmuseum.aspx

Heritage Lines

Gamle Vossebanen ❺
(Norway) (Garnes–Midttun)
PO Box 638 Sentrum,
N 5807 Bergen
Open: June–mid-Sept, Sun only
Features: steam, museum
Nearest station: Arna
Length: 18 km (11¼ miles)
Gauge: 1,435 mm (4 ft 8½ in)
Tel: 5591 7780
http://home.no.net/tgrindhe

Krøderbanen ❻ (Norway)
(Vikersund–Krøderen)
3535 Krøderen
Café, shop, historic station,
museum
Open: steam late June–Aug Sun
Features: Norway's longest
museum line
Nearest station: Vikersund
(local trains from Oslo)
Length: 26 km (16¼ miles)
Gauge: 1,435 mm (4 ft 8½ in)
Tel: 32 14 76 44
www.kroderbanen.museum.no

Rjukanbanen ❼ (Norway)
(Rjukan–Mæl)
Café, museum, railway ferry
Open: contact for schedule
Nearest station: Notodden
Gauge: 1,435 mm (4 ft 8½ in)
Tel: 35 08 15 31

Setesdalsbanen ❽ (Norway)
(Grovane–Røyknes)
Grovane, N 4700 Vennesla
Open: mid-June–end Aug Sun;

also Tue–Fri in July
Features: only remaining
3 ft 6 inch gauge line
Length: 12 km (7½ miles)
Gauge: 1067 mm (3 ft 6 in)
Tel: 38 15 64 82
www.setesdalsbanen.no

Urskog-Hølandsbanen ❾
(Norway) (Sørumsand–Fossum)
Open: Sun late June–end Aug,
Wed in July
Nearest station: Sørumsand
Length: 4 km (2½ miles)
Gauge: 750 mm (2 ft 5½ in)
Tel: 63 86 81 50

Museijärnvägen i Mariefred
❿ (Sweden) (Läggesta–
Mariefred/Taxinge Näsby)
Café, shop
Open: certain days, May–Sept
Features: connects with 1903
steamship to Stockholm
Nearest station: Läggesta
Length: 3.2/7 km (2/4.4 miles)
Gauge: 600 mm (1 ft 11⅝ in)
Tel: 0159-210 00/06
www.oslj.nu

Skara-Lundsbrunns Järn-vägar ⓫ (Sweden); Tullporta-gatan 1, S-53230 Skara
Open: late June–Aug Sun, Tue
and Thur afternoons
Features: roundhouse at Skara
Length: 11.2 km (7 miles)
Gauge: 891 mm (2 ft 11 in)
Tel: 0511 136 36
www.sklj.se

Jokoinen Museum Railway
⓬ (Finland) (Jokioinen–
Minkiö–Humppila)
PO Box 1, FI 31601 Jokioien
Open: June–Aug Sun
Features: museum at Minkiö
Nearest station: Humppila
Length: 14 km (9 miles)
Gauge: 750 mm (2 ft 5½ in)
Tel: 03 433 3235
www.jokioistenmuseo
rautatie.fi

OTHER EUROPEAN ROUTES

Maps on pages 312/335

With a dense network of lines snaking through unspoiled country-side to the remotest corners of little-known lands, rail travel in the East of Europe can be a rewarding adventure

Railway journeys in Eastern Europe are not as straightforward as those in the West. Trains are not as well-appointed or as comfortable, and there are various idiosyncracies and inconveniences to contend with, although these are disappearing fast. On the plus side for the railway enthusiast – with plenty of time – most of the countries of the former Soviet bloc (particularly the Czech Republic, Hungary, Romania and Bulgaria) have a few narrow gauge branch lines winding their way into remote rural backwaters. For convenience, Greece has been included in this section of the book.

Much of the Eastern European railway network developed later than that in the West; lines connecting Vienna and Budapest with their domains in the Austro-Hungarian Empire arrived in the 1870s, spreading gradually east and south towards Istanbul. The first Orient Express to complete the journey from Paris entirely by rail did so in 1889. Railway construction was hindered by the mountainous topography of much of southeastern Europe, as well as the chronic political instability caused by the decline of the Ottoman Empire. In Russia, however, the Moscow to St Petersburg line was completed by 1851.

A commitment to railways

Eastern Europe's railways took a battering in World War II, after which the Communists set about a large-scale rebuilding operation with gusto; the Soviet authorities always gave railways a high priority, as a symbol of development and progress alongside industrialisation and electrification. Many of the branch lines across a broad swathe of the Hungarian *puszta* date from this period. Previously, many Hungarian towns on the grasslands were isolated and the peasants lived off the land. This was anathema to the Soviet idea of modernisation; throughout the 1950s and 1960s new industrial plants were built in rural areas, linked by the extensive rail system that remains today.

The density of the region's railway network is in part due to the fact that Western Europe's long-standing tradition of closing down uneconomic branch lines never caught on. The Soviets were committed to railways, and this mentality has endured, as has a certain pride in the railway system. The fact that car ownership remains considerably lower than in Western Europe, and the motorway network is non-existent in many areas, has also discouraged any cost-cutting measures. With increased prosperity and EU membership for the Baltic States, Poland, the Czech Republic, Slovakia, Hungary, Romania, Bulgaria and Slovenia, this is sadly now changing.

PRECEDING PAGES: the High Tatras from Poprad Tatry, Slovakia. **LEFT:** paint job at Cierny Balog, Slovakia. **BELOW:** outside Moscow's Belorusskaya station.

North Central Europe

N

0 _____ 100 km

0 _____ 100 miles

BALTIC SEA

Łeba Wejherowo Hel Kaliningrad

Ustka Gdynia Bałtiysk RUSSIA

Słupsk Lębork Sopot Chernyakhovsk

Rostock Gdańsk

Greifswald Kolobrzeg Koszalin Elbląg Bartoszyce Giżycko

Ahlbeck Bialogard Tczew Malbork Kętrzyn

Güstrow Kamień Pomorskie Olsztyn Ełk

Neubrandenburg Świnoujście Laskowice Iława Ostróda

Pasewalk Stargard Szczeciński Wisła Działdowo Mława

Waren Szczecin Choszczno Bydgoszcz Ciechanów

Neustrelitz Goleniów Piła Toruń St Petersburg

Pritzwalk Löwenberg Wronki Inowrocław Włocławek Bug ④

Wittenberge Oranienburg Eberswalde Noteć Rogozno Legionowo Tłuszcz

Stendal Angermünde Poznań Gniezno Wisła (Vistula) Warszawa (Warsaw) Mińsk Mazowiecki

Rathenow Berlin Kostrzyn Konin Kutno Otwock

Brandenburg Fürstenwalde Rzepin Zbąszyń Września Łowicz Żyrardów Skierniewice

Burg Potsdam Frankfurt Zbąszynek ⑭ Kolo Łódź Dęblin

GERMANY Wolsztyn Kościan Zduńska Wola Koluszki

Dessau Lutherstadt Wittenberg Lübben Zielona Góra Leszno Jarocin Kalisz Pabianice Pulawy

Doberlug-Kirchhain Odra Sieradz Piotrków Trybunalski Radom

Bitterfeld Weißwasser Głogów Ostrów Wielkopolski Skarżysko-Kamienna

Halle Żary Bolesławiec Olesnica Radomsko Kielce

Leipzig Elsterwerda POLAND Częstochowa

Naumburg Riesa Bautzen Görlitz Legnica Wrocław Kluczbork Sandomierz

Gera Altenburg Löbau Jelenia Góra Oława Opole Myszków Zawiercie Jędrzejów

Zwickau Chemnitz Liberec Wałbrzych Kłodzko Kamieniec Ząbkowicki Bytom Kozłów Wisła

Plauen Erzgebirge Teplice Turnov Hradec Králové Gliwice Sosnowiec Rzeszów

Hof Chomutov Most Sudety Katowice Tarnów

Cheb Kladno Nymburk Pardubice Zabrze Chorzów Kraków

Mārktredwitz Karlovy Vary Praha (Prague) Kolín Česká Třebová Ostrava Tychý Bochnia Dębica

Weiden Mariánské Lázně Příbram Benešov Petrovice Sucha Beskidzka Nowy Sącz Jasło

Domažlice Plzeň CZECH REPUBLIC Olomouc Zwardoń Nowy Targ Krynica

Schwandorf Klatovy Tábor Jihlava Přerov Hranice Čadca Zakopane Plaveč

Cham Strakonice Vsetín Žilina Tatry 2655 Poprád Prešov

Regensburg České Budějovice Třebíč Brno Otrokovice Púchov Ružomberok Margecany

Straubing Deggendorf Gmünd Břeclav Hodonín Trenčín Banská Bystrica ⑧ Košice

Landshut Vilshofen Summerau Kúty SLOVAKIA Rožňava

Simbach Donau Linz Melk Wien (Vienna) Trnava Zvolen Slovenské Rudohorie

Braunau Wels Enns Nové Zámky Levice Lučenec Miskolc Tokaj

Traunstein Steyr Amstetten St Pölten Bratislava Komárno Štúrovo Szilvásvárad ⑫ Nyíregyháza

Rosenheim Salzburg Gmunden Wiener Neustadt Bruck an der Leitha Stúrovo Vác Hatvan Eger Mezőkövesd

Kitzbühel Schwarzach-St Veit Mariazell Sopron Győr Tatabánya Budapest ⑥ Jászberény Debrecen

Krimml Liezen Leoben Bruck an der Mur Szombathely Pápa ⑥ Cegléd Karcag

Großglockner 3797 Knittelfeld Veszprém Székesfehérvár Kecskemét Szajol

Spittal AUSTRIA Graz Zalaegerszeg Ajka Siófok Mezőtúr

Millstättersee Klagenfurt Balaton HUNGARY Kiskunfélegyháza Gyula

Villach Maribor Nagykanizsa Dombóvár Kiskőrös Békéscsaba

Pieve di Cadore Jesenice Pragersko Kaposvár Kiskunmajsa

ITALY Triglav 2863 SLOVENIA Celje Koprivnica Szekszárd Kiskunhalas Szeged Arad

Udine Gorizia Pécs Subotica ROMANIA

Pordenone Ljubljana ⑦ Zagreb Virovitica Drava

Treviso Sežana Dugo Selo Osijek Novi Sad

Venezia (Venice) Trieste Sisak CROATIA Vinkovci Dunav Timișoara

Chioggia Rijeka Novska Slavonski Brod Privlaka Šid SERBIA Vršac

① Museums and Heritage Lines Karlovac Ogulin Sava Ruma Pančevo

Featured route

Poiezierze Pomorski

VENICE TO ZAGREB

Map on page 315

This is a journey that takes travellers from one of Europe's most slickly packaged tourist cities right into the heart of a region that has recovered from the turmoil of the early 1990s to re-emerge, albeit slowly, as one of Europe's most attractive and unspoiled destinations. It follows a route that takes in swathes of spectacular scenery as it skirts the fringes of the Adriatic Sea, climbs to the southeastern edge of the Alps and furrows its way through rugged mountain gorges.

Like all great journeys it begins in a flush of romance, on the very edge of the **Grand Canal**, crowded with gondolas, tourist-clogged *vaporettos*, water taxis and the sirens of whizzing police boats. Above the aquatic mayhem lie the façades of the grand palaces and the sweeping spires of Canaletto's Venice. In the midst of it all is the functionalism of Venice Santa Lucia railway station where the journey into the Balkans begins.

Venice to Monfalcone

Pulling away from La Serenissima the train eases over the causeway that links the slowly sinking city with the urban sprawl of **Mestre**. The waters stretch away on either side of the track, which appears to be floating over the Venetian Lagoon. Mestre is the adjunct of Venice, where the "real" people live, an unlovely town, but a major railway junction with lines continuing west on to Padua, Verona and Milan. To the north the track is divided between the line to Treviso and on to the Dolomites, and the second fork that runs eastwards into the Balkans.

One daytime train, the "Casanova", operates along the 4-hour route to Ljubljana. A connection allows a late evening arrival in Zagreb, the capital of Croatia, but a stay in the Slovenian capital is more pleasant.

Trains between Venice and Budapest continued to run even through the dark days when Slovenia and, to a much greater extent, Croatia were in the grip of a war of independence with the former Yugoslavia. Even when civilians were killed by Serb missiles in Zagreb, and Yugoslav war planes were bombing the late President Tudjman's palace, the Venezia Express continued to ferry in passengers, although they were often UN staff and military personnel, rather than the civilians and the occasional tourists who come today.

Striking north from Mestre the line runs along the flat plains that are bordered by the waters of the Adriatic on one flank and the looming peaks of the Dolomites on the other. Even in summer, the sweeping views of Italy's Alpine spine that open up before you on a clear day show that it is still tipped with a sprinkling of snow. The line studiously avoids tackling both the coast and the mountains and the only natural obstacles are the Livenza, Piave and Tagliamento rivers, which are all easily straddled.

Monfalcone is the large port that heralds the line's arrival on the shores of the Adriatic Sea. As the train rolls into town, the uglier face of the Adriatic appears.

ESSENTIALS

Thomas Cook timetable nos. 89b/91

Distance: 444 km

Duration of journey: 7 hrs 50 mins

Frequency of trains: 1 per day, change in Ljubljana
1 overnight direct train

BELOW: views from a gondola.

Star Attractions:
Venice
● **Grand Canal**
● **Doge's Palace**
● **St Mark's Square**
   and Basilica
● **Rialto Bridge**
● **Colleoni Monument**
● **Santa Maria**
   Gloriosa church
● **Bovolo Palace**
● **Scuola Grande di**
   San Rocco

BELOW: Lake Bled
in the Julian Alps
of Slovenia.

The cranes and clatter of the port precede the billowing sails and idyllic coves that accompany the short run from here to Trieste. After decades of decay this much ignored corner of Italy is starting to re-emerge; trade with the new Balkan states is a key part of the growth. Thankfully, the train soon leaves behind both Monfalcone and the bustle of the port.

A quiet Riviera

The line now hugs tighter to the Adriatic on the approach to **Trieste**. The wide Gulf of Trieste comes into view and remains there all the way into the city. This is the little visited northernmost corner of the Mediterranean, but despite its relative obscurity, it is every bit as spectacular as the French Riviera, albeit without the glamour and the bustling crowds. Cliffs and wooded slopes hug the northern side of the track, while the waters to the south are full of marinas and yachts, with the shadows of larger freighters in the distance out in the gulf.

The direct train is now routed via Villa Opicina and longer stops in Trieste but the city can be reached by local connections from Venice. You might consider spending a day or two in Trieste, which is both an intriguing modern port town and a delightful backwater. With its unique collage of Austrian, Slavic and – very loosely – Italian influences, the ambience is of a raffish "Vienna on Sea" with grand façades and boulevards that date back to Trieste's proud days as the main port of the Austrian Habsburg Empire. It was the headquarters of the Italian high command in World War I, and after a turbulent World War II it did not come under Italian administration until 1954.

Trieste's generous waterfront is centred on the 19th-century Piazza dell'Unità d'Italia (Italy's largest sea-facing piazza), surrounded by a series of handsome

buildings. The city is also home to what the locals claim is Italy's finest coffee; you can enjoy testing this claim in the *belle époque* cafés that grace the city-centre streets.

Into Slovenia

Once back on the main line east the train quickly crosses the narrow coastal strip of Italian territory to reach the **Villa Opicina** border station, before the **Sežana** stop signals entry into the Republic of Slovenia, one of Europe's smallest nation states. Slovenia only came into being in 1991, after a relatively painless divorce from Yugoslavia. The two borders on this line are a world away from the clichéd images of gruff Eastern European border guards roughing up unsuspecting travellers and charging dubious spot-fines. Both Slovenia and Croatia – with the former now a member of the European Union, and the latter hoping to join – are keen to stress their modern European credentials and here it shows in polite, efficient passport and customs checks.

Ljubljana is a lively and attractive city, and a good base from which to explore the rest of the country.

    The charms of Slovenia are soon apparent as the track starts to climb through the wooded slopes of the Julian Alps. As the scenery becomes more and more rugged, tiny mountain villages and church spires pepper the landscape in scenes reminiscent of Switzerland or Austria. National divisions so often blur in this part of Europe, as is the case here, with the Alpine ranges of Austria, Italy and Slovenia all merging into a continuous whole.

    After the effort of negotiating the Julian Alps, the train descends to **Ljubljana**, Slovenia's compact and enjoyable capital. The history of this city of 300,000 inhabitants is apparent in the collage of Italian and Austro-Habsburg architectural styles set out on the banks of the sleepy Ljubljanica River. Italian café culture fills the cobbled streets by the water during the warmer months, while the warmth of beer cellars dominates in winter as the icy temperatures take hold. An eminently walkable city, Ljubljana is easy to explore and its tourist board is happy to point visitors towards the museums, the leafy parks, and the castle that hangs omnipresent over the city.

    Ljubljana is also a good base for exploring the rest of the country. To the north is some tremendous Alpine scenery, particularly around Lake Bled, with its picture-perfect church standing serene on an island in the middle of the lake, and Lake Bohinj, a less touristy mountain resort. There is plenty of opportunity for hiking, climbing or just lazing around admiring the mountain views.

    From Ljubljana, the railway follows the roaring waters of the Sava, an important waterway that connects the Slovenian capital with its erstwhile compatriots, Zagreb and Belgrade. This is the most spectacular part of the

Star Attractions:
Zagreb
● *Belle époque*
  boulevards
● Cathedral
● The Old Town
● Hotel Esplanade

journey as the carriages swing around the tight curves, skip through numerous tunnels, and rumble through the deep rock cuttings necessary to steer the track through this difficult terrain. For much of the journey towards Zagreb the express hugs the fast-flowing river, with towering mountains on each side. Occasionally a waterside village looms into view before the train swings away into another tunnel or cutting, to emerge in view of another hamlet with a ramble of houses clustered around a picturesque old church.

Dobova to Zagreb

The border is reached at **Dobova**, where the voltage is switched to the Croatian standard. Border formalities are relatively straightforward these days. For all its ambition to be regarded as a progressive part of modern Europe, much of Croatia is still heavily reliant on small-scale agricultural production, and in the short stretch from the border to Zagreb you will see horse-drawn carts driven by cloth-capped old men, while head-scarfed labourers work the fields; this corner of Europe is still a world away from the modern, mechanised farming further west.

The approach into **Zagreb** passes the usual sprawl of uninspiring apartment blocks and decaying industrial buildings. Yet this city of almost one million inhabitants has come a long way since being bombarded by Serb rockets in 1991, and has wholeheartedly embraced capitalism. The city has a scenic location, with an old town reminiscent of Prague or Riga and an elegant central business district. On a warm evening when the cafés are full to bursting point with style-conscious young Croatians, it is an invigorating place to be. This is a symbolic end to a journey that takes today's rail travellers across the tracks of the new map of Europe.

BELOW: following the Sava River through the Slovenian mountains.

BERLIN–BUDAPEST

Maps on pages 312/318

This journey from the North European Plain to the heart of central Europe includes some stunning river scenery, notably along the Elbe and the Danube, and beautiful rolling landscapes. The Hungaria train is operated by the Hungarian State Railway (MAV). It has comfortable carriages, and the restaurant car is the real thing – proper sit-down service with a waiter, a menu and a wine list. The line passes through four countries, taking in the superb cities of Dresden and Prague en route to one of Europe's most enjoyable destinations.

Berlin to the Czech border

Having arrived from Hamburg, our train leaves the lower level of the shiny new Hauptbahnhof – a central station built on land freed by the clearing of the Berlin wall, and conveniently close to the Reichstag and Brandenburg Gate. From here the tracks head south across the pancake-flat plain, where there are large tracts of forest and fields stretching into the distance. Settlements are few and far between; this is the middle of the old East Germany, and the few towns and villages are perceptibly poorer than those further west.

About 1½ hours out of Berlin the land begins to rise, and soon changes character completely. Vines appear on south-facing hillsides, cows and horses graze lush pastures. Soon the train is nearing **Dresden**, "the Florence of the Elbe", with excellent views over the city, none more so than when crossing the river. South of Dresden the track follows the river's course (try to get a seat on the train's left side). This is a beautiful stretch, the river running between craggy, forested hills, with an occasional picturesque town strung along the riverside;

ESSENTIALS

Thomas Cook timetable no. 60

Distance: 996 km

Duration of journey: 11 hrs 50 mins

Frequency of trains: 2 per day (direct)

BELOW: Berlin's spectacular Reichstag building.

Star Attractions:
Berlin

● **Reichstag**
● **Cathedral**
● **Brandenburg Gate**
● **Charlottenburg**
● **Museum Island**
● **Friedrichstrasse**
● **Potsdamer Platz**

Schöna is particularly striking, with a long line of market stalls leading to two tall rock pillars positioned either side of a tributary. **Königstein Fortress** can be seen on the right, perched 360 metres (1,160 feet) above the river. The border station of **Bad Schandau** is a centre for hiking trails into Sächsische Schweiz National Park – the area is known as the "Switzerland of Saxony".

Bohemia and Moravia

As the train continues southwards into the Czech Republic, the Elbe (known as the Labe on this side of the border) becomes less visible, although the scenery is no less ravishing, with broad, grassy slopes leading up to extensive stands of forest. Passengers are treated to a fine view over the first town in the Czech Republic, **Děčín**, with a handsome *zámek* (castle). As the train heads into central Bohemia the landscape opens up. Just 30 km (18 miles) before arrival in Prague, the train passes through the tiny village of Nelahozeves, birthplace of Dvorak, a life-long train enthusiast.

A return to river and hills heralds the approach of **Prague**, where most passengers get off; the train stops at the modern Holesovice station in the northern suburbs before cutting through tunnels to the east – views of the old city are limited. From here the route heads east into the heart of Bohemia, the flattest part of the Czech Republic, where the line passes through forests and fields of maize and sunflowers. Many towns are rendered invisible by solid fences running beside the track – which benefits residents suffering noise pollution, but is bad news for passengers interested in their surroundings. The big-sky country is interrupted by wooded hills after Chocen and again around **Brezova**, a tranquil-looking hill town. We are now in Moravia, the other, less-visited half of the Czech Republic.

BELOW: the dome of Esztergom with the Danube in the background.

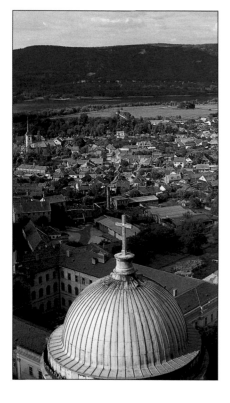

In the hills north of **Brno** we pass peaceful little waterways flanked by pretty gardens. Brno itself is a large city, its historic centre surrounded by belching chimneys and, in common with all the other large towns along the way, overlooked by a gigantic TV tower. South from here to **Břeclav** the train picks up speed (most of the previous five hours have been slow going). There are huge, empty fields, A-frame huts, gaggles of geese, and grassy hills in the middle distance. The land begins to assume a fertile, southern flavour – summers are warmer here than elsewhere in the country, and vines appear along the sides of the track. The lake of Chko Palava can be seen on the right, close to the Austrian border.

Slovakia and the Danube

The Slovak border is crossed north of **Kúty**, and the train continues south to **Bratislava**, with good views down to the Danube on the right. Formerly known as Pressburg, the city has, at various times in the past, been under German, Habsburg and Hungarian ownership. Despite its status as a national capital (since 1993), Bratislava is a small city and still feels provincial – the railway station certainly lacks the grandeur of its big-city counterparts.

After passing the steep slopes of the Little Carpathians on the left, the stretch from Bratislava to the Hungarian border is flat and empty. At the border the Danube is regained, and the final stretch from here to Budapest features wonderful scenery as the river, and the track, are squeezed between the Börzsöny and Pilis hills. We pass **Esztergom**, where the giant basilica's 100-metre (330-ft) green dome can be seen for miles; and **Visegrad**, with its citadel perched high on a hill. Finally, just under 12 hours after leaving Berlin, the train pulls into **Budapest's Nyugati terminus**.

Maps
on pages
312/318

Star Attractions:
Prague
● Hrad (Castle)
● Charles Bridge
● Old Town Square
● Astronomical Clock
● Jewish Quarter
● National Gallery
● Waldstein Palace
● Mala Strana back
streets

BELOW: the Grand Colonnade at Mariánské Lázné.

EXCURSIONS WEST OF PRAGUE

The rolling countryside of Western Bohemia is crisscrossed by a maze of branch lines, many of which make rewarding day trips from Prague.

The main line to Plzen and Germany emerges abruptly from the grimy Prague suburbs into delightful countryside, following the River Berounka as it winds its way up into the craggy hills of the Cesky Kras. Karlstejn Castle can be glimpsed briefly on the right, a short distance before its station. After the town of Beroun the terrain flattens out, with sweeping vistas across cornfields to distant manor houses and castles perched on rocky outcrops. West of Plzen the land becomes hilly, wooded and sparsely populated – this part of the Czech Republic was depopulated after World War II, when ethnic Germans were expelled, and remains conspicuously empty today. There are tremendous views into the river gorge on the right before, just over an hour from Plzen, the train pulls into Mariánské Lázné (Marienbad), one of the three famous spa towns of the region that have preserved their 18th- and 19th-century glory. Take the branch line north to Karlovy Vary (Carlsbad), the largest and best-known of the spas. Trains are outstandingly slow (53 km/33 miles in 1 hour 40 mins), but the route passes through pristine (and protected) forested hills teeming with wildlife.

Looking down on Budapest from the top of Gellert Hill.

HUNGARY: ROUTES FROM BUDAPEST

Budapest makes an excellent base for some enjoyable railway excursions. Hungarians are proud of their railways, and within the extensive network there are several preserved lines and other routes of special interest. *(For more details, see page 342.)*

The Children's Railway

High in the hills above Budapest is the Gyermekvasút (Children's Railway), a narrow gauge line that trundles through the woods between Széchenyi-Hegy (accessed by funicular railway from near Moskva Tér in Buda) and Hüvösvölgy. The railway was set up in the late 1940s to encourage children to develop an interest in railways, and is still run by 10- to14-year-olds, with smart uniforms and serious attitudes. Happily, the trains themselves are driven by adults, and cover the distance of 11 km (7 miles) in about 40 minutes.

From mid-March until mid-October trains run on a daily basis (departures every 45 minutes); in the winter months there are fewer departures and the railway is closed on Monday. From the halt at János-Hegy a path leads to the hill of the same name, at 529 metres (1,735ft) the highest point around Budapest, with tremendous views over the city. From here you can take a chair lift back down to the city, or after seeing the museum at the Huvösvölgy terminus, catch a bus for the short ride back downhill.

BELOW:
recruit on the Children's Railway.

The Szalajka Forest Railway

From the attractive town of **Eger** (two hours northeast of Budapest by train), you can head north into the Bükk Hills, taking an hour to reach the town of Szilvásvárad, jumping-off point for the **Szalajka Forest Railway** (be sure to alight at Szilvásvárad Szalajkavölgy, which precedes the main station). From here, follow the road about 600 metres (650 yds) down the hill, past the Peter Kovacs stud farm, where the white Lippizaner horses for which the region is famous are bred; when the main road swings left, a right turn takes you to the Forest Railway. A tiny steam locomotive strains uphill into the dense beech and alder forest, passing trout pools and the *szikla-forrás* spring before arriving at the lovely, grassy glade at Fatyolvizesés. Most people walk the short distance back to Szilvasvarad. The steam train service is somewhat sporadic; see www.kisvasut.hu or check with the tourist office before setting out.

South of Budapest

A unique railway line runs through the middle of the riverine forest of **Gemenc**, a protected area on the Danube, famous for its red deer. The starting point for the line is the small town of Pörböly, a few kilometres west of Baja. There are also boat trips through the park.

Another interesting line runs from the town of **Kecskemét** (depart from the "KK" station) through Bugac to **Kiskunmajsa**. Trains are infrequent and slow, but this backwater journey gives an opportunity to see an unspoilt part of the *puszta*, the Great Hungarian Plain.

SLOVAKIA: ZVOLEN–KOŠICE VIA BREZNO

Map on page 312

This quiet branch line through the hills and forests of Slovakia to the pleasant city of Košice is one of the most enjoyable rail journeys in Eastern Europe. The route can be completed in a little over four hours on the Horehronec Express (which starts in Bratislava). Alternatively, you may choose to break your journey in places like Brezno or Dedinky and take time to explore the Low Tatras, or the Slovenský Raj. There is another line between Zvolen and Košice, which runs on a more southerly track via Jesenské. In common with almost all the railways in Slovakia, this line has its fair share of attractive mountain scenery.

The Slovak heartland

Zvolen grew rich on profits from the nearby silver mines during the middle ages, although prosperity is far less evident today. The main sight here is the impressive castle, at the base of which stands a replica of the armoured train used in the 1944 Slovak National Uprising. From Zvolen the track follows the wide Hron Valley for an uneventful half hour to **Banská Bystrica**, the administrative capital of central Slovakia and famous as the centre of the 1944 uprising. Get off at the Mesto station, which is reached a couple of minutes before the main station, to have a look around the large, sloping main square. As in the majority of Slovak towns, this roomy, open space is edged with old merchants' houses – mostly dating from the 17th or 18th century – painted in a rainbow of pastel shades.

From Banská Bystrica the railway continues to follow the Hron River as it turns to the east, flanking the long ridge of the Low Tatras to the north. These

ESSENTIALS

Thomas Cook timetable no. 1190

Distance: 235 km

Duration of journey: 4 hours 25 mins

Frequency of trains: 1 per day (direct)

LEFT: repairs at Čierny Balog.
BELOW: looking north from Mt Dumbier in the Low Tatras.

Mannequin in the Čierny Balog museum.

hills are far more extensive than their loftier namesakes to the north, but less well known and a good deal wilder; this is where Slovakia's remaining populations of bears and wolves can be found.

The train continues past lush meadows, one-horse towns with small wooden stations (all of which are manned) and the occasional concentration of heavy industry, usually in a state of dramatic rusting decline. **Brezno** is a typically attractive little Slovak town, with a typically remote station – a brisk 20 minutes' walk from the centre. The town makes a good base for hiking in the Low Tatras, with the highest peaks, Chopok (2,024 metres/6,640 ft and Dumbier (2,043 metres/6,702 ft), accessible from the nearby trailheads at Bystrá or, higher up the valley, the hotel at Srdiecko (where a chair lift operates to the top of Chopok).

The Hronrec Forest Railway

The village of **Čierny Balog**, in the green hills 8 km (5 miles) south of Brezno, is the terminus of the Hronec Forest Railway, Slovakia's leading preserved narrow gauge line and the result of a momentous effort by *Strom Života* (Tree of Life), a local environmentalist group which campaigned against the scrapping of the line in the 1980s. In common with many heritage lines in this corner of Europe, this Lilliputian railway was created for forestry purposes, one of around 40 such lines in Slovakia.

There is a museum and a café at the station here. Most trains are steam-hauled and run the 10 km (6 miles) up to Hronec, close to the station at Chvatimech on the Zvolen–Brezno line, from the beginning of May until mid-September.

BELOW: typical Slovakian scenery.

Map on page 312

The railway from Brezno south to Tisovec and Jesenské was built to transport iron ore and timber. The section between Pohronská Polhora and Tisovec was so steep that it required a rack section; now that it is no longer put to heavy industrial use, the rack section is closed.

As the main line heads east from Brezno the industry peters out and after Hel'pa there are good views of the mountains to the left. If you are tempted to stick your head out of the window, be careful, as the trees and bushes along the tracks are often very close to the train! The temperature starts to drop as the line climbs through pine and spruce forests on the approach to **Červená Skala**, another good base for walking in the hills.

After Telgárt the railway exercises a 360° loop to reach the highest point on the line, at 999 metres (3,277 ft), after which the train enters a new kind of landscape as the Low Tatras give way to the limestone pinnacles and gullies of the Slovenský Raj. Passing the famous ice cave of Dobšiná, with its 20-metre (65-ft) thick frozen lake, the train arrives at the hill resort and hiking centre of **Dedinky**, photogenically edging the waters of the artificial Palcmanská lake.

East to Margecany and Košice

Soon the Slovenský Raj is left behind and the landscape turns drier as the train heads towards Košice, remaining hilly but with beech trees replacing the dense stands of conifers. The highest peaks here are several hundred metres lower than those further west. The Hnilec and Hornad rivers meet to create Ruzin lake just before **Margecany**, the junction with the line to Poprad and Žilina. The lake is a popular holiday area and is surrounded by wooden A-frame *chata* (chalets). From here it is a speedy half-hour run to Košice *(see following page)*.

BELOW: a Roma family in central Slovakia.

ESSENTIALS

Thomas Cook
timetable no. 1180

Distance: 242 km

Duration of journey:
fast train 2 hrs 44
mins, slow train
3 hrs 12 mins

Frequency of trains:
two hourly

SLOVAKIA: KOŠICE–ŽILINA

The scenic railway line running across northern Slovakia was completed in 1872, when the line from the town of Bohumín, now on the Czech border with Poland, met the track running north from Košice to Prešov, which had opened a couple of years earlier. The line provides tremendous views of the High Tatras and other mountain ranges, and the frequent departures and relative speed of the trains make it particularly accessible. Most services continue on from Žilina to Bratislava, which is reached in a further 2 hours 40 minutes.

Košice to the High Tatra

The centre of Košice, Slovakia's second city, has been beautifully restored, and the exceptionally long, main square is reached from the station by a 10-minute stroll through a leafy park. Perched on the northeastern edge of the Hungarian Plain, Košice was Magyar for most of its history, and has retained its separateness from Bratislava and the Slovak heartland.

Heading north, the train passes the giant, rusting skeleton of the steelworks, which, in common with much of Eastern Europe's heavy industry, closed in the 1990s. Almost immediately the hills begin to close in, and before long the junction of Margecany is reached, where the line to Brezno and Banská Bystrica *(see page 321)* branches off to the west.

Soon after Margecany the railway enters the Spiš region – an area settled by Germans from Saxony in medieval times, after which it was granted trading privileges and became wealthy. The Spiš area is full of wide open spaces, enormous fields and grand sweeping vistas across to the mountains – the Low Tatras

BELOW: Spiš castle towers over the town of Spisské Podhradie.

to the south, and the spectacular High Tatras to the north; glimpsed from afar, the jagged peaks seem to float surreally above the plain. The range may be high but it is not extensive – only about 30 km (18 miles) from east to west. This compactness means that hiking paths are often crowded, in contrast to those of the Low Tatras.

Map on page 312

Scenic branch lines

Before reaching Poprad, the main jumping-off point for the mountains, there are a couple of branch lines leading north through the verdant Spiš country-side to noteworthy attractions; the wonderful castle ruins at **Spisske Podhradie**, and the handsome town of **Levoča**. Trains, however, are few and far between.

From the upper level of **Poprad's** extraordinary station, small electric railcars wind up into the hills. There are regular services to **Stary Smokovec**, the main resort, which is full of half-timbered lodges – notably the aptly-named Hotel Grand – as well as several 1970s monstrosities, and on to Strbske Pleso from where a steep rack railway rejoins the main line at **Strba**. The railcars are of the Swiss type (used on all Europe's highland railways), the new ones equipped with extra large windows to allow passengers to admire the view. Unfortunately, this doesn't amount to much as all the lines run through thick forest with only fleeting glimpses down to the plain and up to the rocky heights. A funicular line runs up to Hrebienok from Stary Smokovec.

Košice is one of central Europe's most delightful cities.

Strba to Žilina

West of Strba, Spiš is left behind as the train crosses a line of wooded hills to descend into the Liptov area. The less-visited western end of the High Tatras still looms large to the north, and the highest peaks of the Low Tatras (including Dumbier, at 2,043 metres/6,702 ft) are clearly visible to the south. Just past **Liptovsky Mikuláš** the large artificial lake of Liptovská Mara (Liptov Sea) comes into view, with alpine panoramas across to the mountains. The line then passes heavy industry at **Ružomberok**; many Slovak valleys are filled with such industry – often rusting away – and during cold, still, winter weather pollution levels can be extremely high. The grim surroundings of Ružomberok are relieved by its unusual station, complete with carved wooden eaves and a small tower painted in a fetching shade of blue.

Soon the River Váh widens out quite suddenly as a dam is approached. The line passes the Velka Fatra mountains to the south; at Kralovany a branch line runs through precipitous mountains to Trstená, close to the Polish border. The Žilina line passes right through the middle of the Mala Fatra range, a popular region for hiking. At the western edge of the mountains, just as the train is passing into the valley around Žilina, there is a great view to the left of the 14th-century castle ruins at **Strečno**. You can also get a glimpse of another ruined castle off to the right – the Stary Hrad.

Žilina itself is an important railway town, where the Košice line meets the line running between Bratislava and Poland.

BELOW:
the rocky peaks
of the High Tatras.

Steam in Poland

Poland is a wonderful place for railway enthusiasts: in addition to more than a dozen narrow gauge lines threading their way through its wide open spaces, the western Wielkopolska region is home to Europe's last-surviving regular steam-hauled service. This unlikely throwback to days of yore is based at the small town of Wolsztyn, where an open-air museum showcases steam engines that are still very much in everyday use.

Steam fanatics can indulge their passion with the ultimate experience: driving a steam locomotive, as part of the engine-driving courses that are held regularly in Wolsztyn. In nearby Poznań, meanwhile, there are also opportunities to learn to drive the old city trams.

At the time of going to press there were two daily return steam-hauled departures between Poznań and Wolsztyn. There is also one daily steam train between Wolsztyn and Leszno. (See the Thomas Cook European Timetable no. 1099 for schedules.)

The massive steam locomotive, puffing and hissing steam, looks oddly out of place in the utilitarian surroundings of Poznań's main station in the morning rush hour. Among the commuters hurrying along the platform there are usually a few steam enthusiasts gathered around the majestic engine, taking photographs.

Steam train passengers can usually expect to travel in attractive bespoke carriages, but such luxury is definitely not available on this working railway. The drab, dark-green PKP rolling stock is basic in the extreme, consisting of split level carriages that are in need of a good clean.

A blast of steam from the engine heralds departure on this unique journey, the train heading slowly westwards through the suburbs, whistle sounding. Before long, open fields have replaced the grey apartment blocks and the train picks up speed. Not too much speed, though – it takes a sedate 1¾ hours to reach Wolsztyn, 80 km (50 miles) to the southwest. The line runs across the northern edge of Wielkopolska National Park, with lakes and forests of birch and pine, before emerging into an open, gently undulating landscape with a scattering of villages. The scenery is not particularly diverting.

Apart from its interest for railway fans, Wolsztyn is also popular with water sports enthusiasts, particularly canoeists, as the surrounding area contains numerous lakes that are linked either by the river or by small canals. The choice of accommodation includes an irresistible opportunity to live like a prince for a fraction of the price, in a tourist hostel, the Dom Turysty, located in a neoclassical building that was once a palace. Another hostel, by the Wolsztyn engine shed, represents good-value, basic accommodation.

The line between Wolsztyn and Leszno crosses a region of lakes and woods south of Wolsztyn. From Leszno there are frequent fast trains to Poznań and south to Wroclaw. ❏

LEFT: the steam engines at Wolsztyn are lovingly maintained.

KRAKÓW–ZAKOPANE

Map on page 312

This railway links Poland's undisputed cultural capital with its premier mountain resort, passing through timeless rolling scenery on its ascent to the rugged peaks of the High Tatra. Trains can be crowded in the peak summer season; the best one to catch is the Warsaw–Zakopane which departs Kraków at 11.23.

The line south from **Kraków** heads across the plain of the Wisła River, past the attractive church at Skawina before climbing into the first outliers of the Beskid hills, part of the lengthy Carpathian chain. It is not long before the large Benardine monastery of **Kalwaria Zebrzydowska** appears on a hilltop to the right, just past the town itself. The site became a pilgrimage centre in the 17th century after locals experienced visions of crucifixes on the hill, with a type of Via Dolorosa leading to the summit. Pilgrims throng to the complex at Easter and during the Festival of the Assumption in mid-August. From here to Sucha Beskidzka there are expansive views of the Beskid Makowski range stretching to the south and east.

There is a good view of the open-air steam museum on the way out from **Chabówka** station, with numerous steam locomotives in varying states of repair. A branch line heads east to the attractive town of Rabka before crossing the Gorce region and the Beskid Wyspowy range to reach Nowy Sącz.

Towards the mountains

The Zakopane line turns south to head directly towards the mountains. On the 30-minute journey to **Nowy Targ** the train passes through timeless scenery – lush, rolling meadows grazed by contended-looking cows, set against a backdrop of dark forests and distant mountains. Nowy Targ marks the start of the Podhale region, home to the Górals, a small ethnic group of highland people. Traditionally farmers and shepherds, they speak their own dialect, and maintain their traditional customs and regional costumes – regardless of living among Poles or, for that matter, the dominant influence of tourism. A distinctive feature of Góral folk culture is the local architecture: ornately carved wooden houses and churches, many of which can be admired in the Tatra villages.

Heading south from Nowy Targ the railway slowly ascends towards the mountains, with increasingly impressive views of the jagged peaks to whet the appetite. Practically the entire southern flank of Poland is mountainous, but none of the summits are a match for the Tatras (known in Poland as *Tatry*). The highest peaks are over the border in Slovakia *(see page 321)*, and the range is of modest length, but this has not prevented the Poles from making the most of their Alpine backyard.

Zakopane and its immediate surroundings are decidedly over-developed, the town now sprawling for miles along the valley in a scruffy mélange of half-finished hotels, billboards and tourist schlock. Yet it is not difficult to escape into the mountains, either on the funicular railway up to Gubałówka hill, or simply on foot.

BELOW: street entertainment in Krákow.

ESSENTIALS

Thomas Cook
timetable no. 60

Distance: 1,678 km

Duration of journey:
38 hrs 15 mins

Frequency of trains:
1 per day (change at
Bucharest)

BUDAPEST–ISTANBUL

For passengers on the Orient Express the exotic east began with Budapest. Travellers from the West still get a sense of leaving familiar territory behind as they pull out of the Hungarian capital on a train bound for the Balkans and that most indefinable of cities, Istanbul.

The shortest cross-continental rail route used to take trains from Budapest to Istanbul through Belgrade and Sofia. However, years of political instability in the former Yugoslavia, and decreased personal security for train passengers, made the alternative route through Romania a more attractive option; although it is again perfectly possible to travel via Serbia, the Romania route is more convenient and faster. As a bonus, the trip through Transylvania and northern Bulgaria has far more of interest both in terms of scenery and of places to stop en route.

Romanian excursions

It is possible to travel from Budapest to Istanbul without breaking one's journey, spending two nights on the same train: a sleeper is preferable to a couchette for this, but requires a change of carriage at Bucharest. It is far preferable, however, to do the journey in stages. The fastest trains from Budapest to Brasov and Bucharest go via **Arad** (from where it is worth making a short detour south to Timişoara, often described as "Little Vienna"). But the most interesting route is to the north, crossing from Hungary into Romania at **Oradea**, which has a handsome city centre of baroque and art nouveau architecture.

Across the Western Carpathians from Oradea the train reaches the Transylvanian plateau and the Romanian-Hungarian city of Cluj Napoca. This being

BELOW: the route retraces the tracks of the original Orient Express.

Transylvania, there is no getting away from its most famous undead inhabitant. Most of the Dracula locations peddled by the Romania tourist authorities are spurious but it can be fun to explore them. In the opening chapter of Bram Stoker's book, written in 1897, the English solicitor, Jonathan Harker, takes a train on the branch line from Cluj to Bistrita en route for the vampire count's castle in the "Borgo" (Bârgau) Pass.

Trains from Cluj also go northeast along a spectacular line to Suceava in the Romanian part of Moldavia where there are monasteries decorated inside and out with frescoes. Another scenic line heads north to Sighetu Marmatiei, centre of the Maramures region. From the wood yards of Viseu de Sus (a bus or taxi ride from Viseu de Jos station) Romania's only working steam train hauls forestry workers over 40 km (25 miles) into the forest, ending up close to the Ukrainian border. Passengers are welcome on this train, but no special comforts are provided for them.

Soon after leaving Cluj the main line climbs onto the Transylvanian heath, an area of bleak, sparsely-settled, flat-topped hills. On the other side of them lie Aiud and Teiuş. Shortly before Blaj the north and south Transylvanian routes join and the line passes through the Tarnave **wine-growing** region.

To the south, easily reached by a change of train at Teius or Alba, is **Sibiu**, whose preserved city centre of cobbled streets, squares and ramparts led to it being described as one of Romania's best-kept secrets, until it became the European Union's Capital of Culture in 2007. Moreover, as it has the country's best railway museum (the other one is in Bucharest station), and stands at the hub of a mini-network of unelectrified, scenic lines, Sibiu has the potential to become a steam centre akin to Poland's Wolsztyn.

Maps on pages 333/335

Star Attractions:
Budapest
● **Vár (Castle)**
● **Matyás Church & Fishermen's Bastion**
● **Gellért Baths and Gellért Hill**
● **Hungarian National Museum**
● **Parliament building**
● **Fine Arts Museum**

BELOW: view from the clocktower, Sighişoara.

After Mediaş the main line reaches **Sighişoara**, the Transylvanian town par excellence that no one should miss. A brisk 10-minute walk uphill from the station takes you to the walled old town, the birthplace of the 15th-century ruler of Wallachia, Vlad the Impaler, the inspiration behind Bram Stoker's 1897 novel *Dracula*.

After Sighişoara, the track winds along the wooded valley of the meandering River Olt. Here and there are several villages with defensive walls and churches with stout, fortified towers, recalling a time when Transylvania, then under Hungarian sway, was settled by German-speaking people who had to defend their lands against incursions by Tartars, Mongols and Turks. Archita, Homorod, Cata and Feldioara are especially worth a look.

Braşov is Romania's second biggest city, a place to change trains or to make your base for excursions to other parts of Transylvania. The station is in the modern part of town but a taxi ride takes you to the old quarter, which is a pleasant place to stroll around. Its chief monuments are the 14th- to 15th-century Gothic Black Church and the remnants of medieval walls and gateways. Almost every visitor makes the bus trip to Bran Castle, which is tenuously associated with Vlad the Impaler.

After Braşov, the main line has to squeeze between the two main parts of the Carpathian mountains, southern and eastern. It climbs steeply out of Transylvania through woods to the 1,057-metre (3,468-ft) Timis-Predeal pass between the Bucegi and Baiului mountains. Predeal is the highest ski resort in Romania.

BELOW: Carpathian scenery around Sinaia.

Sinaia, another ski resort, is the next place worth getting off the train. The first Orient Express, in 1883, made a detour here so that passengers could traipse up

a muddy path in the rain to pay their respects to the king and queen of Romania. The extravagantly decorated 19th-century royal summer palace of Peleş Castle is now one of the country's top tourist attractions.

The line gradually drops down from the hills onto the great plain of Wallachia that forms the south of Romania. In between the mountains and Bucharest is Ploieşti, the centre of what remains of an oil industry that was once so important that saboteurs were sent to disable it in World War I and US Liberator bombers to do the same in World War II.

There is little else of interest before arriving at the Romanian capital of Bucharest, which, like almost every where else on this route, should not be judged by its station (where the whole population of the city seems to congregate) or by its immediate surroundings.

The line from Bucharest travels straight and level across the Wallachian plain to the frontier town of **Giurgiu**, where there is a long halt for passport and customs checks. Slowly the train draws near the Danube to cross the 3-km (2-mile) long double-decker bridge (the main road runs above the railway), built in 1954 and still the only fixed link between Romania and Bulgaria.

Several trains often depart from the same platform within a few minutes of each other. Make sure you are on the right one!

Into Bulgaria

The line sweeps around **Ruse**, yet from the train nothing can be seen of the pleasant Danube port, which has a cosmopolitan and cultural history and deserves a visit. The town flourished in the late 19th century when it had the first newspaper, bookshop and public pharmacy in Bulgaria. The country's first iron ship was built in Ruse and the first motion picture was screened here. In 1866 Bulgaria's first railway station was built near the bank of the Danube as the

BELOW: houses cling to the hillside at Veliko Târnovo.

VELIKO TÂRNOVO

Built on a series of hills curving around a tight loop of the River Yantra, Veliko Târnovo is Bulgaria's most picturesque town as well as being the country's former capital and a shrine to national identity.

To the east of the present town, the partially ruined citadel of Tsarevets sprawls over an impregnable site all but surrounded by the river and entered by a causeway. This was the stronghold from which Tsar Petar proclaimed the birth of the Second Bulgarian kingdom in 1185. The best of the town's many restored churches are in the Asenova quarter beneath the citadel.

From the citadel gate the old town creeps west along a ridge and down to the edge of a cliff that fringes the river. Many of the attractive houses date from the 19th-century National Revival period, of which Bulgarians are enormously proud. One characteristic building is the so-called House of the Monkey, slightly set back from the main street. The Constituent Assembly, where Bulgaria's first constitution was formulated in 1879, is another Revival building. There is a pleasant downhill walk from here along cobbled Gurko Street, where No. 88 is a museum that preserves the furnishings of a typical, 19th-century bourgeois house.

The gigantic Palace of the Parliament in Bucharest is the world's second-largest public building (after the Pentagon in Washington DC).

BELOW: folk music on a Bulgarian local train.

western terminus of the Balkans' first railway, which ran to the Black Sea town of Varna. The station is now a Transport Museum displaying antique rolling stock and steam engines.

The passengers of the very first Orient Express took the Varna route. Without a bridge across the Danube in those days the luxurious Wagons-Lits cars could only get as far as Giurgui, from where the passengers were ferried across the river and put on a chartered train from Varna, from where they would ship to Constantinople (Istanbul). Henri Opper de Blowitz, a journalist on board the train, described "a countryside of most barren and melancholy monotony. The fields appeared untilled; we saw only stunted underbrush and sandy soil. Here and there was a little hamlet with a few miserable cottages, hovels built of mud and timber, many riddled with bullet holes – reminders of some past skirmishes of war and bandit attacks." On the way to Varna is **Madara** where an 8th-century figure of a horseman is carved in the hillside.

From Ruse the north–south main line crosses Bulgaria and winds its way through the Balkan ranges via Gorna Oryakhovitsa, Veliko Târnovo, Dryanovo, Tryavna, Raduntsi, Dabovo (between these last two it climbs in two spirals) and Tulovo, to reach the city of Stara Zagora before meeting the Sofia–Istanbul line at Dimitrovgrad and continuing to the border at Svilengrad.

There are several possible detours to be made in Bulgaria. The easiest is to **Veliko Târnovo** *(see box on previous page)*, the country's most picturesque town, which is reached by train or minibus from Gorna Oryakhovitsa. A trip east takes you to Varna and the Black Sea; west to the capital of Sofia. If you want to explore Bulgaria's railways further it is worth catching a train on the narrow gauge railway from Septemvri to Bansko *(see page 335)* – although you'll need

to allow time as it is a slow journey. Another scenic line runs southwest from Sofia to Kyustendil through the gorge of the River Struma.

When you have finished exploring, there is a direct train from Sofia to Istanbul, passing through the rail junction of Plovdiv, where the old quarter is well worth visiting. The line from Sofia and Plovdiv converges with the one from Ruse and Stara Zagora at Dimitrovgrad and as one they head for the Turkish border. Svilengrad is the last station in Bulgaria. Engineers on the Orient Express must have been relieved when they crossed a frontier and left Bulgaria because two of that country's monarchs, Ferdinand I and his son Boris III, often insisted on driving the train themselves when it was crossing their kingdom.

Turkey and Istanbul

Kapikule, across the Turkish border, is the only frontier town on the journey between Budapest and Istanbul where you have to get off the train – in this case to buy a Turkish visa. The delay can seem interminable but once the train is moving again, time 15 minutes then look out for **Edirne**, where the old quarter is crowned by a famous mosque, designed by Sinan, imperial architect of the Ottoman "Renaissance". The mosque comes into view five minutes before the train arrives at the station. From here, it's a fast, straight journey across the farmlands of Thrace, planted with maize and rice.

The stretch of line between Muratli and Corlu features twice in railway history because disasters befell the Orient Express here on two different occasions. On 31 May 1891, the train was held up here and partially derailed, and its passengers politely robbed. Then, in the severe winter of 1929, the Orient Express ground to a halt in an ever-increasing snow drift where it was lost to the world for five and a half days. At first the impeccable Wagons-Lits service was maintained, but before long water, food and fuel for heating had to be rationed.

At last the train makes its way around a sea inlet to the coast of the Sea of

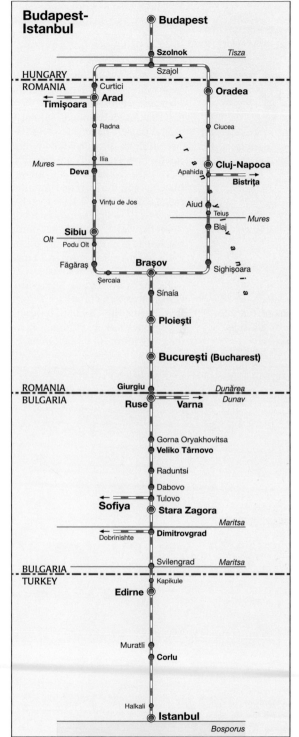

Bulgarian Railways safety poster.

Marmara for its approach to Istanbul. Arriving by train in Istanbul is perhaps even more exciting than arriving by sea and no less thrilling today than it must have been to passengers on the Orient Express. Be ready to rush between the two sides of the train – if you can – as sights flash past.

After the airport (on the right) the city is suitably announced by the old Theodosian Walls that protected Byzantium and by Yedikule Castle guarding their southern end. These great double walls, built of alternating tile and limestone, stretch all the way from the Sea of Marmara to the Golden Horn. The train passes through Kumkapi station, a fishing quarter with many lively restaurants, and on the left-hand side you have a view of the historic district of Sultanahmet crowding up the hill. Standing proud of the mass of wooden Ottoman houses (many now restored) are the Blue Mosque and the Haghia Sophia. Immediately next to the railway line is the 6th-century church of SS Sergius and Bacchus (on the left) and fragments of the Great Palace of Byzantium (to the right) – although it is hard to make sense of the many stretches of ruined, overgrown wall in this part of Istanbul.

All the while you only get glimpses of the Sea of Marmara to the right but in the last few minutes of the journey the Asian side – Hydarpasa Station, the great Selimye Barracks, and Leander's Tower (standing on an islet) can all be seen – and Princes' Islands, out in the Sea of Marmara, come into view.

As the train rounds Seraglio Point it passes underneath the walls of the Ottoman sultans' Topkapi Palace (above the railway line, to the left). The Bosphorus, the Golden Horn and Galata Tower can all be seen as the train approaches Sirkeci Station, which was built in 1890 to welcome passengers on the early journeys of the Orient Express.

BELOW: Istanbul's majestic Hagia Sophia.

Septemvri to Dobriniste on a narrow gauge railway

A picturesque narrow gauge railway ascends into the mountains of southern Bulgaria from **Septemvri** station (on the main line between Sofia and Plovdiv). Five trains a day serve the bottom half of the line as far as Velingrad but there are only four daily trains to the upper stations of Razlog, Bansko and Dobrinishte, the first leaving at 2.45am. The track begins by climbing up the wooded valley of the River Cepinska, passing through a series of tunnels and almost doubling back on itself to gain height. Leaving the valley behind, the train follows the edge of a plateau to arrive at the spa of **Velingrad**. After Tzvetino station it crawls through a series of looping tunnels to reach the highest station in the Balkans, **Avramovo**, at 1,267 metres (4,156 ft).

From here the line descends again, crossing over itself once more, before coming to Yepha Mecta station. The towns along the upland valley here have minarets protruding into the sky and tobacco drying under plastic awnings in the farmsteads of their outskirts – signs of Bulgaria's minority Muslim community, which produces one of the country's most important industrial crops.

After Razlog, the train reaches the penultimate station of **Bansko**, which is a better place to stay overnight than the end station of **Dobrinishte**. The only out-and-back journey possible in one day is 9.05am from Septemvri, returning at 8pm. Located at the meeting point of the Rila, Rhodope and Pirin mountains, Bansko is a centre for winter sports and mountain hiking in the **Pirin National Park**. It has a range of hotels and is known for its *mehanas* or inns, many of them old stone buildings standing in cobbled streets. In the Rila mountains to the north, Bulgaria's highest, is the famous Rila Monastery. Despite its relative proximity to Bansko, however, the monastery is more easily accessed from Sofia.

Maps
on pages
333/335

Star Attractions:
Istanbul

- Topkapi Palace
- Blue Mosque
- Hagia Sophia
- Grand Bazaar
- Chora Monastery
- Hippodrome
- Archaeological Museum
- Sunken Palace

BELOW: Tzvetino station on the Dobrinishte line.

ESSENTIALS

Thomas Cook
timetable no.1400

Distance: 502 km

Duration of journey:
4 hrs 15 mins to 6 hrs

Frequency of trains:
8 per day (+ 3 night
trains)

THESSALONIKI–ATHENS

Travelling by train between Greece's two major cities, Thessaloniki and Athens, is a great way of discovering fascinating and relatively unspoilt parts of mainland Greece. Eight daily trains – limited-stop expresses and all-stops local trains – cover the route. Of the overnight services, one continues from Thessaloniki to Sofia but there are currently no through trains to Western Europe.

Just after leaving the northern Greek metropolis of **Thessaloniki**, trains cross a wide, flat, marshy plain that is the river delta for the Axios and Aliakmon rivers. Platy station, the rail junction to Western Macedonia, is the first important stop on this line. Further south, the significant Macedonian archaeological site of **Pella**, with its tombs, is 16 km (10 miles) from Adendron station.

Continuing south, the line skirts the Thermaic Gulf. Passengers who can take their eyes off the sea will get inspiring views of snow-capped **Mount Olympus** on the other side. If the blue waters are enticing enough, you could get off at Platamon station, which is also a good place to organise treks up Olympus.

The north–south Greek main line is being modernised and rebuilt, and new cutoffs are, sadly, removing much of its charm: sections along the sea front at Platamon and the climb through the Vale of Tempi have been sacrificed in order to gain precious time.

BELOW: Greek
Orthodox priest.
RIGHT: Russanu
Monastery,
Meteora.

Travelling through classical landscapes

Once out of the canyon, trains immediately pick up speed as they descend onto the fertile Thessaly plain. Though the large city of Larissa is of little interest, the junction station offers rail transfers to **Vólos** and the Pelion Peninsula. In addition

to being a major port with frequent sailings to the Sporades Islands of Skiathos and Skopelos, Volos has a twee, 600-mm gauge steam railway line that winds its picturesque way high above the waters of the Pagasitic Gulf from Ano Lechonia through Pelion spectacular mountain country to the stone village of Milies.

South from Larissa, trains race along the country's fastest track to the isolated station of Paleofarsalo. Connections can be made here for Trikala and Kalambaka at the base of the Meteora pinnacles, where Greek Orthodox monasteries defy gravity and cling, seemingly by faith alone, to sheer rock outcrop.

Beyond Paleofarsalo, the main line leaves Thessaly and starts to wind up into rugged **Mount Parnassos** high country. Lianokladi station offers rail transfers for Lamia and the small port of Stylis as well as being the jumping-off point for treks to the Agrafa and Brallos natural reserves. Look out for the multi-arched stone bridge high over the **Gorgopotomos River** (15 minutes from Lianokladi). Here, in November 1942, British commandos and Greek partisans destroyed the bridge in a dramatic raid that disrupted Nazi supply lines.

South of the river, trains continue on the mountain-hugging line, calling at Cheronia (bus and taxi transfers to Thermapoli pass) and Livadhia (for Delphi) then to **Thira** (Thebes), before starting the long descent to the Attica plain. Travellers will notice a distinct change in the journey south of Thebes, where massive investments have paid off handsomely and trains whisk across Northern European-style fast tracks through Oinoi (the junction with the Eubia rail line).

Arriving at **Athens** is almost anti-climatic after the dramatic ride from Thessaloniki. For those continuing by rail, there are frequent transfers to the Peloponnese line and to the major seaport of Pireaus. For those visiting the capital, the metro has a convenient station not far from the railway station.

Map on page 335

Star Attractions:
Athens
● **Acropolis**
● **Agora**
● **Archaeological Museum**
● **Small Mitropolis**
● **Flea Market**
● **Hadrian's Arch & Temple of Olympian Zeus**
● **Herod Atticus Theatre**

BELOW: the rocky Vale of Tempi.

ESSENTIALS

Thomas Cook
timetables no. 1440,
1450, 1455

Distance:
Athens–Kalamata via
Patras 460 km;
Kalamata–Athens via
Arghos 327 km

Duration of journey:
Athens–Patras 3 hrs
21 mins
Patras–Kalamata 4 hrs
Kalamata–Athens via
Arghos 6–7 hrs

Frequency of trains:
Athens–Patras 8 daily
Patras–Kalamata
3 daily (direct);
Kalamata–Athens via
Arghos 4 daily

BELOW: supplies for
the journey at
Athens station.

AROUND THE PELOPONNESE

A train ride around the Peloponnese is a real pleasure, although the landscape suffered terribly from the brush fires in 2007. The charm of the narrow gauge is gradually being replaced by an efficient modern line from Athens to Patras, so make the journey as soon as possible. Whereas a few years ago the exit from Athens was by a quaint narrow gauge train, the first part of the journey is now on modern direct trains on standard track. Transfer to the narrow gauge takes place at Corinth and Kiáto.

Just before **Megara**, favoured by swimmers despite its sharp rocks, the sea comes into view on the left and for an hour until Corinth the railway, with the highway below it, clings to the high cliffs as it skirts the waters of the Saronic Gulf, with tremendous views of the Peloponnese.

In the blink of an eye, the train passes over the **Corinth Canal**, a spectacular waterway cut 6.5 km (4 miles) through the limestone cliffs to give access to the Gulf of Corinth without having to sail around the entire Peloponnese. In 67 BC, the Roman emperor Nero attempted to drive a canal through here, but died before it was completed. It was 1893 before the canal finally came into being. If you want a closer look at this marvel of engineering, get off at Isthmus station; a short walk brings you to the pedestrian bridge over the canal.

Flanked by the sea north and south, modern **Corinth** is a bright, shining city with a lengthy waterfront, that long ago outlived its reputation for licentiousness and the worship of Aphrodite, goddess of love. Prostitutes regarded her as their patron and her cult practised sacred prostitution. The allegedly loose morals of Corinth prompted censure from St Paul, who founded a church here.

To the north is **Loutraki**, an attractive hot springs resort whose bottled mineral water is sold throughout Greece. The train continues westwards, through the Corinth suburbs. Beside the track are gardens thick with bougainvillaea and citrus groves full of bees. Akrokorinthos castle can be seen on a rocky outcrop to the left. At Kiáto, passengers must change from the standard gauge train to the narrow gauge. After the low hills south of Xilokastro, cars towing boats are a reminder that the sea is never far away, and at the red-roofed little town of **Derveni**, the sandy beaches are well populated. For miles the train never strays from the shore.

Kalavrita rack railway

A popular stopping-off point is **Diakofto**, the start of a memorable side trip by rack railway to the mountain-top village of **Kalavrita**. Ascending 550 metres (1,800 ft) up the deep gorge of Vourek River, through delightful groves of trees and past enormous boulders gnawed and shaped by time, the train pauses at two villages. At the second stop, **Zekloron**, a footpath leads to the immense, fortress-like monastery whose 4th-century origins are recalled by exhibits and manuscripts in the adjoining 17th-century church.

Back on the main line, the train passes through Aigion, which suffered a major earthquake in 1995, and Rio, before arriving in **Patras**, the largest city on the Peloponnese. The extensive depots the train passes on its way in offer a good chance of seeing a variety of vintage rolling stock and locomotives. Heading south of Patras, orchards line the track which, after Achaia, heads inland. Everywhere there are fields of corn, tomatoes under plastic, and the ubiquitous olive groves. At Andhravidha, sheep and goats graze beneath sheltering trees.

Map below

BELOW: crossing the Corinth Canal.

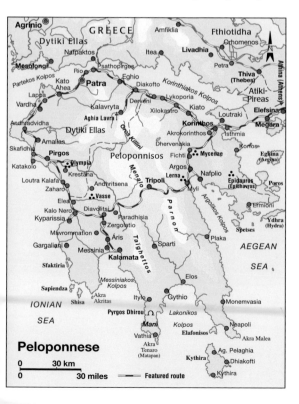

Excursion to Olympia

At Pirgos, most tourists alight to take the line up to **Olympia**, a delightful 27-minute ride through wooded countryside on a small train that has been restored after a lengthy absence.

A road leads from the nearby market town of Krestana via Andhritsene (with a folk museum and celebrated library of centuries-old books) to **Vasse**, where, in a remote, mountainous region, the **Temple of Apollo** is one of the best-preserved in Greece. Its architect in 420 BC was Ictinus, who also worked on the Acropolis in Athens at the time of Pericles. Friezes on the Apollo temple depict Heracles and the Greeks fighting the Amazons and Lapiths fighting Centaurs.

Back on the Kalamata line, the scenic stretch of railway south from Pirgos to Kyparissia (a 1-hour journey) runs along the shores of the Ionian Sea, renowned for its pristine beaches. We are in **Messinia**, the most extravagantly-praised of the six Peloponnese prefectures, which claims superlative sunsets. Adulation of Messinia has a long tradition beginning with Euripides who referred to it as "a land of fair fruitage [suffering from] neither the blasts of winter nor yet made too hot by the chariot of Helios". Approaching Kyparissia through the olive groves there are excellent views of a 13th-century castle. Many trains terminate here; the line to Kalamata retraces the Patras route as far as Kalo Nero, then heads inland, along a valley hemmed in by harsh mountains. After Zergolatio the line runs south across the fertile plain to Kalamata.

BELOW: railcar for Olympia at Alfios junction.

The station at **Kalamata** is at the edge of town with a decent, inexpensive hotel, the Byzantion (a few air-conditioned rooms) conveniently across the street. Within a couple of blocks you come to Aristomenous, a broad, pedestri-

anised boulevard lined with pavement cafés. A short taxi ride away are the spacious ruins of the 13th-century castle, open only in the morning, but on most summer nights the venue for concerts and dance performances. Don't be misled by signs pointing to the seafront, which can lead the unwary to the acres of scorching concrete of the docks. The town beach, with a plethora of lively seafood restaurants, is a lengthy walk east of the harbour.

Map
on page
339

Kalamata to Athens

The cultivated land between Kalamata and Aris is green with succulent cactus and palm trees and after Zergolatio much of the line is a solitary track where the train sounds its raucous horn every few moments all the way to Diavolis. Winding around verdant mountains, in probably the prettiest section of the trip, it overlooks a wide, tree-filled valley to the east with a little stream far below.

An occasional short tunnel or bridge over a ravine punctuates the scenery before the greenery ends, as the train emerges from the hills. The briefest of stops is made at Paradhisia, a strangely unsuitable name for a dusty whistle-stop in the middle of nowhere. Then, at the end of a broad valley, in the centre of a wooded plateau, is **Tripoli**, the capital of the central prefecture of Arcadia.

The track descends 610 metres (2,000 ft) towards the east coast, bypassing the lovely seaside town of Napflio for a stop at **Argos**, whose place in history derives mainly from the Argive school of sculptors. Its star was Polyklaitos (*circa* 550 BC), some of whose works are at Olympia. His gigantic statue of Zeus' wife Hera, which was much praised by the Roman historian, Strabo, has long since disappeared but reliefs of it survive on ancient Argolid coins.

Northeast of Argos and southeast of Nemea, are the impressive ruins of **Mikines** (Mycenae) its name derived from the Greek for "rich in gold", referring to the spoils of war piled up behind the Lion Gate and its immense Cyclopean walls by Mycenaean warriors. But by 1100 BC, Mycenae had been destroyed by fire, its legendary history a later subject for the playwrights, Aeschylus and Sophocles. Some of its ancient treasures, including the golden mask said to have been owned by Agamemnon, are preserved in the Archaeological Museum in Athens. Aeschylus (525-456 BC), who fought at Marathon, where his brother was killed, tells the story of Agamemnon in his drama, *Oresteia*, which depicts the fall of Troy.

Preserved steam on the Kalavrita line.

BELOW: exhibit at the Olympia Archaeological Museum.

A diversion to Epidaurus

After the abandoned greenhouses beside the olive groves of Aradhritsa, comes the first distant glimpse of the sea at Myli. Soon we shall be back in the familiar precinct of Corinth. But, although the train does not go there, there is one last Peloponnese landmark that must be visited. This is the beautifully preserved amphitheatre of **Epidaurus**, on the coast, where the works of the immortal dramatists, such as Aeschylus and Sophocles (496–406 BC), are still performed every summer. At Epidaurus, the acoustics are so perfect that even the most distant of the 12,000 spectators can hear the words spoken on stage without any form of amplification. ❑

Museums and Heritage Lines

Heritage railway lines and museums are few and far between in the eastern parts of Europe – partly because many of the considerable number of forestry and mining lines are still in use as regular passenger services. The numbers relate to the maps on pages 312 and 335.

Museums

Camlik Outdoor Museum ❶
Camlik Buharli Lokomotif Muzesi, Camlik Köyu, Selçuk, Izmir, Turkey
Open: daily 8am–8pm
Features: a collection of 31 steam locomotives on the premises of the former Camlik station, near the ancient site of Ephesus. Visitors are allowed to clamber on board the engines and get a feeling for the running of them from the inside.
Nearest station: Camlik
Tel: 232 894 8116
www.trainsofturkey.com

OSE Railway Museum ❷
4 Siokou Street, 10443 Sepolia, Athens, Greece
Open: Tue–Fri 9am–1pm, weekends 10am–1pm.
Features: small but delightful museum giving the history of railways in Greece with beautifully preserved engines and carriages. Royal carriages, antique Athenian tramways, instruments, tickets, uniforms and

mechanics' tools of the 19th century.
Nearest station (metro): Agios Nikolaos.
Tel: 210 4903163, 5246580, 5126295

Railway Museum of the Municipality of Kalamata ❸
DEPAK, 241 00 Kalamata, Greece
Open: Tue–Fri 9am–1pm, weekends 10am–1pm.
Features: exhibits include an entire station and its area, with a small double-storeyed building for the station-master, four platforms and an entrance pavilion with fixed benches for waiting passengers. Seven steam engines and one diesel engine, two draeseners (one foot-and one hand-operated), a manually operated crane (1890), three first class passenger carriages and five first and second class carriages (1885) and eight freight cars of various types (1885–1947).
Nearest station: Kalamata
Tel: 27210 26464 or 29909
www.odysseus.culture.gr

St Petersburg Museum of Railway Transport ❹
Address: 50 Sadovaya Ulitsa, St Petersburg, Russia
Open: Sun–Thur 11am–5.30pm, closed last Thur of each month
Features: one of the oldest technical museums in the country, illustrating the history or railway transport in Russia from the very beginning; some models are still in working order
Nearest station: (metro) Sadovaya or Sennaya Ploshad
Tel: 812 315 1476
www.saint-petersburg.com/museums

Steam Locomotive Museum, Sibiu ❺, Str. Dorobantilor, nr. 22, Sibiu, Romania (opposite the main railway station).
Open: daily 8am–4pm
Features: 23 standard gauge locomotives, 10 narrow gauge, snow ploughs and steam cranes. Seven of the locomotives are active and used in special train rides for tourists. There are also collections of active and preserved locomotives at several depots. Part of the depot area is still used so care should always be taken. A narrow gauge steam locomotive based at the depot of the narrow gauge Sibiu-Agnita railway (follow the narrow gauge lines east from the station)
Tel: 269-431685
www.enzia.com/Pages/Railpg6.html
www.sibiu.ro/turism

Urban Public Transport Museum ❻, Szentendre, Hungary
2000 Szentendre, Dózsa Gy. út, suburban railway station (in front of Volán bus station)
Open: Apr–Oct Tue–Sun 10am–5pm
Features: the history of public transport in Budapest and other Hungarian cities.
www.bkv.hu/english/muzeum/szentendre.html

Železniški Musej (Museum of Slovenian Railways) ❼
Parmova 35, SI-1000 Ljubljana, Slovenia
Open: Mon–Thur 9am–1pm
Features: over 60 locomotives and in excess of 50 other railway vehicles, plus rail-related artefacts.
Tel: 01 291 2641
www.burger.si/MuzejiIn Galerije/ZelezniskiMuzej

Heritage lines

Horonec Forest Railway Čierny Balog ❽

Clt 2, 976 52 Čierny Balog, Brezno, Slovakia (see page 322)
Open: May–mid-Sept daily
Features: narrow gauge steam railway with museum
Gauge: 760 mm (2 ft 5⅞ in)
Length: 10 km (6 miles)
Tel: 421 48 619 1500
www.chz.sk

Istanbul Railway Museum

❾; Rahmi Koç Müzesi, Hasköy cadessi, Hasköy 80320, Istanbul, Turkey
Open: Mon–Fri 9am–noon, 1–5pm
Features: a small but unique collection of rolling stock including rare industrial equipment formerly used in Turkey. The museum also has a collection of models and pictures. Other exhibits include the carriage used by Sultan Abdülaziz during an 1867 trip to Toulon, Paris, London, Berlin, Vienna and Budapest.
Tel: 212 256 71 73
www.trainsofturkey.com

The Pelion Railway ❿

(Ano Lehonia–Milies) Greece
Open: Sat–Sun dept 11am from Ano Lehonia, returning 4pm from Milies
Features: the only regularly operating steam railway in Greece, with locomotives and rolling stock dating back to 1903; wonderful views down over the Pagasitic Gulf.
Nearest station: Volos
Length: 28 km (18 miles)
Gauge: 600 mm (1 ft 11⅝ in)
www.pelion.org

Sargan Mountain Railway – Mokra Gora ⓫

Omladinska b.b. 31000 Užice, Serbia
Open: various weekends
Features: this remarkable railway is surrounded by rough terrain that forced engineers to construct an eccentric figure-of-eight loop through the hills. The railway is at the heart of a tourist development scheme that also includes a 600 mm (1 ft 11⅝ in) gauge line into the forest. There is a museum at Mokra Gora station.
Length: 15.4 km (9½ miles)
Gauge: 760 mm (2 ft 5⅝-in)
Nearest station: Užice
Tel: 381 31 511 784
www.geocities.com/travel_astra/sargan_mokra_gora.htm

Szilvásvárad–Szalajka Forest Railway ⓬

(see page 320)
Szalajka ut. 6, Szilvásvárad 3348, Hungary
Open: Apr–Oct daily
Features: narrow gauge steam line in the pretty Bükk hills of northern Hungary; forest walks
Length: 4.5 km (3 miles)
Gauge: 760 mm (2 ft 5⅝ in)
Tel: 06 36 355 197
www.kisvasut.hu

Targu Mures Railway ⓭

Romania
Operates three routes: Targu Mures–Sovata; Targu Mures–Mihesu de Campie; and Targu Mures–Lechinta
Features: steam locomotives haul refurbished carriages through beautiful scenery; the lines to the north are especially interesting as they climb up into the Band hills. Several enthusiasts trains have run as far as Band and there is still an option to repair and reopen the line as far as Mihesu de Campie if demand increases. The Chrzanow Px48 "Duna" type locomotive 764.053 is the main steam loco used for hauling preserved trains. Other Romanian heritage railways include the line from Sibiu to Agnita, and the scenic Aries valley line from Turda to Abrud.
www.enzia.com

Wolsztyn Steam Railway

⓮ Poland (see page 326)
Unique in Europe, the steam trains running between Poznan and Wolsztyn, as well as Zbasnyek and Leszno, operate a regular scheduled service. It is possible to arrange driving courses.
Tel: 01628 524876 (UK number) for details
www.wolsztyn.co.uk

Zuin Railway (ZKP) ⓯

Poland
Open: Apr–Aug
Features: tourist passenger trains returned to the Znin–Wenecja–Biskupin–Gasawa line in 1976. The Wenejca railway museum opened four years earlier, and contains a collection of 17 steam locomotives and a variety of rolling stock and other items. The museum area (all outdoors) is being extended. The railway passes the archaeological museum at Biskupin
Gauge: 600 mm (1 ft 11⅝ in)
Tel: 052 30 20 492
www.cleeve.com/znin
www.paluki.pl/ciuchcia (Polish)

INSIGHT GUIDES

TRAVEL TIPS

GREAT RAILWAY
JOURNEYS OF EUROPE

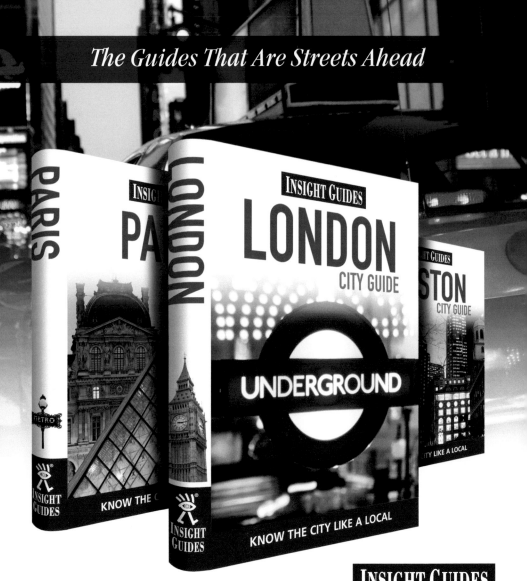

TRAVEL TIPS

European Rail Travel

Booking Agents **348**
Tickets/Reservations **348**
European Rail Passes........ **348**
Visas and Passports.......... **348**
EU Customs Regulations.... **349**
What to Bring **349**
Finding Your Train **349**
Cruise Train Operators **350**
Types of Train................... **350**
Luggage Services **350**
Travel for the Disabled **350**
Taking Bicycles................. **351**
EU Health Coverage **351**
Tour Operators **351**
Timetables....................... **351**
Useful Websites **351**
Hotel Price Categories **351**

A – Z

Austria

The Place **352**
Public Holidays.................. **352**
Telephones **353**
Business Hours **353**
Train System **353**
Ticket Details................... **353**
Where to Stay **354**

Belgium

The Place **354**
Public Holidays **354**
Telephones **355**
Business Hours **355**
Train System **355**
Ticket Details................... **355**
Where to Stay **356**

Central & Eastern Europe

The Place **356**
Public Holidays.................. **357**
Telephones **360**
Business Hours **361**
Train System **361**
Ticket Details................... **362**
Train Talk **364**
Where to Stay **365**

France

The Place **366**
Public Holidays.................. **367**
Telephones **367**

Business Hours **367**
Train System **367**
Ticket Details................... **368**
Train Talk **368**
Where to Stay **369**

Germany

The Place **369**
Public Holidays.................. **369**
Telephones **370**
Business Hours **370**
Train System **370**
Ticket Details................... **370**
Train Talk **371**
Where to Stay **371**

Greece

The Place **372**
Public Holidays.................. **372**
Telephones **373**
Business Hours **373**
Train System **373**
Ticket Details................... **373**
Train Talk **373**
Where to Stay **373**

Ireland

The Place **373**
Public Holidays.................. **374**
Telephones **374**
Business Hours **374**
Train System **374**
Ticket Details................... **375**
Where to Stay **375**

Italy

The Place **375**
Public Holidays.................. **375**
Telephones **376**
Business Hours **376**
Train System **376**
Ticket Details................... **376**
Train Talk **377**
Where to Stay **377**

Portugal

The Place **378**
Public Holidays.................. **378**
Telephones **378**
Business Hours **378**
Train System **378**
Ticket Details................... **378**
Train Talk **379**
Where to Stay **379**

Scandinavia

The Place **379**
Public Holidays.................. **379**
Telephones **380**
Business Hours **381**
Train System **381**
Ticket Details................... **381**
Train Talk **382**
Where to Stay **382**

Spain

The Place **383**
Public Holidays.................. **383**
Telephones **384**
Business Hours **384**
Train System **384**
Ticket Details................... **384**
Train Talk **385**
Where to Stay **385**

Switzerland

The Place **386**
Public Holidays.................. **386**
Telephones **386**
Business Hours **386**
Train System **386**
Ticket Details................... **387**
Where to Stay **387**

Turkey

The Place **388**
Public Holidays.................. **389**
Telephones **389**
Business Hours **389**
Train System **389**
Ticket Details................... **389**
Train Talk **389**
Where to Stay **389**

UK

The Place **389**
Public Holidays.................. **389**
Telephones **390**
Business Hours **390**
Train System **390**
Ticket Details................... **390**
Where to Stay **391**

Further Reading

Railway Books **392**
Other Insight Guides **392**

EUROPEAN RAIL TRAVEL

COUNTRY BY COUNTRY A – Z

E UROPEAN RAIL TRAVEL

ESSENTIAL INFORMATION FOR PLANNING YOUR RAIL JOURNEY

Booking Agents

The following booking agents sell rail passes, such as the InterRail Pass, for European rail travel. Some agents also sell individual tickets for main-line train journeys in most of Europe (but not for journeys wholly within Eastern Europe). Agencies are increasingly internet-based.

UK
Rail Europe
1 Regent Street
London SW1Y 4XT
Tel: 08448 484 064
www.raileurope.co.uk
Deutsche Bahn UK Booking Centre
PO Box 687a
Surbiton KT6 6UB
Tel: 0871 880 8066
www.bahn.co.uk
Rail Pass Direct
Chase House
Gilbert Street, Ropley
Hants SO24 0BY
Tel: 0870 084 1413
www.railpassdirect.co.uk
TrainsEurope
4 Station Approach, March,
Cambridgeshire PE15 8SJ
Tel: 0871 700 7722
www.trainseurope.co.uk
Rail Choice
Chase House
Gilbert Street, Ropley
Hants SO24 0BY
Tel: 0870 165 7300
www.railchoice.co.uk
Eurostar
Tel: 0870 518 6186
www.eurostar.com
Tickets can be booked online. In the UK, you can book by telephone or at London St Pancras, Ebbsfleet International or Ashford International stations.

US
Rail Europe Inc.
Westchester One
44 South Broadway
White Plains, NY 10601
Tel: 1-888-382-RAIL
www.raileurope.com

Tickets and Reservations

If possible, always buy your ticket before boarding the train – not doing so can result in a fine. The same is true of reservations; where a train is marked with an "R" in a square on the timetable, a reservation is required (for more details on reservations see the individual country listings starting on page 352; a list of the types of train which automatically require reservations is on page 350). Travelling on the faster or busier trains may incur a supplement on top of the standard fare; the reservation fee payable on these trains is normally included in this supplement. As a general rule, children under 4 travel free, and those under 12 travel half price.

European Rail Passes

There is a bewildering array of passes available for rail travel in Europe, valid either for a single country, a group of countries, or the entire continent. Most passes only cover the cost of ordinary services, with supplements required for high-speed trains and overnight services.

InterRail Pass
InterRail passes can only be bought by European nationals or anyone who has lived in one of the countries covered for at least six months. You can buy an InterRail pass a maximum of three months before its start date.

Telephone Numbers

All telephone numbers have the area code included in brackets where applicable. We have not bracketed area codes in those countries, such as Italy and Norway, where the code must always be dialled. For numbers which do not include an area code, such as toll-free "0800" numbers in the UK and the US, brackets are not included.

The initial "0" of the area code is omitted if you are dialling that number from another country. This does not apply to Italian numbers.

Several formats are available: the **InterRail Global Pass** version allows travel in almost all European countries, plus Turkey. Exceptions are Russia and other ex-Soviet states, plus Albania; travel within the country where you bought the ticket is excluded, as is travel on certain privately-run railways – notably in Switzerland and Italy. The InterRail Global Pass is available for 5 days in 10, 10 days in 22, 22 days or one month continuous.

The **InterRail One Country Pass** version is valid for one country for 3, 4, 6 or 8 days in a month and replaces the EuroDomino Pass. You cannot use this Pass for travel in your own country of residence. Substantial discounts on many European ferries are included. 1st class and 2nd class passes are available. Prices are about 30 percent lower for those under 26 in second class.

Eurail Pass
Eurail Passes are available to people living outside Europe. They can be

bought up to 6 months in advance outside Europe, or after arrival in Europe, though the latter costs more. The basic pass has no age limit and covers many of the supplements needed for travel on express or deluxe trains. Passes are valid for periods ranging from 15 days to 3 months, offering unlimited 1st-class travel on the national railways of Austria, Switzerland, Hungary, Germany, France, Belgium, Luxembourg, the Netherlands, Denmark, Finland, Norway, Sweden, Portugal, Spain, Italy, Greece, and the Republic of Ireland. Many private railways and ferries are included in the price. Those aged under 26 qualify for the cheaper **Eurailpass Youth**, which is valid for 2nd-class travel.

The **Flexipass** and **Youth Flexipass** allow travel on any 10 or 15 days in a two-month period. The **Eurail Select Pass** is similar but restricted to a specified number of adjoining countries (this means linked by a direct train). Supplements are available to include more countries. Like the other passes, there is a cheaper youth version for those under 26 which covers only second-class travel. Good for families is the **Eurailpass Saver** that allows a group of 3–5 people to travel together for a cheaper rate.

Regional Passes

Balkan Flexipass: unlimited 1st- or 2nd-class travel in Romania, Bulgaria, Turkey, Greece, Macedonia, Serbia and Montenegro for 5, 10 or 15 days in a month.
Benelux Pass: allows unlimited travel

(except on Thalys trains) throughout Belgium, Luxembourg and the Netherlands for any five days in a month. Under-26 rate available.

The **European East Pass** is available to non-European residents, and offers unlimited rail travel throughout Austria, Czech Republic, Hungary, Poland and Slovakia for any 5 days within a month.

Various other passes combining two countries – such as the **France-Italy Pass**, valid for use on four days within a two-month period with extra days available at extra cost – are available to people resident outside of Europe. Individual countries also offer their own passes for domestic use – see country listings for details.

Visas and Passports

Citizens of **European Union Countries** (UK, Ireland, Belgium, the Netherlands, Luxembourg, Germany, France, Italy, Greece, Spain, Portugal, Austria, Denmark, Sweden, Finland and – since 2004 – Poland, Czech Republic, Slovakia, Hungary, Slovenia, Latvia, Lithuania, Estonia, Malta and Cyprus and since 2007, Bulgaria and Romania) only need an identification card or passport for travel between member states. Canadian, US, Australian and New Zealand citizens require a valid passport.

Non-EU citizens planning to stay over six months should consult their nearest British embassy as a consultation paper has been issued by the Home Office proposing tourist visas be restricted to three months.

EU Customs Regulations

People entering EU countries from non-member states are allowed to bring in (or take out) 200 cigarettes or 50 cigars or 100 cigarillos or 250g tobacco, 2 litres of alcohol of max. 22 percent proof, or 1 litre of more than 22 percent proof, and 2 litres of wine. People travelling between EU countries are theoretically permitted to take up to 3,200 cigarettes, 10 litres of spirits and 90 litres of wine.

What to Bring

For long rail journeys, bring a lightweight towel, earplugs, and an inflatable cushion.

Theft can be a problem, particularly on night trains and particularly in Eastern Europe. Make sure your compartment door is locked if possible, and remember to always padlock/chain belongings.

Finding your Train

The majority of stations have electronic departures, and arrivals timetables prominently displayed in the main station concourse, with the words "departures" and "arrivals" clearly marked in English. Otherwise, departures are usually yellow, and arrivals white. Timetables will indicate from which platform the train departs. For the local words for "departures", "arrivals", "platform", etc, see the "Train Talk" section within the individual country listings

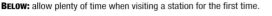

BELOW: allow plenty of time when visiting a station for the first time.

starting on page 352. Larger stations will also have printed timetables with all train departure and arrival times arranged by destination.

Station platforms are clearly marked and numbered, but things can get complicated when letters are used to sub-divide a particular platform. For example, "13A" may indicate the far end of (the very long) platform 13. If you get on the first train you see (undoubtedly the 13B train) you may find yourself whisked off in the wrong direction.

Finding your seat/berth

Make sure you are in the correct carriage – some carriages at the front or rear of the train may be for a different destination, and split off from the rest of the train at some point down the line. This shouldn't be a problem as a guard will normally check your ticket soon after departure, but it pays to be safe. To make things easier, European stations carry train composition boards on the platforms; all you have to do is to find the carriage number on your ticket and then consult the boards to find out if your carriage is in the front, rear or middle of the train. In most countries signs on the platform will help you to find the approximate place at which your carriage will arrive – particularly important when the train is only making a very brief stop.

A board on the side of each carriage indicates the destination of the train as well as its principal stops. A further sign near the doors indicates the carriage number. Seat/berth numbers are clearly marked by the compartment door or, with open-plan seating, next to the seats themselves.

Types of Train

Throughout Europe a standardised set of letters is used to denote the type of train. This feature on all timetables and departures/arrivals notice boards: Any train marked with an "R" in a box requires a seat reservation, to be made in advance. Trains requiring reservations and fare supplements include:

AVE – Spanish high speed train
ICE – German Intercity Express
TGV – French Train à Grande Vitesse
EC – Eurocity international express train
Eurostar – high speed train from London to Paris and Brussels
Eurostar Italia – high speed trains in Italy
IC – Intercity; standard express train, usually on domestic routes only
Talgo – Spanish express train
Thalys – High-speed train between France, Belgium and Germany
CIS – Cisalpino tilting trains (Italy and Switzerland)
EN – Euronight
CNL – CityNightLine
NZ – German NachtZug night train
Trenhotel – Spanish luxury night train
See individual country listings for more details on the types of trains used in each country.

Night trains

The basic form of berth on overnight trains is the **couchette**, simple bunk beds – usually six per compartment in two tiers of three. Sheets and pillows are provided, with toilets and wash basins at both ends of each carriage.

Standard sleeping cars cost quite a lot more than couchettes, and have two, three or four berths plus basic washing facilities. Full bedding is provided. First-class sleeping accommodation means one or two berths and usually includes breakfast.

The most luxurious options are the so-called **Hotel Trains** (principally the CityNightLine services in Germany, Austria and Switzerland, and the Trenhotel services in Spain). These have fewer berths per compartment, armchairs, and private toilets plus showers in first class. Breakfast is included.

Luggage Services

It is possible to arrange to have your luggage sent by train and to pick it up from a particular station. For information, contact the relevant railway company (details in the Railways Across Europe section starting on page 352). Practically all large stations, and many smaller ones, have left luggage facilities – either in the form of lockers or a staffed baggage room.

Travel for the Disabled

The majority of large stations in Western Europe have wheelchair facilities, with staff available to provide assistance. Most fast trains have spaces for wheelchairs.

Information is available from:
Mobility International (UK/USA) Offers a travel information service, tours and exchange programmes for people with disabilities.
Unit 12, City Forum
250 City Road
London EC1V 8AF
Tel: (020) 7250 3222
In the US:
PO Box 10767
Eugene OR 97440
Tel: (541) 343 1284
Fax: (541) 343 6812
www.miusa.org
SATH (Society for the Advancement of Travel for the Handicapped)
347 5th Avenue Suite 610
New York, NY 10016
Tel: (212) 447 7284

Tourist offices can also provide information for disabled travellers.

Cruise Train Operators

Royal Scotsman *(see page 100)* Part of Orient Express group *(see below)* www.royalscotsman.com.

El Transcantábrico *(see page 166)* Transcantábrico, Plaza de los Ferroviarios, 33012 Oviedo, Spain; tel: +34 985 981 711, fax: +34 985 981 710, www.transcantabrico.feve.es.

Venice Simplon-Orient Express *(see page 80)* Venice Simplon-Orient Express, Sea Containers House, 20 Upper Ground, London SE1 9PF; tel: 0845 077 2222, fax: 020 7921 4708. Venice Simplon-Orient Express Inc, 1 Financial Centre Plaza, Suite 500, Providence, Rhode Island 02903; tel: 800-524 2420, www.orient-express.com. Orient-Express Hotels, Trains and Cruises, Central Reservation Office, 205 Meeting Street, Charleston, SC 29401; tel: 800 524 2420, www.orient-express.com.

Trans-Siberian Express *(see page 90)* Russia Experience, Research House, Fraser Road, Perivale UB6 7AG, UK; tel: 020 8566 8846, fax: 020 8566 8843, www.trans-siberian.co.uk.

Trains Unlimited Tours 1105 Terminal Way, Suite 111 Reno, Nevada 89502; tel: (775) 852 4448 or 1-800 359 4870, fax: (530) 836 1748.

Inlandsbanan *(see page 303)* Inlandsbanan AB, Box 561, 831 27 Ostersund; tel: (46) 63 19 44 00, fax: (46) 63 19 44 06, www.inlandsbanan.se. Travel information: Grand Nordic Travel, tel: (46) 771 53 53 53, www.grandnordic.se.

Taking Bicycles

Most European trains allow bicycles on board, but advance notice and an extra payment is often required. Bicycles are not allowed on many high-speed trains, however, and in some countries such as Sweden they are not allowed on any long-distance route; for details see individual country listings. A guard will tell you where to store your bike on the train.

Bike hire is often available at stations and some even allow you to return the bike at another station.

If cycling is going to be a large part of your trip, consider joining the **Cyclists' Touring Club** in the UK, which has fact sheets full of information on all aspects of cycling throughout Europe. Contact the CTC at 69 Meadrow, Godalming, Surrey GU7 3HS, tel: (01483) 417217, www.ctc.org.uk

Reciprocal Health Coverage in the EU

Citizens from EU countries are entitled to medical treatment in other EU countries under a reciprocal arrangement. Visitors from EU states should obtain the European Health Insurance Card (EHIC) from their local post office or visit; www.ehic.co.uk and make a free online application (your card will be delivered in seven days), or tel: 0845 606 2030 (your card will be delivered in 10 days). This entitles the holder to free treatment by a doctor and free medicines on prescription. Only treatment under the state scheme is covered.

Tour Operators

Some tour operators run sumptuous five-star trains along famous routes, such as the Trans-Siberian railway line, often using old steam trains. These "Cruise Trains" *(see tinted panel)* cost about the same as a cruise on a ship, and offer a similar level of opulence.

There are many tour operators around Europe who arrange a wide variety of railway tours ranging from afternoon excursions to epic journeys through wonderful scenery.

Abercrombie and Kent
St Georges House
Ambrose Street
Cheltenham GL50 3LG
Tel: 0845 618 2200
www.abercrombiekent.co.uk
In the US:
1520 Kensington Road

Suite 212, Oak Brook
Illinois 60523-2141
Tel: (630) 954 2944
Fax: (630) 954 3324
www.abercrombiekent.com
This worldwide tour organisation offers luxury train tours to Russia, the Swiss Alps, Italy, Austria, Great Britain, France, Eastern and Pan-European packages.

Ffestiniog Travel
First Floor, Unit 6
Snowdonia Business Park
Gwynedd LL48 6LD
Tel: (01766) 772050
Fax: (01766) 772056
www.festtravel.co.uk
In addition to booking rail journeys in Europe and North America, Ffestiniog also offers escorted rail journeys throughout the world.

Great Rail Journeys Ltd
Saviour House
9 Saviourgate
York YO1 8NL
Tel: (01904) 521936
Fax: (01904) 521905
www.greatrail.com
Great Rail offers exciting trips to nearly all European countries, including an Arctic Circle explorer.

Railtours Ireland
Railtours House
16 Amiens Street
Dublin 1
Tel: (01) 856 0045
Fax: (01) 856 0035
www.railtoursireland.com
Railtours provides a comprehensive variety of rail options in both Northern Ireland and the Republic.

Enthusiast Holidays
146 Forest Hill Road
London SE23 3QR
Tel: (020) 8699 3654
Fax: (020) 8291 6496
www.enthusiasthols.com

BELOW: most European trains allow bikes on board, but check beforehand.

Part of Trainseurope limited, Enthusiast Holidays offers worldwide escorted journeys for the dedicated steam railway traveller.

Voyages Jules Verne
21 Dorset Square
London NW1 6QG
Tel: 0845 166 7003
www.vjv.co.uk
Well-established upmarket travel company with a wide variety of luxury rail holidays.

Thomas Cook Timetable

The *Thomas Cook European Timetable* is published monthly and is an essential for any European rail odyssey. There is also a quarterly version with more background information. The *Thomas Cook Rail Map of Europe* is a useful addition. All are available from large bookshops and all branches of Thomas Cook, as well as by post from Thomas Cook Publishing, PO Box 227, Peterborough PE3 8SB, UK. Alternatively, tel: (01733) 416477, or visit www.thomascookpublishing.com.

For recommended further reading *see page 392*.

Hotel Price Categories

A list of selected hotels (convenient for access to railway stations) appears under each country's A–Z section. Prices are for a double room in high season:
€ under 50 Euros (under £40)
€€ 50–100 Euros (£40–80)
€€€ 100–150 Euros (£80–120)
€€€€ 150–250 Euros (£120–200)
€€€€€ over 250 Euros (over £200)

Useful Websites

National rail companies' websites are listed under "Information" in the country by country listings. Most of these sites provide timetables, most of which work reasonably well. Ticket agents sites' appear on page 348.

"The Man in Seat Sixty-One" is a well-organised site, tremendously useful for planning a European rail journey with links to all national rail companies: www.seat61.com

The European Railway Server provides links to thousands of railway websites across Europe: www.railfaneurope.net

UK heritage railways are well catalogued at www.ukhrail.uel.ac.uk

There is a similar site for French heritage railway at www.trains-fr.org

For a reliable, comprehensive European timetable, visit Deutsche Bahn's site at www.deutsche-bahn.co.uk

EUROPEAN RAIL TRAVEL

COUNTRY BY COUNTRY A – Z

A – Z

A SUMMARY OF PRACTICAL INFORMATION ARRANGED ALPHABETICALLY BY COUNTRY

A Austria 352

B Belgium 354

C Central and Eastern Europe 356

F France 366

G Germany 369

Greece 372

I Ireland 373

Italy 375

P Portugal 378

S Scandinavia 379

Spain 383

Switzerland 386

T Turkey 388

U United Kingdom 389

AUSTRIA

The Place

Area: 83,871 sq. km (32,382 sq. miles)
Capital: Vienna
Population: 8.3 million
Language: German
Time zone: GMT +1. Clocks advance 1 hour from late March until late October.
Currency: Euro
Telepone dialling codes:
International code: 43. Area codes: Vienna 1 (from abroad; when dialling from elsewhere in Austria use 0222); Salzburg 662; Innsbruck 512
Visas and passports: *see page 349*
Customs: *see page 349*

Public Holidays

January 1 – New Year's Day; January 6 – Epiphany; March/April – Good Friday, Easter; May 1 – Labour Day; May 12 – Whit Monday; May – Ascension Day; May/June – Corpus Christi; August 15 – Assumption; October 26 – National Holiday; November 1 – All Saints' Day; December 8 – Immaculate Conception; December 25 – Christmas Day; December 26 – Boxing Day.

Tourist Offices

In Vienna

Österreich Werbung,
Margaretenstrasse 1,
1040 Vienna
Tel: (1) 588 660
Fax: (1) 588 6640

In the UK

9–11 Richmond Buildings,
off Dean Street,
London W1D 3HF
Tel: (020) 7440 3830
Fax: (020) 7440 3848
www.austria.info

In the USA

120 West 45th Street, 9th floor,
New York, NY 10036
Tel: (212) 944 6885
Fax: (212) 730 4568
www.austria.info

UK/US Embassies

UK

Jaurèsgasse 10, 1030 Vienna
Tel: (1) 716 130
Fax: (1) 716 130 5900
www.britishembassy.gov.uk/austria

US

Boltzmanngasse 16, 1090 Vienna
Tel: (1) 313 390
Fax: (1) 310 0682
www.usembassy.at

Money

The main credit cards and travellers' cheques are accepted by major hotels and many shops in cities. ATMs are by far your best option for obtaining local currency; cash dispensers at most banks acceptthe major European debit card. When travelling to remote destinations in rural areas you might need to change money at a train station.

Post offices (indicated by a golden horn symbol) charge little commission but give bad rates of exchange. Banks (usually open Monday–Friday 8am–12.30pm and 1.30–3pm, often to 5.30pm Thursday) and exchange offices will change foreign currency at the current rate of the Viennese stock market exchange.

Health and Emergencies

Austria is a very safe place to travel; nevertheless, it's always prudent to buy health and travel insurance with medical cover prior to a trip. EU citizens need to have their EHIC *(see page 351)*. It doesn't cover private treatment, but does entitle you to reduced cost, sometimes free, emergency medical treatment (see www.dh.gov.uk for more info).

Austria's standard of medical care is good. Visit the local pharmacy for minor problems; most stay open to

6pm weekdays and noon on Saturday and usually post a list of 24-hour pharmacies nearby for night and Sunday duty.

Safety and Crime

Austria is safe, except for a few areas in Vienna, and the chief threat here is the pickpocket. Keep a hand on your wallet in such crowded and/or seedy areas as the West-bahnhof, Naschmarkt, the Prater and especially Karlsplatz – a noted haunt of thieves and drug-dealers at night. Keep valuables in your hotel safe.

Telephones

Telephone calls may be made from post offices and telephone kiosks. Some public telephones require the use of a telephone card, obtainable from post offices and tobacconists. To make an international call, dial 00 + the country code. Access codes for US phonecards are: Sprint 0800 200 236; MCI 0800 999 762; AT&T 0800 200 288.

Business Hours

In general, shops and businesses open Monday–Friday 9am–6pm (grocery stores from 8am) and Saturday 9am–1pm or 5pm. Only small family businesses in rural areas take a 2-hour lunch break. Some supermarkets and basic provisions stores in larger stations offer late night opening. Banks open Monday–Friday 8am–12.30pm and 1.30–3pm, and often until 5.30pm on Thursday.

Train System

Austria's rail network is run by Österreichische Bundesbahnen (ÖBB). The usual European services are in operation; **EC** (EuroCity international express), **IC** (InterCity internal express), **EN** (Euronight) international express services, as well as **ÖEC** (ÖBB EuroCity), **ÖIC** (ÖBB InterCity), **CNL** (City Night Line) international overnight train, and **ICE** German high-speed services. Trains marked "**D**" are ordinary express trains (Schnellzug), those marked "**E**" (Eilzug) or "**SPR**" (Sprinter) are semi-fast regional trains. The usual fare supplements apply for fast trains. Reservations are not compulsory except on night trains (**CNL**), but are recommended.

BELOW: coffee culture at Café Central in Vienna.

Useful Phone Numbers

Fire Brigade: 122
Police: 133
Ambulance: 144
International Operator: 1616
Local Operator: 1161
Directory Enquiries: 11811
International Enquiries: 118 877

Ticket Details

All trains except most "E" and all "R" trains have 1st and 2nd class. Most local trains have non-smoking coaches only. Passengers are required to pay a surcharge on certain InterCity trains; the price of reserved seating is within this additional charge. "EN" and "CNL" trains require supplements for couchettes and sleeping cars. ÖBB and most private railways accept InterRail and Eurail passes.

Discount Passes

InterRail, **Eurailpass**, **European East Pass**, **Switzerland–Austria** and **Austria–Czech Republic** passes are all good for travel in Austria.

The **Vorteilscard** annual card entitles the user to a 45 percent reduction (50 percent at ticketing machines) on most regular train fares. The classic version is available to everyone but there are cheaper cardsfor families, senior citizens, and those under 26. Children under 15, in the company of at least one parent or grandparent travel free with the **Vorteilscard Family**.

The **1-PLUS-Freizeitticket** offers a 25–40 percent discount within Austria for small groups (2–5 persons) travelling over 101 km. **Gruppenticket** offers discounts of 30–40 percent for 6 or more persons. The **Austrian Railpass** is for non-Europeans and must be purchased outside Europe; you may travel on 3–8 days out of a 15 day period. Children aged 6–11 travel half price.

Reservations

No supplements or compulsory seat reservations are required for any train category within Austria except CNL. An extra fee is collected for seat reservations (except in first class). If you travel from Austria to neighbouring countries which impose supplements for EC trains these supplements include the fee for seat reservation inside Austria. Seat, couchette and sleeping car reservations can be made at any ÖBB ticket office. Ticket offices at major railway stations accept credit cards.

Reservations can be made up to 2 months in advance, 3 months for sleeping cars. Tickets may be bought via station ticket offices or at the Österreiches Verkehrsbüro travel agency.

Information

Trains are operated by the Österreichische Bundesbahnen (ÖBB). (Austrian Federal Railway), Felberstrasse 1, A-1150 Vienna, tel: (0)1 93000 50412 (custome3 service office); www.oebb.at.
For local train details call the Mobility Call Centre on 51717, no need to dial an area code.

Stations in Vienna

Vienna has two main stations; Südbahnhof and Westbahnhof. Both are located a few kilometres outside of the Ringstrasse which runs around the city centre. Südbahnof serves southern Austria, Italy, the Balkans, Greece, the Czech Republic, Slovakia and Hungary, and some trains to Germany; Westbahnhof serves much of Austria, Germany, Switzerland, France and Belgium. A third station, Franz-Josefs-Bahnhof serves some, mostly domestic, routes to the north and west of Vienna.
There is also Bahnhof Wien Nord and Wien Mitte station (Vienna Central Station) from where trains depart to the north and south of Austria.

Train Talk

See Germany section on page 371.

BELOW: Hotel Der Salzburger Hof, Salzburg.

Taking Bicycles

Austria is very bicycle-friendly. With over 500 km of cycle paths in the Vienna area, the tourist office makes a special effort to let travellers know about bike-friendly accommodation. Bike hire is available at most stations.
On regional trains you can take your bicycle if there is a free bicycle place on the train, but not all trains transport bicycles.

Where to Stay

For price categories *see page 351*.

Innsbruck

Grand Hotel Europa
Südtiroler Platz 2, A-6020 Innsbruck
Tel: (05) 12 5931
Fax: (05) 12 587 800
www.grandhoteleuropa.at
19th-century hotel opposite the railway station, in the heart of the city. Bombed in World War II, this historic hotel has hosted Queen Elizabeth II, General Patton, and the crew of Apollo 14. Handsomely furnished rooms. €€€€€
Hotel Mozart
Müllerstrasse 15, A-6020 Innsbruck
Tel: (05) 12 595 38
Fax: (05) 12 595 386
www.mozarthotel.com
Central location, but quiet, and away from the tourist crowd. Ten minutes' walk from the railway station, this no-frills hotel has small, inexpensive rooms. From the station, walk down Salurner Strasse, crossing Leopoldstrasse which will lead you to Müllerstrasse. €€

Salzburg

Austria Trend Hotel Europa
Rainerstraße 31, A-5020 Salzburg
Tel: (06) 62 889930
Fax: (06) 62 889938
www.austria-trend.at
Centrally located just 50 metres from Salzburg Hauptbahnhof. Most rooms have good views. €€€
Hotel Der Salzburger Hof
Kaiserschützenstraße 1,
A-5020 Salzburg
Tel: (06) 62 469700
Traditional family hotel in the centre of Salzburg, only 200 metres from the Hauptbahnhof. €€€€

Vienna

Hotel Dorint am Europaplatz
Felberstraße 4, A-1150 Wien
Tel: (1) 981110
Part of a popular German chain, within 50 metres of the Westbahnhof. €€€
Hotel Fürstenhof
Neubaugürtel 4, A-1070 Wien
Tel: (1) 5233 2670
www.hotel-fuerstenhof.com
A family-run hotel, with some en-suite rooms. Close to the Westbahnhof. €€€
Hotel Prinz Eugen
Wiedner Gürtel 14, A-1040 Wien
Tel: (1) 5051 741
Fax: (1) 5051 74119
www.hotelprinzeugen.at
Opposite the Belvedere Palace and within 200 metres of the Südbahnhof. €€
Hotel Westbahn
Pelzgasse 1, A-1150 Wien
Tel: (1) 9821480
www.westbahn.hotels.or.at
A large family-run establishment with a friendly service, close to the Westbahnhof, with an old Viennese inner yard and fountain. Historic atmosphere. €€€€

BELGIUM

The Place

Area: 30,528 sq. km (11,787 sq. miles)
Capital: Brussels
Population: 10.5 million
Languages: Flemish, French and German
Time Zone: GMT +1; EST +6. Clocks advance 1 hour from late March until late October
Currency: Euro
Telephone Dialling Codes:
International code: 32. Area codes: Brussels 2; Bruges 50
Visas and passports: *see page 349*
Customs: *see page 349*

ABOVE: a pharmacy sign in Belgium.

Public Holidays

January 1 – New Year's Day; March/April – Easter Sunday and Easter Monday; May 1 – Labour Day; Ascension Day; Whit Sunday; Whit Monday; July 21 – Independence Day; August 15 – Assumption; November 1 – All Saints' Day; November 11 – Armistice Day; December 25 – Christmas Day.

Tourist Offices

In Brussels

Brussels International Tourist Information Desk
Town Hall, Grand-Place, B-1000 Bruxelles
Tel: +32 (0) 2513 8940
Fax: +32 (0) 2513 8320
www.brusselsinternational.be

In the UK

Tourism Flanders-Brussels
31 Pepper Street, London E14 9RW
Tel: (020) 7867 0311
Fax: (020) 7458 0045
www.visitflanders.co.uk
Belgian Tourist Office for Brussels and Wallonia
217 Marsh Wall, London E14 9FJ
Tel: 0906 3020 245
www.belgiumtheplaceto.be

In the USA

Belgian Tourist Office
780 Third Avenue, New York, NY 10027
Tel: (212) 758 8130
www.visitbelgium.com

UK/US Embassies

UK

85 Aarlenstraat (Rue d'Arlon), 1040 Brussels
Tel: (02) 287 6211
Fax: (02) 287 6270
www.britishembassy.gov.uk/belgium

USA

Regentlaan 25 (Boulevard du Régent) B-1000 Brussels
Tel: (02) 508 2111

Fax: (02) 511 2725
www.belgium.usembassy.gov

Money

All banks in Belgium exchange foreign money. Most open Monday–Friday 9am–4pm, with some closing for an hour during lunch. As a rule, exchange offices in larger railway stations maintain longer hours than banks. Many open on Sunday. Most international credit cards are widely accepted, and there are ATMs all over the country.

Health and Emergencies

All visitors are strongly advised to take out private medical insurance. You may be expected to pay after admittance in case of emergency. It is only possible to claim back 75 percent of the cost with the EHIC; this applies to hospital treatment, doctor and dentist appointments and prescriptions. After regular hours and during holidays you will find the name and address of the nearest chemist on night duty posted at all chemists.

Safety and Crime

Bag snatching and pickpocketing are the main threats for travellers.

Telephones

Coins are accepted by public telephones; make sure you have plenty to hand before making a call; "telecards" are available from post offices and supermarkets. To call other countries first dial the international access code 00, then the country code. US phonecard access codes are as follows: MCI 0800 100 12; Sprint 0800 100 14; AT&T 0800 100 10.

Business Hours

Most shops open Monday–Saturday 10am–6pm, with grocery stores frequently remaining open until 9pm.

Some shops close for a lunch break from noon–2pm. Antique and flea markets are generally open Saturday and Sunday.

Train System

Belgian railways are operated by the Societé Nationale des Chemins de fer Belges (SNCB); www.b-rail.be, known in Flemish as the Nationale Maatschappij der Belgische Spoorwegen (NMBS). Trains include the standard European designations of **EC** (international InterCity), and **EN** night trains, as well as high-speed **Thalys** and **Eurostar** services.

Ticket Details

Considerable price reductions apply to children's fares and some deals include discount entry into tourist attractions. The usual supplements are payable on fast trains. Various discounts are available on weekend return journeys.

Useful Phone Numbers

Accident Aid and Fire Brigade: 100 or 112
Police: 101 or 112
National Telephone Information: 1207
Operator: 1324
English Speaking Operator: 1405
International Enquiries: 1304
International Operator: 1307

Discount Passes

InterRail and **Eurailpasses** are both accepted. The **Benelux Pass** offers unlimited travel on any 5 days within a one month period using the railway network in Belgium, Luxembourg and the Netherlands. If sold in the USA, a second pass is half price. **Rail Pass** (26+) and **Go-Pass** (under 26 years) allow 10 single journeys, 2nd class (made at any time of day); they are valid for one year and may be shared.

Reservations

Reservations are not available for any journeys wholly within Belgium. They are available for EC and night trains operating international routes and are compulsory for Thalys and ICE services, and can be arranged at main stations and travel agents.

Information

Belgian Railways (SNCB/NMBS) can be contacted on tel: (02) 528 28 28 This is also the number to ring for all national and international rail infor-

EUROPEAN RAIL TRAVEL

COUNTRY BY COUNTRY A – Z

mation, including lost property, timetables and advance reservations. Their website is www.b-rail.be The Thalys website is www.thalys.com. Thalys provides transport to Paris, Brussels, Amsterdam and Cologne.

Stations in Brussels

Brussels has three main railway stations, usually marked in both French and Flemish: Nord/Noord; Central/Centraal; and Midi/Zuid.

Midi/Zuid station is the largest of the three, and the departure/arrival point for Eurostar services to/from London. All three stations are connected by the metro system.

Train Talk

See the France section on page 368. In the Dutch- and German-speaking areas of Belgium, you will find that most people speak good English.

Taking Bicycles

Cycling in Brussels is not for the faint-hearted: although cycle lanes do exist, the city is not particularly cycle-friendly. In rural Belgium, by contrast, cycling has long been one of the best ways of getting around. Tourist offices can supply details and maps of local cycle routes. You can rent bicycles from 12 railway stations around the country (not in Brussels), open 7am–8pm, but you must return them to the same station.

It is also possible to take your own bike on the train by buying a ticket for a one-way trip or for the whole day. There are various restrictions on the use of these services; visit www.b-rail.be for details.

Bear in mind if travelling with your bike through Brussels that you cannot load or unload it at Central Station; Midi/Zuid or Nord/Noord stations are recommended instead.

Where to Stay

For price categories *see page 351.*

Brussels
NH Grand Place Arenberg
15 Rue d'Assaut
Tel: (02) 501 1616
www.nhhotels.com
Close to Central/Centraal station; a comfortable four-star hotel. €€
Welcome Hotel
23 Quai au Bois à Brûler
Tel: (02) 219 9546
www.brusselshotel.travel
Small, friendly hotel in city centre; each room is decorated in the style of a different part of the world. €€–€€€

Ustel Hotel
6–8 Square de l'Aviation, Brussels
Tel: (02) 520 6053
www.brusselshotelustel.com
Attractive family-run hotel five minutes' walk from Midi/Zuid station. €€€

CENTRAL AND EASTERN EUROPE

The Place

Bulgaria
Area: 110,910 sq. km (42,822 sq. miles)
Capital: Sofia
Population: 7.7 million
Language: Bulgarian
Time Zone: GMT +2; EST +7
Currency: Lev
Telephone Dialling Codes:
International code: 359. Area codes: Sofia 2; Veliko Tarnovo 62; Plovdiv 32

Croatia
Area: 56,542 sq. km (21,830 sq. miles)
Capital: Zagreb

BELOW: rural life in Troyan, Bulgaria.

Population: 4.3 million
Language: Croatian
Time Zone: GMT +1; EST +6
Currency: Croatian Kuna (Kn)
Telephone Dialling Codes:
International code 385. Area codes: Zagreb 1; Rijeka 51; Split 21; Dubrovnik 20

Czech Republic and Slovakia
Area: Czech Republic, 78,886 sq. km (30,458 sq. miles), Slovakia, 49,035 sq. km (18,932 sq. miles)
Capital: Czech Republic, Prague; Slovakia, Bratislava
Population: Czech Republic 10.2 million, Slovakia 5.4 million
Language: Czech and Slovak
Time Zone: GMT +1; EST +7
Currency: the crown (koruna česká/Kč in the Czech Republic, Slovenská koruna/Sk in Slovakia)
Telephone Dialling codes:
International code: Czech Republic; 420, Slovakia: 421. Area codes: Prague 2; Brno 5; Karlovy Vary 17; Bratislava 7; Banská Bystrica 88; Poprad 92; Kosice 95

Hungary
Area: 93,030 sq. km (35,919 sq. miles)
Capital: Budapest
Population: 10.1 million
Language: Hungarian (Magyar)
Time Zone: GMT +1; EST +6
Currency: Forint
Telephone Dialling Codes:
International code: 36. Area codes: Budapest 1; Eger 36; Miskolc 46.

Poland
Area: 312,685 sq. km (120,728 sq. miles)
Capital: Warsaw
Population: 38.6 million
Language: Polish
Time Zone: GMT +1; EST +6
Currency: Zloty
Telephone Dialling Codes:
International code: 48. Area codes Warsaw (6 digits) 22, (7 digits) 2; Kraków 12; Poznan 61; Zakopane 18

Romania
Area: 237,500 sq. km (91,700 sq. miles)
Capital: Bucharest
Population: 22.4 million
Language: Romanian; minorities speak Hungarian and German
Time Zone: GMT +1; EST +6
Currency: Leu
Telephone Dialling Codes:
International code: 40. Area codes: Bucharest 1; Brasov 68

Russia
Area: 17.1 million sq. km (6.59 million sq. miles)

Capital: Moscow
Population: 145.4 million
Language: Russian
Time Zone: Russia has 8 time zones. Moscow and St Petersburg are GMT +3; EST +8
Currency: Rouble
Telephone Dialling Codes: International code: 7. Area codes: Moscow 095; St Petersburg 812

Slovenia

Area: 20,253 sq. km (7,819 sq. miles)
Capital: Ljubljana
Population: 1.9 million
Language: Slovene
Time Zone: GMT +1; EST +6
Currency: Euro
Telephone Dialling Codes: International code: 386. Area codes Ljubljana 01; Maribor 02.

Visas and Passports

Bulgaria, **Czech Republic**, **Hungary** **Poland**, **Romania**, **Slovakia** and **Slovenia** are all now members of the European Union. Citizens of other EU countries can visit these countries with a valid passport or ID card for up to 6 months or longer. US, Canadian, Australian, New Zealand and South African nationals can stay for up to 90 days without a visa in these countries.
Croatia: EU passport holders and US, Canadian, Australian and New Zealand nationals don't need visas for short stays.
Russia: To obtain your visa from a Russian embassy or consulate, you will need a valid passport, an official application form, confirmation of your hotel reservations (for business travellers and tourists) and 3 passport photographs. If you apply personally, rather than through a travel agency, allow ample time, as it can take up to a month. Carry your passport and visa at all times in Russia: the police have the right to check your identity at will.

Customs

Customs regulations for **Bulgaria**, **Czech Republic**, **Hungary**, **Poland**, **Romania**, **Slovakia** and **Slovenia** are similar to those in other EU countries *(see box on page 349)*.

Croatia

Duty-free allowances for visitors are: 1 litre of spirits, 2 litres of wine, 200 cigarettes or 50 cigars. Don't be alarmed by random "everybody off" spot-checks at the border – these searches tend to be for smuggled black-market goods.

Public Holidays

Bulgaria

1 January – New Year's Day; Orthodox Easter; 1 May – Labour Day; 6 May – St George's Day; 24 May – Culture Day; 6 September – Union Day; 22 September – Independence Day; 1 November – All Saints' Day; 24–26 December – Christmas.

Croatia

30 May – National Day; 22 June – Anti-fascist Day; 15 August – Assumption Day; 1 November – All Saints' Day; 26 December – St Stephen's Day.

Czech Republic

1 January – New Year's Day; Easter Monday; 1 May – May Day; 8 May – Liberation Day; 5 July – Feast Day of Sts Cyril and Methodius; 6 July – Anniversary of Death of Jan Hus; 28 October – Independence Day; 17 November – Freedom and Democracy Day; 24–26 December – Christmas.

Hungary

1 January – New Year's Day; 15 March – National Holiday; Good Friday; 1 May – Labour Day; 24 May – Emancipation Day; 15 August – Assumption Day; 20 August – St Stephen's of Hungary Day; 1 November – All Saints' Day; 25/26 December – Christmas.

Poland

1 January – New Year's Day; Easter Monday; 1 May – May Day; 3 May – Constitution Day; June – Corpus

Christi (variable); 15 August – Assumption Day; 1 November – All Saints' Day; 11 November – National Independence Day; 25–26 December – Christmas.

Russia

2 January – 2nd day of New Year; 7 January – Russian Orthodox Christmas; 23 February – Defenders of the Motherland Day; 8 March – International Women's Day; Good Friday; 1 May – Labour Day; 9 May – Victory Day; 12 June – Independence Day; 7 November – Day of Accord and Reconciliation; 12 December – Constitution Day.

Romania

1 January – New Year's Day; Good Friday; Easter Monday; 1 May – Labour Day; 1 December – National Day; 25–26 December – Christmas.

Slovakia

1 January – Origin of the Republic; 6 January – Epiphany; Good Friday; Easter Monday; 1 May – Labour Day; 8 May – Liberation Day; 5 July – Sts Cyril and Methodius Day; 29 August – National Day; 1 September – Constitution Day; 15 September – Patron Saint's Day; 1 November – All Saint's Day; 24–26 December – Christmas.

Slovenia

8 February – Cultural Day; Good Friday; 27 April – National Resistance Day; 1 May – Labour Day; 15 August – Assumption Day; 31 October – Reformation; 26 December – Independence Day.

Russia

It is best to check with the Russian consulate or embassy in your home country about restrictions and limitations before travelling. It is prohibited to export antiquities and art or cultural objects except for those imported and declared on entry. As a general rule anything of value including personal jewellery and electronics should be declared to avoid a hassle when leaving. Computers, electronic notebooks and related hardware must be presented for scanning at the airport at least 2 hours prior to departure.

Tourist Offices

Most Eastern European countries operate official tourist offices in the UK and US, but in some cases it is necessary to contact the embassy.

Bulgaria

In Sofia
Balkantourist
Stambolijski Bulevard 27
Tel: (02) 87 72 33
In the UK
Embassy of the Republic of Bulgaria
186–188 Queens Gate, London
SW7 5HL
Tel: (020) 7584 9400/9433
www.bulgarianembassy-london.org
In the US
Balkantourist
41 East 42nd Street, Suite 508,
New York, NY 10017
Tel: (212) 573 5530

Croatia

In Zagreb
Croatian National Tourist Board
Iblerov trg 10/4, 10000 Zagreb
Tel: (01) 469 9333
www.croatia.hr

In the UK
Croatian National Tourist Office
2 The Lanchesters, 162–164 Fulham
Palace Road, London W6 9ER
Tel: (020) 8563 7979
www.visit-croatia.co.uk

Czech Republic
In Prague
Sprava Caskych Centre
Rytirská 12, Prague 1
Tel: (02) 2421 2209
In the UK
Czech Tourist Authority
320 Regent Street, London W1B 3BJ
Tel: (020) 7631 0427, or 09063
640641 for 24-hour enquiries
www.visitczech.cz
In the US
Czech Tourist Authority
1109 Madison Ave, New York 10028
Tel: (212) 288 0830
www.czechcenter.com

Hungary
In Budapest
Tourinform
Süto utca 2 (off Deák tér)
Tel: (01) 317 9800
In the UK
Hungarian National Tourist Office
46 Eaton Place, London SW1X 8AL
Tel: (020) 7823 1032
In the US
Hungarian Tourist Board
150 East 58th Street, 33rd floor,
New York, NY 10155
Tel: (212) 355 0240
www.gotohungary.com

Poland
In Warsaw
PTTK, ul Swietokrzyska 36, Warsaw
Tel: (022) 20 82 41
In the UK
Polish National Tourist Office
Westec House,
West Gate,
London W5 1YY
Tel: 08700 675 010
www.visitpoland.org
In the US
Polish National Tourist Office
5 Marine View Plaza, Hoboken,
New Jersey, NJ 07030
Tel: (201) 420 9910
www.polandtour.org

Romania
In Bucharest
ONT Carpati
Bulevardul General Magheru 7
Tel: (01) 614 0759
In the UK
**Romanian National Tourist
Office**
22 New Cavendish Street,
London W1G 8TT
Tel: (020) 7224 3692
www.romaniatourism.com

In the US
**Romanian National Tourist
Office**
355 Lexington Ave, New York,
NY 10017
Tel: (212) 545 8484

Russia
In Moscow
Intourist
Milyutinsky Pereulok 13/1
Tel: (095) 3000/30
In the UK
Intourist
Orchard House, 7 Wellington Terrace,
London W2 4LW
Tel: (020) 7727 4100
In the US
Russian National Tourist Office
130 West 42nd Street, Suite 412,
New York, NY 10036
Tel: (877) 221 7120
www.russia-travel.com

Slovakia
In Bratislava
Bratislava Tourist Office
Klobucnicka 2
Tel: (07) 54 43 37 15
In the UK
Slovakian Tourist Centre
16 Frognal Parade, Finchley Road,
London NW3 5HG
Tel: 0800 026 7943
www.czech-slovak-tourist.co.uk

BELOW: festival time in Bulgaria.

Slovenia
In Ljubljana
Tourist Information Centre
Stritarjeva, 1000 Ljubljana
Tel: (01) 306 1215
In the UK
Slovenian Tourist Office
New Barn Farm, Tadlow Road,
Tadlow, Royston, Herts SG8 0EP
Tel: 0870 225 5305
www.slovenia-tourism.si

In the US
Slovenia Travel Inc.
345 East 12th Street, New York,
NY 10003
Tel: (212) 358 9686

UK/US Embassies

In Bulgaria
UK
9 Moskovska Street, Sofia 1000
Tel: (02) 933 9222
www.britishembassy.gov.uk/bulgaria
US
Kapitan Andreev 1, Sofia
Tel: (02) 80 10 12
www.bulgaria.usembassy.gov

In Croatia
UK
Vlaska 121/111 Floor, PO Box 454,
1000 Zagreb
Tel: (01) 455 5310
www.britishembassy.gov.uk/croatia
US
Andrije Hebranga 2, Zagreb
Tel: (01) 45 55 500
www.zagreb.usembassy.gov

In the Czech Republic
UK
Thunovska 14, 11800 Prague
Tel: (02) 5740 2111
www.britishembassy.gov.uk/czechrepublic
US
Tziste 15, Prague
Tel: (02) 24 51 08 47
www.prague.usembassy.gov

In Hungary
UK
Harmincad u.6, 1051 Budapest
Tel: (01) 266 2888
www.britishembassy.gov.uk/hungary
US
V Szabadság tér 12, Budapest
Tel: (01) 267 4400
www.hungary.usembassy.gov

In Poland
UK
Warsaw Corporate Center,
ul. Emilii Plater 28, 00688
Warsaw
Tel: (22) 625 30 30
US
Al Ujazdowskie 29/31, Warsaw
Tel: (22) 628 30 41
www.poland.usembassy.gov

In Romania
UK
24 Jules Michelet, Sector 1,
Bucharest
Tel: (01) 312 0303
www.britishembassy.gov.uk/romania
US
Strada Nicolae Filipescu, Bucharest
Tel: (01) 210 4042
www.bucharest.usembassy.gov

In Russia

UK
Pl. Proletarskoy Diktatury, 5
193124 St Petersburg
Tel: (812) 320 3200
www.britishembassy.gov.uk/russia
US
Bolshoy Devyatinskiy Pereulok No 8,
12 1099 Moscow
tel: (095) 728 5000
www.stpetersburg.usconsulate.gov

In Slovakia

UK
Panská 16, 811 01 Bratislava
Tel: (07) 5441 9632
www.britishembassy.sk
US
Hviezdoslavovo nám 4, Bratislava
Tel: (07) 533 0861
www.slovakia.usembassy.gov

In Slovenia

UK
Trg republike 3, 1000 Ljubljana
Tel: (01) 200 3910
US
Prezernova cesta 31, 1000 Ljubljana
Tel: (01) 200 5500
www.slovenia.usembassy.gov

ABOVE: vineyards in the Ljutomer-Ormuz hills, Slovenia.

Money

Bulgaria

Banks open Monday–Friday
8–11.30am and 2–6pm. Some open
Saturday 8.30–11.30am. ATMs are
common only in the capital and
coastal resorts. Travellers' cheques
are rarely accepted and charged a
high commission. Private exchange
offices offer better rates than banks.
Credit cards are not widely accepted,
except in top hotels and resorts.

Croatia

Most hotels, restaurants and shops
accept the major credit cards. Banks
in large towns and resorts have
ATMS.

Czech Republic and Slovakia

Cash is still used for most
transactions in the Czech and Slovak
republics. Travellers' cheques are
accepted by some souvenir shops,
hotels and restaurants as well as by
banks, but rates are often poor. Credit
cards are now widely accepted. Don't
change money on the street.

Hungary

Banks open Monday–Friday 9am–
4pm; bureaux de change are open
longer and also at weekends. Most
banks will change money and
travellers' cheques, including
branches of the OTP savings bank.
ATMs are ubiquitous. Hotels, travel
agencies, tourist offices and

campsites change money at
reasonable rates. Don't change
money on the street.
Most restaurants, businesses and
petrol stations in cities accept the
main credit cards, but few in country
areas will be familiar with them.

Poland

Cash can be changed in some travel
agents and hotels. Privately run
bureaux de change (*kantor*, found in
hotels, large railway and bus stations
and main streets) give better rates
than banks, but don't usually change
travellers' cheques. Most hotels,
petrol stations, car-rental firms and
large shops accept credit cards.

Romania

Banks open Monday–Friday 9am–
4pm. ATMs exist even if they are
often out of service. Very high rates
are charged for travellers' cheques, if
they are accepted at all. The best
deals are at bureaux de change.
Official tourist offices also exchange
currency. Credit cards are becoming
more accepted at upmarket
establishments.

Russia

It is illegal to make payments in
foreign currencies; they should be
made in roubles or with credit cards.
Most tourist-related businesses and
restaurants accept major credit
cards.

Slovenia

Banks offer the best rates and are
generally open Monday–Friday
8.30am–12.30pm and 2–4pm.
Some open Saturday 8.30–11am.
Some ATMs do exist in the bigger
banks. Travellers' cheques are

widely accepted. Money can also be
exchanged at tourist offices, post
offices, travel agencies and bureaux
de change. Credit cards are widely
accepted by upscale
establishments.

Health and Emergencies

Medical insurance is essential. If you
need special medication it is best to
bring it with you. Doctors and
hospitals often expect immediate
cash payment.

Poland

Most standard drugs are available
without a prescription. Protection
against tetanus, polio and diphtheria
is recommended. If you are planning
to spend a lot of time in country
areas, particularly close to the
Russian, Lithuanian or Belarus
borders, get your doctor's advice
about Lyme Disease before leaving
home.

Russia

Visitors from the US, Canada,
European countries and Japan do not
need a health certificate, but
vaccinations against tetanus and
diphtheria are recommended. It is
also advisable to be inoculated
against Hepatitis A. Tourists who
intend to stay in Russia for more
than 90 days, or Russian visitors who
have multiple entry visas, must have
a certificate showing that they are
HIV negative.
It is recommended that you wash
fruit and vegetables before you eat
them. You should not drink tap water,
especially in St Petersburg, even in
small quantities. Bottled mineral
water is available everywhere.

ABOVE: bright lights in Red Square, Moscow.

Other Countries

Dentistry is a Hungarian speciality, with many visiting the country to benefit from lower prices.

A vaccine for tick-borne encephalitis is recommended in Slovenia.

Croatian doctors and hospitals may expect cash payment, so take out insurance. Public hospitals are of good quality, but often lacking many medicines. Pharmacies are better stocked and operate during normal hours with a coverage rota for evenings and weekends.

Insurance is vital before a trip to Romania. Health care outside of major cities is of dubious standards. Pharmacies are generally well-stocked and will have a notice for a nearby 24 hour service. Beware of the street dogs and seek medical advice immediately if bitten.

Safety and Crime

Don't carry all your cash in one place, and avoid displaying large sums of money. Behave sensibly and be aware that street crime in the cities of Central and Eastern Europe is generally as rife as it is in any big city in the world. Crime against foreigners has increased in recent years.

Be sure to lock your door securely if on an overnight sleeper train.

In Poland, Gdyina, Sopot and Gdansk are particularly dangerous cities. In the Czech Republic, fraud and larceny have increased. Deposit any valuables in the hotel safe, and if you are the victim of a theft, report it immediately to the reception desk at your hotel.

Telephones

Bulgaria

It is easy to make an international direct call from Bulgaria. All large post offices have international phone facilities. US phonecard access codes are as follows: Sprint 00800 1010; MCI 00800 0001; AT&T 00 800 0010.

Croatia

It is possible to make direct international calls from blue public phone booths on the street using a phonecard available from newspaper kiosks. However, these can be noisy. Alternatively, call from a cabin at HPT, and pay when you have finished. Calls are cheaper 10pm–6am. Or head to the nearest post office where there are plenty of booths.

Dial 00 to call outside Croatia, followed by the country code and then the number you wish to reach. US phonecard access codes are as follows: Sprint 0800 220 113; MCI 0800 22 01 12; AT&T 0800 220 111.

Czech Republic

You can use coins or phonecards, which are available in most newsagents. Public phones are not infrequently out of order. There are rows of telephones at most meter stations as well as on the streets. As ever, bear in mind that hotels will charge considerably more than public telephones. US phonecard access codes from the Czech Republic are as follows: Sprint 0042 087 187; MCI/Connect 0042 000 112; AT&T 0042 000 101.

Hungary

Public telephone boxes in Hungary come in various colours: the metallic ones are for local calls only and calls within Hungary; the red ones are more suitable for international calls. It's a good idea to buy a phonecard at the post office rather than battle with the numerous coins needed for calls. Telephoning is less expensive between 6pm and 7am and at weekends.

To make an international call, dial 00 and wait for the tone. US phonecard access codes are as follows: Sprint 00 800 01877; MCI 00 800 01411; AT&T 00 360 111.

Poland

Public telephones are relatively few in number. It's probably best to go to the post office to make international phone calls. It is worth buying a phonecard, as they can be used for domestic and international phone calls. Newer telephones only accept phone cards. US phonecard access codes are as follows: Sprint 00 800 111 3115; MCI 00 800 111 21 22; AT&T 00 800 111 1111.

Romania

Avoid making telephone calls in Romania. If you must, try to use a private phone or a new orange payphone. Telephone centres are inefficient and expensive. US phonecard access codes are as follows: Sprint 01 800 0877; MCI 01 800 1800; AT&T 01 800 4288.

Russia

Most pay phones take pre-paid phonecards (available from post

Useful Phone Numbers

Bulgaria
Ambulance: 150
Police: 166
Directory Enquiries: 144
Operator: 121
International Operator: 0123

Croatia
Police: 92
Fire: 93
Ambulance: 94
International Directory Enquiries: 902
Local Directory Enquiries: 988
International Operator: 115

Czech Republic and Slovakia
Emergency: 155
Ambulance: 373, 333
Fire: 150

Police: 158
Prague Information: 187
International Enquiries: 0149
Operator: 0102
International Operator: 01315

Hungary
Ambulance: 104
Fire: 105
Police: 107
Directory Enquiries: 117 0170
International Enquiries: 267 5555
Operator: 01
International Operator: 09

Poland
Police: 997
Long-distance Operator: 900
International Operator: 901
International Enquiries: 908
Directory Enquiries: 913

Romania
Ambulance: 961
Fire: 981
Police: 955
International Operator: 971
Operator: 991

Russia
Fire: 01
Police: 02
Ambulance: 03
Directory Enquiries: 927
Operator: 09
International Operator: 8194

Slovenia
Ambulance: 112
Fire: 112
Police: 113
Directory Enquiries: 1188
International Enquiries: 1180

offices and metro stations), and you can make international calls on some of them. Some only accept tokens (available at metro stations and kiosks); these are not suitable for international calls. Local calls made from hotels are free, but international calls are expensive. Dial 810 to make an international call. Internet access is increasingly easy to find and is a good information source; ask at your hotel. US phonecard access codes are as follows: Sprint 747 3324 (Moscow), 8 10 800 110 2011 (St Petersburg), 8 10 800 110 3011; AT&T 755 5042 (Moscow), 325 5042 (St Petersburg).

Slovenia

It is best to make a telephone call from a post office or call centre. These both also send faxes. Public phone boxes require phonecards or tokens. US phonecard access codes are as follows: MCI 080 8808; for Sprint and AT&T in Slovenia, call the operator (tel: 981).

Business Hours

Business hours in Russia are unpredictable, but as a general rule you can expect businesses to operate from 8 or 9am until 5 or 6pm, and to shut for anything between 1 and 3 hours for lunch.

In Eastern Europe in general, hours are as follows:
Shops: most open Monday–Friday 9am–7pm, with speciality stores open 10am–6pm; most shops also open 9am–1pm on Saturday.
Banks and Exchange Bureaux: most banks open Monday–Friday

9am–3.30pm, although larger branches may stay open until 5pm. Exchange bureaux open 8am–7pm or later – some until 10pm. Most hotels will change money around the clock, but at slightly higher rates than at a regular exchange bureau or bank.

In Croatia and Slovenia, clothes shops, bookshops, etc, close in the middle of the day. Opening times can be unpredictable in Romania and Bulgaria, particularly in rural areas.

Train System

Bulgaria

Bulgarian trains are classed as **express** (ekspres) – marked **Ex** on timetables; **fast** (burz); and **regular** (puticheski). Reservations are required for the express trains, and a

BELOW: the domes of Alexander Nevski cathedral in Sofia, Bulgaria.

fare supplement payable. Some other trains also require reservations – these are marked with a boxed "R" in timetables. The Cyrillic alphabet is used and while names of larger stations may also appear in Latin script, be prepared to decipher timetables with the aid of a dictionary.

Croatia

Croatian railways are run by Hrvatske Željeznice (HŽ). **IC** and **ICN** trains are the fastest, some requiring reservations (see below).

Czech Republic

The Czech Republic's extensive railways are run by České Dráhy (CD). The fastest trains are the **SC**, **IC** and **EC** expresses, followed by the **Ex** trains (supplement payable and reservations required). Semi-fast trains are called spesný, slow trains are osobny. Fast trains are marked in red on timetables.

Hungary

Hungarian passenger trains are operated by MÁV Start. Departures are displayed on yellow timetables, arrivals on white. The fastest trains are **EC** (EuroCity), **IC** (InterCity) and **IP** (InterPici), all of which require fare supplements and seat reservations. These trains are marked in red on timetables. Standard express trains (gyorsvornat) are significantly slower. The slowest trains are the local személyvonat services.

Poland

The national rail operator is Polskie Koleje Panstwowe (PKP). The fastest trains are marked in red on

EUROPEAN RAIL TRAVEL

COUNTRY BY COUNTRY A – Z

timetables and designated **IC** (InterCity; domestic routes) or **EC** (EuroCity; international routes). Other fast trains (slower than the IC/EC trains) are marked **Ex** *(ekspresowy)*; **IR** fare supplements apply and reservations are required for all these trains. Semi-fast trains *(pospiezne)* do not require reservations or supplements. Local stopping trains *(osobowe* or *normalne)* are very slow. Night trains offer first- and second-class sleeping cars as well as couchettes.

Fast trains are listed in red, the slower in black. An "ex" on the timetable denotes an express service; IC is for intercity trains. A boxed "R" means seat reservations are compulsory. Departures are listed on a yellow board and arrivals on a white board. Main stations are called *glowny* (abbreviated to Gl).

Romania

The Romanian rail network is relatively dense, linking all major towns. Most trains are electrified and fairly punctual but branch line services are slow. Fares are cheap by Western standards and 1st-class travel is inexpensive – although don't expect luxury.

There are three classes of train in Romania: the fastest are the **IC** (InterCity; domestic) and **EC** (EuroCity; international) trains, on which a sizeable supplement is payable. **Overnight trains** generally carry first- and second-class sleepers as well as couchettes; reservations are required. Standard express trains are known as **rapid**; slower are the **accelerat** semi-fast trains; the slow, frequently stopping, **Persoane** trains are only suitable for shorter journeys.

Russia

The national train operator is RZhD (Rossiskiye Zheleznye Dorogi; R‰ D). The top Russian train is the fast **ER200** that runs between Moscow and St Petersburg. Most trains operate over long distances and seats convert to berths – there are 3 categories: Spalny (CB) 1st-class 2-berth; Kupeiny (K) 2nd-class 4-berth; and Platskartny (P1) 54-berth dormitory-style couchettes. There are also cheap "hard seat" carriages known as Obshchi (O), best avoided for anything other than short journeys.

Slovakia

Železnična Spoločnost Slovensko (ŽSSK) operates Slovak passenger trains. Categories of train are similar to those in the Czech Republic, with

IC and EC trains being faster and requiring a supplement and seat reservations. *Rychlik* are semi-fast trains; *osobny* are slow local trains. Timetables are in Slovakian, but pictograms help to make meaning clear. Departures are on the usual European departure posters in yellow and arrivals on white. Fast trains are marked in red on timetables.

BELOW: Hungarian stamps

Slovenia

The national rail operator is Slovenske Železnice (SZ). Travel on the express **ICS** trains requires reserved seats and carries a fare supplement. **IC** trains have a lower fare supplement and reservations are not compulsory for journeys within Slovenia.

Bulgaria

RILA Travel Agency sells tickets and handles reservations and can provide information on travel routes, connections and fares, tel: 987 07 77. Information is also available at the Transport Service Centre at the National Palace of Culture. **Eurail Select Pass**, **InterRail** and **Balkan Flexipass** are all recognised.

Croatia

Tickets are inexpensive and can be bought in advance. Trains are not usually crowded. Modest supplements are payable on internal express (IC and ICN) trains. **Eurail Select Pass** and **InterRail** passes are recognised.

Czech Republic

Tickets bought at the station must be paid for in Czech currency: go to Czech Railways travel agencies to pay by cheque or credit card. The Czech Republic maintains a well-

developed railway network. Travelling either first- or second-class is quite comfortable as well as relatively inexpensive. If you get on the train without a ticket, go and find the conductor before he finds you. The **Kilometrická Banka 2000 (KMB)** pass allows 2,000 km of second-class travel in 6 months. **Eurail Regional Pass**, **InterRail** and **European East Pass** are recognised *(see Poland).*

Hungary

Tickets can be purchased on the day of departure at the station, although it is advisable to buy them at least 36 hours prior to departure for international services and for all trains in the summer months when demand is heavy. You may buy your ticket on board for certain services, but this carries an additional modest fee.

The **European East Pass** *(see Poland)* is valid; fast train supplements still apply. The following passes are valid: **InterRail**, **Eurail**, **Hungary plus Romania Flexipass** and **Balkan Flexipass**.

Poland

Tickets may be purchased from Orbis Polish Travel Bureau offices, rail stations or the conductor. In the last case, make sure you find him before he finds you. If purchasing at the station, arrive at least 30 minutes before departure to allow time for queuing. Assume the cashier will not speak English and write down your destination, class of travel and time of departure to ease the transaction.

A **European East Pass** (available to non-European residents only) offers unlimited travel on the railways of Poland, the Czech Republic, Slovakia, Hungary and Austria for any 5 days in a month; 1st- or 2nd-class versions are available. Selected **Eurail** and **InterRail** passes are recognised.

Romania

Tickets may be bought in the Agentia SNCFR offices or at the station, though the latter is often crowded. **Eurail**, **InterRail**, **Balkan Flexipass**, **Hungary plus Romania Flexipass** are recognised.

Russia

The ticket must have a cover and a coupon (it is valid only with both these components). You will need a valid passport and visa when purchasing tickets. InterRail and Eurail passes are not recognised in Russia. In order to avoid long queues it's easier to buy tickets at central ticket-office booths designated for foreigners, such as the Central Railway Agency at 5 Komsomolskaya Ploshchad.

Slovakia

Slovakia maintains a well-developed railway network. Tickets can be bought in advance or on the day of departure. It is best to write down your destination and the time you want to depart when you are buying a ticket. Travelling either first- or second-class is quite comfortable as well as very inexpensive. Eurail passes are not recognised but the **European East Pass** *(see Poland)* is valid, as are **InterRail** and the **Kilometrická Banka 2000** pass *(see Czech Republic).*

Slovenia

Tickets may be bought in advance or on the day of travel at stations, or on board the train for an additional charge. Prices are quite low. **Eurail Slovenia Pass** and **InterRail Pass** are valid.

Reservations

Bulgaria

Reservations are essential and first class is recommended. Odysseia-IN, tel: (02) 989 0538; www.odysseia-in.com, email: odysseia@omega.bg is a special-interest travel operator which can book hotel rooms in selected small hotels throughout Bulgaria. Its English-speaking staff are knowledgeable about Bulgaria but note that Odysseia-IN is not an official, state-run tourist information office.

Croatia

Reservations are not possible on local trains; a boxed "R" on timetables indicates that a particular train requires seat reservations – the Zagreb–Split IC train, for example, as well as most international expresses.

Czech Republic

Seats on express trains should be reserved at least 1 hour in advance; go to the counter marked "*místenku*" or "R" in the station. Cashiers rarely speak English. It is best to present them with the destination and date on a piece of paper. Their computers can usually print out your train information in English.

Hungary

You can make your reservations at the customer service office of MÁV at VI, Andrássy út 35, tel: (36) 1 461 5500 (international travel) or (36) 1 461 5400 (domestic travel). The office is open 9am–5pm Monday to Friday. Info lines operate 24 hours a day, and usually with English speakers present.

Poland

Reservations can be made 3 months in advance. See www.intercity.com.pl, where bookings can be made and tickets paid for and collected at the station or on the train. Tickets can be purchased from the Orbis offices or the Polres offices (Warsaw, tel: 365055). It is well worth booking a seat particularly on express services and paying 50 percent extra for a 1st-class ticket, as prices are inexpensive and second class may be very cramped.

The Wolsztyn Experience company can organise steam-train trips, as well as help with information on the steamdriving courses near Poznan *(see page 330)*; tel: +1-972-239-8198 (in USA) or see www.steam-training.com.

Romania

Reservations are obligatory for most services, and it is best to book 1st-class tickets to avoid overcrowding. Bookings may be made online at www.cfr.ro. You can only make a reservation 24 hours in advance or

less than 1 hour before the train departs – the latter usually means joining a flustered queue at a ticket window. Ask to make sure you are in the right queue for the right train. In larger stations there is usually a separate 1st-class reservation window.

The excellent Transylvania Uncovered, tel: (0)1539 531258; www.beyondtheforest.com, can make bookings on most trains in Romania or put you in touch with a local agent. They also make hotel bookings and can arrange pick-ups from stations, transfers and city tours. Their website has detailed information about interesting and scenic railway lines.

Russia

For all but local trains reservation is necessary and passports and visas must be presented. You should make your reservation several days ahead, especially for second-class seats, which are cheap but fairly comfortable. You can reserve through a travel agent, at the Intourist counter at the station, or at the Intourtrans Office, Ul. Petrovka 15, Moscow, tel: (095) 929 8743/8848/8741. There are booking offices in the railway stations of every major city. Ticket booking to all destinations, tel: (095) 266 9333/262 0319. UK-based Destination Russia can also make bookings; see www.destinationrussia.com.

Slovakia

As for the Czech Republic above.

Slovenia

For details contact Slovene Railways (Slovenske Zeleznice), tel: (01) 291 3312 or (01) 291 3380.

Information

Bulgaria

Bulgarian railways are operated by BDZ (Bâlgarski Dârzhavni Zheleznitsi); www.bdz.bg/www.razpisanie.bdz.bg). For tourist information, visit www.travel-bulgaria.com.

Croatia

Contact Hrvatske Zeljeznice (Croatian Railways), tel: (01) 4573 238; www.hznet.hr.

Czech Republic

Timetable information can be obtained around the clock in Prague by dialling (02) 264930. Announcements in stations are repeated in English. Departures are grouped by destination. A useful website is www.vlak.cz, or contact České Dráhy (CD) Czech Railways:

BELOW: travelling over the Danube

V Celnici 6 110 00 Praha 1, tel: (02) 2423 9464/5438; www.cd.cz

Hungary

For timetable information, tel: (01) 461 5000. The MÁV website is www.mav.hu.

Poland

For timetables and reservations contact Polres, Al. Jerozolimskie 4400-024 Warsaw, tel: (022) 825 6033/827 2588. For timetables and ticket information visit www.intercity.com.pl or tel: (+48) 22 94 36 or (+48 42) 94 36.

Romania

Romanian railways are run by CFR (Cailor Ferate Române), tel: (21) 223 9060; www.cfr.ro. Tourist information is available at www.romaniatravel.com.

Russia

In Moscow the telephone number for enquiries about train arrivals and departures from all stations is (095) 266 9000/9333. In St Petersburg, the telephone number for all enquiries is (812) 168 0111.

For information on all trains and routes within Russia and the CIS see www.poezda.net/en/index. For more information on travel within the CIS and on the Trans-Siberian railroad check out the website of G&R International at www.hostels.ru/rail.

Slovakia

Contact Zeleznice Slovenskej Republiky (ZSR), Generalne Riaditelstvo, Klemensova 8, 813 61 Bratislava, tel: (07) 5058 7009; www.zsr.sk.

Slovenia

Contact Slovene Railways (Slovenske Zeleznice), tel: (01) 29 13 332; www.slo-zeleznice.si. Alternatively, contact the tourist office at Stritarjeva, 1000 Ljubljana, tel: (01) 306 1215, www.slovenia.info.

City Stations

Czech Republic

Prague: Most express trains use the main station (Hlavní nádrazí), not far from Wenceslas Square. Trains from Berlin arrive at Holesovice station in the north of the city. Other stations are for local services only.

Hungary

Budapest: Trains to/from Germany, the Czech Republic and Slovakia, and the Danube Bend, generally use Nyugati station; trains to/from Austria, Italy, Slovenia, Croatia, former Yugoslavia, Romania, Bulgaria, Greece and Turkey operate

from Keleti station, as well as some trains to/from Germany, the Czech Republic and Slovakia. The third station, Déli, located west of the Danube in Buda, serves routes to/from western parts of Hungary including Lake Balaton.

Romania

Bucharest: Gara du Nord is the main international station (tel: 134563/64/65).

Russia

Moscow: There are several stations in Moscow. Belorusskaya serves Belarus, Poland, the Czech Republic, Slovakia, Austria and Germany; Oktyabrskaya (also known by its former name, Leningradskaya) serves routes north to Helsinki and St Petersburg; Kiyevskaya serves routes running south and southwest to the Ukraine, Moldova, Hungary, former Yugoslavia, Croatia, Romania and Bulgaria. The Trans-Siberian Express operates from Yaroslavskaya.

St Petersburg: Finlyandski serves Finland; Glavny (also known as Moskovsky), serves Moscow and Murmansk; Vitebski serves the Baltic States, Ukraine, Belarus, Poland, the Czech Republic, Hungary and Germany.

Train Talk

Bulgaria

arrivals preesteeganye pristigane
departures zameenavanye zaminavane
first class p'rvoklasen p"rvoklasen
platform peron peron
railway station stantsiya stanci
reservation rezervatsiya rezervaci
return beelyet za oteevanye ee vr'shchane bilet za otivane i vr"wane
second class vtoreeklasen vtoriklasen
single ednopocochen ednopoco en
sleeping car spalen vagon spalen vagon
ticket beelyet bilet
train vlak vlak
when...? koga...koga...?

Croatia

arrivals dolazak
departures odlazak
first class prvu klasu
platform platforma
railway station stanica
reservation reserviranje
return povratnu kartu
second class drugu klasu
single kartu u jednom pravcu
sleeping car spavaca kola
ticket kartu

train vlak
what time does the train leave?
kada vlak dolazi?

Czech Republic

arrivals prijezd
departures odjezd/odchod
first class první trída
platform nastupiste
railway station nádrazí
reservation místenku
return zpáteca jízdenka
second class druhé triídy
single jízdenka tam
sleeping car spací vuz
ticket jízdenka
train rodeni
when is the next train to...? kdy jede dalsí vlak do...?

Hungary

arrivals érkezés
departures indulás
first class else osztály
platform vágány
reservation helyjegy
return ticket to egy retur jegyet... ra/re
second class másodrendi/kettes érdemjegy, másodosztályú
single ticket please egy jegyet kérek...-ra/re csak oda
sleeping car hálókocsi
ticket jegyet
train vonat
railway station vasútállomás
when? mikor?

Poland

arrivals przyjazd
departures odjazd
first class bilet pierwszej klasy
platform peron
railway station dworzec, samochód, stacja
reservation miejscówka
return bilet powrotny
second class drugiej klasy
single w jedną strona
sleeping car wagon sypialny
ticket bilet
train pociag
when does the train leave for...?
kiedy odjezdza pociag do...?

Romania

arrivals sosire
departures plecare
first class clasa intii
platform peron
railway station gara
reservation resevatie
return a returna
second class de clasa a dova
single bilet simplu
sleeping car vagon de dormit
ticket bilet
train trenul
what time does the train leave? la ce ora trenul pleaca?

Russia

arrivals *priyezd* priezd
departures *otyezd* ot"ezd
first class *pervoklassnee*
pervoklassnyj
platform *plataforma* platforma
railway station *vokzal* vokzal
reservation *zakaz* zakaz
return *obratnee bilyet* obratnyj
bilet
second class *vtoroy klass* vtoroj
klass
single *bilyet v odeen konyets* bilet
v odin konec
ticket *bilyet* bilet
train *poyezd* poezd
when does the train depart for...?
kogda otkhodeet poyezd v kogda
otxodit poezd v...?

Slovakia

arrivals *príchod*
departures *odchod*
first class *prvotriedny*
platform *nastupiste*
railway station *zeleznicná stanica*
reservation *místenku*
return *spiatocny gestovny listok*
second class *sekunda*
single *jednosmerny listok*
sleeping car *lehátkovy vozen*
railway station *zeleznicná stanica*
ticket *lístok*
train *vlak*
when..? *kedy..?*

Slovenia

arrivals *prihod*
departures *odhod*
first class *prvorazreden*
platform *platforma*
railway station *kolodvor*
return *povratna (vozovnica)*
second class *drugorezreden*
single *enosmerna (vozovnica)*
sleeping car *spalnik*
ticket *vstopnica/karta*

train *vlak*
what time does the train leave?
o kateri uri vlak odpelje?

BULGARIA Hotels

For price categories *see page 351.*

Sofia

Sofia Princess Hotel
131 Maria Louisa Boulevard
Tel: (02) 933 8888
Fax: (02) 933 8777
www.sofia-princess-hotel.com
The closest hotel to the train station
and considered one of the best in
Sofia. €€€€

CROATIA Hotels

Zagreb

Hotel Central
Branimirova 3
Tel: (01) 484 1122
Fax: (01) 484 1304
www.hotel-central.hr/gb.htm
Large hotel located opposite the train
station. Doubles are en-suite and
include breakfast. €€
Regent Esplanade
Mihanoviceva
Tel: (01) 435 666
www.regenthotels.com
The only 5-star hotel in Zagreb and
located just outside the train station.
Also has a casino. €€€€

CZECH REPUBLIC Hotels

Prague

Esplanade
Washingtonova 19, 110 00 Praha 1
Tel: (02) 2450 1111
Fax: (02) 2422 9306
www.esplanade.cz
Just off Wenceslas Square, in the
heart of the old historic centre of

town and close to the State Opera
and Hlavní station. €€€€
Hotel Ametyst
Jana Masaryka 11, 120 00 Praha 2
Tel: (02) 2292 1921
Fax: (02) 2292 1999
www.hotelametyst.cz
In the Vinohrady quarter above
Wenceslas Square; within easy
walking distance of the centre of
town. Less than 2 km from Hlavní
station. €€
Palace
Panská 12, 110 00 Praha 1
Tel: (02) 2409 3111
Fax: (02) 2422 1240
www.palacehotel.cz
Just off Wenceslas Square, the Art
Nouveau Palace dates from 1906.
Years of renovation have restored it
to its original splendour. €€€

HUNGARY Hotels

Budapest

K+K Hotel Opera
Révay utca 24
Tel: (01) 269 0222
Fax: (01) 269 0230
www.kkhotels.com
Next to the Opera House. Less than
1 km from Nyugati railway station.
€€€
Nemzeti Hotel Mercure
Jószef körut 4
Tel: (01) 477 2000
Fax: (01) 477 2001
www.mercure.com
Small elegant rooms in an Art
Nouveau building. Half a kilometre
from Keleti station. €€
Radisson SAS Béke
VI, Teréz körut 43
Tel: (01) 889 3900
Fax: (01) 889 3915
www.radissonsas.com
The 247 rooms are nicely furnished.
Nyugati station is less than 1 km
away. Don't miss the cakes in the
first-floor Zsolnay Café. €€€€

POLAND Hotels

Krakow

Francuski (Orbis Hotel)
ul. Pijarska 13
Tel: (012) 627 37 77
Fax: (012) 627 37 00
Only 200 metres from the train
station, this elegant old hotel has
been recently renovated. €€€€
Polski Bialym Orlem
ul. Pijarska 17
Tel: (012) 422 11 44
Fax: (012) 422 14 26
Best hotel near the train station (only
200 metres away) and located right
in the city centre. Standards are
improving now that it's in private
hands. €€€

BELOW: Polski Bialym Orlem Hotel in Krakow

EUROPEAN RAIL TRAVEL

COUNTRY BY COUNTRY A – Z

Poznan
Lech
ul. Sw. Marcin 74
Tel: (061) 853 01 51
Fax: (061) 853 08 79
www.hotel-lech.poznan.pl
This 3-star hotel has been around a while. Half a kilometre from the train station. **€€**
Novotel Poznan
pl Gen Andersa 1
Tel: (061) 858 70 00
Fax: (061) 833 29 61
About 1 km from the city centre and the train station, the hotel houses the head office for Orbis, Poland's National Tourism Agency. **€€**

Warsaw
Metropol Hotel
Ul Marszalkowska 99a
Tel: (022) 32 53 100
Fax: (022) 628 6622
www.hotelmetropol.com.pl
Located near the central railway station and the Palace of Culture and Science. **€€€**

ROMANIA Hotels
Bucharest
Hotel Bucegi
Witing, 2
Bucuresti 77121
Tel: (021) 212 7154
Fax: (021) 212 6641
Next to the the station, noisy but clean. **€**
Hotel Cerna
B-dul Binicu Golescu, 29
Tel/fax: (021) 311 0721
Thirty metres from the station. **€**
Hotel Dunarea
Grivitei, 140
Tel: (01) 222 9820
The nicest of the railway hotels, less than 100 metres from the station. **€**

BELOW: Grand Hotel Union, Slovenia

RUSSIA Hotels
Moscow
Arbat
Plotnikov per., 12
Tel: (495) 244 7640
Fax: (495) 244 0093
Three-star hotel in the heart of the city, 5–10 minutes' drive from the Kremlin, and just 150 metres from the pedestrianised Arbat. The nearest metro station is Smolen-skaya, a 3-minute walk. **€€€€**
Baltschug Kempinski
Ul. Balchug, 1
Tel: (495) 230 6500
Fax: (495) 230 6504
www.kempinski-moscow.com
Luxury hotel on the river bank, 5 minutes' walk from the Kremlin, Nearest metros are Novokuznetskaya and Tretyakovskaya. **€€€€**
Marriott Grand
Tverskaya Street, 26/1
Tel: (495) 937 0000
Fax: (495) 937 0001
www.marriott.com
Comfortable Art Nouveau 5-star hotel in the heart of the city centre, surrounded by traditional 18th-century buildings. Facilities include sauna and pool. The nearest metro is Mayakovskaya – about 5 minutes' walk. **€€€€**
Radisson SAS Slavyanskaya
Berezhkovskaya Nab, 2
Tel: (495) 941 8020
Fax: (495) 941 8000
www.radissonsas.com
Luxury hotel in the west of the city with several fine restaurants and a good view of the river. Next door to Kievsky railway terminal and metro. **€€€€**

St Petersburg
Corinthia-Nevsky Palace
Nevskij Prospekt, 57
Tel: 812 380 2001
Fax: 812 380 1937
www.nevskypalace.com
Comfortable 5-star hotel in the centre of town, which has preserved its original historical style façade. The nearest metro is Ploschad Vosstanya/Mayakovskaya. **€€€€**
Grand Hotel Europe
Ulitsa Mihailovskaya, 1/7
Tel: (812) 329 6000
Fax: (812) 329 6001
www.grand-hotel-europe.com
A 5-star hotel dating to the beginning of 19th century and in the heart of the city. Tchaikovsky spent his honeymoon here, and George Bernard Shaw dined with Maxim Gorky. The nearest metro is Gostiny Dvor. **€€€€**
St Petersburg
Pirogovskaya Nab, 5/2

Overlooking the River Neva, close to Finlyandsky station. **€€€€**

SLOVAKIA Hotels
Bratislava
Crowne Plaza
Hodzovo námestie 2
Tel: (02) 59 34 81 11
A business person's hotel, but this still bridges the distance from the train station and the old town nicely. The former is a kilometre away, the old town less than half that. **€€€**
Perugia
Zelená 5
Tel: (02) 54 43 18 18
Fax: (02) 54 43 18 21
www.perugia.sk
The best of the old town's new hotels. Over a mile from the train station, but superbly located in the centre. **€€€**

Kosice
Centrum
Juzná trieda 2a
Tel: (055) 678 3101
Fax: (055) 678 4380
www.hotel-centrum.sk
Accommodation in Kosice is a short stick and this is probably the longest straw you can draw. On the edge of the centre and about 1 km from the train station. **€**
Penzión pri radnici
Bacikova 18
Tel: (055) 622 8601
The most welcoming stay in the city. 1.5 kilometres from the rail station. **€€€**

SLOVENIA Hotels
Ljubljana
Grand Hotel Union
Miklosiceva cesta 1
Tel: (01) 308 1270
Fax: (01) 308 1015
www.gh-union.si
Pleasant hotel in the city centre, not far from the railway station. **€€€**
Hotel Emonec
Wolfova 12
Tel: (01) 200 1520
Fax: (01) 200 1521
www.hotel-emonec.com
Just 10 minutes from the station. Simply furnished, self-service breakfast. **€**

FRANCE

The Place
Area: 543,965 sq. km (210,026 sq. miles)
Capital: Paris
Population: 61.6 million

Language: French
Time Zone: GMT +1; EST +6. Clocks advance 1 hour from late March until late October
Currency: Euro
Telephone Dialling Codes:
International code: 33
Area codes: Paris 1; northwest 2; northeast 3; southeast and Corsica 4; southwest 5
Visas and passports: *see page 349*
Customs: *see page 349*

Public Holidays

January 1 – New Year's Day; March/April – Easter Monday; May 1 – Labour Day; May 8 – commemorates the end of World War II; Whit Monday; Ascension Day (always a Thursday); July 14 – Bastille Day; August 15 – Assumption Day; November 1 – All Saints' Day; November 11 – Armistice Day; December 25 – Christmas Day.

Tourist Offices

In Paris

20 avenue de l'Opéra, 75001 Paris
Tel: (01) 42 96 70 00
Fax: (01) 42 96 70 71

In the UK

178 Piccadilly, London W1V 0AL
Tel: 0906 8244 123
Fax: (020) 7493 6594
www.franceguide.com

In the US

444 Madison Avenue, New York, NY 10022
Tel: (212) 838 7800
Fax: (416) 838 7855

UK/US Embassies

UK

18 bis rue d'Anjou, 75008 Paris
Tel: (01) 44 51 31 00
Fax: (01) 44 51 31 27
www.britishembassy.gov.uk/france

US

2 avenue Gabriel, 75382 Paris
Tel: (01) 43 12 22 22
Fax: (01) 42 66 97 83
www.france.usembassy.gov

Money

Banks open Monday–Friday in Paris 10am–5pm. In the rest of France banks open Tuesday–Saturday 10am–1pm and 3–5pm, often closing earlier the day before a public holiday. Only banks displaying a change sign will exchange foreign currency. They charge the best rates. French cash machines accept most

ABOVE: fields of lavender in Provence.

international credit and debit cards. Travellers' cheques are widely accepted. Hotels and bureaux de change also exchange currencies but at a higher commission rate. Credit cards are widely accepted, but often require your PIN instead of a signature.

Health

Health insurance is highly recommended. In emergencies you will be admitted and then charged. For minor ailments it may be worth consulting a pharmacy (recognisable by its green cross sign), which has wider prescribing powers than its UK or US counterparts. They are also helpful in cases of snake or insect bites and can recommend doctors.

Safety and Crime

Sensible precautions with personal possessions are all that should really be necessary when visiting France. Theft and other crime exists here as elsewhere. Tourists are frequently targeted on the rail link to and from Charles de Gaulle airport and should never lose sight of their bags.

Telephones

Public phones in Paris can only be operated with *télé-cartes* (which come in 50- and 120-unit versions). They can be purchased at post offices, Metro ticket counters and newsagents.

Foreign calls are cheaper in the evening, but the rate will depend on which phone company you are using. They can be made from any public telephone box *(cabine publique)*. To call abroad, first dial the access code

00 followed by the national code. If using a US corporate calling card, call the company's access number: AT&T 0800 99 00 11; MCI 0800 99 00 19; Sprint 0800 99 00 87.

Business Hours

Shops: 9am–6pm or later, Tuesday–Saturday. Majority of shops shut on Monday, and Sunday opening is uncommon. Long lunch hours (from noon or 12.30 for two hours) are still traditional in banks, shops and other public offices; shops in larger towns and cities open continuously.
Post offices: in cities, generally open continuously 8am–6pm weekdays and 8am–noon Saturday – the main post office in Paris is open 24 hours every day, at 52 rue du Louvre, 75001 Paris; in the provinces post offices are open Monday–Friday 9am–noon and 2–5pm, Saturday 9am–noon.

Train System

The majority of long distance trains, particularly those to and from Paris, are operated by TGVs (Trains à Grande Vitesse) which operate at up to 320 km/h (200 mph). This means that on most routes they are faster between city centres than air services. TGVs are comfortable, air-conditioned and have a buffet/bar car except on services from Paris Gare du Nord to northern France. On certain services, passengers can reserve a full meal in advance of travel. However, in a country renowned for its gastronomy, many trains over relatively long distances have no catering facilities at all and it is important to check this before undertaking a long journey.

Fast and comfortable Thalys trains operate between Paris, Brussels, Amsterdam and Cologne. Most other long distance trains are composed of Corail coaches which offer a high standard and a quiet journey. These trains operate at up to 200 km/h (125 mph). In general, trains are most heavily loaded and may be full on Friday afternoons, Saturday mornings and Sunday evenings and just before and after public holidays.

Reservations are compulsory, and higher fares payable, on all TGV and

Useful Phone Numbers

Ambulance: 15
Police: 17
Fire: 18
Directory Enquiries: 12
Operator: 3123

EUROPEAN RAIL TRAVEL

COUNTRY BY COUNTRY A – Z

ABOVE: strolling through the Marais district, Paris

Thalys services; reservations are recommended on all but local trains in the summer peak season.

Ticket Details

Ticket purchases can be made at the usual ticket windows but also on touch-screen terminals in major stations. These are easy to use and accept major credit cards.

Before boarding the train, tickets must be validated by stamping them in a *composteur* – yellow columns at the entrance to station platforms. A return ticket must be stamped before each journey. This is not necessary for hand-written tickets or passes and does not apply to tickets bought outside France. The ticket must be used on the day and in the train indicated but an exchange can be made if there is a change of plan. If the passenger misses a reserved train, it is usually possible to take the next service. If the passenger forgets to validate the ticket or boards the wrong train, it is advisable to immediately seek the on-board *contrôleur*.

Fares are divided into three categories: peak (red), standard (white) and off-peak (blue). You can obtain a calendar of these times from SNCF.

Discount Passes

Euroilpass, France–Italy, France–Spain and **France–Switzerland** are all valid. **InterRail** is a "rover" ticket, which allows unlimited rail travel for periods from 3 days to 1 month, and can be purchased for travel in France. It should be noted that these tickets do not exempt the traveller from paying for some seat reservations, supplements and

overnight accommodation on the train. Reservations must be made before travel on TGVs, otherwise the traveller will be charged on the train, with an additional fine added on. **France Railpass** (anyone resident outside France) vaild for 3–9 days within 1 month. **Carte 12-25 and Carte Sénior** are youth and senior citizen railcards respectively; they are valid for 1 year and give 25–50 percent reductions. The **Carte Escapades** is available to 26–59 year-olds and gives reductions on weekends.

Cheaper tickets are available at weekends and holidays in some regions.

Reservations

Most reservations are only possible 3 months or less before departure. A special procedure exists for reservations up to 6 months in advance. TGV and Thalys reservations are made automatically when the ticket is purchased, and included in the ticket price. The passenger can specify the position of the seat and even the direction of travel on certain trains.

Reservations on other trains, including overnight services, may become a necessity during peak travel times and on international routes. If you hold a domestic pass, the reservation fee should be waived. However, pass-holder seats are often limited, so be sure to book early. Reservations can be made directly from SNCF, or at any station. The SNCF website now has a facility to deliver a ticket free to almost any country in the world if booked a week or more in advance. In the UK tickets can be booked from Rail Europe *(see page 348)* or at many of the larger stations.

Information

Trains are operated by the Sociéte Nationale des Chemins de Fer Français, commonly known as SNCF. Information and bookings are available on 0844 848 5848 (in UK) or (0) 892 688 266 (in France). Their website (in English) is at www.sncf.com/en_EN/flash.

Stations in Paris

Paris has several stations: St Lazare for Normandy; Gare du Nord for Calais, Belgium, Cologne, the Netherlands and the UK; Gare de l'Est for northeast France, Luxembourg, Germany and Switzerland; Gare de Lyon for east and southeast France, the Rhône-Alpes, Provence, the Côte d'Azur, Switzerland and Italy; Austerlitz for south and southwest France, Spain and Portugal; Montparnasse for Tours, Bordeaux, Chartres, the Loire Valley and Nantes. Trains for the Loire Valley and points southwest to Bordeaux can depart from either Austerlitz or Montparnasse station.

Train Talk

approximately *environ*
arrival, arrives *arrivée, arrive*
calls at *s'arrête à*
change at *changer à*
connection *correspondance, relation*
daily *tous les jours*
delay *retard*
departure, departs *départ, part*
fast(er) *(plus) rapide*
first class *première classe*
hourly *toutes les heures*
journey *voyage, trajet*
journey time *temps de parcours*
platform *quai*
reservation *réservation*
return ticket *aller-retour*
second class *deuxième classe*
single ticket *aller simple*
station *gare*
ticket *billet*
through train *train direct*
timings *horaires*
train *train*
when does the next train depart for...? *à quelle heure part le prochain train pour...?*

Taking Bicycles

Bicycles can be carried on the majority of SNCF trains including TGVs. Depending on the train, they can be carried free in the baggage compartment, or as packaged luggage on payment of a fee; free of charge on local, regional and non-TGV express trains (except during Mon–Fri peak hours on Paris commuter routes). On most TGV trains you can put your bike in the luggage van if you reserve space in advance and pay a small fee – this is the same for most overnight trains.

Where to Stay

For price categories *see page 351.*

Clermont-Ferrand

Hôtel des Puys
16 place Delille, 63000
Tel: (04) 73 91 92 06
Fax: (04) 73 91 60 25
www.hoteldespuys.fr
At the heart of Clermont-Ferrand, close to the railway station. €€
Kyriad Hôtel Coubertin
25 ave de la Libération, 63000
Tel: (04) 73 93 22 22
Fax: (04) 73 34 88 66
In the centre of Clermont-Ferrand. A terrace on the roof offers an unrestricted view of the Puy de Dome. €€

Marseille

La Résidence du Vieux Port
18 Quai du Port, 13002
Tel: (04) 91 91 91 22
Fax: (04) 91 56 60 88
www.hotelmarseille.com
A first class, classic-style hotel, situated in the Old Port area of Marseille. All rooms have outstanding views of the port and Notre-Dame de la Garde. The railway station is less than 1 km away. €€€
Sofitel Marseille Vieux Port
36 Boulevard Ch.-Livon, 13007
Tel: (04) 91 15 59 00
Fax: (04) 91 15 59 50
This modern, comfortable hotel is convenient for sightseeing around the old port district. Just over a kilometre from the railway station. €€€€

Nice

Boscolo Hôtel Plaza
12 avenue de Verdun, 06004
Tel: (04) 93 16 75 75
Fax: (04) 93 88 61 61
www.boscolo-hotel-plaza-nice.cote.azur.fr
Overlooking the Baie des Anges and shaded by magnificent palms, less than 5 km (3 miles) from Nice Côte d'Azur Airport; the railway station is only 3 minutes away by car. €€€€€
Négresco
37 promenade des Anglais, 06000
Tel: (04) 93 16 64 00
Fax: (04) 93 88 35 68
www.hotel-negresco-nice.com
Nice's most glorious hotel with its great pink dome dominating the promenade des Anglais. It offers every luxury, and impeccable service. €€€€€

Vendôme
26 rue Pastorelli, 06000
Tel: (04) 93 62 00 77
Fax: (04) 93 13 40 78
www.vendome-hotel-nice.com
A first class hotel in the heart of Nice, close to the beach and the Acropolis Congress Centre; the railway station is 1 km away. €€

Nîmes

Best Western L'Orangerie Hotel Nîmes
755 rue de la Tour Evêque, 30900
Tel: (04) 66 84 50 57
Fax: (04) 66 29 44 55
www.bestwestern.com
Friendly hotel just outside the centre with pretty garden, small pool and good restaurant. €

Paris

Marignan-Champs Elysées
12 rue Marignan, 75008
Tel: (01) 40 76 34 56
Fax: (01) 40 76 34 34
A luxury hotel between the Champs Elysées and the fashionable avenue Montaigne, with an Art-Deco façade and modern interior focused round La Verrière, the glass-roofed reception and bar. The restaurant, La Table du Marché, is a favourite with personalities from the worlds of fashion, film and media. All stations easily accessed by Metro. €€€€
Le Méridien Étoile
81 boulevard Gouvion St Cyr, BP 75848
Tel: (01) 40 68 34 34
Fax: (01) 40 68 31 31
Situated on the Right Bank between La Défense and the Champs Elysées, this recently renovated hotel is a 10-minute walk to the Arc de Triomphe. All stations easily accessed by Metro. €€€€€
Waldorf Madeleine
12 boulevard Malesherbes, 75008
Tel: (01) 40 35 87 25
Fax: (01) 40 35 06 83
www.hotelwaldorfmadeleine.com
The fabulous Waldorf Madeleine is within walking distance of the Madeleine Metro station, which offers easy access to all parts of Paris. €€€€

GERMANY

The Place

Area: 357,027 sq. km (137,849 sq. miles)
Capital: Berlin
Population: 82.5 million
Language: German
Time Zone: GMT +1; EST +6. Clocks

advance 1 hour from late March until late October
Currency: Euro
Telephone Dialling Codes:
International code: 49. Area codes: Munich 89; Frankfurt 69; Cologne 221; Berlin 30; Dresden 351; Nürnberg 911
Visas and passports: *see page 349*
Customs: *see page 349*

Public Holidays

January 1 – New Year's Day; March/April – Good Friday, Easter Monday; May 1 – Labour Day; May (Thursday) – Ascension Day; May – Whit Monday; October 3 – Day of German Unity; December 25 – Christmas Day; December 26 – St Stephen's Day.

Tourist Offices

In Berlin

Europa-Center
Budapester Strasse 45
Tel: (030) 25 00 22
www.berlin-tourist-information.de

In the UK

PO Box 2695, London W1A 3TN
Tel: (020) 7317 0908
Fax: (020) 7495 6129
www.germany-tourism.de

In the USA

122 East 42nd St, 52nd Fl, New York, NY 10168
Tel: (212) 661 7200
Fax: (212) 661 7174
www.germany-info.org

BELOW: window boxes in Bavaria.

UK/US Embassies

UK

Wilhelmstraße 70
Berlin 10117
Tel: (030) 20 45 70
Fax: (030) 20 75 74
www.britischebotschaft.de/en

US

Pariser Platz 2
10117 Berlin
Tel: (030) 2385 174
www.germany.usembassy.gov

Money

Banks, post offices and bureaux de change *(Wechselstuben)* change money. Airports and major railway stations have electronic currency changing machines, used to exchange foreign currency for euros. Banks in major railway stations tend to open every day until 10–11pm. All major credit cards are accepted in department stores and many high-quality shops, plus hotels, airlines, and fuel stations.

Many smaller establishments and most restaurants refuse them, though, so carry plenty of cash. There are ATMs everywhere which give cash for credit cards. You cannot use travellers' cheques as payment, as they have to be cashed at a bank beforehand.

Health and Emergencies

All non-EU foreign nationals should ensure that they have adequate health insurance before they leave their home country as, without this, medical fees can be very expensive in Germany. For EU citizens, the EHIC only covers public health care, but this is of excellent quality in Germany. For more information on EHICs, *see page 351*.

If you need a doctor, contact the nearest consulate for a list of English-speaking doctors (most doctors speak English). In emergencies either go straight to the nearest hospital's casualty unit or phone for an ambulance. For less major ailments GPs *(Arzt für Allgemeinmedizin)* work 9am–noon and 3–6pm weekdays; some are closed on Wednesday.

Pharmacies *(apotheken)* normally open 8am–6.30pm, and some until noon on Saturdays. They all carry a list on the door of neighbouring pharmacies that are open at night and over the weekend. All accidents resulting in injury must be reported to the police.

Useful Phone Numbers

Police: 110
Fire: 112
Ambulance: 112
Directory Enquiries: 11833
International Enquiries: 11834

Safety and Crime

Crime exists in Germany as it does all over the world, but it is only in the larger cities that visitors need to be especially cautious. Pickpockets seek their opportunities in crowds. Do not leave luggage unaccompanied at stations or near hotels.

Telephones

For most public pay phones you need a telephone card which can be bought in post offices or at newspaper kiosks. Some booths still take coins while credit cards can be used from a small number. For long-distance calls you can also dial direct from most public phone boxes or the operator at the post office will make a connection for you. Since the privatisation of German Telecom there has been competition from companies offering cheaper tariffs. Prepaid cards from other providers are used by dialling a PIN.

Every place of any size in Germany has its own dialling code, which is listed under the local network heading. Access numbers for US phonecards are as follows: MCI 0800 888 8000; Sprint 0800 888 0013; AT&T 0800 225 5288.

BELOW: the Berlin Hauptbahnhof.

Business Hours

Most shops in cities open 9am–8pm Monday–Saturday; in smaller towns they tend to close at 6pm, but are often open later on Thursdays and Fridays. Some small shops might close for lunch; shops close on Sundays with the exception of bakeries on Sunday mornings.

Banks usually open Monday–Friday 9am–4pm (possibly closed at lunchtime), and are closed Saturday and Sunday. Again, hours are often longer in the large cities. Exchange bureaux *(Wechselstuben)* open until 6pm, sometimes until 8pm Monday–Friday, and also on Saturday though for fewer hours.

Restaurants and pubs close at midnight or 1am. Nightclubs and some bars have licences for extended hours. Only in Berlin are there no late-night restrictions.

Train System

Germany's efficient railway network is run by Deutsche Bahn (DB). The usual European **EC** (EuroCity international express), **IC** (InterCity internal express), and **CNL** (CityNightLine) and **EN** (EuroNight international express) services are in operation. The fastest services are operated by the impressive **ICE** high-speed trains, with superbly designed and appointed interiors. German night trains operating on domestic routes are designated **NZ** (NachtZug); Talgo-designed trains operate on the Hamburg–München and Berlin–München routes. **Thalys** high-speed trains operate between Cologne, Brussels and Paris.

Other trains are **IRE** regional express trains, **RE** semi-fast trains, **D** standard express trains, **RB** stopping trains and **S-Bahn** suburban trains.

Fare supplements apply on ICE, Thalys, CNL and NZ services. Lower supplements are charged on EC and IC trains. Reservations are not compulsory except on night trains, Thalys and trains marked R in the timetable, but they are advisable at busy times on inter-city trains.

Ticket Details

Children under 4 years of age travel free of charge, those aged 4 to 11 pay half fare. There are many reduced-fare schemes and passes, including the **BahnCard 25** and **BahnCard 50**, which offer 25 and 50 percent discounts respectively, for rail travel on all routes. There are reduced versions for children, young people, married couples, families and senior citizens. Advance purchase **Savers** are available for return journeys with varying discounts according to the day(s) of travel. **Länder-Tickets** are available for unlimited travel between 9am and 3am the following day within a state of your choice, by second class only, for up to 5 people. The **Schönes-Wochenende Ticket** (Happy Weekend Ticket) is valid on Saturday or Sunday from midnight until 3am the following day on all local trains, second class only. Up to 5 people may travel together at no extra charge.

Reservations

It is advisable to make a seat reservation for trains, which costs a little extra. The German national travel agency, DER, has information and booking services in its offices at main railway stations and some tourist offices. To buy tickets from the UK contact Deutsche Bahn's UK Booking Centre, tel: 0871 880 8066 (PO Box 687A, Surbiton KT6 6UB).

Information

The information number for Deutsche Bahn is the same in all German cities, tel: 11861. From outside Germany, tel: 01805 996633. Their website is www.bahn.de.

Stations in Berlin

There are two main stations, Zoologischer Garten (usually abbreviated to Zoo), formerly the main terminus in West Berlin, and Ostbahnhof, its former East Berlin counterpart. Almost all trains stop at both these stations. Trains bound for Russia and Ukraine depart from Berlin Hauptbahnhof. Night trains from all over Germany terminate at Lichtenberg Station. Some other main line trains also stop at the smaller Berlin stations of Friedrichstrasse and Alexanderplatz. The spectacular Berlin Hauptbahnhof, opened in 2006, handles north-south traffic.

Train Talk

arrival, arrives *Ankunft, kommt an*
change at *umsteigen in*
connection *Anschluß, Verbindung*
daily *täglich*
delay *Verspätung*
departure, departs *Abfahrt, fährt*
entrance *Eingang, Einfahrt*
every xx minutes *alle xx Minuten*
except *außen*
excuse me *entschuldigen Sie, bitte*
exit *Ausgang, Ausfahrt*
fast(er) *schnell(er)*

ABOVE: working out the best route.

first class *erste Klasse*
from (a town) *von xx*
hourly *stündlich*
how far is the station? *Wie weit ist es zum Bahnhof?*
how much is it? *Wieviel kostet das?*
journey *Reise*
journey time *Reisezeit*
later *später*
left *links*
platform *Gleis*
right *rechts*
reservation *die Platzreservierung*
return (ticket) *die Rückfahrkarte*
second class *zweiter Klasse*
single (ticket) *einfache Fahrkarte*
station *Bahnhof*
stopping trains *Nahverkehrszüge*
stop *hält*
straight on *geradus*
supplement *zuschlagpflichtig*
through train *durchgehender Zug*
ticket *Fahrkarte*
to (a town) *nach xx*
train *der Zug*
valid *gültig*
when is the next train to ...? *Wann geht der nächste Zug nach ...?*
where do I get a ticket? *Wo kann ich eine Fahrkarte kaufen?*
where is platform one? *Wo ist Gleis eins?*

Taking Bicycles

It is possible to take your own bicycle on all local and many IC/EC trains for a small additional fee, but because of limited space it is advisable to call the Fahrrad-Hotline in advance, tel: 01805 151415.

The alternative to taking your bicycle is the Call a Bike scheme (a service of DB), whereby cycles can be hired at Munich, Berlin, Frankfurt-am-Main, Cologne, Stuttgart, Karlsruhe and Hamburg although

there are plans for expansion and introduction of the scheme to over 100 stations in Germany. Register on the internet at www.callabike.de or call 07000 522 5522 whereby you will be charged €5 and given a customer number. After initial registration, just call whenever you want to hire a bike. Call the phone number in the red box on the cover of the Call a Bike lock to receive an opening code. Key in the number on the input display underneath the cover to release the lock, then remove the bolt. €15 for 24 hours; €60 for 7 days; in Stuttgart, first ½ hour is free.

Where to Stay

For price categories *see page 351.*

Berlin

Hotel Palace
Europa Centre, Tauentzienstrasse, Charlottenburg
Tel: (030) 25020
Fax: (030) 2502 1197
www.palace.de
This 1960s-built hotel is right in the centre of the city, and next door to Zoo Garten station. The first floor restaurant is excellent. €€€€
Kempinski Hotel Bristol
Kurfurstendamm, 27 Charlottenburg
Tel: (030) 884340
Fax: (030) 883 6075
www.kempinski-berlin.de
Famous luxury hotel, very convenient for Zoo Station. €€€€€
Pension am Park
Sophie-Charlotten Strasse, 57–58 Charlottenburg
Tel/Fax: (030) 321 3485
www.pension-ampark.com
Attractive pension, conveniently located for Zoo station. €€€

Cologne

Brandenburger Hof
Brandenburgerstrasse 2–4, Köln 50668
Tel: (0221) 122889
Fax: (0221) 135304
www.brandenburgerhof.de
Family-style budget hotel with shared bathrooms on each floor. Full cooked breakfast served in the garden in summer. Close to the river and within walking distance of the cathedral and the Hauptbahnhof. €
Dom Hotel
Domkloster 2A, Köln 1 50667
Tel: (0221) 20240
Fax: (0221) 202 4444
www.domhotel.de
Unbeatable location right beside Germany's most famous cathedral, and less than 100 metres from the Hauptbahnhof. Five-star service and facilities. €€€€€

Dresden

Hotel Burgk
Burgstrasse 15, Dresden (löbtau)
Tel: (0351) 432510
Fax: (0351) 4325140
www.hotel-burgk.de
Just to the west of the main station, only 5 minutes by car from the old town. Small, friendly hotel; impressive breakfast buffet €€
Kempinski Hotel Taschenbergpalais
Am Taschenberg, Dresden 01067
Tel: (0351) 49120
Fax: (0351) 4912812
www.kempinski-dresden.de
Originally an early 18th-century royal castle, which was all but destroyed in World War II, the Kempinski was transformed into Dresden's finest hotel in the 1990s. Rooms are the most opulent in town. Today, a tiny portion of the bombed ruin has been artfully retained. Less than 1 km from the main station. €€€€€

Frankfurt

Carlton
Karlstrasse 11
Tel: (069) 241 8280
Fax: (069) 241 82801
www.carlton-frankfurt.de
Family-run hotel located in the heart of Frankfurt's business metropolis, with easy access to the railway station and the city's shopping area. €€€€

Munich

Hotel Am Markt
6 Heiliggeiststraße
Tel: (089) 225014
Fax: (089) 224017
www.hotel-am-markt.eu
Bavarian, cosy, very quiet, directly on the Viktualienmarkt just 700 metres from the Hauptbahnhof. €€
Hotel Bayerischer Hof
2–6 Promenadeplatz
Tel: (089) 21200
Fax: (089) 212 0906
www.bayerischerhof.de
Exclusive family-run grand hotel, famous for its nightclub and Trader Vic's. 500 metres from the Hauptbahnhof. €€€€€
Blauer Bock
9 Sebastianplatz
Tel: (089) 231780
Simple, good location at the Viktualienmarkt, only 700 metres from Hauptbahnhof. Breakfast served in restaurant next door. €€
Königshof
Karlsplatz (Stachus)
Tel: (089) 551360
Fax: (089) 5513 6113
www.geisel-privathotels.de
Elegant luxury hotel in the centre, 2 minutes from the Hauptbahnhof. €€€€€

Nürnberg

Carlton Hotel Nürnberg
Eilgutstrasse 13–15,
Nürnberg 90443
Tel: (0911) 20030
Fax: (0911) 200 3111
www.carlton-nuernberg.de
A block away from the train station, the Carlton is one of the best value hotels in Nürnberg, with service and facilities to match more expensive competitors. Popular restaurant, the Zirbelstube, plus lunch on the stone terrace. €€
Dürer-Hotel
Neutormauer 32, Nürnberg 90403
Tel: (0911) 238 890
Fax: (0911) 238 89100
www.altstadthotels.com
Situated right under the eponymous castle, and near all the major sightseeing attractions. Modern amenities don't rob the hotel of character. Bistro Bar, fitness centre, laundry. Only 1.5 km from the main railway station. €€€

GREECE

The Place

Area: 131,950 sq. km (50,946 sq. miles)
Capital: Athens
Population: 10.2 million
Language: Modern Greek
Time Zone: GMT + 2; EST +7. Clocks advance 1 hour from late March until late October.
Currency: Euro
Telephone Dialling Codes:
International code: 30. Area codes: Athens 1; Patras 61, Kalamata 721, Thessaloniki 31
Visas and passports: see page 349
Customs: see page 349

Tourist Offices

In Athens
NTOG Headquarters
2 Amerikis Street
Tel: (01) +30 210 870 7000

In the UK
Tourist Office (and rail representative)

Useful Phone Numbers

Ambulance: 161
Police: 100
Tourist police: 171
Operator: 151
International Operator: 161
Directory Enquiries: 132
International Enquiries: 162

ABOVE: the Acropolis, Athens.

4 Conduit Street, London W1S 2DJ
Tel: (020) 7495 9300

UK/US Embassies

UK
1 Ploutarchov Street, 10675 Athens
Tel: (01) 0727 2600
Fax: (01) 0727 2720
www.british-embassy-gr

US
91 Vassilissis Sophias Avenue,
10160 Athens
Tel: (01) 0721 2951
www.usembassy.gr

Money

All banks and most hotels are authorised to buy foreign currency at the official rate of exchange fixed by the Bank of Greece. It is worth carrying a limited sum in US dollars or pounds sterling. Travel agencies give poor rates but charge less commission. Post offices charge a low commission to change cash but don't change travellers' cheques; hotels and agents charge a higher commission than banks. Most banks have ATMs.

Many of the better hotels, restaurants and shops accept major credit cards. The average pension or taverna does not. You will find that most brands of card are accepted by the numerous ATMs (different cards in different banks).

Public Holidays

6 January – Epiphany; 25 March – Independence Day; 1 May – May Day; 15 August – Assumption Day; 28 October – "Ohi" Day; 25–26 December.

Health and Emergencies

Citizens of the USA, Canada and the UK do not need any immunisations to enter Greece.

EU residents are entitled to free medical treatment as long as they carry an EHIC *(see page 351)*. Provision is not of the highest quality, however, plus you will be admitted to one of the lowest-grade state hospitals and have to pay for your own medicine, so it is advisable to take out private medical insurance. Keep receipts for any bills or medicines in order to make a claim. There are long waits for treatment in public hospitals.

On the islands, baby pit vipers and scorpions are a problem in spring and summer. Do not put hands or feet in places that you haven't checked first. If you swim in the sea, beware jellyfish.

The drinking water is safe, though brackish on certain islands.

Hotel staff will give you details of the nearest hospital or English-speaking doctor. Or contact the Tourist Police, who are always extremely helpful. Advice is also given by the International Association for Medical Assistance to Travellers (IAMAT), 34 Themistokleous St, GR-106 78 Athens; tel: (01) 0381 6404.

For minor ailments there's usually an English-speaking pharmacist *(farmakío)* in larger towns and resorts. If you need medication bring the prescription and generic name of the drug.

Safety and Crime

Greece is one of the safest countries in Europe. Crime is rare and but petty theft does sometime occur, but is more likely to have been committed by tourists than by locals.

Telephones

International calls can be made from OTE offices or from the many card-operated booths. Phonecards *(tilekarta)* are available from kiosks. For international calls dial 00, then the country code. US credit phonecard access codes are as follows: Sprint 00-800-1411; MCI/Worldphone 00-800-1211; AT&T 00-800-1311.

Business Hours

All banks open Monday–Thursday 8am–2pm, closing at 1.30pm on Friday. In tourist areas you may find banks open additional late-afternoon hours and on Saturday mornings.

Businesses open at 8.30am and close on Monday, Wednesday and Saturday at 2.30pm. On Tuesday, Thursday and Friday most businesses close at 1.30pm and reopen in the afternoon from 5–8.30pm. Schedules are very flexible in Greece.

Train System

The fastest express trains are the **IC** (InterCity) expresses, which are air-conditioned and require a fare supplement – reservations are only needed on certain trains; normal express trains *(Taxeia)* are less reliable; local trains *(Topiko)* are very slow. Endorse your ticket at the station before departure if you wish to break your journey.

Ticket Details

Ticket offices close 5 minutes before the departure of the train; if the office is closed, get your ticket on board – find the conductor, don't wait for him to find you. A **Multiple Journey Card** offers unlimited second-class rail travel for 10, 20 or 30 days, but does not include supplements on IC trains. The **Greek Flexipass Rail 'n' Fly** offers 1st-class rail travel for 3 days in 1 month, plus two flight coupons for selected Olympic Airways flights. **InterRail**, **Eurailpass**, **Balkan Flexipass**, **Greece–Italy Pass** are all valid.

Reservations

Reservations are recommended, but not essential, on many inter-city trains, although you could have a fight on your hands if someone takes your seat because reserved seats aren't marked. They can be made at any OSE office.

BELOW: fresh fish from the market.

Information

Greek railways are run by Organimós Sidiródromon Éllados (OSE), 1 Karolou Street, tel: 1110; recorded information on 1440. Many travel agents in Greece can book tickets. The OSE website is www.ose.gr

Stations in Athens

Larissa Station (Laríssis) serves trains to Thessaloniki, northern Greece and Bulgaria as well as to Korinthos.

Train Talk

arrivals *afixis*
departures *anahorisis*
first class *próti thési*
platform *platforma*
railway station *strathmós*
reservation *kratisi*
return *i sitírio me epistrofí*
second class *défteri thési*
single *aplo isitírio*
sleeping car *kabines*
ticket *isitírioone énna*
train *tréno*
when is the next train? *póte févyi to tréno?*

Where to Stay

For price categories *see page 351.*

Athens

Candia
Diligianni Street, 40, Athens 10438
Tel: (021) 0524 6112
Fax: (021) 0524 6117
www.candia-hotel.gr
A short walk from the railway station, with a roof-top swimming pool and bedroom balconies, some with views of the Acropolis. **€€**

Titania
Panepistimiou Ave, 52,
Athens 10678
Tel: (021) 0332 6000
Fax: (021) 0330 0700
www.titania.gr
Large hotel near the train station. Roof garden. **€**

IRELAND

The Place

Area: 70,182 sq. km (27,097 sq. miles)
Capital: Dublin
Population: 4.3 million
Language: English and Irish (Gaelic)
Time Zone: GMT; EST +5. Clocks advance 1 hour from late March until late October.

ABOVE: the decorative Ha'penny Bridge, Dublin.

Currency: Euro
Telephone Dialling Codes:
International code: 353. Area codes:
Dublin 1; Cork 21; Tralee 66
Visas and passports: see page 349
Customs: see page 349

Public Holidays

January 1 – New Year's Day; March
17 – St Patrick's Day; March/April –
Good Friday, Easter Monday; May 1 –
May Day; June first Monday; August
first Monday; October last Monday;
December 25 – Christmas Day;
December 26 – St Stephen's Day.

Tourist Offices

In Dublin

Baggot Street Bridge, Dublin 2
Tel: (01) 602 4000
Fax: (01) 602 4100
www.ireland.travel.ie

In the UK

150 New Bond St, W1 0AQ
Tel: (020) 7493 3201
Fax: (020) 7493 6439

In the USA

345 Park Ave, New York, NY 10154
Tel: (212) 418 0800 or
800 223 6470
Fax: (212) 371 9052

UK/US Embassies

UK

29 Merrion Road, Dublin 4
Tel: (01) 205 3700
Fax: (01) 205 3890
www.britishembassy.ie

US

42 Elgin Road,
Ballsbridge, Dublin 4
Tel: 3531 668 8777
Fax: 3531 668 9946
www.dublin.usembassy.gov

Money

Banks open 9.30am–4.30pm,
Monday–Friday. Branches in small
towns may close from 12.30–
1.30pm. Most Dublin banks open
until 5pm on Thursday. Travellers'
cheques are accepted at all banks,
money-change kiosks and many
hotels. Banks generally offer the best
rates for cash but bureaux de change
open later. ATMs are plentiful and
accept credit and debit cards.

Health

UK and other EU visitors need only
go to a doctor (or, in an emergency, a
hospital), present some proof of
identity (e.g. driving licence) and
request treatment under the EU
health agreement. EU travellers will
need their EHIC card for this. Medical
insurance is highly advisable for all
other visitors. Local health boards
arrange consultations with doctors.
Pharmacies only dispense limited
medicines without prescription. They
open during normal shopping hours,
though some open until 10pm in
larger towns.

Safety and Crime

The Republic of Ireland is little
affected by the "Troubles" in
Northern Ireland. Pickpocketing is a

Useful Phone Numbers

Emergencies: 999 (North), 112
(Republic)
International Operator: 155
(North), 114 (Republic)
Local Operator: 100 (North), 10
Republic
Directory Enquiries: 118 500
(North), 11850 (Republic)
International Enquiries: 11818

problem on crowded shopping
streets, and it's not advisable to
wander around late at night north of
the River Liffey. If you get into trouble,
contact the Gardaí or Guards (police).

Telephones

The majority of public telephones
take phonecards: cards in various
denominations are sold at post
offices, newsagents and
supermarkets.
   To call the republic from Great
Britain or Northern Ireland dial 00
353. To call the UK from the Republic
dial 00 44. US credit phonecard
access codes from the Republic are
as follows: MCI Connect 1-800 551
001; AT&T 1-800 550 000; Sprint 1
800 552 001. From Northern Ireland
the numbers are: MCI Connect 0800
279 5088; AT&T 0800 890 011;
Sprint 0800 890 877.

Business Hours

Banks: 10am–4pm Monday–Friday.
Branches in small towns may close
from 12.30pm–1.30pm. Most Dublin
banks are open until 5pm on
Thursday.
Shops: generally 9am–5 or 6pm,
9pm on Thur; many smaller
newsagents will stay open later and
in Dublin mini supermarkets and 7-
11s are open until late in the
evening.
Post offices: 9am–5.30pm Monday–
Friday; 9am–1pm Saturday.

Train System

Trains are operated in the Irish
Republic by Iarnród Éireann (IR); in
Northern Ireland by Northern Irish
Railways (NIR). Cross-border services
are jointly operated. Services are
limited on public holidays, especially
at Christmas, New Year and Easter.

Ticket Details

Trains offer second-class tickets as standard, and some also provide "Super Standard" (1st-class) tickets. A City Gold premium class (with supplementary fare) replaces Super Standard on some Dublin–Cork express services. Tickets can be bought from any bus or train station in the Republic, or through a travel agent abroad.

Discount Passes

InterRail and **Eurail Passes** are valid for bus and train travel in the Republic, excluding city services. A free ferry link is provided by Irish Continental from Le Havre and Cherbourg in France to Rosslare. These tickets must be bought in advance from offices of the participating railways.

Various rail and bus passes are available. Reduced-rate **Rambler** passes are available providing unlimited travel on intercity bus and/or train services. The **Irish Explorer** is valid for rail travel (or rail and bus) in the Republic of Ireland for 5 days within a 15 day period. The **Irish Rambler** allows travel by bus only within Republic of Ireland. The **Irish Rover** is similar but covers all Ireland any 5 days in 15. The **Emerald Card** covers rail and bus throughout all Ireland and is valid for 8 days within 15 days, or 15 days within 30 days. Ask about the **Freedom of Northern Ireland** pass also.

Reservations

1st-class, First Plus, City Gold, and Classic customers are advised to reserve seats. You can reserve at the station or at Iarnród Éireann travel centres. Be in your seat at least 5 minutes before departure.

Information

For timetable and fare information, tel: (0) 1 850 366 222, or one of the several regional 24-hour talking timetables: a list of numbers can be found at www.irishrail.ie in the FAQ section.

Stations in Dublin

Connolly Station for trains to the north, although some start at Pearse Station and go through Connolly. Heuston Station for trains to the west and south. Bus no. 90 is an express service between Connolly and Heuston. Connolly and Pearse are connected by DART suburban rail.

Heuston Station has cafés and other refreshments. Pearse and Connolly are less well equipped. There are Lost and Found offices in Heuston, tel: (01) 703 2102, and Connolly, tel: (01) 703 2358. For assistance for the disabled tel: (01) 703 2634.

Taking Bicycles

Bicycles are not allowed on the DART or other suburban trains unless folded and suitably covered. On Intercity trains, unfolded bicycles can be conveyed in the guard's van (caboose) or the cycle racks where provided. You need to buy a separate ticket for your bike, which is very cheap.

Throughout the Republic, specially appointed Rent-a-Bike dealers hire out sturdy Raleigh Tourer bicycles: a list of them is available from the Irish Tourist Board and the bikes can sometimes be delivered to airports. Killarney Rent-a-Bike offers cycle hire around the country, rates from €80 per week (tel: 064 31282).

Where to Stay

For price categories *see page 351.*

Dublin

Jurys Christchurch Inn
Christchurch Place, Dublin 8
Tel: (01) 454 0000
Fax: (01) 454 0012
Newish, less expensive addition to a long-established chain of hotels. Well located for the old city and Temple Bar. €€€€
Othello Guesthouse
Lower Gardiner Street, Dublin 1
Tel: (01) 855 4271
Fax: (01) 855 7460
www.athelloguesthouse.com
Handy, inner north-city location near Connolly Station. Well equipped for the price. €€
The Parliament Hotel
Lord Edward Street, Dublin 2
Tel: (01) 670 8777
Opposite Dublin Castle and adjacent to the lively Temple Bar district, the Parliament's Edwardian façade veils a contemporary interior. Facilities include a bar and international restaurant. €€€
Shelbourne Hotel
St. Stephen's Green, Dublin 2
Tel: (01) 676 6471
Fax: (01) 661 6006
www.shelbourne.ie
Long established as Dublin's most prestigious hotel, with plenty of old-world atmosphere. The lounge is a great place for afternoon tea, or enjoy a pint of Guinness in the Horseshoe Bar. €€€€€

Killarney

Great Southern Hotel
East Avenue, Killarney, Co.Kerry
Tel: (064) 31262
Fax: (064) 31642
www.gsh.ie
Monumental Victorian railway hotel adjacent to town centre. Swimming, tennis, sauna and Irish entertainment nightly from May to September. €€€€

ITALY

The Place

Area: 301,338 sq. km (116,346 sq. miles)
Capital: Rome
Population: 58.9 million
Language: Italian
Time Zone: GMT +1; EST +6. Clocks advance 1 hour late March–late October
Currency: Euro
Telephone Dialling Codes: International code: 39. Area codes: Palermo 091; Florence 055; Pisa 050; Genoa 010; Rome 06; Milan 02; Naples 081; Venice 041. Area codes are included in all calls, including those made from within the same area. The initial 0 is never omitted.
Visas and passports: *see page 349*
Customs: *see page 349*

Public Holidays

January 1 – New Year's Day; January 6 – Epiphany; March/April – Easter Sunday, Easter Monday; April 25 – National Day of Liberation; May 1 – Labour Day; Whit Sunday; August 15 – Assumption; November 1 – All Saints' Day; December 8 – Immaculate Conception; December 25/26 – Christmas Day and St Stephen's Day.

Tourist Offices

In Rome

Italian Government Tourist Office (ENIT)
Via Marghera 2
Tel: 06 49711
Fax: 06 446 3379
Provincial Tourist Office (APT)
Via Parigi 5
Tel: 06 448 991; fax: 06 481 9316

In the UK

ENIT (Tourist Information)
1 Princes Street, London W1B 2AY
Tel: (020) 7408 1254
Fax: (020) 7493 6695
www.enit.it

EUROPEAN RAIL TRAVEL

COUNTRY BY COUNTRY A – Z

Italian Rail Travel, Wasteels, Platform 2, Victoria Station, London SW1V 1JT
Tel: (020) 7834 7066

In the USA
ENIT
Suite 1565, 630 Fifth Avenue, New York, NY 10111
Tel: (212) 245 5618
Fax: (212) 586 9249
www.italiantourism.com (in English)
Italian Rail Travel
CIT Tours Corporation,
594 Broadway, Suite 307
New York, NY 10012
Tel: (212) 697 2100

UK/US Embassies

UK
Via XX Settembre 80a (Porta Pia), 00187 Roma RM
Tel: 06 4220 0001
www.britishembassy.gov.uk/italy

USA
Via Vittorio Veneto 119/A, 00187 Roma
Tel: 06 46741
Fax: 06 488 2672
www.usembassy.it

Money

Banks are generally open 8.30am–1.30pm, and for an hour in the afternoon (usually 3–4pm) Monday–Friday. Given the long queues for money changing in Italy, it is simplest to get cash from cashpoint machines, which are now widely available. Be aware when using credit cards as many banks charge large fees for cash advances. Travellers' cheques are easily exchanged at banks, which offer the best rates. Hotels and bureaux de change also exchange currencies.

In cities, most of the restaurants, hotels, shops and stores will take major credit cards, but in some rural areas especially, you may be able to pay only in cash.

Health and Emergencies

Health insurance is recommended. Most hospitals have a 24-hour emergency department called Pronto Soccorso. For more minor complaints, seek out a *farmacia*, identified by a sign displaying a red cross within a white circle. Normal opening hours are 8.30am–12.30pm and 3–7.30/8pm Monday–Saturday. Outside these hours the address of the nearest *farmacia* on duty is posted in the window.

Safety and Crime

Tourist-targeted crime consists mainly of pickpocketing and bag snatching. Be extra cautious in Rome, Naples or any train and do not leave bags unattended. Also always ask for ID before surrendering a ticket or paying any so-called fine.

Telephones

In Italy it is *always* necessary to include the area code, even if you are calling from within that area. Another oddity is that you must always include the initial 0 in the area code when calling Italy from abroad. Public phones are found in bars and shops displaying a yellow dialling symbol. They require a phonecard (Carta Telefonica), available from tobacconists and newsstands. Note that some phones accept only coins.

To make an international call from Italy, dial 00, followed by the country code. Then dial the number, omitting the initial 0, if there is one. The SIP telephone ofices on the Piazza San Silvestro and the main station are open 24 hours. US credit phonecard access codes from Italy are as follows: MCI Connect 172 1022; AT&T 172 1011; Sprint 172 1877.

Useful Phone Numbers

General Emergency Assistance and police: 113 (24-hour service)
Carabinieri (Police): 112
Fire Brigade: 115
Ambulance: 118
Directory Enquiries: 12
International Directory Enquiries: 176

Business Hours

Shops open 9am–1pm and 3.30 or 4–7.30 or 8pm although department stores and shops in cities tend to open 9.30am–7.30pm. Almost everything closes on Sunday. Shops often also close on Monday (sometimes in the morning only) and some shut on Saturday.

Train System

Italian trains are operated by the Ferrovie dello Stato (FS) under brand name Trenitalia. Internal **IC** (InterCity) and international **EC** (Eurocity) trains require reservations and fare supplements, as do **EN** (EuroNight; international) and **ICN** (InterCityNight; internal) trains. Seat reservations and (higher) fare supplements are required on **CIS** Cisalpino tilting trains (to/from Switzerland), and normally on the high speed tilting **ES** Eurostar Italia trains.

Other services, where reservations are not required (but recommended in peak season) are classified as:
D: Diretto – in theory, these internal services are semi-fast, but in reality they tend to stop at most stations
E: Espresso – semi-fast, sometimes operating international routes
IR: Interregionale – internal cross-country trains.

Ticket Details

Queues at stations can be long so it's best to buy tickets at travel agents, or on the internet at www.ferroviedellostato.it (or from a ticket agent such as Rail Europe – *see page 348*). Fares are calculated per kilometre. Passengers must stamp local tickets in the station before boarding and if, for some reason, that is not possible, try to find the conductor before he finds you.

Discount Passes
InterRail, **Eurail Pass**, **France–Italy**, **Greece–Italy** and **Italy–Spain** passes are all good for travel in Italy. The **Trenitalia Pass** provides unlimited travel for 3–10 days within 2 months.

BELOW: showing you the way to the station in Venice.

There is a 15 percent discount for groups of 2–5 adults. Available in the UK from Railchoice (www.railchoice.co.uk); in the USA, and from major Italian stations.

Reservations

Reservations can be made at most travel agencies as well as at stations.

Information

Trains are operated by Ferrovie dello Stato (FS), except for 20 or so local lines. For train information, call the same number from anywhere in Italy: 89 20 21, or check timetables on the official railway website: www.trenitalia.com. Train information is available from staff at Uffici Informazioni at most major stations.

City Stations

Rome: Termini station handles most main national and international traffic. Ostiense and Tiburtina serve some long-distance north–south trains. Tiburtina is currently being redeveloped as a hub for high-speed rail services.
Milan: most long-distance trains terminate at Centrale. Some trains terminate at Porta Garibaldi station.
Naples: Most long-distance trains terminate at Napoli Centrale, which has undergone modernisation work and is connected to the new high-speed interchange, Stazione Napoli-Afragola. Mergellina and Campi Flegrei stations are further west and handle mainly local trains. Trains to Pompeii and Sorrento depart from Stazione Circumvesuviana.

Train Talk

arrival, arrives *arrivo, arriva*
calls at *ferma a*
change at *cambiare a*
departure, departs *partenza, parte*
every xx minutes *ogni xx minuti*
first class *la prima classe*
how much is it? *quanto costa?*
journey *viaggio, percorso*
platform *binario*
railway station *stazione (ferroviaria)*
return *un biglietto di andata e ritorno*
second class *seconda classe*
single *un biglietto di andata sola*
sleeping car *vagone letto*
ticket *biglietto*
train *treno*
when does the train depart for...? *quando parte il treno per...?*
where? *dove?*

Taking Bicycles

It is possible to carry bicycles in the luggage cars on R *(Regionale)*, IR *(Interregionale)* and D *(Diretto)* trains, for a small fee. They are not generally permitted on fast IC, EC or EuroNight trains. You can board all regional, inter-regional, direct and suburban trains bearing a bicycle symbol but you will need a ticket. Transport is free for bikes when they are in a bike bag.

Where to Stay

For price categories *see page 351.*

Cagliari

Sardegna Hotel Cagliari
Via Lunigiana 50, Cagliari I-09122
Tel: 080 70 286245
Fax: 080 70 290469
www.sardegnahotelcagliari.it
A good three-star hotel situated only 2 km from the train station. €€€

Milan

Mennini
Via Napo Torriani 14
Tel: 02 669 0951
Fax: 02 669 3437
www.hotelmennini.com
A first class hotel, located only 150 metres from central railway station. The hotel is located close to the Castello Sforzesco, La Scala Opera Theatre, Via Montenapoleone, and Piazzo dell Scala. €€€€
Le Meridien Gallia
Piazza Duca d'Aosta 9,
20124 Milano
Tel: 02 67851
Fax: 02 6671 3239
www.milan.lemeridien.com
Located beside Stazione Centrale, with many superb rooms which are gracious and appealing, most featuring original Art Deco marble bathrooms. The staff are friendly and professional. The hotel also has an excellent restaurant. €€€€€
Michelangelo
Via Scarlatti 33
Tel: 02 67551
Fax: 02 669 4232
www.milanhotel.it
Set close to the Stazione Centrale, the Michelangelo is one of the best-run hotels in Milan, and, despite its anonymous setting in a tower, it has not lost the personal touch. Sound facilities and efficient service. €€€€

Naples

Grand Hotel Vesuvio
Via Partenope 45
Tel: 081 76 40 044
Fax: 081 76 44 483
www.vesuvio.it

Located in a sunny waterfront position overlooking the Bay of Naples and dominating the Santa Lucia harbour. Most rooms have a balcony or terrace with an excellent view of the Mediterranean and Vesuvius. Just over 500 metres from the rail station. €€€€€
Jolly Hotel
Via Medina 70
Tel: 081 410 5111
Fax: 081 551 8010
Italy's tallest hotel gives panoramic views of Naples. Located in the heart of the city close to the Piazza del Municipio. Less than 500 metres from the railway station. €€€€

Palermo

Hilton Villa Igiea
Salita Belmonte 43
Tel: 091 631 2111
Fax: 091 547 654
www.hotelvillaigieapalermo.com
Overlooking the Bay of Palermo and set in splendid terraced gardens of jasmine with a swimming pool, the Villa Igiea is one of Sicily's best hotels. €€€€€
Jolly Hotel
Via Foro Italico 22b
Tel: 091 616 5090
Fax: 091 616 1441
A first-class hotel with a magnificent swimming pool in luxuriant gardens. The hotel is located on the seafront and just a few steps from the gardens of Villa Giulia. The harbour and the railway station are just 500 metres away. €€€

Rome

Hotel Doria
Via Merulana 4, 00185 Roma
Tel: 06 446 5888
Fax: 06 446 5889
A simple hotel just five minutes' walk from Stazione Termini. Small and clean, it has a TV and mini-bar in some rooms. €€€€
Le Grand Hotel Roma
Via Orlando Vittorio Emanuele 3,
00185 Roma
Tel: 06 47091
Fax: 06 4201 4201
Between the railway station and the Via Veneto area, this exclusive, dignified hotel is very well run and stylish. It is set in a patrician palace and graced with Chinese and Japanese rugs, chandeliers and antiques. €€€€€
Select
Via V Bachelet 6
Tel: 06 445 6383
Fax: 06 4441 086
www.hotelselectgarden.com
Close to the station, this small friendly hotel has the feel of a secluded villa. Good value. €€

EUROPEAN RAIL TRAVEL

COUNTRY BY COUNTRY A – Z

Venice

Abbazia
Priuli dei Cavaletti, 66–8 Cannaregio
Tel: 041 717 333
Fax: 041 717 949
www.abbaziahotel.com
Converted monastery with 39 rooms and the hotel is framed by a garden. Within easy reach of the railway station (150 metres) and Piazzale Roma. €€€€

Hotel Carlton and Grand Canal
Santa Croce, 578
Tel: 041 718 488
Fax: 041 719 061
www.carlton.hotelinvenice.com
Well-equipped hotel on the Grand Canal, conveniently located for the station. €€€€

PORTUGAL

The Place

Area: 92,345 sq. km (35,655 sq. miles), including Madeira and the Azores
Capital: Lisbon
Population: 10.6 million
Language: Portuguese
Time Zone: GMT (summer time GMT + 1); EST +6; the Azores are 1 hour behind continental Portugal. Clocks advance 1 hour from late March until late October
Currency: Euro
Telephone Dialling Codes: International code: 351
All domestic calls are 9-digit numbers, with no area codes.
Visas and passports: see page 349
Customs: see page 349

Public Holidays

January 1 – New Year's Day; mid to late February – Carnival (preceding Lent); March/April – Good Friday, Easter; April 25 – Anniversary of the Revolution (1974); May 1 – Labour Day; June 10 – Portugal and Camões Day; early June – Corpus Christi; August 15 – Day of the Assumption; October 5 – Republic Day; November 1 – All Saints' Day; December 1 – Restoration of Independence; December 8 – Day of the Immaculate Conception; December 25 – Christmas Day.

Tourist Offices

In Porto

Rua Clube dos Fenianos, 25, 4000-172 Porto
Tel: (22) 339 3470
Fax: (22) 332 3303
www.portoturismo.pt

In the UK

22–25A Sackville Street, London
W1X 1DE
Tel: 09063 640610
Fax: (020) 7494 1868

In the USA

590 Fifth Avenue, 4th Floor,
New York, NY 10036-4704
Tel: (212) 354 4403/4404
Fax: (212) 764 6137

UK/US Embassies

UK

Rua São Bernardo 33,
Lisboa 1249-082
Tel: (21) 392 4000
Fax: (21) 392 4185
www.uk-embassy.pt

USA

Av. das Forças Armadas,
1600-081 Lisbon
Tel: (21) 727 3300
Fax: (21) 727 9109
www.american-embassy.pt

Money

There are banks in all but the smallest towns. Changing cash at a bank or cashpoint is far cheaper than paying the higher rate of commission on travellers' cheques. Visa, AmEx, Maestro and MasterCard are acceptable. ATMs, usually called *Multibanco*, take all major cards. Travellers' cheques are accepted in banks, but in shops – if they are accepted at all – they are charged at a high rate.

Health

Private treatment must be paid for, so it is best to take out health insurance. For minor complaints, consult a pharmacy – a list of those opening late for emergencies is in the window of each and also in newspapers. As part of the EU, emergency medical treatment is free or reduced-cost provided you have an EHIC and your passport or ID card. Beware of sunburn. Use sunscreen and wear a hat. Tap water is generally drinkable, but it is best to use bottled water (*água mineral*).

Safety and Crime

Portugal has a well-deserved reputation for non-violence, though petty theft is becoming a problem in some areas of Lisbon and Porto, and close to larger shopping centres. Report theft to the police within 24 hours in order to claim insurance.

Telephones

Call boxes accept coins and phone cards (sold in Telecom shops, post offices and kiosks), and newer phones also accept credit cards. For long distance and international calls a phonecard *(credifon)* is recommended. US credit card access codes are as follows: Sprint 800 800 187; MCI 800 800 123; AT&T 800 800 128.

Business Hours

Shops: 9am–1pm and 3–7pm Monday–Friday, 9am–1pm Saturday. Large supermarkets remain open all day Saturday and half-day Sunday and holidays.
Banks: main branches open 8.30am–3pm Monday–Friday; closed Saturday, Sunday and holidays. Some in Lisbon open till 6pm.
Post Offices: 9am–6pm Monday–Friday. Some central offices have extended opening hours.

Train System

The main categories of train in Portugal are:
AP: Alfa Pendular – high-speed tilting train *(rápido)* between Lisbon and the Algarve, and in the North, Oporto and Braga.
IC: Intercidades – intercity trains *(directos)*
IR: Interregional – semi-fast trains *(semi-directos)*
Regionais and *Suburbano* services are local stopping trains. **Sud-Express** trains are international train services to Vigo, Madrid and Paris.

Ticket Details

Tickets cost very little, with a choice of first- or second-class, smoking or non-smoking. A seven-day national pass is valid on most trains throughout the country. Because everyone who takes the Douro line on a regular basis knows the "glamour view", i.e. the Douro River, is on the right-hand side (going to Pocinho, on the left side coming back) seats in these coveted positions fill up early. Late-comers are advised to go for one of the

Useful Phone Numbers

Police, Fire, Ambulance: 112
International Operator: 098
European Operator: 099
Directory Enquiries: 118
International Directory Enquiries: 177

relatively empty and still-inexpensive 1st-class compartments. Look for the sign that says *bilheteiras* (tickets). There are fines for boarding the train without a ticket or pass.

Discount Passes

The **InterRail**, **Eurail Pass** and **Spain–Portugal** are all available *(see page 360 for more details)*. **Tourist tickets** *(bilhetes turisticos)* are available for periods of 7, 14 and 21 days (valid for both first- and second-class). The **Portuguese Flexipass** for non-Europeans gives 4 days of travel in first class within 15 days (Madrid hotel train not included). The **Intra-Rail** card gives 12–30 year olds 3 or 10 days travel in four pre-defined zones, and includes nights at youth hostels.

Reservations

Seats must be reserved in advance on AP and IC trains, plus international services. Fare supplements are also payable. Bookings can be made at any CP office or through selected ticket agents.

Information

Caminhos de Ferro Portugueses (CP) is the national operator. For their main office in Lisbon, tel: 808 208 208. Their website is at www.cp.pt.

Stations in Porto/Lisbon

Porto: Fast trains to Lisbon depart from Campanhã station outside the city centre; most other trains depart from the central São Bento station, calling in at Campanhã as they exit the city.
Lisbon: There are four railway stations in Lisbon plus Barreiro on the south side of the River Tagus. Trains for the north of Portugal, Spain, France and beyond depart from Santa Apolónia and the ultra-modern Oriente station. Those heading for Sintra and Figueira da Foz on the coast north of Lisbon depart from Rossio station, while local trains to Cascais and Estoril depart from Cais do Sodré station. Trains to the Algarve depart from Barreiro, on the other side of the Tagus and reached by ferry from Lisbon; buy inclusive ferry/train tickets at Sul e Sueste station.

Train Talk

arrivals *chegadas*
daily *cadadia*
departures *partida*
exit *a saída*

first class *primeira classe*
how much is it? *Quanto custa?*
platform *plataforma*
railway station *estação*
reservation *reserva*
return *retorn-bilhete/bilhete de ida e volta*
second class *segunda classe*
single *bilhete de ida*
sleeping car *uma couchette*
ticket *bilhete*
train *comboio*
when does the train depart for...? *a que hora parta el comboio para...?*
where is the...? *Onde é...?*

Taking Bicycles

Bicycles may be carried on many Portuguese trains, but not on the fast AP and IC expresses. Coimbra Urban, Inter-regional and Regional services charge a fee to carry bicycles at weekends, on public holidays and off-peak times – ask the ticket inspector for a bicycle ticket.

Where to Stay

For price categories *see page 351.*

Porto
Hotel Infante de Sagres
Praça D. Filipa de Lencastre, 62
Tel: 351 223 398 500
Fax: 351 223 398 599
www.hotelinfantesagres.pt
Splendid old hotel right in the centre; full of character. Less than 500 metres from São Bento station.
€€€€€
Hotel Mercure Batalha Porto
Praça de Batalha, 116
Tel: 22 204 3300
Fax: 22 204 3499
Overlooking the old centre of Porto, and just 250 metres from São Bento station; 140 air-conditioned rooms.
€€€

SCANDINAVIA

The Place

Finland
Area: 338,145 sq. km (130,559 sq. miles)
Capital: Helsinki
Population: 5.3 million
Language: 92 percent Finnish, Swedish
Time Zone: GMT +2; EST +.7 Clocks advance 1 hour late March until late October
Currency: Euro
Telephone Dialling Codes:
International code: 358. Area codes: Helsinki 09; Tempere 03; Turku 02

Public Holidays

General
January 1 – New Year's Day; March/April – Good Friday, Easter Day; May 1 – Labour Day; December 25 – Christmas Day, December 26 – St Stephen's Day.

Additional holidays in Finland
January 6 – Epiphany; May – Ascension Day; Whitsun; June – Midsummer's Day; November 1 – All Saints' Day; December 6 – Independence Day; December 24 – Christmas Eve.

Additional holidays in Norway
March/April – Palm Sunday; Maundy Thursday; May 17 – National Independence Day; Ascension Day; Whitsun.

Additional holidays in Sweden
January 6 – Epiphany; June 6 – National Day; June – Midsummer's Eve; November 1 – All Saints' Day; December 24 – Christmas Eve; December 31 – New Year's Day.

Norway
Area: 323,759 sq. km (125,004 sq. miles)
Capital: Oslo
Population: 4.7 million
Language: Norwegian
Time Zone: GMT + 1; EST +7. Clocks advance 1 hour from late March until late October
Currency: Krone
Telephone Dialling Codes:
International code: 47. All numbers are 8-digit – no area codes required

Sweden
Area: 449,964 sq. km (173,732 sq. miles)
Capital: Stockholm
Population: 9.1 million
Languages: Swedish, Finnish, Sami
Time Zone: As for Norway
Currency: Swedish krona, split into 100 öre
Telephone Dialling Codes:
International code: 46. Area codes: Stockholm 8; Göteborg 31; Malmö 40; Ostersund 63

Visas and Passports

Scandinavian citizens may freely move between their countries without a passport, but still need some form of ID. Citizens of most other countries require a passport for stays of less than three months.

Customs

Finland

As for other EU countries – *see page 349.*

Norway

Customs allowances are very similar to those of the EU countries. On top of the tax-free quota you may bring in 4 litres wine or liquor against payment of duty.

Sweden

As for other EU countries – *see page 349.*

Tourist Offices

Finnish

In the UK
3rd Floor, 30–35 Pall Mall
London SW1Y 5LP
Tel: (020) 7930 5871
Fax: (020) 7321 0696
www.finland-tourism.com
In the US
PO Box 4649
Grand Central Station
New York, NY 10163-4649
Tel: (212) 885 9700
Fax: (212) 885 9739

Norwegian

In the UK
Charles House, 5th Floor,
5 Lower Regent Street, London
SW1Y 4LR
Tel: (020) 7839 6255
Fax: (020) 7839 6014
www.visitnorway.com
In the US
655 Third Avenue, Suite 1810, New
York, NY 10017
Tel: (212) 885 9700
Fax: (212) 885 9710
www.norway.org

Swedish

In the UK
Travel and Tourism Council
Swedish Embassy
11 Montagu Place, London W1H 2AL
Tel: (020) 7724 5868
Fax: (020) 7724 5872
www.visit-sweden.com
In the US
Tourism Council: PO Box 4649
Grand Central Station, New York
NY 100163-4649
Tel: (212) 885 9700
Fax: (212) 855 9710
www.gosweden.org

UK/US Embassies

UK

Finland
Itäinen Puistotie 17
00140 Helsinki

Tel: (09) 2286 5100
Fax: (09) 2286 5284
Norway
Thomas Heftyesgate 8
0244 Oslo
Tel: 23 13 27 00
Fax: 23 13 27 41
www.britishembassy.gov.uk/norway
Sweden
Skarpögatan 6–8
Box 27819
11593 Stockholm
Tel: (08) 671 3000

US

Finland
Itäinen Puistotie 14B
FIN-00140 Helsinki
Tel: (09) 171 931
www.usembassy.fi
Norway
Drammensveien 18
0244 Oslo
Tel: 22 44 85 50
www.usa.no
Sweden
Dag Hammarskjölds Väg 31
SE-115 89, Stockholm
Tel: (08) 783 53 00
Fax: (08) 661 19 64
www.usis.usemb.se

Money

Finland is the only Scandinavian country to adopt the Euro. Credit cards are widely accepted, with Visa, Access, American Express, Mastercard and Diner's Club the most common. Travellers' cheques and common currencies can be exchanged easily in banks. ATMs are ubiquitous.

Useful Phone Numbers

Finland

National Emergency Number: 112
Police: 10022
International Operator: 020 208
Operator: 118
Directory Enquiries: 020 202
International Enquiries: 020 208

Norway

Fire: 110
Police: 112
Ambulance: 113
Directory Enquiries: 1881
International Enquiries: 1882
Operator: 1881
International Operator: 1882

Sweden

Police, Fire, Ambulance: 112
Directory Enquiries: 118 118
International Enquiries: 118 119
Operator: 90130
International Operator: 0018

Health and Emergencies

The standard of health provision is very high, and even in remote areas you should have no problem getting medical help. In Norway and Finland, if you are ill ask your hotel, tourist office or a pharmacy for the address of an English-speaking GP. There is no GP system in Sweden, so the place to go for any type of treatment is the nearest hospital. Casualty (*akutmottagning*) deals with serious problems, but *Vårdcentral* or *Husläkarmottagning* out-patients clinics are a better option since you will normally be seen within an hour. Take your passport with you and your EHIC if applicable (although you will still need to pay part of the cost which is non-refundable). Make sure you keep receipts if you have medical insurance.

For minor problems, head for a pharmacy. Most larger cities have all-night pharmacies (a list will usually be posted on the door of each one). Mosquitos in the far north in high summer can be vicious.

Safety and Crime

Scandinavia is generally a law-abiding region. Crime figures are low, and the streets of the cities are by and large safe. Petty theft is the most likely danger so keep an eye on your passport and cash. Lone female travellers rarely encounter problems.

Telephones

Finland

Telephones are dependable and quick in Finland and rarely out of order. Most public telephones operate using a pre-paid card. These can be bought at post offices, kiosks and tourist offices. International call rates go down in the late evening. Hotel phone calls are very expensive. US phonecard access codes are as follows: Sprint 0800 110 284; MCI 0800 110 280; AT&T 0800 110 015.

Norway

Phone calls abroad can be dialled from hotel rooms (but include a surcharge) or from booths; you can also send faxes to other Nordic countries from the main post office in Oslo. Payphones take coins and phonecards, which can be bought in Narvesen kiosks, 7–11 kiosks and at post offices. US phonecard access numbers are as follows: Sprint 800 198 77; MCI 800 199 12; AT&T 800 190 11.

Sweden

Post offices do not have telephone facilities, but there are plenty of payphones, credit card phones (signposted CCC) and special telegraph offices (marked Telia or Telebutik). Most payphones operate only with a telephone card *(Telia telefonkort)* available in Pressbyrå, kiosks and supermarkets. US phonecard access codes are as follows: Sprint 020 799 011; MCI 0200 895 438; AT&T 020 799 111.

Business Hours

Finland

Shops: generally 9am–8pm; in Helsinki many open until 9pm weekdays and 6pm on Saturdays. Large foodstores 9am–8pm weekdays, until 4pm Saturday. Late opening in the tunnel under the Helsinki railway station daily until 10pm.
Banks: 9am–4.15pm Monday–Friday. Some exchange bureaux open later, particularly at travel points such as the airport and main rail stations, and at international ferry terminals.

Norway

Shops: Monday–Friday 9am–5pm, Thursday until 7pm, Saturday from 9am–3pm. Shopping centres Monday–Friday until 8pm, 6pm on Saturday.
Banks: weekdays 8.30am–3.15pm (until 4.30 or 5pm Thursday).
Pharmacies: Monday–Friday 8am–3, 3.30 or 4pm, Saturday mornings and on a rota basis in larger cities. Pharmacies in shopping malls follow the mall opening hours.

Sweden

Shops: Monday–Friday 9.30am–6pm, Saturdays until 3 or 4pm. In larger cities many open on Sunday, usually noon–4pm.
Banks: Monday–Friday 10am–3pm (4pm Thursday, 6pm in some larger cities), closed Saturday. The Exchange bureau in terminal 5 at Stockholm Arlanda Airport's arrival hall is open daily 5.30am–10.30pm and at the departure hall daily 5.30am–6pm.

Train System

Finland

Finland's railways are run by VR Ltd. There are five main types of train. The **Pendolino (S)** is a high-speed tilting train. A fare supplement is payable and there are first- and second-class compartments. The new double-decker **InterCity (IC)** expresses have first- and second-

ABOVE: Södermalm, Stockholm.

class, provide service for wheelchair users, have a play space for children, a booth for mobile-phone use, a smokers' booth, luggage lockers, bicycle and ski locks and designated compartments for families, passengers with pets and allergy sufferers. **Express** *(pikajunat)* and **Regional** *(taajamajunat)* trains have second-class compartments only. **Sleeper trains** operate between Helsinki, Tampere, Oulu and Rovaniemi.

Norway

Norwegian railways are operated by the Norges Statsbaner (NSB). Express trains are either tilting **Signatur** services or the standard **Ekspresstog (Et)**; other tilting trains are designated **Agenda**. Other trains generally only have second-class seating. Signatur and some other express trains have "family" carriages with a play area for children. Night trains with couchettes and sleepers (first/second-class) operate on the Oslo–Stavanger, Oslo–Bergen, Oslo–Trondheim and Trondheim–Bodø routes. Supplement fares are payable on Signatur and Et trains.

Sweden

Swedish trains are run by Swedish State Railways (Statens Järnvägar; SJ); several local lines are run by smaller companies – rail passes are not always valid on these lines; check with a tourist office. 95 percent of Swedish trains are electric. High-speed **X2000** trains are the most prestigious, operating on most long-distance routes in the country. Other fast trains are called

InterCity, on which a smaller fare supplement is payable. X2000 and some InterCity trains have a Family coach with a play area for children. Overnight trains with first- and second-class sleepers and couchettes operate on the Stockholm–Malmo–Copenhagen route, and between Stockholm and northern Sweden.

Ticket Details

Finland

Tickets are sold at railway stations, travel agencies, by other VR agents and on trains. Vending machines sell train tickets and issue tickets and sleeping-berths booked by phone; tickets purchased aboard the train are subject to commission.
Several train passes are valid for travelling in Finland. The **Finnrailpass** is good for unlimited travel on all trains in Finland for 3, 5 or 10 days within 1 month. Further information is available at VR stations. Under 17s pay half price. The **Eurail Scandinavia Pass** offers you unlimited travel in Denmark, Finland, Norway and Sweden for 4–10 days travel (second-class) within a 2-month period. Special fares are available for 16–25 year olds. **InterRail Pass** is also valid *(see page 348)*.

Norway

The **Eurail Norway Pass** offers 3–8 days of second-class travel within 1 month. For non-Europeans it also qualifies you for additional discounts on several ferries. **InterRail, Eurail Scandinavia Pass** and **Eurailpass** are valid *(see page 348)*.

Sweden

An adult passenger (not using a rail pass) can be accompanied by 2 children (under 16) at no extra charge on X2000 and InterCity trains. Under 26s pay 70 percent of the full fare. The **Eurail Sweden Pass** offers unlimited first- or second-class rail travel within Sweden. Choose between 3–8 travel days within 1 month; buy it from Sweden Booking *(see Reservations)* or other booking agents *(see page 348)*. A **Tågplus** ticket enables you to use rail, bus and ferry networks. **Eurail Scandinavia Pass** and **InterRail Pass** are all valid *(see page 348)*. There are trains equipped for wheelchairs on all major routes.

Reservations

Finland

Advance tickets on S220 (Pendolino), InterCity (IC) and Express (P) trains indicate a seat reservation. A 1-year advance reservation of train tickets, sleeping-berths and car-sleeper spaces is possible. Seats may be booked for allergic or disabled passengers, and in Express trains a seat in the children's playroom car or video car. No seat booking is possible on Regional trains.

Norway

Seat reservations are compulsory on Signatur and Et trains, and on other trains marked with a boxed "R" on timetables. An additional fee has to be paid for reservation of seats, couchettes and sleepers.

Ticket sales are from the main hall of the train station or a local travel agent. Tickets for ordinary trains may be bought on board but a supplement is payable unless you boarded at an unstaffed station without ticket machines.

Blind passengers do not pay supplements from unstaffed stations. Tickets can be bought through NSB agents in Norway or from an agent such as Rail Europe in the UK (see page 348).

You can book tickets on www.nsb.no and collect them on the train, or have them sent to an address in Norway. Seat reservations can be made up to 90 days before travel.

Sweden

Seat reservations are advisable on all services: they are necessary on X2000 and overnight trains, but not on InterCity services. Reservations can be made on most long-distance journeys. Reserved seats must be claimed no later than 15 minutes after departure. Contact Sweden Booking, tel: (0498) 20 33 80; fax: (0498) 20 33 90; www.sweden booking.com. X2000 and some InterCity trains have a special carriage with a wheelchair lift and a bookable space for a wheelchair.

Information

Finland

VR Ltd, Finnish Railways, tel: +358 9 231 92 902 (from abroad); 0600 41 902 (in Finland); www.vr.fi

Norway

For timetables, ticket prices and bookings see the Norwegian State Railways (NSB) website at www.nsb.no, or call 81 500 888 and dial 4 for an English-speaking operator.

Sweden

Statens Järnvägar's site is at www.sj.se. Information, tel: (0)771 75 75 75.

Train Talk

Finland

arrivals *saapuvat*
change here for *matkustavat vaihtavat junaa*
daily *päivittäin*
departures *lähtevä*
first class *primaarinen kurssi*
how much is it? *paljonko tämä maksaa?*
platform *ulkoportaat*
railway station *rautatieasema/asema*
reservation *reservaatti*
return *korko*
second class *sekunti kurssi*
sleeping car *makuuvaunu*
thank you *kiitos*
ticket *lippu*
train *juna*
when? *j?*
where is...? *missä on...?*

Norway

arrival *ankomst*
daily *daglig*
departure *avgang, avvik, avreise*
first class *første klasse*
how much is it? *hvaor mye koster det*
platform *perrong*
railway station *stasjon*
reservation *reservasjon*
return *tur-retur*
second class *andre klasse*
single *en vei*
sleeping car *sovevogn*
ticket *billet*
train *tog*
where is...? *hvor er...?*

Sweden

arrival hall *ankomsthall*
change here *byter om tåg*
daily *daglig*
departure hall *avgångshall*
first class *förstklassig*
how much is it? *vad kostar det?*
platform *kateder/läktare*
please *tack/var så god*
railway station *station*
reservation *reservera*
return journey *återfärd/tur och retur*
second class *andraklassbiljett*
single *enda/enkel/ogift*
sleeping car *sovvagn*
ticket *biljett*
train *tåg*
when? *när?*
where is ...? *var är ...?*

Bicycles

Finland

To transport a bicycle on Pendolino and IC trains you need to book in advance. One bicycle per passenger is admitted for transportation in the guard's van, for a fee. Bicycles

cannot be taken on Helsinki region commuter trains during rush hour Monday–Friday (7–9am and 3–6pm).

Norway

Bicycles can be taken on most trains (on fast trains look for the bicycle symbol on timetables) but a charge is made for carrying bikes on the Bergen and Flåm railways. Reservations for transporting bikes can only be made in Norway and should be made well in advance for long distance and intercity trains (tel: 815 00888); on most local trains, you can't reserve: if there is space, you can take your bike.

Sweden

Bicycles are only permitted on the Øresund line serving Gothenburg–Copenhagen and Kalmar–Alvesta–Copenhagen routes, for half the price of a standard ticket. Microcycles and children's cycles may be taken aboard as hand luggage without charge. You can also take your bicycle on a train in Skåne as the local transport provider (Skånetrafiken) reserves space on the Pågatågen trains (tel: 0771 777 777). To send bicycles between other destinations, contact a coach-operated transit courier at the station.

FINLAND Hotels

For price categories see page 351.

Helsinki

Grand Marina
Katajanokanlaituri 7, 00160
Tel: (09) 16661
Fax: (09) 664764
Designed in 1911 by noted Finnish architect Lars Sonck, each of the 462 rooms is exquisitely decorated and well-equipped. A 10-minute walk from the railway station. **€€**
Radisson SAS Royal
Runeberginkatu 2, 00100
Tel: 358 (0) 20 1234 701
Fax: 358 (0) 20 1234 702
Sunny, open dining and bar areas and the usual good service. About a 10-minute walk from the centre. **€€€€**

NORWAY Hotels

For price categories see page 351.

Bergen

Grand Hotel Terminus
Zander Kaaesgate 6
Tel: 55 21 25 00
Fax: 55 21 25 01
www.ght.no
In a great location across from the

station, this elegant hotel has been a popular stopover for wealthy tourists since 1928. The comfortable rooms are beautifully decorated and the restaurant serves fine Norwegian cuisine with many dishes unique to Bergen. Closed at Easter. €€€

Radisson SAS Hotel Norge
Nedre Ole Bulls Plass 4
Tel: 55 57 30 00
Fax: 55 57 30 01
www.norge.bergen.radissonsas.com
One of Bergen's most famous and best-loved hotels. Four restaurants, night club, indoor pool, winter garden; 1 km from the railway station. €€€

Best Western Victoria Hotel
Kong Oscarsgate 29, 5017 Bergen
Tel: 55 21 23 00
Once a staging-post inn, this now has 43 comfortable, modern rooms with own facilities. Full of character and an admirable art collection. Fully licensed lobby bar. Central location, just 500 metres from the railway station. €€€€

Oslo

Bristol
Kristian IV's Gate 7
Tel: 22 82 60 00
Fax: 22 82 60 01
www.bristol.no
Famous hotel, with ornate lobby and antiques in the bedrooms. Less than 500 metres from the station. €€€

Grand Hotel
Karl Johans Gate 31
Tel: 23 21 20 00
Fax: 23 21 21 00
www.grand.no
On Oslo's main thoroughfare since 1874, this exclusive hotel has been the site for many Nobel Prize celebrations and where visiting heads of state tend to stay. Less than 500 metres from Sentral station. €€€€€

Clarion Royal Christiania Hotel
Biskop Gunnerusgaten 3, N-0106
Tel: 23 10 80 90
Fax: 23 10 80 80
www.royalchristiania.no
Magnificent atrium, spacious rooms, wonderful service and breakfasts; convenient location less than 100 metres from Oslo Sentral station. €€€€€

Trondheim

Ambassadeur
Elvegate 18
Tel: 73 52 70 50
One of Trondheim's most reasonably priced hotels, with a roof terrace. Only 500 metres from the station. €€

Clarion Grand Olav Hotel
Olavskvartalet
Tel: 73 80 80 80

Fax: 73 80 80 81
www.choicehotels.no
Top-class hotel in the heart of Trondheim. Close to shops, bars and restaurants. Less than 1 km from the railway station. €€€

Radisson SAS Royal Garden Hotel
Kjøpmannsgt 73
Tel: 73 80 30 00
Fax: 73 80 30 50
www.radissonsas.com
Well-appointed rooms plus solarium, indoor pool, gymnasium, sauna and several good restaurants. Only 300 metres from the railway station. €€€

SWEDEN Hotels

For price categories *see page 351.*

Östersund

Radisson SAS Hotel
Prestgatan 16, Östersund, S-831 31 SE
Tel: (063) 55 6000
www.radissonsas.com
Luxury hotel with sauna, cable TV, heated pool and restauant. €€€€

Scandic Hotel South
Krondikesvagen 97, Östersund, 83146
Tel: (063) 12 75 60
Fax: (063) 68 58 611
www.scandichotels.com
First-class hotel with satellite TV, gymnasium, sauna and solarium. €€€

Stockholm

Radisson SAS Royal Viking Hotel Stockholm
Klarabergsgatan and Vsagatan
Tel: (08) 50 65 40 00
Fax: (08) 50 65 40 01
www.royalviking-stockholm.radissonsas.com
Modern and tastefully designed rooms in the very heart of Stockholm; convenient for the station. €€€€

Continental Hotel
Vasagatan S-101, 22 Stockholm
Tel: (08) 51 75 17 00
Fax: (08) 51 75 17 11
A first-class hotel located in the city centre. Facilities include a sauna and relaxation room. €€€€

SPAIN

The Place

Area: 505,988 sq. km (195,363 sq. miles)
Capital: Madrid
Population: 44.2 million
Language: Spanish (Castilian), plus Catalan, Basque and Galician
Time Zone: Except for Canary Islands

(which is GMT): GMT +1; EST +6. Clocks advance 1 hour from late March until late October
Currency: Euro
Telephone Dialling Codes:
International code: 34
All numbers should be dialled with their area code, for local, long-distance and international calls.
Madrid 910-918; Barcelona 930-938; Seville 854; Alicante 865; Palma de Mallorca 971; San Sebastián 943; Bilbao 94
Visas and passports: *see page 349*
Customs: *see page 349*

Public Holidays

January 1 – New Year's Day; March 19 – St Joseph; March/April – Good Friday, Easter; May 1 – Labour Day; 15 August – Feast of the Assumption; October 12 – Columbus Day or Día de la Hispanidad; November 1 – All Saints' Day; December 6 – Constitution; December 8 – Immaculate Conception; December 25 – Christmas Day. These are all national holidays – numerous other regional ones occur.

Tourist Offices

In Madrid
Duque de Medinaceli 2, Madrid 28014
Tel: (91) 429 4951
Fax: (91) 429 0909

In the UK
22–23 Manchester Square, London W1M 5AP
Tel: (020) 7486 8077
Fax: (020) 7486 8034
www.spain.info/uk

In the US
666 Fifth Ave, 35th Floor, New York, NY 10103
Tel: (212) 265 8822
Fax: (212) 365 8864

UK/US Embassies

UK
Fernando el Santo 16, Madrid 28010
Tel: (91) 700 8200
Fax: (91) 700 8272

USA
Serrano 75, Madrid 28006
Tel: (91) 587 2200
Fax: (91) 587 2303

Money

Banks give the best rates for travellers' cheques and foreign currency, but you can also use the numerous currency exchange shops, *casas de cambio,* which open later. Shop around. Airport bureaux, travel agencies and hotels also change money, at bad rates – although commission is low. Banks give cash against your credit card. Personal cheques are not readily accepted in shops, but may be drawn on local banks. Always carry ID when you go to the bank.

Even small towns usually have ATMs. Credit cards are accepted in most shops and businesses and for long-distance train tickets. You will need to produce your passport or ID card on these transactions.

Health and Emergencies

Spain has countless pharmacies *(farmacias)*, each with a white sign with a flashing green cross. They open 9.30am–1.30pm and 4.30–8pm Monday–Friday; 9am–1.30pm Saturday. In most towns a system operates whereby there is one pharmacy open round-the-clock in each area. A sign in front of each should indicate which are open on which nights.

If you have a serious problem get the number of an English-speaking doctor from your consulate, the police, Turismo or closest pharmacy. The EHIC card only covers emergency public, not private health care. You are advised to take out insurance before travelling.

Safety and Crime

Bag-snatching and pickpocketing are probably the worst problems – and tourists are a major target, so take care in crowds and busy tourist areas, especially the big cities. Avoid flashing money around. Keep valuables in the hotel safe and don't carry large sums of money or your passport (take a photocopy instead). If robbed, contact the local police station – the Policía Municipal are the most sympathetic. Most insurance companies require an official statement *(denuncia)* before they will accept a claim.

Useful Phone Numbers

Police: 091
Municipal Police: 092
Emergency Medical Care: 061
Fire Department: 080
International Operator: 1005
Directory Enquiries: 11818
International Enquiries: 025
Local Operator: 11818

ABOVE: the palm garden at Estación de Atocha, Madrid.

Telephones

There are many coin-operated telephone booths throughout the country, though many either don't work or have been vandalised. Wait for the tone, deposit the coins and dial the number. It is possible to place a long-distance call by depositing a handful of coins. Most bars have coin-operated or meter telephones available for public use as well. A phonecard can be purchased at a tobacconist's. For overseas calls, it's probably better to go to the offices of Telefónica, where one can talk first and pay later and not have to worry about having enough coins. US phonecard access codes are as follows: Sprint 900 99 0013; MCI Connect 800 099 357; AT&T 900 99 00 11.

Business Hours

Banks: hours vary. Most open 9am–2pm Monday–Friday, and some on Saturday until 1pm, though not usually between June–Sept or on Thursday afternoons. All close on Sunday and holidays. Several branches in the business districts open until 6pm or later.
Shops: open 9.30 or 10am–1.30 or 2pm and then reopen in the afternoon from 4.30 or 5 until around 8pm Monday–Saturday. Many close on Saturday afternoons in summer and all day Sunday. Large stores tend to open 10am–9pm Monday–Saturday and on a fixed number of Sundays.
District post offices: 9am–2.30pm Monday–Friday; all close on Sunday.
Principal post offices: open daily 9am–2pm and 4–7pm.

Train System

Spanish trains come in many categories. Fare supplements are payable on InterCity, Arco, Talgo, Alaris and Euromed trains. Reservations are compulsory on all these trains.
D: Diurno – ordinary long-distance daytime train
Talgo/InterCity (IC)/Arco: all three are quality express trains; the Talgo is the most comfortable, with video entertainment
T200: Talgo trains equipped to run on high-speed lines as well as the broad gauge system
Estrella (Estr): night trains with couchettes and sleepers
Trenhotel: high quality night express trains
AVE: Alta Velocidad Española, the Madrid–Seville high-speed line, RENFE's pride and joy, whisking you from Madrid to Seville in just 2½ hours *(see page 177).* You are entitled to a refund if the train arrives more than 5 minutes late.
Em: Euromed – high-speed trains operating between Barcelona, Valencia and Alicante

Local trains don't have an indication of category, except for the fast Tren Regional Diesel (TRD) services. Suburban trains are called *cercanías.*

Ticket Details

Most trains offer first class *(Preferente)* and second class *(Turista)*; a Super first class *(Club)* is available on AVE trains. Ticket price depends not on distance, but on category of ticket and time of travel – costing more at peak times.

Sleeping berths will require payment of a supplement.

Discount Passes

There are many ways to save money on rail travel in Spain, among them **InterRail**, **France–Spain** and **Spain–Portugal Pass**. The **Eurail Spain Pass** is for non-residents of Europe; it allows unlimited travel on main-line services for 3–10 days within a 2-month period (supplements are needed for AVE, Talgo 200 and the Trenhotel).

Reservations

Seats on all except local trains need to be reserved, and a reservation fee paid to the conductor on board costs more than one bought in advance. Tickets can be delivered to you for a small fee, or bought at RENFE offices, railway stations or most travel agencies. RENFE's computerised system is fast and efficient. Credit cards are accepted for payment but not reservations.

Information

Spanish railways are run by the Red Nacional de los Ferrocarriles Españoles (RENFE). For information and bookings, tel: (+34) 902 240 202; international: (+34) 93 490 1122; www.renfe.es. In the UK, call Spanish Rail, tel: 0207 725 7063; www.spanish-rail.co.uk.

Stations in Madrid/Bilbao

Madrid: has two main railway stations. Trains for the north, northeast and northwest of Spain operate from Chamartín in the north of the city. The station also handles the slower trains for southern and eastern Spain. Fast trains for the east, west and south, including AVE trains, operate from Puerta de Atocha near the city centre. Trains for the southwest and Portugal mostly use Puerta de Atocha, although the direct rail service to Lisbon departs from Chamartín.
Bilbao: Abando station for trains to Irún, Zaragoza and Madrid; Concordia station for trains to Santander and points west. EuskoTren services from San Sebastián use Atxuri station, about 1 km from Concordia.

Train Talk

arrival, arrives *llegada, llega*
change at *cambiar en*
confirmation *confirmación*
connection *correspondencia, enlace*
daily *diario*
delay *retraso*

departure, departs *salida, sale*
excuse me *perdón*
exit *salida*
first class *primera clase*
how much is this? *cuánto es?*
platform *andén*
railway station *estación de tren*
reservation *plaza reservada*
return *ida y vuelta*
single *ida solo*
second class *segunda clase*
sleeping car *coche/carro cama*
straight on *todo recto*
this way to... *por aquí a...*
ticket *billete*
to the left *a la izquierda*
to the right *a la derecha*
train *tren*
when does the train depart for...? *¿a qué hora sale el tren para...?*
where is the...? *¿dónde está el ...?*

Taking Bicycles

Bicycles may be carried on many Spanish trains, but not the fast expresses such as AVE, IC and Talgo.

Where to Stay

For price categories *see page 351*.

Bilbao

Carlton
Plaza Federico Moyúa, 2
Tel: (94) 416 2200
Fax: (94) 416 4628
www.aranzazu-hoteles.com
Orson Welles, Ernest Hemingway, Ava Gardner, and many great bullfighters have stayed here. The Republican Basque Government headquarters were here, and later, Franco's general staff. The place breathes history. Less than 1 km from Abando station €€€€
Ercilla
Ercilla, 37–39
Tel: (94) 470 5700
Fax: (94) 443 9335
www.hotelercilla.es
A highly popular hotel with a fine restaurant, the Bermeo. Less than 1 km from Abando station. €€€
Nervión
Paseo Campo Volantín, 11
Tel: (94) 445 4700
Fax: (94) 445 5608
Located beside the estuary, this monolithic operation offers up-to-date comforts and is 5 minutes from the Guggenheim Museum. Less than 1 km from Abando station. €€
Villa de Bilbao
Gran Vía, 87
Tel: (94) 441 6000
Fax: (94) 441 6529
www.nh-hotels.com
Centrally located with excellent service, this business hotel offers a

fine breakfast and La Pergola, a gourmet dining choice. Less than 500 metres from Abando station. €€€€

Madrid

Chamartín
Agustín de Foxá, s/n
Tel: (91) 334 4900
Fax: (91) 733 0214
www.hotelhusachamartin.com
Comfortable hotel close to Chamartín station in the northern suburbs. €€€€
Eurobuilding
Padre Damián, 23
Tel: (91) 353 7300
Fax: (91) 359 0017
www.hotelnheurobuilding.com
In the heart of the business district of northern Madrid, handy for Chamartín station. Has many facilities including shops, restaurants, swimming pool. €€€€
Prado
Prado, 11
Tel: (91) 369 0234
Fax: (91) 429 2829
www.pradohotel.com
Recently remodelled and centrally located hotel, about 1 km from Atocha station. €€€
Wellington
Velázquez, 8
Tel: (91) 575 4400
www.wellington.com
An old-fashioned, stylish hotel. Close to good shops, and across the Parque del Retiro from Atocha station. €€€€€

San Sebastian

Londres y de Inglaterra
Zubieta, 2
Tel: (94) 344 0770
Fax: (94) 344 0491
www.hlondres.com
Lovely hotel by the beach, across from the old part of town. €€€
María Cristina
Paseo República Argentina, 4
Tel: (94) 343 7600
Fax: (94) 343 7676
Originally opened in 1912, it has been entirely remodelled and is the top hotel in the city. Close to Donostia Station. €€€€
Monte Igueldo
Paseo del Faro 134
Tel: (94) 321 0211
Fax: (94) 321 5028
www.monteigueldo.com
A romantic retreat, with beautiful sea views. €€
Niza
Zubieta, 56
Tel: (94) 342 6663
Fax: (94) 344 1251
www.hotelniza.com
One block in from La Concha, San

Sebastián's wonderful beach, this is a handy spot at a reasonable price. €€

Seville
Alfonso XIII
San Fernando, 2
Tel: (95) 491 7000
Fax: (95) 491 7099
www.hotel-alfonsoxiii.com
Old-style elegance in this classic hotel, built in neo-Mudéjar style in the 1920s. Handy for the station. €€€€€
Simón
García de Vinuesa, 19
Tel: (95) 422 6660
Fax: (95) 456 2241
www.hotelsimonsevilla.com
One of the best-value choices in the centre of the city, offering pleasant but no-frills lodgings in an 18th-century house around an Andalucían patio. Within a kilometre of the railway station. €€

SWITZERLAND

The Place

Area: 41,284 sq. km (15,940 sq. miles)
Capital: Bern
Population: 7.4 million
Languages: Swiss-German, French, Italian, Romansch
Time Zone: GMT +1; EST +6. Clocks advance 1 hour from late March until late October
Currency: Swiss franc (SFr)
Telephone Dialling Codes:
International code: 41. Area codes: Zürich 43; St Moritz 81; Lucerne 41; Geneva 22
Visas and passports: No visa is required for citizens of EU countries, the US, Australia, New Zealand, Canada or Japan for stays of up to 3 months.
Customs: Customs allowances are very similar to those of the EU countries (see page 349).

Public Holidays

January 1 – New Year's Day; January 2 – St Berchtold's Day; March/April – Good Friday and Easter Monday; May 1 – Labour Day; Ascension Day; May 12 – Whit Monday; August 1 – National Day; December 25 – Christmas Day; December 26 – St Stephen's Day.

Tourist Offices

In Zürich
Tödistrasse 7, CH-8027 Zürich

Tel: (01) 288 1111
Fax: (01) 288 1205

In the UK
30 Bedford St, London WC2E 9ED
Tel: (020) 7420 4900/
00800-1002 0030 (Europe toll-free)
Fax: (020) 7420 4922/
800-1002 0031
www.myswitzerland.com

In the USA
608 Fifth Avenue, New York, NY 10020
Tel: (212) 757 5944/877-794 8037
Fax: (212) 262 6116
www.switzerlandtourism.com
(also branches in Chicago and LA)

UK/US Embassies

UK
Thunstrasse 50, 3005 Bern
Tel: (031) 352 1442
Fax: (031) 352 1455
www.britishembassy.gov.uk/switzerland

US
Sulgeneckstrasse 19, 3007 Bern
Tel: (031) 357 7011
www.bern.usembassy.gov

Money

Travellers' cheques and currency (only bank notes) can be changed at banks, bureaux de change, airports, travel agents, main train stations – which stay open late and at weekends and charge no commission – and major hotels which offer the worst rates. Travellers can often settle bills in larger hotels, shops and restaurants with foreign money, at a bad rate of exchange, change is likely to be in Swiss francs. Swiss Bankers Travellers' Cheques can be used as cash, and in Switzerland can be exchanged free of charge. ATMs are easy to find.

Health and Emergencies

The quality of medical treatment in Switzerland is very high, but also very expensive; take out health insurance. Although Switzerland is not an EU member, under the EHIC scheme, nationals of EU countries are entitled to emergency medical treatment. In case of emergency, go to the nearest doctor or to the Emergency Station in the nearest hospital. You will have to pay up front for treatment and claim it back later. Larger towns have an emergency doctor's number printed in the local press, or dial 111, which can also give you contact details of 24-hour pharmacies.

Safety and Crime

Switzerland has little crime. Nevertheless, it is better not to walk alone at night in some parts of bigger cities. Be alert for pickpockets in crowded places.

Telephones

Telecommunications are excellent. Be careful when using hotel phones: the charge is much higher than from elsewhere. Be aware that some public phones no longer accept small change. It is easier to use phonecards.
  The Swiss phonecard, called Taxcard, allows cashless phone calls to be made from public payphones which are equipped with card readers. PTT Taxcards are on sale at post offices, newsagents, railway stations, etc.
  US phonecard access codes are as follows: Sprint 0800 899 777; MCI 0800 890 222; AT&T 0800 890 011.

Business Hours

Expect local deviations from this general pattern:
Shops: daily 8 or 9am–6.30pm, and until 4pm on Saturday. Once a week (Thursday or Friday) shops open until 9pm. Outside city centres businesses close for 1–2 hours for lunch. In tourist areas shops have longer hours and often open on Sunday.
Banks: city banks 8am–5pm Monday–Friday, once a week they extend their hours; elsewhere 8.30am–noon and 1.30–4.30 or 5.30pm Monday–Friday.
You can find bureaux de change at major SBB rail stations and banks.

Train System

Swiss trains are extremely punctual, so arrive on the platform on time. Trains you may encounter in Switzerland are:
ICE: German high-speed trains
CIS: Cisalpino high-speed tilting trains operating routes into Italy
EC: EuroCity international express

Useful Phone Numbers

Ambulance: 144
Fire: 118
Police: 117
Directory Enquiries: 111
Operator: 111
International Operator: 1141
International Directory Enquiries: 1818

IC: InterCity domestic express
EN: EuroNight express night train
CNL: CityNightLine luxury night train
IR: InterRegio fast regional train
RE: RegioExpress semi-fast regional train
R: Stopping trains, at all stations

Ticket Details

Inter-city trains have first- and second-class compartments and leave every hour. The larger lakes are serviced by boats; tickets are usually covered by a rail pass.

Discount Passes

Discount Gruppenfahrkarten are tickets for groups of 10 or more. The **Swiss Pass** is a personal network ticket issued for 4, 8, 15 or 22 days, 1 month, or for 3, 4, 5 or 6 days within a month (referred to as a *Flexipass*), which enables its bearer unlimited mileage on SBB and many private railways, post buses and boats (and in 38 cities and towns on buses and trams too). The **Swiss Card** is good for a round trip ticket from one of the Swiss borders or airports to a holiday resort area located in Switzerland. Valid for a month, it also gives 50 percent reduction on all other journeys you make (some mountain railways might not be included). The **Swiss Transfer Ticket** is a return ticket from the border or airport to your holiday resort, valid for one month. You have to buy it outside Switzerland, ideally at the tourist office in your own country. Some regions offer **Regional Passes**, valid for a varying number of days within a set period during which you can travel for free in a limited region. The **Swiss Half Fare Card** offers 50 percent reduction on normal tariffs for trains, boats and mail buses throughout Switzerland for a 1-month period.
Direct information from the rail company SBB: tel: 0900 300 300; visit: www.sbb.ch

Reservations

Switzerland is unusual in that reservations and fare supplements are not generally required, except on international routes and night trains. Reserve tickets for trains, post buses and boats at railway stations or tourist offices; you can buy tickets on post buses and Intercity trains, but it's more expensive to do it this way.

Information

Swiss Railway (SBB/CFF/FFS): place an order by calling +41 512 25 7800 and collecting the ticket at the SBB

ABOVE: Devil's Bridge, Andermatt, Switzerland.

station in Bern. Office open 5.45am–9.40pm Monday–Sunday; www.sbb.ch/en.
The principal source of general tourist information are Swiss Tourist Information Centres. The website www.switzerland.com has the latest train schedules. You can book online or contact the Swiss Travel Centre (in the UK), tel: 020 7420 4900.
Swiss Railway has its own travel agency with special offers on holidays by train. Packages include train tickets, hotels and special offers for the region you wish to stay in. For details contact SBB Reisebüro Bern, Bahnhofplatz 10a, 3011 Bern,
Tel: (051) 220 2334; www.sbb.ch/en.

Stations in Geneva

In Geneva, Cornavin is the main station; Gare Geneve Eaux-Vives in the east services trains to Annecy and St Gervais. Other main Swiss cities each have one principal station.

Train Talk

See France, Italy, and Germany sections on pages 368, 377 and 371.

Taking Bicycles

It is possible to carry bicycles on most Swiss trains but check the timetable – if nothing is written in the "comments" section you can take a bike on the train. You only have to make a reservation for a bike if taking ICN trains. Generally on international trains (ICE and Cisalpino) you are not allowed to take bikes as trains are narrow, so there is no space. Note: on S-Bahn trains in Zurich Monday–Friday you can only take bicycles 8am–4pm and

7pm–6am; on Intercity tilting trains March–October reservations are compulsory for bicycles. Bicycles can be rented from Rent-A-Bike at many railway stations; their website is at: www.rent-a-bike.ch.
Every station that is a starting-point in the large network of bike-hiking-routes has top condition, modern bicycles for rent. It's best to make bookings in advance. If you are in possession of a Swiss travel pass you are entitled to a discount. There are also bikes for children and child seats to attach to adults' bikes.
In some cities, such as Zürich and Bern, you can get free bike rental when you leave your ID card and a small cash deposit with the hire company.

Where to Stay

For price categories *see page 351.*

Geneva

Balzac
Rue de l'ancien Port 14
Tel: (022) 731 0160
Fax: (022) 738 3847
www.hotel-balzac.ch
Large, comfortable rooms, near the lake and a 5 minute drive from the station. €€€€
Kipling
Rue de la Navigation 27
Tel: (022) 544 4040
Fax: (022) 544 4099
www.manotel.com/kipling
Colonial-style decoration in a quiet street 5 minutes' walk from the station. €€
Strasbourg
Rue Pradier 10
Tel: (022) 906 5800
Fax: (022) 738 4208
www.hotelstrasbourg.ch
Pleasant hotel with a good location on a quiet street close to the station, just a 2 minute walk. €€€

Luzern

Goldener Stern
Burgerstrasse 35
Tel: (041) 227 5060
Fax: (041) 227 5061
www.goldener-stern.ch
Small hotel 500 metres from the
railway station. Family rooms
available. €€

Hotel Monopol
Pilatusstrasse 1
Tel: (041) 226 4343
Fax: (041) 226 4344
This elaborate 19th-century grand
hotel is convenient for the railway
station (less than 1 km) or the lake.
Rooms are individually furnished –
some modern and some period.
Room service, laundry, baby-sitting.
€€€€

Wilden Mann Hotel
Bahnhofstrasse 30
Tel: (041) 210 1666
Fax: (041) 210 1629
www.wilden-mann.ch
Seven antique houses (the oldest
dating from the 16th century) make
up this cosy, higgledy-piggledy hotel
right on the Bahnhofstrasse. The
beauty of the original houses is
combined with modern amenities.
Less than 100 metres from the
station. €€€€

St Moritz

Carlton Hotel
Via J. Badrutt 11
Tel: (081) 836 7000
Fax: (081) 836 7001
www.carlton-stmoritz.ch
Just 1 km from the railway station,
this elaborate ochre-coloured
château has a view of the lake
and the mountains and is one
of the loveliest hotels in St Moritz.
€€€€€

Waldhaus am See
Via Dim Lej 6
Tel: (081) 833 6000
Fax: (081) 833 6060
www.waldhaus-am-see.ch
Overlooking the lake, this large three-
star hotel offers reasonably-priced
rooms, but prices rise in the high
season. Only 200 metres from the
station. €€€€€

Zurich

Du Théâtre
Seilergraben 69
Tel: (044) 267 2670
Fax: (044) 267 2671
www.hotel-du-theatre.ch
Designer B&B hotel in the heart of
Zürich, close to the railway station.
€€€€

Hotel Montana
Konradstrasse 39
Tel: (043) 366 6000
Fax: (043) 366 6010
www.hotelmontana.ch
Close to the station and old town.
Includes a highly-rated French
restaurant. €€€

Leoneck
Leonhardstrasse 1
Tel: (044) 254 2222
Fax: (044) 254 2200
www.leoneck.ch
Near the main shopping area and
just 200 metres from station.
Restaurant offers Swiss food. €€

TURKEY

The Place

Area: 779,452 sq. km (300,948 sq.
miles)
Capital: Ankara
Population: 74.8 million
Language: Turkish
Time Zone: GMT +2; EST +7. Clocks
advance 1 hour from late March until
late October
Currency: Turkish lira
Telephone Dialling Codes:
International code: 90. Area codes:
Istanbul European (Throce) side
0212; Istanbul Asian (Anatdia) side
0216

Visas and Passports

Tourists from Australia, Canada,
Ireland, the UK and the USA require
visas and can obtain a sticker-type
entry visa at the point of entry or from
the Turkish consulate in their own
country before departing. Prices are
dependent on nationality (for British
nationals, the cost is £10, and for US
nationals, the cost is US$45).

Customs

You are allowed to bring into
the country up to 200 cigarettes, 50
cigars, 200g pipe tobacco, 5 litres
wine or spirits. Possession of
narcotics is treated as an extremely
serious offence; penalties are harsh.
  It is strictly forbidden to take
antiques, including rugs and carpets,
out of the country. Should you buy
anything old or old-looking, be sure to
have it validated by the seller, who
should get a clearance certificate
from the Department of Antiquities.
Respectable carpet dealers should
be familiar with the procedure.

Tourist Offices

In Istanbul

Karaköy Harbour
Tel: (0212) 249 5776 or
Hilton Hotel

Tel: (0212) 245 6876 or
Sultanahmet Square
Tel: (0212) 518 1802

In the UK

170–173 Piccadilly (First Floor),
London W1J 9EJ
Tel: (020) 7629 7771
Fax: (020) 7491 0773

In the US

821 United Nations Plaza, New York,
NY 10017
Tel: (212) 687 2194
Fax: (212) 599 7568

Turkish Embassies

In the UK

43 Belgrave Square, London
SW1X 8PA
Tel: (020) 7393 0202
Fax: (020) 7393 0066
www.turkish-embassy-london.com

In the US

Massachusetts Avenue NW, Ste 306,
Washington DC 20008
Tel: (202) 612 6700
Fax: (202) 612 6744
www.turkey.org

UK/US Embassies

UK

Sehitersancadno 461A,
Cankaya Ankara
Tel: (0312) 455 3344
Fax: (0312) 455 3356
Email: britembank@fco.gov.uk

US

110 Ataturk Boulevard, Ankara
Tel: (0312) 455 5555
Fax: (0312) 468 6131

Money

Banks open Monday–Friday
8.30am–noon and 1.30–5pm. Some
stay open at lunchtime and some
are open daily in transit areas.
Almost all banks have 24-hour ATMs.
Travellers' cheques are accepted,
for a charge, at the majority of
banks as well as at private
exchange offices.
  Major credit cards are widely
accepted by shops, restaurants,
hotels and petrol stations.

Useful Phone Numbers

Ambulance: 112
Police: 155
Fire: 110
Emergency: 112
Tourism Police: (0212) 527 4503
International Operator: 118
Operator: 131

ABOVE: the Ortaköy Mosque, Turkey.

Public Holidays

January 1 – New Year's Day; 23 April – National Sovereignty and Children's Day; 19 May – Atatürk's Commemoration and Youth and Sports Festival; 30 August – Victory Day; 29 October – Republic Day.

Health and Emergencies

If you fall ill the standard of health care is not high, so it is essential to have medical insurance. Most drugs are available without prescription from pharmacies *(eczane)*. Traveller's diarrhoea is the main hazard. Drink only bottled water, wash and/or peel all fruit and vegetables, and ensure cooked food is piping hot. It's safest to eat freshly prepared local produce.

Safety and Crime

Turkey has an enviably low crime record. Tourists are regarded as guests, so are very well treated. Tourist areas are regularly patrolled by special Turizm or Foreigners' Police, who should do their best to help you and should speak some English.

Telephones

Phone calls can be made from the post office (PTT) or telephone booths using tokens *(jeton)*. You can also use a phonecard for lengthy calls. To call other countries, first dial the international access code 00, then the country code. If using a US credit phonecard dial the company's access number: Sprint 0811 288 0013; MCI 00 800 11177; AT&T 0811 288 0001. You can also send fax messages from the post office.

Business Hours

Shops generally open Monday– Saturday 9.30am–7pm; some only shut for the night at midnight. Shops are usually closed on Sunday, but increasing numbers of large shops stay open all week.

Train System

This book only deals with Turkish railways in Europe. For journeys beyond Istanbul consult the *Thomas Cook Overseas Timetable*. Trains to Istanbul from Hungary, Romania and Bulgaria are assigned a different train number in Turkey.

Ticket Details

Tickets are sold at TCDD stations and appointed agents. Purchase tickets and reserve seats or sleepers in advance, preferably from the station at which your journey will begin.

Reservations

Istanbul: Sirkeci Station (European side), tel: operator (0212) 520 6575; information (0212) 527 0050. Haydarpasa Station (Asian side), tel: operator (0216) 336 8020; information (0216) 336 0475/2063; reservations (0216) 337 8724/336 4470.

Information

Türkiye Cumhuryeti Devlet Demiryollari (TCDD) is the national operator, tel: (0312) 309 0515. Their website is www.tcdd.gov.tr

Stations in Istanbul

Trains from Europe arrive at Sirkeci station in Eminönü, in the heart of old Constantinople. Those from the east come in to the Haydarpaşa Station on the Asian side of Istanbul, from where you can take a ferry or taxi across the Bosphorus to the centre.

Train Talk

arrivals *varis*
departures *birakmak*
first class *birinci sinif*
platform *peron*
railway station *gar/istasyon*
reservation *salkama*
return *gidis-dönüs*
second class *ikiuci sinif*
single *biletinde*
ticket *bilet*
train *tren*
what time does it leave? *kaçta kalkiyor?*

Where to Stay

For price categories *see page 351.*

Istanbul
Hotel Romance
Ebusuud Caddesi, 32
34410 Sultanahmet
Tel: (0212) 512 8676
Fax: (0212) 512 8723
www.romancehotel.com
Very close to Istanbul's main attractions, and less than 500 metres from Sirkeci station. €€
Hotel Saba
Sehit Mehmet Pasa Yokusu, 8
34400 Sultanahmet
Tel: (0212) 458 0262
Fax: (0212) 638 2002
www.saba.com
Comfortable hotel in the historic centre of Istanbul and less than 1 km from Sirkeci station. €€

UNITED KINGDOM

The Place

Area: 242,514 sq. km (93,638 sq. miles)
Capital: London
Population: 60.7 million
Language: English
Time Zone: GMT; EST +5. Clocks advance 1 hour from late March until late October
Currency: Pound sterling
Telephone Dialling Codes:
International code: 44. Area codes: London 020; Edinburgh 0131; York 01904; Glasgow 0141.
Visas and passports: *see page 349*
Customs: *see page 349*

Public Holidays

January 1 – New Year's Day; March/ April – Good Friday, Easter Monday; first Monday in May; last Monday in May; last Monday in August; December 25/26 – Christmas.

Money

Banks open 9.30am–4.30pm Monday–Friday, and often Saturday morning in shopping areas. Most have ATMs where international credit or cashpoint cards can be used. There is no commission on sterling travellers' cheques, but a charge for changing cash into British currency.

Travel agents, such as Thomas Cook, operate bureaux de change at comparable rates. Privately run bureaux de change (many open 24 hours) often have low exchange rates but high commissions. Post offices

UK Tourist Offices

Edinburgh
4 Rothsay Terrace
Edinburgh EH3 7RY
Tel: (0131) 473 3666
www.visitscotland.com

Inverness
Castle Wynd
Inverness 1V2 3BJ
Tel: (01463) 234 353
www.visithighlands.com

London
Britain and London Visitor Centre
1 Regent Street, Piccadilly Circus,
London SW1Y 4XT.
Tel: (020) 8846 9000
Fax: (020) 8563 0302
www.visitlondon.com

York
20 George Hudson Street
York YO1 6WR
Tel: (01904) 550 099
www.visityork.org

and Marks & Spencers bureaux de change do not charge commission when purchasing foreign currency. International credit cards are accepted in most shops, hotels and restaurants.

Health and Emergencies

Most visitors have to pay for medical and dental treatment and should have health insurance. In the case of minor accidents, your hotel will know the location of the nearest hospital with a casualty department.

Boots, the largest chain of pharmacies, sells over-the-counter and prescription medicines.

Safety and Crime

UK cities are no more dangerous than any others; unfortunately, many of the rougher spots are around train stations. If arriving on a late train when there is no public transport available, use only an official black cab from a marked taxi rank. Keep a vigilant eye on your bags in the station and beware of pickpockets.

Telephones

There are three different types of public phone boxes; those that take coins only, those that take phonecards or major credit cards, and those that take both coins and cards. You can telephone abroad from all phone boxes. Phonecards can be purchased from post offices and shops and are available in £1, £3, £5, £10 and £20 varieties. Coins are usually inserted before dialling,

but not all coins are accepted. It is possible for public call boxes to receive calls. US credit phonecard access codes from the UK are as follows: Sprint 0800-89 0877; AT&T 0800 89 0011; MCI/Worldphone 0800-89 0222.

Business Hours

Shops: mostly Monday–Saturday 9am–5.30pm, but larger shops stay open later; also Sunday 10am–4pm.
Pubs: mostly Monday–Saturday 11am–11pm (later in Scotland); noon–10.30pm on Sunday.
Post offices: Monday–Friday 9am–5.30pm; Saturday 9am–12.30pm.

Train System

The railway system in the UK has several idiosyncracies to distinguish it from the rest of Europe. A major difference is that the British system was privatised in the 1990s and is run by many different operating companies. This has proved a mixed blessing and some people blame it for the poor state of the rail system in Britain. Another peculiarity is the extent to which timetables vary between weekdays and weekends. Unlike the rest of Europe, Britain's trains are not labelled on timetables by number – but rather by their final destination.

BELOW: St Pancras, London.

Ticket Details

From 2008 a multiplicity of ticket types and names has been simplified into three basic tickets, in ascending

order of cost: **Advance** are single fares for a specific train booked in advance; **Off-Peak** and **Super Off-Peak** fares can be bought at any time but cannot be used during the busiest times of the day; and **Anytime** tickets which can be used on any train. Tickets can generally be bought 3 months in advance, and the further ahead you book an Advance ticket the cheaper it will be. It is best to buy tickets from a station ticket office or the train operator itself, either by telephone or online; third-party websites (www.thetrainline.com and www.raileasy.co.uk) add various charges and do not always make clear the best choice of ticket for a journey. The best point of entry is the National Rail Enquiries website www.nationalrail.co.uk which not only passes you to the train operator for booking but also has useful links for complementary services such as PlusBus and Traintaxi.

Most Eurostar tickets can be bought 120 days before the date of travel.

Discount Passes

There is a wide variety of BritRail passes for use in the UK and Ireland, covering different areas and days of travel. They are only for the use of visitors to Britain (where the railways are not part of Eurail) and must be bought before arrival in the UK. From the US, tel (toll free): 1-866-BRITRAIL; in Canada 514-733-5247, ext 319.

Reservations

Reservations are not necessary on most trains, but are advisable for long distance services, especially Friday to Sunday. They are always required on sleeper trains, obviously. Reservations can be made online, in person or over the phone with a credit card.

Information

National Rail Enquiries are available on 08457 484950; the online version, where you can also buy tickets, is at www.thetrainline.com The www.rail.co.uk site is a useful alternative.

Eurostar information is available on 08705 186186 (0044 1233 617 575 from outside the UK) and online at www.eurostar.com.

Useful Phone Numbers

Emergencies: 999
Operator: 100
Directory Enquiries (UK): 118 500/118 118/118 888

For North American and other travellers, the following sites are useful: www.britainontrack.com; www.britrail.com.

Stations

London: There are 10 major termini in London: London Bridge for Kent; Charing Cross for East Sussex and Kent; Waterloo for Surrey, Hampshire and Dorset; Victoria for Gatwick and West Sussex; Paddington for Oxford, Bristol, the West Country and south Wales; Marylebone for Stratford and Birmingham; Euston for the West Midlands, Manchester, Liverpool and Glasgow; St Pancras for the East Midlands, Sheffield and Eurostar services; King's Cross for Cambridge, Peterborough, Leeds, York, Newcastle and Edinburgh; Liverpool Street for East Anglia and Cambridge.

Glasgow: Queen Street (Edinburgh and northern Scotland) and Glasgow Central (London, Glasgow and southern services).

Taking Bicycles

Most lines allow bicycles, but many limit it to non-peak times. Check your timetable for more detailed information. Bicycles are often prohibited on trains running through city centres.

Where to Stay

For price categories *see page 351*.

Edinburgh

Holyrood Aparthotel
1 Nether Bakehouse, EH8 8PE
Tel: (0131) 524 3200
Fax: (0131) 524 3210
www.holyroodaparthotel.com
A deluxe hotel located in the heart of Edinburgh. The hotel is near the Palace of Holyrood and the Scottish Parliament Building. Over a mile from Waverley Station. €€€€

Howard Hotel
34 Great King Street, EH3 6QH
Tel: (0131) 557 3500
Fax: (0131) 557 6515
www.thehoward.com
Quiet, luxuriously decorated 16-room hotel in the new part of town. First-class restaurant. Just over half a mile from Waverley Station. €€€€€

Salisbury Hotel
45 Salisbury Road, EH16 5AA
Tel: (0131) 667 1264
Fax: (0131) 667 1264
www.the-salisbury.co.uk
Upmarket B&B in listed Georgian house. About a mile from Waverley Station. €€€

ABOVE: St James' Park, London.

Glasgow

Euro Hostel
318 Clyde Street, G1 4NR
Tel: (0141) 222 2828
Fax: (0141) 222 2829
www.euro-hostels.com
Reasonably priced, en-suite hostel, with a range of rooms suitable for families as well as backpackers. Close to Central Station. €

Malmaison
278 West George Street, G2 4LL
Tel: (0141) 572 1001
Fax: (0141) 572 1002
www.malmaison.com
Smart hotel, with decor inspired by the Paris Malmaison and an excellent brasserie. Less than half a mile from Central Station. €€€€

Inverness

St Ann's Guest House
37 Harrowden Road, IV3 5QN
Tel/Fax: (01463) 236157
www.scotland-inverness.co.uk/stanns
Well maintained family-run guesthouse, 10 minutes' walk from the city centre, rail and bus stations. €€

Westbourne Guest House
50 Huntly Street, IV3 5HS
Tel/fax: (01463) 222700
www.westbourne.org.uk
Situated on the west bank of the River Ness, 5 minutes' walk from the centre and rail and bus stations. €€€

London

Crescent Hotel
49–50 Cartwright Gardens, Bloomsbury, WC1H 9EL
Tel: (020) 7387 1515
Fax: (020) 7383 2054
www.crescenthoteloflondon.com
Attractive family-run hotel with 27 rooms, handily situated for Euston and King's Cross/St Pancras stations. €€€

Elizabeth Hotel
37 Eccleston Square, Victoria, SW1V 1PB
Tel: (020) 7828 6812
Fax: (020) 7828 6814
www.elizabethhotel.com
Friendly hotel in elegant period square, two minutes' walk from Victoria station. There are 40 rooms, 22 with bath. €€€€

The Mad Hatter Hotel
3–7 Stamford Street, SE1 9NY
Tel: (020) 7401 9222
Fax: (020) 7401 7111
www.fullershotels.com
Good value small hotel south of the river, conveniently situated for Waterloo Station. €€€

Strand Palace
372 The Strand, WC2R 0JJ
Tel: 020 7379 4737
www.strandpalacehotel.co.uk
In the heart of Theatreland, with easy access to Waterloo, Euston, King's Cross/St Pancras International and Victoria stations. €€€€€

The Waldorf Hilton
Aldwych, WC2B 4DD
Tel: (020) 7836 2400
Fax: (020) 7759 2408
www.hilton.co.uk/waldorf
Recently restored and steeped in history, the Waldorf is situated in the heart of Theatreland in sophisticated surroundings. Convenient for all the main line stations. €€€€€

York

Dean Court
Duncombe Place, YO1 7EF
Tel: (01904) 625 082
Fax: (01904) 620 305
www.deancourt-york.co.uk
Comfortable 40-room traditional hotel close to the Minster and in its own traffic-free zone. Less than half a mile from the station. €€€

FURTHER READING

RAILWAY BOOKS

Allen, Peter, and Whitehouse, P.B. *Narrow Gauge Railways of Europe* (Ian Allan, 1959)

Balkwill, Richard and Marshall, John. *The Guinness Book of Railway Facts and Feats* (Guinness, 1993)

Behrend, George. *Railway Holiday in Switzerland* (David & Charles, 1965)

Biddle, Gordon, and Nock, O.S. *The Railway Heritage of Britain* (Michael Joseph, 1983)

Bryson, Bill. *Neither Here Nor There: Travels in Europe* (Black Swan, 1998)

Burton, Anthony. *The Railway Empire* (John Murray, 1994)

Carr, S. *The Poetry of Railways* (Batsford, 1978)

Eisenbahnatlas Deutschland (Schweers & Wall, 2007)

Eisenbahnatlas Österreich (Schweers & Wall, 2004)

Eisenbahnatlas Schweiz (Schweers & Wall, 2005)

Faith, Nicholas. *Locomotion* (BBC, 1993)

Faith, Nicholas. *The World the Railways Made* (Pimlico, 1994)

Fletcher, Malcolm, and Taylor, John. *Railways: The Pioneer Years* (Studio Editions, 1990)

Huntley, John. *Railways on the Screen* (Ian Allen, 1993)

Kalla Bishop, P.M. *Mediterranean Island Railways* (David & Charles, 1970)

Kennedy, Ludovic (ed.) *A Book of Railway Journeys* (Collins, 1980)

Kichenside, G.M. *150 Years of Railway Carriages* (David & Charles, 1981)

Lambert, Anthony J. *Heritage Railways of the British Isles* (Grange Books, 1999)

Lambert, Anthony J. *Living Steam* (New Holland, 2005)

Lambert, Anthony J. *Settle to Carlisle* (Paragon, 1995)

Lambert, Anthony J. *Switzerland: Rail, Road, Lake* (Bradt, 2008)

Morgan, Bryan. *The End of the Line* (Cleaver-Hulme, 1955)

Nock, O.S. *Railway Holiday in Austria*

(David & Charles, 1965)

Page, Martin. *The Lost Pleasures of the Great Trains* (Weidenfeld & Nicholson, 1975)

Richards, Jeffrey, and MacKenzie, John M. *The Railway Station: A Social History* (Oxford University Press, 1986)

Rolt, L.T.C. *George and Robert Stephenson* (Longman, 1967)

Simmons, Jack. *Railways: An Anthology* (Collins 1991)

Simmons, Jack and Biddle, Gordon. *The Oxford Companion to British Railway History* (Oxford University Press, 1997)

Simmons, Jack. *The Victorian Railway* (Thames & Hudson, 1995)

Smith, Martin. *British Railway Bridges & Viaducts* (Ian Allan, 1994)

Talbot, Frederick A. *The Railway Conquest of the World* (Heinemann, 1911)

Send Us Your Thoughts

We do our best to ensure the information in our books is as accurate and up-to-date as possible. The books are updated on a regular basis using local contacts, who painstakingly add, amend and correct as required. However, some details (such as telephone numbers and opening times) are liable to change, and we are ultimately reliant on our readers to put us in the picture.

We welcome your feedback, especially your experience of using the book "on the road". Maybe we recommended a hotel that you liked (or another that you didn't), or you came across a great bar or new attraction we missed.

We will acknowledge all contributions, and we'll offer an Insight Guide to the best letters received.

Please write to us at:
**Insight Guides
PO Box 7910
London SE1 1WE**
Or email us at:
insight@apaguide.co.uk

OTHER INSIGHT GUIDES

Other **Insight Guides** to Europe include: *Continental Europe, Austria, Belgium, France, Germany, Greece, Italy, Portugal, Scandinavia, Spain, Switzerland, Turkey, Great Britan* and *Ireland.*

Insight Guides to Central and Eastern Europe include: *Bulgaria, Croatia, Czech and Slovak Republics, Hungary, Russia, Poland, Romania* and *Russia.*

Salzburg is one of the titles in the Insight's **Smart Guide** series. These books pack information into an easily portable and convenient format. Arranged in handy A–Z sections, the comprehensive listings allow the visitor to make their own decisions about where to go and what to see.

ART AND PHOTO CREDITS

INDEX

Numbers in italics refer to photographs

Letters in brackets denote countries:
A: Austria
B: Belgium
BG: Bulgaria
BY: Belarus
CH: Switzerland
CZ: Czech Republic
D: Germany
DK: Denmark
E: Spain
F: France
FIN: Finland
GB: United Kingdom
GR: Greece
H: Hungary
HR: Croatia
I: Italy
IRL: Ireland
N: Norway
NL: Netherlands
P: Portugal
PL: Poland
RO: Romania
RUS: Russia
S: Sweden
SK: Slovakia
SLO: Slovenia
TR: Turkey

A

Aachen (D) 87
Abbaye de Hautecombe (F) 141
Achenseebahn (A) *245*
Achnasheen (GB) 103
Adams, Charles Francis 21
Agay (F) 144
Agrigento (I/Sicily) 228
Aguessac (F) 136
Aigle (CH) 190, 204
Airolo (CH) 193
Ais Gill (GB) 112
Aix-en-Provence (F) 131, 148
Aix-les-Bains (F) 141
Ajaccio (F/Corsica) 154, 157
Ål (N) 293
Alassio (I) 223
Albenga (I) 223
Albula Pass (CH) 199
Albula Tunnel (CH) 199
Alès (F) 135
Aletsch Glacier (CH) 196
Alexisbad (D) 272
Algeciras (E) 171
Alicante (E) 177
Allport, James 28
Almería (E) 163
Alp Grüm (CH) 205
Alpnachstad (CH) 207
AlpTransit project (CH) 202
Altdorf (CH) 193
Altea (E) 177
Almoraima (E) 171
Alnmouth (GB) 107

Älvros (S) 303
Amantea (I) 226
Amarante (P) 181
Ammanford (GB) 114
Andermatt (CH) 193, 197
Andernach (D) 263
Annot (F) *147*, 148
Anthéor (F) 144
Antibes (F) 144
Anulu (I/Sardinia) 232
Appenzell (CH) 204
Appleby (GB) 112
Arad (H) 328
Aranguen (E) 168
Arbatax (I/Sardinia) 233
Arco de Baúlhe (P) 182
Arctic Circle 289, 293, 298, 301
Ardez (CH) 201
Argos (GR) 341
Arisaig (GB) 102
Arlbergbahn (A) 241–2
Arlberg Tunnel (A) 40, 84, 241, 242
Armathwaite (GB) 112
Arona (I) 191
Arosa (CH) 204
Artengill Beck (GB) 111
Arth Goldau (CH) 192
Arvant (F) 139
Arvidsjaur (S) 301–3
Arzana (I/Sardinia) 233
Asarna (S) 303
Aschaffenburg (D) 283
Aßmannshausen (D) 266
Aspres-sur-Buëch (F) 140
Athens (GR) 337, 338
Attnang-Puchheim (A) 248
Aubagne (F) 142
Aumont-Aubrac (F) 137
Aurillac (F) 139
Aurlandsfjord (N) 292
Aviemore (GB) 108
Avignon (F) 131
Avramovo (BG) 337
Azpeitia (E) 167

B

Bacharach (D) *264*
Bad Ems (D) 268–9
Bad Gastein (A) 254
Bad Godesberg (D) 263
Bad Hofgastein (A) 254
Bad Hönningen (D) 265
Bad Kohlgrub (D) 278
Bad Schandau (D) *318*
Baedeker, Karl 268
Bagheria (I/Sicily) 229
Balduinstein (D) 269
Banassac-La Canourgue (F) 136
Bandol (F) 142
Banská Bystrica (SK) 321–2
Bansko (BG) 335
Barbagia (I/Sardinia) 231
Barcelona (E) 163

Barlow, W.H. 44
Barmouth Bridge (GB) 36
Barrême (F) 147
Bartlett, Thomas 39
Basel (CH) 92, 191
Bassin de Thau (F) 135
Bastia (F/Corsica) 154, 155
Battersby (GB) 115
beast of Gévaudan (F) 135, 136
Bédarieux (F) 136
Beeching, Dr 32
Belém (P) 165
Belgodere (F/Corsica) 157
Bellinzona (CH) 193
Benaoján (E) 172
Bengel (D) 267
Benidorm (E) 177
Benneckenstein (D) 271
Bergen (N) *291*, 292
Berlin (D) 87, 261, 317, 318
Bermeo (E) 167
Beroun (CZ) 319
Berwick-upon-Tweed (GB) 107
Betten (CH) 196
Bever (CH) 199, 200
Bex (CH) 190, 204
Bezau (A) 241
Béziers (F) 135, 136
Biasca (CH) 193
bicycles 193, 242, 249, 293, 351, 354, 356, 368, 371, 375, 377, 379
Bilbao (E) 163, *164*, 165, 166, 167, 168
Bingen (D) 264
Bischofshofen (A) 255
Blair Atholl (GB) 108
Blankenburg (CH) 211
Blea Moor Tunnel (GB) 110, 111
Bludenz (A) 84, 241
Böckstein (A) 254
Bocognano (F/Corsica) 157
Bodø (N) 298
Bolna (N) 298
Bolquère-Eyne (F) 153
Bolzano/Bozen (I) 219
Bonn (D) *263*, 265
Bonn-Oberkassel (D) 265
Booch, Thomas 37
booking agents 348
Boppard (D) 263
Borrodale Viaduct (GB) 102
Bourg-Madame (F) *152*, 153
Bourg-St-Maurice (F) 41
Brasov (RO) 330
Brassey, Thomas 23, 24, 36, 39
Bratislava (SK) 319, 321
Břeclav (CZ) 319
Bregenz (A) 241, 279
Brennero (I) 221
Brenner Pass (A/I) 85, 221, 239
Bressanone/Brixen (I) 221
Brest (BY) 89
Bretenoux-Biars (F) 139
Brezno (SK) 322

Brezova (CZ) 318
Brie (F) 131
Brienz (CH) 207
Brig (CH) 191, 195
Bright, John, MP 21
Brioude (F) 133
Brive-la-Gaillarde (F) 138
Brno (CZ) 319
Brohl (D) 263
Broome (GB) 113
Bruck (A) 247
Bruck an der Mur (A) 250
Brunel, Isambard Kingdom 35, 44, 48
Brünig-Hasliberg (CH) 207
Brusio (CH) 205
Brussels (B) 41, 87, *127*
Bucharest (RO) 86, 331, 332
Buchloe (D) 279
Buchs (CH) 84
Bucknell (GB) 113
Budapest (H) 86, 319, *320*, 328, 329
Builth Wells (GB) 113
Bullay (D) 267
Bunyola (E/Mallorca) 182
Burgos (E) 163
Burgundy (F) 131
Byron, Lord 190

C

Cagliari (I/Sardinia) *230*
Cagnes-sur-Mer (F) 144
Calabria (I) 226
calanques (F) 142
Calatrava, Santiago 48, 131
Caledonian Canal (GB) 103
Calenzana-Lumio (F/Corsica) 157
Calp (E) 178
Calvi (F/Corsica) 157
Campiglia Marittima (I) 223
Campocologno (CH) 205
Cannes (F) *143*, 144
Cantábrica (E) 168
Cape Palinuro (I) 225
Capologo-Riva San Vitale (CH) 193
Capo Orlando (I/Sicily) 227
Caronte Bridge (F) 38
Carlisle (GB) 99, 112
Carrara (I) 223
Carroll, Lewis 116
Casamozza (F/Corsica) 154, 155
Cascais (P) 165
Cassis (F) 142
Castelvetrano (I/Sicily) 228
castles of the Rhine (D) 263-4
Causey Arch (GB) 22
Causse de Séverac (F) 136
Causse de Larzac (F) 136
Caux (CH) 210
Cavaillon (F) 131
Cecina (I) 225
Cefalù (I/Sicily) 229
Celerina (CH) 199, 203
Červená Skala (SK) 323
Česky Kras (CZ) 319
Cévennes (F) *132*, 137
Chabówka (PL) 327
Chamalières (F) 138

Chambéry (F) 141
Chamborigaud Viaduct (F) 134
Chamby (CH) 210
Chamonix (F) 149, *150*, 190, 204
Channel Tunnel (GB/F) 24, *34*, 41, 44, 48, 82
Chanteuges (F) 133
Chapeauroux (F) 133
Chaplin, Charlie 189, *190*
Château d'Oex (CH) 211
Chemnitz (D) 284-86
Chiasso (CH) 191, 193
Children's Railway (H) *320*
Chirac, Jacques 138
Christie, Agatha 15
Chur (CH) 198, 204
Church Stretton (GB) 113
Churchward, G.J. 58
Cierny Balog (SK) *310*, *321*, *322*
Cilento (I) 225
Cilmery (GB) 113
Cinque Terre (I) 223
Cinuos-chel-Brail (CH) 200
Clelles-Mens (F) 140
Clermont Ferrand (F) 132, 138
Cluny (F) 131
Cochem (D) 267
Col-de-Bretaye *204*
Col de la Croix Haute (F) 140
Collognes-la-Rouge (F) 139
Cologne (D) 87, *260*, 263, 264
Commondale (GB) 115
Conan Doyle, Sir Arthur 207
Conca d'Oro (I/Sicily) 229
Concoules (F) 134
Conwy bridge (GB) 97
Cook, Thomas 25, 26, 79
Córdoba (E) 175
Corinth (GR) 338
Corinth Canal (GR) 338
Corniche de l'Esterel (F) 144
Corrour (GB) 99
Corsica 154-7
Corte (F/Corsica) 40, 154, 156, 157
Costa Viola (I) 226
Craven Arms (GB) 113
Crianlarich (GB) 98
Cully (CH) 189
Culoz (F) 141

D

Dale (N) 292
Danby (GB) 115
Daumier, Honoré 27
de Chirico, Giorgio 46
Děčín (CZ) 318
Dedinky (SK) 323
Défilé de Chaudan (F) 146
Delvaux, Paul 46
Dénia (E) 182
Dent (GB) *111*
Derveni (GR) 339
Dettingen (D) 283
Deva (E) 167
Diakofto (GR) 339
Diez (D) 269
Digne-les-Bains (F) 140, 143, 147-9

Dingwall (GB) 103, 108
disabled travellers 350
Disentis (CH) 198
Disneyland Paris by Eurostar 41
Dix, Otto 281
Dobova (HR) 316
Dobrinishte (BG) 335
Dolau (GB) 113
Dombås (N) 296
Domodossola (I) 91, 191, 204
Doncaster (GB) 106
Dornbirn (A) 241
Dovre (N) 296
Dovre Railway (N) 294
Drachenfels railway (D) 265
Drahtzug (D) 272
Drammen (N) 293
Drei Annen Hohne (D) *271*
Dresden (D) 282, 317
Dromod (IRE) 117
Druimuachdar (GB) 107
Dublin (IRE) 117, *118*, 119
Dunbar (GB) 107
Dunkeld & Birnham (GB) 108
Dunrobin (GB) 108
Durham (GB) 107

E

Eben (A) 245
Ediger-Eller (D) 267
Edinburgh (GB) 100, 105
Edirne (TR) 333
Egton (GB) 115
Ehrenbreitstein (D) 265
Eibsee (D) 277
Eidsvoll (N) 294
Eiffel, Gustave 24, 38, 137, 156, 163, 184
Eigergletscher (CH) 209
Eiger Wall (CH) 209
Eigg (GB) 102
Eisfelder Talmühle (D) 270, *271*
Eismeer (CH) 209
Elba (I) 223
El Campello (E) 177
El Cremallera (E) 180
Elend (D) 271
Eleusis (GR) 338
Elizabeth II 24
Eltville (D) 266
Engelberg (CH) 204
engineering 35-41
Entrevaux (F) *146*
environmental issues 16, 32, 205, 248, 322
Epidauros (GR) 341
Ercolina/Herculaneum (I) 224
Erpel (D) 265
Erstfeld (CH) 193
Eschenlohe (D) 275
Eschhofen (D) 269
Esterzili (I/Sardinia) 231
Estoril (P) 165
Esztergom (H) *318*, 319
European Federation of Museum & Tourist Railways (FEDECRAIL) 66
European Union
customs regulations 349

reciprocal health coverage 351
Eurostar and Eurotunnel 40, 41, 217; *see also* **Channel Tunnel**
Évora (P) 165

F

Fades Viaduct (F) 38, 138
Faido (CH) 193
Fauske (N) 298
Favre, Louis 39
Feldkirch (A) 241
Ferrol (E) 166, 170
Fiesch (CH) 196
Filisur (CH) 199
Finse (N) 292–4
Firth of Forth (GB) 105
Flå (N) 293
Flåm (N) 292
Flims Gorge (CH) 198
Flüelen (CH) 192
Follonica (I) 223
food on trains 27, 81, 83, 100, 129, 171, *197*, 258–9, 304–5, 321
Font-Romeu-Odeillo-Via (F) 153
Four Solaire d'Odeillo 153
Forsinard (GB) 108
Forth Bridge (GB) *33*, 37, 100, 107
Fort William (GB) 99, 101
Francardo (F/Corsica) 155
Frankfurt (Oder) (D) 87
Frankfurt-am-Main (D) 264, 266
Freiberg (D) 282
Freital-Hainsberg (D) 282
French Riviera (F) 143–5
Freidrichshafen (D) 285
Friedrichssegen (D) 268
Frith, William Powell
The Railway Station 30
Ftan (CH) 201
Fulpmes (A) 244
Furka Base Tunnel (CH) 194, 196–7
Fürth (D) 261, 283

G

Gairu (I/Sardinia) 232
Gais (CH) 204
Gällivare (S) 299, 300–1, *303*
Garabit Viaduct (F) 38, *137*
Garmisch-Partenkirchen (D) 243, 274–5, 279
Zugspitzbahn 276–7
Garnell, Graham 186
Garsdale (GB) 111–2
Garth (GB) 113
Gasawa (PL) 88
Gata de Gorgos (E) 182
Gautier, Théophile 46
Geilo (N) 293
Gemene (H) 320
Geneva (CH) 141, 187, 189, 190
Genoa (I) 223
Genolhac (F) 134
Georgemas (GB) 108
Gernika (E) 167
Gernrode (D) 270, 271, 272

Giessen (D) 269
Giscard d'Estaing, Valéry 138
Gioiosa Marea (I/Sicily) 227
Giornico (CH) 193
Gisclard Suspension Bridge (F) 153
Giswil (CH) 207
Giurgiu (RO) 331
Glacier Express (CH) *8–9, 194*, 195–196, 259
Glaisdale (GB) 115
Glasgow (GB) 98
Gleneagles (GB) 49, 107
Glenfinnan (GB) 101, *102*
Glion (CH) 210
Gloggnitz (A) 250
Glovelier (CH) 204
Gmunden (A) 248
Goethe 269, 270
Gonfaron (F) 143
Gorges de la Carança (F) 153
Gorges du Cians (F) 146
Göschenen (CH) 39, 193
Gossau (CH) 204
Gotthard Tunnel (CH) 39, 193
Grafrath (D) 279
Grainau (D) 277
Granada (E) 163, 170
Grantham (GB) 106
Great Ayton (GB) 115
Grenoble (F) 140
Grimshaw, Nicholas 48
Grong (N) 297
Grosmont (GB) 113
Gstaad (CH) 211
Guarda (CH) 201
Guyer-Zeller, Adolf 208

H

Hackås (S) 303
Hallein (A) 255
Hall in Tirol (A) 245
Hamar (N) 295
Hardangervidda (N) 293, *293*
Hardwick, Philip 44
Harzer Schmalspurbahnen (D) 270–2
Hatfield House (GB) 105
Hattenheim (D) 266
Haugastøl (N) 293
Heilingenstadt (A) 239
Heine, Heinrich 270
Hell (N) 297
Hellifield (GB) 109–10
Helmsdale (GB) *108*
Helsinki (FIN) 304, 305
Hendaye (F) 165
Herculaneum (I) 224
Hergatz (D) 281
Hergiswil (CH) 207
Herisau (CH) 204
heritage railways 16, 57–66, 95, 97, 102, 127
Achensee (A) 61, *245*
Baie de Somme (F) 64
Biskupin (PL) 63, 88
Blonay–Chamby (CH) 66
Bluebell (GB) 60, 62, 97
Bochum-Dahlhousen (D) 65

Bruchlausen-Vilsen–Asendorf (D) 65
Cavan and Leitrim (IRE) 117
Dampfbahn Furka Bergstrecke (CH) 194
Ffestiniog (GB) 61–2, 97
Furka Pass (CH) 66
Great Central (GB) 63
Hronec Forest (SK) *63*, 326
Kassel-Wilhelmshöhe–Naumburg (D) 65
Keighley & Worth Valley (GB) *62*, 109
La Mure (F) 64, 141
Middleton (GB) 60
Mokra Gora–Sargan (YU) 63
Murtalbahn (A) 251
North York Moors (GB) 62–3, 115
Paignton & Dartmouth (GB) 63
Preßnitztalbahn (D) 65
Prien–Stock (D) 65
Puchberg–Hochschneeberg (A) 61
St Wolfgang–Schafberg (A) 61
Sargan Mountain (YU) 63
Snowdon Mountain (GB) 62, 94
South Devon (GB) 63
Strathspey (GB) 108
Swanage (GB) 63
Szalajka Forest (H) 63
Talyllyn (GB) 57, 60, 62, *67*
Train à Vapeur des Cévennes (F) 64, *159*
Train des Pignes 148
Vale of Rheidol (GB) 97
Vivarais (F) 64
Volos Tramway (GR) 63
Welsh Highland (GB) 62
West Somerset (GB) 63, 97
Wolsztyn (PL) 63, 88, *326*
Hersbruck (D) 283
high-speed services 16, 32, 41, 51–5, 80–86, 127, 129, 140, *145*, 163, *179*, 217, *219*, 258, 259, 261, 289, 294
magnetic levitation technology 55
tilting trains 53–4, 189, 217, 289
Hilbersdorf (D) 282
Hjerkinn (N) 296
Hochschneeberg (A) 250
Hof (D) 283
Hohenstadt (D) 283
Hønefoss (N) 293
Hoptonheath (GB) 113
Horseshoe Viaduct (GB) 98–9
Horton-in-Ribblesdale (GB) 110
Hospental (CH) 197
Hotel Schreiber (CH) *49*
Hoting (S) 305
Hrabal, Bohumil 46

I

Ifield (D) 271
Iggejaur (S) *302*
Ilanz (CH) 198
Ile-Rousse (F/Corsica) 157
Immenstadt (D) 280
Inlandsbanan (S) 299–305

Innsbruck (A) 84–5, *221, 243–4,*
  244, 245, 273, 279
Interlaken (CH) 211
Inverness (GB) 103, 107
Iselle di Trasquera (I) 191
Isole Eolie (I/Sicily) 227
Issoire (F) 132–3
Istanbul (TR) 86, 234, *334,* 335

J

Jenbach (A) 245, *246*
Jimena (E) 175
Jokkmokk (S) *301*
Jörn (S) 302
Juan-les-Pins (F) 142
Jungfraubahn (CH) *74,* 208
Jungfraujoch (CH) 206, 208–9

K

Kalamata (GR) 300–1
Kalavrita (GR) 339
Kalwaria Zebrzydowska (PL) 327
Kapikule (TR) 333
Kaprun (A) 247
Karlovy Vary (Carlsbad) (CZ) 319
Kaub (D) 266
Kauffmann, Angelica 198
Kecskemét (H) 320
Keighley (GB) 109
Kempten (D) 280
Kerkerbach (D) 269
Kildare (IRE) 118
Killarney (IRE) 119
Kingussie (GB) 108
Kirchenlaibach (D) 283
Kirkby Stephen (GB) 112
Kirkoswald (GB) 112
Kiskunmajsa (H) 320
Kitzbühel (A) 246
Kjosfossen (N) 292
Klagenfurt (A) 252
Klais (D) 274
Kleine Scheidegg (CH) 208, 209
Knighton (GB) 113
Knucklas Viaduct (GB) 37, 113
Kobern-Gondorf (D) 268
Koblenz (D) 263, 265, 268
Kongsvoll (N) 296
Königsbach (D) 263
Košice (SK) 321, 323, 324, *325*
Kouvola (FIN) 306
Kraków (PL) 327
Kreuzeckbahn (D) 277
Krimml (A) 247
Kristinehamn (S) 303
Kyle of Lochalsh (GB) 100, 102

L

La Bastide (F) 132
La Bourboule (F) 138
La Chaux-de-Fonds (CH) 204
La Ciotat (F) 142
La Grand-Combe (F) 133
Lahti (FIN) 305
Lairg (GB) 108
Lamezia Terme (I) 226
La Motte d'Aveillans (F) 141

La Mure (F) 141
Landeck (A) 243
Landwasser Viaduct (CH) *14, 198,*
  199
Langeac (F) 131
Langen (A) 242
Längenfeld (A) 242
Langogne (F) 132
Lanusei (I/Sardinia) 233
La Punt-Chaumes (CH) 200
Laredo (E) 164
La Rhune (F) 16, *151*
La Rochette (F) 140
Laroquebrou (F) 139
La Seyne (F) 142
La Spezia (I) 223
Lassemoen (N) 297
Latour-de-Carol (F) 153
Laurenburg (D) 269
Lausanne (CH) 189
Lauterbrunnen (CH) 208
La Vésubie (F) 146
Lawrence, D.H. 223, 230, 231
Lazonby (GB) 112
Le Breuil sur Couze (F) 133
Leeds (GB) 109
Le Fayet (F) 150
Le Fugeret (F) 147
Leithen (A) 272
Le Lioran (F) 139
Le Mont-Dore (F) 138
Lempdes (F) 139
Lenin, Vladimir Ilyich Ulyanov 305,
  306
Lenk (CH) 211
Leoben (A) 250
Leopold I 22
Le Prese (CH) 205
Le Puy-en-Velay (F) 132, 133
Les Arcs (F) 143
Les Avants (CH) 211
Les Diablerets (CH) 202
Leszno (PL) 326
Levoča (SK) 325
Liechtenstein 85, 241
Liechtensteinklamm (A) 254
Ligne à Grande Vitesse (F) 32, 54
Ligne des Causses *see* Béziers
Lille (F) 41
Lillehammer (N) 295
Limburg (D) 269
Limerick Junction (IRE) 118
Limpias (E) 168
Lindau (A) 241, 281
Lingostière (F) 146
Linz (A) 248
Linz (D) 265
Liptovsky Mikuláš (SK) 325
Lisbon (P) 48, 163
Livorno (I) 223
Livracão (P) 180
Ljubljana (SLO) *315,* 316
Llanbister Road (GB) 113
Llandeilo (GB) 114
Llandovery (GB) 114
Llandrindod Wells (GB) 113
Llanelli (GB) 114
Llanes (E) 169
Llangammarch Wells (GB) 114
Llangunllo (GB) 113

Llanwrtyd Wells (GB) 114
Llívia (E) 153
Locarno (CH) 204
Löhnberg (D) 269
Lohr (D) 283
London (GB) 41, 44, 45, 47, 48,
  49, 57, *80,* 105
Longniddry (GB) 107
Lønsdal (N) 298
Lorch (D) 266
Loreley (D) 263–4, *265*
Loschwitz (D) 283
Lötschberg Tunnel (CH) 38, 40,
  191
Loughor estuary (GB) 114
Loutraki (GR) 339
Luc (F) 134
Lugano (CH) 193
luggage services 350
Lumière brothers 22, 142
Lus-la-Croix-Haute (F) 140
Luzern (CH) *46,* 66, **204,** 206, *207*

M

Mâcon-Loché (F) 131
Madrid (E) 163, 173, 176
Mägdesprung (D) 272
Mainz (D) 264
Majavatn (N) 298
Málaga (E) 163
Mala Rijeka Viaduct (Serbia) 38,
  40
Mallaig (GB) 101, 102
Mallnitz (A) 253
Mallorca (E) 178–9
Malmö (S) 289
Manchester (GB) 48
Mandas (I/Sardinia) 230, *231*
Mann, Colonel William 29
Manosque (F) 140
Maratea (I) 225
Margecany (SK) 323
Mariánské Lázné (CZ) *319*
Maria Worth (A) *252*
Marinella (I/Sicily) 228
Marktredwitz (D) 283
Marseille (F) 131, 140, 142, 148
Martigny (CH) 190
Martinszell (D) 280
Marton (GB) 115
Marvejols (F) 136
Mascarat gorge (E) 178
Mataró (E) 163
Maugham, Somerset 142
Maurach (A) 245
Mauterndorf (A) 252
Mayrhofen (A) 61, 246
Méailles (F) 147
Meersburg (D) 281
Megara (GR) 338
Meiringen (CH) 207
Menai bridge (GB) 97
Menton (F) 222
Merano (I) 220
Messina (I/Sicily) 227, 229
Messinia (GR) 340
Mestre (I) 313
Meteora (GR) *336*
Meymac (F) 138

Middlesbrough (GB) 115
Mikines (GR) 341
Milan (I) *45*, 58, 193, 193, *246*
Mllazzo (I/Sicily) 227
Millau (F) 136
Millay, Edna St Vincent 25
Minsk (BY) 89–90
Mirador del Pujol den Banya
 (E/Mallorca) 178
Miralgo (CH) 205
Mirandela (P) 182
Mittenwald (D) 274
Mitterrand, François 24
Monaco *143*, *144*, 145, 222
Monasterevan (IRE) 118
Monestier-de-Clermont (F) 140
Monet, Claude 45, 48
Monfalcone (I) 314
Monistrol d'Allier (F) 133
Montbovon (CH) 211
Mont Cenis Tunnel (F/I) 39
Monte Carlo (Monaco) 145
Montélimar (F) 131
Montenvers (F) *149*, 52
Mont-Louis-La-Cabanasse (F) 153
Montpellier (F) 135
Montreux (CH) 189–90, 210
Moorcock Viaduct (GB) *110*, 112
Mora (S) 299, 303
Morar (GB) 102
Moray Firth (GB) 103, 108
Morges (CH) 189
Morteratsch (CH) 205
Morton, Sir Alastair 41
Moscow (RUS) 45, 87, *88*, *311*
Mosel (D) 283
Moselkern (D) 268
Mosjøen (N) 298
Moskosel (S) 301
Mosteirô (P) 181
Muck (GB) 102
Mulhouse (F) 59, 127
Munich (D) 58, *274*, *275*, 276,
 279, 280
Murat (F) 139
Murau (A) 251
Murnau (D) 275
Mussolini, Benito 217
Myrdal (N) 292

N

Nagelmackers, Georges 28–9,
 77
Namsskogan (N) 297
Naples (I) 217, *224*, 225
Napoleon *154*, 157
Nassau (D) 269
national and regional parks
 Bolgheri reserve (I) 223
 Cévennes (F) 134, 135
 Dovrefjell (N) 296
 Nebrodi (I/Sicily) 229
 North York Moors (GB) 115
 Parc du Gévaudan (F) 136
 Pirin (BG) 335
 Sächsische Schweiz (D) 318
 Swiss National Park (CH) 200
 Volcans d'Auvergne (F) 138
 Wielkopolska (P) 326

Yorkshire Dales (GB) 110, 112
navvies 36, 111, 292–3
Neef (D) 267
Nesbit, Edith
 The Railway Children 46
Netzkater (D) 271
Neuschwanstein (D) 278
Neuhaus (D) 283
Neussargues (F) 137, 139
Newark (GB) 106
Newcastle-upon-Tyne (GB) 35, 97,
 107, 283
Nice (F) 144–5, 146, 222
Nicholas I (Tsar) 22
Niederhaimbach (D) 264
Niederlahnstein (D) 265, 268
Niederwald (CH) 196
Nîmes (F) *134*, 135
Nordhausen (D) 270, 271
Norena (E) 169
Norwegian Stationmasters'
 Association 57–8
Novella (F/Corsica) 157
Nowy Targ (PL) 327
Núria (E) 176–7
Nürnberg (D) 52, 261, 283
Nyon (CH) 189

O

Oberalp Pass (CH) 197
Oberalppasshöhe (CH) 197
Oberammergau (D) 272, 275, 277,
 278
Obergurgl (A) 242
Oberlahnstein (D) 265
Oberhof (D) 269
Oberstaufen (D) 280
Oberwald (CH) 196
Oberwesel (D) 264, *266*
observation cars 100, 149, 194,
 195, 203, 206, 210, 270–1
Oederan (D) 282
Offa's Dyke (GB) 113
Olympia (GR) 340, *341*
Oppdal (N) 296
Oradea (RO) 328
Orange (F) 131
Øresund Bridge (DK/S) 38, 289
Orient Express ("real") 29–30, 31,
 234, 332, 333
 see also **Venice Simplon-Orient
  Express**
Orsa (S) 303
Oslo (N) 55, 293, 294, 295
Ospizio Bernina (CH) *203*, 205
Osterspai (D) 265
Östersund (S) 299, 303
Otta (N) 295
Ötz (A) 242
Ötztal (A) 242, 243
Oviedo (E) 165, 166, 169–70

P–Q

Padua (I) 85
Paestum (I) 225, 228
Pagnol, Marcel 142
Palasca (F/Corsica) 157
Palermo (I/Sicily) 227, 228, 229

Palma (E/Mallorca) 178–9
Páola (I) 226
Pardubice (CZ) 318
Paris (F) 16, 41, 45, 48, 80, 83,
 86, 87, *127*, 130, 234
Patras (GR) 339
Patti Tyndaris (I/Sicily) 227
Pella (GR) 336
Peloponnese (GR) 338–41
Pen-y-Bont (GB) 113
Perth (GB) 107
Pertisau (A) 245
Peterborough (GB) 107
Pfaffenberg–Zwenberg Bridge (A) 40
Pians (A) 242
Picasso, Pablo, 167
Pickering (GB) 115
Pietralba (F/Corsica) 157
Pinhão (P) 182
Pirgos (GR) 340
Pisa (I) 223
Pitlochry (GB) 108
PK79+800 station (F/Corsica) 157
"Plandampfs" (D) 66
Plateau de Gergovie (F) 132
Plauen (D) 283
Plockton (GB) *104*
Plzeň (CZ) *319*
Pocinho (P) 179, 182
Poliakoff, Stephen 15
Polminhac (F) 139
Pompeii (I) 224, *225*
Pontardulais (GB) 114
Pont de la Reine Jeanne (F) 147
Pont du Vecchio (F/Corsica) 156
Ponte Gardena/Waidbruck (I) 220
Ponte Leccia (F/Corsica) 154,
 155, 157
Ponte Nuovo (F/Corsica) 155
Pontgibaud (F) 138
Poprad (SK) 325
Portarlington (IRE) 118
Port de Sóller (E/Mallorca) 179
Portico (I) 221
Porto (P) 163, *183*, 184
Portofino (I) *222*, 223
Portuguese Traction Group 181, 182
Poschiavo (CH) 205
Potter, Beatrix 21
Poznań (PL) 88, 326
Prague (CZ) 318, 319
Praia a Mare (I) 226
Pravia (E) 170
Prévencheres (F) 134
Puchberg (A) 249
Puertollano (E) 179
Puget-Théniers (F) 146, 146
Pullman, George Mortimer 28, 29,
 77
Punt Muragl Staz (CH) 203
Queralbs (E) 176

R

rail passes 77, 191, 206, 210,
 289, 348
 Inter-Rail pass 77, 348
Railway Heritage Trust 47–8
Rannoch Moor (GB) 99
Rattenberg (A) 246

Realp (CH) 197
Reggio di Calabria (I/Sicily) 227
Régua (P) 181, 182
Reichenau-Tamins (CH) 198
Reichenbach (D) 283
Reinunga (N) 292
Reisz, Edgar 267
Reith (A) 272–3
Remagen (D) 263
Rhône Glacier 194, 196
Ribadeo (E) 166
Ribadesella (E) 169
Ribes-Enllaç (E) 176
Ribes Vila (E) 176
Ribblehead Viaduct (GB) 111
Riffelriß (D) 277
Riihimäki (FIN) 305
Rila Monastery (BG) 335
Ritter von Ghega, Carl 250
Rivoli (I) 219
Roc de Peyre (F) 137
Rognan (N) 298
Rome (I) 86, 223
Ronda (E) 171, 172–3
Roquefavour Aqueduct (F) 131
Roquefort (F) 136
Rosarno (I) 226
Rossinière (CH) 211
Röthenbach (D) 281
Rougemont (CH) 211
Route Napoléon (F) 147
Rovereto (I) 219
Royal Scotsman 95, 97, 99, *100*, 258
Rudesheim (D) 266
Rum (GB) 102
Runkel (D) 269
Ruse (BG) 331–2
Ružomberok (SK) 325

S

Saanen (CH) 211
Saanenmöser (CH) 211
Saarinen, Eliel 45, 304
Sachseln (CH) 207
Sádali (I/Sardinia) 231
Sant'Agata di Miletello (I/Sicily) 227, 229
St-André-les-Alpes (F) 147
St Anton (A) 84, 242
St-Auban (F) 148
Ste-Cécile d'Andorges (F) 134
Ste-Croix (CH) 204
St-Cyr-sur-Mer (F) 142
St-Denis-lès-Martel (F) 139
St-Exupéry (F) 131
St-Flour (F) 137
St Gallen (CH) 191, 204, 279
St-Georges-de-Commiers (F) 140, 141
St-Gervais (F) 149–50, 194, 204
  Tramway du Mont Blanc 149–50
St Goarshausen (D) 265
St Johann im Pongau (A) 254
St-Martin-du-Var (F) 146
St Moritz (CH) *199*, 200, 203
St Neots (GB) 106
St Petersburg (RUS) 306
St-Raphaël (F) 143

San Remo (I) 223
San Roque (E) 171
San Sebastián (E) 165
Santo Stefano di Camastra (I/Sicily) 229
St Veit an der Glan (A) 252
Salerno (I) 223
Saltaire (GB) 109
Salzburg (A) 248, 257
Samedan (CH) 199
Sangatte (F) 41
Santander (E) 166, 169, 170
Santillana de Mar (E) 166
Sardinia (I) 230–33
Sargans (CH) 84
Sarnen (CH) 207
Savaggio (F/Corsica) 157
Scharnitz (A) 274
Schierke (D) 271
Schmiedinger Kees (A) 247
Schöna (D) 318
Schwarzach-St Veit (A) 247, 254
Schwyz (CH) 192
Schynige-Platte railway *208*
Scilla (I) 226
Scott, Sir Gilbert 44
Scuol-Tarasp (CH) 199, 201–2
Seefeld in Tirol (A) 243, 274
Semmering (A) 250
Semmering Pass (A) *250, 251*
Sens (F) 131
Septemvri (BG) 335
Serres (F) 140
Sète (F) 135
Settle (GB) 110
Settle & Carlisle Railway (GB) 35, 109–10
Seui (I/Sardinia) 231
Séverac-le-Château (F) 136
Seville (E) 16, 163, 173–5
Sežana (SLO) 315
Sherwood, James B. 234
Shipley (GB) 109
Shrewsbury (GB) 111
Sibiu (RO) 329
Sicily (I) 226–9
Sighişoara (RO) *329*, 330
Sihlbrugg (CH) 192
Simplon Tunnel (CH/I) 39–40, 191, 234
Sinaia (RO) 86, 330–1
Sion (CH) 190–1
Siracusa (I/Sicily) 229
Sisteron (F) 140
Skipton (GB) *109*
Skye Railway (GB) 103–4
Sleights (GB) 116
Smolensk (RUS) 90
Snåsa (N) 297
Sognefjord (N) 292
Sölden (A) 242
Sóller (E/Mallorca) 178
Sommeiller, Germain 39
Sorsele (S) 302
Spiš *324*
Spisske Podhradie (SK) 325
Spittal an der Drau (A) 253
"Stairway of Giants" (F) 132
Stalden-Saas (CH) 195
Stams (A) 243

Stanier, Sir William 58
Starnberg (D) 275
Stary Smokovec (SK) 325
Steinerne Renne (D) 272
Steinkjer (N) 297
Stensele (S) 302
Stephenson, George 22, 35, 51, 95, 250
Stephenson Locomotive Society 59
Stephenson, Robert 22–3, 35, 36, 51, 95, 294
Sternhaus-Haberfeld (D) 272
Stevenson, Robert Louis 15, 99, *135*
  Kidnapped 99
Stevenson Historic Trail (F) 135
Stiege (D) 272
Stirling (GB) 107
Stjørdal (N) 297
Stockholm (S) 289, 299, 303
Stoker, Bram 116, 329, 330
  Dracula 116, 329, 330
Stoke Summit (GB) 106
Storuman (S) 302
Strba (SK) 325
Strečno (SK) 325
Stresa (I) 191
Strömsund (S) 302
Susch (CH) *200*, 201
Sutcliffe, Frank Meadow 116
Sveg (S) 299, 303
Swansea (GB) 114
Szalajka Forest Railway (H) 320

T

Tamsweg (A) 251–2
Tangen (N) 295
Tarasp (CH) 202, 203
Täsch (CH) 195
Tattone (F/Corsica) 157
Tavannes (CH) 204
Temple Route (I/Sicily) *228*
Teufenbach (A) 251
Thalkirchdorf (D) 280
Thalwil (CH) 192
Tharandt (D) 282
Theroux, Paul 15
Thessaloniki (GR) 336
Thira (GR) 337
Thirsk (GB) 105
Thues-les-Bains (F) 151
Thurles (IRE) 117
Thurso (GB) 108
Thusis (CH) 201
tickets 348
Tiefencastel (CH) 199
time differences 306
Tirano (I) 199, 205
Tortolì (I/Sardinia) 233
Touët-sur-Var (F) 146
Toulon (F) 142
Tournemire (F) 136
tour operators 351
Train Bleu 31
Tralee (IRE) 119
Transcantabrican route (E) 165–71
Transylvania (RO) 328–30
Trento (I) 85, 219
Trevithick, Richard 95

Trier (D) *267*, 268
Trieste (I) 314–5
Tripoli (GR) 341
Trondheim (N) 294, *296*, 297
Trondheimsfjord (N) 297
Tropea (I) 226
Trubia (E) 170
Tua (P) 182
Tulle (F) 138
Turenne (F) 139
Turnberry hotel (GB) 49
Turner, J.M.W. 23
Tutzing (D) 279
Tzvetino station (BG) *335*

U

Ulriksfors (S) 302
Ulsberg (N) *296*
Ussel (F) 138
Ustaoset (N) 293

V

Vainikkala (FIN) 306
Vajkijaur (S) *289*, 301
Valença (P) 163
Valence (F) 131
Vale of Tempi (GR) 336, *337*
Valpolicella (I) 219
Vantini, Zenoni 49
Varjistrask (S) 301
Vasse (GR) 340
Velden (A) 252
Veliko Târnovo (BG) *331*, 332
Velingrad (BG) 335
Venaco (F/Corsica) 156
Venice Simplon-Orient Express 16,
   29, 66, 80, *81–86*, 234, 260
Venice (I) 80, 86, 217, 313, 314
Veneto (I) 85
Ventabren (F) 131
Ventimiglia (I) 222
Verbania-Palanza (I) 191
Verdal (N) 297
Vernègues (F) 131
Verona (I) 85, 219, 221
Vevey (CH) 189, *190*

Viareggio (I) 217, 223
Vicenza (I) 85
Vic-le-Comte (F) 132
Vic-sur-Cère (F) 139
Victoria, Queen 21, 24, 35
Vienna (A) 57, 239, 249, 250
Vif (F) 140
Vignoles, Charles 189
Vila Real (P) 185, 186
Villach (A) 252, 253
Villagrande (I/Sardinia) 232–3
Villajoyosa (E) 177
Villanueva de Córdoba (E) 175
Villa Opicina (I) 315
Villars-sur-Var (F) 146, 204
Villa San Giovanni (I) 226
Villefort (F) 134
Villefranche (F) 222
Villefranche-de-Conflent (F) 152–3
Villeneuve (CH) 190
Vinstra (N) 295
Visegrad (H) 319
Visp (CH) 191
Vivario (F/Corsica) 156
Vivero (E) 166
Vizzavona (F/Corsica) 157
Vöcklabruck (A) 248
Vólos (GR) 336-7
Volvic (F) 138
von Röll, Dr Baron 57
von Zeppelin, Graf Ferdinand 281
Vorra (D) 283
Voss (N) 292

W

Wagons-Lits 29, 31, *78*, 82–3,
   124, 234
Wanner, Jakob Friedrich 47
Warsaw (PL) 89
Watkin, Sir Edward 41
websites 351
Weilburg (D) 269
Wels (A) 248
Welwyn Garden City (GB) 105
Wengen (CH) 208
Wengernalp (CH) 209
Werningerode (D) 270, 271, 272

Werningerode Westerntor (D) 272
Wetzlar (D) 269
Whitby (GB) *115*, 116
Wick (GB) 108
Wiener Neustadt (A) 249
Wiesbaden (D) 266
Wild Boar Fell (GB) 112
Wilderswil (CH) 208
Williams, Stephen 186
Wolsztyn (PL) 63, 88, 326, 329
Wörgl (A) 246
Würzburg (D) 283
Wyatt, Matthew Digby 44

Y–Z

York (GB) 27, 106–7
   National Railway Museum 27,
      53, 59, *60*, 95, *106*, 107
Yverdon (CH) 204
Zagreb (HR) 316
Zakopane (PL) 327
Zbąszynek (PL) 326
Zekloron (GR) 339
Zell am See (A) 247
Zell am Ziller (A) 246
Zermatt (CH) 191, 194–5
Zernez (CH) 200
Žilina (SK) 325
Zillertalbahn (A) 245–6
Zirl (A) 243
   Martinswand 243
Znin (PL) 63, 88
Zola, Emile 45
Zug (CH) 192
Zugspitzplatt (D) 277
Zumaia (E) 167
Zuoz (CH) 200
Zürich (CH) 47, 191, 192, 193,
   279
Zvolen (SK) 321
Zweilütschinen (CH) 208
Zweiselstein (A) 242
Zweisimmen (CH) 211
Zwickau (D) 283

European Railways:
Featured Route Maps

0 ____ 200 km
0 ____ 200 miles

N

page 98
page 116
page 113
page 265
page 133
page 181
page 152
page 177

NORWAY

Stavanger

Fred

DENMA

Esbjerg

Ham

NORTH

SEA

Inverness

Edinburgh

Glasgow

Londonderry

Belfast

Irish Sea

York

Dublin

Manchester

Leeds

Holyhead

UNITED

KINGDOM

Cork

Norwich

Swansea

NETHERLANDS

Amsterdam

Den Haag

Utrecht

Arnhem

Cardiff

London

Rotterdam

Duisburg

Essen

Norddeich
Mole

Hannov

Southampton

Dover

Calais

**Bruxelles
(Brussels)**

Düsseldor

Köln (Colog

BELGIUM

GER

Celtic Sea

ATLANTIC

OCEAN

Penzance

Brighton

English Channel

Lille

Liège

Fra

Cherbourg

Amiens

**LUXEM-
BOURG**

Ma

Channel
Islands

le Havre

Rouen

Luxembourg

Brest

Caen

Seine

Paris

Metz

Strasbourg

St

Rennes

Orléans

Besançon

Basel

Freiburg

Angers

Loire

Dijon

Zürich

SWITZERL

Nantes

Tours

Bern

F   R   A   N   C   E

Limoges

Genève

Milan
(Mila

Transcontinental Routes

VSOE   page 82
Paris/Amsterdam-Moscow   page 89
Berlin-Budapest
Budapest-Istanbul   page 333

Clermont-
Ferrand

Lyon

Grenoble

Torin
(Turin

Bay of Biscay

Bordeaux

Garonne

Rhône

Avignon

Monte
Carlo

Gen

Nice

A Coruña

Gijón

Santander

Bayonne

Toulouse

Nîmes

MONACO

Oviedo

Bilbao

**Donostia-
San Sebastián**

Marseille

Toulon

*Corse
(Corsica)*

Vigo

**Gasteiz-
Vitoria**

ANDORRA

Andorra la Vella

Perpignan

Ajacci

Porto

Douro

Valladolid

Ebro

PORTUGAL

Salamanca

Zaragoza

Barcelona

Sassari

Madrid

Tarragona

Tajo

S   P   A   I   N

Islas Baleares

Menorca

Macome

Lisboa
(Lisbon)

Valencia

Mallorca

Palma

Sardegna
(Sardinia)

Setúbal

Albacete

Ibiza

Córdoba

Murcia

Alacant

MEDITERRANEAN SEA

Huelva

Faro

Sevilla

Granada

Cartagena

Cádiz

Málaga

Almería

Algeciras

Gibraltar
(UK)

**Alger
(Algiers)**

M O R O C C O

A L G E R I A

Rabat